REMEMBERING JESUS

REMEMBERING JESUS

Christian Community, Scripture, and the Moral Life

ALLEN VERHEY

WILLIAM B. EERDMANS PUBLISHING COMPANY
GRAND RAPIDS, MICHIGAN / CAMBRIDGE, U.K.

Wm. B. Eerdmans Publishing Co.
255 Jefferson Ave. S.E., Grand Rapids, Michigan 49503 /
P.O. Box 163, Cambridge CB3 9PU U.K.

Printed in the United States of America

www.eerdmans.com

06 05 04 03 02   7 6 5 4 3 2 1

Library of Congress Cataloging-in-Publication Data

Verhey, Allen.
Remembering Jesus: Christian community,
Scripture, and the moral life / Allen Verhey.
p.   cm.
Includes bibliographical references and index.
ISBN 0-8028-0323-7 (alk. paper)
1. Christian ethics.   2. Ethics in the Bible.
3. Jesus Christ — Ethics.   4. Bible.
N.T. — Criticism, interpretation, etc.   I. Title.

BJ1251.V47 2002
241 — dc21

2001040681

To
Jacob E. Nyenhuis

Contents

vii

CONTENTS

Contents

Acknowledgments and Dedication

More than a decade ago Union Theological Seminary in Virginia invited me to give some lectures for its summer program in continuing education. I spoke on "Remembering Jesus in the Moral Life," and I thought there might be a book in those lectures if I kept working on them. This, finally, is that book.

I can only begin to list the institutions and the people who have supported me and this project over the course of the past decade.

I am grateful to Union Theological Seminary in Virginia for that initial invitation long ago, and I am grateful to those pastors who listened so patiently to the lectures, praised them so generously, and challenged them so thoughtfully.

There were many other invitations to teach a class, or to give a lecture, or simply to have a conversation in which I had an opportunity to test some of the material that found its way into this book. I do not even remember them all, and I would not dare to attempt to list them all if I did. Even so, I am grateful.

And there have been invitations to publish versions of parts of this material before. I make some use of the following previously published material:

"In Defense of Theocracy," *Reformed Review* 34, no. 2 (Winter 1981): 98-107.
"The Holy Bible and Sanctified Sexuality: An Evangelical Approach to Scripture and Sexual Ethics," *Interpretation* 49, no. 1 (January 1995): 31-45. Used with permission.
"A Protestant Perspective on Access to Healthcare," *Cambridge Quarterly of Healthcare Ethics* 7, no. 3 (Summer 1998): 247-53. Used with permission of the Cambridge University Press.
"Ethique Medicale," *Dictionnaire Critique de Theologie,* ed. Jean Yves Lacoste

(Paris: Presses Universitaires de France, 1998), pp. 718-20. Used with permission.

"Moral Formation — and Difference: A Theological Perspective," in *K-12 Education: The Cultural Context* (Grand Rapids: The Van Andel Education Institute, 1999), pp. 121-44. Used with permission.

"The Practices of Piety and the Practice of Medicine: Prayer, Scripture, and Medical Ethics," in *Seeking Understanding: The Stob Lectures, 1986-1998* (Grand Rapids: Eerdmans, 2001).

As I read through the completed manuscript, I realized again how much I owe to others. I have learned much from the scholars whose works are cited in the notes, of course, and I hope those notes are a way of saying "thank you" to those scholars, even when we disagree. But I also realized how much I owe to a host of people — scholars, teachers, friends, and family — whose names are not cited in the notes.

Indeed, as I read through the manuscript, I wondered sometimes in whose debt I was for what struck me again as a good idea or a felicitous phrase. Was this idea something I heard at a Society of Christian Ethics meeting? Was that phrase something I picked up from hearing a sermon? Was this line of argument suggested by one of my students long ago? Was that formulation of the question presented by one of my teachers long, long ago? I seldom had confident answers to such questions, but I did recognize just how indebted I am to others and how grateful it is right to be. So, I want to acknowledge my gratitude also to those whose names and whose gifts to me I may have forgotten.

It is a pleasure, however, to acknowledge at least a few of those whose names and gifts to me have not been forgotten.

Thanks to Richard Verhey, my dad, who first insisted that Scripture mattered and then allowed some puzzlement about how it mattered. He is ninety now; he misses my mom; but he loves the "think tank" at Sunset Manor.

Thanks to my teachers (and I have been privileged to have some outstanding ones), who nurtured my efforts both to read Scripture and to think about how it is used (and abused) in the common life of Christian communities.

Thanks also to my students (and, again, I have been privileged to have some outstanding ones). Thanks especially to those students who have assisted me with this project over the years: Court Buchanan, Shirley Heeg, Jon Hofman, Seth Kaper-Dale, and especially Amy Rife.

Thanks to my colleagues in the Religion Department at Hope College, for reading drafts of parts of this manuscript, and for making me a better scholar and teacher than I could possibly be without them.

Thanks to Jon Pott, friend and editor-in-chief of Eerdmans Publishing Company, for his patience with this project and for his support for it. There was a long time between our first conversation about this project and this final draft; the project kept getting shoved to the back of my desk as other projects (and their deadlines) demanded attention. But Jon never gave up on either me or the project.

Thanks, of course, to Phyllis. Her support for and patience with the project were of a different sort than Jon Pott's — and harder. They cost her many an evening's companionship. She is, I know, pleased that it is done; I am, she knows, pleased to be her husband.

Finally, I want to acknowledge and thank Jack Nyenhuis, former provost of Hope College and my friend. He came to Hope College in 1975 to be the Dean for the Arts and the Humanities. That same year I accepted an invitation to come to Hope as a visiting assistant professor. I cannot begin to thank him for the contribution he has made to Hope College, first as dean and then as provost. His commitment both to the academy and to the church has been a model for me and for many others. His discerning appreciation of the work of artists, writers, teachers, and scholars has been a source of wonder to me and to others. Hope College is a better place for his presence and for his leadership. He makes it possible for teachers and scholars to do well what they love to do, and he encourages them to do it all in the service of God. If I cannot begin to thank him for the contribution he has made to Hope College, it is still more difficult to thank him adequately for the many and various ways he has supported my work. He supported removing that loathsome "visiting" from my title in 1976. He supported my tenure at Hope, and my promotions, sabbaticals, and grant proposals for summer research over the years, including more than one dedicated to this project. He supported my return to Hope College in 1994 and my appointment to the Blekkink Chair in Religion. And if I owe him much for his support of my work, I owe him more for his faithful friendship. I am, like many others at Hope, a better scholar and teacher because of Jack, but I am also, like many others in Holland, Michigan, a better person because I count Jack a friend.

Therefore, on the occasion of his retirement from Hope College in the summer of 2001, and in appreciation of both his service to Hope College and his friendship, I dedicate this book to Jacob E. Nyenhuis.

φίλος πιστὸς φάρμακον ζωῆς

ΣΟΦΙΑ ΣΙΡΑΧ 6:16

PART ONE

CHOICES, CHURCHES, AND SCRIPTURE

A Continuing Tradition of Discourse and Discernment

Ethics "by Way of Reminder"

Choices

"What should I do?" That's the question with which Christian ethics frequently begins and to which it always finally returns. Christian ethics aims to be a practical discipline, to help people think about the choices they face. Since this is a book about Christian ethics, it is — almost inevitably — a book about choices.

We all make choices, and we all wish we could make (or had made) better ones. We choose to marry or not. We choose to be faithful to our spouses or not. We choose to have children or not. And although we do not choose our children (or our parents), life with them is full of choices. We choose how to earn a living, and then we face choices about how to conduct ourselves with colleagues and customers, with employers or employees, and with the money we earn. We choose to vote or not, and we make choices about particular candidates and policies. We choose whether or not to lie when our hosts serve a lima bean and eggplant casserole and ask whether we like it. We choose to go to the doctor or not, and then we choose whether or not to follow the doctor's advice. We choose our words and our deeds. We choose how to act in the presence of lovers and friends, strangers and enemies. We choose how to behave in response to sickness and sexual attraction, poverty and violence. The list of our choices could, of course, go on and on. It is as long as our cares extend and our powers reach. A book about Christian ethics is, as I said, a book about choices, and no book about choices could presume to be about all of them.

"What should I do?" We pause to ask that question when a choice seems agonizingly difficult. Some choices are like that. They can tear a person or a community apart. Other choices, however — indeed, sometimes the most important choices — are surprisingly easy, almost unnoticed as choices. Such choices seem to "make themselves." When people know who they are and what integrity requires of them, then it is almost as though they have no choice. Like Martin Luther or Thomas More, they "can do no other." Such "easy" choices, however, as both Luther and More knew, can be "hard" choices in their own way, difficult to bear because of the costs. When choices are hard to make, we long for knowledge, for the wisdom to see the right. When the consequences of the right decision are hard to take, we long for goodness, for the strength, the virtue, to do the right. This is a book about choices, but no book in Christian ethics is likely to satisfy such longings for wisdom and virtue.

Humility requires of those who would undertake the task of writing a book on Christian ethics that they warn readers not to expect too much. So, let me (and the readers' expectations) be modest. Do not look here for simple answers to difficult questions of conduct. Do not expect this book to dispense moral wisdom and virtue like some ethical vending machine.

People facing choices and longing for wisdom and virtue have, in fact, sometimes asked my advice. I have been flattered, of course, and I have tried to help them to think clearly and carefully about the choices that are hard to make, and to face courageously the consequences of the right decision when those consequences are hard to take. But I have always wondered and sometimes asked, "Why me? Why ask me?" The answer I keep hoping for is that my advice is sought because I am so wise and virtuous — but I seldom get that reply! The answer I usually get is, "Well, you're a Christian ethicist, aren't you? I thought choices were the sort of thing Christian ethicists were supposed to be good at." That answer always troubles me a little — in spite of the fact that I take Christian ethics to be a practical discipline. It troubles me because I know better: choices are not the sort of thing I'm particularly "good at," and wisdom and virtue are things I'm still working on.

In such consultations I frequently answer the question "What should I do?" with questions of my own: "Who are you?" "Who do you want to become?" "What kind of narrative do you want to tell with the life you are authoring?" It is a way, of course, of recognizing that the question — like most serious moral inquiries — was set in the first person, "What should I do?" In class discussions of moral quandaries we sometimes ask, "What would a reasonable person do in a case like this one?" When we face hard choices of our own, however, we usually ask, "What should I do in *this* case?" The "I" in this case is not just some generic "reasonable person" but a particular person, bound by ties of loyalty to other particular persons, related by history and by covenant to concrete communities, burdened by specific grievances inflicted or endured, sustained by and identified with others. And the choices in such cases

4

are never just about some discrete action cut off from our own past and future; they are choices about our very selves, about our whole lives.

Frequently the best advice I can give people in such consultations is that they go talk with someone else. Sometimes I suggest a conversation with someone who knows more about psychology or sociology or economics or medicine or something else relevant to the choices the people face. Sometimes, that is, I point them toward an expert; more often, however, I point them toward someone who possesses a wisdom that has been learned in a similar experience or toward someone who has displayed a strength of character that has been tested by a similar choice and its suffering. Frequently the best advice I can give people is that they go talk with some other member of one of the communities within which they live and with which they identify. Such communities, after all, are important to who they are and to their vision of who they should become. Such communities are resources of wisdom and virtue for each of us. For Christians, of course, one such community, the decisive such community, is the church.

Such advice is not an admission that, although Christian ethics is a practical discipline, I personally fail to meet some minimal professional standard. It is rather to acknowledge that Christian ethics itself — precisely as a practical discipline — is not independent and self-sufficient. Often the best a Christian ethicist (or a book about Christian ethics) can do is to point beyond Christian ethics as a narrowly defined academic discipline and toward the community out of which it lives and speaks, toward the community of those who gather periodically in the name of Christ and who disperse again in Christ's service. That may finally be the best service to Christian moral discernment.[1]

---

1. This introduction began with the claim that Christian ethics begins and always returns to the question, "What should I do?" It should be noted that there are some who say that this focus on moral choices is what is wrong with ethics in general and with Christian ethics in particular. Edmund Pincoffs, for example, has written a widely quoted essay entitled "Quandary Ethics" (reprinted in *Revisions: Changing Perspectives in Moral Philosophy*, ed. Stanley Hauerwas and Alasdair MacIntyre [Notre Dame: University of Notre Dame Press, 1983], pp. 92-112), in which he objects to a focus on moral dilemmas, or quandaries, not only because it has no classical roots, not only because little argumentation can be found to defend it, but also because what is a moral problem, a quandary, to one person might not be one to another. Pincoffs and others have made the point that a person who confronts a situation does not confront it simply as a rational agent but as a rational agent qualified by his or her communities and history and character. Moreover, the situation itself is not described from an altogether impartial perspective but from the particular perspectives of the participants in it. A number of moral theologians, including my friend Stanley Hauerwas, have adopted this criticism of both a focus on moral quandaries and the "rational" principles used to solve them. (See, for example, the criticism of "decisionism" in James Wm. McClendon Jr., *Systematic Theology: Ethics* [Nashville:

Churches

This is a book, then, not only about choices but also about churches. To put it differently, this is a book about churches *because* it is a book about choices. It was not, after all, a book about Christian ethics that Paul described as "full of goodness, filled with all knowledge, and able to instruct one another" (Rom. 15:14); it was the church at Rome. People facing choices and longing for wisdom and virtue are more likely to find help in such a community than in a book on Christian ethics. Precisely as a practical discipline Christian ethics depends upon such a community, relies upon its "goodness" and "knowledge," and points to it to help people think and talk about their choices. The task of Christian ethics is to serve such communities and their moral discourse and discernment, not to attempt to be a substitute for them.

Even so, there is evidently at times a problem with the suggestion that

Abingdon, 1986], pp. 48-62; the criticism of "punctualism" in John Howard Yoder, *The Priestly Kingdom: Social Ethics as Gospel* [Notre Dame: University of Notre Dame Press, 1984], pp. 35-36; the criticism of "juridical ethics" in Craig Dykstra, *Vision and Character: A Christian Educator's Alternative to Kohlberg* [New York: Paulist, 1981], pp. 7-62. And see especially the work of Stanley Hauerwas, including particularly "The Self as Story: A Reconsideration of the Relation of Religion and Morality from the Agent's Perspective," in *Vision and Virtue* [Notre Dame: University of Notre Dame Press, 1981], pp. 68-89, and *The Peaceable Kingdom: A Primer in Christian Ethics* [Notre Dame: University of Notre Dame Press, 1983], pp. 1-49.)

I am sympathetic with these complaints about quandary ethics. That sympathy is revealed in this introduction by its attention to the church. Nevertheless, the complaints about quandary ethics go too far rhetorically when they seem sometimes to prohibit attention to questions of conduct. The issue, I take it, is not whether ethics should attend to questions of conduct. The issue is, rather, whether ethics can properly attend to such questions of conduct if it supposes that either we or our choices can be (or should be) uninformed by the communities in which we live and independent of the vision and character that those communities form. My indebtedness to those who complain about quandary ethics will be seen, then, in my attention to issues of community and character on the way toward dealing with choices. I take some comfort in the fact that Stanley Hauerwas finally returns to "Decisions, Decisions, Decisions" (in *The Peaceable Kingdom*, pp. 121-30). I might also mention the remarkable essay by James M. Gustafson, "A Protestant Ethical Approach" (reprinted in Stephen E. Lammers and Allen Verhey, eds., *On Moral Medicine*, second ed. [Grand Rapids: Eerdmans, 1998], pp. 600-611). One year before Pincoffs's essay appeared (1970 as opposed to 1971) Gustafson criticized a style of approaching a quandary about abortion which adopted the perspective of an external judge with only universal and rational principles at one's disposal and which focused only on the features of the situation that were physical and could be described objectively. Gustafson's criticisms, however, were put in the service of attention to the case, not set in opposition to it.

people should be in conversation with members of their Christian community, a problem captured in the uncomprehending reaction of some of those to whom I have made such a suggestion. People sometimes reply to that suggestion with a look intimating that they would rather not, or that they think a serious moral conversation would be unwelcome at church. And they sometimes reply to such a suggestion with words that leave little doubt that they dare not talk to anyone at church about the choice they face.

A young woman was considering an abortion. It was "date rape," she said, and now her life and her dreams were "in ruins." An abortion seemed the only choice. She could not talk to anyone at church, she said. "They would just condemn me for being pregnant. Right now, they think I'm little Miss Perfect. I don't want those people to know I'm pregnant, even if it is because of date rape. That's one of the reasons abortion seems like my only choice; otherwise, they'll know. Why would I tell them about it? Besides, I already know what they'll say about abortion." There were a lot of things in those remarks that we talked some more about: whether she could be certain the church would condemn her for being pregnant, whether she wanted to continue a pretence of being little Miss Perfect, whether there were not in fact some other choices, choices that fit who she truly was and wanted to be better than abortion did, whether she really knew what the community would say about abortion, and if she really did know, whether the teaching of her community was important to the choice she had to make. But I could not convince that young woman to talk to someone in her church. And I remember similar remarks by a homosexual young man who was trying to decide whether to come out of the closet, and by a young wife and mother who was considering divorce. They were each willing to talk with other people about their choices, but not with members of their church. I hope that the conversations I had with these young people were helpful to them, but I wish they could have trusted the Christian community where they lived more than they did.

Such examples make it clear that if Christian ethics does sometimes seem a substitute for the moral discourse and discernment of Christian communities, the problem is not necessarily the presumption of people trained to study Christian ethics. The problem is sometimes a failure of people to trust congregations with their choices and their lives, a failure to trust their communities to care for them, to trust them not to despise or condemn them for the choices they face. And sadly, sometimes the problem is that the churches are not worthy of such trust, pretending a perfection that does not allow hard choices, inhospitable to suffering, ready to despise or condemn those who find themselves suddenly on the margins of congregational life. Sometimes churches would simply prefer to avoid hard conversations about hard choices; hard moral choices, after

7

all, can sometimes tear a community apart. No wonder, then, that churches are sometimes inhospitable to conversations about those choices.

No wonder, but still lamentable — for Christian congregations are, both by tradition and vocation, communities of moral discourse and discernment. It seems almost as though churches have no choice about whether to be communities of discourse and discernment. This is a choice that should "make itself." If churches know who they are and what fidelity to their tradition and vocation requires of them, then they "can do no other" than to struggle with the hard tasks of moral discourse and discernment. Such "easy" choices, however, as we have observed, can be hard in their own way, costly and difficult, requiring not just knowledge but virtue, the strength to be such a community.

It is easy enough, of course, to criticize the churches. Some people seem to take sport in "prophetic" indictments of them. To be sure, the churches need repentance and renewal, but that acknowledgment is a part of every church's liturgy. I have little taste for the sort of criticism that is neither very repentant nor very constructive. For the sake of those who face hard choices Christian ethicists must not just criticize the churches but nurture the renewal and reform of congregations as communities of moral discourse and discernment.[2]

But how is that renewal to be accomplished? Where are the resources for reform to be found? Close at hand, it seems. The Spirit of God was poured out at Pentecost as the presence of a risen Christ, as the "first fruits" of God's good future. It was the birthday of the church. And that same Spirit still dwells among us — or to use Paul's phrase, still "dwells in" us (see, for example, Rom. 8:11). The Spirit still reminds us of Jesus and of his future, and is still the power of God to make things new, even us.

But how does the Spirit work among us to renew and to reform? Well, one answer would surely be, "Any way the Spirit will!" "The wind blows where it chooses" (John 3:8), and we cannot tie the Spirit down any more than we can the wind. Still, there are some paths along which the Spirit often moves. When the Spirit was poured out and dwelt among that community in Jerusalem, it was surely no accident that "They devoted themselves to the apostles' teaching and fellowship, to the breaking of bread and the prayers" (Acts 2:42). These things — attentiveness to the apostles' teaching, sharing a common life, breaking bread together, and prayer — are still paths along which the Spirit often moves, still resources for the renewal of the continuing church. There are no guarantees, of course. These resources do not work like magic to manipulate the free Spirit of God. They are not technologies that can be used to achieve

---

2. The converse is also true, of course: Christian communities should nurture the renewal and reform of Christian ethics as an ecclesial discipline.

whatever ends we choose. Still, if we search for resources for the renewal of the church, we need not look far.

Set first in Luke's little list is his observation that the early church devoted itself to the apostles' teaching. Think of that. These were ordinary men and women — eager to be taught. It is not that these ordinary men and women happily assembled to hear long and academic and dull lectures about the relationship of, say, Peter's preaching and Stoic moral teachings. They were eager, I think, simply to hear the apostles talk of Jesus. They had known him. They had walked with him when he had done signs and wonders. They had talked with him about life and about death. And now they could not get over the fact that this Jesus continued to abide with his continuing church.

With people gathered in their work clothes, I imagine, Peter reminisced about an occasion on which Jesus had said this or that about life and the meaning of life, or about anxiety and the power to be carefree. Or, when some complained about the cheap, flashy woman who had joined their little assembly, John took five or six of the complainers aside to tell them about a long, hot, wearying walk the disciples took with Jesus one day just so Jesus could talk with just such a woman, a cheap Samaritan woman. Jesus told her, John said, about the "living water." Or, in another part of town, Andrew — in his halting, stumbling way — told a companion what Jesus had said about a person's daily work, words unfortunately never written down. In quite mundane conversations the Spirit reminded the continuing church of what Jesus had done and said (cf. John 14:25) in the apostles' teaching.

It must have been wonderful to hear the apostles teach. It's too bad that so much of what they taught surely died with them. But much of what they taught has remained with us, too. We have our own access to the apostles' teaching in Scripture. There is more than enough to fill our lives with study — not simply that we might be better informed, but that we may live our lives and our common life with more courage, with more discipline, with more faith and hope and love. To be attentive to the apostles' teaching, to Scripture, continues to mark the continuing church. It continues to provide access to the power and life of Pentecost not only two weeks or two decades but two millennia after Pentecost.

Scripture

As attentiveness to the apostles' teaching is set first in Luke's little list, so we may recognize Scripture as having a certain priority among the continuing resources of the continuing church. In this book, at any rate, we will look especially to Scripture as the place in which the Spirit reminds us of Jesus. We will look to Scripture as a resource for nurturing, sustaining, renewing, and reforming the church as a community of moral discourse and discernment.

It is not that the other paths along which the Spirit moves are unimportant; indeed, reading Scripture in Christian community takes place in the context of these other practices, in the context of sharing a common life, in the context of the sacraments, and in the context of prayer. In the absence of such practices Scripture might be read simply as an interesting little library of ancient Near Eastern religious texts. The Bible is that, of course, but it is also mysteriously, as the church has consistently said, something more than that, something infinitely more, the Word of God. The Bible is the church's canon, the "rule" *(kanon)* for faith and practice. When churches consider (and live) their common life, when they consider (and celebrate) the sacraments, when they consider prayer (and pray), they do so in the light of Scripture. And when they consider their life as a community of moral discourse and discernment, they should do so in the light of Scripture. Because this is a book about choices, it must also be a book about the church; and because it is a book of the church, it must also be a book attentive to Scripture.

Indeed, as David Kelsey has shown, "Scripture" and "church" are correlative concepts. Part of what we mean when we call a community "church" is that this community uses Scripture *somehow* as essential to its identity and common life. And part of what we mean when we call certain writings "Scripture" is that these writings ought to be used *somehow* in the common life of the church to nourish and reform it.[3] Scripture is the book of the church, and the church is the community that somehow uses that book to preserve its identity and reform its common life.

It was, of course, the church that decided to canonize certain writings and not others. That decision was obviously of critical importance to the construction of Scripture. And it was of no less critical importance to the identity of the church! Still, it may be observed that the churches that made this decision had already received these writings, had made a habit of reading them, had discovered in them the authority they acknowledged in the decision to canonize them. The church did not so much create Scripture as acknowledge it as the texts within which the Spirit moved to give life and to guide.

If we would look to the Spirit to sustain and renew the church, then we

---

3. David Kelsey, *The Uses of Scripture in Recent Theology* (Philadelphia: Fortress, 1975), pp. 89-119. Of course, as Kelsey also makes plain, to say that Scripture ought to be used "somehow" does not say precisely how it should be used to shape the church's faith and life. The agreement *that* Scripture has authority does not entail agreement about *how* Scripture should function as authoritative.

must look to Scripture. It is not that we can tie down the free Spirit of God; it is, rather, that we can trust the Spirit to be true to itself and can "test the spirits" (1 John 4:1) against the paths along which the Spirit moved in the prophets and apostles. It is as Calvin said: "[Christians] know no other Spirit than him who dwelt and spoke in the apostles."[4] And we know no other Jesus than the one of whom the apostles taught.

Scripture remains the church's best resource for the constant renewal of its life. It is finally in that book, in Scripture, not in this book (or in any other book on Christian ethics), that the church may find both wisdom and virtue for hard choices.

Ethics "by Way of Reminder"

Paul commended the Roman churches as "full of goodness, filled with all knowledge, and able to instruct one another" (Rom. 15:14). His confidence in the churches, however, did not prevent him from writing them a letter, "boldly" addressing them "on some points" (15:15) and about some choices. His commendation of the churches was not complacency, and his confidence in the churches only reflected his greater confidence, his faith, in the gospel of God. So, he wrote "boldly" and "by way of reminder" (15:15) to the very congregations he praised, reminding them of "the gospel of God" (1:1) in order to bring about "the obedience of faith" (1:5; 16:26).

A Christian ethics that aims to be a practical discipline will nurture the renewal and reform of the moral discourse and discernment of the churches. It may undertake that task not presumptuously but "boldly" when, like Paul, it proceeds "by way of reminder." Christian ethics "by way of reminder" will always be an evangelical discipline,[5] remembering and telling "the gospel of God." If it fails to be an evangelical discipline, then it fails to be *Christian* ethics and fails to nurture "the obedience of *faith*." And if it fails to be a practical discipline, then it fails to be Christian *ethics* and to nurture "the *obedience* of faith."

This book understands its task as both evangelical and practical. It will not

---

4. John Calvin, *Institutes of the Christian Religion*, I.ix.3, ed. J. T. McNeill, trans. Ford Lewis Battles (Philadelphia: Westminster, 1960), p. 96. See also *Institutes of the Christian Religion*, p. 95: "By a kind of mutual bond the Lord has joined together the certainty of his Word and of his Spirit . . . that we may in turn embrace the Spirit with no fear of being deceived when we recognize him in his own image, namely, in the Word."

5. No one has made this point quite so elegantly and forcefully as Oliver O'Donovan, *Resurrection and the Moral Order: An Outline for Evangelical Ethics* (Grand Rapids: Eerdmans, 1986), pp. 11-27.

begin with the choices we confront, although it will surely circle back to some of them. It will not pretend to have the last word about a thousand and one choices. It hopes, however, to speak both boldly and gladly by proceeding "by way of reminder." A Christian ethic that proceeds "by way of reminder" will read Scripture, the "collective scribal memory"[6] of the churches. By reading Scripture churches are reminded of "the gospel of God" and of Jesus of Nazareth at the center of it. A Christian ethic that proceeds "by way of reminder" will remember Jesus.

Some of my students wear bracelets bearing the legend "WWJD?" The idea for the bracelets originated some years ago in a youth group in Holland, Michigan, where I live; perhaps inspired by the line "What would Jesus do?" in Charles Sheldon's *In His Steps,* the teens suggested that the group's members should make and wear bracelets bearing the WWJD legend. The bracelets, of course, became remarkably popular, and "WWJD" moved from bracelets to T-shirts and bumper stickers. There are reasons, I suppose, to be suspicious of a piety that can be worn on someone's sleeve — or on someone's arm. There are reasons to be suspicious of the moral sentiments that one can find on the bumpers of cars. Even so, when young people choose to identify themselves — and to remind themselves of their identity — in this way, there are also reasons to celebrate their choice of accessories.

The question itself, of course, is hardly a new one: "What would Jesus do?" And there are reasons to be suspicious of the question, too. It is sometimes asked with the anachronistic pretence that we can (or should) do precisely what a first-century Jew would do. And it is sometimes asked with the sort of naiveté that prompted Norman Maxwell, the newspaper editor in *In His Steps,* to reject a story on a boxing match and to discontinue a Sunday edition.[7] Even so, it is an important question, a question that can hardly be avoided if the Christian life is to be regarded as a life of discipleship.

Sometimes in the midst of a class discussion about some hard case I have playfully turned to a student sporting such a bracelet to ask, "WWWJD?" or "Well, what *would* Jesus do?" The replies have ranged from embarrassed silence and empty platitudes to wonderfully astute observations. Frequently prefaced by some disclaimer like "I don't know exactly, but . . . ," the astute observations proceed "by way of reminder," calling upon the church's memory of Jesus in Scripture, invoking some story or saying of Jesus, and exercising what William Spohn calls "the analogical imagination."[8]

6. Yoder, *The Priestly Kingdom,* p. 31.

7. See Charles M. Sheldon, *In His Steps* (Nashville: Broadman, 1935), pp. 20-26, 30-34.

8. William C. Spohn, *Go and Do Likewise: Jesus and Ethics* (New York: Continuum, 1999).

Sometimes the little classroom conversation about "WWJD?" leads to another question, "How do we go about figuring out WJWD?" Students have reported that they try to figure out what Jesus would do by reading the Bible, by praying, by talking with Christians whom they trust and respect, or by consulting consciences and intuitions formed within Christian community. There seems to be no recipe, nor is there any substitute for the hard work of moral deliberation. Even so, it seems to me that these students have hold of something important — and important not only to them but to the church's effort to live in the glad obedience of faith. They understand that the Christian life is a life of discipleship. They understand that the test for conduct and character in Christian community is the church's memory of Jesus. They understand that to follow Jesus one has to remember him. And they understand that remembering Jesus requires participation in — and formation by — practices of the church, like reading Scripture, prayer, and moral discourse.

This book shares the affirmations of my students. It proceeds in subsequent parts "by way of reminder." By remembering Jesus — and by remembering the early churches remembering Jesus — it will seek to contribute to the efforts of Christian congregations to discern the shape and style of lives "worthy of the gospel" (Phil. 1:27) and "in memory of Jesus" (cf. 1 Cor. 11:24-25). It will ask what it means to live the story of Jesus that Christians still love to tell. It will speak gladly and boldly of Christian integrity in the strange worlds of our sickness (Part Two), our sexuality (Part Three), our economy (Part Four), and our politics (Part Five).

The remaining chapters of this first part will look more carefully at those churches that Paul commended as "full of goodness, filled with all knowledge, and able to instruct one another." It will find in them a tradition and a vocation for contemporary communities of faith — to be communities of moral discourse, deliberation, and discernment by being communities of memory. And it will consider more carefully how the practice of reading Scripture in Christian community is a resource for that vocation.

CHAPTER ONE

"Able to Instruct One Another": The Early Church as a Community of Moral Discourse

I myself feel confident about you, my brothers and sisters, that you yourselves are full of goodness, filled with all knowledge, and able to instruct one another.

ROMANS 15:14

It was no small compliment that Paul paid to the churches in Rome. The commendation was, to be sure, also subtly a commandment. When my mother used to say, "I am confident, Allen, that you are a well-behaved young man," I knew I had been not only praised but alerted to certain expectations and obligations. The Roman churches doubtless heard these words not only as praise but also as a vocation. Paul had, in fact, just urged them not to be conformed to the present evil age but to be transformed by the renewal of their mind[1] so that they could discern the will of God (Rom. 12:1-2). Still, it was a remarkable commendation of the Roman churches.

It was not just the Roman churches, however, that were commended as "able to instruct one another" — or called to the task of communal discernment. That commendation and calling were implicit in Paul's correspondence with all the churches. Although Paul could write with apostolic authority (e.g.,

---

1. Although the NRSV translates it as a plural, "the renewing of your minds," the word is singular. It is a communal "mind" that is to be renewed.

1 Cor. 5:3-5), he seldom did. He rather "appealed" to the communal judgment of his readers (e.g., 1 Cor. 10:15; Philem. 8, 9). He used the language of polite request rather than the language of command, and he thus conveyed to the churches a sense of their ability and responsibility to be communities of moral discourse and discernment. Paul respected and nurtured the churches as communal contexts for moral deliberation and judgment.

Moreover, this expectation that the churches could and would practice mutual admonition was not unique to Paul. The author of Hebrews, for example, exhorted his (or her)[2] readers to "exhort one another" (Heb. 3:13). The *Didache,* a second-century manual for the churches, encouraged participation in the practice of mutual admonition:

> Every day you should seek the company of saints to enjoy their refreshing conversation. You must not start a schism, but reconcile those at strife. "Your judgments must be fair." You must not play favorites when reproving transgressions. You must not be of two minds about your decision. (4.2-4)[3]

And the *Epistle of Barnabas,* another second-century text, urged its readers to "be good lawgivers to each other, remain faithful counselors to each other" (21:4).[4] Indeed, Celsus, the learned opponent of the early Christian movement, evidently complaining about this practice of mutual admonition, poked fun at Christian communities that treated "stupid and uneducated yokels" as though they could learn and teach moral philosophy. When Origen wrote his massive reply to the charges of Celsus, the Christian philosopher and theologian from Alexandria accepted this particular charge — and delighted in it![5]

The Early Church as a Community of Moral Discourse

The early churches were communities of moral discourse.[6] They talked together about what they should do or leave undone. When Christians met to-

2. Adolf von Harnack, "Probabilia über die Addresse und den Verfasser des Hebräerbriefs," *Zeitschrift für die Neutestamentliche Wissenschaft* 1 (1900): 16-41, argued that the most likely author was Priscilla.

3. Translated by Cyril C. Richardson in *Early Christian Fathers,* ed. Cyril C. Richardson (Philadelphia: Westminster, 1953).

4. Translated by Kirsopp Lake, in *The Apostolic Fathers,* ed. Kirsopp Lake (Cambridge, Mass.: Harvard University Press, 1952).

5. Origen, *Contra Celsum,* 6.1-2. See further Wayne A. Meeks, *The Origins of Christian Morality: The First Two Centuries* (New Haven: Yale University Press), pp. 102-3.

6. Concerning the church as a community of moral discourse, see especially the

gether in Rome — or in Corinth or Antioch or Jerusalem or elsewhere — they talked about the choices they faced. They asked each other — and instructed each other — about their personal and communal responsibilities.

Their questions about personal responsibilities are frequently right on the surface of New Testament texts. They asked, for example, "What should I do about meat once offered to idols now offered to me?" (cf. 1 Cor. 8:1), "What should I do about sexual intercourse now that Christ has been raised and the ages have turned?" (cf. 1 Cor. 7:1), "What should I do about a runaway slave?" (cf. Philem. 8-20). It takes only a little imagination to penetrate the surface of such texts to the community's conversation about personal responsibilities. Questions about communal responsibilities are also there. They asked, for example, "What should *we* do about ordering our communities now that Gentiles are joining?" (cf. Acts 15:5, 6), "How should *we* conduct ourselves during worship?" (cf. 1 Cor. 14:26), "What should *we* do about our relations with other communities — with the Roman Empire" (cf. Rom. 13:1), or "with the poor in Jerusalem?" (cf. 1 Cor. 16:1). And beneath these questions, too, were the conversations of the churches.

They were — and were to be — communities of moral discourse, "able to instruct one another," but it was not easy. Their vocation led them along a narrow path with temptations on either side. When personal choices had to be made, there was a temptation on the one side to deny or neglect the individual's responsibility, to surrender it to the group. The same Paul, however, who commended the Roman church as a community of moral discourse also insisted that "all be fully convinced in their own minds" (Rom. 14:5) and observed that "each of us will be accountable to God" (Rom. 14:12). A community of moral discourse was not a substitute for *personal* responsibility; instead, the community nurtured and respected the freedom and responsibility of each member.

There was, however, also a temptation on the other side, to treat personal

---

work of James Gustafson: "The Church: A Community of Moral Discourse" and "Two Requisites for the American Church: Moral Discourse and Institutional Power," in *The Church as Moral Decision Maker* (Philadelphia: Pilgrim, 1970), pp. 83-95 and 151-63; and *Treasure in Earthen Vessels* (New York: Harper & Brothers, 1961). On the ecclesial context for Christian ethics see especially Thomas Ogletree, "The Ecclesial Context of Christian Ethics," *The Annual of the Society of Christian Ethics, 1984,* ed. Larry Rasmussen, pp. 1-17; James B. Nelson, *Moral Nexus: Ethics of Christian Identity and Community* (Philadelphia: Westminster, 1971); Stanley Hauerwas, *The Peaceable Kingdom: A Primer in Christian Ethics* (Notre Dame: University of Notre Dame Press, 1983), pp. 96-115; John Howard Yoder, *The Priestly Kingdom* (Notre Dame: University of Notre Dame Press, 1984), pp. 15-45; and Bruce C. Birch and Larry Rasmussen, *Bible and Ethics in the Christian Life,* revised edition (Minneapolis: Augsburg, 1989), pp. 17-34, 120-40.

choices as simply "private" matters, as no one else's business, as properly settled by the tastes and preferences of the free person, and therefore as outside the appropriate range of the community's discourse and mutual instruction. Personal choices remained personal, and individual responsibility was not surrendered to the group, but personal choices were made and individual responsibility was exercised *within* the community, not secretly and privately. The advice of Paul to the owner of Onesimus concerning what he should do about his runaway slave, for example, dealt with what was clearly (in the first century, at any rate) a very personal responsibility. The little letter we call Paul's Letter to Philemon, however, was not a private letter;[7] it was addressed to the church (v. 2). The personal choice concerning Onesimus was open to the review of the whole church — a church, it should be noted, which surely included other slaves. The personal decision was not private. Church members were "able to instruct one another" because personal responsibility was not denied but exercised within community.

When they faced decisions about the life of the community, there was a temptation on the one side to deny the community's responsibility for such decisions, to surrender it to a charismatic leader or to an ecclesiastical official. There must be leadership in any community, of course, and there was leadership in the early church. If the leaders circumvented or disregarded the moral discourse and mutual instruction of the Christian community, however, they subverted the community's vocation as a community "able to instruct one another." And if a church surrendered its responsibility to its leaders, it failed to honor its calling. Even while urging the Thessalonian church to "respect" its leaders and not to "despise the words of prophets," Paul insisted that the people "test everything" (1 Thess. 5:12, 20, 21).

When the church faced decisions about the life of the community, there was a temptation on the other side, too. The church might surrender such choices not to a leader within the community but to some other and larger community. The church might regard such decisions as properly settled simply by the application of the generally accredited political wisdom of some broader community, some larger "public" — the conventional wisdom of life in the Greek city, the moral tradition of the *polis,* for example, or the generally accepted rules for life in the household. Or the church might regard such decisions as escaping the realm of morality altogether, as governed simply by the group's interest in survival, as in a moral contest for power neither fit for nor subject to a community's moral discourse. Whether communal decisions were

---

7. See the illuminating study by Theo Preiss, "Life in Christ and Social Ethics in the Epistle to Philemon," in *Life in Christ* (London: SCM Press, 1957), pp. 32-42.

surrendered to another community or to a power struggle, the vocation of the church to be a community of moral discourse would be undercut, for there would be no call for a conversation about the identity and integrity of the particular community whose decision it was. The received political wisdom did function within the Christian communities, of course, but their communal decisions were not to be made on the basis of some other community's self-understanding. Their communal decisions were to be made in the name of the Lord whose people they were. They were "able to instruct one another" because communal responsibility was neither surrendered to the leadership nor given up to a different community.

The Early Church as a Community of Moral Deliberation

The early churches were communities of moral discourse by being communities of moral deliberation. It was also as communities of moral deliberation that they were commended as "able to instruct one another." They talked together not only about *what* they ought to do but also about *why* they ought to do it. They asked *why* they ought to do one thing rather than another or something rather than nothing. The concrete advice of moral discourse led inevitably in these communities to the giving and hearing of reasons. Their moral discourse was not simply the exercise of rhetorical or social power; it involved deliberation, reason giving, and reason hearing. Paul himself addressed the Corinthians as capable of deliberation, as "sensible," and invited them to "judge for yourselves what I say" (1 Cor. 10:15).

It was as communities of moral deliberation that they found their way through the thicket of temptations that threatened their vocation to be "able to instruct one another." By their practice of giving and hearing reasons, they were able to honor personal responsibility without surrendering it to the group and to protect communal responsibility without surrendering it to the leadership. By their readiness to give reasons and to hear reasons they could resist the reduction of personal responsibility to secret and private preferences and the reduction of communal responsibility to the public standards of other communities. By giving reasons and hearing reasons concerning personal and communal choices, the churches could protect the *unity* of human life when a cleavage into a secret private life and an anonymous public life threatened to break it.

To be sure, a charismatic prophet in the community sometimes provided the answer to the question of what a person or the community should do. Such prophets evidently had the gift of knowing and making known in plain, intelligible speech the will of God for some concrete problem that the community or

18

its members faced. Even so, the prophetic word had to be tested by the whole community in the light of the Christian tradition and confession (see, for example, 1 Thess. 5:20-21; 1 John 4:1-2). And that testing involved the church as a community of moral deliberation, giving and hearing reasons.

To be sure, the official leadership of the community also sometimes provided the answer to the question concerning what a person or the community should do. But just as the charismatic advice required testing and deliberation, so did an official's pronouncements. There was no one in the community authorized to say, "Do as I say because I say it." Paul himself seldom invoked his own apostolic authority to put an end to the discourse of the churches; he rather "appealed" to his readers and to their deliberative judgment. He respected and honored the churches he addressed as communities of moral deliberation, as communities where reasons were given and heard, as communities where each was supposed to respect the other as a giver and hearer of reasons. Without that regard for one another the churches could not be communities of moral deliberation, and they would not be "able to instruct one another."

Sometimes the reasons given were simply the moral commonplaces of a Jewish or Hellenistic culture, of the synagogue or the *polis* or the household. Sometimes the reasons involved an appeal to the Law or the prophets or the writings, to the Scripture of the synagogue and the early church. Sometimes the reasons were simply what nature teaches (1 Cor. 11:14-15) or what convention requires (1 Cor. 11:16; 14:33b). There was no wooden scheme for deliberation, no simple checklist for determining what should be done and what left undone, no fixed set of first principles to be applied deductively to questions of conduct. Reasons were given and heard in the community, but even the reasons had finally to be tested in the community — and defended or discarded or qualified by their coherence with the gospel. Exhortation was always "in Christ" (Phil. 2:1), "in the Lord Jesus" (1 Thess. 4:1), "by the meekness and gentleness of Christ" (2 Cor. 10:1), "by the mercies of God" (Rom. 12:1). This was more than pious rhetoric. Discourse and deliberation took place in this community in the service of the people's communal attempt to discern the shape and style of a life "worthy of the gospel of Christ" (Phil. 1:27). Every judgment and every reason was to be tested and qualified by the truth that was the possession not of the church but of its Lord. The church, like Paul, was to "take every thought captive to obey Christ" (2 Cor. 10:5).

As moral discourse prompted moral deliberation (for conversation about choices led inevitably to the giving and hearing of reasons), so moral deliberation in these communities required moral discernment, for the reasons themselves had to be tested by "the gospel of Christ." The churches not only asked what they should do (discourse) and why they should do it (deliberation) but also whether their choices and the reasons for them "fit" the gospel (discernment). It was also as communities of moral discernment that they were commended as "able to instruct one another."

The Early Church as a Community of Moral Discernment[8]

There is no theory of discernment in the New Testament, and surely no recipe for it. Nevertheless, it is clear in the New Testament that discernment is neither simply a spontaneous intuition nor simply a deductive application of either philosophical principles or the prescriptions and prohibitions of Torah. Discernment, or the perception of what is fitting, is a complex human enterprise, involving different elements in different people in different communities in different proportions. Moral discernment in the community of Matthew, for example, almost certainly gave greater place and priority to the interpretation and application of the Law of Moses than moral discernment in the community of Mark. And different people in any one community — the Roman churches, for example — had different strengths and weaknesses in discernment, different gifts and blind spots for the perception of what was fitting. Some were gifted with moral sensitivity; some, with intellectual clarity; some, with passion; some, with reason; but each, with his own experience. Some were blinded by fear; some were blinded by duty; but the perception of each was abridged by investments in his culture or class. As a community of moral discernment the church could capitalize on this variety of individual strengths and gifts and compensate for individual weaknesses and blind spots.

But more than that can and must be said, for communal discernment in the church was not just sharing the little moral wisdom each knew well and compensating for the abridgements (major or minor) of each one's moral vision. Communal discernment, or the perception of what is fitting, in the church was always to be the discernment of what is fitting to, or worthy of, *the gospel*. It was the gospel that made them a community, and it was the gospel, the "mercies of God," which called them to a discernment not conformed to this age, but transformed by the renewal of their mind (Rom. 12:1-2).

8. On discernment see James Gustafson, "Moral Discernment in the Christian Life," in *Norm and Context in Christian Life*, ed. Gene H. Outka and Paul Ramsey (New York: Charles Scribner's Sons, 1968), pp. 17-36; also Gustafson, *Ethics from a Theocentric Perspective*, vol. II: *Ethics and Theology* (Chicago: University of Chicago Press, 1984), pp. 302-19. On Paul's "new discernment," see Allen Verhey, *The Great Reversal: Ethics and the New Testament* (Grand Rapids: Eerdmans, 1984), pp. 106-13.

There were other assemblies and associations in the first century, of course, where there was moral discourse and deliberation, where there was talk together about what should be done and why. There were Jewish sects and Greek philosophical schools. There were synagogues and initiatory cults. There were voluntary associations or clubs. A first-century observer of a Christian community might easily have mistaken it initially for one or another of these associations.[9] But the church was *not* one or another of these associations. The church was a new and distinctive community by its members' common conviction that Jesus of Nazareth was the Christ, the anointed one of God, that he had made the Father known and disclosed the intentions of God with and for the world, that he had made humanity known and disclosed what human life could and should be like. The communal discernment of the church was a new and distinctive discernment because it finally transfigured questions of conduct and character into questions of the deeds and dispositions fitting to that gospel. As a community of moral discernment each church tested all the reasons given in deliberation (including the appeals to Scripture!) against the story of Jesus of Nazareth. Its members transformed the question of what they should do into the question of how they might live the story they loved to tell.

And they did love to tell the story. They were a community of memory,[10] and it was always *as* a community of memory that they were *also* a community of moral discourse, deliberation, and discernment.

The Early Church as a Community of Memory

The early churches were communities of memory. Nowhere does the New Testament pause to reflect on the nature of memory or its function in community. There is no more a theoretical account of memory than there is of discernment. There is nothing to compare, for example, with Aristotle's ancient account of

9. See the masterful work of Wayne A. Meeks, *The Moral World of the First Christians* (Philadelphia: Westminster, 1986), pp. 97-123.

10. On the church as a community of memory see especially Gustafson, *Treasure in Earthen Vessels*, pp. 71-85, and Stanley Hauerwas, "The Moral Authority of Scripture: The Politics and Ethics of Remembering," in *A Community of Character* (Notre Dame: University of Notre Dame Press, 1981), pp. 53-71. On memory in the New Testament see especially Nils A. Dahl, "Anamnesis: Memory and Commemoration in Early Christianity," in *Jesus in the Memory of the Early Church* (Minneapolis: Augsburg, 1976), pp. 11-29 (also pp. 167-75); Luke T. Johnson, *The Writings of the New Testament* (Philadelphia: Fortress, 1986), pp. 114-41; Verhey, *The Great Reversal*, pp. 34-61; and Richard J. Ginn, *The Present and the Past: A Study of Anamnesis* (Allison Park, Penn.: Pickwick Publications, 1989).

memory in *De Memoria*. But everywhere in the New Testament there is remembering.

The gospels, for example, obviously proceed by way of remembrance.[11] They give literary expression to the oral tradition in which the church's memory of the words and deeds of Jesus was handed down. Hardly simply retrospective historical accounts, they nevertheless situated the lives of their readers in relation to the living Christ, the *present* Christ, by way of reminding them of Jesus.[12] By remembering Jesus, they oriented their readers to a future in which the sovereignty of God and of this Christ would be unchallenged. They nurtured and sustained communities of discernment by nurturing and sustaining the memory of the community. It is surely no literary accident that in Luke's Gospel the disciples at the empty tomb are instructed to "remember" (Luke 24:6, 8) or that in John's Gospel it is said that the Paraclete, the promised Holy Spirit, will "bring to your remembrance all that I have said to you" (John 14:26 RSV; cf. John 2:22; 12:16; 16:4). Each gospel is a "remembrance," a literary commemoration of the crucified and risen Lord, forming character and shaping conduct into something worthy of the gospel.

In the epistles, too, there is remembering. Paul explicitly says that he writes to the Romans "by way of reminder" (Rom. 15:15; cf. also 2 Peter 3:1). The epistles bear the tradition of the churches, and they ask their readers to remember it (1 Cor. 15:1; even the epistles to the seven churches of Asia Minor within Revelation, Rev. 3:3). From 1 Thessalonians (e.g., 4:2),[13] which was very likely the first letter, to the later epistles (e.g., 2 Tim. 2:8, 14; 2 Peter 1:12, 13; 3:1-2; Jude 5), discourse, deliberation, and discernment are evoked and sustained by the memory of Jesus. "Remember Jesus Christ, raised from the dead, a descendant of David — that is my gospel" (2 Tim. 2:8) was not a call to preserve, like an archivist, some historical data; it was a call to preserve Christian identity and community and to sustain a common life worthy of the gospel.

---

11. Justin Martyr in his *Dialogue with Trypho* regularly referred to the gospel material as "memoirs of the apostles" (sections 12, 18, 32, 49, 76, 78, 103, 112, 125, 133). One may object against the denotation of an ancient literary form which contained episodes from the lives of famous men and against the connotation of a retrospective historical account, but one must appreciate the continuity of the gospels with the churches' memory of Jesus (cf. also Papias in Eusebius, *Ecclesiastical History*, 3.39, and, of course, Luke 1:1-4).

12. The "remembered" Jesus is thus not to be identified with "the historical Jesus" sought by the Jesus Seminar. The "remembered" Jesus is not simply a figure out of the past whose life ended with his death but the risen Lord.

13. On the place of the tradition in 1 Thessalonians see Meeks, *The Moral World of the First Christians*, pp. 125-30.

The epistles frequently remind their readers of the worship of the community, and it is little wonder, for worship itself was remembrance. Hymns of the early church, themselves forms of remembrance and celebration, were remembered (e.g., Phil. 2:6-11; Col. 1:15-20) and used to nurture discernment of a way of life fitting to the convictions the church expressed in worship. Readers of the epistles were frequently reminded of baptism (e.g., Rom. 6:1-11; 1 Cor. 1:12-16; 12:13; Gal. 3:27-28; 1 Peter 3:21-22). Baptism in the name of Jesus and "into his death" was itself a remembrance — and not merely as a historical recollection — of the death and resurrection of Christ. Baptism established identity, initiated one into a community of common memory, and required fitting conduct. The Lord's Supper, too, was remembered, and the explicit instruction was that it be done "in remembrance" (Gk. *anamnēsis*) of Jesus the Christ (1 Cor. 11:24, 25; Luke 22:19). Again it will not do to construe this remembrance as merely historical recollection, as the preservation of historical data. In remembering that past, they owned the story of the suffering and death of a risen Lord as their own story. The Lord's Supper involved a "pleading guilty" to the death of Jesus, to be sure, but it was also a sharing, "a participation" (1 Cor. 10:16 RSV; Gk. *koinōnia*) in the body of Christ. The memory of Jesus was constitutive of identity and community and decisive for discernment and deliberation. When the rich humiliated the poor, as they did in Corinth (1 Cor. 11:22), when community was broken, as it was in Corinth, then "it is not the Lord's supper that you eat" (1 Cor. 11:20 RSV), then the church eats the bread and drinks the cup "in an unworthy manner" (11:27), then the meal is not truly "remembrance."

There may be no theory of memory, then, but there surely is remembering. Memory is crucial, and this much else is clear: in the New Testament and the churches it addresses memory cannot be defined as "the preservation of perception"[14] or "the permanence of an image regarded as a copy of the thing it images."[15] Such definitions fail to do justice to what we have seen. In the New Testament memory is not simply a mental process of recollection, not just disinterested remembrance of objective historical data; memory is to own a particular history as one's own, to own a past and to own it as constitutive of identity and determinative for discernment. In the New Testament and in the church there is no identity apart from memory, and no community apart from common memory.

14. Plato, *Philebus*, 34a, trans. Harold N. Fowler, in *Plato*, vol. 3, Loeb Classical Library (Cambridge, Mass.: Harvard University Press, 1952), p. 281.

15. Aristotle, *De Memoria*, 451a, in *Aristotle: De Sensu and De Memoria*, trans. G. R. T. Ross (Cambridge: Cambridge University Press, 1906), p. 107.

This usage of remembrance was hardly remarkable. Ordinary Greek was quite capable of analogous usage; the Greek term *anamnēsis* (*an-amnēsis;* Luke 22:19; 1 Cor. 11:24, 25) captures quite nicely the fact that memory is the antidote for amnesia and its attendant loss of identity. The New Testament and its churches, however, are especially indebted to the Hebrew Scriptures and to Jewish communities of faith for this usage of remembrance. The Hebrew Scriptures, too, are full of remembrance (Hb. *zākhar; zikkārôn*) and construe it as that which constitutes identity and determines dispositions and deeds. Again and again and yet again in the Old Testament God says to the people of Israel, "Remember." "Remember that you were a slave in the land of Egypt" (Deut. 5:15). "Remember the wonderful works [the LORD] has done" (Ps. 105:5). "Remember the days of old" (Deut. 32:7). "Remember. . . ." The greatest danger to the Israelites' identity was forgetfulness, and the remedy for forgetfulness was usually a wonderful and lively story. "Take care that you do not forget" (Deut. 8:11) was a summons to remember the stories your father and mother had told you about God and God's works of power and grace. "Remember the LORD your God" (Deut. 8:18) was an invitation to tell those stories to your children and to your children's children. "We were slaves in Egypt and God rescued us from oppression by his powerful hand. Then in the wilderness we wandered and we wondered, hungry, thirsty, and anxious, and God gave us manna, enough for each, for none too much, for none too little." Story after story was told generation after generation. Sometimes the people very nearly forgot the stories — or forgot to tell them — and they very nearly lost their memory and their identity. But the remedy for forgetfulness was always to tell the old, old story — and a new generation would remember and own the story as their story and God as their God.[16]

The art of remembering always involved storytelling — and it always had the shape of obedience. To remember the Lord, to own the stories of God's glory, of God's works of power and grace, always meant in Israel to discern God's will and to do it. To remember God's rescue from Pharaoh's oppression took shape in obedience to a commandment not to oppress a hired hand or to cheat him out of a living (Lev. 19:13). To remember God's gift of manna, enough for all to share, took shape in not piling up lands upon lands or riches upon riches and in leaving the edges of the field unharvested for the poor (Lev. 19:9-10). To remember the stories took shape in Jubilee dispositions to restore

---

16. Notice, for example, in Deuteronomy 5:3 that to remember the covenant was to own it, to be identified by it, to have life shaped by it: "Not with our ancestors did the LORD make this covenant, but with us, who are all of us here alive today." Thanks to my colleague Barry Bandstra for calling attention to this passage.

the slave to freedom, to share the land, to do justice, and to love kindness (Lev. 25). To remember the stories was to let them form and inform discernment. To remember the stories was to live them, not just to recall them.[17]

As it was with Israel, so it was with the church. It learned from the Hebrew Scriptures no theory of memory, but it learned to remember. Forgetfulness was still the greatest danger. The art of remembering still involved storytelling, and remembering still took the shape of discerning and doing the will of God. The people were a community of discernment because they were a community of memory. They were "able to instruct one another" because they could remind one another of the story.

---

17. The remembered story provided the context for the legal traditions of Israel. The story provides, of course, the literary context. The story of Sinai is part of the larger story that moves from Abraham to slavery in Egypt to the exodus to the entry into the Promised Land. The story of Sinai comes after the exodus and before the entry into the Promised Land, and it is the story of Sinai in which the collections of laws are gathered. The story of Sinai stretches from Exodus 19:1 to Numbers 10:10. In that context diverse collections of laws are gathered. The story, moreover, provides the covenantal context for the legal stipulations. The suzerainty treaties of the ancient Near East began with the identification of the great king and a recital of the past history of the relationship of that king and his vassals, before they recounted the stipulations concerning loyalty to the suzerain and living peaceably with other vassals. And the covenantal literature of Israel follows the same pattern — as, for example, in the preface to the Decalogue, "I am the LORD your God, who brought you out of the land of Egypt, out of the house of slavery . . ." (Exod. 20:2). The story, finally, provided the context for discernment in revising the laws of Israel. The Israelites could not simply create social legislation *ex nihilo*. Like us, they received traditions, but they set the received traditions in the context of the story, and the story nudged the legal traditions in the direction of something closer to what was fitting to the story. Perhaps the best illustration of this process is the variety of legal traditions concerning slavery. In the oldest biblical code, the Covenant Code of Exodus 20:22–23:33, the received tradition may be presumed to be something like the Code of Hammurabi, but Israel's code, under the pressure of the story, is somewhat more generous with slaves (Exod. 21:2-6). A later code, the Deuteronomic Code of Deuteronomy 4:44–28:44, revisits the received tradition, revising it into an instrument of reform. The law for the release of slaves in Deuteronomy 15:12-18 revisits the law of Exodus 21:2-6 and revises it. It includes now an explicit reminder of the story: "Remember that you were a slave in the land of Egypt" (15:15). It is made more generous: "you shall not send him out empty-handed" (15:13). And it is expanded to include female slaves as well as male slaves (15:12, 17). And in the still later legal tradition, the Holiness Code of Leviticus 17–26, the law concerning slavery is revised again, made more fitting to the story, forbidding making a fellow Israelite a slave (25:39): "For they are my servants, whom I brought out of the land of Egypt; they shall not be sold as slaves are sold" (25:42). The laws are not given or received as a timeless code; they are open to reform and revision until the story is lived as well as told.

There were a variety of contexts, of course, within which the church was a community of memory. It is not my claim that the church was *only* a community of moral discourse; the church had other functions and intentions when it gathered in memory of Jesus. However, it *is* my claim that the community gathered in memory of Jesus, whatever else it was, was *also* a community of moral discourse, deliberation, and discernment. And it *is* my claim that whatever else the church was nurtured and sustained its identity and vocation as a community "able to instruct one another" in the name of Jesus.

It was a community of memory, for example, in the task of evangelism. But to announce that this Jesus is Lord and to invite others to share in that profession was always also to summon them to a revising of the whole of life with Christ at the right hand of God, to invite them to join in the communal task of discerning the shape and style of life befitting his lordship.[18]

It was a community of memory also, of course, in its services of worship. In preaching and prayer and hymn and sacrament the people remembered Jesus and owned his story as their story, his life as their life, the "mind of Christ" as their mind (cf. Phil. 2:5, with reference to the hymn that follows). In worship they owned an identity and a vision which evoked and sustained communal discernment of the deeds and dispositions which belonged to a life of service, a life of praise.[19]

In whatever way it remembered Jesus, the community also always bore a moral tradition that was never quite reducible to applying a code or trusting an intuition but always called forth discernment. In whatever way it remembered Jesus, the community formed character, nurtured certain dispositions, directed certain intentions, renewed minds and a common mind, and equipped a community for the vocation of being "able to instruct one another."

The Lord's Supper is a case in point. It was done "in remembrance" of Jesus (Gk. *anamnēsis*). Paul reminds the Corinthians of the story he had told them before, "that the Lord Jesus on the night when he was betrayed took a loaf of bread, and when he had given thanks, he broke it and said, 'This is my body that is [broken] for you. Do this in remembrance of me'" (1 Cor. 11:23-24). That story — and the Sacrament — was a remedy for forgetfulness. To tell it, to

18. On the connection of evangelism and Christian ethics see Richard Mouw, *Political Evangelism* (Grand Rapids: Eerdmans, 1973).

19. On the connection of worship and Christian ethics see James M. Gustafson, "Spiritual Life and Moral Life," in *Theology and Christian Ethics* (Philadelphia: Pilgrim, 1974), pp. 161-76; see also William H. Willimon, *The Service of God: Christian Work and Worship* (Nashville: Abingdon, 1983). On worship as a context for early Christian moral discernment and literary activity see C. F. D. Moule, *The Birth of the New Testament* (New York: Harper & Row, 1962), pp. 210-14.

hear it, to own it as their story, had the shape of obedience. So they gathered obediently around the table — and remembered. They took bread — and remembered. They drank the cup — and remembered. Around the table Jesus prepared for them, they remembered Jesus. And because remembering involved storytelling, they told the stories of Jesus.

There were the stories of his *birth*. He did not count equality with God a thing to be grasped. He emptied himself and took the form of a servant. He was content to be subject to his parents, the child of a poor man's home. They remembered Jesus, and the memory formed discernment in them and in the mind of Christ, formed their character and conduct into something *fitting* such stories, filled them with knowledge and goodness.

There were the stories of his *ministry*. He walked among us, mighty in deed, healing the sick and the disordered, using for others the powers he would not use for himself. He walked among us, mighty in word, speaking with authority, announcing the good future of God, the coming cosmic sovereignty of God. He walked among us, making that good future present in his words and in his deeds. He exalted the humble, and humbled the exalted. He ate with sinners, fellowshipped with outcasts, was friend to the despised. He was master and Lord of his disciples, and yet he walked among them as a friend and as one who served. They remembered Jesus, and the memory provided a vision of what the world was and would be by God's power. They remembered Jesus, and the memory formed dispositions and deeds that "fit" such stories. They remembered Jesus, and they were filled with knowledge and goodness.

There were the stories of his *faith*. He observed good customs, and it was his habit to go to synagogue on the Sabbath. But he defied conventions that did not serve the cause of God. He plucked grain and healed the sick on the Sabbath. He made fun of the careful observance of rules while justice, charity, and purity went ignored. He prayed for his disciples — and for his enemies. He remembered to give thanks even as they broke the bread that was his body. They remembered Jesus — and the memory filled them with knowledge and goodness, transformed them by the renewal of their mind so that they could instruct one another.

There were the stories of his *death*. He suffered for the sake of God's cause in the world. He suffered for the sake of his own integrity. He suffered for the sake of humanity. He made the human cry of lament his own cry. And when he suffered, he did not threaten. When he was reviled, he did not return the insults. He knew the dark caves of loneliness in which people have cried out in anguish; he was there. He knew the oppression of the powerful and the power of oppression; he felt them. They remembered Jesus — and they owned his death as their own; they learned whose world it was and whose world it would be. They remembered Jesus — and they learned the meaning (and the cost) of love (1 John 3:16). They remembered Jesus — and they learned who they were and were called to be as a community. Because they were a community of memory, they were — and were to be — a community of patient love. And because they were a community of patient love, they were — and were to be — a community of discernment (Phil. 1:9-10), "able to instruct one another."

There were the stories of his *resurrection*. When the powers of sin and death had done their damnedest, God raised this Jesus up. The humble one was exalted; the humiliated one raised up. The powers which had put him down were themselves led away captive. He was raised, and the disciples were glad. He was raised, and the ages had turned. He was raised, the first fruits of the dead, and the Spirit he sent was the first fruits of God's good future. New songs were sung, for he lives. New hopes were founded, for he lives. A new covenant was assured, for he lives. A new community was formed, for he lives. A new humanity was created, for he lives. A new world was promised, for he lives. They remembered Jesus — and they owned his new life as their life. Because they were a community of memory, they were a community of hope. Because they were a community of hope, they dreamed of all things made new by the power of God and of the lamb; and they were made new themselves in their vision and identity, in their dispositions and intentions, in their discernment. The memory of Jesus, and the Spirit he poured out, filled them with knowledge and goodness and made them "able to instruct one another."

And there were the stories of his *return*. The Jesus whom they remembered they awaited. Even as they remembered in the bread and the cup the broken body and shed blood of Jesus, they rejoiced in them as tokens of a heavenly banquet. In the supper they proclaimed the Lord's death "until he comes" (1 Cor. 11:26). In the meantime there was the rent to pay and equipment to be kept in repair.[20] In the meantime conventional standards passed for wisdom: "The first shall be first, and the last, well, left." "Blessed are the rich." "Caesar is Lord." "Love those who love you." In the meantime sins of pride and greed and enmity asserted their doomed reign. In the meantime even the Lord's Supper could be — as in Corinth — a place of division; the body was broken where one was hungry and another had too much, and the cup of blessing became a cup of judgment where the poor were humiliated (cf. 1 Cor. 11:17-34). In the mean-

---

20. Cf. W. H. Auden, *For the Time Being: A Christmas Oratorio* from *Religious Drama 1: Five Plays*, selected and introduced by Marvin Halverson (Cleveland: Meridian Books, The World Publishing Company, 1957), p. 67: "In the meantime/There are bills to be paid, machines to be kept in repair,/Irregular verbs to learn, the Time Being to redeem/From insignificance."

time forgetfulness still threatened the church and the church's discernment. But also in the meantime a watchful church remembered to tell the story, and in remembering the story, it still formed and transformed identity, still informed and reformed perspective. The memory of Jesus still took form in the dispositions and deeds of the watchful community and its members.

Because Jesus had been raised, because the ages had turned, communal discernment was *possible* in memory and hope. Because Jesus had not yet appeared in glory, because it was not yet the good future of God's unchallenged sovereignty, communal discernment was *necessary* to watchfulness. So Paul both commends the Roman churches and exhorts them (cf. Rom. 12:1-2). They were — and they were called to be — "full of goodness, filled with all knowledge, and able to instruct one another."

One Church and One Choice: Corinth and Eating Meat Sacrificed to Idols[21]

Consider one concrete example of an early church engaged in moral discourse. There are, of course, no transcripts or recordings of the conversations of the early Christians. But there are letters from which one can infer something of a church's discourse and something more of the way a Christian teacher nurtured and sustained both the conversation and the communal discernment of a congregation.

In 1 Corinthians 8–10 Paul replied to a question put to him by the Corinthian church. "Now concerning food sacrificed to idols" (8:1), he began. The question was this: shall Christians eat meat that has been sacrificed to one of the pagan gods? The great pagan festivals would provide one occasion in which this choice might be faced (cf. perhaps 10:20), but it would also be faced routinely at the meat market (cf. 10:25) and at the dinner table when a pagan host served his guests meat (cf. 10:27). To many Jews of the Diaspora — including Christian Jews — such meat, of course, could hardly be counted *kosher,* and to eat it would surely be counted participation in the worship of idols. The Jerusalem Council (Acts 15:1-21) had ruled that Gentile Christians need not be circumcised or observe the Jewish law, but it did urge Gentile Christians to abstain "from things polluted by idols," that is, "from what has been sacrificed to idols" (Acts 15:20, 29; 21:25). That so-called "apostolic decree" may indeed have prompted the question in the largely Gentile church at Corinth. The Corinthi-

---

21. This account is indebted especially to Meeks, *The Moral World of the First Christians,* pp. 130-36.

ans had evidently argued about this issue, and some wanted Paul to settle the matter.

Not all of the Corinthians, however, wanted Paul's advice. Some of the "spiritually gifted" members of the Corinthian church thought they no longer needed Paul — or anyone. These arrogant elitists asserted their independence from Paul, boasted about their own wisdom, and berated Paul's weakness. Paul spent the first four chapters of this letter defending his right to speak. The defense was vigorous, but curious in a way. Paul did not so much deny the charges of his folly and weakness as associate them with the way of God in the world, with the memory of Christ and his cross. The memory of Christ was used to help the church discern the wisdom of the choice to give Paul a hearing.[22]

Having defended his right to speak by associating his words with the weakness and folly of Christ crucified, who is nevertheless "the power of God and the wisdom of God" (1 Cor. 1:24), Paul — in what is still more striking — did not then simply tell the Corinthians what to do about meat sacrificed to idols. Instead he nurtured their discourse; he gave voice to the different views within the Corinthian church. He nurtured their deliberation; he gave ears to hear the voices and the reasons of others. He nurtured their discernment by reminding them of his own way among them, which he had already defended by reminding them of Christ and of his cross.

He gave voice first to the point of view of the "spiritually gifted," whose knowledge, they claimed, freed them from such foolish scruples about food and authorized them to go wherever invited and to eat whatever they pleased. "We know," Paul said, joining his own voice to theirs and citing their slogans, "that 'all of us possess knowledge'" (8:1). And he repeats and affirms their "knowledge": "that 'no idol in the world really exists,' and that 'there is no God but one'" (8:4). Paul did not contradict the argument or the claims of this group; he gave it voice and added his voice to theirs, defending it as faithful to the Christian tradition (8:6) and, indeed, to the radical monotheism of the *Shema* (Deut. 6:4). The pagan construal of the world as full of divine powers to be placated and pleased had been destroyed, and Christians were liberated from anxiety about pagan deities — or about food sacrificed to them.

Paul did not contradict their arguments, but he did qualify them — and at the very beginning. He would not endure arrogance, the proud refusal to attend to others in the community. "Knowledge puffs up, but love builds up," he said (8:1; cf. 4:6, 18, 19; 5:2; 13:4). Moreover, those "spiritually gifted" with "knowledge" still had a thing or two to learn; "he does not yet know as he ought

22. Nils Alstrup Dahl, "Paul and the Church at Corinth," in *Studies in Paul* (Minneapolis: Augsburg, 1977), pp. 40-61.

to know" (8:2 RSV; cf. 13:8-12). There is an eschatological qualification to our knowledge; we still "know only in part" (13:12), and such knowledge doesn't count for much apart from love (cf. 13:2).

It comes as no surprise, then, that, having given them voice, Paul drew the attention of these "gifted" individuals to those they thought spiritual clods, to the members of the community who were not gifted with this "knowledge," to those with scruples about food offered to idols, to the "weak," calling them "believers for whom Christ died" (8:11). Paul would not permit the "spiritually gifted" to deny the real existence of members of the community whose conscience was not yet "liberated." The pagan construal of the world had been destroyed, but when acting on such knowledge threatened also to destroy the conscience of other members of the community, then another voice had to be heard. And Paul spoke in his own voice when he said, "Therefore, if food is a cause of their falling, I will never eat meat, so that I may not cause one of them to fall" (8:13).

Paul not only gave the "spiritually gifted" a voice; he also gave them ears to hear the voice of the "weak." That voice, too, must be heard in the community's deliberation. It must not be muted by the strength of the argument of the "spiritually gifted." In the tenth chapter Paul gave voice to the Jewish Christian tradition that repudiated any form of idolatry, and again he joined his voice to that of the "weak," of those concerned about violations of Jewish righteousness, in a learned argument based on the experience of "our ancestors" (10:1) in the exodus and in the wilderness. The argument in 10:6-14 is one of which any rabbi could have been proud and by which even the "spiritually gifted" could not but be impressed. Gathering together texts from the account of the wilderness experience, including the infamous golden calf episode of Exodus 32:6 (1 Cor. 10:7), this Jewish Christian argument moved compellingly toward the conclusion, "Therefore, my dear friends, flee from the worship of idols" (10:14). The Jewish Christian tradition which urged Gentiles to "abstain" "from things polluted by idols" (Acts 15:20)[23] now seemed the course of wisdom, not foolish scruples from which Christians had been liberated. Moreover, the argument of the strong — to which Paul had just lent his own voice — that "no idol in the world really exists" (1 Cor. 8:4) was here answered by identifying idols with "demons" (10:19-20). The world is, after all, filled with threatening and unearthly powers hostile to God.

Those opposed to eating meat sacrificed to idols were given voice — but not the last word in the discourse. In an abrupt shift Paul returned to the slo-

---

23. Consider also the allusions to this "apostolic decree" (Acts 15:20, 29) in 1 Corinthians 10:8 and 6:18.

gans of those gifted with and freed by knowledge — and to the Pauline qualifi-cations. "'All things are lawful,' but not all things are beneficial" (10:23). Christians may eat "whatever is sold in the meat market" (10:25), may eat "whatever is set before you" at a dinner hosted by an unbeliever (10:27) — and now on the grounds of another citation of Scripture, "the earth is the LORD's, and all that is in it" (Ps. 24:1; cf. 1 Cor. 10:26). Those opposed to idolatry were not to condemn or denounce those who ate meat sacrificed to idols any more than those gifted with knowledge were to despise or repudiate those with scruples against such meat. Where the legitimate anxiety about idolatry in a world that was not yet God's unchallenged reign threatened the (equally) legitimate liberty of other members of the community, then another voice must be heard. And Paul again spoke in his own voice, "If I partake with thankfulness, why should I be denounced because of that for which I give thanks?" (1 Cor. 10:30).

Paul, having defended his right to speak to the Corinthians, did not simply tell them what to do. He nurtured their discourse, giving voice to members of the community. Personal responsibility was not here denied but exercised in the context of community; it was neither surrendered to the community nor rendered simply "private." He nurtured their deliberation, giving ears to hear other members of the community. Reasons were given and heard, the arguments were spelled out elegantly, and attention was directed to those who disagreed and to their arguments. And he nurtured their discernment. The arguments, the rights, the rules were all finally tested and qualified by the memory of Christ. "Be imitators of me, as I am of Christ," Paul finally said (11:1). Once before in this letter he had invited the Corinthians to "be imitators of me" (4:16) and reminded them of "my ways in Christ Jesus" (4:17) — at the conclusion of his defense of his right to speak to them. Now again in the context of these arguments he reminded them of his own conduct. Against the arrogant, against those who insisted upon their rights, against those who boasted about their knowledge or their law and used them to despise or to condemn, Paul pointed to himself as one who did not make the claims that were his to make (9:15-18), as one who served all, both Gentile and Jew (9:19-23), and as one who exercised self-control and endured suffering for the sake of God's good future (9:24-27). In pointing to himself, however, he pointed beyond himself to Christ. It was Christ who was their "wisdom from God, and righteousness and sanctification and redemption" (1:30). It was the memory of Christ that gave them their identity, not simply their circumcision or their uncircumcision, their knowledge or their law. It was the common memory of Christ that made them a community, not simply their rights or their rules, and surely not each asserting those rights or rules. Apart from Paul's reminder, they were simply "quarreling" (1:11); with Paul's reminder of "his ways in Christ Jesus," they were and were called to be a community of moral discourse and deliberation and discernment, "able to instruct one another."

This does not mean, of course, that they suddenly and magically agreed about everything; it does mean, however, that even in their disagreements they could learn from each other and come a bit closer to a way of life "worthy of the gospel." It does not mean, either, that any and every choice or reason was simply to be tolerated in a Christian community of moral discourse and deliberation. The test for discernment was the memory of Christ; and in the name of Christ Paul pronounced judgment against the sexually immoral (e.g., 5:1-5; 6:12-20) and against the rich who "humiliate those who have nothing" (11:22). With respect to the choice of eating meat, too, some limits were found, it seems, in the giving and hearing of reasons. Besides the requirements of regard for the conscience of the weaker brother for whom Christ died and respect for the liberty of the stronger sister whom Christ set free, it seems clear that participation in the pagan cultic festivals themselves was forbidden (10:20-21). The result was a kind of compromise. The point, however, is not to enshrine this compromise as a part of a developing code in the church; the point is rather the process of communal discourse and deliberation and discernment governed and qualified by the memory of Christ. The Corinthian Christians were — and were called to be — "able to instruct one another."

The question of eating meat that has been sacrificed to idols is not one that troubles many churches any longer. The process, however, is still instructive for us. Hard choices, choices that threatened to tear a person and a community apart, were talked about. Reasons were given and heard — and tested against the memory of Jesus. It was that memory, not their liberty, not their law, that gave them identity and kept them a community.

CHAPTER TWO

"Able to Instruct One Another" Still: The Continuing Church as a Community of Moral Discourse

The Roman churches were, Paul said, "full of goodness, filled with all knowledge, and able to instruct one another" (Rom. 15:14). It is the claim of this chapter that churches today are *still* "full of goodness, filled with all knowledge, and able to instruct one another." Let it be admitted that such a commendation seems extravagant. Let the counterevidence of scandals and willful ignorance and bickering be acknowledged. Paul's compliment must have seemed extravagant to the Romans, too. And there was more than a little evidence counter to Paul's commendation of the Roman churches, as well. Romantic notions of the early church may prompt an easy acceptance of Paul's praise, while we presume that realism requires us to deny any such commendation of contemporary churches. It is easy — too easy — to say, "The Roman churches must have been wonderful communities. But that was the early church. My church is just not that gifted with knowledge and goodness, and we surely are not able to instruct one another." It is easy — but it is also wrong.

It is wrong, in the first place, because the Roman churches — or the Corinthian Christians, or any of the other early Christian communities — were made up of quite ordinary people. There was not a halo to be seen. There is no reason to think that moral discourse and mutual instruction came more naturally to those churches than it comes to contemporary churches. Can we really suppose that the Roman Christians had some "natural" readiness to be patient with the thoughts, words, and deeds of others? Or that they had a "natural" disposition to respect other members of their community as givers or hearers of reasons? On the contrary, those Jewish and Gentile Christians in Rome did not even have a "natural" reason to regard themselves as members of the same community, and they had, therefore, no "natural" reason to care enough about each other to encourage or to admonish one another.

Indeed, what came "naturally" to those Roman Christians seems to have been accusations and epithets, suspicion and animosity. Jews had traditionally regarded Gentiles as idolaters and as "sinners"; Roman Gentiles had long regarded Jews as "superstitious";[1] and that traditional animosity and suspicion evidently seemed "natural" to many of the Christians in Rome. Some Jewish Christians at Rome condemned the Gentiles as "sinners," and some Gentile Christians despised the Jews for their scruples about Sabbath and festivals and food. The "righteous" Jews called the Gentiles "sinners"; the Gentiles thought of themselves as "strong" and called the Jewish Christians "weak." The epithets, however, were only part of the problem. There were serious and substantive disagreements between Jewish Christians and Gentile Christians about the place of the Law and about the meaning and scope of Christian freedom. These disagreements allowed Jewish Christians to use the Hebrew Scriptures like a weapon against Gentile "sinners," and allowed Gentile Christians to flaunt their freedom in order to spite those Jewish legalists. Such moral differences — and the boasting and judging and enmity that surrounded them — may make one wonder not how I could make the claim that contemporary churches are *still* "full of goodness, filled with all knowledge, and able to instruct one another," but how Paul could have made that extravagant claim about the Roman Christians in the first place.

Paul's confidence was not founded on any "natural" saintliness of those Roman Christians. It was founded on the extravagant grace of God. It was founded on the gospel, "the power of God for salvation to everyone who has faith" (Rom. 1:16), both Jew and Gentile. It was founded on what God had done in Christ to create such community and on what God had done in the Spirit to equip them for mutual instruction. Paul wrote "boldly" of that gospel. He reminded the Jewish Christians not only of the verdict of Scripture that "there is no one who is righteous" (Rom. 3:10, citing Ps. 14) but also of the gospel of God in which both Jew and Gentile are justified (Rom. 3:21-26). "There is no distinction" (Rom. 3:22). There is no room in the gospel for boasting (3:27-31), and there is no room for condemnation (8:1). Paul reminded the Gentile Christians of their baptism. They had died with Christ in his death to sin so that, as Christ was raised from the dead, they too "might walk in newness of life" (6:4),

---

1. See Robert L. Wilken, *The Christians as the Romans Saw Them* (New Haven: Yale University Press, 1984), pp. 50-67.

so that they might be no longer sinners but "righteous" (6:1-23). There is no room in the gospel for the flaunting of one's freedom. Paul reminded them all that Christ had died for the "weak" and for "sinners" and for "enemies" (5:6-11), so that the "weak" might be "strong in faith," so that "sinners" might be "righteous," so that enemies might be reconciled both to God and to each other. He reminded them, in sum, that the gospel of God had made them a community, that they were members of "one body in Christ, and individually . . . members one of another" (Rom. 12:5; cf. 1 Cor. 12:27; Eph. 4:25; 5:30). And having reminded them of the gospel of God, Paul invited them to the "obedience of faith" (Rom. 1:5; 16:26). He called upon them to "welcome one another" (Rom. 15:7). On the foundation of the gospel of God, he expressed his confidence that they were "able to instruct one another."

The second reason, therefore, that it is wrong to regard Paul's commendation of the Roman churches as inappropriate to the continuing churches is simply this: the extravagant grace of God is still at work. God continues to create community and to equip the continuing churches for moral discourse.

The "knowledge" of the Roman churches was not simply a collation of what individual members knew that they knew; their "goodness" was not merely a sum of the little good individual members were proud of doing well. The Roman churches were full of "knowledge" and "goodness" because they remembered Jesus and shared in the knowledge and goodness of Christ. And because the continuing churches still remember Jesus, there continue to be reasons to commend them as "full of goodness, filled with all knowledge, and able to instruct one another." They are still able to be — and they still are called to be — communities of moral discourse, deliberation, and discernment.

A Continuing Tradition of Discourse, Deliberation, and Discernment

Paul's commendation may still seem extravagant. And acknowledging that the grace of God is the foundation of Paul's confidence may make it seem a commendation of God rather than a commendation of the Roman — or the continuing — churches. Permit me, therefore, to begin again with a more modest claim and to support it by calling attention to some very mundane features of the common life of Christian community. The modest claim is this: Christian communities continue to be communities of moral discourse. Members of the churches still sometimes talk together about what they should do or leave undone.

The discourse can be quite informal. Conversations after worship, for example, are frequently about the prospects for a favorite team or a recent graduate, but I have overheard conversations that could prompt something like Paul's compliment. A father was sick and a mother had lost her job, and a conversation concerned how that family could be helped. A morning paper had a headline about homelessness in the city, and the conversation concerned how the congregation could respond. Such informal conversations are not all at church, of course. Individuals sitting together at a block party may have a conversation about whether and how to make a special effort to welcome some new (and different) neighbors. When they happen to meet in the market, they may talk about medical care for their aging parents or about parental care for their adolescent children. The discourse continues.

And it continues in more formal contexts, too, in contexts more intentionally committed to moral discourse. In a church's educational program, for example, there will be conversations about moral responsibilities. In one class there may be talk about choices that affect the air and the water that sustain life. In another class there may be a discussion of the violence in some distant part of the world, or of the violence in the church's neighborhood. A hospice nurse from the congregation may lead another class in reflection about decisions we need to make about our dying and our care for the dying. And in yet another class there may be a conversation about being young and single and sexual. The discourse continues.

And it continues in institutional settings. In a congregational meeting, for example, there may be a discussion of the fund for "benevolence," the fund to help the poor. In a committee for building expansion there may be a conversation about whether to take a loan from a bank that regularly refuses loans to minority businesses. In a committee to consider hiring someone to minister among them there may be talk about recognizing and utilizing the gifts of women. The lists could go on, of course, for the discourse goes on. The modest claim surely stands: Christian communities continue to be communities of moral discourse.

The discourse continues, but so do the temptations. With respect to personal choices it remains tempting to surrender personal responsibility to the group, to neglect or to disown one's own responsibility. In Western culture, however, it has become considerably more tempting to treat personal choices as purely "private" matters, as nobody else's business, as matters to be decided by the secret tastes and preferences of autonomous individuals. It is tempting, for example, to treat divorce as a purely "private" matter, as no business of the Christian community. The Christian tradition, however, contains convictions and practices about marriage that should make the community reticent to treat a personal decision by one of its members to divorce as a purely "private" choice. Moreover, Christian churches have reasons to think that a vision of autonomous selves, linked only by contract, is unable to give an adequate account of our common life — or of our marriages. If these things are so, then Christian communities may and must recognize that to treat personal decisions as purely "private" choices is a temptation, and they may and must resist temptation.

With respect to communal decisions, it is still tempting simply to surrender them to an ecclesiastical official, to some institutional leadership, but in our society it is still more tempting to treat communal choices as purely "public" matters to be decided by the generally accredited wisdom of some broader community. It is tempting, for example, for churches to make decisions about their investments simply on the basis of security and yield, the conventional wisdom about investments. But churches have some particular convictions that make them distinctive communities. They regard themselves as stewards, for example, and stewardship in Christian community entails more than getting top dollar; it means using our investments — and our borrowing and our buying and our selling, as well — in ways that honor God and serve God's cause. If churches are serious about being disciples of Christ and stewards of God's good gifts, therefore, they may recognize that to make communal decisions by the unqualified application of another community's standards — even if they are prudent and sensible standards — is a temptation. And they may and must resist temptation.

Churches are only able to resist these temptations when they continue to be not only communities of discourse but also communities of deliberation. There must be conversation not only about what should be done but also about *why* it should be done. It is critically important that members of Christian communities continue to give and to hear reasons. Giving voice to a rationale for a certain choice, and giving ear to it as well, is not, however, sufficient. Churches must also continue to test reasons by their coherence with the gospel, to defend or reject or qualify reasons by their congruity with the story of Christ. Churches must continue, that is to say, to be communities of discourse and deliberation by being communities of discernment and memory.

There are, after all, other communities in which there are conversations about what should be done and why. There are professional associations and labor unions, neighborhoods and political precincts, countries of which we are citizens, and many others. Each of these communities bears a tradition and forms character and, to some extent at least, influences the choices and decisions of its members. Indeed, for many of us participation in other communities is more determinative of our decisions than our membership in the church.[2] Nev-

2. James M. Gustafson, "Christian Ethics and Social Policy," in *Faith and Ethics: The Theology of H. R. Niebuhr*, ed. Paul Ramsey (New York: Harper & Row, 1957), pp. 119-39, especially p. 133.

ertheless, churches can and sometimes do test and qualify these other traditions, call for the re-formation of character and conduct, and sustain discourse and deliberation in the service of discernment of a way of life "worthy of the gospel of Christ." The churches are not to be confused with any of the other associations. They continue to be distinctive communities of discourse and deliberation and discernment by remembering Jesus and by transforming questions of character and conduct into the question of how they may live the story they still love to tell.

Contemporary churches, then, continue to be — and to be called to be — communities of discourse, deliberation, and discernment in memory of Jesus. They remember Jesus not simply as an object of historical recollection but as the living Lord who continues to abide with his continuing church and continues to call them to repentance and discipleship. Such remembrance still fills the church with goodness and knowledge and makes its members "able to instruct one another."

The Danger of Forgetfulness in Moral Discourse Today

Contemporary churches are not exempt from Paul's remarkable commendation of the Roman churches, or from its subtle vocation to be such communities. But it isn't easy, and the greatest danger is still forgetfulness. In the context of moral differences, there are at least two ways in which the churches — and their ethicists — stand at particular risk of forgetfulness today: first, by their confidence in and enthusiasm for an impartial perspective, for universal rational principles, and second, by their confidence in and enthusiasm for certain partial and parochial values.

The Danger of Forgetfulness in Moral Esperanto

The enthusiasm for an impartial perspective is not hard to understand. The moral pluralism of contemporary culture seems to require it. Christians can, of course, witness to their deepest convictions in a pluralist society, but they can hardly expect a non-Christian to find those Christian convictions persuasive grounds for doing something or for leaving something else undone. Therefore, many Christian ethicists have sought moral principles that all persons do or can and should hold on the basis of reason alone, quite apart from their membership in particular communities with specific moral traditions, and have attempted to use those principles persuasively. To convince the non-Christian

39

physician not to treat abortion as a morally trivial matter, to persuade a legislative body (which, although it may have Christians in it, is constitutionally prohibited from the "establishment" of a religion) to protect the rights of the poor in the land, to argue before a corporation's board of directors that they should sacrifice some profit to protect against pollution from their factories — all such contexts for moral discourse seem to require not Christian conviction but pure and practical reason.

Theologically, the quest for an impartial perspective and for universal principles seems warranted by the conviction that the God who called a cosmos from chaos also established a certain moral order in the universe and wrote certain moral principles on human hearts (Rom. 2:15). All persons, then, whatever their loyalties and identities, can be expected to know certain moral principles and to know they are obligated by them, and many Christian ethicists have tried to articulate, defend, and apply such principles.

Philosophically, the quest for impartial reasons and universal principles has seemed not only permitted but also required. Kant's first formulation of the "categorical imperative," after all, was "Act only on that maxim whereby thou canst at the same time will that it should become a universal law."[3] Kant's project for morality, shared by many philosophers since, was to identify and to justify an impartial and rational principle for morality, a principle that *all* people can and must hold independently of their particular circumstances and conditions, independently of their particular communities and histories, quite apart from their specific loyalties and identities, quite apart from any particular narrative or story that they remember and from any putatively partial vision of human flourishing for which they hope.[4] Many philosophers since Kant have identified the

3. Immanuel Kant, *Fundamental Principles of the Metaphysic of Morals* (Grundlegung zur Metaphysik Der Sitten), trans. Thomas K. Abbott (New York: Liberal Arts Press, 1949), p. 30.

4. Kant's maxim has some obvious problems: (a) Maxims that can be universalized are not necessarily moral duties. It is possible to universalize the maxim "Put your left shoe on first," but it is not a moral duty. (b) Different and conflicting maxims might be universalizable. For example, although Kant argued that breaking any promise was prohibited by his first maxim, others have argued that one could will, "I will break a promise when it is necessary to help someone in need" as a universal law. (c) It is insufficient for the moral life. It is quite plausible, for example, that the rich fool of Luke 12:13-21 could universalize the maxim on which he evidently acted, "Let each one look out for himself." Kant responds to this objection by saying that "many cases might occur in which one would have need of the love and sympathy of others" (41). It is true that the rich fool later found himself inconsistently willing to abrogate that rule when he was in torment and needed a drop of water to cool his tongue, but for one who is sure of his fortune and of his future universalizability will not establish the duty to be benevolent

moral point of view with an impartial perspective. But because universalizability is a formal and empty principle, they have usually supplemented it with a principle taken to be required by it. Kant himself offered a second formulation of the categorical imperative: "So act as to treat humanity, whether in thine own person or in that of any other, in every case as an end withal, never as a means only."[5] That formulation has been critically important in public discourse in pluralist societies, for it insists upon respect for autonomy. Kant may have had a richer notion of "humanity" than many Kantians, but the richer notion was hard to sustain on purely rational grounds. At any rate, the principle has often been translated in pluralist societies into the universal principle of equal freedom, which assures people have the right to do as they please as long as it does not interfere with other people's equal right to do as they please.

The chief competitor to this general way of articulating a universal and rational principle has been utilitarianism, which requires all people to do whatever will bring the greatest good for the greatest number. The attraction of the good is universal, indeed analytical (since to call anything "good" is to say we are or should be attracted to it), and Bentham's dictum "everyone to count for one, nobody for more than one" preserves impartiality.[6] The utilitarians have themselves argued about what is "good," and particularly about whether it is sufficient to say that pleasure or happiness is "good,"[7] but it is hard to defend a richer notion of the good on the basis of reason alone. At any rate, the principle of utility has often been translated in pluralist societies into a universal principle of preference satisfaction: so act as to maximize the satisfaction of the preferences of the most people.

Many contemporary philosophers have challenged the "Enlightenment project,"[8] the striving for a "moral Esperanto," "an artificial moral language invented in the (unrealistic) hope that everyone will want to speak it."[9] But the arguments most frequently made and credited in public discourse still seem to

---

or to prohibit self-centeredness. See William K. Frankena, *Ethics* (Englewood Cliffs, N.J.: Prentice-Hall, Inc., 1963), pp. 25-28.

5. Kant, *Fundamental Principles of the Metaphysic of Morals*, p. 46.

6. Jeremy Bentham (1748-1832) was the founder of classical utilitarianism.

7. John Stuart Mill already questioned Bentham's account of the pleasure principle, attempting to distinguish between "higher" and "lower" pleasures. "It is better to be a human being dissatisfied than a pig satisfied; better to be Socrates dissatisfied than a fool satisfied." Mill, *Utilitarianism*, in *Utilitarianism, Liberty, and Representative Government* (London: J. M. Dent & Sons, Ltd., 1910; *Utilitarianism* was first published in 1863), p. 9.

8. Especially noteworthy is Alasdair MacIntyre, *After Virtue* (Notre Dame: University of Notre Dame Press, 1981).

9. Jeffrey Stout, *Ethics After Babel* (Boston: Beacon, 1988), p. 294.

be that someone's freedom is being infringed upon or that the pursuit of pleasure (or of satisfying preferences) is being hindered even though no one is being harmed. Evidently the public has not been persuaded which impartial principle is the *right* impartial principle, whether freedom or utility, but it has evidently been convinced that public discourse — including discourse in the church — should be limited and governed by impartial rational principles. And many Christian ethicists have evidently also been persuaded, for many speak and write more like followers of Kant or Mill than like disciples of Jesus.[10]

The enthusiasm for an impartial perspective within a pluralistic society is not hard to understand. I do not say, and I do not mean, that an impartial perspective is morally unilluminating or that there are no universal principles knowable by reason. I do not claim that "the Enlightenment project" has altogether failed.[11] I hold no brief for a "theological veto" of natural morality,[12] not even within the church. For Christians to dismiss arguments based "on reason alone" strikes me as an *argumentum ad hominem* on the scale of an *argumentum ad humanum*.[13] In the New Testament itself "natural morality" and moral commonplaces evidently enter into moral deliberation.

I do say, however, that the impartial perspective is not to be identified with the Christian perspective, that the impartial perspective can provide only a *minimal* account of the moral life, and that if its minimalism is not acknowledged, the church and its moral discourse will suffer forgetfulness.

The minimalism of the impartial perspective can be seen in the account it gives of relationships of covenant and community. The relationship of husband and wife, for example — or of parent and child, or of pastor and parishioner, or

10. One might note, for example, how the Christian notion of love can sometimes be reduced to either a Kantian notion of respect for persons or a utilitarian notion of beneficence. The point is made persuasively in Stanley Hauerwas, "Love's Not All You Need," in *Vision and Virtue: Essays in Christian Ethical Reflection* (Notre Dame: Fides, 1974), pp. 111-26.

11. That "the Enlightenment project" has failed is MacIntyre's claim in *After Virtue*, pp. 35-39. The more modest claim would be that its successes have been minimal. In a conversation with a pluralist society we might do better as Christian ethicists to give up the pretentious attempt to construct what Stout calls "Moral Esperanto" and be satisfied to learn "Moral Pidgin."

12. See Karl Barth, *Church Dogmatics*, II/2, trans. G. W. Bromiley, J. C. Campbell, et al. (Edinburgh: T. & T. Clark, 1957), pp. 509-42; Karl Barth, "No!" in *Natural Theology: Comprising "Nature and Grace" by Professor Dr. Emil Brunner and the reply "No!" by Dr. Karl Barth,* trans. Peter Fraenkel (London: The Centenary Press, 1946), pp. 67-128.

13. An *argumentum ad hominem,* of course, is the fallacy that pretends to have discredited an argument by attacking the character of the person who made the argument. An *argumentum ad humanum* would be an argument that pretends to have discredited an argument by the observation that the person who made the argument is a human being.

simply of being "members one of another" — can from an impartial perspective only be construed as *contractual* relationships between autonomous individuals or as *instrumental* relationships to achieve some extrinsic good. The impartial perspective will not build or sustain or nurture *community*.

The minimalism of the impartial perspective can be seen in another way. It requires of people a certain alienation from themselves,[14] from the passions and loyalties that give them moral character and from the histories and community that give them moral identity, in order to adopt the impartial point of view. It is legitimate, indeed salutary, for people to attempt to see themselves as objectively as they can, as others see them. No one, however, can *live* that way, transcending his links with others in time and place, denying his mortal identity — at least, no one can live that way with integrity. The impartial perspective will not build or sustain or nurture *character*.

The minimalism of the impartial perspective can also be seen in its reticence to instruct anyone about values or, indeed, about what should be done. The standard of equal freedom prefers the question "who should decide?" to the question "what should be decided?"; and utilitarianism prefers to find procedures for satisfying the preferences of the greatest number while treating such preferences as matters of private taste. The impartial perspective by itself will not build or sustain or nurture moral conversation. It threatens to sunder the unity of life into a private realm of autonomy and preference and a public realm of impartiality.

The identification of Christian ethics with an impartial perspective and the failure to acknowledge the minimalism of such a perspective, then, threaten the ability of the church to form moral communities, to form moral character, and to be a community of moral discourse, deliberation, and discernment. They condemn the church — and her ethicists — to forgetfulness.

The Danger of Forgetfulness in Parochialism

It is not just enthusiasm for an impartial perspective and universal principles that tempts us to forgetfulness and threatens the ability of members of the Christian community to instruct one another, however. So do parochialism and provincialism and chauvinism and any narrowness of vision or abridgment of perspective that may belong to particular communities as well as to individual members of the community. It is clear, I suppose, that whenever Christians

14. Stanley Hauerwas, *The Peaceable Kingdom: A Primer in Christian Ethics* (Notre Dame: University of Notre Dame Press, 1983), p. 18.

identify or confuse the story of Jesus with "rags to riches" stories or stories of success through possibility thinking, they are in danger of forgetfulness. Surely, whenever they celebrate the story of America as the story that gives them identity and makes them a community in the church, they are at risk of forgetfulness. When the Lord's Supper is a place of happy division of denominations or happy segregation of races or happy separation of classes, then certainly the church is at risk of forgetfulness.

Christians also stand at risk of forgetfulness when any one good is made absolute, whether the sanctity of life, or the sanctity of truth, or any other genuine but partial good. They stand at risk of forgetfulness when they identify any one good with the cause of God and the triumph of that good with the reign of God.

I do not say, and I do not mean, that congregations of socially homogeneous people cannot be the church. I do not claim that the assimilation of particular loyalties and identities and histories and values and causes is forbidden to particular congregations in their particular times and places. Christians need not and should not dismiss the particular cultural histories of people from the reason giving and reason hearing of moral deliberation; the New Testament itself doesn't. And I do not say, and I do not mean, that the particular and partial goods sometimes identified with the cause of God are not *genuine* goods, that it is inappropriate to seek them, or that we may ever turn against them.

But I do say that the community that fails to acknowledge its parochialism is doomed to forgetfulness. I do say that all the particular histories of persons in the church must be submissive to the story of Jesus, which gives the church identity and makes the church a community. All of our little certainties and all of our little virtues must be not only assimilated but also made submissive to Jesus, whose memory still fills the church with knowledge and goodness. All of our political and social and economic and national loyalties must be opened to question and criticism by our loyalty to Christ. All our genuine but partial goods must kneel before the one who is the way, the truth, and the life, in whom the fullness of God and the fullness of good was pleased to dwell, and whose cosmic sovereignty we await. Then it will be the reign of *shalom*, even among the diverse goods that are part (but not the whole) of God's cause, but here and now genuine goods can come into genuine conflict. Here and now *part* of what we know from the memory of Jesus to be God's cause can come into tragic conflict with another part of what we know from the same memory to be God's cause. Here and now watchfulness is required lest our defense of God's cause on one front leaves it open to attack on another. Watchfulness requires memory — and discourse with those who are different from us in the church.

44

We *need* those whom it is too much our impulse to shun and despise. Without them we stand at risk of an abridged perspective, at risk of confusing our particular ethnic, economic, professional, or other tribal identities with our identity in Christ, at risk of identifying our particular but partial good with the reign of God, at risk of forgetfulness. It was not accidental that Paul commended the Roman churches, which included both Jewish and Gentile Christians. The Jewish Christians could remain Jewish Christians and the Gentile Christians could remain Gentile Christians, but they were nevertheless one in Christ and able to instruct one another. The very differences that made discourse difficult made it mutually instructive, too. They had to remember Jesus, in whom there is "neither Jew nor Gentile." To be sure, they told the story somewhat differently, but it remained one story behind the different tellings.[15] It was not incidental that the church to which Paul wrote with advice to the master of the runaway slave Onesimus (see Philem.) included slaves.

Even if, or especially if, a congregation is socially homogeneous, it needs to be in conversation with the heterogeneity of Christ's body, with *all* those who tell the story of Jesus and own it as their own. Without them and without the self-critical reflection, the repentance, nurtured by remembering Jesus in the context of the whole church, a church may nurture certain virtues, say, middle-class respectability or, more nobly, reverence for life. It may even discern what is fitting, say, fitting to (and worthy of) American individualism, or more nobly, the truth about American individualism. But it will not be the community which remembers Jesus and which, full of knowledge and goodness, possesses members able to instruct one another in the great variety of goods and in the conflict of goods.

Such discourse will not always result in unanimity — and it need not. It may not — and often will not — resolve dilemmas or produce judgments that have the force of law in the Christian community. But it can — and sometimes does — bring conflicting interests, values, and perspectives under the judgment and renewal of the one Christ whose story Christians celebrate. Mutual admonition and mutual accountability can encourage and help all Christians to make every partial good, every political opinion, every social strategy, every economic goal and tactic, and every heritage captive to the Lord of the story.

---

15. The Gospels of Matthew and Mark may be taken as illustrative of this point. Mark, the earlier of the two, is written for a community of Gentile Christians; Matthew, for a largely Jewish Christian community. See Allen Verhey, *The Great Reversal: Ethics and the New Testament* (Grand Rapids: Eerdmans, 1984), pp. 74-92.

A Diversity of Gifts

The community that remembers the story of Jesus and would live it recognizes not only a variety of goods but also a variety of gifts. Discernment, or the perception of what is fitting to the story we love to tell, is not the task of the ethicist or the pastor alone. It is the task of the church in discourse. Christian ethics is not a substitute for that discourse. Discernment involves the diversity of gifts of the congregation — the gifts of wisdom and creativity, of indignation at injustice and sympathy with the suffering, of knowledge of people and places, of awareness of opportunities and obstructions, of technical knowledge and special skills — all enlightening the way to the particular and specific deeds that are worthy of the gospel in the places and times in which we live. Each gifted member of the church (and each member of the church *is* gifted) can only speak out of his own perspective and her own experience, but each is also willing to recognize the gifts of others, to listen to the reasons of others, and to see things differently because of the body of Christ.

There are a *variety* of gifts, but it is also important to say that this diversity is a variety of *gifts*. Two things follow from this. The first is that there is no room for boasting in the community of discourse, neither by one member over-against another, nor by the Christian community over-against other communities. This language of "gift" should be enough to keep us from claiming moral superiority for Christians or for ourselves in comparison with other Christians. As Paul says, "If then you received it, why do you boast as if it were not a gift?" (1 Cor. 4:7). If that isn't enough to keep us from boasting, then we may need to be reminded also of the blemished history of the church, marred as it is by religious hatred, holy killings, pious self-righteousness, and sanctified complacency with slavery and apartheid and the oppression of women and other injustices. When the church gathers for worship, it neither storms nor strolls into the presence of God; it always comes in repentance and confession; it always longs to hear again the assurance of pardon. The gift of forgiveness permits no self-righteousness, but it does permit persons and communities to begin again to discern and to do God's will, and it does permit persons and communities to make the ambiguous choices courageously, confident of God's good gift of forgiveness.

Christians and Christian communities that remember Jesus and remain alert to his call to repent and believe the gospel are unlikely to indulge in comparisons between their own righteousness and the righteousness of their neighbors; in memory of Jesus such comparisons are unworthy and unfitting. A focus on the distinctiveness of the Christian life may very well contain a temptation to such comparisons and to such boasting. It should not surprise us

46

— and it surely should not dismay us — if non-Christians make decisions similar to those Christians make or if they make them for some of the same reasons. The Christian community does not have a corner on moral truth. Indeed, it acknowledges that the Truth is not its possession but its Lord. It receives and celebrates (however imperfectly) the gifts the Lord gives to his church, including this one, that the Lord fills it with goodness and knowledge and enables mutual instruction. The church is *given* a particular identity to which it may and must be faithful. The gift does not provide a place for pride or room for sloth. It calls us to discernment. The church remembers Jesus. It owns his story as its own story and gives thanks to God for the gift of Christ and of his body.

The second thing that follows from the recognition of a variety of *gifts* is, well, gladness. "The disciples were glad when they saw the Lord" (John 20:20), and the church is still glad when it remembers him. The gospel is good news still, a story we should love to tell — and to live. A life worthy of the gospel — and a discernment worthy of the gospel — will be marked by a certain felicity. The gifts of God may be received with gratitude and joy, including the gifts for discourse and deliberation and discernment in the church. We may delight to be — to be gifted to be — "full of goodness, filled with all knowledge, and able to instruct one another." The choices, to be sure, are sometimes serious ones, and the task of discernment is sometimes sobering, but there is a joy that runs along our choices, a joy which enables us to make the hard choices and to bear the sufferings of the right choices without taking either them or ourselves too seriously. It is upon God — not upon us or our hard choices — that the good future of the world depends; we may be glad for that. And while we wait for that good future and watch for it, while we strive already to let its power be felt, if we must suffer a little for the right choices, then we only share in the suffering of Christ; and we may be glad for that as well. The gifts of God are demanding, but the demands of God are not burdensome but light with joy.

Paul's words to the Roman churches are a remarkable compliment and a demanding vocation, but they are also a commendation and a calling in which churches today may also delight. If we can recover this vision of the church, if we can receive with gratitude the gifts of God to the church for discourse and discernment, and if we can receive joyfully the demands upon us correlative to God's gifts, then perhaps the church will look less like an archaic museum piece to some of our contemporaries and more like a confident community that knows why it exists and why it acts, more like its Lord, whose story is its story, whose life is its life.

In subsequent parts of this book we will return to some of the choices Christians face today. I do not presume to have the last word about any of them. As a member of the Christian community and as a moral theologian, I simply hope that my attention to medical ethics, sexual ethics, economic ethics, and political ethics will contribute to the moral discourse of the churches. It is the church, not this little book, that is "full of goodness, filled with all knowledge." Nevertheless, I will proceed "boldly," for I will proceed "by way of reminder" (Rom. 15:15). Each of the subsequent parts of this book will remember Jesus and the early church remembering Jesus in an effort to contribute to the formation of community and character congruent with the story we love to tell, and to the communal discernment of conduct worthy of the gospel.

To proceed "by way of reminder" will mean to attend to Scripture, that "collective scribal memory, the store *par excellence* of treasures old and new,"[16] and especially to the New Testament and its memories of Jesus. The next chapter, therefore, must attend to the practice of reading Scripture in Christian community and to the place of Scripture in the churches' moral discourse, deliberation, discernment, and memory.

---

16. John Howard Yoder, *The Priestly Kingdom: Social Ethics as Gospel* (Notre Dame: University of Notre Dame Press, 1984), p. 31.

CHAPTER THREE

"Useful . . . for Training in Righteousness": Scripture, Churches, and the Moral Life

All scripture is inspired by God and is useful for teaching, for reproof, for correction, and for training in righteousness, so that everyone who belongs to God may be proficient, equipped for every good work.

2 TIMOTHY 3:16-17

With these words an early Christian leader commended Scripture to his readers. The churches have always agreed; like this early Christian leader, they have affirmed that Scripture is "inspired by God and . . . useful for teaching, for reproof, for correction, and for training in righteousness." That commendation has echoed down the centuries and across the divisions of the Christian churches.[1]

Christian churches, called to the tasks of teaching, reproof, correction, and training in righteousness, have always considered Scripture "useful" for those tasks. Attentive to their tradition and vocation as communities of moral discourse, deliberation, and discernment, they have always counted Scripture among the gifts of God that equip them for faithfulness to that tradition and vocation. When members of Christian churches face choices, or when they would "instruct one another" about the concrete shape of integrity with their Christian identity, they turn quite naturally to Scripture. And Christian

---

1. Indeed, the church has read that commendation to include not just the Hebrew Scriptures but also — and especially — the writings gathered together as a New Testament after Paul (or an early Paulinist) penned the words of 2 Timothy 3:16-17.

ethicists — at least those who consider their work part of the common life of the Christian community — have also shared this affirmation of the authority of Scripture for moral discernment in the church. This chapter, therefore, will attend to the usefulness of Scripture in the churches' moral discourse, deliberation, and discernment.

Some Problems

It may be "useful," however, to begin by acknowledging that there are some problems when Christians turn to Scripture for moral instruction, reproof, correction, and training. There are some problems with Scripture, and there are some problems with us, with those who would use Scripture in moral discourse. There are reasons to be cautious and also, perhaps, a little suspicious when Scripture is "used" in moral discourse.

One obvious problem is the *silence* of Scripture. Scripture simply does not deal with many of the moral questions contemporary Christians find themselves asking. When we contemplate our choices, including those choices encountered in our medicine, our sexual lives, our economic concerns, and our politics, we frequently face options not considered in the Bible. And when we turn to Scripture for instruction about such choices, we find it silent about them.

The Bible is silent, for example, on the question of artificial organs. No scribe ever asked Jesus about contraceptives. Nor did any congregation ask Paul about removing the medical equipment keeping someone alive. And it is not just with respect to new medical technologies that Scripture is silent. Although Paul called for a collection for the poor, there is no "Chapter 11" that deals with bankruptcies in a capitalist economy. And no vision of Revelation foresaw the question about whether the contributions of political action committees to political campaigns should be limited. This is not to say that Scripture is irrelevant to the questions about which it is silent; it is simply to admit that it does not directly address many of the particular moral questions that contemporary Christians confront. Contemporary questions frequently seem alien to Scripture.

The silence of Scripture, however, is not the only reason — or even the main reason — to be cautious about its use as a source of moral wisdom. In addition to the silence of Scripture, there is its *strangeness*. Not only do contemporary questions often seem alien to Scripture; the strange worlds of Scripture also frequently seem remote and alien even to those who would speak with Christian integrity and candor. When Christians consult Scripture for advice concerning medical ethics or sexual ethics or economic ethics or political eth-

50

ics, they confront quaint and strange worlds of sickness, embarrassingly patriarchal cultures, alien economic orders, and quite different political realities and
assumptions.

When, in 2 Chronicles 16:12, the Chronicler rebukes Asa for having
sought the help of medical practitioners, it is a strange world of sickness in
Scripture. The Chronicler reports, "In the thirty-ninth year of his reign Asa was
diseased in his feet, and his disease became severe; yet even in his disease he did
not seek the Lord, but sought help from physicians." Few of us today would
chide a friend for consulting a physician about a gangrenous leg. When Deuteronomy 23:19 prohibits charging interest on a loan (or when, in Luke 6:35, Jesus
reiterates the prohibition while commanding his disciples to "lend, expecting
nothing in return"), it is a strange economic world in Scripture. The words of
Scripture are human words, we are driven to admit, words we may not simply
identify with timeless truth dropped from heaven or repeat without qualification as Christian counsel today. Still, they are the Word of God, our faith reminds us, and words we may not simply discredit at our convenience.[2]

Scripture is sometimes silent; it is sometimes strange; and sometimes one
part of Scripture seems to disagree with another part. That is the third problem
with Scripture as a resource for moral instruction: the *diversity* within it. Scripture does not always speak with one voice concerning the moral questions that
it does address. To give but one example, there is considerable diversity with respect to the question of divorce. Moses evidently allowed men to divorce their
wives (Deut. 24:1). Jesus, however, issued a prophetic denunciation of all divorce (Mark 10:2-12), except that in Matthew's Gospel he does evidently permit men to divorce their wives in cases of "unchastity" (Matt. 19:9). And Paul,
speaking for himself, seems to permit Christian men or women to divorce unbelieving spouses who had abandoned them (1 Cor. 7:15). Efforts to reduce
these diverse voices to one, or at least to get these voices into harmony, have
sometimes been ingenious but also frequently disingenuous. The diversity of
Scripture must be acknowledged, and it should give us pause when we consult
Scripture as a source for moral instruction.

Moreover, it is frequently difficult to figure out just what Scripture

2. In the famous 1916 address of Karl Barth, "The Strange New World within the Bible," the "strangeness" of Scripture is recognized on a number of levels, historical, moral,
and religious. Nevertheless, in the Bible Christians find "the Word of God" (p. 43). This is
the "strange new world within the Bible": "The Holy Spirit establishes the righteousness of
heaven in the midst of the unrighteousness of earth and will not stop nor stay until all that
is dead has been brought to life and a new *world* has come into being" (p. 50). Barth, *The
Word of God and the Word of Man*, trans. Douglas Horton (New York: Harper & Row,
Harper Torchbook edition, 1957), pp. 28-50.

means. What did Matthew mean by "unchastity," for example? What kinds of things did he intend to include as justification for divorce and remarriage in Matthew 19:9? We must therefore add the *difficulty* of Scripture to the problems we face when we consult it as "useful" for moral instruction. When we turn to Scripture as useful for moral instruction it is wise to remember these problems: the silence of Scripture, the strangeness of Scripture, the diversity within Scripture, and the difficulty of Scripture.

It is also wise, however, to admit that there are problems not only in Scripture but also in us. Indeed, the difficulty of interpreting Scripture can be attributed to us as well as to the text. We are *unfamiliar with Scripture.* That may be too kind to some of my students. Some of them are biblically illiterate, even when they have grown up within the church, even when they have some vague idea that the Bible ought to be important to them. A colleague at the college where I teach tells of a student, for example, who wrote in an essay that Jesus must have been a Roman Catholic because he was, after all, born before the Reformation. Our lack of familiarity with Scripture makes understanding any part of it difficult. This problem, thankfully, can be remedied. That student, I hope, became a good deal more familiar with Scripture by the end of the course in which he was enrolled, and we can all invest a little time in becoming familiar with Scripture.

I do not mean, of course, that we all have to become experts in Scripture. Some scholars in the church should learn Hebrew and Greek so that the community has access to Scripture in its original languages, but it is not necessary that everyone do so. Some scholars should study the history, literature, and culture of the ancient Near East and of the Mediterranean region during the biblical period, but it is not necessary that we all invest our lives in such scholarship. Some scholars should study the history of the interpretation of Scripture, but it is not necessary that everyone be familiar with classical or contemporary debates about hermeneutics. What is necessary, however, if the church is to be attentive to Scripture as "useful" for moral discourse and discernment, is that members of the Christian community be familiar with Scripture.[3]

3. The church gathers around Scripture, after all, and not around the conclusions of its biblical scholars concerning Scripture. The church may be grateful for the contributions of biblical scholarship to its communal effort to understand Scripture, but it must not substitute some scholar's reading of Scripture for its own. Just as the work of a moral theologian must not substitute for the moral discourse of the Christian community but serve it, so the work of the biblical scholar must not substitute for the community's reading of Scripture but serve it. Its vocation as a community of moral discourse, deliberation, and discernment requires members who are familiar with Scripture. The community should be hospitable to scholars but not surrender its communal obligation to gather together around Scripture rather than around scholars.

The problems with us as readers go deeper than ignorance, however. Programs of instruction may easily enough remedy our lack of familiarity with Scripture, but the deeper problem is our refusal to be formed by Scripture. What we need is not just information about Scripture or from Scripture but a readiness to be formed by Scripture in Christian community. Call it *pride,* or "interpretative arrogance," but we too frequently "use" Scripture, just as some Jewish Christians in Rome used the Law, to judge others as "sinners" and to defend ourselves as the "righteous." We use Scripture as a weapon against others and in defense of our own interests. Such habits of reading Scripture leave us, rather than it, in charge, and should make us not only careful but also perhaps a little suspicious when Scripture is "used" in moral discourse.

There is a story told in more than one pious Dutch Calvinist household of great-great-grandpa in the Netherlands. He was famous for his piety and especially for his ability to recite a Scripture verse appropriate to any occasion. He was not unfamiliar with Scripture. People would come from the surrounding villages to consult with him about a verse to use at a particular funeral or wedding or baptism. He was, however, infamous as a horse trader. None of the villagers who so admired his ability to quote Scripture would deal with him when they needed a horse. One day a stranger's horse went lame, and great-great-grandpa sold the stranger an old nag to get home for about four times its value. Great-great-grandma complained about this behavior, giving great-great-grandpa a little nag of her own, calling attention to her husband's reputation among the villagers. Great-great-grandpa retorted quickly, "But great-great-grandma, I did it by the command of the Lord: I saw a stranger, and I took him in."

The story is surely apocryphal. The phrase "took him in" is an American idiom, not a Dutch idiom, for "took advantage of him." The story is told in pious households like the one I grew up in to amuse, surely, but also as a cautionary tale. There are reasons to be suspicious of the "use" of Scripture in moral arguments — especially when its use is self-serving.

We need not resort to bad jokes, however, to be reminded of the possibilities for abusing Scripture. We need only remember our histories. Dutch Calvinists like me should remember that Dutch Calvinists in South Africa used Scripture to defend apartheid. All American Christians ought to remember that Scripture was used to defend slavery. It must simply be admitted that appeals to Scripture have sometimes done a great deal of harm. When some people pointed to the Bible to claim that AIDS was God's punishment for homosexual behavior, a great deal of harm was done. And when some Dutch Calvinists refused to have their children immunized against polio because Jesus said, "Those who are well have no need of a physician" (Matt. 9:12), a great deal of harm was done. It may be said, and rightly said, that these uses of Scripture are all abuses of Scripture, but people have nevertheless sometimes been harmed by appeals to Scripture — notably, usually women or children or those on the margins, seldom "righteous" adult males.

Such abuses of Scripture may make us a little suspicious when we hear appeals to it in moral argument, and they should surely make us careful about the way we use Scripture ourselves. As soon as we make an effort to be methodologically careful, however, we encounter another problem. There is not only moral diversity within Scripture but also methodological diversity among interpreters about how to read and use Scripture as "useful" to moral instruction. This is hardly a problem we can avoid if we would be careful about reading and using Scripture. The silence and the strangeness of Scripture, its diversity and the difficulty, the widespread lack of familiarity with it, the habitual abuse of people by the abuse of Scripture, and the methodological diversity among interpreters, all conspire to suggest that it might be best simply to ignore Scripture when we think about the moral life.

On the other hand, there is that commendation of Scripture by the author of Second Timothy that Scripture is "useful." And there is the commonplace affirmation of the confessions of the churches that Scripture is somehow normative for the churches' faith and life.[4] There is, moreover, the practice of Christian communities that continue to read the biblical materials not simply as curious literary artifacts but as canon, not only as scripted, as written, but also as script to be somehow performed.

If we allow the problems we have identified to overwhelm us, if we push Scripture to the margins of congregational life because of them, we put ourselves at risk of forgetfulness. Ignoring Scripture is not an option for the church, not at least if it is to continue to be the church. There is no Christian life that is not shaped *somehow* by Scripture. There is no Christian moral discernment that is not tied *somehow* to Scripture. There is no Christian ethic — no Christian medical ethic or sexual ethic or economic ethic or political ethic — that is not formed and informed *somehow* by Scripture.

Granted that Scripture is sometimes silent about the particular moral questions Christians face today. Granted that the worlds of sickness and sex and money and politics in Scripture are sometimes strange and alien. Granted that

---

4. To give just one example, the Belgic Confession, Article 7: "We believe that this Holy Scripture contains the will of God completely and that everything one must believe to be saved is sufficiently taught in it. . . . Therefore we reject with all our hearts everything that does not agree with this infallible rule. . . ." Quoted from *Psalter Hymnal* (Grand Rapids: CRC Publications, 1987), p. 821.

Scripture is sometimes diverse and sometimes difficult. In spite of the problems Christian communities turn again and again to Scripture, and they find in it a resource to renew their life, to retrieve their identity and vocation, and to re-form their practices. The central problem is finally not whether to continue to read Scripture as "useful for teaching, for reproof, for correction, and for train-ing in [the moral life]" but how. A contemporary Christian ethic will not sim-ply be identical with Scripture, but it must somehow be informed by it. Some-how — but how? That is the problem.

It is not the sort of problem, however, that, given a little time and giving a little effort, we can figure out and set aside as solved. It is more a mystery than a puzzle. The formation of a community and its moral life by the reading of its Scripture is a mystery that transcends our puzzling over it, eludes our efforts at mastery, and evokes not just curiosity but wonder. The mystery is admitted and celebrated when Christians point toward the Spirit of God as the One who in-spires Scripture and illuminates it.

The mystery keeps methodological reflection humble, but it does not eliminate the need for it. The Spirit did not simply overrule the human authors of Scripture. They spoke and wrote with their own voices. And the Spirit does not simply overrule the human readers of Scripture. We hear and interpret with our own ears. And as there were many prophets who claimed to speak a word from the Lord, so there are many interpreters who claim to hear a word from God in Scripture. The community that gathers around Scripture needs to think hard and humbly about how Scripture is "useful" for the moral life.

Somehow — but *How?* A Proposal

"Humbly" would indeed seem to be the first rule for the use of Scripture. *We must read and use Scripture humbly.* That first rule, of course, applies to propos-als for the use of Scripture as well: if we must read Scripture humbly, then surely we must make proposals for the use of Scripture humbly. This proposal is not offered as the last word about the use of Scripture in Christian ethics, as if this problem were merely a puzzle waiting for solution. It is offered in recogni-tion of the mystery at work in creating and reading Scripture. It is not intended to be the last word but a helpful word, a humble contribution to the Christian community that gathers around Scripture in the conviction that it is "useful" to its conversations about the moral life.

Reading Scripture Humbly

To read Scripture humbly is to read it with a readiness to be formed — and re-formed — by it. To read Scripture humbly is to reject the pride or the "interpre-tative arrogance" that reads Scripture to defend our own righteousness and to condemn others as "sinners." When we use Scripture as a weapon against others and in defense of our own interests, we do not read it humbly. When we called attention to the "problem" of "interpretative arrogance," we called attention to the fact that the abuse of Scripture frequently led to the abuse of people, and we observed that it was usually women, children, and those on the margins who ended up hurt. Let the rule that we read Scripture humbly, therefore, make us suspicious of those readings, including those that claim to be "objective," which hurt or abuse those a particular culture assigns to the margins. Let the rule that we read Scripture humbly prompt us to identify with the powerless and those on the margins in our readings. At the very least, let this rule prompt us to listen carefully to them and to *their* readings of Scripture.

Scripture is "inspired by God," the author of Second Timothy reminds us, but all our efforts to "use" it in moral instruction remain human efforts. We may not substitute our reading of Scripture for Scripture itself. We may not presume to speak the divine Word, or the last word, simply because our argu-ment makes some use of Scripture. And we may not be so arrogant as to insist upon our own way in reading it, claiming for ourselves some "right to private interpretation." Love "does not insist on its own way" (1 Cor. 13:5), even when it is a way of reading Scripture. We read Scripture humbly when we read it in community with those who are different from us. We read it humbly when we are part of a community that silences neither Scripture nor each other, part of the whole people of God attentive to the whole of Scripture.

The temptations we encountered in moral discourse are encountered once again in interpretation. There was, you recall, a temptation to regard per-sonal choices simply as private matters, as no one else's business. That tempta-tion is encountered here in the insistence upon the "right to private interpreta-tion." But that is not to read Scripture humbly. There was also, you recall, a temptation to surrender personal choices to the group, denying personal re-sponsibility for one's choices. That temptation is encountered here in the ne-glect of our own responsibility to read Scripture humbly, surrendering the re-sponsibility for interpretation to others. The community is not a substitute for personal responsibility, even when we are reading Scripture; it nurtures and sustains that responsibility. With respect to communal decisions, we noted pre-viously the temptations to surrender such choices either to the church's leaders or to some other community. We encounter those temptations here when communities surrender the interpretative task either to the ecclesiastical hierarchy or to the academy. It is not easy to find our way through this thicket with temptations on every side, but we will not find our way by ourselves. *We must read and use Scripture in Christian community.* That is the second rule for our use of Scripture, and all the rest are simply implications of it.

Reading Scripture in Christian Community

This second rule comes as no surprise, I suppose, for we have observed that "Scripture" and "church" are correlative concepts. Part of what we mean when we call a community "church" is that this community uses Scripture *somehow* as essential to its identity and to its common life. And part of what we mean when we call certain writings "Scripture" is that these writings ought to be used *somehow* in the common life of the church to nourish and reform it. Without the church, as was noted earlier, the writings we call "Scripture" are simply a little library of ancient Near Eastern religious texts. And without the Scripture the church loses its identity and its way.

Reading the Scripture as "Canon"

If without the church these writings are simply a little library of ancient Near Eastern texts, within it they are "canon." To read Scripture within Christian community means, therefore, that *we must read it as canon.*

"Canon" is correlative to "church," not to the university. Within the university, at least within the university formed by the Enlightenment of the eighteenth century, these writings *are* simply a miscellaneous collection of ancient religious texts. Within such universities the interpretation of Scripture was required to be "scientific." A "scientific" reading of Scripture required objectivity and neutrality; it required that Scripture be treated like any other text. The historian's inquiry was limited to the historical situation about which (or in which) the texts were written. When historians assume hegemony over the reading of Scripture, they conscientiously bracket consideration of the contemporary significance of the text.

The historical study of these texts has, to be sure, provided important information about them, information that those who read Scripture in Christian community may not simply dismiss. The historian's methods have provided quite valuable information and quite interesting theories about the history of Israel and of Jesus and of the early church, about the historical circumstances of the texts. "Objective" historians, however, are, ironically, always at risk of forgetfulness. There is plenty of recollection of data, but — without surrendering "objectivity" and joining the confession of the church that these writings are canon — there is no owning this story as our story, no remembering in which we can find identity and community. The "objective" historians are always at risk of reducing the memory of the church to a (biased) recollection of historical data. The methods and results of post-Enlightenment historians fragmented the canon and drove a wedge between the historical meaning of Scripture and its continuing significance, and the wedge quickly opened up an ugly ditch between the past and the present.

Moreover, because the Enlightenment regarded public order as founded on rational and universal principles rather than on the particular traditions of specific communities, the university formed by the Enlightenment undercut the "public" significance of Scripture. Part of that rational public order, after all, was the guarantee of freedom of choice in things "publicly indifferent." And the Enlightenment regarded the interpretation of Scripture as one such "publicly indifferent" thing. Individuals were authorized to interpret it in a publicly indifferent way — to see it as being addressed, for example, as Hobbes insisted, to the "inward man" about the inward man,[5] or to regard it, following Kant, as a naive and mythical account of a morality that the "enlightened" could now recognize and approve as rational.[6] Thus the Enlightenment sanctioned and sustained "the right of private judgment."[7]

Against "the right to private judgment" we have insisted on the importance of reading Scripture in Christian community. And one implication of reading Scripture in that social context, rather than in the social context of the Enlightenment university, is that we must read Scripture as "canon." It was, as we have noted, the church that decided which writings to canonize. If we are to read Scripture as "canon," then, we may be instructed by the story of the church's decision.

The history of the canon is, of course, a complicated history, but any account of it that fails to acknowledge the significance of Marcion is a flawed account. Marcion came to Rome around 140 A.D. There he proclaimed the gospel as he understood it, and there the church said that he misunderstood it, misunderstood it so thoroughly as to destroy it. Marcion (mis)understood Paul's con-

---

5. Thomas Hobbes, *Leviathan* (Harmondsworth: Penguin, 1968), IV, ch. 47, pp. 710-11.

6. Immanuel Kant, *Religion within the Limits of Reason Alone*, bk. 3.

7. See John Milbank, *Theology and Social Theory: Beyond Secular Reason* (Oxford: Basil Blackwell, 1990), pp. 17-20.

trast between Law and gospel to entail an antithesis between the Hebrew Scriptures and the good news of Jesus. Indeed, Marcion proclaimed that Jesus, far from being an agent of the God who had created the world and covenanted with Israel at Sinai, had delivered humanity from that Creator God, from Israel's Lawgiver, from that vindictive judge. Jesus, Marcion insisted, had delivered us from the world that God made and from the hold that God has on us through our bodies. Marcion rejected the Hebrew Scriptures and proposed instead a new Scripture, a collection of the ten Pauline epistles and an abridged Gospel of Luke. Correlative with such a canon and such a view of God was Marcion's anthropology. He (mis)understood Paul's contrast between "flesh" and "spirit" to imply a dualism between body and spirit and to entail indifference, indeed, animosity, toward the body. Accordingly, his version of Luke's Gospel left out the nativity narratives and began when Jesus "came down to Capernaum" (from heaven presumably). It comes as no surprise that Marcion demanded of his followers a rigorous asceticism.

The church said "no" to Marcion — "no" to his theology, "no" to his anthropology, and "no" to his canon. And when Marcion insisted on his own Scripture and on his own way of reading it, the church excommunicated him in 144. The response hastened the development of both canon and creed. The canon would (continue to) include the Hebrew Scriptures as Christian Scripture, and it would include a larger collection of "New Testament" writings. The creed summarized the story of that Scripture and guided the reading of it.

To read Scripture as canon is to *read it without Marcion's dualism.* We must read Scripture without animosity toward the world God made or toward the bodies God created. We must read Scripture not as good news about deliverance *from* the world God made but as good news about deliverance *for* the world God made. We must not reduce its significance to an address to "the inner man" about some otherworldly realities. We must acknowledge its worldly and "public" significance. And we must remember the rootedness of Christian proclamation in Hebrew Scripture.

This also is entailed in the story of the canon: To read Scripture as canon is to *read it according to the "Rule of Faith,"* according to the creed. The creed is the "short story" of the canon. What came to be called the Apostles' Creed, for example, begins, as the canon begins, with the Creator. The Creator is the Redeemer; the God who made this world, these bodies, and covenantal promises is the very God who sent Jesus. The center of the creed, and the center of the Christian canon, is the story of Jesus, who "suffered under Pontius Pilate, was crucified, died, and was buried. . . . On the third day he arose again from the dead. . . ." And the end of the story is the work of the Spirit; the creed, like the canon, concludes with the confident hope for the resurrection of the dead. The creed is a Cliff's Notes for our reading of Scripture. It may not be substituted for Scripture, but it may and must guide our reading of it.

The churches that made the decision to canonize these writings had already received them, had made a habit of reading them, and had discovered in them the authority they acknowledged in the decision to canonize them. The church did not so much create Scripture as acknowledge it as the texts within which the Spirit moved to give life and to guide. And we must remember not only that without the church there is no Scripture but also that without Scripture the church loses its identity and its way. The church is the community that interprets and performs Scripture.

As "canon" Scripture is recognized both as scripted and as script.[8] It is scripted — that is to say, it was written. The texts of Scripture were written once upon a particular time by authors who did certain things with words. And it is script — that is to say, it is to be performed. Scripture is performed again and again by those who set these writings apart as "canon." It is performed again and again in the life of the churches, in their worship, in their organization, in their moral choices. Indeed, as Nicholas Lash has observed, "the fundamental form of the *Christian* interpretation of Scripture" is the life of the believing community.[9]

Every performance of any script is, of course, an interpretation. A performance can be improved if someone in the troupe attends carefully to what the author once did with the words at his or her disposal. To be sure, such study is hardly a guarantee of a good performance. Lacking other gifts, a troupe will give a wooden and spiritless performance of a carefully studied text. Moreover, careful study of the script is not even strictly necessary for an excellent performance. A troupe may have seen (or heard) enough fine performances in the past to perform not just adequately but splendidly. Even so, even though careful study of the original script is neither sufficient nor strictly necessary, it remains important — and important both for those who would check the "integrity" of a performance and for the troupe, those who have the responsibility to perform. Moreover, because there are different performances, and because no performance definitively captures the meaning of the script, study of the script as scripted, as written, remains critically important as a test for and guide to per-

8. Or, to use a distinction made by Nicholas Wolterstorff, Scripture is both "object" and "instrument"; it is the effect of the action of writing texts and the instrument that we use to perform certain other actions. See Nicholas Wolterstorff, *Art in Action: Toward a Christian Aesthetic* (Grand Rapids: Eerdmans, 1980), p. 80.

9. Nicholas Lash, "Performing the Scriptures," in *Theology on the Way to Emmaus* (London: SCM Press, 1986), p. 42.

formance. I might be talking about Shakespeare's *Hamlet* in this paragraph, but I'm not. I'm talking about Scripture as canon and the interpretation and performance of that script in the life of the church. And I am making a case for careful exegesis, for consideration of what the authors of Scripture did with the words at their disposal. To read Scripture as script to be performed we must read it carefully as scripted, as written once upon a particular time by authors who did certain things with words. The rule that we must read Scripture in Christian community is not a license to neglect exegesis, as though we could simply substitute some particular tradition of performance and interpretation for the script. On the contrary, to read Scripture in Christian community requires that we nurture and sustain biblical scholarship as an important contribution to the communal effort to understand and perform Scripture. *We must read Scripture with exegetical care and skill.*

Reading Scripture with Exegetical Care

The canon itself recognizes that the writings gathered there have a history. Scripture is quite candid about the fact that it did not simply fall from heaven as some timeless document. Luke, for example, reported that he made use of the oral tradition and of other narratives in putting together his Gospel. Paul's letters are quite clearly letters, concrete addresses to particular congregations dealing with specific problems in a timely way. To read Scripture with exegetical care and skill will mean to attend not only to the grammatical construction of the words authors had at their disposal but also to literary issues like genre, to issues of audience and occasion, to the use of sources and traditions, and to the social and historical location of the text as written.

To read Scripture with exegetical care and skill is a daunting task, and as we have said, careful attention to the script as scripted does not insure a lively and spirited performance. So, we come back to the rule about reading Scripture in Christian community, now to celebrate the diversity of gifts within the community. Some are gifted with exegetical learning and skills. They bring their knowledge of Hebrew and Greek, or their training in the tools of historical, literary, or social investigation, not just to the texts but to the community. And the community may be glad for their contribution to the communal task of interpretation and performance. Others are gifted with an awareness of the tradition of interpretation and performance within that particular community — or within a different particular community. Some are gifted with moral imagination. Some are gifted with a passion for righteousness, a hunger for justice. Some are gifted with sweet reasonableness, peacemakers among us. Some are gifted with intellectual clarity, and some with simply piety. Such gifted people — including those gifted with exegetical learning — must not boast of their gifts, or claim to have no need of the other members of the community. The task of interpretation and performance is a communal one. We must read Scripture in Christian community.

There is a diversity of gifts within the interpretive community. And there is also a diversity of interpretations, diverse ways of using Scripture as morally instructive. Reading Scripture in Christian community does not mean that we will always agree. There have been diverse ways of using Scripture in moral discourse for as long as there have been Christian communities. Jewish Christians did not all read Scripture one way, but they read it differently than Gentile Christians did. Within the New Testament canon there are diverse ways of interpreting the Hebrew Scripture, of using it for moral instruction. Matthew has Jesus say of the Torah that "whoever breaks one of the least of these commandments, and teaches others to do the same, will be called least in the kingdom of heaven" (Matt. 5:19). Mark, on the other hand, reports not only that Jesus broke the Sabbath commandment (Mark 2:23–3:7; cf. Matt. 12:1-14) but also that he taught others to disregard the commandments concerning kosher (Mark 7:18-19). To read Scripture in Christian community, to read Scripture as canon, is not to insist upon unanimity in reading it. It is to insist that, together with those with whom we differ, we continue existing traditions — *and continue to assess existing traditions* — of interpretation and performance of those works created by authors and recognized as canon.

Reading Scripture Prayerfully

To read Scripture in Christian community is to read it in ways informed by the practices of Christian community. Consider, for example, the practice of prayer. There is an obvious — but often overlooked — connection between reading Scripture and prayer. The churches recognize the connection in the intimate association between Scripture and prayer in most Christian liturgies. When Scripture is read, a prayer for illumination is close at hand. We read Scripture in the context of prayer. Wisely so, for *we must read Scripture prayerfully.*

Moreover, to pray is itself a performance of Scripture. When we say the Lord's Prayer, following the advice of Scripture, "Pray then in this way . . ." (Matt. 6:9), and when we cry "Abba!" (Rom. 8:15) or "Maranatha" (1 Cor. 16:22), or when we simply groan in pain toward God's good future (Rom. 8:22-27), we perform Scripture. We pray in the context of reading Scripture, and we must read Scripture in the context of the practice of prayer.

Prayer is a part of the Christian life. Indeed, it is, as John Calvin said, the most important part, "the chief exercise of faith,"[10] the part of the whole Christian life that cannot be left out without the whole ceasing to *be* the Christian life. And as Karl Barth said, the Christian life is a life of prayer, a life of "humble and resolute, frightened and joyful invocation of the gracious God in gratitude, praise, and above all, petition."[11] Since prayer is a practice for Christians, we could also quote Alasdair MacIntyre; in an important but difficult set of clauses he defines a practice as a "form of socially established cooperative human activity through which goods internal to that form of activity are realized in the course of trying to achieve those standards of excellence which are appropriate to, and partially definitive of, that form of activity with the result that human powers to achieve excellence and human conceptions of the ends and goods involved are systematically extended."[12] Not many Christians at prayer are likely to quote Calvin or Barth or MacIntyre, but some Christians at prayer would be likely to make Calvin and Barth and MacIntyre nod their heads and say, "Yes, that's what I meant."

Prayer is learned in Christian community, and it is learned not only as an idea but also as a human activity that engages one's body as well as one's mind, one's affections and passions and loyalties as well as one's rationality. Prayer is an activity that focuses one's whole self on God. In learning to pray, one learns the good that is "internal to that form of activity"; one learns, that is, to attend to God, to look to God.[13] To attend to God is not easy to learn — or painless. Given our inveterate attention to ourselves and to our own needs and wants, we frequently corrupt the practice. We corrupt prayer whenever we turn it to a means to accomplish some other good than the good of prayer, whenever we make of it an instrument to achieve wealth, happiness, health, or even moral improvement. In learning to pray, we learn to look to God; and after the blinding vision, we begin to look at all else in a new light.

---

10. John Calvin, *Institutes,* III.xx.1.

11. Karl Barth, *The Christian Life: Church Dogmatics,* IV/4, trans. Geoffrey Bromiley (Grand Rapids: Eerdmans, 1981), p. 43.

12. Alasdair MacIntyre, *After Virtue: A Study in Moral Theory* (Notre Dame, Ind.: University of Notre Dame Press, 1981), p. 175. On prayer as a practice, see further Allen Verhey, "The Practices of Piety and the Practice of Medicine: Prayer, Scripture, and Medical Ethics," in *Seeking Understanding: The Stob Lectures, 1986-1998* (Grand Rapids: Eerdmans 2001), pp. 191-250.

13. On prayer as attention see especially Iris Murdoch, "On 'God' and 'Good,'" in *Revisions: Changing Perspectives in Moral Philosophy,* ed. Stanley Hauerwas and Alasdair MacIntyre (Notre Dame, Ind.: University of Notre Dame Press, 1983), pp. 68-91; Craig Dykstra, *Vision and Character* (New York: Paulist, 1981), pp. 45-98; and Simone Weil, *Waiting on God,* trans. E. Craufurd (London: Collins, Fontana Books, 1959), p. 51.

In learning to pray, we learn as well certain standards of excellence[14] that belong to prayer and its attention to God, standards of excellence that are "appropriate to" prayer and "partially definitive" of prayer. We learn *reverence*, the readiness to attend to God as God and to all else in relation to God. We learn *humility*, the readiness to acknowledge that we are not gods, but the creatures of God, cherished by God but finite and mortal and, yes, sinful creatures in need finally of God's grace and future. We learn *gratitude*, the disposition of thankfulness for the opportunities within the limits of our finiteness and mortality to delight in God and in the gifts of God. We learn *hope*, a disposition of confidence and courage that comes not from trusting oneself and the little truth one knows well or the little good one does well, but from trusting the grace and power of God. And we learn *care*; attentive to God, we grow attentive to the neighbor as related to God. These standards of excellence form virtues not only for prayer but also for daily life — and for the reading of Scripture. Prayer-formed persons and the prayer-formed communities — in the whole of their being and in the whole of their living — will be reverent, humble, grateful, hopeful, and caring. One does not pray in order to achieve these virtues. They are not formed when we use prayer as a technique. They are formed in simple attentiveness to God, and they spill over into new virtues for daily life and discernment.

What would a prayer-formed reading of Scripture look like? There are some hints, I think, in these standards of excellence, but consider also the forms that such attention to God takes. Prayer attends to God in the form of invocation and adoration, confession, thanksgiving, and petition. *Invocation* requires remembrance.[15] We invoke (and revere) not just any old god, not some nameless god of philosophical theism, not some idolatrous object of somebody's "ultimate concern." We invoke the God "rendered" in Scripture, and a prayer-formed reading of Scripture will serve remembrance and invocation. So the practice of prayer both performs Scripture and forms the practice of reading Scripture in Christian community. We remember God; and, as we do, we are reoriented to God and to all things in relation to God.

This reorientation to all things is called *metanoia*, repentance. Invocation evokes repentance. Attention to God in prayer, therefore, also takes the form of

14. Consider, for example, John Calvin's attention to the "rules" of prayer in *Institutes*, III.xx.4-16. Calvin's "rules" are reverence, a sincere sense of want (that is, to pray earnestly), humility, and confident hope.

15. On prayer as an act of remembrance see Nicholas Wolterstorff, *Until Justice and Peace Embrace* (Grand Rapids: Eerdmans, 1983), pp. 152-56. Donald Saliers, "Liturgy and Ethics: Some New Beginnings," *Journal of Religious Ethics* 7 (Fall 1979): 173-89, also emphasizes that "the shape and substance of prayer is anamnetic" (p. 178).

(humble) *confession.* Prayerful readings of Scripture will serve confession. Prayer will form a readiness to read Scripture "over-against ourselves"[16] and not just "for ourselves"; "over-against" our lives and our common life and not simply in self-serving defense of them; "over-against" even our conventional readings of Scripture, subverting our efforts to use the texts to boast about our own righteousness or to protect our own status and power. Confession is good for the soul, but it is also good for hermeneutics; it can form a hermeneutic humility. Such humility will attend carefully but without anxiety to the readings of saints and strangers (especially to the readings of the poor and the powerless and those whom it has been too much our impulse to shun and neglect), and it will attend to the whole church attending to the whole Scripture.

Attention to God also takes the form of (grateful) *thanksgiving.* Gratitude to God can form in readers the readiness not to count what is given as "ours to dispose of as if we created it nor ours to serve only our own interests."[17] Prayers of thanksgiving can train us to stewardship of our gifts, including Scripture and the skills to read it. They train readers to share their gifts, to use them in service to the community, without the conceit of philanthropy. The conceit of philanthropy divides the community of readers into two groups, the relatively self-sufficient benefactors (or scholars) and the needy beneficiaries of their interpretative skill. Prayer-formed readers of Scripture (including those readers with scholarly gifts) will share their gifts and serve the community, acknowledging that we are all recipients of God's gifts. Such service is no less a response to these gifts than the prayers of thanksgiving themselves. Gratitude, moreover, trains readers to gladness, to delight in the gifts of God, including Scripture. It forms an attitude toward Scripture that is itself a "performance" of the psalmists' delight in Torah. Moreover, as prayers of thanksgiving are a form of attention to God, the gifts are celebrated not so much because they serve our interests but because they manifest God's grace and glory and serve God's cause. Prayers of thanksgiving, then, this form of attention to God, form in the community of readers a readiness to reform their reading habits and their "performances" that God may be manifest and his cause served.

Finally, simple attentiveness to God takes the form of (hopeful and caring) *petition.* It is easy, of course, to attend to ourselves in petition rather than to God, to our wishes rather than to God's cause. The practice of prayer is cor-

---

16. Dietrich Bonhoeffer, *No Rusty Swords: Letters, Lectures, and Notes, 1928-36,* ed. Edwin H. Robinson, trans. Edwin H. Robinson and John Bowden (New York: Harper & Row, 1965), p. 185.

17. James M. Gustafson, "Spiritual Life and Moral Life," in *Theology and Christian Ethics* (Philadelphia: Pilgrim, 1974), p. 170.

rupted when we use it as a kind of magic to get what we want, whether a fortune, or four more healthy years, or a resolution to an interpretative or moral dispute. When petition is a form of attention to God, however, then we pray — and pray boldly — that God's cause will be displayed, that God's good future will be present. We pray — and pray boldly — as Jesus taught us, for a taste of that future, for a taste of it not so much in an ecstatic spiritual experience but in such ordinary things as everyday bread and everyday forgiveness, in such mundane realities as tonight's rest and tomorrow's work, in such earthy stuff as the health of mortal flesh and the peace and justice of our communities. We govern our petitions — and our deeds, including the acts of reading and interpreting Scripture — by a vision of God's good future and by the aching acknowledgment that it is not yet. That vision is evoked by remembrance and formed by reading Scripture, but it also must govern our readings. A prayer-formed reading of Scripture attends to God and to the cause of God, and it forms in turn both our words in petition and our works in everyday attention to God. So, the practice of prayer may form both the practice of reading Scripture and the Christian life.

Prayer is not a technique to get what we want. It does not rescue us from ambiguity. It does not free us from the necessity of thinking hard about moral cases, sorting out various principles, identifying the various goods at stake, and listening carefully to different accounts of the situation. It does not liberate us from the tasks of reading texts carefully, attending to genre and to grammar, to historical and social contexts. Prayer does not rescue us from all of that, but it does permit us to do all of that while attentive to God and to be attentive to all of that as related to God. Moreover, the standards of excellence for prayer — reverence, humility, gratitude, hope, and care — may spill over into both our reading and our living when our reading is remembrance and our lives are attentive to God.

The Practice of Reading Scripture

As we noted, to read Scripture in Christian community is to read it in ways informed by the practices of Christian community. Prayer is such a practice, but so is reading Scripture itself.[18] Christians learn to read Scripture (and to read Scripture as important to the moral life) by being initiated into the practice of reading Scripture in Christian community, not by being taught that a creed

18. On reading Scripture as a practice, see further Verhey, "The Practices of Piety," pp. 41-51, and "The Holy Bible and Sanctified Sexuality," *Interpretation* 49, no. 1 (1995): 41-45.

calls Scripture an "infallible rule," nor by being taught by a biblical scholar that the Bible is a little library of ancient Near Eastern literature. The creed and the scholar may both be right, and Christian communities should affirm their creeds and be hospitable to scholars, but Christians learn this practice of reading Scripture in Christian community.

In learning to read Scripture as a practice of Christian community, Christians learn as well the good that belongs to reading Scripture, the "good internal to that form of activity." They learn, that is, *to remember*.[19] They learn to remember not only as an intellectual exercise, not just as a mental process of recollection, not only as disinterested recall of historical facts. They learn to own a past as their own past in the continuing church, and to own it as constitutive of identity and determinative for discernment.

That remembered past is not simply a series of events that can be described objectively but rather events to be celebrated in repentance and jubilee, to be rehearsed in ritual and festival. That past, moreover, is not simply gone; we do not live in the past, but it lives in us. Neither we nor our communities live in simple transcendence over time. Against Kant and Kierkegaard, we do not discover ourselves as "noumenal" selves in moments of radical freedom cut off from past and future. On the contrary, we find ourselves by remembering. By remembering we interpret the present, make sense of it. And by remembering we sustain certain possibilities and nurture certain expectations; by remembering we learn to hope. Without memory there is no hope. We are not "fated" by our past (not as long as repentance remains a possibility sustained by our memory, at any rate). On the contrary, the freedom we have we have by marshalling memories, by learning to tell a different story of our lives, to interpret our present situation differently, and by sustaining other possibilities.

Without remembering, there is no identity. In amnesia, one loses oneself. In memory, one finds an identity. And without common remembering, there is no community. It is little wonder that the church sustains this practice of reading Scripture and is itself sustained by it. The practice of reading Scripture is not the only way the church has to remember, but Scripture is surely the critical document for the church's remembering.

There are temptations to forgetfulness in public life, when Enlightenment assumptions demand generic principles and "scientific" knowledge, pushing

---

19. For the notion of remembrance as the "good" of reading Scripture, I am indebted to Stanley Hauerwas, "The Moral Authority of Scripture: The Politics and Ethics of Remembering," in *A Community of Character* (Notre Dame: University of Notre Dame Press, 1981), pp. 53-71. See also James Gustafson, *Treasure in Earthen Vessels* (New York: Harper & Brothers, 1961), pp. 71-78.

"god" to the margins. There are temptations to forgetfulness in personal life, when the private realm is construed as a space for the self-centered quest to satisfy desire. And there are temptations to forgetfulness, ironically, in the sort of historical reading of Scripture that treats these writings simply as the (more or less reliable) record of a figure of the past whose life ended with his death. Then the memory of Jesus is "merely a memory,"[20] an intellectual process of recollection, a disinterested reconstruction of some historical facts, not the memory that is constitutive of identity and community and determinative for discernment. In Christian community Scripture is read on the Lord's day, in celebration of resurrection, and in the confidence that the remembered Jesus lives. Forgetfulness threatens a loss of identity, but the remedy for forgetfulness is remembrance, and remembrance is served by reading Scripture.

Moreover, in learning to read Scripture and to remember, Christians learn as well certain standards of excellence "appropriate to" and "partially definitive" of this practice — three pairs of virtues for reading Scripture: holiness and sanctification, fidelity and creativity, discipline and discernment. *Holiness* is the standard of excellence for reading Scripture in Christian community that sets these writings apart from others, and also sets apart a time and a place to read them and to remember.[21] The church sets these writings apart as "holy" Bible, sets them apart as a whole as canon. To read any text as canonical is to read it in Christian community and in the light of that "whole." The canon itself, however, reminds its readers that texts have genre, authors, and audience, that they involve a process of tradition, that they have social and historical location. To read any text as canonical, therefore, does not license reading it as if it stood in timeless transcendence over its own time and place. On the contrary, holiness invites and welcomes attention to the textual, grammatical, literary, historical, and social investigations.

Sanctification is the standard of excellence in reading Scripture that is ready to set this canon alongside our lives and our common life as their rule and guide. It is the readiness to set the remembered story alongside all the stories of our lives — stories of sexual desire, stories of sickness and healing, stories of wealth and poverty, stories of politics — until our conduct and character and communities are judged and made new by the power of God, are formed in remembrance and hope, and themselves render the story rendered by Scripture. Sanctification invites and welcomes attention to the saints as the best interpreters.

---

20. See Luke Timothy Johnson, *Living Jesus: Learning the Heart of the Gospel* (San Francisco: HarperSanFrancisco, 1999), pp. 3-11.

21. See Stephen E. Fowl and L. Gregory Jones, *Reading in Communion: Scripture and Ethics in Christian Life* (Grand Rapids: Eerdmans, 1991), pp. 31-33.

Remembrance provides identity, and *fidelity* is simply the standard of excellence in reading and performing Scripture that is ready to live with integrity, ready to live faithfully in the memory that the church has owned as its own and in the hope that memory endues. Fidelity, however, requires a process of continual change, of *creativity;* for the past is past and we do not live in it, even if we remember it. We do not live in David's Jerusalem or in Pontius Pilate's, and an effort to "preserve" the past is doomed to the failure of anachronistic eccentricity. Nicholas Lash makes the point quite nicely with respect to the traditions and ecclesiastical dress of the Franciscans: "If, in thirteenth-century Italy, you wandered around in a coarse brown gown, . . . your dress said you were one of the poor. If, in twentieth-century Cambridge, you wander around in a coarse brown gown, . . . your dress now says, not that you are one of the poor, but that you are some kind of oddity in the business of 'religion.'" Fidelity to a tradition of solidarity with the poor requires creativity and change.[22] Moreover, God's good future is not yet, still sadly not yet. We do not live in John's "new" Jerusalem either, and an effort to read Scripture that neglects the continuing power of sin is condemned to the failure of utopian idealism. Creativity is the standard of excellence (nurtured in and limited by particular communities and traditions) that is ready to find words and deeds fitting both to Scripture and to our own time and place, so that we may live in the present with memory and hope and fidelity.

Discipline is the standard of excellence for reading Scripture that marks one as ready to be a disciple in a community of disciples, ready to submit to and to contribute to the mutual admonition and encouragement of Christian community, to its interpretive and moral discourse. Discipline is the humility not to insist that Scripture be read "for ourselves," either by insisting on a "right to private judgment" in interpretation or by demanding that any interpretation serve our interests. It is the humility to read Scripture over-against ourselves and our communities. Discipline holds both individuals and their ecclesial communities to their responsibilities to read and to perform Scripture, to form their lives and their common life by the truth of the story they love to tell.

Yet, the shape of that story and of lives formed to it requires *discernment,* the ability to recognize "fittingness."[23] In reading Scripture, discernment is the ability to recognize the plot of the story, to see the wholeness of Scripture, and to order the interpretation of any part toward that whole. It is to recognize how

22. Lash, *Theology on the Way to Emmaus,* p. 54.
23. On discernment see especially James M. Gustafson, "Moral Discernment in the Christian Life," in *Norm and Context in the Christian Life,* ed. Gene H. Outka and Paul Ramsey (New York: Charles Scribner's Sons, 1968), pp. 17-36.

a statute, a proverb, or a story "fits" the whole story. And in reading Scripture as "useful . . . for training in righteousness" (2 Tim. 3:16), discernment is the ability to plot our lives to "fit" the whole of Scripture, to order our lives toward that whole.

Discernment is a complex but practical wisdom. It does not rely on the simple application of general principles (whether of hermeneutics or of ethics) to particular cases by neutral and rational individuals. There is no checklist for discernment, no flow chart for how to read and perform Scripture in "fitting" ways. Still, there is discernment. It is learned and exercised in the community gathered around the Scriptures, and it involves the diversity of gifts present in the congregation. Some, as we said, are gifted with the scholarly tools of historical, literary, and social investigation; others, with moral imagination or with a passion for justice or with sweet reasonableness. But all are gifted with their own experience, and each is gifted with the Spirit that brings remembrance (John 14:26). Discernment requires a dialogue with the whole church gathered around the whole of Scripture; it requires reading Scripture with those whose experience is different from our own and whose experience of the authority of Scripture is different from our own. It requires a dialogue in which people listen both to Scripture and to one another, muting neither Scripture nor one another. In that dialogue and discernment, the authority of Scripture is "nonviolent."[24] The moment of recognition of Scripture's wholeness and truthfulness comes before the moment of submission to any part of it and prepares the way for it. Discernment enables us to see in the dialogue with Scripture and with saints and strangers that our readings of Scripture do not yet "fit" Scripture itself, and that our lives and our communities do not yet "fit" the story we love to tell and long to live. Then discernment is joined to discipline again, and the recognition of a more fitting way to tell the story and to live it prepares the way for humble submission and discipleship.

To be sure, in the community some are blinded by fear, and some by duty, and the perception of each is abridged by investments in his culture or class. To be sure, whole communities are sometimes blinded by idolatrous loyalties to their race, their social standing, or their power. Witness, for example, many Christians in Germany during Hitler's rule or the Dutch Reformed Church in South Africa during apartheid. And to be sure, the practice of reading Scripture is corrupted then. Frequently the habits of reading Scripture do not measure up

---

24. Margaret Farley, "Feminist Consciousness and the Interpretation of Scripture," in *Feminist Interpretation of the Bible,* ed. Letty M. Russell (Oxford: B. Blackwell, 1985), pp. 41-51; see esp. pp. 42-44. She cites Paul Ricoeur, *Essays in Biblical Interpretation,* ed. L. S. Mudge (Philadelphia: Fortress, 1980), p. 95.

to the standards of excellence given with the practice, and communities can stand at risk of forgetfulness even when they call Scripture an "infallible rule."

The remedy for forgetfulness is still to hear and to tell the old, old story, and to hear it now and then from saints and now and then from strangers.[25] In the struggle against forgetfulness we read Scripture in Christian community and struggle to meet these standards of excellence for reading it, both holiness and sanctification, both fidelity and creativity, both discipline and discernment.

Scripture and Moral Discourse in the Church

The practice of reading Scripture is not a substitute for the practice of moral discourse, but by now it should be clear that the two are intimately related. As in prayer we learn to be attentive to God and to all things as related to God, so in reading Scripture we learn to remember the story of God's work and way and to exercise discernment. In reading Scripture we remember a story that stretches from the creation of all things to "all things made new" (Rev. 21:5) through the story of Jesus of Nazareth, and we learn to do ethics "by way of reminder."

The practice of moral discourse is, as we have seen, evidently as old as the church itself. Paul described the Christian churches at Rome as "full of goodness, filled with all knowledge, and able to instruct one another" (Rom. 15:14). Nevertheless, he wrote "boldly" to the congregations he praised "by way of reminder" (Rom. 15:15), reminding them of the "gospel of God" (Rom. 1:1) in order to encourage "the obedience of faith" (Rom. 1:5; 16:26). The reading of Scripture in the context of moral discourse will also proceed "by way of reminder." Its good is remembrance. Its form is evangelical, remembering and telling "the gospel of God." And the standards of excellence are holiness and sanctification, fidelity and creativity, discipline and discernment.

Continuing churches are still — by tradition and vocation — communities of moral discourse. They talk together about what they ought to do. And not only about *what* they ought to do, but also about *why* they ought to do it. They give and hear reasons. And they weigh the reasons, they test them against the story they love to tell and long to live. That is to say, continuing churches are also still — by tradition and vocation — communities of moral deliberation, discernment, and memory.

The churches' moral discourse, of course, frequently integrates delibera-

25. Fowl and Jones, *Reading in Communion,* pp. 62-64, 111-30.

tion, discernment, and memory into one conversation. They are not a set of sequential steps, as though any conversation had to proceed through these stages in sequence in order to count as a good conversation. Even so, permit me to divide them into stages or levels of discourse for the sake of analysis, for at the different stages of the churches' discourse Scripture is "useful" in different ways. At the different levels of its conversation Scripture's authority is different.

When we are simply talking about our concrete choices, about what we should do or leave undone, Scripture is hardly "useful." We do not live in the first century. Our choices are different. Even a choice that would have some external similarity to a choice in the first century will be a different choice because the social context for it is different. The choice, for example, to take interest on a loan is a different choice in our world than it was in the economic world of the first century. At the stage of deliberation, however, when reasons are given and heard, Scripture can be cited (and frequently is cited) as part of the process of deliberation in Christian communities. It is "used" to say why something was done or left undone. And, of course, among the passages of Scripture which can be cited (and frequently are cited) there are rules and "prescriptions." When we are talking about why something should be done, we sometimes appeal to one or another of these biblical rules. We may appeal to a particular piece of advice that Paul gave to the Corinthian Christians, for example — in ways not unlike the ways some members of that early church appealed to the Hebrew Scriptures. We may appeal to some biblical rule as a reason that something should be done or left undone in the contemporary church — say, to Matthew's prohibition of divorce "except for unchastity" as a reason to license (or prohibit) a certain divorce.

Notice, however, that at the deliberative stage there are also appeals to a wide variety of other sources of moral insight and wisdom. As in the early church, Christians today may give reasons that appeal to the witness of a charismatic prophet or to the authority of an official leader of the community. They may appeal to the moral commonplaces of the surrounding culture or to the traditions of the community, to conventional wisdom or to sociological information. They may appeal to their own experience, or to what they know that they know in some other way than that it is found in Scripture.

It is altogether appropriate that deliberation involve a variety of sources. In the deliberative dialogue, we may not demand that people violate what they know that they know in other ways. We may not use the slogan *sola scriptura* to silence other voices and other sources, to discount the experience of oppression or natural science or "natural" morality. We may not use the "authority of Scripture" to put a stop to conversation, to beat those who speak from some other experience or from some other source into silence and submission. Of course, in the community gathered around Scripture it will always be appropriate to invite each and all to the reconsideration of what we know that we know, but that is an invitation to the next level, to discernment. In the Christian community it will always be appropriate to exhort each other to interpret our experience, or the "assured results" of science, or some minimal notion of morality, in the light of Scripture, but that is a call to engage in the next stage, in discernment.

At the deliberative stage it is appropriate that there be appeals to a wide variety of sources — and at the deliberative stage it is also altogether appropriate that Scripture be counted simply as one of many sources! The rules and laws of Scripture have a limited "usefulness" and authority at the level of deliberation. The prescriptions and prohibitions that are found within Scripture ought to be considered in deliberation, but the ability to cite a biblical rule does not put a stop to the community's deliberative conversation. Fidelity to Scripture requires creativity. We may repeat Paul's word to the Corinthians, "Does not nature itself teach you that if a man wears long hair, it is degrading to him?" (1 Cor. 11:14), but we may not repeat it as the last word in a conversation about proper coiffure for men. We may repeat Matthew's account of Jesus' word concerning divorce, "whoever divorces his wife, except for unchastity, and marries another commits adultery" (Matt. 19:9), but we may not repeat it as a timeless rule that puts a stop to a community's conversation about, for example, divorce following abuse. To be sure, there are many biblical rules that we do well to regard as normative rules for ourselves. But we do well to regard them as such not because they have the status of biblical rules but because they have been tested and validated by the community's experience and discernment. *The point is this: that appeals to Scripture at the deliberative level remain subject to the communal process of discernment, just as subject as appeals to the wide variety of other sources.* A prescription or prohibition lifted from Scripture may be and must be tested and accepted or qualified or rejected by the discernment of the community gathered around Scripture and exercising discernment. Reasons are given and heard in the community, but any and all reasons must finally be tested in the community and defended, discarded, or qualified by their coherence with the gospel. Every judgment and every reason given in deliberation — *even when they involve the citation of Scripture* — are to be tested and qualified by a communal discernment of the shape and style of life "worthy of the gospel of Christ" (Phil. 1:27).

At the stage of discernment, when we are testing the reasons, Scripture is "useful" and authoritative because by reading Scripture we remember the story against which we test all the little good we do well and all the little wisdom we think we know well. Discernment, or the perception of what is "fitting" or "worthy," is — as already noted — a complex human enterprise, and there is no recipe for it in Scripture or in the community. Discernment is clearly neither simply reliance on intuition nor simply the deductive application of generic principles. Communal discernment is not just a matter of sharing the little moral wisdom each member knows well or of compensating for the abridgments (major or minor) of each one's moral vision. Discernment is always in the church to be the discernment of what is fitting or worthy of the story Christians love to tell and long to live. It is that story which makes them a community, and it is that story which calls them to a discernment not conformed to this age, but transformed by the renewal of their mind (Rom. 12:1-2).[26] It is that story which forms community and character, identity and perspective, fundamental values and commitments, into something coherent with the remembered story and capable of testing the reasons given in deliberation, even "scriptural" ones.

I do not deny the presence of prescriptions in Scripture, nor do I propose that they be torn from the canon, from that collection of writings (in all their "great variety") which (as a whole) can and should rule the churches' life and speech. I do not deny that citations of scriptural prescriptions can be appropriate in the deliberative process of giving reasons for specific moral judgments and rules. What I deny is this: that the fact that one can cite a scriptural prescription or prohibition is *sufficient* for the justification of a contemporary judgment or rule. One cannot simply and definitively answer the question "What ought I (or we) do?" by citing a scriptural prescription or prohibition. The Christian community is a community of discernment by testing rules — even rules that are formally identical to scriptural prescriptions — by their creative fidelity to the whole story, by their ability to nurture and sustain a contemporary "performance" not of a little piece of the canon but of Scripture as a whole. Indeed, the rules within Scripture are finally normative for the church less as rules than as part of the whole story.

The churches are communities of moral discourse and moral deliberation, "able to instruct one another," because they are communities of moral dis-

26. Wayne A. Meeks, *The Origins of Christian Morality: The First Two Centuries* (New Haven: Yale University Press, 1993), p. 17:

> The moral life has a plot, and it is a plot that implicates not merely each individual, but humankind and the cosmos. It may be that what most clearly sets Christian ethics apart from all the other ethical discourse of late antiquity, with which it otherwise shares so much, is just the creation of this peculiar story in which each of us is called on to be a character, and from which character itself and virtue take their meaning.

See further pp. 189-210.

cernment, and they are communities of moral discernment by being communities of memory. Discernment in Christian community depends finally on
remembering the story of Jesus. And Scripture is "useful" for that remembering. It is by reading Scripture that the church remembers! Remembering is the
good that the Christian community aims at in its practice of reading Scripture.
The greatest danger for the Christian life is still forgetfulness, and reading
Scripture together is still the remedy for it.

Somehow — but how? That is the question. It is less a puzzle to solve than
a mystery to live with. Even so, we can hardly avoid making some effort to answer it. Christians must read and use Scripture humbly. We must read and use
Scripture in Christian community. We must read it as canon. We must read it
without Marcion's dualism. We must read it according to creed, the "rule of
faith." We must read it with exegetical care and skill. We must continually assess
existing traditions of interpretation and performance. We must read it prayerfully. A prayer-formed reading of Scripture will serve invocation and remembrance. It will serve repentance by reading Scripture over-against ourselves. It
will serve thanksgiving to God by the sharing of gifts (including the scholarly
gifts of some readers). And it will serve petition by governing both our petitions and our readings by the vision of God's good future born of remembrance — and by the aching acknowledgment that that future is not yet. We
must read Scripture in order to remember. We must set these writings aside as
"holy" and set aside a time and a place to read them. We must set all the stories
of our life alongside the story of Scripture that they may be made new. We must
read Scripture and perform it both faithfully and creatively. We must read it
with a readiness to be disciplined by it, to be disciples of the remembered Jesus.
We must read it with (and for) discernment. We must read it not as a timeless
moral code but as the story of our lives.[27]

The subsequent parts of this book are an effort to read Scripture within
the context of the Christian community and for it, and especially within the
context of the churches as communities of moral discourse and for their discernment. We will return from time to time to some of the choices Christians
face today. I do not presume to have the last word about any of them. It is still
the church, not this little book, that is "full of goodness, filled with all knowledge." Nevertheless, I will proceed "boldly," for I will proceed "by way of re-

---

27. Interested readers will find this proposal worked out in conversation with the
proposals made by others interested in the contribution of Scripture to Christian ethics in
Allen Verhey, "Scripture and Ethics: Practice, Performances, and Prescriptions," in *Christian Ethics: Problems and Prospects*, ed. James F. Childress and Lisa Sowle Cahill (Cleveland:
Pilgrim, 1996), pp. 18-44.

minder." The subsequent parts of this book will attempt to read Scripture for the sake of remembrance. Together we will remember Jesus, and we will remember the early church remembering Jesus, in the strange worlds of medicine, sex and gender, the economy, and politics. The good we seek in reading Scripture is remembrance. The standards of excellence we aim at are holiness and sanctification, fidelity and creativity, discipline and discernment.

PART TWO

REMEMBERING JESUS
IN THE STRANGE WORLD OF SICKNESS

A Continuing Tradition of Care for the Suffering

CHAPTER FOUR

"Disciples of the Saving Christ" in Sickness and in Healing

Walter Rauschenbusch is one of my heroes of faith. He lived a century ago and spent many years of his life in a little church on the edge of Hell's Kitchen in New York City. There he served a community of poor immigrants just before the turn of the twentieth century. There he witnessed the economic exploitation of the poor and the tragic consequences of injustice. And there he remembered Jesus. He spoke boldly against exploitation and injustice "by way of reminder," and he wrote gladly of the hope he found for society in the memory of Jesus. I number him among that "cloud of witnesses" (Heb. 12:1) that surrounds us in the church, encouraging us to remember the story of Jesus and to live it by "looking to Jesus the pioneer and perfecter of our faith" (Heb. 12:2). Medical ethics was not Rauschenbusch's primary concern, but he did write this prayer for doctors and nurses and included it in his little book of "prayers for a social awakening."

> We praise thee, O God, for our friends, the doctors and nurses, who seek the healing of our bodies. We bless thee for their gentleness and patience, for their knowledge and skill. We remember the hours of our suffering when they brought relief, and the days of our fear and anguish at the bedside of our dear ones when they came as ministers of God to save the life thou hadst given. May we reward their fidelity and devotion by our loving gratitude, and do thou uphold them by the satisfaction of work well done.
>
> We rejoice in the tireless daring with which some are now tracking the great slayers of mankind by the white light of science. Grant that under their teaching we may grapple with the sins that have ever dealt death to the

race, and that we may so order our communities that none may be doomed to an untimely death for lack of the simple gifts which thou hast given in abundance. . . .

Strengthen in their whole profession the consciousness that their calling is holy and that they, too, are disciples of the saving Christ. May they never through the pressure of need or ambition surrender the sense of a divine mission and become hirelings who serve only for money. Make them doubly faithful in the service of the poor who need their help most sorely, and may the children of the workingman be as precious to them as the child of the rich. Though they deal with the frail body of man, may they have an abiding sense of the eternal value of the life residing in it. . . . Amen.[1]

Walter Rauschenbusch penned that prayer nearly a century ago. During the twentieth century some things changed. The "white light of science" has indeed tracked some of "the great slayers of mankind." (God does evidently answer prayer.) Developments in medical research and technology have given medicine powers it never had before, powers Rauschenbusch never dreamed of, powers at once fascinating and terrifying, promising and threatening. Human beings can now intervene in quite extraordinary ways into the quite ordinary human events of giving birth and suffering and dying.

We may indeed "rejoice" about such progress, as Rauschenbusch did in his prayer — but we may also worry a little, for with the new powers have come new problems and new causes for prayers. The powers are medical powers, but the problems are inevitably moral problems. Now that we can keep the dying alive, must we? Now that we can diagnose a fetus with Down's Syndrome and abort it, may we? Now that we can utilize the tissue of an anencephalic baby in transplant surgery, should we? The "white light of science" has provided medicine with remarkable new powers, but science does not and cannot tell us how to use them. It does not tell us what ends to seek with the powers it gives us or how to use them without violating the human material on which they work. It is little wonder that medical ethics has become the growth industry of the academy.

In the years since Rauschenbusch wrote that prayer, however, many things have *not* changed. The sense of gratitude evoked by a gentle and skillful nurse or by a patient and knowledgeable doctor has not changed. The fact that life and health depend most upon the order of our communities and upon simple things like clean air, pure food and water, periodic rest from labor, and security from violence — that has not changed. Physicians are still tempted to be-

1. Walter Rauschenbusch, *For God and the People: Prayers of the Social Awakening* (New York: Pilgrim, 1909), pp. 77-78.

come "hirelings who serve only for money." The quality of care for the poor remains a problem. The children of the uninsured and underinsured still need medical care as much as — or more than — "the child of the rich." And, finally, neither the fragility nor the sanctity of human life has changed.

The simple fact that Rauschenbusch penned this prayer nearly a century ago may remind us that Christians have been thinking about medical ethics for a very long time. Long before medical ethics became a distinct field of inquiry in the last third of the twentieth century, long before it became a growth industry in the academy (indeed, long before Rauschenbusch), Christians were thinking about Christian integrity in the strange world of sickness. Christian doctors and nurses conscientiously tried to bring their practice into line with their Christian profession. Christian patients tried to make decisions about medical care with Christian integrity. And ministers and other leaders struggled to find a Christian word of admonition or encouragement for both medical professional and patient.

It is little wonder, then, that thirty-five years ago, when new medical powers raised some (apparently) novel moral problems, the first voices in the public discussion belonged to theologians. Theologians had at their disposal traditions and resources for selective retrieval that others simply did not have. When medical ethics became a growth industry, however, many of the Christian ethicists who wrote on medical ethics and contributed to public discussion of these new powers seemed to suffer theological amnesia.[2] They were more easily identified as followers of some moral philosopher — of John Stuart Mill, say, or of John Rawls — than as "disciples of the saving Christ."

To be sure, there are sometimes good reasons for silence about one's religious convictions. When the professional group one wants to persuade is composed of both Christians and non-Christians, then one may look for more generic principles on which to base an argument. Or, when the policy-makers one hopes to convince have sworn to protect freedom of religion and not to establish a peculiarly Christian policy, then one may look for legal precedents rather than religious justifications. Or, when the society within which one tries to form a consensus is overwhelmingly secular, then arguments based candidly on Christian convictions may be regarded as insufficient or even as irrelevant.

---

2. See especially the lament of James Gustafson in 1978 that although "persons with theological training are writing a great deal about technology and the life sciences," "the relation of their moral discourse to any specific theological principles, or even to a definable religious outlook, is opaque." "Theology Confronts Technology and the Life Sciences," *Commonweal* 105 (June 16, 1978): 386-92, 396. The essay is anthologized in *On Moral Medicine,* ed. Stephen Lammers and Allen Verhey, second ed. (Grand Rapids: Eerdmans, 1998), pp. 46-52.

Such contexts seem to require arguments based on universal and rational, even if minimal, principles of morality, on legal precedents, and on an objective and impartial point of view — and such are the arguments one frequently finds in the literature on medical ethics.

Silence about our religious convictions and the enthusiasm for a universal and impartial perspective, however, puts the Christian community at risk of forgetfulness, and Christians then fail even to render full service to a pluralistic society. A genuinely pluralist society profits from the candid articulation and vigorous defense of particular points of views. If Christians never speak candidly as Christians when they speak publicly of medical morality, the silence is lamentable for the pluralistic society in which they live.[3] It puts that society at risk of reducing morality to a set of minimal expectations necessary for pluralism, of reducing morality to legality. Moreover, the silence leaves the culture bereft of the human wisdom that is to be found in particular religious traditions. And, finally, when a pluralistic society, for the sake of its pluralism, requires a secular and religiously neutral moral language, a moral Esperanto, it requires people to deny that they belong to particular communities — at least in public. The irony of universal languages like Esperanto, of course, is that hardly anyone really speaks them. And the irony of pluralism's requirement of a moral Esperanto for public discourse is that it is inhospitable to differences. After all, the requirement of a secular and religiously neutral moral language is a requirement that people who would engage in public discourse disown or disregard the particular convictions and loyalties that give them their moral identities and their moral passions — and this for the sake of moral discourse. At its best it is the discourse of people who, in spite of their differences, resolve to live together as peaceful strangers. But it can hardly nurture any other form of community than that of wary and spiteful strangers who want to be protected from each other.

The enthusiasm for an impartial perspective may be chastened by the recognition that medical ethics is as morally fragmented as our culture.[4] In addressing both the novel questions posed by the extraordinary new powers of medicine and the old questions still posed by finitude and mortality, medical ethics has not transcended the diversity of perspectives adopted in our pluralistic society in order to deal with the ordinary human events of giving birth and suffering and dying, with the questions about the meaning and value of

3. Daniel Callahan, "Religion and the Secularization of Bioethics," *Hastings Center Report* Special Supplement, "Theology, Religious Traditions, and Bioethics," July/August 1990, pp. 2-4.

4. Stanley Hauerwas, *Suffering Presence* (Notre Dame: University of Notre Dame Press, 1986), pp. 1-2.

"life" and "health" and "freedom," with the questions about the goals worth striving for and the limits to be imposed on the means to reach them, with the questions about what human persons and human communities are meant to be and to become. Perhaps this is not surprising, but it ought not be overlooked either, for it suggests the public importance of particular points of view, the public significance of Christians' witness to their deepest convictions. More modest claims about the possibilities of fashioning one common moral language, a moral Esperanto, may free religious persons and communities to discover their own voices and to speak more eloquently in their own moral languages about medicine and medical ethics.

If Christians never speak candidly as Christians about medical ethics, the silence is still more lamentable for the communities of faith with which they identify. Communities of the faithful continue to be and to be called to be communities of moral discourse, deliberation, and discernment about, among other things, the new medical powers. The silence of Christians puts the church at risk of forgetfulness. Faithful members of Christian communities want to live and die — and give birth and suffer and care for the suffering — with Christian integrity, not just with impartial rationality. They want to talk together and think together and pray together about how Christian convictions can guide and limit these new medical powers, about the shape of Christian integrity in the middle of the new powers over life and death and in the muddle of the technological apparatus that surrounds our dying, about the form of Christian response to the old issues of allocation of health care to the poor and the social disorder that threatens life and health.

Finally, and most importantly, however, Rauschenbusch reminds us also to attend to God in the world of sickness and health, in the world of medicine and nursing. It is, after all, a prayer. That is obvious, I suppose, but it ought not be overlooked. And it might also be observed that prayer remains commonplace in hospitals — as commonplace, I dare say, as bedpans. In spite of that, contemporary medical ethics has paid little attention to prayer.

When prayer is discussed in the literature on medicine, it has frequently been regarded either as "alternative medicine" or as a supplemental technique. There are justifications for this, of course. Christian Science practitioners regard their prayers and their practice as an alternative to medicine. And there is the bad joke about the doctor who reports to her patient that the only thing left to do is to pray, to which the patient replies, "I didn't even think it was serious." After all, we tend to think of prayer as a technology of last resort, to be used when medical technologies have failed. If prayer were simply another medical technology, then we could be satisfied with empirical studies of the effectiveness of the technology, but it isn't. When we use prayer as an instrument, a technology, to achieve health — or wealth or happiness or even moral improvement — we corrupt the practice of prayer.[5]

In prayer Rauschenbusch did not attend to something beyond God which God — or prayer — could be used to reach; he attended to God. That's what prayer is: simple attentiveness to God. And in attending to God, Rauschenbusch learned to attend to all else — including doctors and nurses, and life and death, and health and suffering — as related to God. In looking to God, he looked at all else in a new light. His prayer begins, like most good prayers, with invocation, with calling upon God. "O God," he says. The significance of invocation should not be measured by its length. To call upon God is to recall who God is and what God has done. Rauschenbusch invoked not just any old god, not the nameless god of philosophical theism, but the God who was remembered and named in the little German Baptist church at the edge of Hell's Kitchen. To invoke God is always an act of remembrance, and such remembrance is not ever just the historical recollection of a good archivist. Rauschenbusch's brief invocation leaves that memory unspoken, but it is implicit. Christian prayer is simple attention to the God made known in Scripture, to the God made known in Jesus of Nazareth.

Reading Scripture serves and instructs that remembrance. It can teach us both how to pray and how to live. The task undertaken in this part of the book is to nurture the moral discourse and deliberation and discernment of the churches as their members face choices in the world of sickness. It will proceed "by way of reminder," calling attention to the memory of Jesus. It is not intended to be a substitute for that discourse. However "boldly" one may speak "by way of reminder," it would be presumptuous to claim to articulate *the* Christian perspective on even one of the central issues involved in the use of the new medical powers — say, *the* Christian perspective on death. And it would be foolhardy presumption not only to attempt to develop *the* Christian perspective on death but also on life, autonomy, technology, the significance of suffering, and much besides.

That may be the task finally, but it is and must be a task for communal discourse and discernment, not the work of a single Christian moralist, however presumptuous the moralist may be. It is a task that will demand the diversity of gifts within the church, including the special skills and contributions not only of moral theologians and clergy but also of physicians, nurses, patients, and those who stand to be patients — which, after all, includes all of us. Each

---

5. This is a risk in the renewed attention to the "therapeutic effects" of prayer; see, for example, Larry Dossey, *Healing Words: The Power of Prayer and the Practice of Medicine* (New York: Harper Collins, 1993).

may and must speak from her own perspective and out of his own experiences, and each may and must be willing to see things differently because we share the memory of a common story. What is undertaken here, then, is not to say the last word on the choices we face in the world of medicine, but to make a modest contribution to communal discourse and discernment by reading Scripture and remembering Jesus. Only by remembering Jesus can we all — both the sick and those who care for them — be "disciples of the saving Christ."

The Case of Coles's Friend

It is conventional that essays in medical ethics consider a case. So, consider this: In his *Harvard Diary*, Robert Coles tells the story of a friend of his, a physician who knows that his own cancer is not likely to be beaten back, a Christian who knows that the final triumph belongs to the risen Christ.[6] The dying man was visited by a hospital chaplain, who asked how he was "coping." "Fine," he said, in the fashion of all those replies by which people indicate that they are doing reasonably well given their circumstances, *and* that they would rather not elaborate just now on what those circumstances are. But this chaplain was unwilling to accept such a reply. He inquired again about how the man was feeling, how he was managing, how he was dealing with the stress. Relentlessly he pressed on to questions about denial and anger and acceptance. But finally he gave up with the suggestion that when the man was ready to discuss things, he should not hesitate to call him. After the chaplain left, Coles's friend got angry — not so much about his circumstances or his dying as about the chaplain. The chaplain, he said, was a psychobabbling fool. And Robert Coles, the eminent Harvard psychiatrist, agreed. What his friend needed and wanted, Coles says, was someone with whom to attend to God and to God's word, not someone who dwelt upon the stages of dying as though they were "stations of the cross."

Coles's friend was not finished with the chaplain. He called for him to return; there were some things, he said, that he wanted "to discuss." When the chaplain returned, Coles's friend had his Bible out, with the bookmark set to Psalm 69, and he simply asked the chaplain to read. Coles quotes the opening words of Psalm 69. It is a prayer, a lament, a cry of anguish and a call for help: "Save me, O God, for the waters have come up to my neck . . . I have come into deep waters. . . ." If the chaplain read on, he would have discovered what Coles

6. Robert Coles, "Psychiatric Stations of the Cross," in *Harvard Diary: Reflections on the Sacred and the Profane* (New York: Crossroad, 1990), pp. 10-12. See also pp. 92-94.

does not mention, that Psalm 69 is an imprecatory psalm, a cry of anguish that vents its anger in curses on those who fail to comfort. And the curse on the enemy may be no small part of the reason this dying man chose this psalm for this particular representative of the church. "I looked for pity," it says, "but there was none; and for comforters, but I found none. They gave me poison for food, and for my thirst they gave me vinegar to drink. Let their table be a trap for them" (Ps. 69:20-22).

Coles's friend, of course, was not complaining about the hospital food. He was complaining about a chaplain who had emptied his role of the practice of piety, who neglected prayer and Scripture, and who filled his visits to the sick with the practices of psychotherapy. And his curse upon the table of his enemies was not intended, I suppose, to suggest that the skills and language of psychology are useless. It was intended, rather, to remind the chaplain that at the table set before us we may eat and drink judgment to ourselves if we forget or ignore the gifts of God for the people of God. And those gifts include not only bread and wine, but also prayer and Scripture and the presence of a suffering and risen Christ. My concern just now is not that the church or its representatives will forfeit their inheritance for a mess of psychology, neglecting or ignoring talk of God for the sake of psychobabbling talk about "stages" and "phases." My concern is rather with medical ethics and with the temptations to forgetfulness when our discourse and deliberation focus on an impartial point of view and the sort of generic principles favored by medical ethicists. So let's create another case.

The Case of Sally Smith

Imagine another physician stricken with cancer, in another hospital. Call her Sally Smith. She, too, is a Christian, and she, too, is visited by a hospital chaplain. Suppose, however, that this cleric had been trained as an "ethicist" rather than as a therapist. Suppose he had been enlisted on some hospital ethics committee and there taught a little Mill and a little Kant, taught to respect and protect a patient's autonomy, taught to regard human relationships as contracts between self-interested and autonomous individuals, taught to speak the language of rights (or utility) as a moral Esperanto, as a universal moral language. This chaplain is anxious not so much with psychological states and stages as with not interfering with the patient's rights — including, of course, the right to be left alone. His enthusiasm for a common moral language, for the kind of Esperanto ethicists like to speak, will make him hesitate to speak in a distinctively Christian voice, hesitate to use and to offer the gifts of prayer and Scripture when people are dying or suffering and face hard medical and moral decisions.

If you can imagine all of that, then you can also imagine that after this visit from the cleric turned ethicist Sally Smith might complain no less bitterly about gall in her food than Coles's friend had, and might curse this chaplain no less legitimately than Coles's friend had cursed his. She too might call the chaplain back with her bookmark set at Psalm 69. Again the point is not that philosophical skills or generic moral principles are useless. But Sally Smith too needs and wants not just to have her autonomy respected and protected, but also to attend to God. She still needs and wants someone to talk of God and of the ways of God, not a conversation in moral Esperanto, a language she little understands and doesn't really care to learn, not now as she lies dying, at any rate. She has decisions to make, to be sure, hard medical and moral decisions about what should be done and what left undone, but she wants to make them prayerfully, oriented to God and to the cause of God, and not just with impartial rationality.

Now imagine something more: Imagine that after his first visit to Sally Smith this chaplain turned ethicist wonders whether there was some test of his theological and religious integrity in that hospital room. And imagine that he is unsure whether he passed that test, unsure whether he was altogether faithful to his identity as a Christian pastor and a Christian ethicist. His agenda as a medical ethicist, he decides, had left no room for the contribution of practices central to Christian community. "A patient might legitimately expect more from a representative of the church, even in this secular world of medicine and medical ethics," he says to himself, and he resolves to make another visit to the room of Sally Smith, this time to pray and to read a little Scripture, perhaps to learn from the pious sick what he had forgotten under the instruction of the medical ethicists.

Though conscious that he had in some way failed, he still doubts that reading Scripture will be useful; he is aware that the many problems we discussed in chapter three regarding turning to Scripture for moral guidance apply in full force to the strange world of sickness. He begins his conversation with Sally by voicing these doubts.

"I've come to read a little Scripture with you — since, I gather, that's what you want," he says. "But you must admit that there are some problems with looking to Scripture for guidance in medical care."

"Problems?" Sally asks. "What could be wrong with turning to Scripture at a time like this?"

"Well, for starters," the chaplain replies, "there's the silence of Scripture. Scripture simply doesn't deal with the new powers of medicine or the new moral problems they create. Israel's law codes didn't need a statutory definition of death in response to technology that could keep the heart beating and the lungs pumping. The sages didn't comment on the wisdom of in vitro fertilization or the prudence of another round of chemotherapy and radiation in cases like yours. The prophets who beat against injustice with their words never mentioned the allocation of scarce medical resources. No scribe ever asked Jesus about withholding artificial nutrition and hydration. And the early Christian communities didn't ask Paul about medical experimentation. The Bible simply doesn't answer many of the questions that new medical powers have forced us to ask; the authors, even the most visionary of them, never dreamed of these new powers. To use any passage of Scripture to answer directly any of the particular problems posed by these new powers isn't possible." Sally looks as though she might say something, but the chaplain is clearly on a roll now and plunges ahead.

"And then, besides the silence of Scripture, there is its strangeness. When Scripture does speak of sickness and the power to heal, its words are . . . well, quaint. You must admit that the world of sickness in Scripture is strange and alien to us. Think of that story in Second Chronicles, when King Asa is chided for consulting the physicians about his diseased feet. There are lots of examples."[7] Sally nods in agreement and the chaplain hastens on.

"And, of course, Scripture is also diverse. That's a third problem. Scripture doesn't speak with one voice about sickness and healing. The Chronicler evidently rejected physicians and their medicines, but the sage Jesus ben Sirach integrated physicians and medicines into a Jewish faith in God without any problem at all." Sally, though a Protestant, recognizes the reference to the book of Sirach (or Ecclesiasticus), a book of the Apocrypha, and even quotes a little bit of it: "Honor physicians for their services, for the Lord created them; for their gift of healing comes from the Most High. . . . The Lord created medicines out of the earth, and the sensible will not despise them" (Sir. 38:1-2, 4; cf. 38:1-15). The chaplain hasn't forgotten his original concern though. "Don't you see," he says, "the diversity of Scripture on medical issues? Shouldn't that diversity give us pause before we attempt to relate the practice of reading Scripture to the practice of medicine?"

Sally is patient with him. "Is there anything else?" she asks. "Well, yes," he replies, "as a matter of fact there is. There is the problem of the abuse of Scripture — and of the abuse of people with Scripture as the instrument. You must admit that appeals to Scripture have sometimes done a great deal of harm.

---

7. See 2 Chronicles 16:12, or the discussion of the example in chapter three of this volume.

When Genesis 3:16, 'in pain you shall bring forth children,' was quoted to oppose pain relief for women in labor, a great deal of harm was done.[8] It would be ridiculous to deny that this sort of use of Scripture is an abuse. And given all of these problems, it's little wonder that in medical ethics even those who know Scripture hesitate to read it as though it were relevant to cases like yours."

Sally can restrain herself no longer. "It may be little wonder, but it's still lamentable! Faithful members of Christian communities long to live and die faithfully. If we must suffer while we live or as we die, we want to suffer with Christian integrity, not just with impartial rationality. If we are called to care for the suffering (which we surely are), we want to care with integrity — not just with impartial rationality. This longing of faith and of the faithful for Christian integrity isn't served by ignoring the resources of the tradition; and it isn't served by silencing the peculiar voices of Scripture either. It *is* served by talking together and thinking together and praying together about the ways in which the Christian story can form and inform a response to the ancient human events of giving birth and suffering and dying. It's served by talking and thinking and praying about how the same story can guide and limit the uses of new medical powers. As a chaplain, you should understand that in Christian community the tradition, including Scripture, doesn't merely exist as an archaic relic in an age of science and reason. In Christian community Scripture continues to evoke loyalties and to form and reform character and conduct into dispositions and deeds 'worthy of the gospel,' as it says in Philippians."

"I take it that Scripture is really important to you," the chaplain concludes. "'Important' hardly covers it," she says. "Scripture is, after all, 'inspired by God' and 'useful . . . for training in righteousness,' as Paul said" (2 Tim. 3:16).

"That seems a long way from where we began," the chaplain remarks, and reminds Sally that she was nodding in agreement when he talked about the silence and strangeness of Scripture. "I don't deny that these words are human words," she says, "and I don't claim that we should simply repeat them as Christian counsel about medical practice and medical ethics today. What you said is true — the world of sickness in Scripture *is* sometimes strange and alien, and a Christian ethic won't simply be identical with it. But it must somehow be in-

8. See Ronald L. Numbers and Ronald C. Sawyer, "Medicine and Christianity in the Modern World," in *Health/Medicine and the Faith Traditions: An Inquiry into Religion and Medicine,* ed. Martin Marty and Kenneth Vaux (Philadelphia: Fortress, 1982), pp. 133-60, p. 134. Numbers and Sawyer also observe, however, that Scripture was also cited to justify the use of anesthetics, notably Genesis 2:21, where God mercifully caused "a deep sleep to fall upon" Adam before removing his rib.

formed by it, don't you think? There is no Christian life that is not tied some-how to Scripture." Sally pauses, and this time it is the chaplain's turn to nod his head in agreement. Finally he asks, "So exactly why — or how — is Scripture important to you?"

"Well, it's important to me," she says, "because the Second Vatican Council calls it 'the supreme rule of faith.'"[9] Well, probably not; she is not Catholic, after all. But she is no more likely to have said, "Scripture is important to me because Article Seven of the Belgic Confession calls it an 'infallible rule,'" or to have cited any other Protestant creed. She has not learned of Scripture or of its significance from a confession or a creed but from participation in the practice of reading it with the people of God. So would Sally reply, "Scripture is important to me because reading Scripture is what Alasdair MacIntyre called a 'practice'"? Well, probably not. She is not a philosopher either. But she *is* a Christian, and she has learned to read Scripture in Christian community. And in learning to read Scripture, she has learned as well the good that belongs to reading Scripture, the good internal to the practice. She has learned, that is, to remember.

Sally may never have read MacIntyre, but she has read John Bunyan's wonderful allegory *Pilgrim's Progress,* and she knows what Great Heart knew. She knows what that marvelous helper and guide said to the son of Christian as he pointed ahead to a place called "Forgetful Green." "That place," Great Heart said, "is the most dangerous place in all these parts."[10] And that's how Sally responds to the chaplain's inquiry, by reminding him of that story and that line. "That's why — and how — Scripture is important to me," she says. "I know the temptation to forgetfulness in the Forgetful Green of health and in the great medical powers to heal. And I know the temptation to forgetfulness in the Forgetful Straits of pain and suffering and in the final powerlessness of medicine. I fear amnesia in this 'world come of age' called a hospital and in this 'religionless' world called medicine. That's why I lament so deeply the failure of those medical ethicists who know Scripture to remind me of it. That's why I long so deeply to connect the remembrance that belongs to the practice of reading Scripture to both suffering and the care for the suffering that belongs to medicine."

"There are some problems . . . ," the chaplain says, ready to rehearse again the silence and strangeness and diversity and abuse of Scripture. The problems

9. "Dogmatic Constitution on Divine Revelation," in *The Documents of Vatican II,* ed. Walter M. Abbott, S.J. (New York: Guild, 1966), pp. 111-28, 125.

10. John Bunyan, *The Pilgrim's Progress* (New York: Washington Square Press, 1957), p. 234. (It was originally published in 1678.)

have not gone away, but they do not seem quite so overwhelming now, at least not overwhelming enough to keep one from the task of remembrance. So, he stops in mid-sentence and says instead, "Let's read a little Scripture together." "Yes, let's," Sally smiles. And bowing his head he says, "Good Lord, teach us what has been done for our redemption, that Christ may form our hearts to faith and our lives to love until we become faithful disciples of the saving Christ."

CHAPTER FIVE

Remembering Jesus
in the Strange World of Sickness

The chaplain visited Sally Smith, the doctor turned patient, every day during her stay in the hospital. Every day they read a little Scripture together. And every day the chaplain in memory of Jesus retrieved a little his role as a representative of the Christian community. Suppose that we went along as a witness to their conversations, their reading of Scripture together, and their effort to discern the shape of faithfulness in the face of death. Suppose that we were there when they confronted again and again the strange world of sickness in Scripture. Suppose that we were there when they began to mark out the way of Jesus through that strange world. Suppose that we were there when they remembered Jesus and remembered the early church remembering Jesus. And suppose that we were there when — in memory of Jesus — they began to discern the path of discipleship in their own strange world of sickness. If you can suppose all that, then you can imagine something like the next three chapters.

In this chapter we report their confrontation with the strange world of sickness in Scripture and, then, their memories of Jesus. In the next chapter we will eavesdrop on their conversation about the early church remembering Jesus, and we will report their effort to retrieve the tradition of the church as a healing community in memory of Jesus. In chapter seven we will bear witness to some of the ways the practice of reading Scripture and the memory of Jesus formed and informed the moral discernment both of Sally Smith as she faced her death and her dying and of the chaplain as he learned to care for her.

Reading Scripture in Christian community is "useful" to a wider range of issues in medical ethics than those faced by our friend Sally, of course, and the memory of Jesus governs discernment over a wider set of cases. The conversations we witness will sometimes hint at the wider relevance of reading Scripture and remembering Jesus, but the focus of these conversations is understandably on the form of faithfulness in the face of death.

The Strange World of Sickness in Scripture[1]

Sally and the chaplain searched the Scriptures, not surprised to find there a strange world of sickness but confident that they would nevertheless find a light upon the path of discipleship. The strange world of sickness was confronted at almost every turn of the page.

There they were in the wilderness, fresh from God's triumph at the Red Sea. And God said, Sally reported, "If you will listen carefully to the voice of the LORD your God, and do what is right in his sight . . . I will not bring upon you any of the diseases that I brought upon the Egyptians; for I am the LORD who heals you" (Exod. 15:26). It all seemed promising enough, but the chaplain was troubled by it. He could not help but think that Sally was a good woman, that she had done "that which is right," and that she still had this horrible disease. And he wondered whether, if he were sick, he would find much encouragement or consolation in this verse.

In the wilderness still, with the people of God they were threatened by serpents that bit and poisoned at the Lord's command. The complaint of the people turned to confession, and the intercession of Moses led to God's instruction to put a bronze serpent on a pole, and the people were healed (Num. 21:4-9). "It's a strange world of sickness in Scripture," the chaplain said, and it grew stranger still when Hezekiah destroyed the same bronze serpent because it had become an idol and a charm (2 Kings 18:4).

Then they were in Ashdod among the Philistines wondering about Dagon's fall and about their own helplessness against a plague of tumors. "Probably hemorrhoids," Sally, still the physician, diagnosed.[2] The diagnosis

1. On sickness and medicine in Scripture and the ancient Near East, see further Darrell W. Amundsen and Gary Ferngren, "Medicine and Religion: Pre-Christian Antiquity" and "Medicine and Religion: Early Christianity Through the Middle Ages," both in *Health/Medicine and the Faith Traditions: An Inquiry into Religion and Medicine*, ed. Martin Marty and Kenneth Vaux (Philadelphia: Fortress, 1982), pp. 53-92 and 93-131; Klaus Seybold and Ulrich B. Mueller, *Sickness and Healing*, trans. Douglas W. Stott (Nashville: Abingdon, 1981); R. K. Harrison, "Heal," in *International Standard Bible Encyclopedia*, rev. ed., vol. II (Grand Rapids: Eerdmans, 1982), pp. 640-47; and Bernard Palmer, ed., *Medicine and the Bible* (Exeter: Paternoster, 1986).

2. Amundsen and Ferngren, "Medicine and Religion: Pre-Christian Antiquity," p. 62.

was not altogether clear, but the cause of the tumors was clear enough. The God of Israel had brought this affliction. It did not happen "by chance"; it was "the hand of the LORD." And the remedy was to send the ark back to the Israelites, loaded with a guilt offering (1 Sam. 5:1–6:9). "It's a strange world of sickness in Scripture," the chaplain repeated.

Next they were in Jerusalem with David, who was worrying about the child born to Bathsheba. "The LORD struck the child . . . and it became very ill" (2 Sam. 12:15), the chaplain read. David knew that he had sinned, and he assumed the posture of penitence while he made petition for his child's life, but the child died.

Then they were at the temple, listening to a dying man's lament, hearing a confession of his guilt, and wondering with the temple's priest whether his supplication for health might yet be granted.

> O LORD, do not rebuke me in your anger,
>   or discipline me in your wrath.
> For your arrows have sunk into me,
>   and your hand has come down on me.
> There is no soundness in my flesh
>   because of your indignation;
> there is no health in my bones
>   because of my sin.   (Ps. 38:1-3)

From their own world of sickness there were many unanswered questions: What was the diagnosis? What was the prognosis? Was there a doctor in the house? In the strange world of sickness in Scripture there was no concern with a medical diagnosis or with securing the aid of a physician or even with getting a couple of aspirin (which the Sumerians had discovered at least a millennium before, as Sally reported[3]). There are different expectations of the sick in Scripture: not to send for the physician or the magician or the medicine man, but simply to be a penitent and a supplicant before God.[4]

Then they were with Job, who suffered not only from his sickness but also from the confidence of his friends in this familiar paradigm that suffering is a punishment for sins. Job held fast to his conviction that God was the healer (and the cause!) of his suffering, but he struggled against the conventional assumption that the role of penitent and supplicant was appropriate to him because he was sick. Instead, he insisted upon his innocence and brought suit against the Lord. ("For malpractice, probably," Sally said).

---

3. Harrison, "Heal," p. 642.
4. See also, e.g., Psalms 6, 39, 69, 88, 102, 107:17-22.

They stood together before the priest with one who suffered from what Sally suggested might later be called "the heartbreak of psoriasis." The priest of Leviticus 13–14 called the condition leprosy. (It could not, however, have been Hansen's disease, or modern leprosy, Sally reported, for that disease was probably first brought to the Near East by the troops of Alexander the Great.[5]) The priest did not use his diagnosis to serve as a basis for medical therapy but as a basis for determining ritual impurity. There was, however, a prescription. They shuddered as the man was told of his exclusion from the community and instructed to cry "Unclean, unclean" to any who passed by (Lev. 13:45). Talk about "the heartbreak of psoriasis"! And this time it was Sally who said, "It's a strange world of sickness in Scripture."

They talked together about the strangeness of Scripture. The chaplain offered the suggestion that there was a "sick role" in Israel as surely as there is a "sick role" today, but it was quite a different role. "Today," he continued, "the sick are largely exempted from normal social responsibilities, largely exempted from blame for their condition, expected to seek competent medical help, and to cooperate in the process of getting well. So, at least, runs Talcott Parson's famous account of the 'sick role.'"[6]

"In ancient Israel," the chaplain continued, "far from being for the most part exempted from blame for one's condition, the sick person was very largely blamed for it. So, the 'sick role' involved assuming the posture of a penitent before God, pleading with God for forgiveness and healing." They noticed also, however, diversity within the tradition, and Sally observed that the book of Job mounted a serious attack against this paradigm within the Old Testament itself.

The chaplain, however, had thought of another contrast between the modern world of medicine and that of ancient Israel. "Far from being expected to seek competent medical advice," he noted, "the sick in Israel had limited access to the developing medical arts because of their faith. Not only were the use of magical incantations and charms forbidden by prophets and law-givers (e.g., Ezek. 13:17-23; Deut. 18:9-14), but the more sophisticated medicine of the Egyptians and Sumerians[7] was also evidently considered a heathen art and hardly welcomed by

---

5. Seybold and Mueller, *Sickness and Healing,* pp. 67-74. See also E. V. Hulse, "The Nature of Biblical Leprosy and the Use of Alternative Medical Terms in Modern Translations of the Bible," *Palestine Exploration Quarterly* 107 (July-December 1975): 87-105.

6. Talcott Parsons developed the concept of the sick role already in 1951 in his *The Social System.* For his more recent account of it see Talcott Parsons, "The Sick Role and the Role of the Physician Reconsidered," *Milbank Memorial Fund Quarterly* 53 (Summer 1975): 257-78.

7. More is known about Egyptian medicine than about Babylonian medicine because several Egyptian papyri concerning medicine have been preserved. One of them, the

the faithful, not even into the court of the king (2 Chron. 16:12). To be sure, there is evidence of folk remedies and salves (e.g., Jer. 51:8) and techniques for treating wounds (e.g., Isa. 1:6) and for setting fractures (e.g., Ezek. 30:21), but the 'sick role' in Israel required the person to seek God's help, not some physician's."

This rejection of medicine was also finally challenged within the tradition, Sally noted. "Remember when we talked about the book of Sirach the other day?" she asked. "Jesus ben Sirach effortlessly integrated physicians and the rational medicine of Alexandria into Jewish faith in God, saying that we should 'Honor physicians for their services.' His wise advice to the Jews dates all the way back to the second century before Christ. He recognized that the gift of healing comes from God, acknowledging the Lord's 'healing monopoly'[8] while making room for the use of the skill of physicians, the power of medicine, and the work of pharmacists" (Sir. 38:1-15).

The chaplain and Sally then observed another contrast between the "sick role" in ancient Israel and the "sick role" today. There was, Sally observed, hardly a guarantee of solicitude toward the sick in ancient Israel. Instead of thoughtful attentiveness to the one in pain, the community was typically anxious about the continued health and well-being of the ones who were not. Far from being relieved and sustained by their society, the social situation of the sick was lamentable. The sick suffered not only from their sickness but also from the attitude of their culture toward them. There were, moreover, evidently no institutions providing for the care of the sick or for the families of the sick. The legal system and the cultic system, in contrast, were quite developed. Chaplains did give aid to some of the sick — not medically, but in their role as medi-

---

Ebers papyrus, presents over eight hundred prescriptions for over two hundred illnesses. Another, the Smith papyrus (James H. Breasted, ed., *The Edwyn Smith Surgical Papyrus* [Chicago: University of Chicago Press, 1930]), has been called "the oldest surgical textbook" (Seybold and Mueller, *Sickness and Healing*, p. 33). In Babylon there were evidently medical professionals who were not identified as priests and who applied a variety of empirically tested methods. In one famous case a baby was delivered by Cesarean section from a woman who had just died. (See Seybold and Mueller, *Sickness and Healing*, pp. 27-34; Amundsen and Ferngren, "Medicine and Religion: Pre-Christian Antiquity," pp. 55-61; John A. Wilson, "Medicine in Ancient Egypt," *Bulletin of the History of Medicine* 36 [1962]: 114-23; Robert Biggs, "Medicine in Ancient Mesopotamia," *History of Sciences* 36 [1969]: 94-105.) It should be said that the rational and empirically based medicine was not tidily separated from sacerdotal medicine in either Egypt or Babylon. Medicine and religion overlapped and blended together in both cultures, making it nearly as difficult to learn medicine without engaging in some act of obeisance to, for example, Tooth, the divine physician among Egyptian gods, as it was to learn agriculture in Canaan without worshipping the Ba'alim of Canaan.

8. See Seybold and Mueller, *Sickness and Healing*, p. 109.

ator for the penitent. Moreover, chaplains excluded some of the sick from community — as unclean, not as contagious. And chaplains also presided over rituals of thanksgiving celebrating rehabilitation to health and to the community. The prophets were consulted by the sick and provided either oracles, as messengers of God, predicting health or sickness and death (e.g., 2 Sam. 12:14; 2 Kings 14:4-16), or miraculous healings, as agents of God (e.g., 1 Kings 17:19-23; 2 Kings 4:18-37; 5:3-14). Institutions and personnel to care for the sick in their suffering or to provide relief for them in their continuing responsibilities, however, were absent from the Old Testament.

The chaplain, finally, made one more observation, one he thought was crucial to all the other observations they had made together. "The Old Testament," he said, "points us to God, the sovereign one, as the cause of sickness and of health. It is God alone who kills and makes alive (Deut. 32:39; 2 Kings 5:7; 1 Sam. 2:6), who says, 'I am the LORD who heals you' (Exod. 15:26). It was not 'by chance' that the Philistines or the Israelites or David's son or anyone who was sick became ill. It was God's 'hand that struck' them (1 Sam. 6:9). That is the strange world of sickness in Scripture: the sovereignty of God."

Even on this point, however, they observed that the tradition was not static — either with respect to the cause of disease or to God's healing power. The view that God directly caused sickness as punishment for sin continued, but it was increasingly modified and challenged by other views. Jesus ben Sirach, who saw a place for physicians and pharmacists, also saw a place for "natural" explanations of sickness (e.g., Sir. 31:20-21; 37:27-31). A less "rational" but more popular perspective attributed disease to demons, who moved from the margins (where they had been in the Old Testament, e.g., Ps. 91:6) to the center in explanations of sickness (e.g., Jub. 10:10, 12-13; Tob. 6:7, 14). Connected to this view was the apocalyptic personification of death, attributing sickness to the power and dominion of death. Sickness and death were viewed less and less as evidence of God's sovereignty and more and more as a challenge to it.

The apocalyptic perspective also affected the view of God's power to heal. According to the apocalyptic view of the world, there are two ages, the present evil age, which since Adam's sin is under the dominion of sin and death, and the age to come, when God will establish an unchallenged sovereignty. On this view God's unchallenged sovereignty is "not yet." In this evil age the demonic powers and the power of death rule. The faithful await God's action to establish unchallenged sovereignty in God's own good future. Then the power of demons and death will be defeated. Then God's power, including the power to heal, will be unchallenged. Then, as the New Testament apocalypse says, "Death will be no more; mourning and crying and pain will be no more, for the first things have passed away" (Rev. 21:4; cf. Isa. 65:17-20).

Jesus and the Strange World of Sickness

During one of the chaplain's visits to Sally, just as they were ready to read a little Scripture, her doctor came into the room. "He's still trying to talk me into another round of chemotherapy," Sally said with more than a hint of impatience. The chaplain offered to return another time, but both Sally and her doctor seemed eager to enlist the chaplain as an ally in the struggle with the other. The doctor expected the chaplain to define his role in terms of the therapeutic ambitions of the medical establishment, and Sally hoped he would be an advocate for the patient's perspective. The chaplain happily reported that he had come to read a little Scripture, to remember the story, not to be a defender either of the authority of physicians or of the autonomy of patients. Sally invited the doctor to sit down for a moment and to read a little Scripture with them — and he did! Then she picked up her Bible, and the chaplain suggested a text. "Perhaps it's time to turn to the story of Jesus," he said. "Perhaps Luke 6," and he quoted a little piece of it: "Love your enemies . . . , bless those who curse you, pray for those who abuse you" (Luke 6:27-28).

Sally smiled at that, because the verse had reminded her of a story, which she quickly began to tell. It was the story of an Armenian Christian woman who was kept for a time by a Turkish officer who had raided her home and killed her aged parents. She escaped from him, and after she had escaped, she trained to be a nurse. Some time later, when the officer became gravely ill, this woman happened to be his nurse. Exceptional nursing care was required, and exceptional nursing care was given. When finally the officer recovered, his doctor pointed to the nurse and told the man that the credit for his recovery belonged to her. When he looked at her, he said, "We have met before, haven't we?" And when he recognized her, he asked, "Why did you provide such care for me?" Her reply was simply this, "I am a follower of the one who said, 'Love your enemies.'"[9]

Sally's doctor was evidently touched by the story. "That makes me a little ashamed of the way I treated the patient I just left. If you'll excuse me, I think I'll go pay him another visit. I'll be back soon." Sally smiled at that, too, thinking perhaps that there was some hope for this physician yet.

When the doctor had left, the chaplain reflected on the story Sally had told. "That woman was a saint," he said, "one of the company of those to whom we must listen when we would read Scripture for the moral life and the medical life. How do you think she read Scripture? She appealed to a command, to be

9. The story is told in Geoffrey Wainwright, *Doxology* (London: Epworth, 1980), p. 434, and in Stephen E. Fowl and L. Gregory Jones, *Reading in Communion: Scripture and Ethics in Christian Life* (Grand Rapids: Eerdmans, 1991), pp. 79-80.

sure, but not as though Scripture were to be regarded as 'a system of divine laws.'[10] She described herself as a 'follower' of Christ. The command to 'love the enemy' coheres with a story, not with some eternal code."

"That's right," said Sally. "Scripture doesn't give us a moral handbook or a medical textbook; it gives us a story we own as our own. In the midst of sickness, we hear a story — a story we should love to remember and tell and must struggle to perform even when we are dying or caring for the dying. And at the center of the story is Jesus of Nazareth, whom God raised from the dead. In that resurrection the God of creation and covenant vindicated Jesus, exalted the crucified one, and established the good future Jesus had announced. In that resurrection there was the *final* revelation, and both our reading of Scripture and our practice of medicine must be made to fit with that final disclosure of God's cause and purpose.[11] It is indeed time to turn to the story of Jesus."

So, they searched the Scriptures again — and remembered Jesus. He came announcing that the good future of God was "at hand." "The kingdom of God has come near," he said, "repent, and believe in the good news" (Mark 1:15). And he already made that future present and its power felt in his works of healing and in his words of blessing. When he healed the sick and preached good news to the poor, he showed what God's good future would be like, and he showed himself to be the agent of that future (Matt. 11:5-6; Luke 7:22-23). He suffered for the sake of God's cause in the world, but when the powers of death and doom had done their damnedest, God raised this Jesus up, "the first fruits of those who have died" (1 Cor. 15:20).

Boldly, then — and gladly — they proceeded by way of reminder. They remembered Jesus as the one who healed the sick and disabled, as the one who preached good news to the poor, as the one who suffered and died under Pon-

---

10. Against John M. Frame, *Medical Ethics: Principles, Persons, and Problems* (Phillipsburg, N.J.: Presbyterian & Reformed, 1988), p. 10. By this judgment about the wholeness of Scripture, Frame provides backing for his appeals to Scripture as a moral code to answer directly questions about conduct. But many theologians, no less convinced of the authority of Scripture, would argue that such an account of the wholeness of Scripture is not a discerning reading of Scripture, that it is a flawed reading, and that, therefore, the use of Scripture as if it were a moral code is also flawed. I count myself among that number. Cf. also Frame, *Medical Ethics*, p. 2: "Scripture says it, we believe it, and that settles it."

11. For resurrection as the key to Scripture see Allen Verhey, *The Great Reversal: Ethics and the New Testament* (Grand Rapids: Eerdmans, 1984), pp. 181-83; David Kelsey, "The Bible and Christian Theology," *Journal of the American Academy of Religion* 68, no. 3 (1980): 385-402, especially pp. 398-402; and the essay by Oliver O'Donovan, "Keeping Body and Soul Together," in *On Moral Medicine*, ed. Stephen E. Lammers and Allen Verhey, second ed. (Grand Rapids: Eerdmans, 1998), pp. 223-38.

tius Pilate, and as the one God raised "as the first fruits of those who have died." It became difficult to sort out who said what, but their conclusions can be reported.

A Healing Ministry[12]

In his healing ministry Jesus made known God's good future, and he made its power felt against death and Satan and sin. And when God raised Jesus from the dead, God healed the healer, vindicated him as the one who had made known God's cause, and established God's own future sovereignty over that same triumvirate of the powers of this age.

First of all, and most obviously, when God raised Jesus, it was a great triumph over the power of *death*[13] — and in the healing ministry of Jesus that future victory of God already made its power felt. The dead were raised, and those who were thought in the first century to be "like dead" or under the power of death — the lepers, the blind, the paralyzed — were healed (Luke 7:22-23).[14] In

12. On the healing ministry of Jesus see especially Seybold and Mueller, *Sickness and Healing*, pp. 114-17; Albrecht Oepke, *"iaomai," Theological Dictionary of the New Testament,* ed. Gerhard Kittel, trans. Geoffrey W. Bromiley, vol. 3 (Grand Rapids: Eerdmans, 1965), pp. 194-215, esp. 204-13; John T. Carroll, "Sickness and Healing in the New Testament Gospels," *Interpretation* 49, no. 2 (April 1995): 130-42. On the miracles of Jesus there is, of course, an enormous literature. Reginald H. Fuller, *Interpreting the Miracles* (London: SCM Press, 1963), remains a very valuable critical but nontechnical introduction. See also Howard Clark Kee, *Miracle in the Early Christian World* (New Haven: Yale University Press, 1983); David Bartlett, *Fact and Faith* (Valley Forge: Judson, 1975); and Charles F. D. Moule, ed., *Miracles: Cambridge Studies in Their Philosophy and History* (Naperville, Ill.: Alec Allenson, 1965). The question of whether Jesus actually did miracles has been much debated. The tradition of Jesus as miracle-worker is attested by every identifiable source for the gospels and in a variety of forms besides the miracle stories themselves. Moreover, the question at issue initially seems not to have been whether Jesus actually did miracles but how to explain his miracles — whether as demonstrations of the future power of God or as collusion with Satan (e.g., Mark 3:22, 23; Matt. 12:27). Leaving aside the question of whether particular stories and their details are historically authentic, the general tradition is well-attested, and it can be discounted as the product of an overly active imagination in the church and the credulity of early Christians only if the reader begins with *a priori* assumptions about a closed universe operating according to fixed laws of cause and effect.

13. See Lloyd R. Bailey Sr., *Biblical Perspectives on Death* (Philadelphia: Fortress, 1979); Leander Keck, "New Testament Views of Death," in *Perspectives on Death,* ed. Liston Mills (Nashville: Abingdon, 1969); Otto Kaiser and Eduard Lohse, *Death and Life,* trans. John E. Steely (Nashville: Abingdon, 1977).

14. Seybold and Mueller, *Sickness and Healing,* p. 123.

the healing ministry of Jesus the power and the purpose of God were disclosed. As Sally observed to the chaplain, "God's cause is life, not death; God's cause is human flourishing, including the flourishing we call health, not sickness. And when God raised Jesus from the dead, that cause was assured."

Jesus' healing ministry and God's future power stand opposed to the domain of death and strive against what diminishes and frustrates human flourishing. To remember this Jesus and to welcome the future sovereignty of God that he announced is to stand with those whose lives or whose flourishing are threatened and to withstand the disorders that threaten them, however we explain those disorders. In memory of Jesus and in expectation of God's final triumph, the Christian community will celebrate and toast life, not death, but also will be able to endure even dying with hope. In memory of Jesus and in hope the Christian community will delight in human flourishing, including the human flourishing we call "health," but also will be able to endure even the diminishing of human strength we call "sickness" with confidence in God.

The Christian community today may still join Rauschenbusch in praise of God for doctors and nurses and for their knowledge and skill. Christians may see medicine as a gift of God the creator, still following the lead of that wise and prudent Jewish teacher, Jesus ben Sirach; and they may also, remembering Jesus, see medicine as a servant of God the redeemer, as a healing ministry today, as a way God's future may still be given token. Physicians and nurses within the Christian community may construe their profession as a "calling,"[15] indeed as a "holy" calling and themselves as "disciples of the saving Christ," as Rauschenbusch prayed they would. To condemn medicine because God is the healer would be like condemning governments because God is the ruler or families because God is the father. Of course, if medicine pretends to be messianic, if it arrogates to itself the role of faithful savior, if it presumptuously thinks of itself as the ultimate healer, then its arrogance may be and must be condemned — as the arrogance of governments and families who make pretentious claims to ultimacy may be and must be condemned. Perhaps doctors and nurses — at any rate good and honest doctors and nurses — are less tempted to this sort of extravagant and idolatrous expectation of medicine than many patients are. At any rate, a modest medicine may be granted its modest — and honorable — place under God and alongside other measures that protect and promote life and health, good nutrition, public sanitation, a clean environment, and the like. Medicine need not be condemned in Christian community — and it may not be "idolized."

15. See James M. Gustafson, "Professions as 'Callings,'" *Social Service Review* 56 (December 1982): 501-15.

If, as we have said, the resurrection of Jesus was a triumph over death, it was also a great victory over the power of *Satan*.[16] And in the healing ministry of Jesus the future reign of God over Satan and his hosts already made its power felt, for that ministry included exorcisms. "If it is by the finger of God that I cast out the demons," Jesus said (Luke 11:20), "then the kingdom of God has come to you."

"Possession" was widespread in the ancient Mediterranean, or, more precisely, the demonological understanding of sickness and psychosis was widespread.[17] Jesus was hardly the only one with the power to "cast out demons." Indeed, one defense Jesus makes against the charge that he casts out demons "by Beelzebul" is the inconsistency of attributing the exorcisms done by "your exorcists" to God and those done by Jesus to the power of Satan (Luke 11:18-19). Jesus evidently shared the demonological understanding of some sickness and psychosis. He explained his exorcisms neither as collusion with Satan nor as magic but as the present power of the future sovereignty of God over Satan (Luke 10:17-18). His exorcisms — and all exorcisms — were of one piece with God's final triumph over the powers of evil and already diminished Satan's dominance.

To remember this Jesus and to welcome the future sovereignty of God he promised is to celebrate his exorcisms and *somehow* to make the stories of exorcism our own. That does not mean that we must account for pathologies and psychoses in the strange and alien terms and categories of the first century, as the power of demons at work. The texts are not addressed to modern scientific and clinical questions and may not be used to prescribe either the way to understand such suffering today or the way to provide therapy.[18] This is not to say

16. The figure of "Satan" is, of course, hardly mentioned in the Old Testament (1 Chron. 21:1; cf. 2 Sam. 24:1). "Satan" — a.k.a. Azazel, Beelzebul, Belial, the devil, "god of this world," "the evil one," etc. — becomes an important figure in the apocalyptic literature as the chief of the demons and as the explanation of a variety of evils. See T. H. Gaster, "Satan," *The Interpreter's Dictionary of the Bible*, vol. IV (New York: Abingdon, 1962), pp. 224-28.

17. Seybold and Mueller, *Sickness and Healing*, p. 116.

18. Seybold and Mueller, *Sickness and Healing*, p. 118; see Bartlett, *Fact and Faith*, pp. 65-83, for one thoughtful account of ways to celebrate these stories and to own them as our own. A good deal of work has been done on the "principalities and powers" in relation to the contemporary church's social and political responsibilities; see, for example, Hendrikus Berkhof, *Christ and the Powers*, trans. John Howard Yoder (Scottdale, Penn.: Herald, 1962); Albert van den Heuvel, *These Rebellious Powers* (Naperville, Ill.: SCM Book Club, 1966); John Howard Yoder, *The Politics of Jesus* (Grand Rapids: Eerdmans, 1972), pp. 135-62; Richard Mouw, *Politics and the Biblical Drama* (Grand Rapids: Eerdmans, 1976), pp. 85-116.

that our scientific and clinical questions always provide access — or the only access — to what is "really" happening in and to patients. There are Christian communities where the power of demons — as quaint and strange as the notion sounds to "rational" and "developed" Westerners — is still experienced as "real," and sometimes in the West attention to "realities" like the "id" and "superego" can hide a "spiritual" struggle in and for the patient. "I have never seen a demon," Sally said, "but I have never seen an 'id' either." And the chaplain, who liked to read Peter De Vries, could not help himself; he rummaged in his briefcase to retrieve a copy of *Forever Panting*, and he read the opening lines.

> Or look at it this way. Psychoanalysis is a permanent fad. A vogue here to stay because it tells an old story in a new way. I mean the traditional conflict between flesh and spirit, as viewed by the Christianity now supposedly outmoded, isn't likely to ease up because we have scrapped the notion of sin and now speak instead of the ego and superego between them riding herd on something called the id. It's the same keg of nails any way you open it. "Id" isn't just another big word, either. Far from it.[19]

"That sounds like something Robert Coles could have written," said Sally.[20] "It's more sarcastic maybe, but there's the same suspicion of psychobabble. Do you happen to know Coles's *Harvard Diary* and the story in it of a friend of his who is visited by a chaplain? I thought about that story the first time you visited." She proceeded to tell the story of Coles's friend and the chaplain who treated the stages of dying as if they were "stations of the cross."

Sally's chaplain laughed and said, "Surely that chaplain didn't remind you of me!"

"Well, a little," Sally admitted, "but I suppose that chaplain would hardly need to be reminded that in some cultures and in some contexts, 'id' is a useful construct to explain what is happening and to help people cope with it."

The chaplain laughed again and responded with some questions of his own: "Do I need to remind you that in other cultures and in other contexts 'demons' may be a useful construct? Seriously, do you think demons are 'real'? Do real demons exist?"

Sally replied, "Frankly, I don't know — but I know this in memory of Jesus: that God will triumph over all that hurts and harms and demeans persons and over all that destroys human community. I know this in memory of Jesus: that if there are demons, they are doomed with all the powers of death and destruction.

19. Peter DeVries, *Forever Panting* (Boston: Little, Brown & Company, 1973), p. 3.
20. See, e.g., Robert Coles, "Psychology as Faith," in *Harvard Diary: Reflections on the Sacred and the Profane* (New York: Crossroad, 1990), pp. 92-94.

'If there are any demons, they are shadow players in the drama of God's action, already doomed to be driven foolishly from the stage with no one to mourn their loss.'[21] And I know this: that it remains a strange world of sickness in Scripture."

Sitting in that hospital room they agreed that the world of exorcisms seemed a strange and alien world to them, but they also agreed that the stories of Jesus could remind even the twenty-first-century scientific clinician of some features of the cause of God. One decisive characteristic of "possession" was precisely possession. The sick did not have control of themselves; they were possessed, subject to the power of the demons; their speech and action had no genuine connection with who they were. And a second decisive characteristic of possession was isolation. The sick were separated from their community, alienated from the very ones who would ordinarily care for them. The strong man of Mark 5, for example, "lived among the tombs; and no one could restrain him any more, even with a chain" (Mark 5:3). But Jesus healed him, restored him to self-control (5:15), and said, "Go home to your friends" (5:19). The exorcisms freed persons to be themselves and to be with others; they restored persons to their own identity and to their community. The cause of God made known in Jesus' healing ministry is human flourishing, and the human flourishing made known in the exorcisms involves integrity and community.

They agreed also that, if a clinician was to be a "disciple of the saving Christ," then she must serve that cause of God. In Christian community and in memory of Jesus, physicians may use their best medical skills and knowledge to explain what is happening in and to the sick. They must use those skills and that knowledge, however, in ways that honor God and serve God's cause, including not only life and health but also the integrity of the sick and their community with those who are well. We remember Jesus and honor God's future sovereignty by standing with those who lack control over their own lives, who lack control over themselves, by standing with the weak and the powerless, and by standing against whatever and whoever hinders and frustrates their freedom to be or to act in ways that have integrity with their identity.

Sometimes sickness threatens such freedom, and then medicine can serve God's cause by using its powers. But sometimes medicine itself can threaten the powers of persons to live (or die) with integrity or within community — and then medicine can only serve God's cause by not using its powers. When, for example, medicine can only prolong one's dying, or when by its technological interventions it can only rob the dying of dignity and separate them from the human companionship of friends and family, then medicine must acknowledge that the moral limit to its powers comes long before the technological limit of its powers.

21. Bartlett, *Fact and Faith*, p. 83.

104

The resurrection of Jesus was also God's great victory over the power of *sin*.[22] In the ministry of Jesus sins were already forgiven in token of God's reign on the far side of the last judgment, and in his healing ministry Jesus already broke the power of sin. Jesus broke the conventional correlation of sin and sickness. To be sure, the stories of Jesus point in more than one direction here. On the one hand (John 9; cf. also Luke 13:1-5), Jesus rejected the assumption that a man's blindness must be caused by either his sin or the sin of his parents. Jesus did not explain the man's blindness as warranted by someone's sin; instead, he simply pointed to the power of God to heal and made that power felt. To remember Jesus is to disown the putative connection of sin and sickness whenever it is used to distance ourselves from the sick, whenever it is used to renege on our obligations of solidarity with the suffering, whenever it is used self-righteously to justify segregating the "sinful" sick from the "righteous" well. Whenever we refuse to be present with the sick or to use our powers against disease because they deserve their sickness, the memory of Jesus will have none of it. It is the disposition to cure the sick, not a readiness to condemn them, which is worthy of the gospel. It is care, not condemnation, which fits the memory of Jesus. When, for example, a person with AIDS is abandoned or neglected or shunned or condemned, then Jesus is not remembered or the Scripture performed.[23]

On the other hand (Mark 2:5), we also have Jesus' astonishing reply to a request for healing, "Son, your sins are forgiven." In this case the connection between sin and sickness was apparently accepted, but it was not used to isolate, segregate, judge, or condemn the sick. On the contrary, God's acceptance of the sick young man was total and unqualified, and the whole person was renewed as a token of God's good future. To remember this remark by Jesus and to hope for the future sovereignty of God it signals is not to disown a duty to care or a desire to cure; it is to recognize and to deal with the whole person, refusing to reduce a person's suffering to its physical manifestations or its clinical symptoms. Many persons with AIDS, for example, sometimes hurt in places no medicine can touch; they have needs that are not simply medical but psychological and social and spiritual. Sometimes they need relief from a sense of isolation and abandonment; always they need to restore and maintain not only certain physiological processes but also certain relationships with others. In memory of

22. Sin is regarded as a "power" in the New Testament and not simply as an individual act which falls short of the mark. Sin "ruled," and expressed its power in the acts of persons. See *"hamartanō," Theological Dictionary of the New Testament,* vol. 1 (Grand Rapids: Eerdmans, 1964), pp. 267-316, especially the sections contributed by Gustav Stahlin and Walter Grundmann, pp. 293-316.

23. On the response to AIDS see Hessel Bouma III et al., *Christian Faith, Health, and Medical Practice* (Grand Rapids: Eerdmans, 1989), pp. 319-42.

Jesus we will not reduce patients to their pathologies — "the heart attack in room 515," for example — nor reduce the practice of medicine to a collection of skills and tools. The Christian community in memory of Jesus should care for the whole person.

Moreover, if Jesus forgives people in token of God's good future, then we ought also to repent and to forgive one another. Sally underscored the point: "Jesus came announcing that the good future of God was near," she said. "He called for repentance in response to it (Mark 1:15), and he forgave sinners in token of it. Remembering Jesus still evokes practices of repentance and forgiveness." It seemed clear to the chaplain that he was not dealing with any major-league sinner here, but he humored her. "What would you confess?" the chaplain asked with a laugh; "Are you a smoker?"

"Not I," Sally replied. "But I see a reflection of my life as a physician in my doctor, and I don't like it. I have been where he is, angry at the patient who refuses another round of therapy, angry at my own powerlessness to save her, eager to use my authority as a physician to convince her to try again, and eager to avoid her when she refuses to try again or dies before we can. It is no great callousness I confess; it is the failure to acknowledge the fallibility and limits of medical care.[24] I need the forgiveness of God — and of my patients.

"And now I find myself where my patients have been; and I don't like it much better, angry at the doctor who cannot deliver a miracle, judging her much too quickly and severely, angrier still that she would try to tell me how to live while I am dying, and eager to render her still more powerless and optionless. It is no great callousness I confess here either; it is the failure to acknowledge the fallibility and limits of my own autonomy. I need the forgiveness of God — and of my doctor."

Confession is good for the soul, of course, but it could also be good for medical ethics, the chaplain thought. It helps us to see the fallibility of both medicine and patients. It helps us recognize the evil we sometimes do in resisting evil, the suffering we sometimes inflict in the effort to banish suffering and those who remind us of it.[25] Both Sally and her doctor had been a little too ready to condemn and to blame; the doctor thought it would be his patient's fault if she died, and Sally thought the doctor's passion for her life impertinent.

24. See Douglas Anderson, "The Physician's Experience: Witnessing Numinous Reality," *Second Opinion* 13 (March 1990): 111-22. Pages 117-22 focus on confession, the freedom it gives from being "blinded by the utopian images arising from uncritical overestimations of technology's power" (pp. 121-22) and the freedom it gives for presence to those who hurt or grieve.

25. See Stanley Hauerwas, *Suffering Presence* (Notre Dame: University of Notre Dame Press, 1986), p. 35.

The doctor had been a little too ready to reduce Sally to her body, to manipulable nature, and then to manipulate her body (and her), a little too ready to reduce Sally to her disease and then to combat it (and to combat her). And Sally had been a little too ready to reduce the doctor to an "animated tool"[26] and then to put it down (and to put him down). Repentance and forgiveness might heal their relation a little, at least enable them to listen to each other a little longer and a little better. The memory of Jesus and his forgiveness would neither render the patient optionless by insisting on a physician's authority nor render the physician optionless by insisting simply on patient autonomy.

The healing ministry of Jesus is remembered in the gospels and still remembered in the churches. It was remembered in the conversation of the chaplain and Sally. And that memory is not merely historical recollection. It formed a people, and it still forms a people — and a medicine among those people — disposed to protect life, not to practice hospitality to death; disposed to sustain health, not to welcome sickness; disposed to respect the embodied integrity of people, not to run roughshod over their freedom and identity; disposed to nurture community, not to isolate and alienate the sick; disposed to cure and, if to cure is impossible, always at least to care, but not to condemn or abandon. The memory of the healing ministry of Jesus still calls Christian doctors and nurses to a humble healing ministry of their own as "disciples of the saving Christ" and still calls the rest of us to gratitude for the presence of such caregivers among us.

Good News to the Poor[27]

Sally and the chaplain remembered Jesus not only as a healer but also as a preacher, as the one who brought good news to the poor (Luke 7:22; Matt. 11:5). The resurrection of Jesus was the vindication of Jesus as the Christ, as "the anointed one" — "anointed," as he said, "to bring good news to the poor" (Luke 4:18). His words to the poor and his compassion for them were no less a token and a promise of God's good future than his works of healing (e.g., Luke 6:20). There is no remembering this Jesus, no calling this remembered Jesus

26. "Animated tool" is Aristotle's definition of a slave. See Paul Ramsey, *Ethics at the Edges of Life* (New Haven: Yale University Press, 1978), pp. 45, 158.
27. On this topic there is again a great deal of excellent literature. The interested reader might consult Martin Hengel, *Property and Riches in the Early Church* (Philadelphia: Fortress, 1974), pp. 22-30; Richard Batey, *Jesus and the Poor* (New York: Harper & Row, 1972), pp. 5-23; Luise Schottroff and Wolfgang Stegemann, *Jesus and the Hope of the Poor,* trans. Matthew J. O'Connell (Maryknoll, N.Y.: Orbis, 1986), pp. 1-37; and part four of this book.

"the anointed" (i.e., the Christ), that may be unmoved by his proclamation of "good news to the poor." There can be no discernment of a way of life — or of the requirements of a common life — worthy of this gospel that is inattentive to the needs of the poor, including their health-care needs.

No evangelist represents this feature of the memory of Jesus more elegantly or emphasizes this requirement of Christian discernment more powerfully than Luke, the physician,[28] so the chaplain and Sally spent a little time together reading Luke's Gospel. From the very beginning, they noted, Luke emphasizes Jesus' solidarity with the poor. Jesus' own parents were poor, offering the sacrifices of the poor (Luke 2:24; cf. Lev. 12:6-8). The chaplain and Sally read together Mary's "Magnificat" (Luke 1:46-55), and saw how she rejoiced in the birth of Jesus as the beginning of the decisive episode of God's activity to exalt the humble, the hungry, and the poor, and to humble the exalted. They read of the visit of humble shepherds, not rich magi, to Jesus, and noted that they found him in an animal stall, not in a house (Luke 2:8-20; cf. Matt. 2:1-12). In Luke's Gospel, they discovered, the Beatitudes announce God's blessing on the poor and hungry, not just upon those who are "poor in spirit" and hungry for righteousness (Luke 6:20-21; cf. Matt. 5:3-6). Luke's memory of Jesus requires love and mercy, carefree generosity toward the poor (6:30), and lending to them without expecting a return (6:34, 35). Then Sally and the chaplain went through Luke's parables together: The parable of "The Good Samaritan" explicates the love command in terms of mercy to the neighbor in need. That kindness includes care for the health of the "half-dead" neighbor whom it is too much our impulse to shun and neglect. The parable concludes with the admonition, "Go and do likewise" (Luke 10:25-37). The parable of "The Rich Fool" condemns both the concern of the wealthy for their own ease and their failure to do justice or to practice kindness to the poor in faithfulness to God (Luke 12:13-21). The parable of "The Great Supper" includes a reminder of God's intention to bless "the poor, the crippled, the blind, and the lame" and follows an exhortation to practice hospitality toward the same (Luke 14:15-24). The parable of "The Rich Man and Lazarus" announces a great reversal of blessings upon the poor and woes upon the ungenerous rich (Luke 16:19-31). In the story of Zacchaeus the choice to do justice and mercy is commended by Jesus in

---

28. Colossians 4:14 mentions "Luke, the beloved physician." The traditional identification of the author of the Gospel of Luke with this Luke who was a physician and a companion of Paul has been vigorously challenged, but it remains in my view quite plausible. For a defense of the tradition see E. E. Ellis, *The Gospel of Luke* (London: Nelson, 1966), pp. 40-51, and Joseph Fitzmyer, *The Gospel according to Luke: Introduction, Translation, and Notes*, Anchor Bible, vol. 28 (Garden City, N.Y.: Doubleday, 1981).

words which suggest that in such justice and mercy toward the poor the future reign of God has "today" begun to take effect (Luke 19:1-10).

Jesus' preaching good news to the poor, like his healing ministry, is remembered in the gospels and still remembered in the churches. It was remembered in the conversation of Sally and the chaplain. And it is worth noting again that that memory is not merely historical recollection. It still forms a people — and a medicine among those people — disposed to insist on justice for the poor and to practice kindness toward them. Poverty can debilitate both soul and cell. There are too many whose spirits are crippled, whose lives are ended, and whose health is destroyed by poverty. The needs of the poor are not all (or even mainly) medical; even their health-related needs are not all (or even mainly) medical. The memory of Jesus should still evoke Rauschenbusch's concern and prayer to "order our communities that none may be doomed to an untimely death for lack of the simple gifts" of clean air and pure water, adequate nutrition, periodic rest from labor, and security from violence.

The need for medical care seems relatively insignificant against the background of that list of more fundamental human needs. But the poor do have needs for medical care, and the need for medical care never seems insignificant when you have it. The poor, however, do not all have secure access to medical care. In the United States, while some of the poor are covered by Medicaid, many others are uninsured and have no assured access to medical care.[29] Medicine, meanwhile, is adopting a corporate image. A marketplace medicine will do great things for those who can pay, but the poor and powerless who are sick will be left to their own resources — and sometimes to despair.

The Christian community in memory of Jesus must still struggle to find words and deeds to form public policies and medical practices that "fit" such a story, that are worthy of "good news to the poor." The memory of Jesus can be honored in political efforts to form a medical-care system that expresses and signals a concern for the poor and for the health of the poor. The memory of Jesus can be honored in community efforts to support hospitals that resist the marketplace story of medicine. As Edmund Pellegrino has said, "The Church in its health ministry has Christ as its model. It must be concerned with those on the margins of society, or they will not receive care."[30] The Catholic Church and

---

29. Nearly 25 percent of the population of the United States is without either public or private insurance. See further Bouma et al., *Christian Faith, Health, and Medical Practice*, pp. 144-75.

30. Edmund Pellegrino, "Competition: New Moral Dilemmas for Physicians, Hospitals," in *On Moral Medicine*, ed. Stephen Lammers and Allen Verhey, first ed. (Grand Rapids: Eerdmans, 1987), pp. 650-52, p. 650.

some other churches are playing an indispensable role in their support of religious hospitals that resist the new competitive ethos of medicine, but that support will have to be increased and other churches will have to join the effort if such hospitals are both to survive and to care for the poor. In memory of Jesus the churches must be concerned about political policy and about institutional programs — and about professionals. The memory of Jesus can be honored in efforts to nurture the professional identities of doctors and nurses so that they have the strength (and the resources) to resist the temptation to become "hirelings who serve only for money," to use Rauschenbusch's still apt phrase.

The chaplain and Sally took note of this feature of the church's memory of Jesus, but time was also a scarce resource, and they left further consideration of it to another day and for a different room, perhaps the board room.[31] But before they moved on to other features of the story of Jesus, Sally called attention to the ending of the story of the Rich Man and Lazarus (Luke 16:19-31). "The tight-fisted rich man died in the parable, too," she said. "Not as soon as the poor man, but he died — and from his torment in Hades he called out to Abraham to send someone from the dead to warn his rich brothers to do justice and to love kindness. Abraham refused, saying that, 'If they do not listen to Moses and the prophets, neither will they be convinced even if someone rises from the dead.' Luke knew, of course, that Jesus had been raised from the dead. The one 'anointed to bring good news to the poor' has been raised from the dead. Are we convinced? Do we remember the resurrection of this Jesus? The greatest danger is still forgetfulness." The memory of Jesus and of his resurrection must govern discernment in the church concerning our responsibilities to and for the poor who are sick.

Suffered under Pontius Pilate[32]

Sally and the chaplain remembered Jesus not only as the healer, not only as the preacher of good news to the poor, but also as the one who "suffered under

---

31. On Scripture and the allocation of health-care resources, see chapter twenty in this volume.

32. On the passion narratives see especially Hans-Ruedi Weber, *The Cross,* trans. Elke Jessett (Grand Rapids: Eerdmans, 1979). For a thoughtful theological reflection concerning suffering which remembers the story of the cross, see Arthur C. McGill, *Suffering: A Test of Theological Method* (Philadelphia: Geneva, 1968). On medicine in the light of such reflection, see especially David H. Smith, "Suffering, Medicine, and Christian Theology," in *On Moral Medicine,* ed. Stephen E. Lammers and Allen Verhey, first ed. (Grand Rapids: Eerdmans, 1987), pp. 255-61; Stanley Hauerwas, *Suffering Presence;* and Bouma et al., *Christian Faith, Health, and Medical Practice.*

Pontius Pilate, was crucified, died, and buried." The passion narrative is remembered by all the gospels; indeed, they decisively tie the memories of Jesus
as healer and as preacher to the story of the passion. "This is the crucial memory," the chaplain concluded. "Apart from it the church is always at risk of dis-
torting the good news into a kind of Pollyanna triumphalism and then of self-
deceptively ignoring or denying the sad truth about our world. But with this
memory of the suffering of Jesus the church is able to face the sad truth about
our world and to respond even to suffering and to death truthfully."

Sally agreed, and as a doctor she reported that medical professionals are
called to respond to suffering and death as a matter of routine. They confront
suffering in the myriad of sad stories people tell with and of their bodies: the
burn victim who endures not only pain but disfigurement, the athlete whose
accident severed her spine and left her a quadriplegic, the parents who grieve
the death of their child of promise, the elderly patient in decline with Alzhei-
mer's, the AIDS patient. It is a sad world medicine witnesses and serves. "The
questions of theodicy," she said, "are hardly theoretical in a hospital. There people cry out in the honesty of grief and pain, 'Why, God? Why?' and they beat
against the heavens with the one great human complaint: 'If you are so good
and powerful, God, how can you let this happen?'"

The chaplain remembered that he had recently been asked that question
by a patient, and that he had not been of much help to her with it. To Sally he
replied, "The Christian community will not find that question or that complaint offensive. How can it? For it remembers Jesus, who cried out from the
cross, 'My God, my God, why have you forsaken me?' (Mark 15:34; Matt. 27:46)
and made the human cry of lament his own cry. It will not find that question or
that complaint easy to answer, either, however. It does not have any tidy theoretical theodicy to give in reply.

"Conventional and traditional theodicies have usually defended God's
justice and goodness by explaining evil as either deserved or as educational.
Some have insisted that God is kind to the good and pays back evil for evil, that
suffering is always in some sense *deserved.* But not only do the wicked sometimes experience God's kindness, as Jonah learned to his chagrin, but also and
more distressingly the innocent sometimes suffer, as Job witnessed to his
doubtful friends. Suffering is sometimes deserved, to be sure, but not always —
and seldom so clearly that we can read God's justice or God's judgment in the
suffering of any. I do not see any justice in your suffering, my friend.

"Some others have insisted instead that suffering is educational, that it
teaches us to rely on God, that it forms character, that it is necessary if we are to
learn to celebrate the good and to be properly grateful for it, that it is always in
some sense *meaningful.* To be sure, the time we have spent together has con-

111

vinced me once again that people can learn and grow by suffering. I know I have grown by being present in your suffering. Even so, this reply is hardly sufficient as a theoretical theodicy. People are as often broken by suffering as they are educated by it. Suffering is sometimes meaningful, to be sure, but not always — and seldom so clearly meaningful that we can be content with the meaning and pedagogical significance of another's suffering. You are paying too high a price for my instruction, my friend.[33]

"Neither account of suffering is finally very satisfying in a hospital — or very honest intellectually. The memory of Jesus does not make liars of us. Much suffering is undeserved; much suffering is pointless. It is a sad world, marked and marred by suffering. Christians do not deny the horrible reality of suffering or their own powerlessness to 'justify' God and God's ways in a theoretical theodicy. In memory of Jesus Christians point to a Roman cross and to an innocent Jewish healer and teacher who suffered there. The cross is no lie. The cross is the truth about our world in its revelation of the reality and power of evil. When Christians remember the cross, they acknowledge the sad truth about our world. This healer, this teacher, this suffering one, however, was raised from the dead and vindicated as God's own Son. And in remembering the cross Christians point to the Son of God who hung there and made the human cry of lament his own cry (Ps. 22:1; Matt. 27:46; Mark 15:34). Jesus shares our suffering, making it his own. The cross is no lie. The cross is the truth about our world not only in its revelation of the reality and power of evil but also in its revelation of God's own compassion, of God's suffering with those who suffer. And when Christians remember the cross, they not only acknowledge the sad truth about our world, but they also celebrate the glad tidings that God cares, that God does not abandon the sufferer, that God 'did not despise or abhor the affliction of the afflicted . . . but heard when I cried to him' (Ps. 22:24). The lament that opens with the great cry of abandonment ends with confidence in God and with a vision of God's good future (Ps. 22:27-31). To those who suffer, then, the first word of the Christian community is not an effort to justify God for sending evil as punishment or as training; it is to remind them of Jesus and of his cross. Remember Jesus, my friend."

Sally was at once touched and amused. The chaplain seemed to have changed quite a bit since their first encounter. She thanked him for his words and confirmed them with her own. "To those who suffer," she said, "the story of Jesus is a glad story, indeed. To be sure, this glad story does not deny the sad truth about our world or about our sickness; it does not announce here and

33. These last paragraphs are indebted to David H. Smith, "Suffering, Medicine, and Christian Theology."

now the end to our pain or an avoidance of our death. Nevertheless, it does provide an unshakable assurance that we do not suffer alone, that we are not and will not be abandoned, that Jesus suffers with us, that God cares. And that is a glad story, indeed. So the suffering may cry out 'My God, my God, why?' and still know that Christ has made their cry his own. The glad story of Jesus is indeed a hard reminder that in a world like this one, no matter how righteous or repentant we are, we cannot expect to be spared pain and sorrow. Certainly life and the human flourishing we call 'health' are goods which belong to the cause of God and which one may and should seek, but 'a disciple is not above the teacher' (Matt. 10:24). In our sad stories we keep good company. That's a part of the good news — and this: that beyond the cross, beyond the sad story of suffering, is the resurrection, the triumph of God over all these diseases.

"The story of Jesus is good news to the suffering," she repeated, and then she looked carefully at the chaplain and added, "and it provides you a vocation, my friend. It is a call to those who would remember him to minister to the suffering, to care for the sick, to have compassion for the dying. Such a calling can nurture and sustain the vocation of medicine to heal and to care, to intervene if possible against the evils of suffering and premature dying, and to be present to the one who suffers even if and when the medical interventions do not provide a happy ending. The good news must be expressed not only in fitting words but in worthy deeds as well. A medicine formed and informed by the memory of Jesus will be able to care even when it cannot cure, to wipe the tears of the dying man away tenderly even when it cannot save his life, to resist the temptation to abandon (or eliminate) the patient when it cannot eliminate her suffering. In those who suffer the eyes of faith are trained to see the very image of the Lord, and the ears of faith are open to that always surprising word, 'just as you did it to one of the least of these . . . , you did it to me' (Matt. 25:40)."[34]

The "Not Yet" Character of Our Life and Medicine

Together they remembered the story of Jesus and celebrated it. God raised this Jesus from the dead in our world and in our history, and our world and our history have, happily, no escape. This healer, this preacher of good news to the poor, this one who suffered under Pontius Pilate, was raised up as the "first fruits of those who have died" (1 Cor. 15:20, 23). The resurrection of Jesus was the promise of God's good future, the guarantee of God's unchallenged cosmic

34. Jan Van Eys, "*Mihi Fecistis:* Thinking Ethically While Giving Care," a lecture at Hope College, November 4, 1986.

sovereignty, the first fruits of a day on which God "will wipe every tear from their eyes. Death will be no more; mourning and crying and pain will be no more, for the first things have passed away" (Rev. 21:4).

But that good future, they both acknowledged, is not yet. God's cause has been made known and its triumph assured, but the powers of death and sin and suffering still assert their doomed reign. "The ancient foe still seeks to work us woe," the chaplain said, and Sally added the next lines from Luther's great hymn, "His craft and power are great, and armed with cruel hate, on earth is not his equal."[35]

It is not yet the promised future of God's unchallenged sovereignty. And it is not within our power — not even within our new medical powers — to establish it. Our powers — including our new medical powers — are not messianic. In memory of Jesus we may and we should delight in any and every token of God's good future in the interim, and medicine can be such a token. But we may not and must not entertain extravagant and idolatrous expectations of any human power, including our new medical powers. It is God in Christ who suffers with us and for us and can sustain us in our suffering and dying, not medical science. It is God in Christ who will bring the good future of God's unchallenged sovereignty, when pain and death shall be no more, not medical technology. The memory of Jesus and the hope that memory evokes sustain and nurture patience, courage, and care — not only in the face of the sad stories of pain and suffering and death, but also in the face of the sad stories of the failure of medical interventions to relieve pain or to remedy suffering or to rescue from death. The memory of Jesus and the hope that memory evokes sustain and nurture both the sick and those who care for the sick in their respective roles.

God's cause is not death — but people die still. God's cause is not suffering — but people suffer still. In memory of Jesus the healer the Christian community will not celebrate death or suffering as good; they will, rather, celebrate the medical powers God gives to intervene in a person's premature dying and to relieve a person's unnecessary suffering. In memory of Jesus, the preacher of "good news to the poor," the Christian community will not delight when such powers — and the simpler things upon which life and health depend — are not shared fairly and generously with the poor. In memory of Jesus who suffered and died, the Christian community will pray boldly not only for some token of the healer's final triumph in the success of medical intervention against death and suffering; it will also pray — and still more boldly — for the presence of the one who suffers with us and died for us, who has compassion on us in our suf-

---

35. Martin Luther, "A Mighty Fortress Is Our God."

fering and who will not abandon us even in our dying. The church that prays for that presence must also practice it, signaling Christ's presence and care to those beyond cure by their own. In memory of the resurrection of this Jesus and in the hope of their own, Christians will not pretend or presume that the final victory over death is within human powers or that this life can be altogether freed from suffering. The victory over death and suffering is finally God's victory, not medicine's. Jesus, not medicine, is the Messiah. In living and in dying, in suffering and in caring for the suffering, Christians remember the resurrection of Jesus and hope for God's good future. So they need not fear death. They need not use all their resources or all human powers against it. They may risk their lives for the sake of other goods that belong to God's good future, trusting in that future. They may permit death its apparent victory, confident of God's final triumph. They need not fear suffering either. In memory of Jesus and in the hope that memory evokes, Christians have the courage not only to risk and to endure their own suffering for the sake of God's cause in the world but also to share the sufferings of others, to be present in care and in prayer for those medicine cannot cure.

There is another mark of the "not yet" character of our life and medicine: moral ambiguity. It is not yet God's future of *shalom;* there is not yet peace even among the goods which all belong to God's cause. Here and now, even as the people of God welcome God's cause and serve it, they face conflicting goods and confront gathering evils. Here and now, even as they seek to consent to God's future rule, part of what they know to be God's cause comes into conflict with another part of what they know to be God's cause. In allocating finite funds, for example, the memory of Jesus as preacher of "good news to the poor" disposes the Christian community to use finite funds to meet basic human needs before it allocates money for expensive medical care, to provide a decent minimum of health care for all before providing the very best medical care for any, but the memory of Jesus the healer disposes people to seek the very best medical care possible for those who need it. In deciding about the care of one patient, to give another example, the disposition to preserve life can come into conflict with the disposition to relieve suffering.

The conflicts are still more commonplace and routine than that. Trade-offs are sometimes necessary between listening to a patient's sighs and listening to a patient's chest, between taking time to be present with the patient and taking time to research new studies of the patient's condition. The medical technology that enables medical professionals to care more effectively than before (though not more profoundly) may also so distance the practitioner from the patient that it is more difficult to nurture and to signal care.

Even when competence is joined to care, the conflict of goods is not transcended, for medical care — even competent medical care — can still abuse. "Taking care of someone" can, in ordinary language and in some sophisticated medicine, be synonymous with doing violence to them. The memory of Jesus will dispose us to care — and so to heal, if possible. The memory of Jesus will also dispose us to preserve, honor, and respect the embodied integrity of those who are patients, even if and when that embodied integrity requires that a medical procedure not be used — and still to care even when we *may* not cure.

Here and now, in these times between the times, the dispositions to heal, to respect integrity, to do justice and to love kindness for the poor, to preserve life, all belong to the memory of Jesus and all can conflict. The memory of Jesus does not provide any neat and easy resolution to such conflict. It does not usher in a new heaven and new earth, either. Here and now there is ambiguity.

Still, already, the memory of Jesus sheds some light on our sicknesses and on our care for the sick and enables the communal discernment and mutual instruction of Christian churches.[36] The memory of Jesus can, should, and sometimes does illumine both the enduring problems and the novel quandaries of medicine, even it if does not tell us precisely what to do.

This chapter has sketched the strange world of sickness in Scripture and marked out the way of Jesus in the context of that strange world. The next chapter will remember the early church remembering Jesus. And, finally, chapter seven will return to the case of Sally and — in memory of Jesus — attempt to discern a form of faithfulness in the face of death.

36. See James P. Wind, "Congregations and Medical Ethics," *Bulletin of the Park Ridge Center* IV, no. 2 (May 1989): 35-37. The congregation is not only a community of discourse about medicine, of course. It is also a community of healing; see Thomas A. Droege, "Congregations as Communities of Health and Healing," *Interpretation* XLIX, no. 2 (April 1995): 117-29; and Abigail Evans, "The Church as an Institution of Health," *Interpretation* XLIX, no. 2 (April 1995): 158-71.

CHAPTER SIX

Remembering the Early Church Remembering Jesus in the Strange World of Sickness

Having marked out the way of Jesus in the strange world of sickness, Sally and the chaplain continued to search Scripture. They continued to confront a strange world of sickness, but they also encountered communities that were called to be communities of healing and of moral discernment — and both in memory of Jesus. Reading the New Testament, they remembered the church remembering Jesus. And recalling the history of the church, they saw sometimes among saints and strangers a performance of the Scripture they read.

The Early Church and the Strange World of Sickness

The early church was a community of healing. In memory of Jesus it could hardly be otherwise. Jesus was a healer, and in his healing miracles the coming rule of God already made its power felt (e.g., Luke 11:20). Remembering Jesus, the church discerned in life and health great goods, gifts of God, and tokens of a good future in which "Death will be no more; mourning and crying and pain will be no more" (Rev. 21:4). With such memory and hope Christianity entered the world as a religion of healing.[1]

The early Christians remembered the stories of Jesus the healer — and, remarkably, they lived the stories. In the early Christian community the healing ministry of Jesus continued — and it continued to be a sign of the good future

1. Henry Sigerist, *Civilization and Disease* (Ithaca, N.Y.: Cornell University Press, 1943), p. 69.

of God. Among their accounts of Jesus' instructions for their mission was this one: "cure the sick . . . and say to them, 'The kingdom of God has come near to you'" (Luke 10:9; cf. Matt. 10:7-8). The miracle stories in Acts (e.g., Acts 3:1-10; 8:4-8; 9:33-34; 14:8-10; 16:16-18; 19:11-17; 20:9-12) and the inclusion of the "gift" of healing in the Pauline list of spiritual gifts (e.g., 1 Cor. 12:9, 30) confirm this impression of the early church as a community of healing. In these healings, too, the good future of God already made its power felt. In the gift of healing the Spirit provided a "down payment" on that future. These healings were done "in the name of Jesus Christ of Nazareth" (Acts 3:6). In memory of Jesus the early church turned toward the sick, attended to them, evidently sometimes healed them, but never abandoned them.

This remarkable healing power was, however, not without its temptations. The "spiritually gifted" members of the Corinthian congregation, some of whom evidently had the gift of healing, needed to be warned against elitism and arrogance, needed to be reminded that the gifts of the Spirit, including the gift of healing, were "for the common good" (1 Cor. 12:7). There was no reason for boasting. There was no justification for the eschatological triumphalism that supposed that the gift of the Spirit provided a magical power by which God could be manipulated and God's cause domesticated. There was no warrant for the Pollyanna optimism that supposed that the gospel provided a charm against sickness or suffering and an escape from dying. And there was no place for the insidious enthusiasm that could suppose that sickness and suffering were signs of "little faith."

"What do you have that you did not receive?" Paul asked them. "And if you received it, why do you boast as if it were not a gift?" (1 Cor. 4:7). The spiritual enthusiasts in Corinth needed to be reminded that the gift of healing was a gift, not a magical technology under the control and at the disposal of the spiritually gifted. They needed to be reminded that the gift of healing, like the other gifts, merely pointed toward God's good future; it did not constitute it. They needed to be reminded that the gift of healing, like the other gifts, is worthless without love. Then, "if one member suffers, all suffer together with it" (12:26). God's good future will be fully known only when God's gracious sovereignty is unchallenged. While they waited and watched for that good future, in memory of Jesus and his cross (2:1-2) they would sometimes have to share and endure suffering with patience and in hope.[2]

2. Consider also the Gospel of Mark. It was evidently written to a largely Gentile Christian community that had experienced suffering (in the form of persecution) and could expect to experience more. The stories of the miracles of Jesus were cherished in that community, but by themselves they could neither explain the suffering nor enable the

118

The spiritually gifted in Corinth may have been tempted to arrogance, but others were tempted to despair. If the Corinthian enthusiasts thought they were already angels, some other Christians were tempted to think that nothing had really changed. In the oldest part of the New Testament, 1 Thessalonians, for example, Paul addressed a crisis of hope in the Thessalonian church, a crisis evidently caused by the deaths of some of the community (1 Thess. 4:13). Timothy had given Paul a good report about the congregation, "the good news of your faith and love" (3:6). But it is not accidental that "hope," the third member of the familiar triad, was absent from Timothy's report (compare 1:3) — for there was a crisis of hope in the congregation. Timothy had also evidently reported that some were troubled "concerning those who are asleep" (4:13 RSV). Paul would not have them despair. The basis for hope, Paul tells them, is not some power we have at our disposal but "that Jesus died and rose again" (4:14). Then, utilizing apocalyptic images (and probably a fragment of the apocalyptic tradition), Paul assures them that even the dead have not been abandoned, that even death cannot separate them from the love and power of God (cf. Rom. 8:38, 39). The powers of death and Satan and sin continue to assert their doomed reign; we still must "wait," wait for the appearance of Christ in glory (1 Thess. 1:10), "wait for . . . the redemption of our bodies" (Rom. 8:23).

To "wait" is not to do nothing. To wait is to delight in what healings there are as tokens of God's future without supposing that either the power to heal or God's good future is simply at our disposal. To wait is to endure suffering and to share it with patience and hope. To wait is to comfort the grieving (1 Thess. 4:18) and to "help the weak" (5:14). In memory of Jesus the church may be confident of God's final triumph and still endure patiently "the sufferings of this present time" (Rom. 8:18).

Paul knew better than to yield to either pride or despair. He had learned better by his own sickness, his "thorn in the flesh."[3] He called the ailment "a

---

community to endure it. Mark ties the miracle tradition to the passion narrative in such a way that the congregation can no longer understand Jesus as "Son of God" only (or even primarily) in his power to heal and to relieve suffering but must now understand Jesus as "Son of God" also (and fundamentally) in his enduring the suffering of the cross (Mark 15:39). In this way they are enabled to understand their own suffering as a "heroic discipleship" (Allen Verhey, *The Great Reversal: Ethics and the New Testament* [Grand Rapids: Eerdmans, 1984], pp. 74-81) and to dare to endure such suffering for the sake of their own integrity and the cause of God in the world.

3. There has been a wide range of speculative diagnoses of Paul's condition — everything from hemorrhoids to epilepsy. See the note on this passage in Philip E. Hughes, *Paul's Second Epistle to the Corinthians* (Grand Rapids: Eerdmans, 1962), pp. 442-48; and Klaus Seybold and Ulrich B. Mueller, *Sickness and Healing*, trans. Douglas W. Stott (Nash-

messenger of Satan" (2 Cor. 12:7); it was a reminder of the continuing power of that which resists God's cause. Still, Paul had learned to be "content with weaknesses" (12:10). There is nothing in Paul's contentment that denies the reality of the evil he suffers bodily; there is no spiritual retreat to inwardness. Sickness is, as Karl Barth has said, a "forerunner and messenger of death,"[4] and faithfulness to God will resist what resists God, including sickness. Paul reports that he had called upon the Lord for healing, but he was not healed. The answer of the Lord is also reported: "My grace is sufficient for you, for power is made perfect in weakness" (12:9). What was — and remains — a "messenger of Satan" now makes known God's power. Sickness is not only the messenger of death but also the reminder that the power of God is not simply at the disposal of human beings, that the grace of God is not simply a human possession, and that our hope is not that God's good future is already in our hands but that we are in God's hands. Paul remembers Jesus, who "was crucified in weakness, but lives by the power of God" (13:4), and he has learned to live the story he loves to tell.

Moreover, he has learned that it must be so, that his story as minister of the gospel must be told and lived as a performance of the story of Jesus' suffering. While it is not yet God's good future, still sadly not yet that future, the conflict with evil continues, and to enlist in that conflict makes one vulnerable to suffering. It is not that Paul deliberately seeks suffering. He is not a masochist. But he is prepared to accept suffering for the sake of God's cause in the world. He is prepared to accept the vulnerability to suffering that comes with compassion, indeed, with any committed relationship of love and with any genuine community with the sick, the outcast, or the oppressed. And he is prepared to suffer for his own integrity as an apostle. As Jesus asked that "the cup" be removed, so Paul prayed that "the thorn" be removed. And as Jesus accepted his suffering and death as a suffering and dying with and for others, so Paul accepted his suffering, his weakness, his vulnerability, as the way of discipleship and ministry while it is

---

ville: Abingdon, 1981), pp. 175-76. The evidence seems to me to suggest an eye condition: After mentioning the "physical infirmity" (Gal. 4:13) which led to an unscheduled stop in Galatia, Paul says of their kind hospitality, "you would have torn out your eyes and given them to me" (4:15). Paul dictated his correspondence rather than writing his letters himself, and to the Galatians he added a postscript in his own hand in "large letters" (6:11). There may not be enough data to make a certain diagnosis, but it does seem clear that the thorn in the flesh is some "physical infirmity" (4:13) and not a personal opponent or a moral temptation.

4. Karl Barth, *Church Dogmatics*, III/4, trans. A. T. Mackay et al. (Edinburgh: T&T Clark, 1961), p. 366; pp. 363-73 are reprinted in Stephen E. Lammers and Allen Verhey, eds., *On Moral Medicine: Theological Perspectives in Medical Ethics*, second ed. (Grand Rapids: Eerdmans, 1998), pp. 242-47.

not yet God's good future. Indeed, Paul had learned somehow to "rejoice" in his suffering for the sake of the communities he loved: "in my flesh I am completing what is lacking in Christ's afflictions for the sake of his body, that is, the church" (Col. 1:24). Others since Paul have done the same; Pope John XXIII, who offered up his suffering during his last illness as community with others who were sick and hurt, comes to mind. The conflict goes on.

The "super-apostles" (2 Cor. 12:11) who opposed Paul in Corinth boasted about the power of God as though it were their own. To them Paul's sickness could only be offensive and scandalous and alienating, but those who remember the story of Jesus and his cross may see in Paul's patient endurance of sickness the very image of their Lord. The sickness is not "good." It is a mark of the "not yet" character of Christian existence. Health and strength are good, but they are not the greatest good. The patient and courageous endurance of sickness can curiously make known the power and grace on which Christians rely but which is never simply under their control.

Paul not only reminded the Corinthians of his sickness; he also reminded them of their own. In the midst of chastening words about the way they celebrated the Lord's Supper Paul says, "For this reason many of you are weak and ill, and some have died" (1 Cor. 11:30). It is a difficult verse, to be sure, but the point is surely *not* that proper partaking of the Lord's Supper provides a medicine against sickness and death, *nor* that those who are weak and ill or dead had failed to partake of the Supper in a discerning way. That could only nurture the boasting of the Corinthian elitists who were healthy, only sustain their claims to be already fully spiritual, only encourage them to partake of the Supper without a sense of community with the "less gifted." Paul surely means to indicate that the destructive powers of this age have not yet laid down their arms in Corinth, have not yet admitted defeat in Corinth.

More than that, however, is clear: Paul ties the sickness and death of the Corinthians to God's judgment.[5] He evidently assumes a connection between sin and sickness — but not to license an inference from any person's illness to that person's sinfulness! That would be to fail to discern a body in which "If one member suffers, all suffer together" (1 Cor. 12:26) and to fail to "proclaim the Lord's death until he comes" (11:26). When he comes, sickness and weakness and death will be no more; until he comes, the pointed reference to his death should prevent the inference from sickness or weakness or death to any person's unworthiness or guilt. To remember the Lord's death is to remember the suffer-

---

5. On judgment in the Lord's Supper, see C. F. D. Moule, "The Judgment Theme in the Sacraments," in *The Background of the New Testament and Its Eschatology*, ed. W. D. Davies and D. Daube (Cambridge: Cambridge University Press, 1964), pp. 464-81.

ing of the innocent, to remember his suffering with and for those who hurt. To proclaim his death is not to judge or condemn, but to care. The Corinthians who eat the Lord's Supper in a worthy manner will not turn against the sick but toward them, will attend to them, will care for them, indeed, will use their powers to attempt to heal them without boasting that the future of God is at their disposal. As long as it is "not yet" God's unchallenged sovereignty, there will be those beyond the reach of human powers to heal. A church that forgets or ignores the crucial story of one who suffered and died would likely also be happy to forget or ignore those among it who are suffering or dying. Churches, however, that are faithful to the memory of Jesus — and hopeful because of that memory — will not forget the sick; they will care for them.

God's cause of life and flourishing was already made known in Jesus' healing ministry and in his resurrection. God's way of compassion, of suffering with those who hurt, was revealed on the cross. God's power to heal was already demonstrated in Jesus' healing ministry and in his resurrection. And in memory of Jesus churches may delight in any and every token of God's good future; they must stand against whatever challenges God's cause and power; and they may gratefully use what powers they have against sickness and death. But God's compassion was decisively revealed in the cross, and we live under the sign of it.

"Are any among you sick?" the letter of James asks, and gives this advice: "They should call for the elders of the church and have them pray over them, anointing them with oil in the name of the Lord" (James 5:14). It is still a strange world of sickness in Scripture. Our advice would very likely be, "They should call for the doctor." Even so, James reminds us both that the church must care for the sick and that the church may make bold petition that the good future of God make its power felt. The promised age has *already* made its power felt in the healing ministry of Jesus and in his resurrection — and James, therefore, confidently and boldly and gladly announces, "the Lord will raise them up" (5:15). Nevertheless, the promised age of God's sovereignty is *not yet* unchallenged — and Paul, therefore, confidently and boldly and gladly shares the weakness and suffering of the crucified one. Hope and contentment, eager expectation and patient watchfulness, like bow and strings play against each other in the memory of Jesus.

The Memory of Jesus in the Life of the Church

The conversations of Sally and the chaplain reached beyond the New Testament into the continuing life of the church performing the Scripture they had read together. They very nearly applauded sometimes when the script had been performed with excellence, and they rued the poor performances, and, in either case, they were instructed concerning the performance they might still be called to give.

Miracle, Magic, and Medicine[6]

Christianity entered the world as a religion of healing — and it inevitably confronted the practices and moral traditions of other communities of healing. Christianity was not, after all, the only religion of healing, nor was religion the only context for healing. The early church accepted miracles, of course, but it claimed that all healing comes from the God of creation and covenant, the God of Jesus and the Spirit. It was not by the power of Asclepius and Serapis that people were healed, but by the power of God.[7] They accepted miracles, but the confidence that God would act miraculously to heal was sometimes guarded; miracles were mentioned infrequently in the literature of the second and third centuries, for example. In the fourth century, however, especially in the hagiographic literature, which began with Athanasius's *The Life of Saint Antony*, there were frequent reports of miracles.[8] The cult of saints and relics (and the reports of associated miracles) was important to the conversion of western Europe[9] and supplanted the superstitious practices of paganism, but it was also influenced by those practices, and it became difficult to distinguish miracle and magic.

Magical practices had been popular in the late Roman Empire and assimilated into many healing communities. Religious figures — including Christ — were invoked in the magical papyri which survive.[10] The early church rejected magical healing practices as associated with "the deceitful rites of demons" and as reliance upon "incantations and charms" rather than upon God — even

---

6. Pages 123-32 are taken in part from my "Ethique Medicale," *Dictionnaire Critique de Theologie*, ed. Jean Yves Lacoste (Paris: Presses Universitaires de France, 1998), pp. 718-20.

7. The cults of Asclepius and Serapis, of course, were important competitors of the early Christian movement. Against these miracle-working cults the church insisted that Jesus was the chosen agent of God's healing power. (In his polemic against Christianity, Celsus also affirmed miracle, but he insisted that Asclepius was the agent of divine healing power and that Jesus was a mere magician [Origen, *Contra Celsum*, 3.22-24, 7.35]).

8. Martin Marty and Kenneth Vaux, eds., *Health/Medicine and the Faith Traditions: An Inquiry into Religion and Medicine* (Philadelphia: Fortress, 1982), p. 103.

9. Darrel W. Amundsen, "The Medieval Catholic Tradition," in *Caring and Curing: Health and Medicine in the Western Religious Traditions* (New York: Macmillan, 1986), p. 71.

10. Howard Clark Kee, *Medicine, Miracle, and Magic in New Testament Times* (Cambridge: Cambridge University Press, 1986), pp. 107-12.

when the name of Jesus was invoked.[11] Voices within the medieval church were regularly raised against the mingling of pagan magical practices with the practices of a people reliant on God's power, even while it celebrated the saints and practiced the rituals of anointing and petition.[12] Indeed, the very regularity with which magic was condemned was eloquent testimony to the popular confusion of miracle and magic.

Greek and Roman medicine could accommodate both miracle and magic.[13] And Christianity accommodated Greek medicine without surrendering its conviction that all healing comes from God. Most Christians followed the sage advice of Jesus ben Sirach, who regarded physicians and their medicines as instruments of God (Sir. 38:1-15).[14]

---

11. See, for example, Augustine, *City of God,* bk. 10, ch. 9. Consider also Peter's rejection of the offer of Simon Magus to pay for the power of the Spirit (Acts 8:9-24). The magician recognized the divine presence and power, but he wanted to commodify it and then to manipulate it in order to serve the cause of the magician, to glorify Simon Magus, not God.

12. Amundsen, "The Medieval Catholic Tradition," pp. 71-74. The Reformers repudiated the popular and magical account of the cult of the saints (Keith Thomas, *Religion and the Decline of Magic* [New York: Scribner, 1971]). Their suspicion of any magical manipulation of a sovereign God and their conviction that the order of the universe and of the body is simply the way God ordinarily works, that "nature" no less than "miracle" comes to us from the gracious hand of God, helped to secure the primacy of medicine among the means of healing in the West.

13. The great Galen, for example, wrote his essay on anatomy as a hymn to Asclepius; he regarded his work as combining a mystical association with the god and the learned traditions of medicine.

14. To be sure, some regarded the use of medicine as a form of faithlessness. Tatian, for example, in the second century, seems to have regarded pharmacology as a bad means to achieve a good end. He warned Christians in the second century against seeking the help of *"pharmakeia"* instead of relying upon God — advice that has seemed to some to be reminiscent of the Chronicler's chiding of Asa. See Tatian, "Address to the Greeks," 18, in *The Ante-Nicene Fathers,* ed. Alexander Roberts and James Donaldson (Buffalo: Christian Literature Publishing Co., 1989-96). Owsei Temkin, *Hippocrates in a World of Pagans and Christians* (Baltimore: Johns Hopkins University Press, 1991), concluded his analysis of Tatian's position by insisting that "Tatian should not be quoted as a witness for early Christian hostility to medicine" (p. 122). Darrell W. Amundsen, "Tatian's 'Rejection' of Medicine in the Second Century," in his *Medicine, Society, and Faith in the Ancient and Medieval Worlds* (Baltimore: Johns Hopkins University Press, 1996), pp. 158-74, agrees with Temkin and explains why Tatian singled out pharmacology for condemnation. At any rate, most early Christian leaders commended medicine as a gift of God, even while they insisted that all healing comes from God and must serve God's cause. Clement of Alexandria, for example, in advice similar to that of Jesus ben Sirach, construed medicine as the provision of God against sickness. See *Stromateis,* 6.17, in *Ante-Nicene Fathers.*

Medical Ethics Owned and Qualified

The church's acceptance of medicine as a form of healing did not mean, of course, that anything and everything "medical" was approved. When the church called Jesus "the great physician" it honored physicians, especially the "Hippocratic" physicians, commending their compassion and their commitment to the patient's good,[15] but it also provided a model for medicine and set it in the context of a story that reached from creation to resurrection and God's good future.

Within that story the body and its health were regarded as great goods, but as part of a larger good, not as the *summum bonum*.[16] And sickness was regarded as an evil, as a feature of the disorder introduced by human sin, as part of a larger evil.[17] Although physical affliction is an evil, it might, by the grace of God, remind people of their finitude, their dependence, their sinfulness, and the disorder that infects the relations of persons to their bodies, to each other, and to God. Within that story to care for the sick was a reflection of God's care for sinners, and to heal the sick was a token of God's triumph over sin. God's cause included health, but it was not to be reduced to it. Basil the Great, for example, insisted that Christians "must take great care to employ this medical art . . . as redounding to the glory of God."[18] Both sickness and health were to be oriented to God's cause; both health and the means to it were to serve God's glory.

The orientation to "the glory of God" did not enable (or require) Christians to create a new medicine — or a new ethic for medicine — out of nothing. Among contending accounts of the appropriate conduct of physicians the Christian community adopted and adapted the medical ethic epitomized by the Hippocratic Oath. The ascendancy of the oath itself in the Western tradition of medicine is probably a result of the rise of Christianity.[19] The church supported

---

15. See Temkin, *Hippocrates in a World of Pagans and Christians*.

16. Some ancient philosophers had argued against some ancient physicians that health was not the *summum bonum* and that medicine was itself unable to determine how to rank health relative to other goods. See Ludwig Edelstein, "The Relation of Ancient Philosophy to Medicine," in *Ancient Medicine: Selected Papers of Ludwig Edelstein*, ed. O. Temkin and C. L. Temkin (Baltimore: Johns Hopkins University Press, 1967), pp. 349-66. The church evidently agreed with the philosophers on this point.

17. E.g., Augustine, *City of God*, bk. 14, ch. 3; bk. 22, ch. 22. See further an excellent piece by George Khushf, "Illness, the Problem of Evil, and the Analogical Structure of Healing: On the Difference Christianity Makes in Bioethics," *Christian Bioethics* 1, no. 1 (1995): 102-20.

18. Basil the Great, *The Long Rule*, 55, in *Fathers of the Church*, vol. 9, p. 334.

19. Ludwig Edelstein, "The Hippocratic Oath," *Bulletin of the History of Medicine*, Supp. 5, no. 1 (1943): 1-64.

this tradition — but also modified it. One result of this revisionary affirmation was a version of the oath "in so far as a Christian may swear it,"[20] and it is probable that by the sixth century this version had been adopted by the church. "The Oath According to Hippocrates In So Far As A Christian May Swear It" stood in obvious continuity with "the doctor's oath," but it also modified it. The Christian version began not by invoking Apollo, Asclepius, Hygeia, and Panacea, but with doxology: "Blessed be the God and Father of our Lord Jesus Christ." It set medical practice and moral principles not in the context of loyalty to the Greek gods and goddesses of healing but in the context of the memory of Jesus and the praise it evoked. That feature of the Christian oath was expressed visibly as well; at least some copies of it were written in the shape of a cross.[21] So it oriented the physician toward doxology, toward the praise of the glory of God, and set medicine in the context of the memory of Jesus.

Despite those changes, many provisions of the Christian oath were like those of the original Hippocratic Oath. In memory of Jesus it reiterated the Hippocratic commitment of fidelity to the sick. Moreover, the Hippocratic prohibitions of euthanasia and abortion, which had stood in sharp contrast to the wide acceptance of abortion, infanticide, and euthanasia in Greece and Rome, were adopted as consistent with the church's condemnations of killing. The Christian version also accepted the prohibition of sexual relationships with patients or members of their households as consistent with the church's concerns about sexual morality. Finally, the Christian version affirmed the obligation of confidentiality; patients (like penitents) were required to reveal what they might prefer to keep secret, and physicians (like priests) were forbidden to use such revelations for any purpose other than the professional end of helping the sick (or penitent).[22]

---

20. See W. H. S. Jones, *The Doctor's Oath: An Essay in the History of Medicine* (New York: Cambridge University Press, 1967), pp. 23-25. See also Allen Verhey, "The Doctor's Oath — and a Christian Swearing It," *Linacre Quarterly* 51, no. 2 (May 1984): 139-58, reprinted in Lammers and Verhey, *On Moral Medicine*, second ed., pp. 108-19. The date of the Christian version is unknown, but it probably goes back to the sixth century; the oldest extant manuscript is from the tenth century.

21. See facsimiles in Jones, *The Doctor's Oath*, frontispiece and p. 26. By the sixth century, it needs to be said, Jews had also entered medical practice and distinguished themselves. See David Feldman, *Health and Medicine in the Jewish Tradition* (New York: Crossroad, 1986), pp. 41-48, for a brief account of "Jews and Medicine," and pp. 15-33 for an account of the way the rabbis dealt with some of the passages treated above as "the strange world of sickness in Scripture."

22. Jerome noted the analogy between the decorum required of physicians and of priests. Indeed, when instructing a priest that it was his "duty to visit the sick," he com-

The changes in the stipulations of the oath, frankly, were few. The Christian version did omit the filial obligations of medical student to the one who taught him the art; instead, there was a commitment to teach the art "willingly and without any indenture." In memory of Jesus medicine was regarded less as an elite guild and more as a form of service to the sick. To be sure, about some matters there were disagreements within the Christian community. For example, although there was a greater concern about telling the truth to a patient than one finds in the Hippocratic tradition, some in the church were much more sympathetic with "therapeutic deception" than others.[23]

---

mended the decorum of the Hippocratic physician when exposed to the intimacies of a household or entrusted with the secrets of the sick:

> Let it therefore be your duty to keep your tongue chaste as well as your eyes. Never discuss a woman's looks, nor let one house know what is going on in another. Hippocrates, before he will instruct his pupils, makes them take an oath. . . . That oath exacts from them silence. . . . How much greater an obligation is laid on us who have been entrusted with the healing of souls! (Jerome, "Epistle 52," section 15, cited in Temkin, *Hippocrates in a World of Pagans and Christians,* p. 182)

The church's experience with the confidentiality of the confessional reinforced the importance of confidentiality in medical practice but also helped identify some of its limits. Most medieval theologians agreed that secrets could be revealed when they involved serious threats to the public good or to innocent third parties; they frequently discussed, for example, the case of a doctor with a patient suffering from an incurable and highly contagious venereal disease who intended not to disclose this fact to his fiancée, and they usually permitted the secret to be told — but only to the person threatened and only that part of the patient's confidence necessary to prevent the harm. Fidelity to the patient (and penitent) required confidentiality, but not complicity in wrongdoing. See further R. E. Regan, *Professional Secrecy in the Light of Moral Principles: With an Application to Several Important Professions* (Washington, D.C.: Augustinian Press, 1943), pp. 104-13.

23. Both the Hippocratic Oath and the Christian version of it were silent concerning veracity. And Plato, of course, had permitted physicians the "useful" lie (*Republic,* 389b). There was, to be sure, support for the tradition of "therapeutic deception" in the early church (e.g., Clement of Alexandria, *Stromateis,* 7.8; Origen, in a fragment cited [and repudiated] by Jerome, *Apology against Rufinus,* 1.18). Augustine, however, rigorously opposed deception and explicitly rejected the lie told by a physician in order to help (or spare) a patient. He resisted, he said, the powerful pull of arguments for deception intended to benefit the patient only by devotion to the One who is "Truth" ("Against Lying," 18, 36). Augustine's challenge to "therapeutic deception" was driven by his loyalty to God, but his rigorous prohibition of any deception was determined by his image of the God to whom he was loyal. Others, no less driven by loyalty to God and no less ready to qualify the received medical ethical tradition in the light of their understanding of God and of God's cause, did not construe God simply or primarily as "Truth," nor construe "Truth" as the conformity of words to thoughts (but as "covenant fidelity"), and took positions closer to

Still, the memory of Jesus hardly left the practice of medicine as it found it. The memory of Jesus prompted what Henry Sigerist has called "the most revolutionary and decisive change" in the tradition of medicine. It was this: the sick were ascribed "a preferential position."[24] Jesus was, after all, not just healer, not just "the great physician"; he was also one who suffered and died. Remembering Jesus' suffering and death, Christians saw in the sick the very image of their Lord and discerned in their care for them (or in their abandoning of them) an image of their care for (or abandonment of) Christ himself. The classic passage, of course, is Matthew 25:31-46, a passage explicitly cited, for example, in the instruction of *The Rule of St. Benedict* to care for the sick "as if it were Christ himself who was served."[25] It remained in many ways a strange world of sickness — but the position of the sick had fundamentally changed. In memory of Jesus the Christian community turned toward the sick, not against them, caring for them in their suffering and attending to them in their dying, practicing hospitality to them rather than ostracizing them from community. In the plague of the third century in Alexandria, Christians distinguished themselves by their heroic care for the sick while the pagans of the city abandoned the sick, deserted their friends, and "cast them out into the roads half-dead."[26] By the ministry of Christians, some of the sick were healed, but many of those who cared for the sick died — their deaths a witness *(martus)* to their memory of Jesus and to their hope in him. Down through the centuries the memory of Jesus echoed in the care of the sick — in the heroism of Alexandrian Christians, in the vow of the Knights Hospitallers of Saint John of Jerusalem in the sixteenth century to "serve our lords, the sick,"[27] in the "holy calling" of Rauschenbusch's prayer. In memory of Jesus the sick have been accorded a preferential position, and in memory of Jesus care for them has been regarded as a duty of Christian community.

Because care for the sick was a duty, the church required competence and diligence of physicians. The medieval penitential literature, for example, re-

---

Clement and Origen. See further Allen Verhey, "The Truth and the Life," *The Reformed Journal* (April 1987), pp. 11-15.

24. Sigerist, *Civilization and Disease,* pp. 69-70.

25. *Rule of St. Benedict,* ch. 36.

26. From a letter of Dionysius, bishop of Alexandria, quoted in Eusebius, *Ecclesiastical History,* 7.20, trans. Christian Frederick Cruse (Grand Rapids: Baker Book House, 1966), p. 293. The remark about those "half-dead" is a reminder of the Jewish traveler attended to by the Good Samaritan (Luke 10:30). The Alexandrian Christians followed Jesus' command to "do likewise" (Luke 10:37).

27. Darrell W. Amundsen, "History of Medical Ethics: Europe: Ancient and Medieval," in *Encyclopedia of Bioethics,* rev. ed., ed. Warren Reich (New York: Macmillan, 1995), 3:1509-37, p. 1524.

quired physicians to confess incompetence and negligence.[28] The same literature made it clear, however, that although care for the sick included competent medical care, it could not be reduced to "medical" care. The Fourth Lateran Council (1215) had also decreed that "physicians of the body . . . admonish [the sick] to call for the physician of souls" to make confession.[29] At the very least the decree stood as a reminder that, although physical health and life are great goods, they are not the greatest goods. Moreover, because life and health are not the greatest good, the means to achieve these goods must not violate the greater or larger good. In the same Fourth Lateran Council physicians were forbidden to "advise a patient to have recourse to sinful means for the recovery of bodily health."[30]

Life and health are great goods, gifts of God the creator and part of the cause of God the redeemer, but they are not "second gods."[31] Life and health may be the goals of "physicians of the body," but those who would remember and follow one who endured suffering and death for the sake of God's cause will hardly count them the law of their being.

28. Amundsen's survey of the penitential literature prompted by the decree of Lateran IV (1215), which required annual confession by all Catholics, reveals that physicians were expected to confess incompetence and negligence. Both rashness and excessive caution were regarded as sins if patients were harmed (or not helped). By requiring competence, the duty of care nurtured medical learning and training, but it also restrained and ordered it, for exposing a patient (especially a poor patient) to unnecessary risk for the sake of an experiment was also mentioned. See Darrel W. Amundsen, "Casuistry and Professional Obligations: The Regulation of Physicians by the Court of Conscience in the Late Middle Ages," in his *Medicine, Society, and Faith in the Ancient and Medieval Worlds*, pp. 248-88.

29. See R. J. Schroeder, *Disciplinary Decrees of the General Councils* (St. Louis: Herder, 1957), p. 236.

30. Schroeder, *Disciplinary Decrees*, p. 236. In the penitential literature the "sinful means," as well as the proper ends for rational creatures, were identified by means of "natural law": they included fornication, masturbation, incantation, and breaking the church's fasts. Natural law, along with the authority of the magisterium, continued to characterize Roman Catholic reflection about medical ethics. (See further Charles Curran, "Roman Catholicism," in *Encyclopedia of Bioethics*, rev. ed., ed. Warren Reich [New York: Macmillan, 1995], 4:2321-31.) By means of the requirement of confession and the penitential literature that guided it, the church exercised a remarkable control over every part of life, including medicine. Luther objected to the penitential system as an invitation to self-justification, as a domestication of the grace of God, and as an offense to the freedom of a Christian. Medicine within the Protestant tradition was a vocation still oriented toward God's cause, but reflection about medical ethics was frequently marked by a suspicion of casuistry and an emphasis on the freedom of both physician and patient. (See further Allen Verhey, "Protestantism," in *Encyclopedia of Bioethics*, 4:2117-26.)

31. Barth, *Church Dogmatics*, III/4, p. 342.

Concern for the Poor

Jesus was not only a healer, not only one who suffered, but also a preacher of "good news to the poor" (Luke 4:18). His words of blessing to the poor were no less a token and a promise of God's good future than his works of healing (e.g., Luke 6:20). The poor along with the sick were accorded a "preferential position" in memory of Jesus, and fidelity to God required that the needs of the sick poor not be forgotten, neither by physicians nor by their communities.

Clergy frequently took the lead in providing medical assistance to the sick and poor. The tradition of clergy physicians stretched from the early Middle Ages into the modern period (with Catholic, Orthodox, and Protestant representatives), and it was largely devoted to the care of the sick poor.[32] There was, moreover, a tradition of medical texts written by clergy in the service of the poor, books like *Thesaurus Pauperum*, a list of simple herbal remedies available to the poor (authored by the priest who became Pope John XXI in 1276), and John Wesley's *Primitive Physick* (1747). And, of course, treatises exhorting physicians to care for rich and poor alike were commonplace.[33]

The hospital itself has its origin in the Christian concern for the poor.[34] Christian hospitality to the sick and care for them led quite naturally to the founding of *xenodocheia* (hospices) to feed and shelter the poor. In 372 Basil the Great founded a vast *xenodocheia*, the Basileias, with buildings to care for the sick poor and with a staff that included physicians. (The buildings, incidentally, included separate buildings for those with contagious diseases and for those with noncontagious diseases.) It quickly became the prototype of many other such Christian institutions. It was followed soon after by others — for example, the hospital in Rome founded by a friend of Jerome, a woman named Fabiola, in the late fourth century.[35] The early hospitals were funded first by bishops themselves, but soon bishops raised funds by calling upon local aristo-

---

32. The tradition was discouraged (but not ended) both by the development of guilds and licensure in the late Middle Ages and by the suspicion of the church that some clergy were practicing medicine "for the sake of temporal gain" and were neglecting "the care of souls" (Lateran II [1139], in Schroeder, *Disciplinary Decrees*, pp. 201-2).

33. Marty and Vaux, eds., *Health/Medicine and the Faith Traditions*, pp. 119-20. The censure of avarice here is the flip side of the concern for the poor — and a staple of Christian commentary on the conduct and character of physicians.

34. T. S. Miller, *The Birth of the Hospital in the Byzantine Empire* (Baltimore: Johns Hopkins University Press, 1985).

35. Darrell W. Amundsen and Gary Ferngren, "Medicine and Religion: Early Christianity through the Middle Ages," in *Health/Medicine and the Faith Traditions*, ed. Marty and Vaux, p. 109.

crats and benefactors to endow the hospital for the community. By the twelfth century the Pantokrator hospital in Constantinople maintained seventeen physicians, thirty-four nurses, and six pharmacists; it served patients on five specialized wards (and provided outpatient services as well) and was used by both rich and poor. Hospitals developed much more slowly in the West but according to the same pattern. The hospital, which had its beginnings in Christian remembrance and charity, developed into a civic responsibility to care for the sick poor.

The Retrieval of Medical Ethics

When, in the middle of the twentieth century, hospitals became showcases for medical technology and patient care became increasingly "medicalized," theologians retrieved important elements of this tradition and played a major role in "the emergence of the field" of medical ethics.[36] Against extravagant and idolatrous expectations of either health or medicine, they reminded their communities that God alone is God. Against the reduction of patients to their pathologies, they retrieved the professional commitment of fidelity to patients (and research subjects) as persons, and underscored consent as a fundamental component of fidelity.[37] Against the reduction of persons to their capacities for agency, they insisted on embodiment.[38] They reiterated the concern for the poor in debates about access to health care.

Beginning in the middle of the twentieth century, advances in medical science and technology prompted a series of dramatic questions, questions about experimentation and the protection of human subjects, questions about transplantation and the definition of death, questions about kidney dialysis

36. See LeRoy Walters, "Religion and the Renaissance of Medical Ethics," in *Theology and Bioethics: Exploring the Foundations and Frontiers*, ed. Earl E. Shelp (Dordrecht: D. Reidel, 1985), pp. 3-16; David H. Smith, "Religion and the Roots of the Bioethics Revival," in *Religion and Medical Ethics: Looking Back, Looking Forward*, ed. Allen Verhey (Grand Rapids: Eerdmans, 1996), pp. 9-18; and Daniel Callahan, "Religion and the Secularization of Bioethics," *Hastings Center Report*, Special Supplement, "Theology, Religious Traditions, and Bioethics," July/August 1990, pp. 2-4.

37. See, for example, Paul Ramsey, *The Patient as Person* (New Haven: Yale University Press, 1970), especially pp. xi-xviii.

38. See, for example, Paul Ramsey, *Ethics at the Edges of Life* (New Haven: Yale University Press, 1978). See also Allen Verhey, "The Body and the Bible: Life in the Flesh According to the Spirit," in *Embodiment, Morality, and Medicine*, ed. Lisa Sowle Cahill and Margaret A. Farley (Dordrecht: Kluwer Academic Publishers, 1995), pp. 3-22.

and the allocation of scarce medical resources, questions about prenatal diagnosis and genetic counseling, questions about reproductive technologies and the use of donated gametes. Such questions were not simply scientific questions. They were obviously and inevitably moral questions. Efforts to answer such questions always invoked judgments about the good to be sought and done, about the ends to seek with the powers medicine gives, about the moral appropriateness of certain means, and about how to use medical powers without violating the human material on which they work. Thus, the new questions led quickly to some very old questions, fundamental questions about the meaning of life and death, health and suffering, freedom and embodiment.

The tradition of Christian reflection about health and healing remains an important resource for efforts to answer such questions, both old and new. And the memory of Jesus continues to govern discernment concerning them. The church continues to confront other communities of healing, qualifying or questioning their practices and powers, joining medicine to a concern for the poor and vulnerable, and setting care for the sick in the context of the church's memory of Jesus.

Our friend Sally and the chaplain were glad for their opportunities to read Scripture together. They were glad for the good news of Jesus, glad for the memory of this Jesus who healed the sick, who proclaimed good news to the poor, who suffered under Pontius Pilate, and who was raised, "the first fruits of those who have died." And they were glad for the church, for the community that has given sometimes stunning performance of the script that they read, for the community that has set that script aside as "holy" and has been willing to test the stories of our lives and all of its performances against it. They were glad for the fidelity and creativity of the church reading Scripture together and struggling to give an adequate contemporary performance of it. They were glad for the discipline and discernment of the community that still considers medical ethics "by way of reminder," that talks together and prays together about how to practice medicine or to use it in memory of Jesus. And they were confident that members of that community were still able to instruct each other, still able to help one another find the path of discipleship through the strange world of our sicknesses and medicine. They did not talk more of many of the issues of that strange world; they did not talk of genetics or assisted reproductive technologies; they did not talk of the allocation of resources or of research using human subjects; they did not talk of the great variety of topics that they were confident the church would speak of. But they did talk of the prospect of death and of faithfulness in the face of it; they did talk of Sally's particular case. The outcome of that conversation is the subject of the next chapter.

CHAPTER SEVEN

The Strange World of Sickness Today:
Toward a Watchful Medicine — A Continuing
Tradition of Care for the Suffering

Sally, the physician turned cancer patient, had some difficult choices to make. She was facing death. Her doctor had visited her earlier in the day. He had reported that the cancer gave no signals of remission. It was the news she had expected to hear. She was a physician, after all, and she had grown almost obsessively attentive to her own body. Her professional skill and knowledge, however, provided no shield against the horror of the news. She had expected it, but she still dreaded it, and when it came, it came as an assault.

She called the chaplain later that day, asking him to stop by. "I'll be glad to," he said. "I was going to stop by today whether invited or not. I want to know what the doctor said about your latest tests." "Well, that's what I want to talk with you about," Sally said, "but I'd like to have you here." "I'll be right there," the chaplain said. The chaplain did not expect the news to be good either, but his own professional skill provided no better shield than his physician friend's had, and when he was told the news, he felt tears fill his eyes.

"The doctor wants me to let him try again, something new, an experimental chemotherapy," Sally said. "We talked about it some. He admitted that it would be pretty toxic, and he admitted that he couldn't confidently say that it would work. But, as he also said, if I do nothing, I will surely die. He thinks I will die within six months if we find no way to beat this cancer back. I thanked him for his honesty and for his concern for my well-being, and I told him that I wanted to think about it some — and to talk with some friends."

The chaplain was glad to be counted a friend, and he squeezed Sally's

133

hand a little, but the feeling was overwhelmed by the sadness of losing a friend. They sat there silently for a long minute. They both may have been thinking about their short but dear friendship, about the chaplain's first visit to Sally and about those subsequent visits in which they had read Scripture together. Just now, however, there were no words.

Sally was the first to break the silence. "So, I've been thinking. You know the Apostles' Creed, right?"

"Yes, of course," the chaplain replied.

"Good. Then you know how it ends?"

The chaplain thought for a moment, and finally answered, "I believe in . . . the resurrection of the body, and the life everlasting."[1]

"Yes, it's a fine ending, don't you think? That truth can be learned from Scripture, of course. I thought about that the other day after we had read Scripture together, how the creed captures the story of Scripture. It's a short story, of course, but it begins with creation, sets Christ in the center, and ends with the work of the Spirit and talk of resurrection. At any rate, the creed has a fine sense of an ending. And Christians claim to know something about endings, about destiny, whenever we recite it."

"Yes," the chaplain said, "It's a fine ending. But how is it related to the decisions you have to make?"

"Well, I'm not sure exactly, but that's what I've been thinking about. It isn't enough simply to recite the creed. This knowledge, this sense of an ending, must, as John Calvin said, 'enter our heart and pass into our daily living, and so transform us into itself that it may not be unfruitful for us.'[2] I want to affirm with the creed and with the church 'the resurrection of the body, and the life everlasting' in my living — and in my dying. And I wish I had paid more attention to this affirmation when I was practicing as a physician; I wish it had been more 'fruitful' in my care for the dying."

1. The Apostles' Creed, in *Creeds of the Churches*, ed. John Leith, third ed. (Atlanta: John Knox, 1982), pp. 24-25. Although the Apostles' Creed was not written by the apostles, it is an ancient confession and the most widely used creed in the Western churches; its predecessors may be traced to the Interrogatory Creed of Hippolytus (c. 215; Leith, *Creeds of the Churches*, p. 23). The Nicene Creed, which was accepted in Nicea in 325 and revised at Constantinople in 381, ends similarly: "We look forward to the resurrection of the dead and the life of the world to come. Amen" (Leith, *Creeds of the Churches*, p. 33).

2. John Calvin, *The Institutes of the Christian Religion*, III.vi.4, trans. Ford Lewis Battles (Philadelphia: Westminster, 1960), p. 688.

Death as Destiny

The chaplain was having a little trouble making sense of this, and he said as much to Sally.

"I have recited the creed more times than I can remember," Sally noted. "I got to that ending all of those times: 'I believe in . . . the resurrection of the body, and the life everlasting.' But on Mondays when I went to the office — or on Sunday afternoons if I got called in — the reality seemed to be that, however the creed ends, our lives evidently end in death. Death, not life, seems to have the last word. First we live, and then we die. Death seems our destiny. Pascal said it well: 'The last act is tragic, however happy all the rest of the play is; at the last a little earth is thrown upon our head, and that is the end forever.'"[3]

"Peter De Vries may have said it better," the chaplain said. "'Like the cleaning lady, we all come to dust.'"[4]

"Ha! That's good! And Scripture may have said it best: 'you are dust, and to dust you shall return'" (Gen. 3:19).[5]

"Right. Scripture acknowledges our mortality. And the creed's talk of resurrection doesn't require — and won't permit — a denial of the reality of death. It doesn't make liars of us. Death is real," the chaplain said.

And as if completing his thought, Sally added, "And it is a real evil! It is intimate with sickness and suffering. Sickness comes, as Barth said,[6] as a forerunner and messenger of death; and suffering threatens the embodied integrity that death inevitably destroys. Death — and sickness and suffering — alienate people from their own flesh, from their communities, and from God.[7] And, you see, if death is our destiny, then so is alienation."

---

3. Blaise Pascal, *Pensées* 210 (New York: E. P. Dutton and Co., 1958), p. 61.

4. Peter De Vries, *Slouching Towards Kalamazoo* (New York: Penguin Books, 1984), p. 23.

5. It is not just human beings, it may be added, who seem to have death as their destiny. Every biological organism is on a trajectory that ends with death; the tiniest air-borne insect and the great redwoods alike will die, though their life spans may be measured respectively by hours or centuries. Both cell and cosmos evidently share this destiny and are on trajectories toward death, each, of course, at its own pace. See Richard Gunderman, "What Can Medical Science Contribute to Theological Ethics?" in *Christian Ethics: Problems and Prospects,* ed. Lisa Sowle Cahill and James F. Childress (Cleveland: Pilgrim, 1996), pp. 152-65.

6. Karl Barth, *Church Dogmatics,* III/4, trans. A. T. Mackay et al. (London: T. & T. Clark, 1961), p. 366.

7. See William F. May, "The Sacral Power of Death in Contemporary Experience," in *On Moral Medicine: Theological Perspectives in Medical Ethics,* ed. Stephen Lammers and Allen Verhey, second ed. (Grand Rapids: Eerdmans, 1998), pp. 197-209,

"Yes, but medicine resists death — and sickness and suffering," the chaplain said.

"To its great credit!" Sally replied. "But if there is no other and better sense of destiny, then its resistance becomes sometimes presumptuous, sometimes desperate, and frequently (if ironically) alienating."

Death and Our Flesh

The chaplain pulled up a chair by Sally's bedside, to continue the conversation in more comfort. "I think I see your first point, about death threatening alienation from our own flesh," he said. "And that's a real and terrible threat; we are, after all, embodied selves, not ghosts.[8] We live and love in the world as embodied selves. We eat, work, play, and worship in our flesh." The chaplain was right, of course. It is in our bodies that we exercise control over ourselves and over the world. In our bodies we discover something of the wonderful variety of color, shape, sound, scent, texture, and taste of the creation. And in our bodies we reveal ourselves to others — in a gesture or a word, in a smile or a tear, in a touch. Sally was right to quote Barth; sickness does come as the forerunner and messenger of death, and suffering does come as the experience already of a threat to the embodied integrity that death destroys.

Thinking of her own experience, Sally went on, "Sometimes it's not until we're sick that we really think about these things. But sickness reminds us, first, of our *identity* with our bodies; it reminds us that we are our bodies, that our 'selves' depend on the integrity of the bodies we otherwise take for granted, that our health and our lives, our 'selves' and our identities, are radically contingent."[9] With a smile at the chaplain, she continued, "But this reminder doesn't come gently; it isn't like listening to some friendly preacher reading from the psalms. In sickness this identification with the body is experienced at the same time as *alienation*."[10]

---

especially pp. 181-84, and William F. May, *The Patient's Ordeal* (Bloomington, Ind.: Indiana University Press, 1991), pp. 9-14, 200-206. I want to acknowledge an indebtedness to the work of Bill May that is hardly captured by the occasional citation of his work in this chapter, and I want to commend especially his attention to resurrection.

8. Allen Verhey, "The Body and the Bible: Life in the Flesh According to the Spirit," in *Embodiment, Morality, and Medicine*, ed. Lisa Sowle Cahill and Margaret A. Farley (Dordrecht, Netherlands: Kluwer Academic Publishers, 1995), pp. 3-22.

9. Arthur Kleinman, *The Illness Narratives: Suffering, Healing and the Human Condition* (New York: Basic Books, 1988), p. 45.

10. Kleinman, *The Illness Narratives*, p. 45.

Death makes its power felt, Sally explained, in serious or chronic illness and in severe pain, when the body is experienced not only as "us," but as "the enemy."[11] It makes its power felt in the weakness that robs the sick of the capacity to exercise responsible control of themselves and of their world. It makes its power felt when the wonderful variety of God's creation is reduced to something barren and sterile or to something putrid and foul. It makes its power felt when the body no longer opens up into a larger and sharable world, when the body — and the world — of the sick shrinks to that place "a bandage hides."[12] Death makes its power felt in the sense of a betrayal of that fundamental trust we have in our bodies. And with another smile at the chaplain, she concluded, "When such a fundamental trust is broken, all trust can become suspect — more important, to be sure, but more questionable, too."

"Medicine resists that death," the chaplain said. "At least you've got to give it that."

"Yes," replied the dying woman, "and its resistance is sometimes heroic.[13] But, as I said a moment ago, without some other and better sense of an ending, its resistance can be presumptuous, pretending to rescue human beings from their mortality and their vulnerability to suffering. Or it can be desperate, laboring under the tyranny of survival or ease. And sometimes — though it is ironic and tragic[14] — death makes its power felt in a hospital and in the sort of medicine that is technologically oriented to biological survival.

"When the sick, at once identified with their bodies and alienated from them, seek medical care, they sometimes find this self-understanding reinforced.[15] I have seen this happen myself, and I have felt it happen to me. Patients are reduced to their pathology, and the body is treated as 'the enemy,' as that manipulable and untrustworthy 'nature' which must, for the sake of my self, be overpowered, but which remains, willy nilly, my self. Patients suffer then not only from the disease but also from the treatment of it — and death makes its power felt not only in sickness but also in medicine."

11. Kleinman, *The Illness Narratives*, p. 45; Elaine Scarry, *The Body in Pain: The Making and Unmaking of the World* (New York: Oxford University Press, 1985), p. 47; M. Therese Lysaught, "Suffering, Ethics, and the Body of Christ: Anointing as a Strategic Alternative Practice," *Christian Bioethics* 2, no. 2 (1996): 172-201, p. 177.

12. W. H. Auden, "Surgical Ward," in *Selected Poetry of W. H. Auden* (New York: Random House, Modern Library, 1958), pp. 45-46.

13. Hessel Bouma III, Douglas Diekema, Edward Langerak, Theodore Rottman, and Allen Verhey, *Christian Faith, Health, and Medical Practice* (Grand Rapids: Eerdmans, 1989).

14. On tragedy see further Bouma et al., *Christian Faith*, pp. 123-43.

15. Lysaught, "Suffering, Ethics, and the Body of Christ," p. 177.

"I think I see what you mean," the chaplain interrupted. "If death has the last word, if alienation from our bodies is our destiny, then desperation against death is reasonable for both patients and physicians, and the ironic result is sometimes the premature alienation from our bodies — for the sake of survival."

Death and Our Communities

The chaplain sat meditating for a minute, and then said, "As I recall, you also noted earlier that death threatens to separate people from their communities. That threat, too, is real and horrible, because we are communal selves, not isolated individuals. Our lives are lives lived with others, and death threatens separation and removal, exclusion and abandonment. That is why the sadness of death is felt most dreadfully by those who contemplate not their own deaths but the deaths of those they love.

"Sickness comes as the forerunner and messenger of this alienation, too. And the sick suffer a sense of betrayal by the communities they trust as a kind of foretaste of the abandonment of death."

"Yes," said Sally. "Death makes its power felt when the sick or dying are removed and separated from those with whom they share a common life. When their environment is inhospitable to family and friends. It makes its power felt when disease so monopolizes attention that there is no space for the tasks of reconciliation, forgiveness, and community. Or when the fear of being abandoned is not met by the presence of others who care. And the silence of death makes its power felt in lonely dumbness, when community and communication have failed. Sickness, with its pain and weakness, pushes people to the margins of public life, forces a withdrawal from the public activities of working and shopping, attending a concert or a ballgame."[16]

The chaplain heard the power and the pain of that remark, and he interrupted to make an admission. "Sometimes those of us who are 'well,'" he said, "provide some of the leverage that moves the sick to the margins, for we are not hospitable to reminders of our own vulnerability and contingency.[17] We are autonomous, in control, in charge, productive; those who are sick are not. We have been successful against the powerful threats of nature; those who are sick

16. Kleinman, *The Illness Narratives,* p. 44; Bradley Hanson, "School of Suffering," in *On Moral Medicine,* Lammers and Verhey, second ed., pp. 328-35; Lysaught, "Suffering, Ethics, and the Body of Christ," p. 176.

17. Lysaught, "Suffering, Ethics, and the Body of Christ," pp. 176-77.

have not. They have been captured by the power of death, by the forces of chaos, by the nature that threatens us all, by the nature against which our best hope is technology, the power knowledge gives, the knowledge most of us do not have. They belong, therefore, in a hospital and under the care of a physician, not in public spaces reserved for strength and beauty, for efficiency and productivity, for life. They belong — elsewhere.'"

Sally acknowledged by a moment of respectful silence that the chaplain had made an important admission, something close to confession. Then she picked up her earlier thought, saying, "Even within our own spaces, we who suffer can be further isolated and alienated, because we have lost our voice.[18] Do you know Auden's wonderful and painful line about sufferers? 'Truth in their sense is how much they can bear;/it is not like ours, but groans they smother.'[19] The point isn't just that those who suffer are sometimes driven back to the sounds and cries human beings make before they learn a language. The point is that there are no words. The person in pain knows it, knows it with a certainty that Descartes might envy, but cannot make sense of it, cannot tell it, cannot communicate or 'share' it.[20] And the silence of death makes its power felt in the lonely dumbness of the sick and the helpless deafness of those who would care!"

"I know that feeling," the chaplain said.

"And so do I," Sally replied. "Medicine resists death, as you said before, and it can sometimes identify the pain, make sense of it, and manage it by creating a language for it. As a doctor I know that is a good thing. As a patient, though, I have learned something more, something I did not see as clearly (or appreciate sufficiently, I fear) in my work as a doctor. Sometimes that language, the language created by medicine, isn't the language of the patient; and where the language of medicine is the official language, the only approved language, there patients find themselves 'strangers in a strange land,'[21] aliens, 'speechless,' and with little hope for making their pain — or themselves — known.

"Medicine resists death, but without another and a better sense of an ending, death sometimes makes its power felt both when a community abandons the sick to medicine and in a hospital when medicine neglects a person's community and a patient's voice."

18. Lysaught, "Suffering, Ethics, and the Body of Christ," p. 178.

19. Auden, "Surgical Ward."

20. This loss of voice is confirmed by the words of a patient: "That's the worst thing about pain. You can't see it. You can't know what it's like unless, God help you, you suffer from it." Cited in Kleinman, *The Illness Narratives*, p. 68.

21. H. Tristram Engelhardt Jr., *The Foundations of Bioethics* (New York: Oxford University Press, 1986), p. 256.

Death and God

The chaplain nodded, and Sally went on to make a third point. "In my work I have seen death make its power felt in the sense of betrayal by our bodies and by our communities, but death also threatens people in their relationship with God — I'm sure you have seen that in your own work." Sally had latched on to an important point here; the threat of death is real and terrible, for human beings are religious, in spite of the denials of secularism. Death threatens any sense that the One who bears down on us and sustains us is dependable and caring. It threatens abandonment by God and separation from God. It threatens human beings in their identity as cherished children of God. Death makes its power felt whenever the sick and dying, or those who care for them, are not assured of the presence of a loving God who cares.

The chaplain, who had recently reread Peter De Vries's *The Blood of the Lamb,* was reminded of the experience of Stein, a character in that novel. He asked Sally if she had read it, and then he observed that Stein surely seemed to experience his daughter's sickness as a betrayal by the God he denied. "I remember how he described his daughter's leukemia as a 'sluggishly multiplying anarchy. . . . A souvenir from the primordial ooze. The original Chaos, without form and void. In de beginning was de void, and de void was vit God. Musn't say de naughty void.'[22] 'God,' Stein said, 'is a word banging around in the human nervous system.' And when Stein was reminded of the martyrs and of their courage in the face of death, I remember that he called it 'part of the horror.' 'It's all a fantasy,' he said. 'It's all for nothing. A martyr giving his life, a criminal taking one. It's all the same to the All.'[23] Then medicine is just, as Stein said, 'the art of prolonging disease . . . in order to postpone grief.'"[24]

"Yes, that's it exactly — *if* death is our destiny, *if* death is the last word," Sally said. "Medicine resists death, as you said, but if there is no other or better sense of human destiny, its resistance is undertaken under the power of death, under the tyranny of survival, and with the desperation of hopelessness — even if it is an assertive hopelessness like Stein's. And then medicine becomes — ironically — a place where death makes its power felt, by alienating patients from their bodies, and from their communities, and from God — before the end of their lives and for the sake of their survival.

"The last word, it seems, belongs to death, and the horror of it isn't simply

22. Peter De Vries, *The Blood of the Lamb* (New York: Little, Brown & Company, Popular Library Edition, 1961), p. 177.

23. De Vries, *The Blood of the Lamb,* p. 178.

24. De Vries, *The Blood of the Lamb,* p. 179.

the termination of existence, but the unraveling of meaning, the destruction of relationships, the lordship of chaos. It's the light that seems ephemeral; it's the darkness that seems to surround and to 'overcome' the light and life. Then we are right to be fearful of death, to tremble in the face of darkness and chaos.[25]

"So the questions I've been thinking about are these: What would have to be the case for it to be otherwise? For it to be possible — without illusion, evasion, or fantasy — to tell the story of the ultimate victory of life? And if it were otherwise, what would our dying and our caring for the dying look like?"

"Good questions," the chaplain said. "And do you have the answers to them?"

To that question Sally promptly replied, "I think the answers are found in the reading of Scripture that we did together and in the church's memory of Jesus."

"Perhaps you're right," the chaplain said. "Why don't we take your first question first? What would have to be the case for it to be otherwise? For it to be possible — without illusion, evasion, or fantasy — to tell the story of the ultimate victory of life?"

Life as Destiny: Resurrection

The chaplain thumbed idly through his Bible for a moment, thinking. "For it to be otherwise," he said finally, "we should have grounds for thinking that we live and die, although *in* darkness, yet not *into* chaos or darkness, but into unconquerable light and eternal life."[26] Sally simply repeated the line from the creed. "I believe in . . . the resurrection of the body." "Yes," the chaplain said, "and life has the last word! Christians don't deny the reality or the evil of death, but they do insist that death isn't the last word, that the last word belongs to God, that the last word is not death but life, not suffering but shalom. In the face of death and its power Christians hope. But what are the grounds for this hope? Is there any basis for this confidence of a different and better destiny? One is reminded, I suppose, of the schoolboy's definition of faith: 'Faith is believin' what you know ain't true.'[27] Hope that has no basis is simply wishful thinking."

25. Nicholas Lash, *Theology on the Way to Emmaus* (London: SCM Press, 1986), pp. 176-77.

26. Lash, *Theology on the Way to Emmaus,* p. 177.

27. Robert McAfee Brown, *The Spirit of Protestantism* (New York: Oxford University Press, 1965), p. 69.

"Right," Sally replied, "but the Christian hope is not just whistling in the dark. The grounds for hope are found in the story the Apostles' Creed tells between its initial 'credo' and the resurrection and the life at its end. The grounds for its sense of an ending are found in the story — and in the faithfulness — of the triune God."

"Yes, of course," the chaplain replied. "The beginning of the story was creation: 'I believe in God the Father almighty, creator of heaven and earth.' At that beginning by God's breath and gift the dust was made 'a living being' (Hb. *nephesh*; Gen. 2:7).[28] From that beginning it was clear that without God human weakness and mortality would make their inevitable way toward death, and that without God great human powers would demonstrate their weakness, their 'flesh,' by their inability to preserve the cosmos from tilting back to chaos."

Sally and the chaplain together had come to realize that the grounds for hope in Scripture are not in some 'soul' that has its immortality independently of God and finds liberation in the death of the body. The grounds for hope are not located in some romantic account of the cycles of nature, as bringing always the return of life and spring. And the grounds for hope are not to be found in the technological mastery over nature. These are the grounds for hope: the powerful and creative word of God that can call a cosmos out of chaos and give light to the darkness and life to the dust.

"The creation, of course, isn't the whole story," the chaplain continued. "The canonical narrative continues with the story of human sin and of a 'curse' that rests on the whole creation and on all life. Sin brings death and alienation in its wake — not mortality, it should be said, which was and is a simple sign that we don't have life the way God has life. Even under the burden of a 'curse,' however, this is the reason for hope: the faithfulness of God to what was the cause of God from the beginning, God's refusal to let sin and death to have the last word in the world.

"Human sin might have smashed the world back to chaos, but God wouldn't let evil have the last word. So, 'the fall' — or the flood — is not the end of the story either. God comes again to covenant and to bless. And the blessing with which God would visit the world is not a rescue from the world but a voca-

---

28. The "living being" (Hb. *nephesh*) was and remained "flesh" (Hb. *basar*); that is, whole selves were and are "flesh" in their creatureliness, in their contrast to God and in their dependence upon God, in their weakness and mortality. To be sure, the *nephesh* is *basar;* but the *basar* is *nephesh,* too. The "flesh" is *not* without God. The flesh, too, is from God. Whole selves — embodied selves, mortal and dependent, creative and powerfully gifted — are "flesh," and that they are flesh is good (but not without God). See further Verhey, "The Body and the Bible," pp. 3-22.

tion within it, a vocation to be a blessing (e.g., Gen. 12:1-4), to restrain and to lift the power of the 'curse' in the world God made and preserves and loves.

"And as we saw in reading Scripture," Sally commented, "the center of the Christian story — and of the creed — is Jesus of Nazareth. He came announcing the good future of God, and he made its power felt in works of healing and in words of blessing. When the dead were raised, the good future of God was revealed. When the sick — those under the power of death — were healed, that good future was present. When demons were cast out and those afflicted were returned to themselves and to their communities, it was made known and made real. When the poor heard good news, it made its power felt. And when sinners were forgiven and forgave, there was a foretaste of God's good future.

"Jesus 'suffered under Pontius Pilate, was crucified, dead, and buried.' He didn't choose suffering, and he didn't choose death; but he endured both for the sake of God's cause in the world and his own integrity."

"True," said the chaplain, "and just think of the contrast between Socrates and Jesus! Socrates drank the hemlock with sublime tranquility, confident that the death of his body would free his immortal soul, but Jesus wept and cried at the prospect of alienation from his flesh, from his friends, and from God (Heb. 5:7).[29] And his death was real and horrible (in contrast to the beautiful death of Socrates); he made the human cry of lament in the face of death his own cry, 'My God, my God, why have you forsaken me?'" (Ps. 22:1; Mark 15:34).

Sally picked up the thread. "But God raised this Jesus up, 'the first fruits of those who have died' (1 Cor. 15:20).[30] The power of God and the love of God reached into death to raise him up, vindicating both Jesus and God's own faithfulness." Sally was right. The powers of death and doom had done their damnedest, but God would have the last word. God raised Jesus up — and established once and for all the good future, the destiny, of which he spoke.

"We seem to have just reviewed our reading of Scripture together," the chaplain said.

They had. And this, they realized, is the reason for the hope that is in us (1 Pet. 3:15): God raised Jesus in this world and in this history and thereby established a destiny from which this world and this history have — happily —

29. See Oscar Cullmann, "Immortality of the Soul or Resurrection of the Dead," in *Immortality and Resurrection,* ed. Krister Stendahl (New York: Macmillan, 1965), pp. 9-53, pp. 12-20.

30. It was a curious body, to be sure, but it was recognizable as Jesus' body — as the body of the one who preached and healed and suffered. His wounds were raised with him. It was no mere "spirit" (Luke 24:40 RSV); this embodied person was identifiable — had an identity — in ways no mere "spirit" could. "It is I myself," he said. "Touch me and see" (Luke 24:39).

no escape. Because of the resurrection of Jesus of Nazareth, God's victory over the powers of death and sin, Christians say, "Therefore, I hope. Therefore, 'I believe in . . . the resurrection of the body, and the life everlasting.'" The New Testament fairly thunders with that sense of victory and expectation.

Moreover, because Jesus has been raised, the Spirit has been poured out, "the first fruits" (Rom. 8:23) and the "guarantee" of God's good future (2 Cor. 5:5), and the Spirit is included in the creed and in the grounds for Christian hope. The Spirit was there at the beginning, of course, brooding on the waters of chaos, the breath that made the dust a living creature. And then, when sin brought death and a curse in its wake, the Spirit that gives life was still there to renew and to bless, still brooding on the waters of human tears, pledging that death would not have the last word.

The Spirit was there in the hurt, there when Israel took notice of its pain in Egypt and gave it voice, there when the psalmist took note of his suffering and cried out to God in lament, there when Jesus joined his voice to theirs on the cross, "My God, my God, why?," there when, as Paul wrote, the whole creation groans in travail (Rom. 8:22 RSV). All of these cried to God in the hope — against hope — that there was someone there to hear their cry.

And the Spirit was there, hearing the cry, feeling the hurt, answering the pain with promise. The Spirit was there in the promise then, and he was there when the promise was given token, when Israel was delivered from its bondage, when the psalmist was assured that he would not be abandoned, when Jesus was raised. And — but this promise is still outstanding — the Spirit will be there when the whole creation is made new, and death shall be no more, and neither mourning nor crying nor pain shall be any more (Rev. 21:4).

The Spirit, as Paul says, "helps us in our weakness" (Rom. 8:26). While we "groan inwardly" (Rom. 8:23), when there are no words, while we wait for "the redemption of our bodies" (Rom. 8:23), the Spirit gives us words, "Abba! Father!" (Rom. 8:15), and makes us "heirs," "joint heirs" (Rom. 8:17), of God's good future. The Spirit is at work where the groaning find words and where God's future makes its power felt: when the sick are healed, when the grieving are comforted, when (like Pentecost and unlike the tower of Babel) people understand each other, and when the threat of death is met with confidence in God and with care for persons as embodied and communal selves.

And the Spirit is at work in the church, in that community where the resurrection is celebrated and where the good future of God is anticipated in practices of friendship and forgiveness, or, as the creed says, "the communion of saints [and] the forgiveness of sins." Such practices of the church, done in memory of Jesus and in anticipation of God's good future, may be counted as among the grounds for Christian confidence in a different and better destiny.

All of this the chaplain and Sally discussed, and the chaplain then provided something of a summary of their discussion that day. "So, there are grounds for thinking that death is not the last word. Christians hope because they know the faithfulness of the triune God. And because they know the story of the One who made all things, because they know the story of one who was raised from the dead, and because they know the story of a life-giving Spirit, they cannot but claim to know something of the end of the story. They cannot but say, 'I believe in . . . the resurrection of the body, and the life everlasting.' The Christian church owns a story in canon and in creed that ends with talk of God's good future — and our own. And when in memory and in hope Christians perform the story, they find their hope confirmed."

"Right," said Sally. "But it is, of course, not yet that good future. The creation and the churches still 'wait' and 'watch' and pray for it" (Rom. 8:19-23).

Living, Dying, and Caring into Such a Destiny

"We began," the chaplain noted, "by acknowledging the reality and the power of death, but we have seen that — in spite of appearances — there are grounds for believing that death isn't the last word, that human destiny is life and light. But if this is true, if death is not the last word, if our destiny is life, then what should our dying and our caring for the dying look like? That was, as I remember it, the second question you identified. So, how would you answer it?"

Sally was glad for the opportunity to answer the question she had been thinking about. "The short answer to that question, I think, is 'watchfulness.'" She paused, like a good teacher confident that a good pupil would ask the right question, and the chaplain measured up to her expectations. "But then," the chaplain asked, "what does 'watchfulness' look like? What does it look like for patients, for the community, and for caregivers?"

"Here I take my cues from Scripture," Sally replied. "In the Gospel of Mark, the call to 'watch' is a call to heroic discipleship. In the book of Revelation, watchfulness takes the shape of 'patient endurance.'"

"And then," the chaplain added, "there are the letters of Paul, which invite Christians to 'rejoice' (and to grieve) 'in hope.'"

"And in the Gospel of Matthew," Sally continued, "the call to 'watch' becomes a call to care for those who are pressed down and crushed by hurt and harm."

With Courage and Patience

"Well, let's start with the first of those, then, with the Gospel of Mark," the chaplain replied. "Tell me about watchfulness as heroic discipleship."

"In heroic discipleship," Sally replied, "neither our own survival nor our own ease is the law of our being. To be sure, life and its flourishing are recognized and celebrated as good. They belong, after all, to the creative and redemptive cause of God. The signs of that cause are breath and a blessing, a rainbow and a commandment, and finally, an empty tomb. We cannot turn against these goods without turning against the cause of God. Acts which aim at death or suffering don't fit devotion to the cause of God or gratitude for the gifts of God. Even so, life and its flourishing aren't the ultimate goods; they are not, to use Barth's term, 'second gods.'"[31] Sally was a big fan of Barth, and she knew her Gospel of Mark pretty well too. Mark's Gospel, she noted, makes it plain that Christ walked steadily and courageously the path that led to his suffering and to his death, and plain that Christians are called to follow him on a path of heroic discipleship, to take up his cross (Mark 8:34). Christians may not live as though either their own survival or their own ease were the law of their being. Sometimes life must be risked and death accepted; sometimes suffering must be endured or shared for the sake of God's cause in the world and for the sake of our own integrity. The refusal ever to let someone die and the attempt to eliminate suffering altogether are not signs of "watchfulness" but of idolatry.

"And if life and its flourishing aren't the greatest goods," Sally concluded, "neither are death and suffering the ultimate evils. They need not be feared finally, for death and suffering are not as strong as the promise of God. One needn't use all of one's resources against them. One need only act with integrity in the face of them. There are goods more weighty than our own ease, duties more demanding than our own survival, goods and duties which must determine how we live, even as we are dying."

Since Sally had cited Barth again, the chaplain interrupted to cite the martyrs. "The martyrs," he said, "knew the story well; they lived it and died into it, 'bearing witness' (martus) to it by choosing neither death nor suffering but by being ready to endure either for the sake of God's cause and their own integrity. Their comfort was that they were not their own but belonged to God, the giver of life, from whom not even death could separate them. And their comfort was their courage."

"Yes," said Sally. "And in more mundane and commonplace ways many Christian patients still display the same comfort and the same courage. They still

31. Barth, *Church Dogmatics*, III/4, p. 398.

bear witness to their hope by their readiness to die but not to kill. They display their comfort and their courage by refusing both offers of assisted suicide and those offers of treatment that may prolong their days but only by rendering those days (or months or years) less apt for their tasks of reconciliation with enemies or fellowship with friends or simply fun with their families. Heroic discipleship and its courage liberate patients from the tyrannies of survival or ease."

"But courage is only part of the picture," said the chaplain. "I mean, you're right that heroic discipleship is the image of watchfulness in Mark, but don't forget what you earlier said, that in Revelation the image is of patient endurance. Of course, the patience formed by watchfulness is not to be confused with Stoic resignation. Stoic 'contentment' *(apatheia)* is accomplished by resigning the passions, quitting desire; the Stoic ceases to fear by ceasing to hope; he learns contentment by unlearning sadness.[32] Stoics had no place for (and little patience with) lament, but they did make place for suicide, for quitting life. Revelation invited the churches of Asia Minor to patient endurance; it didn't invite them to contemplate a world of reason without passion but to join already the acclaim of the lamb that had been slain and enthroned. It called them not to be passionless but to share, in hope, the passion of Christ."

Such patience, the chaplain and Sally agreed, is capable of lament, but it doesn't permit suicide. For the fathers, at least, patience puts suicide out of the question.[33] Cyprian, Tertullian, and others used the patience of Job (and of Christ) to urge patients to be patient rather than to curse God or choose death, to endure suffering patiently rather than to "dare death impatiently," as Saint Augustine put it.[34]

The patience formed by watchfulness does not deny that death and sickness and suffering are real. And it does not pretend that they are not real evils. But such patience knows that all resistance to sickness, all human affirmation of embodied and communal life, is necessarily in vain if God is not God — and if Jesus has not been raised. More than that, such patience knows that — because God is God and because Jesus has been raised — sickness and suffering

---

32. Martha Nussbaum, *The Therapy of Desire: Theory and Practice in Hellenistic Ethics* (Princeton: Princeton University Press, 1994), pp. 388-99.

33. Darrel W. Amundsen, "Suicide and Early Christian Values," in *Suicide and Euthanasia: Historical and Contemporary Themes,* ed. Baruch A. Brody (Dordrecht, Netherlands: Kluwer Academic Publishers, 1989), pp. 77-154, pp. 109-115; Stanley Hauerwas and Charles Pinches, "Practicing Patience: How Christians Should Be Sick," *Christian Bioethics* 2, no. 2 (1996): 202-21, p. 208.

34. Augustine, "On Patience," 18; cited by Hauerwas and Pinches in "Practicing Patience," p. 209.

and weakness and withering signal not just the power of death and chaos but also our human limits and our dependence upon God. And because God is God and Jesus has been raised, at those limits and in that dependence we live and die into the hands of God; at those limits and in that dependence God may still be trusted. Sally quoted Barth again, this time to say that we do not live "under the intolerable destiny" of having to give wholeness and duration to our lives by our own efforts and technological achievements,[35] and we need not, therefore, (hopelessly) assert and attain our own life or our own dignity.

"The desire to be limitless and totally independent is a Promethean desire and quite hopeless," Sally concluded, "even if it is assertively hopeless. We should, rather, accept our limits — in spite of death — as not simply accidental but as from God, and we should, indeed, accept our dependence as ordered — in spite of death — not to our destruction but to 'the redemption of our bodies' (Rom. 8:23). Then sickness will be not only 'the forerunner and messenger of death' but also 'the forerunner and messenger' of God's grace.[36] Watchfulness can 'rejoice in hope' and 'be patient in suffering' (Rom. 12:12), not by resignation, but by living and dying toward the God who is coming. In patience the Christian can 'let herself go' toward the good future of God. And I can let myself go toward that good future."[37]

With Lament and Joy

Sally paused just then, as if to let register with the chaplain that she had just announced her decision to refuse the physician's suggestion of another round of chemotherapy. It evidently did register, for the chaplain asked, "So you've decided not to go through with the experimental treatment?" Sally nodded, and

---

35. Barth, *Church Dogmatics*, III/4, p. 372.

36. Barth, *Church Dogmatics*, III/4, p. 373.

37. Eberhard Jüngel, *God as the Mystery of the World*, trans. Darrell Guder (Grand Rapids: Eerdmans, 1983), pp. 394-95. The patience formed by watchfulness is not passivity. One need not worry that this emphasis on the patience of patients will only increase the asymmetry of power between a physician and a patient. Patience is not a spineless submission to the evil that fate dishes out; it is the confidence that death and evil will not have the last word; it is the lively integrity of a hope that looks to God's good future; and the twin of the patience formed by watchfulness, as we have said, is courage. A "patient" patient would not necessarily be "compliant" with an institution or a medicine that alienates her from her flesh or from her community. A "patient" patient may be a bone crossways in the throat of a medical establishment that is technologically oriented to biological survival.

there was a silence. "Sally, you have become my teacher and my friend since you first called me back to this room to read a little Scripture," he said. "I don't want to let you go."

Sally smiled at the remark and at the friendship displayed in it, but when she spoke again, she took up her discourse where she had paused, as though she had been reminded of the next point she wanted to make. "Watchfulness forms in patients courage and patience. I think we have been clear about that, and I hope it is clear to you how such watchfulness has also formed my decision. But let's also be clear about this: watchfulness forms in Christian community a readiness both to 'rejoice in hope' (Rom. 12:12) and to mourn, to grieve, in hope (1 Thess. 4:13-18). Watchfulness, like Jesus, still blesses 'those who mourn' (Matt. 5:4), blesses the aching visionaries who long for God's future and who weep because it is not yet.[38] Watchfulness is not inconsistent with grief; indeed, watchfulness evokes lament — for it is not yet God's good future. Paul made it clear to the Thessalonian Christians that — because Jesus has been raised — they may hope (1 Thess. 4:14). He didn't tell them, however, not to grieve, but not to grieve as those 'who have no hope' (1 Thess. 4:13)."

"True," said the chaplain. "It's like the contrast between a lament and a dirge. The dirge moves from glory to shame, from strength to powerlessness: 'How are the mighty fallen!' as it says in Second Samuel (1:19-27). The decisive feature of a dirge is the contrast between past glories and present misery. In a dirge, to be sure, the suffering or the grieving find a voice — but not hope. In lament, however, the suffering and grieving find a voice addressed to God, and lament — by its attention to God and its confidence in God's faithfulness, by watchfulness — reverses the tragic reversal of the dirge. Lament moves from distress to wholeness, from powerlessness to certainty, from anger to confidence in God's future."

The chaplain understood well the concept of lament. The form itself moves from invocation to the complaint to the prayer for help to the certainty of a hearing.[39] But notice also the process. The sufferer is struck dumb. There

38. Nicholas Wolterstorff, *Lament for a Son* (Grand Rapids: Eerdmans, 1987), pp. 84-86.

39. On lament see A. R. Johnson, "The Psalms," in *Old Testament and Modern Study*, ed. H. H. Rowley (Oxford: Clarendon, 1951), pp. 162-82, for a summary of the form-critical approach pioneered by Hermann Gunkel; and see Walter Brueggemann, "From Hurt to Joy, From Death to Life," *Interpretation* 28, no. 1 (1975): 3-19, for an account of the theological significance of lament. Lament is without embarrassment dialogical and communal. Psalms, the songbook of the second temple, included them — and not just for "private" reading. The ones who suffered had to do with God, and God had to do with them. The ones who suffered had to do with the community, and the community had to do with them. It is in the presence of God and in the presence of the community that the suffering

are no words. But if he is to recover from his suffering — or even to cope with it — he must find words that express his pain and encompass it in some pattern, some meaning. The first words may simply be those cries of anguish which belong to the dirge: "Alas, alas." But to those cries may also be added the pattern of the dirge, and the grieving may express the tragic reversal of his experience, that he has gone from joy to mourning. Then, invoking God in lament, the distress, the anxiety, the anger, the loss, the loneliness are given voice no less than in the dirge, but the pattern changes.

Lament does not disallow the sorrow. To look to God is not to look away. Lament, too, gives the sufferers voice, but it allows them to begin to reconstruct their identity, to hold to a meaning and a covenant that promises that the tragic reversal is not the last word. The sufferer may be helped to find words that hold hope for a saving reversal and nurture the reconstruction of a faithful identity, a faithful direction. And even if the sufferer does not find his way to the certainty of a hearing, the direction itself has changed.[40]

There is no pretense in lament, no denial, no withdrawal to some other-worldly reality. There is no romantic effort to reduce the hurt to some domesticated account of nature. And there is no presumptuous claim to secure human well-being by the mastery of nature. The watchfulness that mourns may provide a corrective to that religious triumphalism that denies the sadness of this world — and to that medical triumphalism that would provide a technical remedy for it.

"Now, watchfulness doesn't always take the form of lament," the chaplain concluded. "It also sometimes takes the shape of a hymn, of 'joy dancing.' Christians are ready to practice hospitality to joy, ready to celebrate merrily the outrageously good news of God's good future, ready to dance with delight wherever God's future makes its power felt in this sad world, whenever the Spirit — or those gifted by the Spirit — establish a little foothold for the presence of the future. But when Christian communities leave aside the language of lament, we marginalize not only suffering but also sufferers. When we leave aside lament in our liturgies, then in our anger or our sense of absurdity we

---

must be — and may be, and can be — dealt with. The one who brought lament knew that one need not face the hurt alone. In the contemporary church, however, by pushing lament to the margins of worship, we have lost something of the capacity for genuine dialogue and community as well. See further a work that I got too late to make any use of in this chapter, Kathleen D. Billman and Daniel L. Migliore, *Rachel's Cry: Prayer of Lament and Rebirth of Hope* (Cleveland: United Church Press, 1999).

40. Allen Verhey, "Is the Last Word 'Darkness'?" in *Religion and Medical Ethics: Looking Back, Looking Forward,* ed. Allen Verhey (Grand Rapids: Eerdmans, 1966), pp. 142-50.

think we sit alone in the congregation. There is a failure of nerve, a refusal to presume on another's humanity, and so we reach for our bootstraps and struggle to lift ourselves to the heights of some triumphant liturgy, or else we reach for our technology and struggle to lift ourselves to immortality and invulnerability to suffering."

With Care, with Reverence, Humility, and Gratitude

"So," Sally summarized, "Mark reminded us that watchfulness takes the shape of courage; Revelation, that it takes the shape of patience; and Paul, that it takes the shape of lament and joy. Notice this yet from Matthew's Gospel, that watchfulness takes the shape of care, of simple acts of compassion for the suffering."

Matthew brings his own account of watchfulness to a climactic conclusion with a story about the last judgment (Matt. 25:31-46).[41] When the Son of Man comes in his glory, he invites some to enter the kingdom — because, as he said, "I was hungry and you gave me food, I was thirsty and you gave me something to drink, I was a stranger and you welcomed me, . . . I was sick and you took care of me. . . ." Those who heard him were surprised, shocked, by the words. "When?" they asked. "We were watching for you, waiting for you, but when, Lord, did we care for you?" And the Son of Man answered them, "Inasmuch as you cared for one of the least of these, you cared for me."

The parable is eloquent testimony that watchfulness takes the shape of care. And it is an elegant reminder to caregivers that the presence of God is mediated to them through their patients, and that patients — in their very weakness and vulnerability, in their hurt and loneliness — (re)present Christ to the caregiver.

Caregivers may still stand there stuttering and sputtering, "Do you mean to say that that was you, Lord? That that fat old windbag was you, Lord? That that irritating buffoon was you, Lord? She certainly had a rough life, and she was you, even so? Do you really mean to say that that broken body was your spiritual presence?" And the answer is always "yes," and the answer calls for a kind of reverence in response.

This reverence requires care for patients as embodied and communal selves. It does not just insist in Cartesian fashion that the patient is also an agent; it does not set the mind (or the will) over and over-against the body; it does not simply demand respect for a patient's autonomy while the body re-

41. Matthew adopts Mark's chapter about watchfulness (cf. Mark 13 and Matt. 25), but he adds to it a collection of parables about watchfulness, which climaxes in the parable of judgment (Matt. 25:31-46).

mains manipulable nature. A watchful medicine, formed to care with rever-ence, is more apt to attend to suffering than either the technical expert who re-duces the sick to manipulable nature or the moral expert who reduces the patient to capacities for choice, for patients suffer neither as ghostly minds nor as biological organisms but as whole persons.[42]

"That parable in Matthew is eloquent testimony that watchfulness calls for care," the chaplain noted, after they had discussed it. "And it is an elegant witness to the humility appropriate to caregivers. There is no place here for Messianic pretension. If anyone is Messiah in this parable, the patient is. The caregiver is not Messiah. A watchful medicine won't deny the not-yet character of our existence or of our medicine, not to itself and not to patients. On the contrary, a watchful medicine will sustain and nurture truthfulness about our finitude and about our limits. Humility, after all, finds its twin in truthfulness."

"And if medicine is not the Messiah," Sally continued, "it is freed by watchfulness and its humility for a more carefree care. A watchful medicine need not bear that finally intolerable burden of being Messiah; it needn't sub-stitute anxiously for a finally powerless God. Watchful medicine need not panic in the presence of suffering and dying.[43] In a watchful medicine caregivers can simply 'be there' with and for patients, present to the suffering and the dying. When there are no words, when the suffering is mute, a watchful caregiver can 'be there' with a silent readiness to listen — and that silent presence can help a patient find words to express the hurt. And when the patient finds those words, a watchful caregiver can 'be there,' ready to join her voice to his in complaintive lament — and that 'expressive compassion' can help a patient find meaning and begin to construct the next chapter of a life, even if it will be the last chapter.[44] Watchfulness can nurture and sustain a more carefree care, and bring calm to chaos."

The chaplain remembered an earlier conversation and the story Sally had told about Coles's friend and the chaplain who dwelt on the stages of dying as though they were "stations of the cross"; he pointed out the irony of Sally's in-structing him about "stages," about the progress from mute suffering (and si-lent compassion) to expressive suffering (and expressive compassion) to the re-construction of an identity and integrity with it.

42. Eric J. Cassell, "Recognizing Suffering," *Hastings Center Report* 21, no. 3 (May-June 1991): 24-31.

43. William F. May, *The Physician's Covenant: Images of the Healer in Medical Ethics* (Philadelphia: Westminster, 1983), p. 60.

44. Warren Reich, "Speaking of Suffering: A Moral Account of Compassion," *Soundings* 72, no. 1 (Spring 1989): 83-108, pp. 93-97; Margaret E. Mohrmann, *Medicine as Ministry: Reflections on Suffering, Ethics, and Hope* (Cleveland: Pilgrim, 1995), pp. 75-88.

"I don't mean that these stages are simply sequential," Sally replied, "as if you have to go through them one after another in order to suffer or to be compassionate in the right way. That would be silly, but you need to be present to others in ways appropriate to their suffering. Besides," she said sadly, "our wounds frequently open up again, and we find ourselves slipping back to mute suffering." She was tired, and it showed in a little exasperation with the chaplain. Nevertheless, she continued. At first it seemed to the chaplain that she just wanted to prove that she was in no danger of slipping back to mute suffering, but soon it was clear to him that she had summoned up her strength in order to bring their long talk that day to a conclusion, to report her thoughts about a "more excellent way" of dying and of caring for the dying.

"Death, we said, threatens alienation from our bodies. A watchful medicine will care — and meet the threat by attention to embodied selves, relieving pain and nurturing the strength of patients to exercise self-control and responsibility; by attention, yes, to the delights of the flesh, to the music patients like and to the flowers they love, to their environment and to their dining (no less than to their diet), and by the human touch that signals compassion.

"Death, we said, threatens alienation from our communities. A watchful medicine will care — and meet the threat by hospitality not only to patients but to those whom patients love and by whom they are loved, by making those visiting the sick and dying comfortable and welcome, by ministering to those who can only stand and wait, for in such hospitality medicine cares for the patient, too. A watchful medicine will care — and help the patient recover her voice, even if only in lament.

"And death, we said, threatens alienation from God. A watchful medicine will care — but not by trying to dispense God, not by trying to provide God in pleasant little doses, convenient tablets, say, designed to make God easier to swallow. A watchful medicine is not undertaken as though God were not present to those threatened by death unless someone produces God; a watchful medicine is undertaken as a sign of a divine love that is always present and as a signal of a human hope that is already real.

"A watchful medicine, it needs finally to be said, requires a watchful community.[45] A watchful community will not abandon the sick or the suffering to medicine, nor will it abandon caregivers to their technology. A watchful community will call the sick and suffering to courage and patience, will comfort them in their lament, and encourage them to heroic discipleship and patient

---

45. Stanley Hauerwas, *Suffering Presence: Theological Reflections on Medicine, the Mentally Handicapped, and the Church* (Notre Dame: University of Notre Dame Press, 1986), pp. 63-83.

endurance. A watchful community will call caregivers to understand their work as a calling, indeed as a 'holy calling,'[46] a form of discipleship of the suffering and saving Christ, a vocation in which and through which they can serve the cause of God, rejoicing sometimes in some little token of God's good future they are able to bring, lamenting sometimes with a patient that it is not yet that future.

"Then we may signal together an other and a better destiny, that death is not the last word, and that God's good future makes its power felt not where the dying cling desperately to life, nor where the dying are deliberately killed, but where dying is faced with courage and accompanied by care. 'I believe in . . . the resurrection of the dead, and the life everlasting.'"

That's the way she finished her remarks that day, and, as if worn out by them, she fell asleep. The chaplain got up to leave after a few moments, hoping for more opportunities to visit her in the hospital, hoping for an opportunity just to be with her a little longer, to pray with her, to thank her. At the door he looked back to his sleeping friend and said, "I do, too." And he had a sense of an ending that still struggles to enter our lives and to shape our living and our dying and our caring for the suffering.

46. Walter Rauschenbusch, "For Doctors and Nurses," in *On Moral Medicine*, ed. Lammers and Verhey (Grand Rapids: Eerdmans, 1987; the prayer was first published in 1909), p. 5.

PART THREE

REMEMBERING JESUS IN GILEAD

A Continuing Tradition of Liberation and Chastity

CHAPTER EIGHT

The Handmaid's Tale of Gilead

"The Republic of Gilead, said Aunt Lydia, knows no bounds. Gilead is within you."[1] Gilead is a land Margaret Atwood invented in her chilling vision of a patriarchal future, a land that not long before was the United States, a land where secret police called Aunts give such advice to women. In spite of such counsel, the heroine of Margaret Atwood's story finally attempts to escape from Gilead and from its powers, leaving behind her tale as a testimony to her struggle.

The name of the story is *The Handmaid's Tale,* and its Gilead is a future made plausible by being educed from the sexism and patriarchy of our past. As Atwood has one expert in Gileadean Studies report in the appended "Historical Notes" (379-95), "there was little that was truly original with or indigenous to Gilead: its genius was synthetic" (389). Gilead is a future artfully reduced to absurdity, but it is no less plausible or terrifying a future for all that. Atwood's story describes a future in which the possibility of resistance is sustained by hope and in which the remnants of hope are preserved in memory. It provides a useful introduction for us not only because it provides an image for the distortions of the patriarchies in which we live and which live in us, but also because the churches' memory of Jesus can preserve a hope for escape from those distortions and sustain the possibilities of resistance to the culture's distorted accounts of gender and sexuality. An ethic by way of reminder will preserve a tradition of both liberation and chastity.

1. Margaret Atwood, *The Handmaid's Tale* (New York: Fawcett Crest, 1985), p. 31. Subsequent page references to Atwood's novel in this and the following chapters are given in parentheses in the text. On Atwood's novel see Janet Karsten Larson, "Margaret Atwood's Testaments: Resisting the Gilead Within," *Christian Century* (May 20-27, 1987), pp. 496-98.

The Handmaid's Tale is a first-person account of a woman conscripted as a surrogate mother, assigned to the household of Fred, one of Gilead's "Commanders." The religious regime that had seized control of what once was the United States used religion to justify stripping women first of their property, then of their access to information, and finally of their identities.

Property was the easiest; the assets of women were frozen or confiscated by a few keystrokes at Compubank. As a friend explained, "Any account with an F on it instead of an M. All they needed to do is to push a few buttons. We're cut off" (231).

Information was harder, but libraries were closed to women, and reading was forbidden to them. Even lettered signs in public places were replaced by pictures; "the lettering was painted out, when they decided that even the names of shops were too much temptation for us" (33).

Identity was the hardest of all, but we know the Handmaid only as "Offred," a patronymic that would change whenever she was assigned a new household. She was reduced to her reproductive capacities and assigned to the service of one of Gilead's elite; Offred was the Handmaid of Fred. In response to "plummeting Caucasian birthrates," the expert in Gileadean Studies reported, the regime "created an instant pool of such women by the simple tactic of declaring second marriages and non-marital liaisons adulterous, arresting the female partners, and on the grounds that they were morally unfit, confiscating the children they already had" (385). So the Handmaid lost her husband Luke and their child and entered the service of Fred. Even her clothes were not her own. All the Handmaids wore long red dresses, which gives the patronymic "Offred" a second meaning, of course, hinting to the reader of her resistance: off-red.

Not all the women of Gilead were Handmaids, naturally, reduced to fertile wombs; but all women were reduced to their utility to men. Some were "Marthas," dressed in dull green and reduced to being the household servants of men. The "Wives" of Gilead were the supervisors of the households of elite men. The "women of the poorer men" were "not divided into functions. They have to do everything; if they can" (32). Their dresses were striped, and they were called "Econowives." Some were "Aunts," like Aunt Lydia; these were the secret police of Gilead, for "the most effective way to control women for reproductive and other purposes was through women themselves" (390). Some were harlots at "the club," which was not officially sanctioned but was allowed to operate in service to the men of Gilead. And some, of course, were simply not useful — or refused to be; these were called "Unwomen" and discarded, sent to the "Colonies" to clean up toxic waste or, if they were lucky, to pick cotton.

The men of Gilead hardly benefited from this patriarchy, except for the ways power feeds the egos of the elite — and the cost was enormous. The reader does not get to know any of the men of Gilead very intimately — but that is just the point in a way; no one does. Fred, Offred's "Commander," longs for intimacy. At the end of a clandestine game of Scrabble, forbidden to women in Gilead, the Commander asks to be kissed. Offred obeys. "'Not like that,' he says. 'As if you meant it.' He was so sad" (181). The Commander hardly wins the sympathy of the Handmaid or of the reader. "Still, it must be hell, to be a man, like that. It must be just fine. It must be hell. It must be very silent" (114).

It is not just intimacy that is lacking; there is no genuine passion either. Sexual intercourse with a Handmaid "is not exciting. It has nothing to do with passion or love or romance or any of those other notions . . ." (122). The Handmaid just lies there during intercourse, thankful that kissing is forbidden, and "the Commander, too, is doing his duty" (122). And it is no better at "the club"; there sexual intercourse is not reduced to a biological means of reproduction, but it is reduced to a technology of pleasure, and very banal pleasure at that.

While Atwood envisions this patriarchal future, she also reminds her readers of the importance of memory. The regime uses — or misuses — the biblical tradition to justify its power and its policies. There are constantly allusions to Scripture. "Gilead," of course, recalls the inheritance of Reuben and Gad (Num. 32:28-32). The surrogacy arrangement itself is authorized by appeal to the story of Rachel, which, as Offred says, the Aunts had "drummed into us at the Center. *Give me children, or else I die. . . . Behold my maid Bilhah. She shall bear upon my knees, that I may also have children by her*" (114).[2] When a Handmaid does give birth, the Wife takes her place on a "Birthing Stool" above and behind the Handmaid, who then gives birth "upon the knees" of the Wife (161). The procedures for giving birth, however, do not include any anesthetics; "Aunt Elizabeth said it was better for the baby, but also: *I will greatly multiply thy sorrow and thy conception; in sorrow thou shalt bring forth children*" (146; Gen. 3:16 KJV). At "Women's Prayvaganzas" part of the ritual is a reading of 1 Timothy 2:9-15 — by a man, of course. "'Let the woman learn in silence with *all* subjection.' Here he looks us over. 'All,' he repeats" (286).

The biblical tradition is remembered, to be sure, but also dismembered in Gilead; little episodes and verses are shorn of their context in a larger narrative. Individual verses are distorted in the service of the powerful. The Pauline cry for equality (2 Cor. 8:14) is revised to the slogan, recited three times after dessert, "From each according to her ability; to each according to his needs" (151). The Beatitudes, played from a tape recording at lunchtime, include "Blessed are

2. The passage is from Genesis 30:1-3 (KJV). It is also cited as a frontispiece to the book.

the silent" (115). Offred knows that this is "wrong, and that they left things out, too, but there was no way of checking" (115). The powerful men have a monopoly on literacy, on reading and interpreting; so memory in Gilead stands in the service of men and is distorted into propaganda for patriarchalism.

But Offred remembers — and by her memory she preserves her identity. She cherishes the memory of her real name, for she is not "Of Fred," not the possession of the head of the household. She cherishes the memory of her husband Luke, with whom she could argue and make love, and of her daughter and of her mother. She remembers her job and reading the paper. All of that is gone now, but the memory preserves her against the powerful. Aunt Lydia may claim that "the Republic of Gilead knows no bounds," that "Gilead is within you" (31), but remembering is Offred's protection. She worries about the young, the little girls who have no memories of the way it was before, of reading books or playing baseball. They have no protection against the Gilead within (283).

Remembering not only preserves identity and protects Offred from the Gilead within; it also makes community and nurtures a resistance to Gilead without. For women to talk together about their memories is forbidden; but just as Offred preserves identity by memory, so the women create community by shared memory, by truthful testimony in snatched and forbidden moments of conversation and intimacy. A Handmaid of Fred before her had left a testimony scratched with a pin on the floor of a cupboard, "in the corner where the darkest shadow fell: *Nolite te bastardes corborundorum*" (69).[3] Offred says, "I didn't know what it meant. . . . Still, it was a message, and it was in writing, forbidden by that very fact. . . . It pleases me to ponder this message. It pleases me to think I'm communing with her, this unknown woman" (69). And she pictures the woman as resourceful and indomitable and takes comfort and courage.

Her own tale, likewise, makes community and nurtures resistance. She addresses an unknown and future reader: "Dear You," she says (53), and creates not only words but the flesh to hear them (53). "I tell, therefore you are," she says (344), and creates as well a relationship that is forbidden in Gilead. To tell the tale, to remember and repeat the story, even to "You," nurtures her own resolve to resist Gilead; and for "You" to hear the story, to commune with the Handmaid, may form character and conduct capable of resistance to Gilead's power, too.

Offred remembers more than the events of her own life. She remembers the biblical tradition too, and it provides both correction and hope. In her room there is one pillow on a window seat big enough for three, and this one

3. Later Offred discovers, in an old Latin textbook the Commander hoarded, that this is schoolboy Latin for "Don't let the bastards grind you down" (242).

pillow has a word printed on it; FAITH, it says. She treasures it for the word, of course, and wonders, "There must have been three, once. HOPE and CHARITY, where have they been stowed?" (141). She remembers the Lord's Prayer, too, and she prays it, or something like it:

> My God. Who Art in the Kingdom of Heaven, which is within.
>
> I wish you would tell me your name, the real one I mean. But *You* will do as well as anything.
>
> I wish I knew what you were up to. But whatever it is, help me to get through it, please. Though maybe it's not your doing; I don't believe for an instant that what's going on out there is what you meant.
>
> I have enough daily bread, so I won't waste time on that. It isn't the problem. The problem is getting it down without choking on it.
>
> Now we come to forgiveness. Don't worry about forgiving me right now. There are more important things. For instance: keep the others safe, if they are safe. Don't let them suffer too much. If they have to die, let it be fast. You might even provide a Heaven for them. We need you for that. Hell we can make for ourselves.
>
> I suppose I should say I forgive whoever did this, and whatever they're doing now. I'll try, but it isn't easy.
>
> Temptation comes next. At the Center, temptation was anything much more than eating and sleeping. Knowing was a temptation. What you don't know won't tempt you, Aunt Lydia used to say. . . .
>
> I think about the chandelier too much, though it's gone now. But you could use a hook, in the closet. I've considered the possibilities. All you'd have to do, after attaching yourself, would be to lean your weight forward and not fight.
>
> Deliver us from evil.
>
> Then there's Kingdom, power, and glory. It takes a lot to believe in those right now. But I'll try it anyway. *In Hope,* as they say on the gravestones.
>
> You must feel pretty ripped off. I guess it's not the first time. (253)

The Lord's Prayer becomes lament in her remembering — but not without hope. Even gravestones can curiously give birth to hope for Offred; once before she had remembered a gravestone with "an anchor on it and an hourglass and the words *In Hope*" (135). The anchor of hope, of course, is the Lord whose prayer Offred remembered (Heb. 6:19). There is hope even in Gilead when Jesus is remembered — remembered well and faithfully.

To remember well and faithfully is not simply to recall historical data, however; Margaret Atwood makes that clear as well when she also envisions for us the time the Handmaid's tale is finally told. A "historical note" is appended to *The Handmaid's Tale* (379-95), a transcript from the proceedings of a symposium of Gileadean Studies at the end of the twenty-second century at the University of Denay, Nunavit. *The Handmaid's Tale* has just been discovered at the site of the last way station of "The Underground Femaleroad." It has been published, and the editor remarks on its significance, of which he can see precious little. Historians are professional rememberers, and this expert does provide some very important data, but the "objectivity" in which the intellectual class takes such pride prevents him from responding with any passion. "Our job is not to censure but to understand," he says (383). The objectivity of the historian, moreover, is belied when he dismembers the Handmaid's tale in search for clues about "the real history" of Gilead — that is, for clues about the influence of powerful men — and when he uses sexist humor to keep his audience attentive, calling the way of escape for women, for example, "The Underground Frailroad" (381). He denies none of it, but he does not understand Offred the way Offred longed to be understood in her tale. He does not "commune" with her. He does not remember well or faithfully. He is not worthy of Offred's "You." Margaret Atwood artfully provides us not only with the story of a handmaid, but also with the story of the interpretation of the Handmaid's story. She envisions not just one chilling future, but two. Gilead is before us — or behind us — but the greatest danger is that it is within us, silencing the women and muting their voices.

A Cautionary Tale: Some Problems

Atwood's story of Gilead provides a useful background for consideration of the use of Scripture in part simply because it serves as a cautionary tale for any who would attend to Scripture as authoritative for the worlds of gender and sexuality. Scripture is used — and abused — in Gilead. It is remembered — but also dismembered and made to serve the patriarchal regime. *The Handmaid's Tale* may remind us that there are problems when we turn to Scripture for moral guidance.

We have already discussed the problems of turning to Scripture — its silence, its strangeness, its diversity, and its potential for harm — in relation to sickness and health. These problems are equally evident when seeking answers to questions about gender and sexuality, however. Scripture is certainly silent concerning many of the concrete social and sexual issues of the world in which we live. No law code of Israel contained a Title IX to prohibit sexual discrimination in athletic scholarships. No sage commented on the wisdom of "the pill" or on the folly of pornography on the Internet. The prophets, always ready to take

162

the side of the vulnerable against the rich and powerful, never mentioned adolescents and the entertainment industry. No scribe asked Jesus whether women could administer the sacraments, or about the possible commodification of women in practices of surrogate motherhood and ova donation (or vendoring). And no early Christian community asked Paul about sexual orientation, although there were plenty of questions about sexual behavior. Revelation, for all its visions, seems never to have dreamt of "women's liberation" or "the sexual revolution."

The strangeness of Scripture is equally evident. When Scripture does speak of human gender and sexuality, its words sometimes seem quaint. Solomon's many wives and concubines hardly seem the course of wisdom today. And, while the Song of Solomon may be great love poetry, "your teeth are like a flock of shorn ewes . . . all of which bear twins" (4:2, 6:6) seems more humorous than passionate. Levirate marriages (Deut. 25:5) strike us as more than a little odd. The story of Jacob's purchase of a bride (Gen. 29:15-30) seems unfair not only to Jacob but to Rachel and to Leah. The story of Bilhah giving birth to Jacob's child while she sits between the legs of Rachel (Gen. 30:1-3) seems no less strange when we read it in Scripture than when we read it in *The Handmaid's Tale*.

If it's a strange world of sex and gender in Scripture, it's also a diverse one. Scripture does not always speak with one voice about gender or about sex and marriage. Galatians 3:28 says, "there is no longer male and female," but when 1 Timothy 2:9-15 (the passage read at the "Women's Prayvaganzas") would "permit no woman to teach or to have authority over a man," then "male and female" seem still to be functioning to divide social roles. "The LORD God said, 'It is not good that the man should be alone'" (Gen. 2:18), but Paul said that to refrain from marriage is "better" (1 Corinthians 7:38). Moses permitted men to divorce their wives (Deut. 24:1-4), but Jesus evidently did not (Mark 10:2-12, although there are different voices about that as well). The Song of Solomon celebrates the mutual delight of a man and a woman, but Proverbs 7 warns that sexual desire can lead to temptation and death. Such diversity should give pause to any who would insist on the authority of Scripture for contemporary sexual ethics.

Moreover, just as appeals to Scripture in other areas have sometimes done a great deal of harm, so have appeals regarding questions of sexuality and gender. Witness Offred, or, for that matter, Hester Prynne of Nathaniel Hawthorne's *The Scarlet Letter*. As we have noted before, when Genesis 3:16, "in pain you shall bring forth children," was quoted — and not only by the Aunts of *The Handmaid's Tale* — to oppose pain relief in labor, a great deal of harm was done. When reports of abuse and incest are hushed by reading texts about submission, then great harm is done. It is true, as we have said, that such uses of Scripture are *abuses of Scripture*. A community formed by the message of "good news to the oppressed" (Isa. 61:1; cf. Luke 4:18) ought not fail to observe that, when Scripture is abused in the areas of sex and gender, as when it is abused in other areas, it is often women and children and those on the margins who are hurt. The abuse of Scripture — and the abuse of persons by citing Scripture — is reason enough to be careful about using Scripture as the basis for an ethic of gender and sexuality.

There are problems in Scripture, but *The Handmaid's Tale* reminds us much more powerfully that there are also problems in the readers of Scripture. The arrogant and fearful Commanders of Gilead assumed control over the interpretation of Scripture. They read it in the service of their own interests and power, in the service of patriarchy. They read it over-against women, not over-against themselves. They rendered women illiterate, unable to read Scripture for themselves, unable to check the readings of men. They silenced women. They did not read the whole Scripture, and they did not read any part of it with the whole community. They read it badly! The practice of reading Scripture was corrupted in Gilead, even if the Commanders set it aside as "holy." They forgot the story. In their proud hands Scripture became a handbook for a fertility cult, a code for patriarchy. They did not remember Jesus. It is not just in Gilead, of course, that men have assumed control over the interpretation of Scripture. And it is not just in Gilead that the expropriation of the memory of the church by powerful men has led to the distortion of the church's memory — and of the community's life.

The remedy for forgetfulness is not to be found in the "neutrality" and "objectivity" of the university. Atwood reminds us of that when she provides us not only with the story of the Handmaid but also with the story of the interpretation of the Handmaid's story. The "historical note" appended to *The Handmaid's Tale* displays the failure of the "objective" historian, that professional rememberer, to read the *Handmaid's Tale* either well or faithfully. The expert did provide some historical data useful and important to the reading of the Handmaid's story, but to simply recall historical data is not to remember. His pretence to "objectivity" kept him from genuinely understanding Offred, from being formed by her story. Moreover, when he read the Handmaid's tale to search for clues about "the real history" of Gilead, that is, for clues about the influence of powerful men, it is clear that his "objectivity" was in fact biased. The "objective" historian was still silencing the women and muting their voices. It is not just in Denay, Nunavit, of course, that "objective" historians have had hidden prejudices and have failed to nurture remembrance.

The Importance of Remembering

There are problems within Scripture and within us as readers. But there is also the promise of remembering. By remembering Offred preserves her identity. By remembering she resists Gilead, resists being fated by the culture without and within. And by remembering she creates a community of shared memory, not only with other handmaids in forbidden snatches of conversation, but also, she hopes, with the reader of her story. The reader who remembers the story well and faithfully (not like that historian in Denay, Nunavit), communes with Offred, and is formed by her story to resist the power of Gilead.

It is not, however, just the general phenomenon of memory that is important to *The Handmaid's Tale* — or to us. Offred remembers also little bits and snatches of the biblical story that she is forbidden to read, and remembering it nurtures her resistance and a little hope. There is hope even in Gilead when Jesus is remembered — remembered well and faithfully. *"In Hope,"* the gravestone said, as Christians remember the story of a risen Lord.

Christians turn to Scripture to remember. Such remembering, as we have noted, is not just a mental process of recall, not just a disinterested recollection of objective historical facts, not just some historian's reconstruction. Christians learn no particular theory of memory by reading Scripture, but they do learn to remember, and such remembering is to own a past as one's own and to own it as constitutive of identity and community and as determinative for discernment. That remembering is the good of the practice of reading Scripture in Christian community. And in that remembering Christians find also the promise for renewal and reform of the Gileads within which we live and which live in us.

As Christians, we turn to Scripture because we long to think and to live our lives — including our lives in the contemporary world of gender and sexuality — in the light and power of the gospel. We are convinced that to think about gender and sexuality and to live with Christian integrity require that we read Scripture together and remember. Moreover, as we have said, in learning to read Scripture Christians learn certain standards of excellence "appropriate to" and "partially definitive" of this practice.[4] We learn, that is, three pairs of virtues for reading Scripture: holiness and sanctification, fidelity and creativity, discipline and discernment.[5]

---

4. Alasdair MacIntyre, *After Virtue: A Study in Moral Theory* (Notre Dame, Ind.: University of Notre Dame Press, 1981), p. 175.

5. For a more in-depth review of these virtues than will follow here, see pp. 68-71 in chapter three of this volume.

These standards apply to the world of gender and sexuality as much as to any other area of life. If, for example, we have described sanctification as the standard that sets the remembered story alongside all the stories of our life, then those stories surely include stories of sexual romance and desire, of sexual fidelity and infidelities, of children and childlessness, of marriage and singleness, and of gender. These times and places of our lives too must be made new by the power of God, made to fit remembrance, made worthy of the gospel.

The virtues of fidelity and creativity remind us that continuity and change are the marks of any living tradition. If remembrance requires fidelity, faithfulness to the memory the church has owned as its own, it also requires creativity, for the past is past, and we do not live in it, even if we remember it. To treat Scripture as a timeless moral code for gender and the sexual life is a corruption of the practice of reading it in accord with these "standards of excellence." It confuses fidelity with an anachronistic eccentricity. And to treat Scripture as simply dated and irrelevant to the contemporary social and sexual world is also a corruption of the practice. It turns remembrance into an archivist's recollection, and runs the risk of alienating the Christian community from its own moral tradition and from it own moral identity. It invites amnesia.

A pilgrim's progress still comes by way of remembering, by the practice of reading Scripture, and the narrow path between anachronism and amnesia requires both discipline and discernment. Discipline, of course, means that we are ready to be a disciple, ready to follow the One of whom the story is told. It requires that we read Scripture over-against ourselves and not just for ourselves, over-against our lives, in judgment upon them and not just in self-serving defense of them, over-against even our conventional reading of biblical texts, subverting our efforts to use Scripture to boast about our own righteousness or to protect our own status. A costly and humble discipleship tests character and conduct by the truth of the story we love to tell. But the shape of that story and of lives formed to it requires discernment, the ability to recognize "fittingness." And in reading Scripture as "useful . . . for training in righteousness," discernment is the ability to plot our lives to "fit" the whole of Scripture, to order every part of our lives — including our gender and our sexuality — toward that whole. To be sure, sometimes our reading can be corrupted by our commitments to our own power and interests. Like Gilead's Commanders, for example, we can be blinded by our investment in patriarchy. And we, too, stand at risk of forgetfulness then, even if we treat Scripture like an icon.

Our reading (and performance) of Scripture can be corrupted, however, not only by patriarchy but also by the culture and assumptions of the Enlightenment. That the Enlightenment had effects on interpretation we have already observed. It moved the social location for the interpretation of Scripture from the church to the university, and shifted the interest from remembering the story to describing the history "scientifically" and "objectively." The "objective" study of Scripture required neutrality; it required that Scripture be treated like any other text. Reading Scripture became the task of those who pretended to transcend particular traditions and communities, and the task was regarded as achieved when the significance of Scripture was confined to a past time and place or to the private realm of individual preferences. Such readers, however, may well remind us of the expert historian who failed to read the Handmaid's tale either well or faithfully. When the "objective" historians are permitted hegemony over interpretation, then Christian communities are put at risk of forgetfulness. When Scripture is read in Christian community, however, there is a remedy for forgetfulness, for in reading Scripture we may learn to remember the story, "the old, old story" that Christians still love to tell and long to live, still today in the post-Enlightenment world of sex and gender.

The Enlightenment has clearly left its mark on our sexual world. It was the expectation of the Enlightenment that reason and its child, science, would play the role of integrating society by providing common standards and interpreting reality. Religion would no longer bind the community together by providing a common interpretation of reality or a shared set of legitimating standards.[6] The result of this Enlightenment project has been a minimal public morality that restrains freedom — including sexual freedom — only by the equal freedom of all others, and that guides freedom only by the moral wisdom of utility, itself reduced to maximizing the satisfaction of arbitrary preferences. The church — with its fuller vision of a good sexual life, with its concerns for additional restraints and its wisdom about life as embodied selves in community — has been pushed to the margins of public life, to an arena marked off as private. And what matters publicly is simply that there be such a private space, not how it is filled.

The Enlightenment may be regarded as the grandparent of the so-called "sexual revolution." The understanding of sexuality once considered normative could hardly be sustained in a public ethos that celebrated freedom and restrained its exercise only by the equal freedom/liberty/license of all others. The sexual ethic of such a culture can only be a minimal one: consent. That is hardly a trivial requirement, but it is nevertheless a minimal one. It is true that "nonconsensual" sex is wrong, but there is more to say about a good sexual life, and if we deny that there is more to say, then we finally destroy and subvert a good sexual life. The sufficiency of consent quickly deteriorates into sexual li-

---

6. See, for example, Peter Berger, *The Sacred Canopy: Elements of a Sociological Theory of Religion* (Garden City, N.Y.: Doubleday, 1967), pp. 132-33.

cense, and it is only fair that the sexual license enjoyed by some in this society be extended to all. A second principle inherited by the sexual revolution from the Enlightenment is the principle of utility. In the absence, however, of any common standards for determining what counts as a "good" to be sought or as a "harm" to be avoided, the principle of utility quickly gets reduced to maximizing the satisfaction of arbitrary preferences (or desires). In the sexual revolution the sexual life itself was reduced to a private arena without public significance, an arena for the exercise of liberty, an arena for the satisfaction of personal (and private) preferences.

The effects of the sexual revolution are cleverly satirized by Peter De Vries in more than one of his novels, but never more cleverly than in *Slouching Towards Kalamazoo*. There De Vries revisits Nathaniel Hawthorne's story of Hester Prynne, but he tells it in a way appropriate to "sexually liberated twentieth-century America."[7] Miss Maggie Doubloon taught *The Scarlet Letter* to her eighth grade class in "the buckle of the Bible belt," and then she lived the story, or one something like it. Having committed Hester's sin, she wore a scarlet letter A on her T-shirt, but with the addition of a little "+" sign. What was Hester's badge of shame was for Miss Doubloon a grade, A+, proclaiming her excellence as a sexual partner, "good in bed" (108). The shameless gag became a commercial success, and Miss Doubloon got rich in the T-shirt business. The identity of the father was kept secret, and De Vries's character Biff Thrasher, like the Reverend Dimmesdale of *The Scarlet Letter*, suffered a little in the silence of suspicion. Thrasher ends up marrying Bubbles Breedlove and entering the ministry. It was hardly a faithful marriage; the allure of adultery was too powerful for that. And it was hardly an evangelical ministry; his expositions were given to "shooting the Bible full of holes and ridiculing prayer" (238). Thrasher's lecture tour is the analogue to Dimmesdale's famous "Election Sermon." Thrasher's "sermons," moreover, far from providing a word from outside to call us all to repentance and renewal in our sexual lives, end up inviting licentiousness. "'And so, dearly beloved,' [he] said, gathering up [his] notes, 'if there's one thing I'd like to drive home tonight, it's the woman who introduced me'" (238).

Christians have frequently been suspicious of the "sexual revolution," unable to render it coherent with the script they read and would perform. Sometimes, to be sure, their resistance to the sexual revolution has been repressive and selective, ready to be "realistic" about divorce but not about the sexual con-

---

7. Peter De Vries, *Slouching Towards Kalamazoo* (New York: Penguin Books, 1984), p. 3. Subsequent page references to De Vries's novel in this paragraph are given in parentheses in the text.

duct of adolescents, ready to be "romantic" about the intimacy of heterosexual lovers but eager to condemn homosexual intercourse. Even so, because we are a community of moral discourse, deliberation, and discernment by being a community of memory, we may (and must) insist that the church — not MTV, not television talk show hosts, not the marketplace, not Kinsey or Masters and Johnson, not the local psychotherapist, but the church — provide the appropriate context for the formation and reformation of our sexual lives. And we may (and must) insist that the goal of such moral development — also for our children — is not Kohlberg's sixth stage but a life — and a sexual life — "worthy of the gospel of Christ" (Phil. 1:27).

Christians have sought to fashion and form such lives by attention to Scripture and by remembering. There are problems, to be sure, but the longing of the faith and of the faithful for sexual lives worthy of the gospel of Christ, worthy of the exhortation of Paul to "glorify God in your body" (1 Cor. 6:20), is not served by silencing either Scripture or each other. It is served by remembering, and by exercising discernment in the community of memory. The greatest danger is still forgetfulness. There are temptations to forgetfulness in the patriarchal cultures from which Atwood imaginatively formed Gilead, and there are temptations to forgetfulness in the division of life formed by the Enlightenment, the division of life into a public realm governed by generic principles and "scientific" knowledge and a private realm reserved for the self-centered quest to satisfy desire. Forgetfulness still threatens a loss of identity and community. And the remedy for forgetfulness is still to read and to tell the old, old story, a lively and wonderful and true story — and to hear it now and then from saints and now and then from strangers for whom Christ also died.[8] That story still has Jesus at its center.

In Christian community Scripture does not merely exist as an archaic relic in an age of science and reason, of Kinsey and Russell, say. That there are problems is not denied; that the words are human words and may not simply be repeated as Christian counsel about sexual and gender ethics today is not denied. Nevertheless, we turn to Scripture to find there the Word of God — and to remember. We read Scripture in Christian community, not in the university, however helpful the scholarly tools and research may be. In Christian community the practice of reading Scripture engages the church in discernment. Together we plot the story of Scripture. Together we talk and argue about how to interpret and shape our lives — and our common life — in remembrance. In that dialogue people must listen to Scripture and to each other, muting neither

---

8. See further Stephen E. Fowl and L. Gregory Jones, *Reading in Communion: Scripture and Ethics in Christian Life* (Grand Rapids: Eerdmans, 1991), pp. 62-63 and 110-34.

Scripture nor each other. And in that communal discernment and mutual discipline, the authority of Scripture is experienced again and anew. In Christian community and in remembrance we test and qualify the judgments (and the reasons for them) that we find in our own Gileads and in our own cultures of Enlightenment. In Christian community we talk together and think together and pray together about our choices in remembrance of Jesus.

The chapters that follow are an effort to do ethics "by way of reminder." They are undertaken in an effort to remember Jesus, and then to remember the early church remembering Jesus, in our strange world of sex and gender. They are written "boldly" but also gladly and humbly. I do not claim that they are the last word, but I hope they are a contribution to the church as a community of moral discernment and discourse.

CHAPTER NINE

Remembering Jesus:
The Handmaid's Son in Gilead

Atwood's story of Gilead does not provide only a cautionary tale for the reading of Scripture as somehow normative. It also provides a revealing background for an effort to remember Jesus — and to remember the church remembering Jesus — for Atwood's Gilead is a future imaginatively drawn out of our past, out of social and sexual worlds not unlike the first-century Palestinian world in which Jesus lived and not unlike the patriarchal worlds in which the church has lived and which have lived in the churches.

The Patriarchal World of Jesus

First-century Palestine was a thoroughly patriarchal world.[1] Women did not count for much outside the home. Indeed, they were not counted at all when

1. On patriarchalism at the time of Jesus, see Erhard S. Gerstenberger and Wolfgang Schrage, *Woman and Man,* trans. Douglas W. Stott (Nashville: Abingdon, 1981), pp. 130-32; Joachim Jeremias, *Jerusalem in the Time of Jesus* (Philadelphia: Fortress, 1969), pp. 359-76; Paul K. Jewett, *Man as Male and Female* (Grand Rapids: Eerdmans, 1975), pp. 86-94; Richard N. Longenecker, *New Testament Social Ethics for Today* (Grand Rapids: Eerdmans, 1984), pp. 73-74; Albrecht Oepke, *"gunē," Theological Dictionary of the New Testament,* ed. Gerhard Kittel, trans. Geoffrey W. Bromiley, vol. 1 (Grand Rapids: Eerdmans, 1964), pp. 776-89; Elisabeth Schüssler Fiorenza, *In Memory of Her: A Feminist Theological Reconstruction of Christian Origins* (New York: Crossroad, 1983), pp. 105-55; and Judith Romney Wegner, *Chattel or Person? The Status of Women in the Mishnah* (New York: Oxford University Press, 1988).

171

checking to see if the number necessary for a synagogue service were present. The *minyah* or "count" necessary was ten adult males. Nine adults plus all the women in Galilee would not constitute the quorum necessary for a proper synagogue service.[2] And in a proper service, of course, the women were silent, neither reading the Scripture nor leading the prayers.[3]

At the temple, too, women did not count for much. They were not required, like the men, to make pilgrimage to the temple, and if they did, their access to the temple was restricted. They were not allowed into the inner court of Herod's temple, not permitted such proximity to the Holy of Holies and the presence of God. The women's court was further removed from the altar of sacrifice and fifteen steps lower than the inner court. During menstruation and for forty days after the birth of a son and eighty days following the birth of a daughter, women were not even allowed in the court of the Gentiles.[4]

Women were not obliged to learn Torah like the men were. There was a permission to learn, in theory at least, but if a woman should seize that permission, she would find her access to the study of Torah restricted as surely as her access to the temple. In Palestine, for example, anyone could become a rabbi — anyone, that is, except a woman. And most self-respecting rabbis would not teach a woman the Law — even if the woman were his daughter. Such, at least, was the view of Rabbi Eliezar, who said, "Everyone who teaches his daughter Torah is as if he taught her promiscuity"[5] and "Better to burn the Torah than to teach it to women."[6] There were exceptions to this refusal to instruct women, notably Rabbi Ben Azzai.[7] And there were women — like Judith and Beruryah — who studied Torah, in spite of the judgment of men like Rabbi Eliezar. Nevertheless, most rabbis evidently held the view that it was best to avoid all unnecessary conversation with women,[8] and since women were not obliged to learn

---

2. Lewis N. Dembitz, "Minyan," *The Jewish Encyclopedia,* vol. VIII (New York: Funk and Wagnalls, 1904), pp. 603-4; Raphael Loewe, *The Position of Women in Judaism* (London: S.P.C.K, 1966), p. 45; Jewett, *Man as Male and Female,* p. 91; but see note 21 below.

3. Tosephta, *Megillah* 3:11; Babylonian Talmud, *Megillah* 23a. On this see Loewe, *The Position of Women,* pp. 44-46, and Wegner, *Chattel or Person?* pp. 145-59.

4. Jeremias, *Jerusalem in the Time,* p. 373.

5. Mishnah, *Sotah* 3:4; cited in Longenecker, *New Testament Social Ethics,* p. 74. On this passage of the Mishnah and on the question of "Torah Knowledge for Women," see Moshe Meiselman, *Jewish Woman in Jewish Law* (New York: KTAV Publishing House, 1978), pp. 34-42.

6. Jerusalem Talmud, *Sotah* 3:4, 19a.7; cited in Jeremias, *Jerusalem in the Time,* p. 373.

7. Mishnah, *Sotah* 3:4.

8. Mishnah, *Aboth* 1:5; Jeremias, *Jerusalem in the Time,* p. 360.

the Law, the effort to teach them was unnecessary conversation. Women were thus assigned to ignorance and then — with marvelous sexist logic — blamed for it. Even the great Hillel said, "Many women — many superstitions."[9]

No, women did not count for very much in first-century Palestine. Indeed, they were sometimes simply counted as possessions.[10] And they were sometimes numbered among the heathen and the illiterate, as in a doxology commended to pious Jewish males for daily use by Rabbi Judah ben Elai (C.E. 150). "Praise God that he did not create me a heathen! Praise God that he did not create me a woman! Praise God that he did not create me an illiterate person!"[11] Women did not count for very much in first-century Palestine. They were numbered among the least, among the last.

Jewish men were expected to learn and to obey Torah. Among other things this meant refraining from the sexual immoralities prohibited by the Law, including fornication, adultery, homosexual behavior, and bestiality. Such immorality was linked with idolatry and Gentile ignorance of God. Obedience to Torah also meant that men had a duty to marry and to have children.[12] Women, on the other hand, although they were not obligated to learn the Law, were subject to the prohibitions of the Torah and to the penalties prescribed for their violation, including the death penalty. Women were not, however, obligated to observe all of the positive commandments;[13] they were not obligated to marry and to have children, for example.[14] Such an obligation would hardly have been practical in any event, for only men "married" in first-century Palestine. Women were "given in marriage." Once "given" in marriage, they were still not directly obligated by Torah to procreate, but they were expected to defer to the husband's obligation to "be fruitful and multiply" (Gen. 1:28). If they failed to have children, they could be blamed and even (after ten years) divorced.[15] Divorce was exclusively a male prerogative. Women "given in marriage" could be expected to bear and nurture children, to satisfy their husbands sexually, and to avoid tempting others to immorality. As

9. Mishnah, *Aboth* 2:7; cited by Jewett, *Man as Male and Female*, p. 91.

10. See Jeremias, *Jerusalem in the Time*, p. 367, on the similarity of the acquisition of a wife and a slave. Also see Wegner, *Chattel or Person?*, whose study demonstrates that women are treated as a "legal hybrid" (p. 8) of chattel (or property) and person in the Mishnah.

11. Tosephta, *Berakoth* 7:18, cited in Jewett, *Man as Male and Female*, p. 92.

12. In obedience to Genesis 1:28, e.g., Mishnah, *Yebamoth* 6:6. Some Essenes eschewed marriage; so Josephus, *War*, II.viii.13.

13. Jeremias, *Jerusalem in the Time*, p. 372.

14. See Loewe, *The Position of Women*, pp. 47-57.

15. Mishnah, *Yebamoth* 6:6.

one rabbi put it, "all we [men] can expect from them [i.e., from women] is that they bring up our children and keep us from sin."[16] In short, home was the place for a Jewish woman, and there her place was under her husband.[17] The social and sexual world of first-century Palestine was thoroughly patriarchal. Women just did not count for very much.

This bleak picture of Palestinian patriarchalism was not unrelieved. Within the patriarchal household, women could be praised and honored. The candid and robust chauvinism of Rabbi Judah ben Elai's doxologies was softened by real appreciation of women *as* wives and mothers. Rabbi Akiba's wife Rachel, for example, was celebrated as a selfless and devoted wife who encouraged and enabled Akiba to become a selfless and devoted rabbi and martyr. What the great Akiba became he owed to Rachel; he said as much.[18] But such appreciation for women does not challenge or even part company with the patriarchalism of first-century Palestine.

It needs also to be said, however, that this patriarchalism was not unchallenged. The sexual and social world of first-century Palestine was not monolithic. There were reform movements within Judaism in the first century.[19] The story of Judith was evidently a popular tale in the first century. Judith was a widowed heroine as remarkable for her intelligence and piety as for her beauty and purity, and she was celebrated for her dedication to Israel's national survival. The very popularity of the story is eloquent testimony that the patriarchalism of the first century was not monolithic. And in the early second century Beruryah would become famous for her knowledge of Torah, her piety, her judgment, her wisdom, and her wit. She put that wit to good use against patriarchalism. A rabbi asked her once, "By which road should we travel in order to reach Lydda?" Her reply was a rebuke, "Did not the rabbis say, 'Talk not overmuch with women'? You should have asked, 'How to Lydda?'"[20] There were voices raised within Jewish piety that called for women to be counted — and to be counted as among the children of God. And there were, indeed, some synagogues where women not only counted but were also "head" or "leader" or "el-

16. Babylonian Talmud, *Yebamoth* 63a; cited in Longenecker, *New Testament Social Ethics*, p. 74.

17. See further, Jeremias, *Jerusalem in the Time*, pp. 363-72.

18. Babylonian Talmud, *Kethuboth* 63a.

19. See especially Schüssler Fiorenza, *In Memory of Her*, pp. 105-18. See also Lillian Sigal, "Images of Women in Judaism," in Phillip Sigal, *Judaism: The Evolution of a Faith* (Grand Rapids: Eerdmans, 1988), pp. 265-92.

20. *Eruvin* 53b, cited by Zvi Kaplan, "Beruryah," *Encyclopedia Judaica*, vol. IV (Jerusalem: Keter Publishing House, 1972), p. 701. See also Henrietta Szold, "Beruria," *The Jewish Encyclopedia*, vol. III (New York: Funk and Wagnalls, 1902), pp. 109-10.

der."[21] Within the Jewish piety of first-century Palestine an alternative and corrective vision was possible. Patriarchalism was not unchallenged.

Finally, it must be observed that the patriarchalism of first-century Palestine was not unparalleled; it was not so different from the patriarchalism of the Greek and Roman world. Indeed, the chauvinism of Rabbi Judah ben Elai's doxologies had a remarkable parallel in the "three reasons of gratitude" attributed to a number of Greek philosophers: "that I was born a human being and not a beast, next, a man and not a woman, thirdly, a Greek and not a barbarian."[22] The authorization might be different, but when Aristotle appealed to "nature" to warrant his view of marriage as the union of a "natural ruler and a natural subject,"[23] it was not less imposingly patriarchal than the Torah. To be sure, the patriarchalism of the Greek and Roman world was not monolithic either. There was evidently some recognition of women as legal persons in the spheres of financial and marriage law. Women could inherit, draw up a will, and file for divorce. Now and then in the first century, a philosopher would speak in recognition of women as full persons; Musonius of Rome, for example, urged that women be taught philosophy.[24] In the literature and in the history of Hellenism one encounters women rulers, women merchants, women property owners, women priestesses. While women were excluded from some cults and festivals, in many others they played a prominent role, notably as ecstatics in the cult of Dionysus and as priestesses of Isis. But patriarchalism was still the rule, and its grip on Hellenistic culture was

21. Bernadette Brooten, *Women Leaders in the Ancient Synagogue,* Brown Judaic Studies 36 (Chico, Calif.: Scholars Press, 1982). Brooten takes note of nineteen inscriptions (from 27 B.C.E. to the sixth century and from Palestine, Italy, Asia Minor, and Egypt) in which women bear the titles of "mother" or "priestess," and she argues convincingly that they are not "honorific" titles but functional titles. I owe this reference to David Deboys, librarian at Tyndale House, Cambridge.

22. This statement is attributed to Thales and Socrates by Diogenes Laertius (*Lives of Eminent Philosophers,* 1.33), to Plato by Plutarch (*Marius* 46.1) and Lactantius (*Divine Institutes,* 3.19.1); cited by Longenecker, *New Testament Social Ethics,* p. 70; see also Wayne A. Meeks, "The Image of the Androgyne: Some Uses of a Symbol in Earliest Christianity," *History of Religion* 13 (1974): 165-208; p. 167, nn. 7-8.

23. Aristotle, *Politics,* I, 1254b; on this see David Balch, *Let Wives Be Submissive: The Domestic Code in I Peter,* SBLM 26 (Chico, Calif.: Scholars Press, 1981), pp. 33-38.

24. Cora E. Lutz, *Musonius Rufus: "The Roman Socrates"* (New Haven: Yale University Press, 1947); see Abraham Malherbe, *Moral Exhortation, A Greco-Roman Sourcebook* (Philadelphia: Westminster, 1986), pp. 132-34, 152-54; also William Klassen, "Musonius Rufus, Jesus, and Paul: Three First-Century Feminists," in *From Jesus to Paul: Studies in Honor of Francis Wright Beare,* ed. Peter Richardson and John C. Hurd (Waterloo, Ont.: Wilfred Laurier University Press, 1984), pp. 185-200.

firm. Just how firm can perhaps be gathered from the letter of a certain Hilarian to Alis, his wife: "When you are delivered, if it is a male, let it live, but if it is a female, cast it out."[25]

The sexual practice of Greece and Rome was also marked by patriarchalism, reducing women to their utility to men. Wealthy men in the Greek world, according to Athenaeus anyway,[26] kept "mistresses for pleasure, concubines for daily concubinage, and wives . . . in order to produce children legitimately and to have a trustworthy guardian of our domestic property." Poor men had fewer options, but there were plenty of lower-class prostitutes and brothels, especially in a harbor town like Corinth.[27] The Jewish suspicion of Gentile immorality was not altogether unfounded. The sexual world of Greek culture was much more tolerant of practices which Jewish piety condemned as immoral. The patriarchalism of the Greek sexual world was also reflected in the double standard that demanded a much higher standard of sexual morality from wives than from husbands. Where there was more freedom for women — and there was more freedom the further west one went — the standard of sexual morality did not improve, even though the double standard diminished.[28]

There were, to be sure, attempts to reform the sexual world of Greece and Rome in the first century. Frequently the attempts at reform had an ascetic impulse, repudiating sexual intercourse as well as sexual immorality, renouncing the flesh as that which tethers the human spirit to this world and prevents it from attaining its essentially divine nature. Apollonius of Tyana, for example, a barefoot wanderer and charismatic teacher and healer who exhorted the common people to improve their sexual morals, himself renounced wine, meat, and marriage.[29] The ascetic view of sex in Apollonius and other Neo-Pythagorean teachers nurtured the ideals of continence and spiritual marriage in first-century Hellenism. The condemnations of sexual immorality by Stoics were also rooted in the attempt to free men from the passions. The most notable of the first-century Stoic reformers, perhaps, was Musonius of Rome, who held that all sexual intercourse outside of marriage was wrong and that marriage,

25. Adolf Deissman, *Light from the Ancient East* (New York: Doran, 1927), p. 168.

26. *Deipnosophistae,* XIII, 573b; see also Pseudo-Demosthenes's speech against Neaira (59, 122) cited by Oepke, *"gunē,"* p. 778.

27. The Greek word coined from the name of that city, *corinthiazesthai,* meant "to fornicate."

28. The decadent behavior of Roman women is satirized by Juvenal, *The Sixteen Satires,* VI.

29. Philostratus, *The Life of Apollonius of Tyana,* trans. F. D. Conybeare, Loeb Classical Library (Cambridge, Mass.: Harvard University Press, 1960).

while including sexual intercourse for the sake of procreation, is sustained by the spiritual communion of equal partners.[30]

The patriarchalism of first-century Palestine was neither without relief by appreciation for women as wives and mothers, nor without challenge by reform movements within Judaism, nor without parallel in the social world of Greece and Rome; but first-century Palestine *was* thoroughly patriarchal.

Remembering the Handmaid's Son[31]

Against the background of first-century Palestine, against the background of the sort of past Atwood's Gilead was drawn from, I would proceed boldly now "by way of reminder" to tell again the tale of a handmaid's son.

Jesus was born of Mary, the "handmaiden" of God (Luke 1:48 RSV). In the song of joy attributed to her by Luke (the "Magnificat," Luke 1:46-55) Mary not only delighted in God's taking notice of "the low estate of his handmaiden" (1:48 RSV) but also in God's regard for all of those who are oppressed. She rejoiced in God's project of humbling the exalted and exalting the humble, of feeding the hungry and sending the rich away empty (1:52-55), and she saw the birth of her son as the beginning of the decisive episode in which God would accomplish that project.

The song of Mary stood squarely within Jewish piety. It was reminiscent of Hannah's song (1 Sam. 2:1-10). It remembered God's mercy to Israel and the promises "to Abraham and to his descendents forever" (Luke 1:54-55). Her song shared the confidence of Jewish piety that God would hear the cries of those who hurt and would answer them. Although her voice was not raised in explicit protest against first-century patriarchalism, it stood against patriarchalism as surely as it stood within Jewish piety. Her confidence in God led her to raise her voice against all the hurt one human being can cause another and to raise her voice *as* a woman. It was within such a Jewish piety that Mary raised her voice, and it was within such a Jewish piety that Mary also raised her son.

This handmaiden's son came preaching that the future rule of God had "come near" (Mark 1:15), and already during his life he made its power felt in his works and words. And in those works and words it was clear that the good

---

30. See note 24.

31. On Jesus' attitude toward women, see also, in addition to the literature in note 1, Michael Cosby, *Sex in the Bible* (Englewood Cliffs, N.J.: Prentice Hall, 1984), pp. 84-102, and Rachel Wahlberg, *Jesus According to a Woman* (New York: Paulist, 1975).

future of a gracious God — and the present power of that future — had consequences for the ways gender and sexuality were understood and practiced.

In God's coming sovereignty, Jesus said, "many who are first will be last, and the last will be first" (Matt. 19:30; Mark 10:31; cf. Luke 13:30). And he not only announced that future; he made its power felt. He made the last first. He exalted the humble and the humiliated. Those who did not count for very much in first-century Palestine counted with Jesus. Women counted with Jesus. The ways in which patriarchal structures ground women down and reduced them to their utility to men were rejected by Jesus, rejected by his vision of the coming cosmic sovereignty of God and by his words and his deeds.

Jesus broke convention simply by talking publicly with women. He talked with a Samaritan woman (John 4:1-26), and the disciples "were astonished that he was speaking with a woman" (John 4:27). It was astonishing and offensive, scandalous, but a future far different from Gilead was making its power felt. And it made its power felt again when the testimony of this woman was heard and believed (John 4:39). Jesus taught women and instructed them. Mary of Bethany welcomed the future Jesus announced and assumed a position of equality with the male disciples, sitting at Jesus' feet in the posture of any good rabbinic student (Luke 10:39; cf. Acts 22:3), listening to Jesus teach. And when Martha complained, imploring Jesus to tell Mary to leave the circle of the disciples and to return to the conventional domestic role of helping with the preparation of the food, Jesus would have none of it (Luke 10:38-42).

The future he promised made its power felt not only when Jesus taught women but also when he was taught *by* a woman. A Syrophoenician woman (Matt. 15:21-28; Mark 7:24-30)[32] came to Jesus (interrupting his rest, according to Mark) to plead for her daughter. Jesus turned her down and turned her away when he said, "Let the children be fed first, for it is not fair to take the children's food and throw it to the dogs" (Mark 7:27). The woman was turned down because she was a Gentile, a dog; God's good future was intended for God's children, for the Jews. Jesus' reply would have silenced most; most would have crept away like rebuked puppies with their tails between their legs. But this remarkable woman answered Jesus, wittily turning his reply to her daughter's advantage. By cleverly switching the image from a frugal father to a richly abundant table she reminded Jesus that the goodness of the God whose future he proclaimed was

---

32. On this story see Sharon Ringe, "A Gentile Woman's Story," in *Feminist Interpretation of the Bible,* ed. Letty M. Russell (Philadelphia: Westminster, 1985), pp. 65-72; Elizabeth Moltmann, "Jesus Christ — the Humanity of God," *Perspectives* 4, no. 7 (Sept. 1989), pp. 7-9; and James Brownson, "Confronting the Text as Alien Object," *Perspectives* 4, no. 7 (Sept. 1989): 11-13.

broad enough and abundant enough to include even those who don't count for much, even the dogs. "Even the dogs under the table," she said, "eat the children's crumbs" (Mark 7:28). And Jesus learned. He learned something more of what it meant to be the sort of Christ who brings a future where the humiliated are exalted, where the last are first, where the outcast and despised are included at the eschatological banquet table. He learned from a woman, and he did not rebuke her for being presumptuous, for forgetting her place as a woman or as a Gentile. And the future he announced made its power felt when he commended the Syrophoenician woman "for this saying" and healed her daughter.

That was one of the many miracles done on behalf of women (Mark 1:30-31; 5:21-43; Luke 13:10-17; and other passages). In the miracles of Jesus the coming cosmic sovereignty of God already made its power felt, and in the miracles of Jesus for women that coming rule of God made itself known as an inclusive rule, blessing women no less — and no less fully — than men. Women counted no less than men did in the healing ministry of Jesus. The woman who was "bent over" by her infirmity was as worthy of being healed on the Sabbath day (Luke 13:10-17) as the man with "a withered hand" (Mark 3:1-5) — in spite of the Sabbath legislation and in token of the future rest and wholeness of God's people. She was a "daughter of Abraham" (Luke 13:16), and that counted no less with Jesus than being a "son of Abraham" (Luke 19:9).

Still more remarkable, perhaps, were the healing of the woman who had "a flow of blood for twelve years" (Mark 5:25-34 RSV) and the raising of a twelve-year-old girl from the dead (Mark 5:21-24, 35-42). The stories are clearly linked together. The story of raising Jairus's daughter provides an envelope for the story of the woman with the flow of blood. The woman had been menstruating for as long as the child had been alive. She had been ritually unclean for twelve years, cut off from the holy congregation of God's people by her flow of blood for all that time. The "little girl" was twelve, the age Jewish girls became marriageable, the age they began to menstruate. In both cases Jesus became ritually unclean himself, in the first by being touched by a menstruating woman (cf. Lev. 15:19-31) and in the second by touching a corpse (cf. Num. 19:11-13); in spite of such violations of ritual purity, the woman was healed and the child was raised. Menstruation was not intended to be pathological, but it was not to be despised either; the good future Jesus made present in his miracles restored the woman to good health, to regular periods, and restored the little girl to life — and to life *as a woman.*

Jesus commended women (e.g., Mark 12:41-44) and defended women (e.g., Mark 12:40; Luke 7:36-50), but never in a patronizing way, never reducing them to their role in a patriarchal household or to their utility to men. To the woman who cried out from the crowd, "Blessed is the womb that bore you and the breasts that nursed you!" he said, "Blessed rather are those who hear the word of God and obey it" (Luke 11:27-28). In that exchange Jesus rejected the reduction of women to reproductive roles, to the sort of role that was conventionally celebrated; and he summoned the woman in the crowd — and all who heard him — to welcome already a future in which women have access to the word and are treated as agents. Offred would have loved it. Mary of Bethany evidently loved it — and others, too. It was little wonder that women heard him gladly, that they celebrated the great reversal he announced and lived, that they accompanied him even in his suffering (Mark 15:40-47), were present at the empty tomb (Mark 16:1), and gave the first testimony to the resurrection.[33]

And it was little wonder, too, that some — especially among those who counted in first-century Palestine — were scandalized by this Jesus and did not welcome the future he announced and enfleshed. To those who were first, after all, the "promise" was that they "shall be last" — and the concrete command was "be last of all and servant of all" (Mark 9:35; cf. Mark 10:43-44; Luke 22:26). To rejoice in the good future Jesus proclaimed was — and is — to welcome the ways he made it known — and to follow him. He was among them as one who served (Luke 22:27; cf. Mark 10:45; John 13:2-17), and he treated women in nonpatronizing and liberating ways. To rejoice in the good future Jesus pronounced was — and is — to welcome the great reversal Jesus envisioned — and to begin to live it. It was — and is — for men joyfully to surrender the rights and privileges conferred by patriarchalism. "You are not to be called rabbi . . . ," Jesus said. "And call no man your father. . . . Neither be called masters. He who is greatest among you shall be your servant; whoever exalts himself will be humbled, and whoever humbles himself will be exalted" (Matt. 23:8-12 RSV). Thus Jesus challenged the patriarchal world of Palestine and envisioned a different future than Gilead. The future reign of God promised — and was already signaled by — social relations of equality and mutual service, not hierarchical patterns of power and obedience. Some were scandalized by this Jesus. All the Gileads of our past and future have had to silence him. But "blessed is anyone," he said, "who takes no offense at me" (Matt. 11:6; Luke 7:23).

33. Jesus' unconventional and liberating treatment of women is confirmed, it is worth noting, by every criterion brought to the gospels in an attempt to reconstruct "the historical Jesus." It is attested by multiple sources (Mark, Q, the material unique to Luke, and John; the only source in which it is not clearly attested is the material unique to Matthew); it is attested in multiple forms (parable, controversy stories, miracle stories, sayings); it is confirmed if we eliminate the tendencies in the tradition; it is confirmed even on the basis of dissimilarity to Jewish and early church traditions. On these criteria see Allen Verhey, *The Great Reversal: Ethics and the New Testament* (Grand Rapids: Eerdmans, 1984), pp. 9-11.

Some of the priestly aristocracy around Jerusalem took offense at Jesus. They had settled into the good life, funded by fees for their priestly service and from the tenant farmers who worked their land. They did not celebrate the future Christ envisioned. Against his promise of God's victory even over death, they appealed to the law of "levirate marriage" (Mark 12:18-23; cf. Deut. 25:5-10). Suppose, they said, that a woman fails to provide her husband an heir before he dies. The law is that she is given to her husband's brother "so that his name may not be blotted out of Israel" (Deut. 25:6). But suppose that he dies, too. Suppose that there are seven brothers, and that they each marry her in an effort to provide an heir for the first. If they are all raised, they said, an impossible and incestuous and offensive situation would result. "In the resurrection whose wife will she be?" (Mark 12:23), they asked. With that question they thought to dismiss the resurrection and the future Jesus proclaimed. But Jesus replied not only by defending the hope for resurrection but also by challenging the patriarchal marriage traditions on which their dismissal of the resurrection was founded. In the next life, Jesus announced, there would be neither marrying nor giving in marriage (Mark 12:25). When "the power of God" (Mark 12:24) makes itself felt, the relations of men and women are not governed by patriarchal marriages or by a man's necessity to secure for himself a name and an heir; they are governed by the mutuality and equality that belong to God's rule.[34]

Jesus announced the coming reign of God as good news, liberating good news, for women — and for men who are willing to let go of patriarchal privilege and to relate to women as equal partners in response to God's cause. And he made its future power felt in his words and deeds. He did not provide some new social program. He did not propose new legislation to take the place of the Torah and its levirate marriages. He did not announce some alternative kinship system to institutionalize God's future. Nevertheless, the good future of God made its power present in relationships of equality and mutuality. Jesus challenged patriarchal systems and summoned people to welcome the good future of God.

That future made its power felt upon sexual morality as well. In God's future, Jesus said, people "neither marry nor are given in marriage" (Mark 12:25), and already singleness or celibacy was an option (Matt. 19:10-13), signaled by Jesus' own singleness.[35] Marriage was no longer to be regarded as a duty of To-

---

34. See further Schüssler Fiorenza, *In Memory of Her,* pp. 143-45.

35. The argument of William E. Phipps, *Was Jesus Married?* (New York: Harper, 1970), that Jesus was indeed married (like any good first-century Jewish male) is quite unconvincing. See Jewett, *Man as Male and Female,* pp. 105ff.

rah nor as a necessary condition for human fulfillment and divine approval. Celibacy was, however, not regarded as a duty either (Matt. 19:12), and marriage remained a legitimate option.

Indeed, marriage itself could be a place the future power of God would already make its power felt — when it was marked by mutuality and equality rather than by patriarchal power, when husband and wife were "one flesh" (Mark 10:8). "One flesh" includes a sexual relationship, but it cannot be reduced to a sexual relationship, or better, sexual relationships cannot be reduced to a technology of pleasure. "One flesh" — and the sexual relations that express that unity and participate in it — connotes a common human life, a full and equal — and enduring — partnership.

Divorce, which was exclusively a male prerogative in first-century Palestine, was not a way the good future of God made its power felt. The Torah permitted men (and only men) to divorce. The passage is Deuteronomy 24:1-4: "Suppose a man enters into marriage with a woman, but she does not please him because he finds something objectionable about her, and so he writes her a certificate of divorce, puts it in her hand, and sends her out of his house." The rabbis debated the interpretation and application of this statute.[36] Hillel and Shammai disagreed about the meaning of "something objectionable" (Heb. 'erwath dabar). Hillel said that the words must mean "some unseemly thing," and that a man might therefore divorce his wife for any "unseemly thing," for burning the morning toast, for example. Shammai said that the words meant "unchastity," and that a man might therefore divorce his wife only if she had been unchaste. Jesus does not enter this rabbinic dispute about divorce or about the statute concerning it in Deuteronomy 24; he brushes aside the statute as not so much Law as dispensation (Mark 10:2-12 RSV).[37]

The statute was given, he says, for "your hardness of heart" (Mark 10:5); it belonged to the present evil age and was, since the ages are turning, no longer the finally decisive thing. Jesus appealed instead to the narratives of creation (citing Gen. 1:27 and 2:24) and insisted that "what God has joined together, let no one separate" (Mark 10:9). The point was not to provide new Torah, not to establish a new and extremely rigorous statute. The point was to announce the future reign of the creator God — and to summon people to welcome it in marriage as in all other matters. He was not formulating a new moral rule but forming the disposition, the readiness, not to divorce even when the Law (or a

36. Mishnah, Gittin IX.10.

37. It is true that in Matthew's Gospel (Matt. 19:3-9) Jesus is represented as providing an interpretation of Deuteronomy 24:1 that is close to that of Shammai. See below, pp. 229-30, and Verhey, The Great Reversal, pp. 84-85.

self-interested and patriarchal reading of the Law) would permit it. The power of God makes itself felt when husband and wife are "one flesh" and when their marriage endures. The power of sin makes itself felt in divorce and in the patriarchal hegemony of husband over wife (Gen. 3:16). The observation of Genesis 2:24 and of Jesus that "a man leaves his father and his mother and clings to his wife" (cf. Mark 10:7) remarkably cut against the patriarchal assumption that the woman is assimilated into the man's family.[38] The coming cosmic sovereignty of God is at hand and already makes its power felt not in nit-picking observance of patriarchal statutes but in the glad faithfulness of couples who are "one flesh."

Within marriage and within the community, having children remained a blessing of God. Jesus made God's good future present also by his hospitality to children (Mark 10:13-16). Children, too, were among those whom Christ exalted and blessed. Those who did not count for much counted with Jesus. And he made it clear that to welcome him was to welcome children, and that to welcome children was to welcome both Jesus and the reign of God made known in his delight in little ones (Mark 9:37; 10:13-16). Nevertheless, to have children was not a duty, nor a condition for human fulfillment and divine approval, and barrenness was surely not a reason for divorce.[39] *The* child had been born — and to the childless, too. The genealogies had been fulfilled. Therefore, sexual relations are not simply *for* procreation. They gesture and nurture the "one flesh" God has made them.

Adultery, of course, was prohibited. The coming of God's future sovereignty demands, however, here too, the response of the whole person, not just external conformity to the Law. The law against adultery holds, but Jesus is not content with the sort of scribal righteousness that merely puts an external limit on human expressions of lust (or anger or revenge or deceit).[40] Such a law could leave the person quite as lecherous as before and render observance of the law grudging and external. Jesus radicalized the prohibition of adultery to a prohibition of lust (Matt. 5:27-28), a prohibition of any readiness to reduce a human being to sexual object, to an instrument of our sexual satisfaction, even in the imagination. Human beings are to be regarded as joint heirs of the kingdom. Again Jesus is not legislating, not formulating a new and impossibly rigorous moral rule; he is forming character, shaping dispositions of chastity rather than of lust (and of reconciliation rather than anger, forgiveness rather than revenge,

38. Lisa Sowle Cahill, *Between the Sexes: Foundations for a Christian Ethics of Sexuality* (Philadelphia: Fortress, 1985), p. 55.
39. Cf. *Yebamoth* 6:6.
40. See further Verhey, *The Great Reversal*, pp. 21-27.

and truthfulness rather than deceit). Jesus reached and challenged the Gilead within by announcing and performing the good future of God.

Self-righteous men found it difficult to welcome such a kingdom, such a Lord, while those the world reduced to sexual function repented eagerly, received the forgiveness of God, and delighted already in a future quite different from Gilead (e.g., Luke 7:36-50).

CHAPTER TEN

Remembering the Early
Church Remembering Jesus in Gilead:
A Continuing Tradition of Liberation

Atwood's story of Gilead should not be forgotten when we turn our attention to the church remembering Jesus. Atwood displayed the corruption of memory when the Commanders of Gilead seized control over it. She reduced the male monopoly over the interpretation of Scripture to absurdity in Gilead's policy of female illiteracy and in Offred's inability to check the uses of Scripture that reduced her to a fertile womb of Fred. Jesus' reply to the woman in the crowd evidently did not make it into the working canon of the Republic of Gilead. Little wonder! Atwood's story of Gilead, however, for all its absurdity, is a story imaginatively drawn from our own past, from the expropriation of the church's memory by its own powerful men. The story of the church includes its resistance to Gilead in memory of Jesus, but it also includes distortions of the church's memory — and, therefore, of the church's life — when males monopolize the interpretation of Scripture.

The Contributions of Feminist Scholarship

Against the expropriation of the church's memory by its own powerful men — and against the distortions and omissions that result — feminist scholarship has made an enormous contribution.[1] It has made that contribution in

---

1. See, for example, Letty M. Russell, ed., *Feminist Interpretation of the Bible* (Phila-

part by close and careful exegetical work, reexamining some texts frequently used to justify patriarchal practices and forcing attention to some forgotten texts that challenge the patriarchalism of the church.[2] As a result of such work, a better understanding of a text has sometimes emerged. At times, to be sure, no new consensus about how to interpret a crucial passage has resulted. And sometimes, indeed, the result has been merely a struggle in the church using competing "proof texts" (or different interpretations of the same "proof text") as weapons.

The contribution of careful exegetical attention to particular texts is necessarily limited because the texts are always part of a whole. Some imaginative construal of the meaning of the whole is necessary for discernment in the midst of competing interpretations and competing texts. A second contribution of feminist scholars has been that they sometimes offered an account of the wholeness of Scripture, of the wholeness that should govern the interpretation and use of any part of Scripture. And sometimes that account has helped us all to grasp the message of Scripture, to remember Jesus, to see in Jesus and in the writings that testify to him a vision of God's reign and of the *shalom* it brings.[3]

In Elisabeth Schüssler Fiorenza's brilliant book, *In Memory of Her,* feminist scholarship took a third step, a step beyond attempting to "rehabilitate" Scripture after the distortion of centuries of patriarchal interpretation, a step beyond attempting to discern a nonpatriarchal wholeness in these writings. Schüssler Fiorenza claims that the expropriation of the memory of the church by powerful men began very early and left its mark on the canon itself. Indeed, she claims that the canon we have is the product of the triumph of patriarchal traditions in the church over the traditions of liberation represented by Jesus and the community of equals which first remembered him.[4] The moral imperative for interpretation, then, according to Schüssler Fiorenza, is to appeal to women's history and women's experience against the text, to work Jesus and his movement of liberation against the church, its patriarchal structures, and its canon.

delphia: Westminster, 1985), and especially the essays by Margaret Farley, "Feminist Consciousness and the Interpretation of Scripture," and Katherine Doob Sakenfeld, "Feminist Use of Biblical Materials," in that volume (pp. 41-51 and 55-64 respectively).

2. Of much literature I mention only Phyllis Trible, "Depatriarchalising in Biblical Interpretation," *Journal of the American Academy of Religion* 41 (1973).

3. Of much literature again I mention only one, Letty M. Russell, *The Future as Partnership* (Philadelphia: Westminster, 1979), with its emphasis on participation in a community which lives in "anticipation" of a new creation.

4. Elisabeth Schüssler Fiorenza, *In Memory of Her: A Feminist Theological Reconstruction of Christian Origins* (New York: Crossroad, 1985), pp. xv, 53-56.

It is a book of enormous learning and courage. Schüssler Fiorenza challenges "'objective' biblical interpretations" and value-neutrality in biblical studies.[5] She rejects the "objectivity" that Atwood satirized through the expert in Gileadean studies who insisted, "Our job is not to censure but to understand" (383), and whose "objectivity" made him deaf to the Handmaid's tale and disguised his own sexism as scholarship. Schüssler Fiorenza reminds the church of its collusion with oppressive patriarchal structures (even if unwitting) in the name of scholarly objectivity (not to mention its collusion with oppression in the name of spiritual transcendence). And she challenges the churches to read and test Scripture in the light of the memory of Jesus and his advocacy for the poor and the oppressed, including women.

The danger, of course, is clear and real. If one brings a compassion for women in their suffering and a commitment to their liberation from patriarchal structures to the text as a "criterion of appropriateness for biblical interpretation and evaluation of biblical authority claims,"[6] then one risks making the Scripture a secondary authority, subject to the test of moral insights drawn from some more fundamental authority. And, no doubt, some theologies of liberation have uncritically surrendered control of the theology and praxis of the church to an ideological perspective that they have adopted.

The issue of authority or control is an important one. If it must be raised with respect to the project of Schüssler Fiorenza, however, then it must also be raised with respect to the theological projects and biblical interpretation of powerful men in the churches. To criticize Schüssler Fiorenza for a lack of self-criticism in aligning her interpretation with the experiences and interests of women is a little like pointing out the sliver in a neighbor's eye while ignoring the log in the eye of the conventional theology of powerful men. The fundamental question Schüssler Fiorenza puts to conventional interpretation must still be answered: If the memory of Jesus is not neutral about patriarchy, then may our reading of the Scripture that tells of him be "neutral"? If Jesus himself and his earliest community were not content to deal with women in ways conventional to patriarchy, then may his continuing community read Scripture in ways conventional within patriarchy? If the memory of Jesus still sponsors the protest of women against sexism and the hope of women for God's good future, then can the people who find their identity and their hope in that memory be faithful in their reading of Scripture in any other way than by reading it with a readiness to be an advocate for women and to protest against patriarchalism?

---

5. Schüssler Fiorenza, *In Memory of Her*, p. 30.
6. Schüssler Fiorenza, *In Memory of Her*, p. 32.

The danger of surrendering control over the interpretation of Scripture to any extra-biblical criterion remains clear and real. It puts us at risk of forgetfulness, of cutting ourselves off from the story that gives us identity and makes us a community. But perhaps we should think of the authority of Scripture less violently. Margaret Farley has argued that the authority of Scripture rests upon a "recognition" of its truth, that Scripture's authority is "nonviolent," that it does not violate the integrity of the self or contradict our deepest sense of what is good or just.[7] If Farley is right, and I think she is, then the appropriate response to Schüssler Fiorenza's proposal is neither to be content with setting women's experience *against* the text nor to insist on the authority of Scripture *against* the experience of women. The appropriate response is rather to attend to the testimony of women concerning their experience *of* the genuine authority of Scripture, to their "recognition" of the truth of Scripture in their lives. It is in the whole community listening to the whole of Scripture — and to each other! — that we have the best protection against self-serving and rationalizing

7. Farley, "Feminist Consciousness and the Interpretation of Scripture," pp. 42-44. Farley argued not only that this is true for all interpretation and use of Scripture but also "that included in a feminist consciousness are some fundamental convictions [she later identifies two of them as equality and mutuality] so basic and so important that contradictory assertions cannot be accepted by feminists without violence being done to their very understanding and valuations" (p. 44). My own work on the case of Scripture in moral argument has pointed in the same direction. In Verhey, *The Use of Scripture in Moral Argument* (Ph.D. Thesis, Yale University, 1975), I described the logic of appeals to Scripture in the work of Walter Rauschenbusch and Carl F. H. Henry. Both affirm the authority of Scripture, but they use it in moral argument in quite different ways. When they would defend their use of Scripture, they can and do provide arguments — appealing to judgments about the nature of Scripture, the questions appropriate to it, its message, the relevance of other sources, and to criteria like consistency and non-idiosyncrasy — but they also appeal finally to their own experience of the authority of Scripture and attempt to evoke a similar experience in their readers. Particular ways of understanding and using Scripture are justified not at the end of an argument as much as in the midst of life, where experience of the authority of Scripture both can make Scripture vivid and alive and can illuminate and unify the moral life in particular ways. How Scripture is used depends not just on whether or not it is acknowledged as an "authority" but also on the "authorizations" one provides for appeal to it — and the authorizations depend not just on arguments about the nature and message of Scripture (and the like) but also on an experience of the authority of Scripture which Farley more elegantly calls a "recognition" of Scripture's authority. In *The Great Reversal: Ethics and the New Testament* (Grand Rapids: Eerdmans, 1984), p. 193, I have proposed some rudimentary sense of justice as a test for moral claims based on Scripture and for authorization for the use of Scripture, and by that I mean the sort of sense of equality and mutuality which Farley spells out much more eloquently.

uses of Scripture, the best protection against the proud reading of Scripture over-against others rather than over-against ourselves, the best protection against forgetfulness.

It is when Schüssler Fiorenza calls for a "church of women" that the danger is upon us. She recognizes, to be sure, that a "church of women does not share in the fullness of church," but she insists that "neither do exclusive male hierarchical assemblies."[8] That is certainly correct, but it hardly makes "separate but equal" an acceptable substitute for one community of mutual commitment and admonition. "Separate but equal" may be understandable as a response to "separated, silenced, and subordinated" (and even indicated as a strategy in response to such a Gilead). It is not, however, to remember Jesus, not at least in the way I judge this handmaiden's son longs to be remembered. And it is not to signal the good future of God. As a strategic decision it signals the "not yet" character of our lives and communities. One whole community of female and male listening to Scripture and to each other — muting neither Scripture nor each other — that is to remember Jesus and to image God's good future.

It cannot be denied that the New Testament is the words of men; indeed, it cannot be denied that it is (at least largely)[9] the words of males, or that the patriarchal world in which they lived lived in them as well. But it also ought not be denied — not in the Christian community, at any rate — that the New Testament is the Word of God. When Schüssler Fiorenza sets her historical reconstruction of Jesus and his community against the text and the patriarchalism it represents, she comes dangerously close to the dismissal of Scripture as merely "the words of men." It must be noted that she does *not* make the move of Elaine Pagels. She and Pagels agree that "the winners write the histories,"[10] and they agree, moreover, that in the church the "winners" were patriarchalists; but Pagels finally prefers the Gnostic traditions to the canonical tradition.[11] Schüssler Fiorenza knows better than this

---

8. Schüssler Fiorenza, *In Memory of Her,* p. 346.

9. A few scholars have expressed an opinion that women wrote certain parts of the New Testament. The most plausible case — and the oldest — is that Priscilla was the author of Hebrews; see Adolf von Harnack, "Probabilia über die Addresse und den Verfasser des Hebräerbriefs," *Zeitschrift für die Neutestamentliche Wissenschaft* 1 (1900): 16-41.

10. Elaine Pagels, *The Gnostic Gospels* (New York: Random House, 1979; Vintage Books Edition), p. 170; Schüssler Fiorenza, *In Memory of Her,* p. xix.

11. Pagels adopts, to be sure, the pretense of historical "objectivity": "the task of the historian, as I understand it, is not to advocate any side, but to explore the evidence" (p. 180). For an extended criticism of Pagels's account of Gnosticism from the point of view of another scholar who prizes "objectivity" in historical scholarship, see Susanne

— and does better than this. She knows that Gnosticism was as thoroughly patriarchal as the patristic theologians who resisted it.[12] She knows that even if Gnostic texts can be found which sound as if they are "for" women, they are "against" the creation, "against" the body, and "against" the church's memory of Jesus, preferring a heavenly revealer who unveils a secret knowledge which saves us *from* the world of our embodiment, our gender and sexuality, not within it. Schüssler Fiorenza does better by attending carefully to the New Testament itself for "a glimpse of the egalitarian-inclusive practice and theology of early Christians."[13] She finds glimpses of an early egalitarian and inclusive community in the very passages that restrain such impulses and retrieve a more patriarchal rule for the community from Jewish or Hellenistic traditions. She utilizes a vision drawn from the canonical New Testament texts in order to criticize the New Testament itself. Schüssler Fiorenza attends to the canon as the place we can learn to remember Jesus, but she would then work the memory of Jesus *against* the canon, dismissing the canonical text as human — and male — words.

I admit that there are (at least largely) male voices in the New Testament, but I claim that these human and male words are, nevertheless, the Word of God. That claim does not license the simple identification of any of the human words with divine words. It will not permit, for example, the simple repetition of a biblical set of rules for a first-century household as an eternal divine code, or the use of those human and male words to silence women today or to mute their voices. Such an understanding and use of the canon, by confusing the human words with the divine word and transmitting the human words into divine words, violates the rule of Chalcedon for the conjunction of the divine and the human.[14] The rule of Chalcedon does not permit the church simply to identify the human words of Scripture with the Word of God (and so to use some patriarchal texts to mute women) — but neither does it allow the church to select some part of Scripture or some revelation behind Scripture as the Word of God and then simply to contrast the human (and male) words of

---

Heine, *Women and Early Christianity,* trans. John Bowden (Minneapolis: Augsburg, 1988).

12. Schüssler Fiorenza, *In Memory of Her,* p. 274.

13. Schüssler Fiorenza, *In Memory of Her,* p. 56.

14. The Definition of Chalcedon (451) said that the divine and human natures of Christ are to be affirmed "without confusing the two natures [*asunkutōs*], without transmuting one nature into the other [*atreptōs*], without dividing them into two separate categories [*adiairetōs*], without contrasting them according to area or function [*achoristōs*]." John Leith, ed., *Creeds of the Churches,* third ed. (Atlanta: John Knox, 1982), pp. 35-36. See further Verhey, *The Great Reversal,* pp. 169-74.

Scripture with that divine word (and so to mute Scripture itself). Chalcedon points toward some "middle way."[15] That there are (largely) male voices in the New Testament cannot be denied, but it is still the place we all learn to remember Jesus. That they are words of men is not to be denied, but they are, I judge, the words of men whose prejudice against the testimony of women has been broken and who struggle against the Gileads within and without. As such human words they are the Word of God.

The Sort of Story Women Tell and Luke's Gospel

The human (and male) words of the New Testament are the words of men whose prejudice against the testimony of women has been broken. Witness, for example, the words of Luke. He tells the story of the empty tomb and of the women who visited it and told their story to the apostles. "But these words seemed to them an idle tale, and they did not believe them" (Luke 24:11). The first crucial question for the apostles was whether to believe the testimony of these women. At first they did not believe it. It seemed an "idle tale," the sort of story women tell, confirmation of the decision of a patriarchal society not to count their testimony in a trial, surely not in a capital trial, where life and death were at stake. But it was a true story, the story on which they and the church finally staked their lives. This testimony of these women was to be believed.

The prejudice against the testimony of women was broken, and the words of this man tell a story in which women — and their testimony — count. It is to Mary, not to Joseph, that the angel appears with the message of Jesus' birth (1:26-38). Elizabeth plays as prominent a role as Zechariah does (1:5-25). Anna, the pious old prophetess, stands alongside Simeon welcoming and announcing the arrival of the one in whom ancient promises would be kept (2:25-38). The widow of Zarephath is mentioned along with the great Naaman as a Gentile to whom God had been gracious in the past (4:25-27). In Luke's remembering of Jesus' healing ministry he adds to the already remarkable number of instances in Mark in which women figure prominently (e.g., 7:11-17; 8:2; 13:10-17, a "daughter of Abraham"). In his account of Jesus' teaching, women are taught (e.g., 10:39; 11:27; 23:27-31, "daughters of Jerusalem"), and their behavior is used to teach (e.g., 15:8-10; 18:1-8; 21:1-4).

Moreover, in Luke's account of the early church, women play an important role (e.g., Acts 1:14). Joel's promise that daughters and sons shall prophesy

---

15. Louis Jacobs, *Principles of the Jewish Faith* (New York: Basic Books, 1964); see Verhey, *The Great Reversal,* pp. 159-60.

is fulfilled (Acts 2:17; cf. Joel 2:28; see also Acts 21:9 and Luke 2:36-38). In the early church, according to Acts, women are ministered to — in charity (Acts 6:1) and in teaching (16:11-15) — and women minister, in charity (like Dorcas, 9:36), in hospitality (like Mary, John Mark's mother, 12:2; and Lydia, 16:14-15), and in teaching (like Priscilla, 18:26).[16]

When Henry Cadbury describes Luke's interest in women as "artistic or domestic or sentimental,"[17] the problem is with Henry Cadbury, not with Luke. Luke's interest in women is governed by his memory of Jesus. Because he remembers Jesus, he is captured by a Spirit that had "anointed" Jesus as the Christ (i.e., as the "anointed one"), "to bring good news to the poor" and "to let the oppressed go free" (Luke 4:18). And in the first century, women were among the poor and the oppressed. When Mary, "the handmaiden of the Lord," is exalted, her "Magnificat" (Luke 1:46-55) can hardly be called "domestic" or "sentimental." Luke, in fact, rejects the domestic sentimentality of the voice from the crowd, "Blessed is the womb that bore you" (Luke 11:27). And when Cadbury describes Luke's account of Mary and Martha as "the characteristic temperamental differences of two spinster ladies,"[18] he ignores the contrast between conventional role assignments and Jesus' unconventional treatment of women. The words of Luke are the words of a man, to be sure, but the words of a man formed and nurtured by the testimony of women and by the story of Jesus. His male interpreters should do so well against the Gileads within.

Luke does not provide legal regulations to govern the place of women in the church. He has no social program. But the testimony of the women at the tomb is to be trusted. Luke owns and tells the story of Jesus, and the readers who make his story their own are called to resist the Gilead within, to attend to the testimony of women; they are no longer determined by conventional role assignments or by sentimental prejudices but formed by Jesus' unconventional and unsentimental behavior toward women.

The prejudice against the testimony of women is broken, but it does not suddenly, automatically, and miraculously disappear. All the gospels agree that it was women (or a woman, Mary Magdalene) who visited the tomb and found it empty, and more than one source (Matthew and John) attest that women were the first witnesses of a risen Christ, but the pre-Pauline tradition in 1 Co-

---

16. Leonard Swidler, *Biblical Affirmations of Women* (Philadelphia: Westminster, 1979), even suggests that Luke's special materials come from a source that may have been written by a woman, giving further evidence that Luke has broken the prejudice against the testimony of women.

17. Henry Cadbury, *The Making of Luke–Acts* (New York: Macmillan, 1927), p. 263.

18. Cadbury, *The Making of Luke–Acts,* p. 264.

rinthians 15:3-6 does not mention women: first "he appeared to Cephas, then to the twelve" (15:5). And Luke himself, evidently to conform to this tradition, preserves the priority of the appearance to Simon Peter, i.e., Cephas (Luke 24:34). These are male words in the New Testament, and they are not empty of the conventional prejudices against the testimony of women.[19] Even so, the prejudice has been broken by the story of Jesus and by the story women told about his resurrection — and that is the decisive thing.

Struggling to Put on Christ in Gilead

The prejudice against the testimony of women was broken, but the New Testament is not altogether empty of it. The social and sexual world in which these men lived — and which lived in them! — did not suddenly and simply vanish. Nevertheless, in memory of Jesus they struggled against the Gilead within, and that struggle left its mark both on them and on the New Testament. And in memory of Jesus the early Christian communities struggled against the Gileads without. The patriarchal world in which these men — and these communities — lived was impossible simply to escape. The early church could not snap its fingers and create *ex nihilo* new role relations and social structures. The social and sexual world in which they lived would not simply go away. But neither would the memory of Jesus. And although Jesus provided no social program, no alternative kinship system, because they remembered Jesus, they envisioned a different world, a world of God's unchallenged cosmic sovereignty, a world with Jesus at the right hand of God, a world in which there "is no longer male and female" (Gal. 3:28). They struggled to bring the world in which they lived into conformity to the world they envisioned, and the struggle was the critical thing.[20] That struggle against the Gilead without left its mark on the New Testament, too.

19. Indeed, here and there in the New Testament this conventional prejudice against the testimony of women seems to be sponsored; e.g., especially 1 Timothy 2:12 and 1 Corinthians 14:34-35; on these passages see below.

20. The model here is the religious transformation of social interactions or, more modestly, the religious qualification of existing structures and relationships. This is the model Elisabeth Schüssler Fiorenza adopts as well; see p. 92 of *In Her Memory*. She presumes, however, that the historical choices open to the churches can be adequately described by simply juxtaposing patriarchy and a community of coequal disciples. These ideal types are simply played off against each other and, in her account, one of them is swallowed up and nearly destroyed in the course of early church history. It is not unlike (or unrelated to) the overly simple contrast between charismatic and institutional authoritarian accounts of the early church's history. That overly simple contrast has been chal-

To be sure, there is always some distance between their vision and the historical realization of their vision. And in some early Christian communities and in some texts of the New Testament there was more distance than in others. Nevertheless, in memory of Jesus and in the hope for the cosmic sovereignty of God that Jesus promised, they continued to envision a community of mutuality and equality, and that memory and hope continued to evoke a struggle against Gilead. And where the church remembers Jesus, the struggle against Gilead continues.

Baptism: Putting on Christ in Gilead

When people were baptized in the early church, they were initiated into Christ and into the body of Christ. They were baptized "into Christ Jesus" (Rom. 6:3), into his death and resurrection, indeed, into his death and resurrection as events that were of one piece with the eschatological events of the final judgment and the resurrection of the dead. Baptism was an act of God; God brought the believer both into judgment (together with Christ) and safely through it (together with Christ)[21] into "newness of life" (Rom. 6:4), into a "new creation" (Gal. 6:15), into a new community in which "there is no longer Jew or Greek, . . . slave or free, . . . male and female" (Gal. 3:28). Baptism was also, of course, an act of the church, an act in memory of Jesus and in hope for God's good future, an act of faith, an act of receiving the grace of God and the promise of God by welcoming those who were different into a community of mutuality and equality. And the ones being baptized acted, too, of course. They

---

lenged by Bengt Holmberg, *Paul and Power: The Structure of Authority in the Primitive Church as Reflected in the Pauline Epistles* (Philadelphia: Fortress, 1980); he concludes that in the Pauline churches one can see not only the authority of "charisma" but also the authority of "office." Moreover, he concludes that the person with charismatic authority is as likely to be the initiator of institutional authority as its victim and that persons with institutional authority are likely still to recognize (and claim) charismatic authority. Charismatic authority seeks institutional realization; institutional authority seeks to retain charism. The real choice for the early church was not either charismatic authority or institutional authority but how to shape and reshape authority in the church both to preserve freedom and to provide a different kind of freedom, freedom from an unstructured common life. Similarly, in my view, the real choice for the early church was not either a community of coequal discipleship or patriarchy but how to shape and reshape a common life that was both historically realizable and faithful to a new vision of equality and mutuality.

21. See further C. F. D. Moule, "The Judgment Theme in the Sacraments," in *The Background of the New Testament and Its Eschatology,* ed. W. D. Davies and D. Daube (Cambridge: Cambridge University Press, 1964), pp. 464-81.

"put off" their old patterns of conduct, and they "put on" Christ. They renounced "all wickedness" (cf. Eph. 4:31; Col. 3:8; James 1:21; 1 Pet. 2:1), and they clothed themselves with Christ, "with the new self, created according to the likeness of God in true righteousness and holiness" (Eph. 4:24; cf. Col. 3:9). Such actions were probably related to the ritual disrobing and robing that accompanied baptism in the early church. The ones being baptized owned the story of Jesus as their own story, owned his death to sin as their death to sin, owned his resurrection as their hope. They remembered Jesus, and in memory of Jesus they assumed a new moral identity in Christ and a new community in Christ. In baptism they "put on Christ" (Gal. 3:27), and in Christ "there is no longer Jew or Greek, . . . slave or free, . . . male and female; for all of you are one in Christ Jesus" (Gal. 3:28).

Galatians 3:26-28 was already a traditional baptismal declaration when Paul reminded the Galatians of it.[22] Paul's citation of the tradition was an instance of "ethics by way of reminder." A new identity was owned in baptism, and a new world was envisioned — an identity and a world in which sexual hierarchies (along with ethnic and class hierarchies) were radically subordinated to community and equality in Christ.

There remained, of course, male and female (and Jew and Greek and slave and free), and the Gilead without did not go away. "No longer male and female" was an eschatological reality, but it made its power felt already in the mutuality and equality of members of the community and in a sexual ethic that honored singleness and chastity. The churches remembered Jesus — and watched for him — and struggled against the Gileads without and within. They struggled to give some communal embodiment, some fleshly consequence, to their eschatological unity and equality in Christ. They struggled to put on Christ in Gilead.

Ministry: Paul's Colleagues

The memory and hope of the church were given communal embodiment when women were colleagues in ministry. Paul, for example, says of Euodia and Syntyche that they worked "side by side with me in the gospel" (Phil. 4:3 RSV), and he counts them among his "co-workers" in the mission of God. And Paul evidently regarded many other women as colleagues: Priscilla (Acts 18:26; Rom. 16:3-5; 1 Cor. 16:19), Phoebe (Rom. 16:1-2), Mary (Rom. 16:6), Tryphaena and

22. See Richard N. Longenecker, *New Testament Social Ethics for Today* (Grand Rapids: Eerdmans, 1984), pp. 30-33; Hans Dieter Betz, *Galatians: A Commentary on Paul's Letter to the Churches in Galatia* (Philadelphia: Fortress, 1979), pp. 181-201.

Tryphosa (Rom. 16:12), Persis (Rom. 16:12), Junia (Rom. 16:7), and others. These women have not always been fairly treated by biblical scholars and translators. Phoebe, for example, is described as a *diakonos* by Paul (like Paul himself and Apollos in 1 Cor. 3:5), but the RSV arbitrarily rendered this masculine form into a special order of "deaconess" (Rom. 16:1). Phoebe is also described as a *prostatis,* as one who "stands before"; the word is sometimes used for a presiding officer, but the RSV translation simply described Phoebe as a "helper" (Rom. 16:2). Junia was treated even less well; she was made into a male. Her identification as a noteworthy *woman* among the apostles was hidden behind the translation: "Greet Andronicus and Junias, my kinsmen and my fellow prisoners; they are men of note among the apostles" (Rom. 16:7 RSV).[23] The early church did better at remembering Jesus against the Gilead within than some subsequent male interpreters and translators.

Praying and Prophesying: 1 Corinthians 11

The mutuality and equality of men and women in this community was also given communal embodiment in the participation of women in worship, praying, and prophesying (1 Cor. 11:2-16). It is well known, of course, that in this passage Paul objected to the behavior of some of the Corinthian women when they prayed and prophesied — and that later (in 14:34) he said, indeed, that women should "be silent." These passages are difficult to reconcile with each other — and more difficult still to reconcile with either Paul's practice of collegiality with women in ministry or his eschatological vision that in Christ there is no male and female. They are not easy to understand, but some attempt must be made.

Paul's advice in 1 Corinthians 11, it must first of all be observed, is far from prohibiting the full and equal participation of women in the life of the church. On the contrary, Paul here assumes that women may exercise leadership in public worship as well as men. The parallel construction of his advice is eloquent testimony to that assumption: "Any man who prays or prophesies . . . , any woman who prays or prophesies . . ." (11:4, 5). No argument is given for the participation of women in worship because no argument is required; Paul and the Corinthian church agree about this fundamental point. Indeed, when at the

---

23. See Schüssler Fiorenza, *In Memory of Her,* pp. 47, 172. The NRSV corrects this translation and acknowledges that Junia was a woman. See also Bernadette Brooten, "Junia . . . Outstanding Among the Apostles," in *Women Priests,* ed. L. and A. Swidler (New York: Paulist, 1977), pp. 141-44.

beginning of this section Paul commends the church for remembering him and for maintaining the traditions which he "delivered" to them, we must surely understand those traditions to include the baptismal tradition that in Christ "there is no longer male and female" (Gal. 3:28). He comes back to that tradition and reiterates it in verses 11 and 12: "Nevertheless, in the Lord woman is not independent of man or man independent of woman. For just as woman came from man, so man comes through woman, but all things come from God." Paul sets this anti-patriarchal tradition before and behind his more narrowly focused argument. It provides the context within which Paul writes and the context within which the Corinthian church — and the contemporary church — must attempt to understand Paul and to discern a fitting response to the gifted women in its midst.

The issue in 1 Corinthians 11, however, is much more narrowly focused than whether women may exercise some role of leadership in the community's worship. Paul's concern is evidently that, when women do pray and prophesy, they must preserve a certain decorum. Just what behavior Paul thought indecorous it is now impossible to say with certainty. The NRSV and the traditional interpretation have taken Paul's concern to be that the women who pray and prophesy should be "veiled." But there is no explicit reference to a "veil" in the Greek, and a full veil, which covers everything but the eyes, was unknown in antiquity. Some[24] have taken the issue to be another form of external covering, like a shawl or a linen cloth to be worn on the head. Partly on the basis of the remark that "her hair is given to her for a covering" (1 Cor. 11:15), some commentators[25] have suggested that Paul's concern was that the women who pray and prophesy should not cut or unbind their hair. Paul's general concern, of course, is that in the worship of the congregation "things should be done decently and in order" (14:40). But what is indecent or disorderly about an uncovered head or unbound hair? The narrow issue, whether an issue of veils or of coiffure, seems to most contemporary readers to be as quaint and strange as blaming Asa for consulting a physician.

We may never know precisely what the particular issue was or precisely

24. Gordon D. Fee, *The First Epistle to the Corinthians* (reprint; Grand Rapids: Eerdmans, 1991 [1987]), pp. 491-530.

25. W. J. Martin, "I Cor. 11:2-16: An Interpretation," in *Apostolic History and the Gospels,* ed. W. W. Gasque and R. P. Martin (Grand Rapids: Eerdmans, 1970), pp. 231-34, takes the view that the issue was that some women were having their hair cut short. Schüssler Fiorenza, *In Memory of Her,* pp. 227-28, and J. Murphy-O'Connor, "Sex and Logic in I Corinthians 11:2-16," *Catholic Biblical Quarterly* 42, no. 4 (Oct. 1980): 482-500, see pp. 488-89, argue, I think compellingly, that the issue was that some women were letting their hair down, loosening it in public.

why Paul objected to the practice of these women, but it does seem clear that he considered their behavior another instance of the elitist spirituality that threatened the Corinthian church. The Corinthian church was disrupted and its worship disordered by the ecstatic behaviors and utterances of certain spiritually gifted individuals. These evidently considered themselves already fully "spiritual," already "angels," on the basis of their spiritual gifts. They looked down on others who were less "gifted," including Paul evidently. Paul did not deny that these individuals were "gifted" — but he objected in the strongest possible terms when they turned God's gifts into occasions for boasting or envy or strife and when they turned worship into an occasion for the self-serving display of their spirituality. Paul did not deny that these individuals were gifted, but he would not let them deny that each other member of the Corinthian church was also gifted. Even that one whom many regarded as a spiritual clod because all she did was join in making the confession of the church, "Jesus is Lord" (1 Cor. 12:3), was gifted by the Spirit of God. Each is gifted (12:7, 11), and to each their own!

By itself that should undercut the pride of the enthusiasts and diminish the envy of the more extraordinary gifts. But Paul makes a second point: "To each is given the manifestation of the Spirit *for the common good*" (12:7, emphasis added). The mark of the Spirit's gifts is not mere ecstasy, but service to the community, ministry. The Spirit that comes from God binds us to Jesus, to his cross, and to his reign. According to the pattern laid down in the memory of Jesus, the greatest gift and the test for any other is love (12:31–14:1). The Spirit's work and gifts enable members of Christ's body to minister to each other and to the world; they do not license elitist assertions of independence. The same baptismal tradition that challenges patriarchalism affirms that "all of you are one in Christ Jesus" (Gal. 3:28; cf. also 1 Cor. 12:12-13). To be in Christ is to be in community. As there are diverse gifts, so there are diverse ministries. Paul permits — and requires — all to minister in their own ways. But he permits no one to boast about his eloquence or knowledge or ecstacy or to deny the gifts and the ministry of simply sharing bread with the hungry or time with the lonely or a laugh with the disheartened or faith with the doubting or a simple rational point within the community in discourse. Such everyday and mundane workings of care and patience and community are also gifts that the one Spirit gives and are much more fitting to the pattern and memory of the one Lord.

Among the spiritually gifted at Corinth there were some women whose display of their gifts during worship was indistinguishable from the ecstatic utterances and behavior of the women in the cults of Dionysus or Isis. Their elitism, their claims to be already fully spiritual, their protestations of independence from the community and from conventional proprieties — all of it evidently worried Paul. He could not abide their eschatological claim that they were already fully "spiritual" or their construal of Christian freedom as license or their denial of Christian community by their displays of independence.

Paul attempts to convince the church not to tolerate the excesses of these women by a wide variety of appeals — to the Torah (1 Cor. 11:7-9), to nature (11:14), and finally to ecclesiastical custom (11:16). The specific arguments are notoriously difficult to comprehend, but the first one is especially important for the support it has been taken to provide to Gilead within the church. In it Paul seems to interpret Genesis 2 (badly) as providing a creation order that requires patriarchal structures. That man is the "head" of woman is taken by some to be a metaphorical way of saying that men should rule over women and that women should be subordinate to men. In Greek, however, *kephalē* ("head") does *not* generally have that meaning; it does, however, frequently refer to "source."[26] Paul is not using Genesis 2 (and the story of the creation of the woman from man as a source) to establish certain hierarchical authority structures. On the contrary, he is using it to say that, when women participate fully and equally in the congregation's life, they should not do so in ways that deny their community with men or their interdependence with men. He distinguishes man and woman to provide some basis for the practice he wants the Corinthians to follow, but he does not defend what has sometimes been called the "headship principle" of male authority and female submission. If he did, he could hardly have authorized the women with bound hair (or with veils) to lead the church.

Paul seems to be worried that some may misunderstand him in precisely the way patriarchal readers have misunderstood him, for he reiterates the tradition of Galatians 3:28 and asserts that the interdependence is mutual, that "in the Lord woman is not independent of man or man independent of woman" (1 Cor. 11:11). And to be quite sure that his argument about the sequence of creation will not be misrepresented to deny the equality of men and women or their unity within the church, Paul adds one more remark: "For just as woman came from man, so man comes through woman; but all things come from God" (11:12; cf. 3:21-23). "In the Lord" and in common dependence upon God they may find a basis for their mutuality and equality in the church and dismiss any boasting elitism.

---

26. Robin Scroggs, "Paul and the Eschatological Woman: Revisited," *Journal of the American Academy of Religion* 42 (1974): 534, n. 8; L. Ann Jervis, "'But I Want You to Know . . .': Paul's Midrashic Intertextual Response to the Corinthian Worshippers (1 Cor. 11:2-16)," *Journal of Biblical Literature* 112, no. 2 (1993): 231-46, esp. pp. 239-41.

Silencing Women?

Paul's advice to the Corinthians concerning the decorum to be observed when women pray and prophesy makes it even more puzzling that in 1 Corinthians 14:34 he says "women should be silent in the churches." The difficulty of reconciling this passage with 1 Corinthians 11 (and with the role of women as "co-workers" with Paul) has led some to the conjecture that 1 Corinthians 14:33b-36 is an addition to Paul's original letter by a later editor, possibly on the model of 1 Timothy 2:11-12.[27] Whether these passages are from Paul's own hand or not, they are still in Scripture, still to be counted among the texts which we read with the whole of it and in the light of the whole of it.

The argument that 1 Corinthians 14:33b-36 is a non-Pauline addition is not unsubstantial, but neither is it compelling.[28] The passage should be read, I think, as intimately related to the pastoral advice Paul gives the Corinthians in chapter 14. There Paul applies his anti-elitist account of spiritual gifts and of love (in 1 Cor. 12–13) to their gatherings. His concern is evidently still that their gatherings for worship should create not an opportunity for the self-serving display of individual gifts but a service that both builds up the church (14:5, 12, 17, 26) and is accessible to the "outsider" (14:23-25, 16). On that basis Paul much prefers the practice of prophecy in these gatherings to the practice of speaking in tongues. And on the same basis he suggests certain rules for the conduct of worship (14:27-35). The first rule concerns those who speak in tongues: If two or three have already spoken, or if there is no one to interpret, let them "be silent in the church" (*sigatō*, 14:28). The second rule concerns those who prophesy (and as we have seen, women with bound hair are authorized to be in this number): Let them speak in an orderly way; if one has something to say, let the others "be silent" (*sigatō*, 14:30). *All* may prophesy, but not all at once. Only by such an order will all "learn" *(manthanōsin)* and all be exhorted *(parakalōntai,* 14:31; NRSV: "encouraged"). Moreover, those who prophesy must exercise self-control *(hupotassetai,* 14:32). The final rule is that "women should be silent" *(sigatōsan,* 14:34; cf. *sigatō* in 14:28, 30). The rule cannot be read as silencing all speech of all

27. Victor P. Furnish, *The Moral Teachings of Paul: Selected Issues* (Nashville: Abingdon, 1986), pp. 90-92; Hans Conzelmann, *I Corinthians* (Philadelphia: Fortress, 1975); and most convincingly, Gordon D. Fee, *The First Epistle to the Corinthians,* pp. 699-708. Some manuscripts place verses 34 and 35 at the end of the chapter, but no manuscripts of the New Testament omit them.

28. For arguments against reading the passage as a non-Pauline interpolation (and for a fine analysis of the passage itself) see L. Ann Jervis, "1 Corinthians 14:34-35: A Reconsideration of Paul's Limitation of the Free Speech of Some Corinthian Women," *Journal of New Testament Studies* 58 (1995): 51-74.

women in the gatherings of the Corinthian church. Paul has just said that *all* may prophesy (14:31), and earlier (11:2-16), as we have seen, Paul explicitly authorized women with bound hair to prophesy and pray. One wishes the text were clearer about what speech of what women was being prohibited. The Corinthians, of course, probably understood the import of Paul's three rules well enough. They lived with the problem of the disruption of their services. They had asked Paul the question "concerning spiritual gifts" (12:1; or "concerning spiritual persons," as the marginal reading of the NRSV translates it). This much seems certain: some "spiritual" women had evidently used the gatherings to display their status as spiritually gifted, as the elite among the Corinthian Christians. Perhaps the particular problem was an elitist display of the gifts of ecstatic utterance.[29] Perhaps it was simply that some women who regarded themselves as "spiritual" were disrupting the meetings with their self-serving speech.[30] Any speech, whether ecstatic or not, that is "envious or boastful or arrogant or rude," that insists upon "its own way," that is "irritable or resentful" (1 Cor. 13:4-5), Paul would regard as unspiritual and uninspired.[31] These women are to be silent — like the others who threaten to disrupt the worship. Like the prophets they should exercise self-control (*hupotassesthōsan*, 14:34; NRSV: "be subordinate";[32] cf. 14:32 *hupotassetai*). This third rule, too, exists that *all* may learn and that mutual exhortation may take place (14:31). Their silence could be the work of the

29. So Verhey, *The Great Reversal*, pp. 116-17, but Jervis, "1 Corinthians 14:34-35," finds such an explanation unlikely.

30. So Jervis, "1 Corinthians 14:34-35," p. 61.

31. See Jervis, "1 Corinthians 14:34-35," p. 61, where she calls attention to the fact that, although "speech" is qualified as "spiritual" in almost every other place it appears in the chapter (e.g., 14:2, 3, 4, 5, 6, 9, 18, 19, 23, 27, 29), in 14:34-35 "speech" is not so qualified. The distinctive unqualified use serves to identify the speech of these women as "unspiritual."

32. Grammarians disagree about the so-called "reflexive" use of the middle voice of the Greek language, but this seems to be an instance of it: *they* are to subordinate *themselves*, that is, they are to exercise self-control. There is no particular object given (except in codex Alexandrinus, a fifth-century copy, which supplies "to their husbands"), and the implicit contrast is between ecstasy and a self-control that is ordered toward the community's edification. If an object is to be supplied here other than "to themselves," let it be that they subordinate themselves to the community's edification. The "law" referred to here (14:34) may well be the public law that, in response to the excesses of women in Dionysian and other festivals that encouraged ecstasy, required self-control of women and prohibited their participation (Richard and Catherine Clark Kroeger, "Pandemonium and Silence at Corinth," *Reformed Journal*, June 1978, pp. 6-11). Paul's irony, then, would be that if some women insist on construing worship as an ecstatic festival, let them play by the public rules for such festivals.

Spirit, the sign that they were spiritually gifted "for the common good" (12:7). The problem was not that women were speaking but that the speech of these women was not moved by love or oriented to mutual edification.[33]

To be sure, Paul seems to lose patience with these ecstatic women when he says that if they want to learn, "let them ask their husbands at home" (14:35). Indeed, let it be said again that the New Testament is not altogether empty of the prejudice against women. The social and sexual world in which Paul lived — and which lived in him! — did not suddenly and simply vanish. Nevertheless, in memory of Jesus he struggled against Gilead, treating women as colleagues, giving them voice in prayer and prophecy. Paul's "rules" for the worship services of the Corinthians may not be read as establishing patriarchal structures as a timeless and eternal order. They make an *ad hoc* response to the ways in which those worship services were threatened by the self-serving and individualistic display of the spiritual gifts of some members of the Corinthian church, including some women. The abiding principle, if we are looking for one, is not patriarchalism but mutual edification. To use this passage today to silence women in the church is to misuse it, to abuse Paul in the service of Gilead, and to forget Jesus, whom Paul would have us remember.

Let it be admitted that there is some distance between the vision of the mutuality and equality of male and female in Christ and the historical realization of that vision in Corinth and in Paul's advice. We do not know how the Corinthians responded to Paul's letter with respect to this particular point. (We do know that after this letter there was a period of alienation between Paul and the Corinthian church, followed happily by reconciliation; 2 Cor. 2:1-4; 7:13-16.) But it ought to be remembered that the response would be worked out in a conversation that involved women as full and equal partners in the community. I suppose that some women — even some women who were not guilty of the self-serving behaviors and individualistic attitudes that riled Paul — were pushed to the margins of the life of the Corinthian church. But in memory of Jesus and in hope for God's good future they — and the whole church — would and should continue to struggle to put on Christ in Gilead and to resist the Gileads within and without.

A word must yet be said about the Pastoral Epistles and especially about the passage read in Gilead at the "Women's Prayvaganzas," by a man, of course.

> Let a woman learn in silence with full submission. I permit no woman to teach or to have authority over a man; she is to keep silent. For Adam was formed first, then Eve; and Adam was not deceived, but the woman was de-

---

33. Jervis, "1 Corinthians 14:34-35," p. 73.

202

ceived and became a transgressor. Yet she will be saved through childbearing, provided they continue in faith and love and holiness, with modesty. (1 Tim. 2:11-15)

It is little wonder that this passage found its way into Gilead's working canon. But it is also in our canon, and it is not easy to figure out what to do with it. We do not read Scripture humbly if we turn Scripture into some literary garage sale, looking over the texts, choosing some things we like that don't cost too much, and discarding the rest. But we do not read it in Christian community or as canon by lifting it out of its context in the story of Scripture in order to render it a timeless moral prescription. In Christian community we continue to assess existing traditions and performances against the whole story, against the story that has Jesus at its center. In Christian community we read Scripture prayerfully, governing our petitions and our readings by the vision of God's good future in the name of Jesus. In Christian community we read Scripture to remember, and recognizing holiness and sanctification, fidelity and creativity, discipline and discernment as standards of excellence. If this passage is appealed to as a "proof text" for defending the silencing of women in the church, then we may and must exercise discernment in memory of Jesus, and in memory of Jesus we may and must insist that that discernment be exercised in the context of a community within which women have a voice.

We may admit that there is considerable tension between this advice and the church's memory of Jesus, and considerable distance between this passage and the church's vision of one new humanity in which "there is no longer male and female." We may even admit that there seems to be little recognition of that tension, of that distance, and little evidence of a struggle. We must, nevertheless, attempt to make some sense of the passage, asking how it coheres with the rest of the story. Permit me to make two points.

First of all, it is important to observe that the Pastoral Epistles are preoccupied by the threat of a heresy that distorts the memory and hope — and the life — of the Christian community. The heresy evidently made some use of the Hebrew Scripture. (There are references, for example, to "teachers of the law" [1 Tim. 1:7], to "Jewish myths" [Titus 1:14], to "quarrels about the law [Titus 3:9], and to "those of the circumcision" [Titus 1:10].) But the greater threat seems to be the sympathy of the heretics with a dualistic form of spirituality not unlike the spiritual elitism of the Corinthian enthusiasts. The heretics had "swerved from the truth by claiming that the resurrection has already taken place" (2 Tim. 2:18; cf. 2 Tim. 4:8 and Titus 2:11-14). The consequences of their claim that they were already fully spiritual, of their denial of the "not yet" character of their lives, included both asceticism (e.g., 1 Tim. 4:1-5) and libertinism (e.g., 1 Tim. 1:19). Moreover, the docetic implication of their dualism, their view that Christ only "seemed" to be an embodied human being, put the gospel at risk (see, e.g., 1 Tim. 2:5; 3:16).

In the struggle of the Pastoral Epistles against this particular heresy and its dualistic spirituality, they insisted that there was "one God" who created all things, that the "one mediator" between God and humanity was the embodied Christ, and that "we wait for the blessed hope" (Titus 2:13). They insisted, that is, upon the story, upon something like the Rule of Faith. In their struggle against the claim to spiritual transcendence over both body and duty, the Pastoral Epistles emphasized not only "sound doctrine" but also sound morality. Against these heretics they soberly reinforced the mundane obligations and ordinary role responsibilities that the heretics rejected. Against the asceticism born of this heretical dualism, against those who "forbid marriage and demand abstinence from foods" (1 Tim. 4:3), the Pastoral Epistles insisted that "everything created by God is good" (4:4). They urged not abstinence but moderation. Against the libertine inferences drawn from the same dualistic premise, the Pastoral Epistles defended the importance of conventional moral obligations.[34] The grace of God does not simply liberate us from this world and its mundane responsibilities; on the contrary, it trains us "to renounce impiety and worldly passions, and in the present age to live lives that are self-controlled, upright, and godly" (Titus 2:12). One may wish that there were some greater sense of the tension between the "sound" and "sober" morality of conventional gender roles and the identity and community of Christians in memory of Jesus. In the struggle against this particular heresy, the struggle to put on Christ in Gilead seems largely forgotten and neglected. Even so, one can appreciate the resistance to these heretics that made it necessary to define and to defend — in however prosaic and pedestrian a way — "sound" doctrine and morality.

Moreover, and this is the second point, in the struggle of the Pastoral Epistles against this dualistic heresy the tension between patriarchy and the Christian hope founded in memory is not altogether forgotten. The dualism of

34. The good future of God seems to qualify very little the traditional and patriarchal sources of moral wisdom that are assimilated and used in the Pastorals. The household code is relatively free from the marks of an explicitly Christian justification or mutuality or equality or attention to the other as a neighbor whom one should love. (See Titus 2:1-10.) The good future of God seems rather to call forth "sober, upright, and godly lives in the world" (Titus 2:12 RSV). Such a "quiet and peaceable life in all godliness and dignity" (1 Tim. 2:2) is identified on the one hand with conventional (and patriarchal) morality and on the other hand with the "good" and "acceptable" (1 Tim. 2:3 RSV). Women (perhaps "wives") are instructed to "learn in silence with full submission" (1 Tim. 2:11; cf. Titus 2:5) and are prohibited from exercising "authority" over men (perhaps "husbands," 1 Tim. 2:12).

the heretics is finally no friend to women. Consider, for example, the claim of the Gnostic *Gospel of Thomas* that women who attain the esoteric knowledge *(gnosis)* of their spiritual origin and destiny become "like males."[35] The claim is fundamentally misogenic, displaying distrust and hatred of women (and their bodies). It sounds to me like something the Aunts of Gilead would like better than Offred would. In the Pastorals, at least, women are not saved *from being* women, as though *that* were the curse. They are not required, for example, to give up their sexual powers of bearing children (as they were in some ascetic Gnostic communities). Rather, women are saved as women. Moreover, if we translate 1 Timothy 2:15 not as "she will be saved through childbearing" (NRSV) but as "she will be brought safely through childbirth" (marginal reading NRSV),[36] then there is at least a recognition that in the good future of God the curse on woman will be lifted. The curse on woman is not that they are women, after all, not that they are embodied. The curse on woman is that "I will greatly increase your pangs in childbearing; in pain you shall bring forth children, yet your desire shall be for your husband, and he shall rule over you" (Gen. 3:16). If we adopt the translation suggested above, then the Pastoral Epistles at least acknowledge that where Jesus is remembered the curse on woman is lifted; she will be "brought safely through childbirth." One may still wish, of course, that there were more of a struggle against the curse in the Pastorals, more of a struggle against Gilead. But Gilead can take no comfort where the curse is being lifted; the lifting of the curse on woman will demand some concrete expression in the world of our flesh.

These words of Paul and of a later Paulinist are the words of men, of males; indeed, they are the words of men who lived in patriarchal cultures and in whom patriarchal cultures lived. For all of that, these words are included in Scripture. They are a part of the whole collection that the Christian community sets aside as "Holy" Bible. That does not mean that we may or must simply repeat these words as a timeless code. That would be to allow the tradition to pet-

35. See, e.g., *Gospel of Thomas,* 114.
36. In defense of this translation there are a number of points: (1) The similar construction of 1 Peter 3:20 is better translated as "brought safely through water" than as "saved by means of water." (2) *Dia* with the genitive can evidently have this meaning. (3) The singular "woman" in 1 Timothy 2:14 and the literary context suggest the reference to the curse in Genesis 3:16. (4) The alternative that "she shall be saved by bearing children" is theologically wrong-headed. It should not be necessary to point out that the curse of Genesis 3:16 is not normative, but the curse has been used as a defense of patriarchalism (see *The Handmaid's Tale,* p. 146). The curse on Adam, of course, has not been used to condemn efforts to increase the fertility of the soil or the ease with which it can be cultivated.

rify and to add weight to the curse instead of lifting it. To own them as part of the formative and normative tradition of the church is to disown Gnostic dualism. We must disown dualism not only when it is expressed as libertinism, as in "The body is of no spiritual significance; therefore, you may do whatever you please in and with your body." We must disown dualism not only when it is expressed as asceticism, as in "The body is of no spiritual significance; therefore, you should have only contempt for the body and its pleasures." We must also disown dualism when it is used to interpret the significance of the memory of Jesus and the hope it evokes, as in "The body is of no spiritual significance; therefore, although the mutuality and equality of men and women is a spiritual reality, in the world nothing has changed — or need change."

To read these words as a code for our embodied life in community today while giving lip service to a "spiritual" equality is a form of dualism — and it falls under the judgment of the Pastoral Epistles themselves. The curse has been — and must be — lifted. In memory of Jesus the vision remains a world where man no longer "shall rule over" woman (Gen. 3:16). The Jesus we remember was no docetic heavenly apparition; the Jesus we remember lived in the world of our flesh. To remember Jesus evokes no Gnostic vision of a disembodied and spiritual equality; it evokes a vision of and a struggle for equality in the "real" world, in the world of our flesh, in the only world we know, in the world where God's own good future is still "at hand" and still "not yet."

The Household Codes: Nudging Received Roles toward the Story

In memory of Jesus the early church envisioned a world in which the curse on women would be lifted, a community in which there would be "no longer male and female" (Gal. 3:28). It was not yet that world, of course, and they were not yet that community. As we have noted, some early Christian communities were further from that vision than others, and in some texts of the New Testament there is more distance between the vision and the historical realization than in others. Nevertheless, in memory of Jesus and in the hope for the good future of God that Jesus promised, the early church continued to envision a community of mutuality and equality, and that memory and hope continued to evoke a struggle against Gilead. They remembered Jesus, and they hoped for the manifestation of his glory, and they struggled against Gilead.

Both the distance and the struggle are on display in "the household codes," or *haustafeln,* within the New Testament.[37] The household codes articu-

37. Ephesians 5:21–6:9; Colossians 3:18–4:1; Titus 2:1-10; 1 Peter 2:13–3:8. See fur-

late a moral tradition that was not native to the church. The church imported these rules for behavior in the household from the Greek philosophical tradition (as Hellenistic Judaism had before it).

There was in the first century a retrieval of the Aristotelian position that the relation of ruler and ruled in the household was "natural."[38] The "natural" role for free men in a household was to rule, and the "natural" role for slaves and children and women was to be ruled. The Christian church entered the social world of the first century. The memory of Jesus and the hope for a community in which there is "no longer . . . male and female" did not (and could not) magically provide new gender roles and household structures; the churches did not (and could not) create *ex nihilo* a new social world. They entered the existing social world, and even if here and there they could (and did) find or make a respite from the power of Gilead, the rules for that social world were already established. The church in large part adopted those commonplace rules and assimilated some of the conventional reflection regarded as important to decisions about choices within the household. They adopted the commonplace rules, but they also adapted them. They assimilated the moral traditions important in the wider culture to reflection about these rules, but they also transformed them. In their adoption of these rules the distance between their vision and its historical realization is displayed. And in the adaptation of these rules, in their transformation of the tradition, the struggle against Gilead is manifest.

With the instructions that wives (and slaves and children) should "be subject," the tradition of the household codes seems to accept and baptize conventional morality and its role assignments. Mary of Bethany might remind them (and us) of Jesus' refusal simply to accept the conventional role assignments. The instruction that wives "be subject" and the acceptance of conventional role assignments for women stood in some tension with the memory of Jesus and at some distance from the baptismal identity and vision of the Christian community. The early church, however, not only adopted the moral commonplaces of the culture, they also put such "wisdom" in the context of their memory of Jesus and their conviction that he was Lord and Christ. To be sure, the effect of that context might have been simply to authorize and legitimate the moral commonplaces of the culture within the church. But the context also served to relativize, challenge, reorient, and qualify those moral commonplaces,

---

ther, David Balch, *Let Wives Be Submissive: The Domestic Code in I Peter,* Society of Biblical Literature Monograph Series, no. 26 (Chico, Calif.: Scholars Press, 1981); Schüssler Fiorenza, *In Memory of Her,* pp. 250-70; Verhey, *The Great Reversal,* pp. 67-69; John H. Yoder, *The Politics of Jesus* (Grand Rapids: Eerdmans, 1972), pp. 163-92.

38. On this see especially David Balch, *Let Wives Be Submissive.*

to form them and to transform them into something more "fitting" to the story they loved to tell and longed to live. The memory of Jesus continued to nurture the struggle against Gilead. No new kinship system was simply given with the story, but the story was not forgotten or the struggle with Gilead neglected when the early church adopted and adapted the rules for a household. The early church exercised discernment in memory of Jesus. It did not simply baptize Hellenistic moral commonplaces as God's law, and it surely did not absolutize them.

There can be no doubt that the tradition of the household codes represented a historical achievement that left the church at some distance from the future it envisioned. There can be no doubt that the household codes have been used to put (and to keep) women (and slaves) at the margins of society. But there can also be no doubt that the struggle against Gilead evoked by the church's memory and vision left its marks on the tradition.

It left its mark, first of all and fundamentally, on the *justification* for submission: "Wives, be subject to your husbands, as is fitting in the Lord" (Col. 3:18). The justification is no longer "nature" but the story of Jesus. The justification is no longer that ruling and being ruled are "natural," simply the way things are, or in accord with some cosmic patriarchal reason. The justification is not that by our willing participation in the "nature" or the "reason" at work in the way things are we can transcend our passions. Where the story of Jesus is the justification and the pattern for submission, there the one who would rule is also called to serve. Where the story of the cross is remembered, the model is not that we should be passionless but that we should own Christ's passion as our own. Where the humility of Christ is remembered, the pattern is that we should not make the claims that are ours to make but humbly serve. Where the resurrection of Christ is remembered, the way things are is not confused with the way things are to be. Where Christ, in whom "there is no longer slave or free, there is no longer male and female," is remembered, there is justification not only for the household code as an accommodation to the social world in which they lived but also for continuing the struggle against Gilead.

Justifications are like that: They not only authorize rules, they guide and limit the application of the rules. For example, if one were to justify the rule that one should tell the truth by saying that truth-telling serves the greatest good for the greatest number, then that justification would also guide *how* the truth is told and limit the duty to tell the truth. It would require us, for example, sometimes not to tell the truth if the greatest good for the greatest number were served by deception. On the other hand, if one were to justify truth-telling by saying that telling the truth is a rational necessity, then the rule will be applied differently and deception will not be justified simply by its utility. Still other

208

reasons for telling the truth might be given,[39] and each justification would not only authorize the rule to tell the truth but also affect the way the rule is applied and limited. The point is this: To appeal to the memory of Jesus to authorize these rules for the household is also to provide for the qualification and limitation of the application of these rules.

The church receives also its own tradition, including its biblical traditions, including the household codes, as justified by the story of Jesus, and as requiring continuing discernment. It continues to assess the tradition and performances of the tradition in the light of its memory of Jesus. The tradition of submission represented by the household codes — justified by the memory of Jesus — also finds its limit and direction in that memory. Where it is used in the service of Gilead, we may and must in memory of Jesus put a limit to it and reorient it.

The memory of Jesus in the early church qualified the way these conventional Greek commonplaces were received in the church and reiterated in the household codes in other ways as well; the different justification created other differences, differences which display the struggle against Gilead. A second mark left on the tradition of the household codes is that submission is *mutual*. Ephesians 5:21 says it best in its preface to its household code: "Be subject to one another out of reverence for Christ." It is not just women and slaves and children who are called to be subject. "Out of reverence for Christ" free fathers and husbands are called to be subject, too. "All of you must clothe yourself with humility in your dealings with one another" (1 Pet. 5:5). Men "put on Christ" in Gilead when they clothe themselves with humility, when they are ready not to make the claims that some "natural" order of ruler and ruled would license. The emphasis on role responsibilities in the tradition is hardly innovative or surprising, but the emphasis on mutuality signals a new chapter in the story of our world of gender. It displays something of the vision born in remembering Jesus.

There is a third mark left on the household codes, an even more surprising one; the biblical codes recognize *equality*. The masters of slaves, for example, are reminded that both slave and master "have the same Master in heaven, and with him there is no partiality" (Eph. 6:9; cf. Col. 4:1). And husbands are reminded that both husbands and wives are members of the same body, the church (Eph. 5:25-30). Men as well as women are members of the church, the bride of Christ. Women as well as men are members of the church, the body of Christ the Lord. Neither slavery nor Gilead can finally endure the recognition of equality that marks not only the baptismal vision of the church but also the household codes.

39. See, for example, Allen Verhey, "The Truth and the Life," *Reformed Journal*, April 1987, pp. 11-15.

Finally, the memory of Christ left a fourth mark on this tradition, a fourth transformation. The biblical codes do not call attention to the self, to the natural nobility of the free husband and father; they call attention instead to the *neighbor* — and to the neighbor *as one who is to be loved* (e.g., Eph. 5:28, 33). Moreover, this duty to love the neighbor is not construed according to the conceit of philanthropy; it is not motivated by a self-serving sense of one's own goodness in nobly granting kindness to those "naturally" under one. It is rather understood as our response to Christ, as a self-forgetful sense of gratitude to this ruler of all who was (and is) among us as one who serves.

The distance between the vision and the historical realization of that vision in the household codes remains — and it remains troubling. But the struggle is the crucial thing. And there is much to be learned from the marks which that struggle left on the household codes as the church continues its pilgrimage toward the good future of God that is still on the horizon, a good future in which the remembered Jesus rules.

The Contemporary Church

The church may never be content with the distance, and it may not today simply repeat the first-century codes as the timeless word of God. That would be to allow the tradition to fossilize and to petrify; it would be to permit the struggle to be forgotten and neglected; and it would put a stop to our pilgrimage. A pilgrim's progress still comes by remembering and by envisioning the future born in memory. The memory of Jesus still does not enable us to create *ex nihilo* new social structures nor permit us to suppose that, even if we could, they would eliminate the distance between any historical realization and the reign of this Jesus. Nevertheless, we are enabled to talk together and pray together and exercise discernment together about the "household traditions" we still receive and assimilate. The memory of Jesus must continue to qualify the way these biblical texts — and the moral commonplaces of our own social world — are received and handed down. And we are required in memory of Jesus to continue to struggle to put on Christ within them, to struggle against the Gileads within them and within us. So we think about our choices together in the community Christ still makes and still marks by mutuality and equality and a self-forgetful love of the neighbor.

That the words of the New Testament are male words is not to be denied, but they are the words of men who, faithful to the memory of Jesus, have broken the Gileads within and challenged and qualified the Gileads without. If we reject these words we cut ourselves off from the church's most critical memory of Jesus and from the early church's struggle to give already some "fleshly consequences" to a future quite different from Gilead. If we use these words to silence women and to mute their voices, if we allow the tradition to fossilize and petrify, we will be serving Gilead, not the alternative future Christ proclaimed and whose power he made known. If we give up the struggle for liberation, we will not be remembering Jesus, even if we have a very sophisticated historical method.

That was Margaret Atwood's final lesson in *The Handmaid's Tale*. When the Handmaid's tale was finally told, it was told by the professional rememberers, the "disinterested historians" who prided themselves on their "objectivity," who insisted that their job was only to understand, not to censure, and who finally dismembered the story of the Handmaid rather than remembering it.

The church is not a historian's convention. To *remember* Jesus is not simply to recollect some historical datum or simply to recall some historical detail or even simply to reconstruct a historical figure; to remember Jesus is to own a particular history as one's own, to *own* a past and to own it as constitutive for identity and community and as determinative for discernment. To remember the tale of this handmaid's son is to struggle to live it. Mary understood her son's story best of all perhaps — and she understood his birth as the beginning of the decisive episode in which God would raise the humble and humble the exalted. Her "Magnificat" may be our *mea culpa*. Perhaps the only way we can begin to live this story is by repentance, but repentance itself practices hospitality to the future Jesus dreamt of and made known. There is no remembering Jesus that does not celebrate his future. There is no remembering Jesus that does not censure oppression, that does not struggle against the Gileads without and within, that does not struggle for some fleshly consequence of the vision of a world in which the curse is lifted, a world in which there is "no longer male and female." To remember the story is not simply to follow a set of rules as though a normative kinship system has dropped from heaven either into first-century Scripture or into post-Enlightenment political philosophy. To remember the story is rather to nurture and cherish a continuing tradition of liberation in the moral discourse and deliberation and discernment of the church. Let our choices be in memory of Jesus. Let our choices be a recognition and celebration of the full and equal participation of women in the life of the churches. Let our choices nudge our communities in the direction of mutuality and equality.

CHAPTER ELEVEN

Remembering the Early
Church Remembering Jesus in Gilead:
A Continuing Tradition of Good Sex

Sex was not good in Gilead. Offred just lay there during intercourse, thankful that kissing was forbidden and that the Commander, too, was just "doing his duty" (122). It was no better at "the club." There sexual intercourse was not reduced to a biological means of reproduction, but it was reduced to a technology of pleasure for the Commanders, and very banal pleasure at that. The only thing that made it exciting was that it was forbidden. What was missing was intimacy, the sharing of human lives in the sharing of their flesh. What was missing was any meaning to the performance of sexual acts beyond technique. The Commander hungered for a little intimacy. When the Commander asked to be kissed after that clandestine game of Scrabble, Offred obeyed, but her obedience was not what the Commander wanted. "'Not like that,' he sa[id]. 'As if you meant it.' He was so sad" (181). The men of Gilead certainly don't win our sympathy, but if sex was not good for the women of Gilead, it was not good for the men either. "[I]t must be hell, to be a man, like that," Atwood writes. "It must be hell. It must be very silent" (114).

Sex was not good in the story Peter De Vries told of Maggie Doubloon, either. She was Biff Thrasher's eighth-grade teacher when she taught him more than grammar, more than Hawthorne's *Scarlet Letter.* Just before she tells him that he is about to be a father, just before she asks that he honor his responsibilities as a father by purchasing some ergot tablets at the local drugstore in order to get rid of his child, she makes a confession (of sorts).

212

I shouldn't have let myself be carried away like that, despite what many of us feel about the self-justifying beauty of life's greatest pleasure. Sovereign cure for the woes of man, the pagan dignity of mating and all that. At my age you too will have learned to gather all the rosebuds you can, and while you may. The question of whether in doing so you "corrupt" someone younger is a problem for hairsplitting casuists.[1]

Maggie wore the "A+" as a badge of honor, but you do not have to be a hairsplitting casuist to know that when an eighth-grade teacher has sexual intercourse with a student, it does not count as "good in bed." The world of sexuality that De Vries satirizes is empty of "Puritan repression" — and also empty of restraint and responsibility and of any meaning to sexuality beyond self-serving pleasure. Sex is reduced to a technology of pleasure; sexual partners are reduced to instruments of our pleasure; and we are reduced to individual (and lonely) pleasure seekers. What is missing is commitment — or fidelity to commitments. What is missing is continuity, the sharing of human lives over time in the sharing of their flesh.[2]

There is a story, however, in which sex is good. It is the story Jesus remembered when he was asked about divorce. It is the story of creation. Some Pharisees, Mark says (10:2-9), asked whether it is lawful for a man to divorce his wife. Moses, after all, had allowed a man to do so (Deut. 24:1-4), and every rabbi worth his salt had some interpretation of this law. But Jesus swept the law aside and reminded the Pharisees of the story of creation. The law, he said, was given "because of your hardness of heart." The *story*, he said, is that "God made them male and female" (Gen. 1:26-28; Mark 10:6) and "For this reason a man shall leave his father and mother and be joined to his wife, and the two shall become one flesh" (Mark 10:7-8; cf. Gen. 2:24).

To remember Jesus in the world of our sexuality is to remember that story of creation. Paul remembered it in his appeals to the Corinthians to reject sexual license (1 Cor. 6:16). The Ephesians were reminded of it as relevant to the relations of husbands and wives and of Christ to the church (Eph. 5:31). And the church, remembering Jesus, has remembered also the story of creation in countless weddings.

1. Peter De Vries, *Slouching Towards Kalamazoo* (New York: Penguin Books, 1984), p. 27.

2. De Vries also satirizes the repression of sexuality in certain conservative Christian communities. The mayor of the town where Maggie Doubloon teaches, upon hearing that Miss Doubloon has assigned *The Scarlet Letter*, exclaims in protest, "We're gonna tighten our Bible Belt! We're gonna show 'em we're the buckle of that belt!" (p. 4).

The Story of Creation and Good Sex

In the story of creation "once upon a time" is "in the beginning." In the beginning, there was love. That's the story. It is a story, first, of God's love. "In the beginning," according to the first creation story (Gen. 1:1–2:4a), God created male and female (Gen. 1:26-28; Mark 10:6). At the climax of creation the triune God[3] made human community. It was a gift and a reflection of a divine love. And in the second story (Gen. 2:4b-25) the divine love was shown in this, that the triune God said, "It is not good that the man should be alone" (Gen. 2:18), and God made of the one human creature two so that the two might be one. In both creation stories our creation as male and female is a gift of God's love.

It is a story of God's love, but it is also a story of human love, of Adam's love for Eve and Eve's for Adam. Indeed, it can be read as a romantic story of human love. In the romantic story we hear of a love evoked by a vision of the beloved as lovely, as wholly lovable, and to that vision the whole self responded with affection and passion. Once upon a time Adam awakened from a deep sleep and saw . . . a vision. He probably pinched himself, thinking, "I must still be sleeping — and dreaming." "She is made for me," he said, or words to that effect. He looked upon this woman and said what God had said over the creation, "It is good, very good." And once upon a time Eve watched Adam wake from sleep, glad for his awakening. "Flesh of my flesh and bone of my bones," she said. "It is good, very good," or words to that effect (cf. Gen. 2:21-23).

If they had known it, they might have sung the song of Solomon, "As a lily among brambles, so is my love among maidens. As an apple tree among the trees of the wood, so is my beloved among young men" (Song 2:2-3) — except, of course, that they knew little yet of brambles and nothing of other young men and maidens. If they had known it, they might have sung the song of U2: "One life, but we're not the same. We get to carry each other, care for each other. One love; one."[4] Whatever song of love they did know, you can bet they sang it, for they delighted in each other and in their love.

There they stood, in the beginning, together: at home in their flesh, "naked, and . . . not ashamed" (Gen. 2:25); at home with each other, vulnerable and not anxious, the vulnerability of their nakedness an occasion for delight and mutuality, not shame and power; and at home with God, the giver of life and love and joy. The vision of the beloved, that romantic vision, called forth affec-

---

3. It should be admitted, of course, that the original authors of Genesis did not have a notion of a *triune* God, but to read Scripture in Christian community, to read it according to the rule of faith, permits us to tell the story in this way.

4. I owe this reference to Timothy Verhey.

tion and passion — and also commitment! "Therefore," the story goes, "a man leaves his father and his mother and clings to his wife, and they become one flesh" (Gen. 2:24; cf. Mark 10:7-8). The vision prompted Adam not only to say, "Eve, I love you," but, "Eve, I *will* love you." Her delight prompted Eve not only to say, "Adam, I love you," but, "Adam, I *will* love you." Adam and Eve made commitments to each other and made love in celebration of those commitments. Marriage, like our creation as male and female, is a gift of God's love.

Sex is good in the creation, very good. It is a story of an embodied relationship, a "one flesh" union, of male and female, begun in vows, carried out in fidelity, and blessed with children. Good sex "in the beginning" involves mutuality and equality, intimacy and continuity, and the blessing of children. Sex is good, but it is not God; nothing God made is God. The story from the beginning cautions against idolatrously extravagant expectations of sexuality, against making it (to use Maggie Doubloon's phrase) "the sovereign cure for the woes of man." When human fulfillment is made dependent on sexual fulfillment, then we have failed to remember creation. Sex is good, and from the beginning it involves whole persons, embodied selves. The story cautions against the dualism that drives a wedge between body and soul. Asceticism is a form of amnesia (cf. 1 Tim. 4:3-5), but so is any reduction of persons to mere physiology (or to disembodied capacities for choice) and of sexual intercourse to a technology of pleasure.

Sex is good, and from the beginning it requires commitment. That was the way God intended it. Love that is good offers itself fully and finally. Love that is good makes promises. So it is with God's love, and so it was with Adam and Eve. There at the beginning commitment was a way to love into the future, a way to give a future to their present love, binding not only Adam to Eve and Eve to Adam but binding present and future together. The romantic moment, the original vision, was not closed in upon itself but open to the future. Their love would have a history. Their relationship would endure — either as fidelity or as betrayal. To remember the story forms one to be ready to keep one's promises, forms one to resist infidelity and divorce; so the remembered Jesus remembered the story.

Even in the beginning, evidently, they knew that the romantic moment, the original vision, would not last, could not last. Perhaps God had told Adam that there would be mornings when he would wake up and look over at Eve and wonder what he could have been thinking that morning long ago. Perhaps God had warned Eve that there would be times when she only delighted in Adam's awakening because it put a stop to his miserable snoring.

At any rate, things soon got much more difficult. Creation is, after all, only the beginning of the story of human sexuality. The story continues under the shadow of human sin. Sin is a dreadful mystery, but this much is clear: the fault was not in God and not in nature. The fault was in human choice. Humanity's free grasping at freedom in the demand to be "autonomous," to be a law to themselves, brought not freedom but bondage, a "voluntary bondage" to the powers of sin and death that usurp God's rule and resist God's cause. In the wake of sin came death and a curse.

Death fell heavy on the story of Adam and Eve, and heavy on their love. Death alienates us from our flesh, and Adam and Eve, once naked and not ashamed, at home in the flesh, felt the power of death in the shame of their nakedness. Death alienates us from each other, and Adam and Eve, once vulnerable and not anxious, confident of their mutuality and community, felt the sting of death in power and patriarchy. Death alienates us from God, and Adam and Eve, who had walked with God in the garden, now hid from God and felt the power of death in their hiding.

Because of human sin, the curse weighed down on them — and on good sex, too. The story of Genesis 3 itself identified the curse with patriarchy and with the pain of childbirth (Gen. 3:16). But the marks of the curse are legion. Other stories made it clear that not just pain in childbirth but barrenness bore the mark of the curse. The curse makes its power felt in the reduction of any to a sexual function and in the reduction of sexual relations to a technology of pleasure. Under the power of the curse sexuality becomes the occasion for lust and for shame, for license and for legislation, for the confounding of expectations of fecundity, for the breaking of covenant, for the betrayal of partners.

It's a sad story, and in the midst of it, that original vision, that romantic moment, must have seemed to Adam and to Eve long ago. And their commitment must have seemed wishful thinking. You can imagine it. Adam, irritated, complains that Eve seems not to understand how hard he has to work to get the miserable ground to yield a crop. And Eve, angered, complains in turn that Adam seems to think that patriarchy is the way it is meant to be, not a curse to be worked against just as vigorously as the stubborn ground. You can imagine it. Each complains to the other and to God — but mostly to themselves — that the original vision in that romantic moment long ago had simply been wrong: "I had not seen these things before." "Now I know the other better than I did then." "How could I have missed what is now so obvious?" "How could I have been such a fool as to bind myself and my future so irrevocably?" "Now I see what the man is really like!" "Now I see what the woman is really like!"

So they grew suspicious of the original vision, and they were right in a way. Each had come to know more of the other than at the beginning: the flaws, the faults, the irritating oddities, the aggravating eccentricities, the wearying habits, the boring routines (even of the other's affection and passion). Such knowledge can make one suspicious of the original vision. A man waking from sleep is seldom entrancing, and the sight of a woman when one awakes is frequently less than enchanting. But they were wrong, too. That first vision was right, still. Eve was a gift of God to Adam. Adam was a gift of God to Eve. And in such gifts there was and remained the vocation of gratitude to God for the other and the calling of faithfulness to the other. In that first vision Adam and Eve saw the other well, for they saw the other as a gift of God. That moment contained a truth about the other that should not be forgotten, but they — like all their children — grew weary of the wonder of those who were near them. They grew tired of beholding beauty; they thought the beauty had faded when their vision had dimmed. It is, I think, a mark of the curse. Such knowledge of the other (and such forgetfulness of the other) made the task of living together with gratitude and fidelity harder still.

So they grew suspicious of commitment, too. And they were right in a way, for commitment, too, can be distorted by the power of death. Where death rules, commitment — when it still exists — can take the form of resisting time, because time leads to death. Commitment under the threat of death insists that some romantic moment last in spite of time, as if there were no time. But, of course, there is time, and it will not be resisted, and the effort to preserve some precious present by cutting it off from any future is futile (and boring). They were right in a way to be suspicious of commitment, but they were wrong, too. For death and the curse were not the end of the story of Adam and Eve. It is a story — not only first, but also finally — of God's love. The grace of God would not let death have the last word in God's creation, or the last word about Adam and Eve and their love. Commitment could be dared and done with hope in God. With hope in God Adam and Eve had courage for commitment, not in order to resist time or to deny it but to embrace time and to embrace each other into the future.

Far as the curse is found, so far the grace of God would reach to restore and to bless, even finally and hilariously to the grave. The grace of God made its power felt in a world now marked and marred by sin and death, by power and patriarchy, by lust and selfishness, but it made its power felt. The grace of God made its power felt when a child was born to Adam and Eve, a token of the promise of another child: that death would not have the last word. The grace of God made its power felt in the tender affection that remembered the first vision, in their forgiveness and faithfulness, in their mutuality and equality, and yes, in their passion, naked again and not ashamed again, vulnerable still, but entrusting themselves to the care of the other and to God. The grace of God made its power felt in the hope that gave their love a history again. It made its power felt in a commitment that celebrated God's love and signaled their confi-

217

dence in God's future. They embraced time, embraced the future, cleaving to each other and to God.

It's a good story, after all, and whatever song of love they knew you can bet they sang it. If they had known it, they might have sung the Song of Solomon, "Set me as a seal upon your heart, as a seal upon your arm; for love is strong as death" (8:6). Not to pretend that the romantic moment was sufficient, not to commit themselves to resist and deny time, but to celebrate the grace of God who would win the victory over death and sin. If they had known it, they might have sung a song of resurrection and of a wedding feast at the end of time.

It's a good story, after all, and countless storytellers have reminded us of it. Human sin might have smashed a cosmos back to chaos — and our sexual world along with it — but God sustained the cosmos and our sexuality, restraining the effects of sin upon them both. The grace of God made its power felt from the beginning. "Now the man knew his wife Eve, and she conceived and bore Cain, saying, 'I have produced a man with the help of the Lord'" (Gen. 4:1; see also Gen. 5:1). The grace of God made its power felt in Sarah's "laughter" (in her Isaac; see Gen. 17:19; 21:6), in Joseph's fidelity against the temptations of Potiphar's wife (Gen. 39), in the tender affection of Boaz and Ruth and in their fecundity, in the forgiveness and faithfulness of Hosea to Gomer, in the mutual passion of the lovers of Solomon's song. The signs of God's grace were in the midst of a fallen world, of patriarchy and polygamy, but there were signs of it. And the signs of it gave hope for the good future of God's unchallenged reign — and for sexuality, too.

It's a good story, and it is still told at Christian weddings, when a community comes together in the presence of God because a couple knows that their story is a part of the story of God's love. The couple comes because they would commit to God their commitments to each other, because they only dare to bind themselves and their future irrevocably to each other by faith in a God who loves and whose love makes and keeps promises. They only dare to embrace each other and time and change with hope in a God who will not allow death and the curse to have the last word. We come, the community comes, to witness their promises, to wish them well, to commit ourselves to help them to cherish each other and their marriage, to pledge ourselves again to God and to God's gifts of life and love and joy, and to celebrate the story. Together we celebrate their love, the delight they take in each other, the vision they have and hold of each other. The romantic vision will not be enough, and it is certain to be doubted at times, but it contains a truth not to be forgotten, that God has given them to and for each other. Together we celebrate the promises of love, the commitments love undertakes with faith and hope. The parents, perhaps, do not exactly celebrate the inevitable change in their own relationship with a child, the separation, the "leaving father and mother," but they endure it and, yes, bless it for the sake of the couple's "cleaving" to each other. There is a something of a new creation here, and together we celebrate it, as Jesus did at a wedding at Cana of Galilee long ago (John 2:1-11).

And, of course, we come together to pray for them. We pray for the community of two who are not the same, but no longer simply two either: "As it was in the beginning, so may it be with them." We pray for the mutuality and equality of their partnership: "As it was in the beginning, so may it be with them." We pray that they may have the courage to embrace not only each other but also time and to give their love a history; we pray for the courage that comes from knowing that God's love is stronger than death, stronger than the curse. And we pray for their happiness — not because happiness is what Christian marriage promises to those who enter it, nor because it is what those who enter Christian marriage promise. We pray for the marital happiness that is put at risk when one insists on one's own rights or on one's own happiness. We pray for the marital happiness that is won in much more costly ways than that — for the happiness that is won in fairness and forgiveness, in compassion and honor, in mutual submissiveness, in a love that is patient and kind, a love that is not jealous or boastful or rude, a love that does not insist on its own way, a love that is not irritable or resentful, a love that can bear and endure the worst while it believes and hopes for the best (cf. 1 Cor. 13:4-7), the sort of love to which we are all called in the one body of Christ and to which they are called in the "one flesh" of marriage.

Good Sex and Celibacy

Remembering Jesus we learn to celebrate not only marriage but also singleness. Jesus of Nazareth came announcing the good future of God and making its power felt in his works and words. He told the story of creation, of course, and he celebrated the wedding at Cana of Galilee. But there was something new, not just the creation revisited, not just the curse restrained, but something new — the coming future of God.

In the good future of God, Jesus said, "they neither marry nor are given in marriage, but are like angels in heaven" (Matt. 22:30; Mark 12:25; cf. Luke 20:35-36 and Matt. 19:10-12). That was something new — and suddenly and already, singleness and celibacy were an option for those who would remember Jesus, an option signaled by Jesus' own singleness. Suddenly and already, marriage was no longer a duty of Torah or a necessary condition for human fulfillment and divine approval. Singleness and celibacy can be a performance of the announcement that the good future of God is "at hand." Remembering Jesus, Paul honored not only marriage as a "gift" (a *charisma*) of God (1 Cor. 7:7), but celibacy as well. Singleness and celibacy were not, however, made into a new duty of some Christian law or into a necessary condition for spiritual fulfillment and divine approval, just as marriage was no longer a duty, but remained a legitimate option on the way to God's good future.

The implication of Jesus' announcement of a new thing was not ascetic denial of our embodiment. The roots of the announcement were not, after all, dualism. It was part of his proclamation that the creator of this world and of these bodies would act to end the rule of sin and death. It was, in fact, part of his reply to the Sadducees (Mark 12:18-27) who dismissed the hope for resurrection by insisting on the patriarchal patterns of "levirate marriage." Jesus announced that when "the power of God" (Mark 12:24) makes itself felt, the relations of men and women are governed not by patriarchal marriages, not by a man's need to secure for himself a name and an heir (Deut. 25:6), but by the mutuality, equality, and fidelity that belong to God's creative and redemptive purpose. There the curse of Genesis 3:16 is being lifted. It is good news, liberatingly good news, for human sexuality, not asceticism.

To be sure, there were some in the early church who made ascetic inferences from the tradition, notably some members of Paul's congregation in Corinth. The spiritual enthusiasts there claimed to participate already fully in the future age, claimed to be already fully spiritual, already "angels." And some of these made the ascetic inference that participation in the life of the body with its sexual pleasures was forbidden to genuinely spiritual Christians; they prohibited sexual intercourse and made celibacy a duty, or at least a mark of the spiritual elite.

"'It is well for a man not to touch a woman'" (1 Cor. 7:1) was probably a slogan of these enthusiasts.[5] Paul did not disagree with the slogan; celibacy is indeed a signal that the ages have turned, that the future age has already made its power felt, that the rule of Christ in whom there is "no longer male and female" is real. But he immediately qualified their enthusiasm — and their elitism — by the recognition that the rule of Christ is "not yet" unchallenged. He

5. This is the opinion of many recent commentators — and some ancient ones (notably Origen, whose judgment that this is an extract from the Corinthians' letter to Paul is cited by F. F. Bruce, *The New Century Bible Commentary: I & II Corinthians* [Grand Rapids: Eerdmans, 1971]). Other quotations of parties in Corinth may be found in 1 Corinthians 6:12; 6:13; 8:1; 8:4; 10:23. In each case Paul does not so much reject the slogan as immediately qualify it.

said, "But because of the temptation to immorality, each man should have his own wife and each woman her own husband" (1 Cor. 7:2 RSV). Paul was capable of providing other — and better — grounds for marriage than that it is a remedy for concupiscence. (Indeed, in 1 Thessalonians 4:5 [RSV], it is the "heathen" who marry "in the passion of lust.") But here, against the eschatological assumptions of the Corinthian enthusiasts, he reminded the Corinthians of the "not yet" character of their existence. The powers of *porneia* (sexual immorality) have not yet laid down their arms and admitted defeat. And until they have, celibacy remains a "gift," not a duty, a "gift," not a reason to boast. Indeed, Paul urged those who would be celibate to be celibate not as a way of boasting that they were already fully spiritual, already "angels," but "in view of the impending crisis" (1 Cor. 7:26).[6]

Paul agreed with the Corinthian enthusiasts that celibacy was an indication that the ages had "already" turned and that it was a "gift" of the Spirit who is the first fruits of that future. But he disagreed with their denial of the "not yet" character of existence. He disagreed with their boast that this "gift" identified them as already "angels" and with their making celibacy a requirement of the truly spiritual. According to Paul, the "not yet" character of the world of our sexuality not only justified marriage (or the permission to marry, 7:2, 36-38); it is also what made celibacy itself sometimes prudent (7:25-35). Let the one who would be celibate be celibate not as a way to boast about being already an angel but as a way to wait and watch for God's good future. Paul's argument was not based on his belief that *only* a brief span of time remained before Christ's unchallenged sovereignty. Rather, it was based on his recognition (contrary to the eschatological assumptions of the Corinthians) that Christ's unchallenged sovereignty is "not yet," that a (brief) span of time still remains *before* Christ's appearance and the general resurrection. It was not founded on some Greek dualism of body and spirit that would justify and require asceticism, as though the body belonged to the old age and God's good future would be purely "spiritual." It was founded rather on the recognition that sin continues to assert its power in the world of our sexuality. The power of sin still threatens to disorder our embodied existence. Against the continuing power of sin celibacy is sometimes a prudent strategy, and sometimes not.

Celibacy is not a duty, but it is a "gift." Marriage is no longer a duty, but it, too, can be a "gift" (1 Cor. 7:7). Marriage may belong to the order of things that will pass out of existence (7:31), as the Corinthian enthusiasts surely believed,

---

6. It is possible, indeed preferable, to translate "the impending crisis" as "the present crisis," but in either case Paul refers to the eschatological situation and to the "not yet" character of existence.

but the new order of things can mark marriage itself as well. Let the celibate be celibate in recognition that it is not yet God's good future, and let the married act in ways that recognize that the ages have already turned. Marriage, and not just celibacy, can be a sign of God's good future. The new identity and community owned in baptism in memory of Jesus prompted a revision of the marriage relationship. The full mutuality and equality of the marriage partnership in 1 Corinthians 7 — including the sexual aspects of that partnership (7:3-5) — is stunning. It was hardly surprising, of course, that in the first century Paul should say, "the wife does not have authority over her own body, but the husband does" (7:4). All the Gileads of our past and present have welcomed and treasured that line. But that Paul should continue then in the first century to say, "likewise the husband does not have authority over his own body, but the wife does" (7:4) was stunning, and it shatters the patriarchal pretensions of Gilead within marriage. The mutuality of authority, of ruling and submitting, within the partnership of marriage is itself a token of God's good future, a sign that the curse is lifted, an indication of a future in which there is "no longer male and female."[7]

Within marriage, moreover, sexual intercourse was not merely tolerated but encouraged. Paul had accepted the Corinthian slogan that "it is well for a man not to touch a woman"; celibacy is good. But marriage is also good, and within marriage "not to touch" your spouse is not good! The sort of "spiritual marriage" some Corinthians were attempting — and sometimes imposing on a partner — was not good. "Do not deprive one another," Paul says, "except perhaps by agreement for a set time, to devote yourselves to prayer" (7:5). Sex is good, even in this chapter where celibacy is called "better," and good sex gestures "one flesh," the unity and the mutuality and the equality of partners committed to each other and to God. Neither Christian identity nor Christian marriage requires asceticism.[8]

7. Attention might also be given to three facts about this passage that are surprising in the first century. First, Paul does not simply assume that a wife's religious identity will be determined by her husband's religious identity (1 Cor. 7:12-13). Second, Paul says "the unbelieving husband is made holy through his wife" as well as "the unbelieving wife is made holy through her husband" (7:14; see also 7:16, and David Daube, "Pauline Contributions to a Pluralistic Culture: Re-creation and Beyond," in *Jesus and Man's Hope*, ed. Donald G. Miller and Dikran Y. Hadidian [Pittsburgh Theological Seminary, 1971], pp. 223-45, 240). And third, Paul addressed both husband and wife with respect to divorce. The equality and mutuality of man and woman is consistently reflected in this chapter in the equality and mutuality of husband and wife.

8. The closest the New Testament comes to asceticism is Revelation 14:4, which describes the faithful (the 144,000) as those "who have not defiled themselves with women, for they are virgins" (Gk. *parthenos*). This verse must surely be taken figuratively, as a sym-

Indeed, the pastoral epistles explicitly rejected asceticism. Some of those whom the author of the pastorals opposed evidently had forbidden marriage (1 Tim. 4:3). The Pastoral Epistles condemned such teaching and the dualism behind it, for "everything created by God is good" (4:4). In opposition to these heretics the author of the Pastoral Epistles seems even to retreat from the Pauline recognition of celibacy as a gift and an option, for he evidently makes marriage a requirement for ecclesiastical office ("husband of one wife," RSV, 1 Tim. 3:2, 12; Titus 1:6). It is possible, however, that "married only once" (NRSV) was not directed against the celibate but against those who engaged in the degenerate Hellenistic practice of successive brief marriages.[9]

Chastity and Embodiment

In memory of Jesus the early church could honor both celibacy and marriage, but it could not abide sexual immorality. In memory of Jesus the early church did not require (or approve) asceticism, but it did require, as we have seen, mutuality and equality and, as we shall now see, chastity and fidelity. Jesus himself had issued a new and radical commandment prohibiting lust (Matt. 5:27-28), and to remember that commandment was to refuse to use another or to think of another simply as an instrument for our own sexual gratification. To remember Jesus and that commandment meant to delight in the other as one who, in his or her sexuality, shares the gifts and callings of the Creator and Redeemer. In remembrance of Jesus the early church formed a tradition urging its members to "abstain" from sexual immorality.

The advice to "abstain" from sexual immorality was part of a very early Christian tradition, reaching back to Jesus' prohibition of lust (Matt. 5:28) and to the "apostolic decree" attributed by Luke to the Jerusalem Council (Acts 15:20, 29; 21:25). The Christian tradition was surely informed by the Jewish tradition of sexual morality, and it was used to instruct Gentile converts (Acts 15:20, 29; 21:25; 1 Thess. 4:3-8; 1 Peter 2:11-18).[10] Sexual immorality was linked in Jewish tradition to the pagan ignorance of God (1 Thess. 4:5; 1 Peter

---

bolic reference to the moral purity of the faithful, and as an image in concert with the description of Babylon (Rome) as "the great harlot" (17:1 RSV), which is obviously figurative. While Revelation 14:4 does not describe or prescribe an ascetic lifestyle for the faithful, however, it does use an image for their faithfulness that is undeniably ascetic.

9. Albrecht Oepke, *"gunē," Theological Dictionary of the New Testament,* ed. Gerhard Kittel, trans. Geoffrey W. Bromiley, vol. 1 (Grand Rapids: Eerdmans, 1964), p. 788.

10. E. G. Selwyn, *The First Epistle of St. Peter* (London: Macmillan, 1947), pp. 369-75.

1:14) and contrasted to the "holiness" to which they were called (1 Thess. 4:3; 1 Peter 1:15-16). The Christian church never retreated from the very Jewish prohibition of sexual immorality.

The lists of vices, another traditional form of moral instruction in the churches, are an index of the unanimity of the Christian tradition on the prohibition of sexual immorality. The Greek word *porneia* (NRSV: "fornication," "immorality") occurs more often than any other word in these lists (eleven times) and frequently stands first in the list (Mark 7:21-22; Gal. 5:19-21; Eph. 5:3-5; Col. 3:5-8).[11]

Yet there were some libertines in the Christian communities. "All things are lawful for me" (1 Cor. 6:12) was probably one of their slogans. Some of them even boasted about their sexual immorality (5:1-2) — as evidence, I suppose, that "all things are lawful." The claim of the Corinthian enthusiasts that what one did in the body was a matter of moral indifference grew out of the same soil as their requirement of asceticism: dualism. The claim that they were already fully in the new age, already altogether spiritual, already angelic, allowed either ascetic or libertine inferences.

In his conversation with such libertines (1 Cor. 6:12-20), Paul quoted their slogans without disagreeing with them, but he immediately qualified them. Paul, "the apostle of liberty," who had exclaimed to the Galatians, "For freedom Christ has set us free!" (Gal. 5:1), could hardly dismiss their slogan, "All things are lawful for me." But he did remind these libertines, "but not all things are beneficial," and he warned them of the counterfeit liberty that masks enslavement to the power of sin (1 Cor. 6:12; cf. also Gal. 5:13). The libertines responded (in Paul's construction of this conversation, at least) with a second slogan, a libertine slogan about the irrelevance of kosher regulations, "'Food is meant for the stomach and the stomach for food'" (1 Cor. 6:13). Paul was no defender of kosher regulations, but he would not allow the libertines to infer from the freedom to eat what was set before you a license for fornication. "The body is meant not for fornication," Paul replied; it is meant "for the Lord, and the Lord for the body" (6:13). What one does in and with the body is not a matter of indifference to God. Paul reminds them then that "God raised the Lord and will also raise us by his power" (6:14). That memory and hope shattered the dualism of the Corinthian enthusiasts, condemned their sexual immorality, and called for chastity.

Paul insisted upon an embodied participation in the redemption wrought by Christ; the resurrection was not simply a disembodied spiritual

---

11. Moreover, *aselgeia* (licentiousness) is mentioned six times; *akatharsia* (impurity), four times; *moicheia* (adultery), three times.

matter, nor is participation in Christ disembodied. It must have some "fleshly consequence," and the fleshly consequence of participation in Christ is not sexual license, not the liberty to use prostitutes for sexual gratification. The Pauline inference is the same conclusion that the Jerusalem Council had drawn: "Shun fornication!" (1 Cor. 6:18). The libertines were allowed one final remark: "Sin is a spiritual matter."[12] Paul's response did not deny that sin is a spiritual matter, but he insisted that it is also an embodied matter. Sin and our slavery to sin, like redemption in Christ and our participation in it, are embodied. "Therefore glorify God in your body" (6:20). Christian freedom is not found in the libertine assertion that we are our own, that what we do in our own bodies is a matter of moral indifference and no one else's business. That way leads to alienation from our bodies, alienation from each other, and alienation from God; that way leads to death. "You are not your own," Paul reminds them; "you were bought with a price" (6:19, 20). Christian freedom is our redemption from our enslavement to sin, not a new excuse for it. Therefore, "shun fornication" and "glorify God in your body."

The dualism of the libertines was capable of treating sexual intercourse as "casual sex" because, if dualism were right, what one does with the body does not involve the "real" person. Paul's reply insists on embodiment, and therefore he insists as well that sexual intercourse may not be reduced to mere physiology. The mystery of our embodiment is related to the mystery of sexuality: "The two shall be one flesh" (1 Cor. 6:16, citing Gen. 2:24).

Sex is not a bowl of buttons. That sounds like an unpromising place to begin a brief commentary on our embodiment, but many Sunday afternoons ago I would play with the bowl of buttons my mother kept in her sewing and mending cabinet. I would dump the buttons out and try to flip them like tiddlywinks back into the bowl. Sunday afternoons were boring in the household of my parents, I thought, and it was sort of fun. The fun was in the tech-

---

12. That, at least, is the way I understand the notoriously difficult line in 1 Corinthians 6:18 which the RSV translates "Every other sin which a man commits is outside the body." The Greek text does not have "other"; it is supplied by most translators because of the difficulty of having Paul say (as in the NRSV), "Every sin that a person commits is outside the body." The problem is overcome, however, if we take this to be another slogan of the Corinthian spiritualists who are libertine. Then it represents their claim that what one does in the body is a matter of indifference, not relevant to one's true spiritual self. The line in verse 18 should have quotation marks around it, like the RSV and NRSV supply in verses 12 and 13. That this verse, too, is to be understood as a slogan of Paul's opponents in Corinth was pointed out by C. F. D. Moule, *An Idiom-Book of New Testament Greek* (Cambridge: Cambridge University Press, 1963), pp. 196-97, but seems not to have been noticed by most commentators.

nique; it took a certain amount of dexterity and skill. Now sex is not like that; it is not a bowl of buttons. It is not simply a technique for getting some pleasure in the middle of a boring afternoon or semester. It is not simply a matter of dexterity, a matter of skill, to secure some small (or large) pleasure. Sex has meaning beyond the quality of its performance. Yet sex as skill, as performance, as dexterity, as a bowl of buttons, is the vision of sexuality one frequently sees in our sex-saturated society. The proper technique and presto: fulfillment. Sex, in this vision, is a happiness technology. The rule is simple enough for bumper stickers: If it feels good, do it.

The person who has to make a choice about whether to "fool around" also has to make a decision about how to envision sex. Is it a technology of plea-sure? Or is it an embodied commitment between two persons? People *have* skills, but they *are* sexual, and there is something as mysterious about sex as there is about persons — and about temples. No matter how much we know about technique, human sexuality remains a mystery. This is the mystery: that two persons become "one flesh" (Gen. 2:24; Mark 10:8; 1 Cor. 6:16). Sexual rela-tions always involve us as whole persons, as embodied spirits or in-spirited bodies, with our capacity to make and keep covenant. The person who has to make a choice about whether to "fool around" has to make a choice finally not only about how to envision sex but also about what sort of person he or she wants to be and to become. We can live our sexual lives as technical experts or as whole (and vulnerable) persons, as pleasure seekers or as covenant makers and covenant keepers (to use Lewis Smedes's nice phrases).[13] It is not quite a matter of making sex one thing or another. There remains in every act of coitus, and perhaps in the vulnerability of nakedness and any clumsy gesture toward lovemaking, a sign of God's intention with sex, for there remains an implicit ex-change of entrusting and commitments. To ask during the intimacies of mak-ing love, "But will you love me tomorrow?" is to impugn the *committal* of the act. Note that one may ask about the depth of one's affection, the intensity of one's affection, but not about *continuity.* "How much do you love me?" does not insult the act. "How long will you love me?" does. Perhaps this is not the way things simply are; perhaps this is simply the way we have been trained in memory of Jesus to think of the mystery of sex; but even the pleasure-seekers know "It's hard to keep sex just plain fun."

Sex is a mystery. We may — and we should — delight in this mystery. Witness the Song of Solomon, and remember that the memory of Jesus does not entail asceticism. And we must — and we may — be sober about this mys-

---

13. See Lewis B. Smedes, *Mere Morality: What God Expects from Ordinary People* (Grand Rapids: Eerdmans, 1983), pp. 157-82.

tery. Witness Proverbs 7, and remember that the memory of Jesus does not allow sexual license. The sexual act celebrates the mystery of "one flesh," one whole and exclusive relationship covenanted of two people who are committed not only to each other but to the cause of the one who creates and keeps covenant and renews all things — including them. The sexual act celebrates not the act itself, not technique, not even the intensity (or depth) of attraction two people can feel for each other in some romantic moment or the fulfillment of desire one person can find in another in a moment of passion. In memory of Jesus good sex is a celebration of the "one flesh" union begun in vows and carried out in fidelity. The union of husband and wife is not *merely* physical, but it *is* physical, and the physical union expresses and evokes the commitments of whole persons. Such is the delight and sobriety — and adventure — of the mystery of sex.

The story of good sex is not simply a romance. In a romance the hero or heroine set out on an adventure in quest of intensity — not continuity. Fidelity is not important — and it may be an impediment — to the romantic. In the story of good sex in Scripture, the adventure is the quest for continuity — and fidelity is crucial. Extramarital sex may provide new romantic intensity when married life and married sex have become routine, but it is ruled out by the heroic quest for continuity. Premarital sex may promise romantic excitement and a relationship deeper and more intense than anything a young person has known before — but for a moment, and that moment must be ordered toward and governed by the heroic quest for continuity.

We may delight in sexuality, but sobriety will keep us from expecting too much from it. Human fulfillment is not found in sexuality; it is found in God's good future. Sexuality is not the "sovereign cure for human woes." In memory of Jesus we will not make sexual relations either a necessary or a sufficient condition for human fulfillment. We may have sober expectations of sexual activity — and we should still delight in it. Sobriety is not prudishness. Indeed, our readiness to delight in sexuality will not condemn technique or pleasure of the fulfillment of the desire of each in the other, but fidelity will subordinate them to the mystery of "one flesh" and to the heroic quest for continuity in acts of covenant-making and covenant-keeping. Technique, after all, may enhance the intensity of delight for a moment, but technique alone quickly becomes boring (witness the bowl of buttons), and sexual relations reduced to technique or to pleasure quickly move from one technique to other more exotic ones in the quest for pleasure. Moreover, our readiness to delight in sexuality will not disown romantic moments with one's partner, but it will order romance to the mystery of "one flesh" and its commitments. Romance is hardly boring, but sexual relations reduced to romance quickly move from one partner to another in the quest for intensity. Good sex is not simply a technology of pleasure, not simply a romantic quest for intimacy; good sex is the "one flesh" union of a man and a woman that signals and seals a covenant undertaken in vows and carried out in fidelity.

Fidelity and Divorce

Jesus remembered a story in which sex is good, and he announced the good future of God. In memory of Jesus and in hope for that future, the early church honored both marriage and celibacy. In memory of Jesus and in hope for that future, the early church rejected both asceticism and license. The good future of God makes its power felt in the "gift" of celibacy. It makes its power felt when marriage is regarded as a "gift" (not as a requirement of Torah or for human fulfillment) and when marriage is marked by mutuality and equality — even in the sexual aspects of the relationship of the spouses (1 Cor. 7:3-5). The good future of God makes its power felt in fidelity, and the gift of good sex requires fidelity. That brings us to the prohibition of divorce — and back to the story with which this chapter began, the story of Jesus remembering the story of "the beginning."

In Mark's story of Jesus (Mark 10:2-12), you remember, some Pharisees asked whether it is lawful for a man to divorce his wife. Jesus set aside the Torah, Moses' dispensation for divorce in Deuteronomy 24:1-4, as having been written "because of your hardness of heart." Instead, he reminded them of the story of the way it was in the beginning. The *story,* he said, is that "God made them male and female" (Gen. 1:27; Mark 10:6) and "For this reason a man shall leave his father and mother and be joined to his wife, and the two shall become one flesh" (Mark 10:7-8; Gen. 2:24). And that story, he said, is the answer to the question of the Pharisees. "Therefore what God has joined together, let no one separate" (Mark 10:9). In "the beginning" there was no divorce. Human sexuality was there, and marriage was there, as the gift of God, but there was — and there was to be — no divorce. Divorce was not what God intended. It is a mark of our fallenness, an effect of the curse. And now that God's future is "at hand," now that it is making its power felt in the works and words of Jesus, the statute of Torah is no longer the finally decisive thing. To those who would follow him, to the disciples, Jesus said, "Whoever divorces his wife and marries another commits adultery against her; and if she divorces her husband and marries another, she commits adultery" (Mark 10:11).

This word to the disciples is noteworthy for a number of reasons. It is noteworthy, first, that in this verse women are regarded as agents in marriage and divorce no less than men. In the Law only men "marry"; women are "given

228

in marriage." And in the statute of Deuteronomy 24:1-4, only men could divorce their wives. This equal standing of men and women is a new thing, not found in the Law, but found in the good future that Jesus announced and made present. Moreover, it is noteworthy that in this verse a man can commit adultery against his wife. In the Law adultery was an offense against a man's property, a matter of taking another man's property. Technically, a man could not commit adultery against his wife but only against other men. But in Jesus' words a stunning new world of sex and marriage is created, a world where the wife is not simply property but partner, a partner who has the same rights over her husband that her husband has over her (cf. 1 Cor. 7:3-5). This, too, is a new thing, and it sweeps the Torah aside much more comprehensively than would the dismissal of a single statute. Finally, of course, it is noteworthy because it says, in effect, that those who would remember Jesus and follow him will renounce divorce. God's good future does not make its power felt in divorce.

The point of Jesus' word to the disciples was not to provide a new Torah, not to establish a new and extremely rigorous statute, not to invent an alternative social system that would institutionalize God's good future. The point was rather to announce the good future of God and the ways it already makes its power felt not only in singleness and celibacy but in sexual relationships of equality and mutuality, where husband and wife are "one flesh," joined to each other in an embodied and enduring relationship. The point was to summon people to welcome God's rule in marriage and sexuality as in all other matters. The power of God makes itself felt when husband and wife are "one flesh," and in their glad faithfulness when their marriage endures. The power of sin makes itself felt in divorce and in the patriarchal hegemony of husband over wife. God's purpose from the beginning is revisited and restored. Good sex is still the embodied love of a man and a woman that expresses and sustains both intimacy and continuity, that signals a covenant undertaken in vows and carried out in fidelity.

If those who would remember Jesus and follow him are to renounce divorce, then Christians may ask — and must ask — whether they may ever choose divorce. To begin to answer that question it should be observed that we face the problem of diversity here. Matthew, Luke, and Paul all handle the question of divorce somewhat differently.

Matthew, for example, tells the story Mark told somewhat differently in Matthew 19:3-12. In Matthew the Pharisees ask whether it is lawful for a man to divorce his wife "for any cause" (19:3); they ask, in effect, for Jesus to comment on the legal dispute about the interpretation of Deuteronomy 24:1-4. Then Matthew artfully changes the order of Jesus' reply. Jesus first takes up the Genesis texts and gives the Marcan conclusion, "Therefore what God has joined together, let no one separate." Then the Pharisees cite Deuteronomy 24:1, and Jesus responds, as in Mark, by saying that the law was a concession to the hardness of the people's hearts; but he does not for that reason brush aside either the law or the necessity of interpretation. Instead, he interprets the law in the light of God's intentions. He gives a legal (or *halakic*) interpretation for his community, an interpretation similar to the interpretation of Rabbi Shammai:[14] "Whoever divorces his wife, except for unchastity, and marries another commits adultery" (Matt. 19:9; cf. also Matt. 5:32).[15] The law holds (Matt. 5:17-20; 23:23), and Jesus is its best interpreter (Matt. 9:9-13; 12:1-8).

This passage *is* a legal ruling. Should we then revise our renouncing of divorce to make allowance for men to divorce their wives "for unchastity" (for *porneia*)? But what of Paul in 1 Corinthians 7:10-16? Paul cites the "command" of the Lord "that the wife should not separate from her husband . . . and that the husband should not divorce his wife" (7:10-11). The church's disposition toward divorce is to be shaped by its memory of Jesus, but Paul does not use that command as the basis for a legal ruling. Instead, faced with the concrete problem of whether marriage to an unbeliever can be dissolved, he exercises discernment. He offers the church his own advice. ("I say," he says, "I and not the Lord.") On the basis of "one flesh" the couple is "holy" if one of the partners is (7:14); therefore, the Christian wife or husband should not divorce an unbelieving spouse (7:12-13). But if the unbelieving partner initiates divorce, then his advice is to "let it be so," for "it is to peace that God has called you" (7:15).

Mark and Matthew and Paul all remember Jesus, and they all remember him faithfully and creatively. They receive and modify the tradition so that Jesus may be remembered — and so that the memory of Jesus may be performed — in their own communities. None of them, nor all of them combined into some elusive harmony, should be read as a timeless code to settle directly and immediately a contemporary Christian community's question asked about a particular choice to end a marriage. But all of them are a part of the whole Scripture that the churches read and struggle to perform.

They read the texts, and reading, remember. They remember the story of Jesus as connected to the beginning of the story, to the creation. They remember Jesus as the remedy for the story of death and a curse that came in the wake of human sin. They remember Jesus as connected to the end of the story, to

---

14. See Mishnah, *Gittin*, IX.10.

15. The passage in Matthew, it should be observed — in no small part because it remains an interpretation of Torah — does not, like the passage in Mark, regard women as agents in marriage or divorce, and it omits the stunning new idea in Mark that a man could commit adultery against his wife.

God's good future. And they set that story alongside the stories of their sexuality, of their marriages, and of their singleness. They read it disciplined by the standards of excellence in reading Scripture: holiness and sanctification, fidelity and creativity, discipline and discernment.

In Christian community Christians set Scripture aside as *"holy,"* and they set their sexual lives alongside the story to be judged, challenged, formed, re-formed, *"sanctified."* *Fidelity* to this text and to its story does not, as we said, require (or permit) us to read Mark (or any other particular text) as a timeless moral code. We do not live in Mark's community (or in Matthew's or Paul's), but we live in memory of Jesus and we test our lives — and our readings — for fidelity. Fidelity requires creativity, and creativity licenses the formation of rules and judgments concerning divorce which need not be identical to Matthew's concession or to Paul's, but which respect both the vows of marriage and the partners of a marriage, which protect both the vulnerability of sexuality and the vulnerable, which honor God's creative and redemptive intentions. In a world like this one — where God's good future is not yet — although divorce is never to be celebrated as a good in itself or as a way God's future makes its power felt, a Christian community may acknowledge that divorce may sometimes be necessary in order to protect either marriage itself or one of the marriage partners. As killing is sometimes allowed with fear and trembling, in, for example, a just war, so a Christian community may permit divorce "between the times" with mourning and repentance. It might, for example, (and given the promise of God to protect the weak and to defend the humiliated, I think it should) permit divorce in cases of abuse. Or, taking a cue from the just war tradition, the Christian community might insist that divorce be "a last resort." Matthew (5:32; 19:9) and Paul (1 Cor. 7:10-16) make such "concessions." Fidelity to Scripture and to its story surely does require a disposition not to divorce, even when the Law (or a self-interested and patriarchal reading of the Law) would permit it. It chastens any effort to read the text of Deuteronomy or the texts of Matthew and Paul as if they provided easily accessible justifications for divorce. The longing to be faithful to Scripture will permit neither treating the text as a manipulable oracle nor treating divorce as if it were a purely private matter. It requires that the community's reading of Scripture *discipline* our dispositions and decisions about divorce. Personal responsibility is not disowned, but it is put in the context of the community that remembers Jesus and is ready to follow him, to be disciples and pilgrims on the way toward God's good future. The longing to be faithful to Scripture will require the community's *discernment,* both that we may see how parts of Scripture fit the whole and that we may learn how our lives and our common life can be made coherent with remembering Jesus.

Homosexuality and Good Sex

Given the current conversations within many denominations, we can hardly conclude this chapter on remembering Jesus in the world of our sexuality without some consideration of homosexuality. The issue of homosexuality never assumes any great importance in the New Testament, and I thought for a time of relegating consideration of it to a footnote as a way to signal that simple truth. It has, however, assumed great importance in many ecclesiastical deliberations. To treat homosexuality in a footnote might be appropriate to Scripture, but it would hardly be appropriate to the continuing church as a community of moral discourse, deliberation, and discernment. Let it be admitted, however, that in reading Scripture we face the problem of silence here — and in two ways. First, if in reading Scripture we focus on the memory of Jesus, it is worth remarking that Jesus says nothing about homosexual behavior. Second, Scripture is silent about what we have learned to call "sexual orientation." No one in the ancient world, including any author of Scripture, had such a notion.

Although the issue of homosexual behavior is never mentioned by Jesus and never assumes any great importance in Scripture, there are texts which count such behavior as sexual immorality (Lev. 18:22; 20:13; Rom. 1:24-27; 1 Cor. 6:9; 1 Tim. 1:10).[16] The passages from Leviticus are clear enough in a way: "You shall not lie with a male as with a woman; it is an abomination" (Lev. 18:22; similarly 20:13). The context, however, should give us pause before we make of these verses anything like a timeless code for the behavior of Christians. These verses are part of the "Holiness Code," which contains not only much legal wisdom but also some curious regulations, regulations that Christians no longer take to be instructive for their choices.[17] Even so, it is clear that these verses provide the foundation for the Jewish tradition that consistently rejected homosexual behavior, regarding it as a form of Gentile immorality.

---

16. The story of Sodom and Gomorrah and its destruction (Gen. 18–19) is sometimes listed among the relevant passages, but it should not be. The sin that brought God's judgment upon these cities was not homosexual behavior. Ezekiel identifies the sin of Sodom quite differently: "This was the guilt of your sister Sodom: she and her daughters had pride, excess of food, and prosperous ease, but did not aid the poor and needy" (Ezek. 16:49). The attempted homosexual rape against the angelic visitors is despicable, but it is hardly the cause of the judgment the angels went to Sodom to announce. Moreover, although the act of homosexual rape is despicable, no party to the conversation in Christian community is defending rape. Homosexual rape is hardly relevant to the question of consensual homosexual relationships.

17. Consider, for example, Leviticus 19:19: "you shall not sow your field with two kinds of seed; nor shall you put on a garment made of two different materials."

The passages in 1 Corinthians 6:9-10 and 1 Timothy 1:10 are lists of vices, two of many in the New Testament but the only ones to mention homosexual behavior. Both of these lists include *arsenokoitai* (NRSV: "sodomites").[18]

Two things seem clear from these lists: First, the Pauline tradition was indebted to the Jewish tradition concerning sexual immorality with its prohibition of homosexual behavior. The very word *arsenokoitai* is probably coined from the Septuagint's translation of Leviticus 20:13 into Greek for Greek-speaking Jews (*meta arsenos koitēn gynaikos:* "lies with a man as with a woman"). The indebtedness of (at least part of) the Christian tradition to the Jewish tradition at this point is hardly accidental. They shared a story of creation. Sex is good in the creation, very good. It is a story of an embodied relationship, a "one flesh" union, of male and female, begun in vows, carried out in fidelity, and blessed with children. Good sex "in the beginning" involves mutuality and equality, intimacy and continuity, and the blessing of children. But the second point is this: the Christian tradition did not emphasize this prohibition — not by frequency of appearance in its lists of vices, not by placement within the vice lists in which it does appear, and not by any gloss. There is nothing in the New Testament or in remembrance to warrant applying this vision prejudicially and oppressively to single out homosexual behavior as especially worthy of condemnation or to shun and stigmatize homosexual persons.

The only other passage that mentions homosexual behavior (and the only passage in Scripture to mention lesbian behavior) is Romans 1:26-27.

> For this reason God gave them up to degrading passions. Their women exchanged natural intercourse for unnatural, and in the same way also the men, giving up natural intercourse with women, were consumed with passion for one another. Men committed shameless acts with men and received in their own persons the due penalty for their error.

The passage, it should be noted, was not prompted by any inquiry concerning homosexual behavior. The problem in the Roman churches, the problem that prompted the letter, was not homosexuality but the tension and enmity between Jewish Christians and Gentile Christians, between the "weak" and the "strong" (to use the terms used by the Gentile Christians), between "the righ-

---

18. Against the effort of John Boswell, *Christianity, Social Tolerance, and Homosexuality* (Chicago: University of Chicago Press, 1980), to suggest some other meaning for this term, see Robin Scroggs, *The New Testament and Homosexuality* (Philadelphia: Fortress, 1983), pp. 106-8. First Corinthians 6:9 also includes a reference to Gk. *malakoi* (NRSV: "male prostitutes").

teous" and "sinners" (to use the terms preferred by the Jewish Christians).[19] Many of the Jewish Christians were all too ready to judge and condemn the Gentile Christians as "sinners" and to boast about their own righteousness. Many of the Gentile Christians were all too ready to despise the Jewish Christians as "weak" and to boast about their own strength and freedom. Paul writes to assert that in Jesus Christ all are "righteous" and that without him all are "sinners." He writes "by way of reminder" to encourage "the obedience of faith." They are not to judge and despise each other; they are to "welcome one another" (Rom. 15:7), to be hospitable to one another, signaling a good future in which there is "no longer Jew and Gentile." Throughout the letter Paul addresses sometimes particularly the Jewish Christians, sometimes particularly the Gentile Christians, and sometimes the whole community.[20] In the passage that begins in Romans 1:18 Paul is addressing the Jewish Christians. ("You" always refers to the Jews [e.g., 2:17]; "they" are the Gentiles.)

In Romans 1:18-32 Paul deliberately makes use of an argument that would have been familiar to the Jewish Christians in Rome as the explanation for Gentile sexual immorality. The Jewish tradition told the story of creation and a fall to explain Gentile immorality (cf., e.g., Wisd. Sol. 13:1-9), and Paul tells that story, too, or something like it. Utilizing the Jewish tradition, Paul traces Gentile immorality to their refusal to honor God as the creator, their refusal to give thanks to God for the creation, their pride in "claiming to be wise" (1:21-22). "They are without excuse" (1:20). This failure to honor God, this refusal to give thanks to God, their pride and idolatry (1:23, 25), has provoked God's wrath. "The wrath of God is revealed . . . against all ungodliness," Paul said (1:18), and those Jewish Christians eager to judge and condemn their Gentile neighbors would have loved it. You can almost hear them, "Amen, brother. Preach it, Paul!" Paul goes on, still utilizing the Jewish tradition, to illustrate how the wrath of God is manifest, how the curse is felt, in Gentile wickedness. Because of their root sin, "God gave them up" to their own depravity, "to a debased mind and to things that should not be done. They were filled with every kind of wickedness, evil, covetousness, malice" (1:28-29). The curse falls not *just* on the sexual life, but the curse falls there as well. "God gave them up in the lusts of their hearts to impurity, to the degrading of their bodies among themselves, because they exchanged the truth about God for a lie and worshiped and

---

19. See Paul Minear, *The Obedience of Faith: The Purposes of Paul in the Epistle to the Romans*, Studies in Biblical Theology, Second Series, 19 (Naperville, Ill.: Alec R. Allenson, 1971).

20. For example, there are explicit markers of the change of audience in Romans 7:1 and 11:13. See further Minear.

served the creature rather than the Creator" (1:24). And the curse makes its power felt in homosexual behavior (1:26-27). That is the setting for these verses in Romans 1:18-32. Those Jewish Christians eager to condemn the Gentiles would have loved it. They read the story over-against the Gentiles, not over-against themselves; they read it to boast about their righteousness and to condemn their neighbors. They were glad when Paul joined his voice to theirs, condemning Gentile immorality and saying that those Gentiles had no excuse.

But Romans 1:18-32 has its own setting in the larger context of Romans. Paul has only set the Jewish Christians up rhetorically for the next sentence: "Therefore you have no excuse . . . when you judge others" (2:1). Those who judge and condemn the Gentiles commit the same root sin. They refuse to honor God as God or to give thanks for the decision to include the Gentiles. In their judging and condemning, in their thinking themselves wise and righteous because they possess the Law (2:17-29), they make themselves fools and resist God's plan to include the Gentiles in his righteousness. Paul finally rejects the reading of Scripture over-against others. He acknowledges, to be sure, that the Jews have a certain advantage over the Gentiles, for "the Jews were entrusted with the oracles of God" (3:2); but he insists that Scripture be read over-against ourselves. Citing a series of passages beginning with Psalm 14:1-2, he claims that the "advantage" of Scripture is that we know we are at no "advantage," for "there is no one who is righteous" (3:10). All are "sinners," both Jew and Gentile; and in Christ all are made "righteous," both Jews and Gentiles. There is no place for boasting about one's own righteousness (3:27). And "there is therefore now no condemnation for those who are in Christ Jesus" (8:1). Romans 1:18-32 was not written as an instruction concerning homosexuality but as part of an argument against the readiness of some Christians in Rome to condemn others.

The context is critically important, and must not be forgotten when we read and use this text in the moral discourse of the churches. Even so, it does seem clear that Paul shares the Jewish tradition's aversion to homosexual behavior, and the content of this passage may not be forgotten in the moral discourse of the church, either. "For this reason," the passage begins, referring to the root sin of the Gentiles, their refusal to honor God as God, their refusal to give thanks to God. (Similarly, the "therefore" of 1:24 and the "since . . ." of 1:28.) Homosexual behaviors are not the root sin; they are one of the consequences of the root sin. But how does Paul understand the sexual behaviors of which he speaks? He talks of persons who "exchange" "natural intercourse" for "unnatural" and of being "consumed with passion for one another." Let's take each in turn.

The language of "exchange" had been used before in this chapter — in

1:23 and 1:25. In those verses the Gentiles "exchanged the glory of the immortal God for [idols]" and "exchanged the truth about God for a lie"; in those verses "exchanged" is a reference to the root sin of idolatry. The first point, then, is simply that in 1:26-27 the language of "exchanged" creates a powerful reminder of the root sin and a rhetorical connection between it and the homosexual acts that are among its consequences. The language of exchange suggests that the acts that are a consequence of the root sin also somehow reflect it. The second point, however, is more important. In 1:23 and 25 this "exchanging" suggests a choice. The Gentiles could have known God in the world of the creation. They should have known God in the manifest works of God in "the things he has made" (1:20). That's why "they are without excuse" (1:20). The knowledge and praise of God were, it might be said, "natural" to them. They were made to know God and to praise him. But they didn't! They "exchanged" the "natural" knowledge of God for a lie. And in 1:26-27 the "exchanging" also suggests a choice. It is possible that we should understand Paul, as Victor Paul Furnish suggests,[21] to refer in this verse to those homosexual behaviors which are freely chosen by people for whom heterosexual relations were "natural" and which are motivated by insatiable lust. If we should understand Paul in this way, as locating one consequence and reflection of "exchanging" the glory of God for an idol in the choices of heterosexual persons to engage in homosexual intercourse in an attempt to satisfy their insatiable sexual appetites, then such behaviors would surely be examples of "shameless acts." And most persons, including most persons who are homosexual and are therefore liable to be exploited by such behaviors, would surely join Paul in finding such behavior reprehensible. The problem, of course, is that Paul knew nothing of a concept of "sexual orientation," so he cannot have been saying precisely that persons *with a heterosexual orientation* chose to engage in homosexual behaviors.

But what does Paul mean by "natural"? "Natural" was surely a critical word in the vocabulary of Greek moralists, and it was familiar to Hellenistic Judaism. Even so, it remains notoriously ambiguous, and it always risks collapsing the distinction between the way things are and the way they ought to be. When Paul describes homosexual acts as "against nature" (*para physin;* Rom. 1:26), he cannot mean that such acts violate a heterosexual orientation which is "natural" to and normative for human beings, or that such acts violate a heterosexual orientation which is "given" by nature to human beings (rather than chosen by them). As has

---

21. Victor Paul Furnish, *The Moral Teachings of Paul,* rev. ed. (Nashville: Abingdon, 1985), pp. 52-82. Furnish usefully displays the similarity of Paul's remark not only to the Jewish tradition but also to the understanding of homosexual behavior in some first-century Stoic moralists, notably Seneca and Dio Chrysostom.

just been observed, the now common and important concept of sexual orientation was unknown to Paul and his contemporaries. Nor does he mean simply that such behavior is unusual.[22] The background to his use of "natural" is not twentieth-century psychology. Nor for that matter, is the background for his thought Greek philosophy, although the terminology is indebted to it. The background for his use of "natural" here, I think, is the biblical story of our creation as male and female, the story of good sex in the beginning. When Paul describes homosexual acts as "against nature," he means that they do not fit the kind of embodied creatures we were created as. It is, after all, the story of the creation and fall — or one something like it — that Paul tells in Romans 1:18-32. The story, rather than some statute considered by itself, formed Paul's vision of good sex. If we understand "natural" as appropriate to the sort of embodied creatures we were created as, then the connection of this verse with the "exchanging" of 1:23 and 25 is clear. The Gentiles exchanged the truth of God that was given with the creation for a lie, for idolatry, and they exchange the "good sex" given with the creation for homosexual behaviors. As the knowledge and praise of God are "natural" in the creation, so are sexual relations of a man and a woman.

This "exchanging," however, still suggests a choice, a conscious and deliberate rejection of the sexual longings and fulfillment in accord with the story of creation. And if there is no choice, then they are not, after all, "without excuse" (1:20). Paul, like other writers of his day, simply assumed that people could control not only their sexual appetites but also the "orientation" of their appetites, ordering those appetites into conformity with the dictates of reason or the laws of nature or the story of creation. That helps to explain the reference to being "consumed with passion." Homosexual behaviors were evidently understood by Paul — as they were by Dio Chrysostom (and others) — as prompted by an insatiable lust, the sort of lust which drives a man first to visit female prostitutes and then, in search of something more exotic, to seduce other men.[23] There is clearly no concept of sexual orientation at work here. It may be an anachronism to import a notion of sexual orientation into the first century and into our reading of Paul, but it requires no anachronism to suggest that Paul refers here to homosexual behaviors freely chosen by people whose appetite for sexual pleasure was once but is no longer sated by heterosexual relationships.

We read these texts and this text in Christian community. There the good

---

22. Against Boswell on this point see Richard Hays, "Relations Natural and Unnatural: A Response to John Boswell's Exegesis of Romans 1," *The Journal of Religious Ethics* 14, no. 1 (Spring 1986): 184-215, especially 192-99.

23. Dio Chrysostom, *Discourse* VII, trans. J. W. Cohoon (Loeb Classical Library, 1932), pp. 151-52; cited in Furnish, *The Moral Teachings of Paul*, p. 63.

is remembrance, not the search for some timeless code. We read these texts as a part of the whole story, with the memory of Jesus in the middle of it. We read these texts in a community that includes homosexual persons as well as heterosexuals, in a community that silences neither Scripture nor each other. We read them attentive to the standards of excellence for reading Scripture: holiness and sanctification, fidelity and creativity, discipline and discernment.

And what then shall we say about the choices homosexuals do have? And about the choices the church faces in response to them? What can be said "by way of reminder"? What can be said in memory of Jesus? There is still much work to be done in discourse, deliberation, and discernment on this issue, and I certainly do not claim to have the last word. But I offer this "by way of reminder."

Remember that in memory of Jesus Paul attempted the reconciliation of those in the Roman churches who boasted about their righteousness while condemning others as "sinners" and those who boasted about their strength while despising others who cherished ancient Jewish traditions. Part of Paul's effort at reconciliation was the reminder that they were "able to instruct one another" — not because of the little good some of them thought they did well nor because of the little knowledge some of them thought they knew well — but because they gathered and dispersed in memory of Jesus. And remember that another part of Paul's effort at reconciliation was to train them to read Scripture over-against themselves and not simply in self-serving defense of their own righteousness.

Remember the story of good sex that Jesus told, the story of "one flesh." The story of our creation as male and female still suggests, I think, that the Christian vision of good sex is the "one flesh" union of a man and a woman that gestures and nurtures the covenant made in vows, carried out in fidelity, and hospitable to children. That story, rather than some statute considered by itself, formed Paul's vision of good sex. And it continues to sustain a moral preference for the "one flesh" union of a man and a woman.

Remember that the good future of God that Jesus announced brought something new. Human fulfillment does not depend on sexual fulfillment. Celibacy is an option, although it should not be undertaken as a way to boast about our spiritual transcendence over our bodies, as though we were already angels. Remember the importance of prudence in the face of temptations while we wait and watch for God's good future.

And remember the effort of the community to remember Jesus in response to other sexual choices that fall short of God's good future. Divorce, for example, is not the way God's good future makes its power felt, but while we wait and watch for God's good future, the church may sometimes allow it to protect marriage or one of the marriage partners. If we read the texts concerning homosexual behaviors less generously than we read the texts about divorce,

238

we must ask why. And consistency may require that we revisit our reading and performance of both.

Remember that it is no longer simply the creation, and it is not yet God's good future. In this interim, our sexual lives all fall under judgment. The story-formed vision of good sex is violated in a variety of ways, by sexual intercourse without a commitment to continuity, by adultery, by divorce, by patriarchy, by abuse, and by homosexual behavior, to name a few. These all may be numbered among the marks of the curse, of our common fallenness.

And consider what Scripture did not know, that people have a sexual orientation that they do not so much choose as discover. Fidelity to Scripture will require creativity in recognition of that fact alone. We are all responsible, of course, for the choices we do have. So what shall we say, then, about some of the choices faced by our homosexual brothers and sisters in Christ? And what shall we say about some of the choices faced by the church in response to them?

Singleness and chastity is an option to be considered by both heterosexual and homosexual persons. It signals that the ages have turned, that human fulfillment does not depend upon sexual fulfillment, and that, until the power of sin lays down its arms and admits defeat, there is restraint against the disorders still threatening human relations in the world of our sexuality.

But what shall we say if celibacy is not one's "gift"? One does not have to be indifferent to the Scripture's story-formed preference for heterosexual intercourse in order to see and to say that intercourse (whether heterosexual or homosexual) within the context of a relationship of commitment and continuity is better than promiscuity and infidelity. That moral preference is also formed by the story. It is still not yet the good future of God, but even in a fallen world — and in a fallen sexuality — fidelity and mutuality can be a mark of God's good future. If we allow divorce in a world like this one for the sake of protecting marriage and marriage partners, and if we allow remarriage after divorce, then we must also consider allowing homosexual relationships for the sake of protecting fidelity and mutuality and the homosexual partners. It does not make divorce a good or homosexual behavior a good. The Orthodox Church has a special liturgy for remarriage after divorce that recognizes that such relationships are marked by our fallenness even while it blesses and consecrates the marriage. Perhaps that would provide a model for homosexual unions.

What shall we say then? There is "no excuse" for homophobia in the church. Let the discipline of the church judge "our" *akatharsia* (our impurity[24])

---

24. *Akatharsia* is used in Romans 1:24, and it is included in the vice lists much more often than *arsenokoitai*. (See 2 Cor. 12:21; Gal. 5:19; Eph. 5:3; Col. 3:5; see also n. 11 in this chapter.)

no less rigorously than "their" *arsenokoitai*. Let the community gathered around the whole Scripture for discernment include those whom it is too much our impulse to shun. Let us silence neither Scripture nor each other. In remembrance and in hope, in repentance and in celebration, together we wait and watch and pray for the good future of God and struggle somehow to live the story we love to read and tell.

PART FOUR

REMEMBERING JESUS
IN THE WORLD OF ADAM SMITH

A Continuing Tradition of Justice and Generosity

CHAPTER TWELVE

A Rich Fool in the
World of Adam Smith

I was born into a Dutch family. It will come as no surprise to those who know and believe the stereotype that my parents were always hard workers, prudent spenders, and thrifty savers. When I was a little boy, they used to give me an allowance, and when I was a very little boy, my allowance was a dime. (As you may guess, I was a very little boy a very long time ago.) My mother would sometimes say, as she pressed a dime into my eager little hand on a Saturday morning, "Now remember, Allen, a fool and his money are soon parted."

It ought to be mentioned, I suppose, that I almost always had that dime spent on candy or baseball cards before the morning was over. (It might also be mentioned that the baseball cards were purchased — and discarded — long before baseball cards became an investment.) At any rate, my reckless habits as a consumer made it only appropriate that my mother caution me, "Now remember, Allen, a fool and his money are soon parted."

Over the years that proverb made quite an impression on me. No one wants to be a fool, after all. For quite some time, while I was growing up, I was convinced that this line about a fool and his money must be a quotation from the Bible. My mother liked to quote Scripture for the instruction of her four sons. (Her favorite was 1 Corinthians 10:12, "Let him that thinketh he standeth take heed lest he fall" [KJV].) But I could never find this proverb in Scripture. Still, I wondered sometimes whether it was not there somewhere, hidden perhaps where only the most devout (like my mother) could find it.

There is, to be sure, a parable in the Gospel of Luke about a fool who is separated from his money — and soon.

The land of a rich man produced abundantly. And he thought to himself, "What should I do, for I have no place to store my crops?" Then he said, "I will do this: I will pull down my barns and build larger ones, and there I will store all my grain and my goods. And I will say to my soul, Soul, you have ample goods laid up for many years; relax, eat, drink, be merry." But God said to him, "You fool! This very night your life is being demanded of you. And the things you have prepared, whose will they be? . . . " (Luke 12:16-20)

The rich man is called a fool, and he and his money are soon parted; nevertheless, the parable seems to be saying something quite different about a fool and something quite different about money than my mother's maxim.

In the following chapters we will try to see that difference — and to see something of the difference it might make in the formation of character and community. We will once again proceed "by way of reminder." We will remember Jesus and remember the early church remembering Jesus in the bold confidence that the memory of Jesus still gives the church identity and still makes it a community of moral discourse and deliberation and discernment, also with respect to money.

It should be acknowledged, however, that the economic world has changed and is changing. Jesus and the first Christians did not live in the same economic world most of us live in, the world of capitalism and corporate profits, the world of Adam Smith. And before we attempt to remember Jesus we might try to recall a more recent past.

The World of Adam Smith

1776 was a revolutionary year. On one side of the Atlantic a new political democracy was born; on the other side Adam Smith published his *An Inquiry into the Nature and Causes of the Wealth of Nations* and became the "father of political economy." Smith would hardly have thought of himself as a revolutionary, but his work ground the prescription lenses through which people learned to see themselves and their tasks differently. The whole of Europe and the infant nation born that year became the world of Adam Smith.

In that world each learned to expect others to do what was in their economic self-interest, and society learned to rely on a free market to direct such self-interested economic activity toward society's benefit. When we deal with "the butcher, the brewer, or the baker," he said, we depend not on their benevolence but on their self-interest.[1] We enter their shops without looking for fa-

1. Adam Smith, *An Inquiry into the Nature and Causes of the Wealth of Nations* (Oxford: Clarendon, 1979), bk. I, ch. 2, p. 26.

vors, offering instead to pay for the goods they offer for sale. If they charge too much or offer inferior goods, they know that we won't be back, that it will be in our self-interest to enter the shop of a competitor instead, relying on the initiative of yet another self-interested party to exploit a commercial opportunity.

In Adam Smith's world the self-interested individual was liberated from the control of tradition and political or religious authorities. The son was no longer simply expected to perform the task his father performed the way his father performed it. The conduct of citizen and Christian was no longer determined economically by the edicts of political or religious authorities. The initiative of this freed and self-interested individual was released to exploit commercial opportunities and to develop industry and technology, and thus — "naturally, or rather necessarily"[2] — the pursuit of economic self-interest in a free market would increase the wealth of the whole society. Such was the vision of Adam Smith in 1776, and such is the prescription for the lenses through which many economists still see the world in capitalist economies.

Adam Smith may have been the first "economist," but he was also a moralist. And as a moralist he was no egoist, simply pronouncing a benediction upon self-interest. When he published *The Wealth of Nations,* he was already famous for a book he had published seventeen years earlier, *The Theory of Moral Sentiments.* In that book Smith argued that human beings could and should put themselves in the position of an objective and impartial observer in any moral case, temporarily suppressing their natural self-interest for the sake of moral judgment. Following his own advice, he tried to adopt that position in his analysis of the economy. In *The Wealth of Nations,* he reported his "objective and impartial" observations of the economic order, including the "observation" of an "invisible hand"[3] which fashioned the competition of self-interested individuals into a socially beneficial harmony. Such assurances gave moral legitimacy to the character and community of economically self-interested individuals, and they helped to suppress (at least temporarily) the moral qualms and scruples about the consequences of this new economic liberty. It was, in Adam Smith's world, finally virtuous to be self-interested in the marketplace.

It might be asked, of course, whether Adam Smith created a new economic order or simply reported one. Medieval culture had disintegrated before

2. Smith, *Wealth of Nations,* bk. IV, ch. 2, p. 454.
3. The famous passage is from Smith, *Wealth of Nations,* bk. IV, ch. 2, p. 456: "[The individual] generally, indeed, neither intends to promote the publick interest, nor knows how much he is promoting it. . . . [H]e intends only his own gain, and he is in this, as in many other cases, led by an invisible hand to promote an end which was no part of his intention."

Adam Smith. A feudal and agrarian economy had been dying — and painfully — for some time. The Reformation had turned the religious calling and asceticism "this-worldly" (according to Max Weber, at least)[4] and thus unleashed forces of industry and thrift. Exploration and colonialism had enriched monarchs and their nations. Commerce had begun to develop before Adam Smith, and power had begun to shift from the nobility to the merchants. Double entry bookkeeping, which became a standard practice only in the seventeenth century, provided a device for rational accounting and made management of large-scale business easier. Other "devices" made an enormous impact; the printing press, the windmill, the paper mill, the clock, and other inventions changed the economy and the culture and signaled a different spirit toward innovation. The Industrial Revolution arrived during Adam Smith's lifetime. There were economic forces and energies at work in 1776 that did not so much await release by an economic theory as simply break the bonds of tradition and convention. Still, the vision of Adam Smith made this complex world seem habitable, even hospitable, and put the conscience of society at rest about the consequences of the economic activity of free and self-interested individuals.

It might be asked as well, of course, whether it is still the world of Adam Smith. Things have changed since 1776. The confidence that an "invisible hand" would fashion social well-being through the competition of a free market could hardly endure the sight of children working fourteen hours a day in sweatshops or the smell of noxious factory smoke. Some moral qualms and scruples have been impossible to suppress. Consider the social legislation enacted in the last century and a half, in areas ranging from child labor laws and the abolition of slavery, that market in human flesh, to the rights of workers to organize, Social Security, safety standards for the workplace, and environmental impact studies. Such legislation has expressed some of those moral qualms and relied on human hands and human resolve to intervene in free markets. Some political control of the economic order is now not only accepted but expected — and not only in response to moral qualms and scruples about the consequences of a free market but also in order to assure that the market works predictably enough for people to have confidence in it.

Things have changed since 1776. No less important than the acceptance of some political restraints and constraints upon markets is the rise of the corporation as an economic agent. The world of Adam Smith, as it exists today, is populated less by free and self-interested individuals than it is by corporations.

Things have changed, and in the midst of change some have envisioned a

4. Max Weber, *The Protestant Ethic and the Spirit of Capitalism* (English trans.; New York: Charles Scribner's Sons, 1958).

different economic world. Karl Marx did much of his work in the world of Adam Smith (in nineteenth-century Britain, more precisely). He didn't like what he saw of that world, and he urged a different vision. The world of Adam Smith, he complained, was a world of inevitable inequity and exploitation. Wealth and power were in the hands of the capitalists, and the workers were beaten down to poverty and powerlessness. Marx trusted no "invisible hand," but he did trust the power of social resentment and the righteousness and grace of a historical dialectic working inexorably in history to judge and destroy the world of Adam Smith and to give birth to a world of communal ownership. The labor pains would be revolution, but the new world would be "the socialization of property." In the real world of communism, however, "the socialization of property" accomplished equity no better than productivity; economic power and political power were concentrated in the hands of a bureaucratic oligarchy. Recently, of course, communism has crumbled. Countries have rushed from the world of Karl Marx; many of the formerly communist countries have struggled to establish free markets and to "privatize" property. And in the world of Adam Smith many point to the crumbling of the world of Karl Marx as the best defense of their own confidence in self-interest and free markets.

To be sure, there are failures in the world of Adam Smith as well, none more spectacular perhaps than the failures of its very successes. Capitalism has indeed generated enormous wealth, but it and its conspicuous consumption exist alongside grinding poverty. Industrial corporations have produced not only products for markets but also pollution for the planet. Commercial advertising has created not only markets for the products but also a joyless and vulgar consumer culture.[5] It is hard to suppress moral scruples in and about such a world, and confidence in Smith's "invisible hand" seems a creed ripe for doubt.

The doubters, however, are met with a number of able defenders of Adam Smith and of his world. They insist not only that the successes of capitalism must be celebrated over-against the failures of communism but also that the best chance for dealing with the failures of capitalism's successes will come not by political regulations and controls but by free individuals in a free world supported by free markets. Robert Benne, for example, insists on "this hard fact of life — that moral, social, and political gains are curiously dependent on the relative autonomy of economic efficiency."[6] The world of Adam Smith, he acknowledges,

5. Tibor Scitovitz, *The Joyless Economy: An Inquiry into Human Satisfaction and Consumer Dissatisfaction* (New York: Oxford University Press, 1976).
6. Robert Benne, *The Ethic of Democratic Capitalism: A Moral Reassessment* (Philadelphia: Fortress, 1981), p. 128. Benne finds both strengths and weaknesses, both virtues and vices, in democratic capitalism. Among the virtues are the encouragement of economic

does not guarantee a just or a good world, but it is necessary for one.[7] The economic process has an important priority to moral questions and an important independence from moral scruples. Michael Novak, similarly, defends both the vision of Adam Smith and the notion of a "virtuous self-interest."[8]

Both Benne and Novak are — like Adam Smith himself — moralists. Both acknowledge and appreciate the importance of moral values like justice and love as well as economic values, and both appreciate the importance of political and moral-cultural systems as well as of economic systems. But both — like Adam Smith himself — provide an account of the economic world which allows (and requires) the temporary suppression of certain moral qualms and scruples as too "costly" to productive capacity, as counter-productive interference with the generation of wealth. Neither is ready to call for removal of the social legislation enacted in the past century and a half; neither wants child labor laws repealed, for example. But each seems to presume that such regulations are simply a part of a decent and respectable capitalist economy, even though such regulations were once innovative interventions into the market and opposed by many of the wealthy and economically powerful as too "costly."

The world of Adam Smith still lives in the vision of moralists like Benne and Novak — and in the rhetoric of those economists and corporate managers who insist that "the business of business is business." Milton Friedman, for example, defends the pursuit of profit not only against government regulatory interventions into the market but also against the social conscience of some other economists and managers. In the world of Adam Smith, in a "free economy," he says, "there is one and only one social responsibility of business — to use its resources and engage in activities designed to increase its profits."[9] Not only are

---

efficiency and growth, the decentralization of power, and a role for government in seeking justice for the weak. Among the vices are the depletion of energy resources, exploitation of poorer countries, and injustice toward the poor within the country. According to Benne, however, democratic capitalism has the resources to address its own weaknesses.

7. Benne, *Ethic of Democratic Capitalism,* p. 135.

8. Michael Novak, *The Spirit of Democratic Capitalism* (New York: American Enterprise Institute, 1982), pp. 92-95. See Daniel Dombrowski, "Benne and Novak on Capitalism," *Theology Today* 42 (April 1984): 61-65.

9. Milton Friedman, *Capitalism and Freedom* (Chicago: University of Chicago Press, 1962), p. 133. He adds the qualifier, "so long as it stays within the rules of the game, which is to say, engages in open and free competition, without deception or fraud." But he does not pause to ask who made the rules or whether they could be modified in the interest of either fairness of competition or the well-being of society or the planet. There seems the same presumption — although not quite as strong — as in Benne and Novak that some "rules of the game" such as child labor laws are simply part and parcel of a decent capitalist economy.

corporations expected to pursue profits single-mindedly and free to do it with an easy conscience, trusting "an invisible hand" to fashion conflicting corporate interests into a socially beneficial harmony,[10] they are prohibited from doing anything else. To accept any other responsibility, to intend anything other than making a profit, to do anything motivated by a social conscience, is "fundamentally subversive."[11] In such an account of business and its responsibility, it is still the world of Adam Smith. Economic activity is still understood fundamentally as the effort to increase wealth, to generate profits, and moral qualms and scruples are still squashed by the confidence in an invisible hand.

But we need not rely on the arguments of moralists or the testimony of economists to know it is still the world of Adam Smith. My mother's maxim has made quite an impression not only on me but also on our culture. "A fool and his money are soon parted." But imagine that the rich fool of Jesus' parable were alive today. (It does not take an enormous stretch of one's imagination.) He might not be a farmer, but he would be rich. If we met him on the street or in the store, we would not be likely to nudge each other and say, "Look, there he is — you know, the fool, the one in the parable." We would be much more likely to say, I think, "Look, he's no fool; he's rich." For, after all, a fool and his money are soon parted — and, therefore, anyone with money is no fool.

Perhaps this is not quite fair. A self-indulgent landowner who hoards his wealth or consumes it is not a hero in the view of Adam Smith. Indeed, Adam Smith would call him a villain and a fool, too. Money is not to be hoarded or wasted; it is to be used to make more money. Adam Smith's advice to this rich fool might be to part with his money to invest it — in order to make more money. That is the sort of advice, however, which a rich fool might readily and happily follow: buying stock, perhaps, instead of building barns. Perhaps buying stock would employ more people than building barns, and perhaps some confidence in an invisible hand could be restored. But the pursuit of profit would demand no change of character; it would require no turn from self-interested prudence as the fundamental motive. It might require contracts, but it would not nurture community. Such advice could be regarded as a "friendly amendment" to the fool's actions and my mother's maxim: A fool and his money are soon parted by stupid investments as well as silly consumption, but a wise man (or woman) parts with money to make more by clever investments. Jesus' parable, on the other hand, seems to call for a more fundamental amendment, for a change in character and community so fundamental one might call it "subversive."

10. Friedman quotes Adam Smith's account of the "invisible hand" (*Capitalism and Freedom*, p. 133).

11. Friedman, *Capitalism and Freedom*, p. 133.

The world of Adam Smith seems to be alive and well in our culture, and the rich fool seems to be alive and well and making "wise" investments in the world of Adam Smith. Notice also that my mother's maxim, as amended by Adam Smith, has made a deep impression on the theories of justice we typically use in our culture to consider issues of wealth and poverty. Suppose again that the fool were alive today and that he were to ask today how to secure his goods. After he had said, "Aha! I will not build barns but buy stock," he might well say, I suggest, "What I must build is a social structure that will protect my rational self-interest." And that is where both John Rawls and Robert Nozick begin their famous theories of justice. There are important differences between their theories of justice,[12] of course; and the fool would still have choices to make about the sort of social structure to build (or support). John Rawls identifies justice with two principles, maximum freedom *and* presumptive equality, whereas Robert Nozick is content to identify justice with historical entitlement. Both theories, however, assume the rational self-interested individual who wants to secure an arena within which to pursue and preserve private goods. Both assume the sort of person Jesus calls a "fool."

Now, I do not mean to suggest that Christians have no stake in the philosophical and theoretical debates concerning whether Rawls or Nozick is right — or that they have nothing to contribute to them. And I surely do not mean to suggest that the concern for justice among these moral philosophers is not an improvement over the temporary suppression of moral questions by some other moralists when considering the economic order. A concern for justice is

12. John Rawls, *A Theory of Justice* (Cambridge, Mass.: Harvard University Press, 1971); Robert Nozick, *Anarchy, State, and Utopia* (New York: Basic Books, 1974). Briefly, the dispute between them is whether the universal standards of justice that agents are obliged to accept by their own rationality and self-interest include a principle of equality as well as of liberty. Rawls argued that there are two principles of justice: "Each person is to have an equal right to the most extensive total system of equal basic liberties compatible with a similar system of liberty for all," and "Social and economic inequalities are to be arranged so that they are both: (a) to the greatest benefit of the least advantaged . . . and (b) attached to offices and positions open to all under the conditions of fair equality of opportunity" (*A Theory of Justice*, p. 301). Nozick accepts only the first of these principles and insists that Rawls's second principle necessarily violates the autonomy of individual agents and their choices concerning the distribution of what they produce and to which they are historically entitled. Nozick's "Historical Entitlement Principle" is "From each according to what he chooses to do, to each according to what he makes for himself (perhaps with the contracted aid of others) and what others choose to do for him and choose to give him of what they've been given previously (under this maxim) and haven't yet expended or transferred." Or, "From each as they choose, to each as they are chosen" (*Anarchy, State, and Utopia*, p. 160).

absolutely essential to publish and protect some boundaries of civility and fairness against rich fools like Michael Milken and Ivan Boesky who bought and sold junk bonds on the basis of insider information and whose pursuit of profit in the market evidently knew no bounds.

I do mean to suggest, however, that such theories of justice — relying on a self-consciously impartial point of view and attempting to articulate and apply presumably universal standards of justice — can and do provide at best a minimal account of what is morally at stake in our economic life. I do mean to suggest that we need a richer account of what is morally at stake in our wealth and our poverty, in our buying and our selling. The minimal accounts of justice do not and cannot form a *character* other than the enlightened and self-interested "fool." They do not and cannot nurture a *community* other than the sort of harmony created by a rough balance of power among individuals competing to secure their rights and their possessions (and so their lives). And they do not and cannot sustain *discourse* about the good economic life, for the good life — in such accounts — is a private matter, and it is only the right to pursue such private visions of the good life that may be talked of publicly and candidly.

We have mentioned the temptations to forgetfulness before, but they are nowhere stronger than in the world of Adam Smith. There is again the danger of forgetfulness in the old story of self-centeredness, here blessed as virtuous with the assurance that an invisible hand will manipulate the conflicting interests of the many toward social well-being. There is again the danger of forgetfulness in the confidence in and enthusiasm for one partial and parochial value, here profit, the production of wealth, to the exclusion of other goods and goals. And there is again the danger of forgetfulness in the confidence in and enthusiasm for an impartial perspective, for universal and rational moral principles, here the principles of distributive justice (which, ironically for "universal" principles, it is necessary to further describe as Rawlsian or Nozickian or utilitarian). If the Christian community starts with such principles of justice, or if it allows them to monopolize its deliberations concerning the economy, then it stands at risk of forgetfulness. And forgetfulness creates the risk of amnesia, of losing the identity and forfeiting the community that is founded in the church's memory of Jesus. And then, of course, the churches will no longer be communities of moral discourse and deliberation and discernment as communities of memory — not about economic issues, at any rate. The calling to instruct one another will go unheard, or unheeded, at least with respect to wealth and poverty. The rational standards of justice are morally important and politically useful, but as long as the church longs to live with integrity and not just with impartial rationality, it will have to live in memory of Jesus.

Things have changed, to be sure, and things will change. The world of

Adam Smith has its fault lines. The vision of Adam Smith has its uncorrected astigmatisms. There are critics who see some other goals for economic activity and who, therefore, justify some other regulations for the economy, some other "rules of the game." There are "socially responsible" economists and managers who hear and speak of morality not only after accumulation of wealth (as the necessary precursor to a good or just society) but during and even before it. These may be "subversive," to use the characterization of Milton Friedman, but they are not silent in the world of Adam Smith. In the context of this economic world and in the context of moral discourse about its fruits and flaws, the Christian community must remember Jesus and struggle to discern the shape of Christian integrity, the bearing of that memory of the formation of character and community and, yes, on the reformation of corporations and of the rules of the game.

Such an undertaking must be a communal one, for it demands a variety of gifts and skills. The next few chapters are only a very modest contribution to that communal task; nevertheless, they are offered "boldly by way of reminder." Such a communal undertaking, it ought to be observed, might be a risky one, for among other things, Christians remember of Jesus that he was accused of being "subversive."

CHAPTER THIRTEEN

Jesus and His Economic Worlds

The economic world in which Jesus lived — and in which the rich fool of his parable lived — was not the world of Adam Smith, but it was in its own way no less complex. If we are to remember Jesus, some attention to that world is required.

To say that it was an agricultural economy is simple enough and certainly true. Agricultural activity was not just a segment of the economy but its foundation. It is no accident that in the stories of Jesus remembered in the gospels there are constantly references to agricultural activity, to sowing seed and harvesting, to herding sheep (and swine in Gentile territory, Mark 5:11-17), and to fishing.

Advances in agriculture — the invention of the iron plow, the domestication of some animals, the harnessing of animal power, and countless other small developments — had over the centuries made agriculture surpluses sufficient to support nonagricultural crafts, commerce, and culture. The villages and the cities of Palestine were the centers of such activity, and it is no accident that the stories of Jesus are filled with references to them as well. There one found markets not only for agricultural products but for the work of potters and weavers and leather workers and carpenters and a variety of other craftsmen.[1] Money could be made at such markets; indeed, with money to invest and a willingness to take some risks, great fortunes could be made. Most of the crafts and commerce, however, were conducted on a small scale to meet local and basic needs. And if a great fortune was made, it was usually invested in the

---

1. John E. Stambaugh and David L. Balch, *The New Testament in Its Social Environment* (Philadelphia: Westminster, 1986), pp. 69-72.

253

purchase of an "estate," a large tract of agricultural land by which the good life could be secured. Such an estate was owned by the rich fool of Jesus' parable.

The model for increasing wealth was not yet deliberate improvements in productivity or distribution — even with respect to agriculture. One desiring wealth aimed less at more production from the land than at control of the land. And control of the land points us back to the villages and cities, for there one found the offices and homes of the wealthy landowners or their stewards, who leased the land to tenant farmers or supervised large farms themselves. And there one found as well the offices and homes of the agents of government and temple who took a tax or a tithe from the produce.

It sounds simple enough: a world of agriculture and pre-industrial cities. What made it complex was that this ancient economy, like other ancient economies, was "embedded" in a cultural context.[2] Every economy, of course, is affected by its cultural context, but modern economies have a degree of independence, of autonomy, from their cultural contexts that ancient economies simply did not have. That is, in a way, what makes modern economies "modern." Adam Smith had liberated the economy from the authority of tradition and from the control of political and religious officials, had separated economic motives from non-economic ones. But the economic world of Jesus was not the world of Adam Smith; the economy was still intimately tied to a whole way of life, enmeshed in culture, "embedded" in a social world.

Moreover, the economic world of Jesus was still more complex because the economy of first-century Palestine was intimately tied to conflicting ways of life, enmeshed in contrasting cultures, "embedded" in differing social worlds. The complexity can only be captured by a plural: Jesus lived in economic *worlds.* There was the world of the Roman Empire with its patronage, the world of the peasant farmer with its ties to family and the land, and the world of Jewish religion with its temple and Torah.

The Roman Empire and Patron-Client Relations[3]

It was proverbial that all roads led to Rome — and along those roads the wealth of the empire was carried to Rome: the spoils of wars, the surplus production of

2. Halvor Moxnes, *The Economy of the Kingdom* (Philadelphia: Fortress, 1988), pp. 27-32; Karl Polonyi et al., eds., *Trade and Market in the Early Empires* (1957; reprinted Chicago: Henry Regnery, 1971), p. 250.

3. See S. N. Eisenstadt and L. Roniger, *Patrons, Clients, and Friends* (Cambridge: Cambridge University Press, 1984); Stambaugh and Balch, *New Testament in Its Social Environment,* pp. 63-81; Moxnes, *Economy of the Kingdom,* pp. 40-47.

great estates in the provinces (not least among the spoils of war), and of course, the taxes. From the epicenter of Roman wealth and power, from that place where the emperor sat enthroned, patronage flowed in the other direction. The emperor named prefects and princes in the provinces and made gifts and loans to support their offices. These in turn provided honors and hospitality to the emperor, the support and resources due patrons from their clients. Being a client of the emperor ordinarily meant one had the status and the funds to be a patron to others. So, for example, in Palestine Herod the Great and his sons depended on the emperor's continued patronage and were patrons themselves to the Palestinian aristocracy, the urban elite. These, in turn, supported the Herods and became patrons themselves to subordinates who acted as stewards of their lands or lesser officials in the government. Again, the emperor was patron to centurions, who provided loyal service in return; centurions in turn won support where they were stationed by being patron to a village or its elders, sometimes even building a synagogue (Luke 7:4-5).

Patron-client relationships were marked by reciprocity. The "generosity" of the patron was reciprocated by the political or military or religious or financial support of the client, and the support of the client was given in expectation of continuing patronage. Patron-client relationships were not, however, marked by stability. To have wealth without power, that is, without the power of one's patrons, was to be in a precarious position. To lose the favor of one's patron was damning, and for one's patron to lose the favor of his patron made one's position almost equally risky. It would indeed be a rich fool in the first century who thought that wealth itself provided security.

Money-lending frequently followed the path of patronage,[4] and it provided a way not only to extract money by interest but to solidify power, for creditors could bind their "clients" into permanent slavery or temporary debt bondage if they could not or would not pay upon demand (e.g., Matt. 18:23-25). Conspicuous displays of wealth were necessary to preserve or to enhance one's status as patron, but any indebtedness was risky.

The land remained the source of wealth, but the crucial issue in Roman patronage was power. The peasants, closest to the land, were far from both power and wealth. And those driven to the margins of the villages, the sick and needy, had neither patron nor hope.

---

4. Stambaugh and Balch, *New Testament in Its Social Environment*, pp. 72-73.

The Way of Life of the Peasant Farmers[5]

The peasants were far from both the power and the wealth of patronage, but they were closest to the land. They worked the land as their fathers had, joined by ties of kinship and loyalty to family and clan. The extended family was both the unit of production and the unit of consumption. The economic world of the peasant was oriented to "subsistence,"[6] to that which was needed by a household for its members to be fully functioning members of the village society. Subsistence included food, to be sure, and shelter and clothing, but also sufficient resources to meet social and cultic requirements. The failure to achieve this objective might mean starvation, but it surely entailed a loss of standing in the village.

When the Hasmoneans defeated the Seleucids and won Jewish independence, they distributed some of the conquered land to Jewish households. The peasants had a patron in Simon, whose rule (145-135 B.C.E.) was celebrated in 1 Maccabees 14:12 as the fulfillment of divine promise, "Each man sat under his vine and his fig tree" (cf. Mic. 4:4). But patrons and powers come and go. The Romans rendered many peasants landless once again, reducing them to the status of tenant farmers, and Herod, who received some of the land from Augustus in patronage, did not return it to the peasants. The first century was a hard time for peasant farmers in Palestine. Many small landholders and tenant farmers had to take loans to farm their land or to pay their rent, to pay their taxes or their tithes and then the interest on their loans, and to subsist. But while patrons and powers came and went, the peasant way of life continued. The focus on "subsistence," however, muted the potential social criticism and resistance of the peasants; the question was not how much was taken but whether enough to subsist was left.[7] Hard times required holding on to what one had, restricting the circle of kinship obligations as much as was socially acceptable, and psychologically distancing oneself from the most needy, from those on the margins of society, in spite of (or because of) one's own proximity to that very margin.

The land remained the source of wealth but the crucial issue for the peasant household was subsistence. Those who could not manage that were reduced to begging or to banditry.[8]

---

5. Stambaugh and Balch, *New Testament in Its Social Environment*, pp. 91-92; Moxnes, *Economy of the Kingdom*, pp. 33-34, 79-83.

6. Moxnes, *Economy of the Kingdom*, p. 80.

7. Moxnes, *Economy of the Kingdom*, p. 81.

8. On "banditry" see R. A. Horsley and J. Hanson, *Bandits, Prophets, and Messiahs:*

Temple and Torah

Religious life and loyalties cannot be neatly separated from the way of life of Roman patronage or peasant farmer — but they must be distinguished. Temple and Torah could be co-opted to the interests of both patronage and peasantry, but they also preserved the memory and the hope of an alternative way of life.

The priestly aristocracy around Jerusalem, the Sadducees, capitalized on their relation to the temple to win for themselves political powers in Jerusalem as patrons and to preserve for themselves control of the temple treasury and great tracts of land. They were in turn patrons to others, to stewards of their lands and to the Levites who gathered the tithes. Their patronage extended into the villages and countryside of Judea and Galilee. The Torah required tithes and offerings, and the priests were happy to call for observance. (One relevant text here, Numbers 18:15-32, was part of the priestly code and appropriate to a priestly government, but such tithes were hardly necessary financially when Romans, with taxes of their own, ruled.) The peasants paid the price, if they could, and many of them willingly, for such financial obligations were included in "subsistence," in the maintenance of the status of full membership in the community. Many peasants shared a religious vision of the ties between temple and land and between both and God, creating one holy space which God ruled from the temple and in which their own place was confirmed.

Some priests and some peasants, however, rejected the Jerusalem priesthood and their temple observance as corrupted and co-opted. The community at Qumran is the most obvious example. They kept alive an alternative vision of the presence of God and of God's ties to the land, a vision that promised judgment against both Roman rulers and Jerusalem priests. In the meantime theirs was a new covenant; their community was a new temple, and they were its priests. It is no surprise, perhaps, that this community shared its goods and its meals and withdrew from the cities.

Torah, too, could be co-opted to the interests of patronage or peasantry, and not just the statutes about tithing. A written Scripture requires interpretation, and the scribal authority to interpret the Law provided the scribes with significant power in the community, and any power made one a valuable client. The scribes sat on the Council, the main body for Jewish self-government (what there was of it) during Roman administration, and they served on lesser judiciaries in their cities and villages and, of course, as officials of synagogues.

Popular Movements in the Time of Jesus (New York: Seabury, 1985), and the different profile of the phenomenon in Sean Freyne, *Galilee, Jesus and the Gospels* (Philadelphia: Fortress, 1988), pp. 163-67.

Joachim Jeremias called them "a new upper class,"[9] and the Gospel of Matthew discloses that they were accustomed to long robes, to seats of honor, and to greetings appropriate to their position and patronage (23:5-7).

Among the scribes the Pharisees were noteworthy (and praiseworthy)[10] for their efforts both to intensify and to democratize observance of the Law. They intensified observance by requiring of all members of their fellowship scrupulous observance not only of the statutes but also of priestly ritual purity. They democratized observance by requiring this priestly purity not only of priests and Levites in the temple but also of *all* members of their fellowships. Cultic purity and priestly holiness were brought to bear on everyday life, and they accomplished an "inner constitutionalism" which enabled Judaism to survive not only Roman occupation and the destruction of the temple but much else besides. They did not withdraw to the wilderness, but they formed a society within a society, small fellowships *(haverim)* with strict requirements.

The very strictness of the requirements, however, also served to limit the social requirements of hospitality and table fellowship, and thereby they rendered the *haverim* susceptible to being co-opted for economic interests. Those peasants who were still fully members of the village could limit their social obligations to those on the margins of village society by undertaking the additional cultic obligations of this smaller and more rigorous fellowship — and could do so without sacrificing their standing in the villages. Even if they did not become members of one of the Pharisaic *haverim*, they might co-opt this righteous separatism in order to hold on to what they had, to restrict the circle of kinship obligations in a socially acceptable way, to distance themselves from those "sinners" at the margins of society.

Temple and Torah might be co-opted by patronage and peasantry, but they also provided the memory and hope of alternative economies. When at the festival of first fruits pious Jewish farmers made pilgrimage to Jerusalem, they would lay at the temple some of the first of their harvest and recite again an ancient creed. It began, "A wandering Aramaean was my ancestor," and it continued with memories of slavery in Egypt, of bondage and oppression, and with memories, too, of God's gracious deliverance and gift of the land (Deut. 26:5-11). The Torah tells the same story, of course; it is the story that shaped not only Jewish faith but also the vision of the economy among the Jewish faithful.

To remember Abraham, that wandering Aramaean, was to remember a

---

9. Joachim Jeremias, *Jerusalem at the Time of Jesus* (Philadelphia: Fortress, 1969), pp. 233-45.

10. See Wayne Boulton, *Is Legalism a Heresy? The Legacy of the Pharisees in Christian Ethics* (New York: Paulist, 1982).

semi-nomadic way of life, patriarchs and matriarchs journeying with flocks and herds and pitching their tents where water and pasture invited. Then there were no rich or poor within the clan, for no one owned the land; flocks and herds belonged to the whole extended family, and the patriarch held them in trust. Such a nomadic economy, however, was already a thing of the past when the first farmer laid his first fruit before the priest. It persisted, to be sure, in the way of life of countercultural clans like the Rechabites, who pledged to own no vineyard, to till no soil, and to build no house (Jer. 35). And it persisted as well in the vision of an economy in which there would be no rich or poor, a no-madic ideal. Few, however, really wanted to return to a semi-nomadic existence, for although there were no rich or poor within the clan, the clan itself could be desperately poor. Even wealthy semi-nomadic families had lived a dangerous and difficult existence, contending against the threats of nature and marauders, and always only a steppe away from disaster.

Their own disaster was remembered, too: the sojourn in Egypt that be-came slavery to Pharaoh, the children of Abraham reduced to a life without place or dignity. Their story included their remembrance of "our affliction, our toil, our oppression" (Deut. 26:7), but it climaxed in their remembrance of the mighty work of God who heard their cries, saw their pain, rescued them from Egypt's slavery, and gave them the land. The land was God's gift, and they were its stewards, responsible to a God who hears the cries of those who hurt. The land was meant for a shared prosperity, not for patronage, not even for a peas-antry that turned its back on those still less fortunate. That story and vision was hardly realized in successive Jewish economies, but that memory and hope did constantly challenge and qualify their historical realities, and they left their mark also on the texts that addressed those historical realities and made their way finally into Torah and the other Hebrew Scriptures.

The settlement in Canaan itself caused profound changes in the Israelite economy. Settled agricultural life required the cultivation of field crops, or-chards, and vineyards; and the arts of cultivation, at least as the Canaanites practiced them, required proper ritual and reverence for the fertility gods, the Baalim, whose favor assured the crops. The struggle between loyalty to God and obeisance before Baal was not only a religious struggle but also an agricultural one. God's victory at Mount Carmel meant that agriculture was desacralized: Israel was free to farm without recourse to fertility rituals. And the religious and agricultural struggle was also an economic struggle. The victory of the God of Abraham and of the exodus meant not only the rejection of fertility gods but also the affirmation of the requirements of the covenant to provide for the poor and protect them from exploitation.

A settled agricultural life was reflected in the ancient Covenant Code

(Exod. 20:22–23:33).[11] There one finds presupposed customs and practices which were familiar to such historical economies: the reduction of some to slavery and property and the reduction of women to chattel (e.g., Exod. 21:1-11, 20-21, etc.). The story and vision of the ancient creed was hardly realized in this code or in the economy it reflected, but it did leave its marks. In the Covenant Code one finds not only the familiar practices legitimated but also a remarkable collection of statutes to protect the stranger (22:21; 23:9), to free the slave (21:2), to care for the widow and orphan (22:22-24), to provide rest and food and a hearing for the poor (23:6-8, 10-11, 12), and to protect the debtors (22:25-27). The very ones left vulnerable by the settled agricultural economy presupposed by the Covenant Code are especially protected by it against exploitation and victimization. Moreover, such protections are the very stipulations supported in the code by reference to the story and to the character of God made known in the story. The story of creed and of Torah was not realized in this economy, nor even in this code that was finally included in Torah, but it left its mark and endured to challenge and qualify the economy that came next.

The transition to monarchy caused economic changes no less profound than the settlement in Canaan. David's reign had marked the beginning of an urban culture and of a commercial prosperity in the land, but the prosperity was not shared equally. The royal court and a standing army were innovations that required taxation and conscription (1 Sam. 8:11-17). While the king and his court favorites grew prosperous and powerful, the poor suffered under a heavy burden of taxation, conscription, and powerlessness. So, while some lived in great luxury, many more fell into poverty, first mortgaging their lands and then losing them, becoming landless tenants or slaves.

In principle the king was subject to laws of the covenant, which he publicly vowed to uphold. In practice, however, royal despotism often displaced the covenant as the basis of social obligation. Ideally, then, the king was a defender of the poor (e.g., Ps. 72), but in reality he was often among their oppressors. The story of Naboth and his vineyard (1 Kings 21) is paradigmatic of the conflict between royal despotism and covenant law, and Elijah's condemnation of Ahab is paradigmatic of the social criticism of the kings by the prophets. With vivid realism the prophets described the violation of covenant, the oppression and injustice within the social order. They condemned the kings and their clients who failed to protect the poor (e.g., Jer. 22:13-17; Mic. 3:9-12). They protested against the professional prophets, priests, and sages who said what their patrons wanted to

---

11. On the Covenant Code see Paul D. Hanson, "The Theological Significance of Contradiction within the Book of the Covenant," in *Canon and Authority*, ed. George E. Coats and Burke O. Long (Philadelphia: Fortress, 1977), pp. 110-31.

hear instead of what the justice of God required (e.g., Jer. 8:8-10; Hos. 4:4-6; Amos 7:10-17; Mic. 3:5-7). They ridiculed rich women who lived in luxury careless of the cries of the poor (Isa. 3:16-26; Amos 4:1-3). They sentenced the dishonest and avaricious merchants (Amos 8:4-6), selfish and heartless creditors (Amos 5:11), covetous landowners (Isa. 5:8; Mic. 2:1-4), and venal judges (Isa. 1:23; 3:13-15; Amos 5:7, 10, 12) to the judgment of God. They beat against oppression and exploitation with their words. They were visionaries, to be sure, but it was a vision of a future made known and sure by God's faithfulness to what God had done in the past, when rescuing them from Egypt, providing for them in the wilderness, and giving them a land for shared prosperity. The prophets were not economists or politicians; they came with no practical political or economic program that could simply be instituted and realized; but they did challenge the economic world of monarchy, and they left their mark. The prophets left their mark, for example, on the reforms of Hezekiah and of Josiah. These were, in part at least, responses to the message of the prophets.

Josiah's reform in 622 is reflected in the Deuteronomic Code, on which it was based. That code, unlike the Covenant Code, presupposed an urban culture and monarchy. It reinterpreted the ancient Law in the light of a new economic and cultural situation, calling, for example, for sacrifices at a single sanctuary (Deut. 12:5, 11; 14:23-24; 16:2, 6, 11; 26:2; contrast Exod. 20:24), and providing statutes for the conduct and character of kings (Deut. 17:14-20). But it also reinterprets the ancient Law in the light of the still more ancient story, insisting now that female slaves as well as male be freed on the sabbatical year (Deut. 15:12) and that, when slaves were released, they be also furnished "liberally" (Deut. 15:14). There was slavery still, but the memory "that you were a slave in the land of Egypt, and the LORD your God redeemed you" (Deut. 15:15) left its reforming mark on this new legislation. The sabbatical year was celebrated as a time not only for the land to lie fallow and for the poor to eat from it (Exod. 23:10-11) but also for the remission of debts (Deut. 15:1-11). The Deuteronomic Code called for judicial reforms (16:20; 24:17) and for consumer protection (25:13-16, by standardized weights and measures). It demanded that the wages of a day laborer be paid at the end of each day (24:14-15). It regulated lending practices (23:19-20; 24:6, 10-13, 17). It provided for gleaning (23:24-25; 24:19-22) and for systematic gathering and distribution of food to the poor and dispossessed. (The second tithe of the produce, to be taken every third year, was stored in each city for the poor [Deut. 14:28-29; 26:12-15]).

The memory of the people of God challenged the economic order, marked the economic reform, and provided a vision of a society in which "there will be no poor among you" (Deut. 15:4 RSV). To that vision was joined both a call to soft-hearted and open-handed generosity to the needy and a re-

Jesus - "the poor will always be among you.

minder that the very reality of poverty in the midst of them disclosed that they were not yet the people God had called them and covenanted them and commanded them to be (Deut. 15:1-11).

Not long after Josiah's efforts at reform the Babylonians conquered Jerusalem. The monarchy was ended. The leaders were exiled. Those who remained in the land lived in desolating poverty (Lam. 5:1-18), their inheritance "turned over to strangers" (Lam. 5:2). The Babylonians were followed by the Persians, and the Persians by the Greeks, and after a little period of Jewish independence, the Romans came, and each exacted a colonial tribute from the land that God had given for a shared prosperity. Sometimes the memory and the vision nearly withered, but never quite. They endured in lament (Lam. 5:19-22) and broke forth in a flash of prophetic hope (e.g., Isa. 58:6-8) and in apocalyptic vision (T. Jud. 25:4; Jub. 23:18-23). They pressed toward partial realization in the reforms of Nehemiah (Neh. 5:1-13) and in the rule of Simon (1 Macc. 14:4-15).

In spite of efforts to co-opt temple and Torah, economies "embedded" in such a world of memory and hope could hardly go unchallenged or unqualified. Those most alienated from the worlds of patronage or peasantry might give expression to this challenge in violence (like some forms of social banditry or religious zealotry) or in the formation of countercultural communities (like "the congregation of the poor" at Qumran; 4Qp Ps 37; cf. also 1Qp Hab. 12:3, 6, 10; 1QS 1:11; 6:19, 22, 25). But even for those struggling to keep their position within those worlds, temple and Torah preserved a memory and a hope that could not be fully and finally co-opted.

That memory and hope not only sustained statutes for the protection of the poor but also sometimes formed a disposition to observe them. They nurtured a readiness to identify not only with a patron or a client, not only with one's extended family, not only with a community of the righteous separated from sinners, but with God who heard the cries of those who hurt, who rescued slaves from oppression, who provided in the wilderness, and who gave them a land for a shared prosperity.

Remembering Jesus

Such were the economic worlds of Jesus and of the rich fool of his parable. Jesus was the child of a poor man. His father was not among the poorest of the poor — he was a craftsman, a carpenter, not a day laborer or a slave — but he was poor. Jesus probably apprenticed at his father's bench in the peasant village of Nazareth, but when he emerged into the public record it was not at market to sell his beds and benches for the sake of subsistence, or to look for a patron for the sake of upward mobility and the dream of an estate one day. He appeared as an itinerant preacher, announcing the coming rule of God. Traveling from village to village with "nowhere to lay his head" (Matt. 8:20; Luke 9:58), dependent upon the generosity of others, upon their hospitality and their gifts, sometimes gleaning in the fields (Matt. 12:1-8; Mark 2:23-28; Luke 6:1-5), he preached that the good future of God was at hand.

The itinerancy of Jesus may be compared with the itinerancy of other wandering moralists and miracle workers.[12] The wandering Cynic philosophers practiced the simple life and demonstrated an alternative to conventional opinions, including conventional opinions about wealth and security. They were deliberately "outsiders" to the ways of life of patronage and peasantry, but they were not hermits. In their style of life with its emblems of cloak, staff, and pouch and in their conversations and instructions, their harangues and diatribes, they challenged their hearers to think again about their lives and to live according to nature rather than according to conventions. Some Cynics held the public and their conventions in utter disdain; these "harsh" Cynics confronted others simply to insult them and to demonstrate their own moral superiority to the masses. Others, the "mild Cynics," were known for their gentleness and patience and confronted others in order to benefit them, frequently accommodating their rigorous message to the capacity of their hearers.[13]

Jesus, too, seems to have been deliberately an outsider to the conventions of patronage and peasantry. He, too, by his style of life and by his instructions challenged his hearers to think again about their lives and to "repent," to turn from conventional assumptions and expectations; but the alternative he provided and proclaimed was not the Greek ideals of freedom and self-sufficiency and life according to nature. Jesus' alternative was, rather, the memory and hope of Israel, addressed again to all Israel and indeed to all, the kingdom of God. The Cynics' deliberate choice to be outsiders was joined to a decision to live according to nature, not according to convention; Jesus' choice was joined to a decision to live according to the coming rule of God. (The itinerancy and poverty of the miracle worker Apollonius of Tyana point in the same direction, for Apollonius's miracles were attributed not to magic and not even to supernatural power directly but to his sensitivity to the gods and to their operations with the natural order, both enhanced by the simplicity of his life.[14])

12. Stambaugh and Balch, *New Testament in Its Social Environment*, pp. 143-45.

13. See Wayne A. Meeks, *The Moral World of the First Christians* (Philadelphia: Westminster, 1986), pp. 52-56; Abraham Malherbe, "Cynics," *Interpreter's Dictionary of the Bible*, Supplementary Volume (Nashville: Abingdon, 1976), pp. 201-3.

14. Howard Clark Kee, *Medicine, Miracle, and Magic in New Testament Times* (Cambridge: Cambridge University Press, 1986), pp. 84-86.

The itinerancy of Jesus may also be compared with the lifestyle of John the Baptist. One would expect to find this son of Zechariah following his father's footsteps, entering into priestly service in Jerusalem. Instead, one finds him "in the wilderness" (Mark 1:4), "clothed with camel's hair, with a leather belt around his waist" (1:6), evoking by his dress memories of Elijah (cf. 2 Kings 1:8), and eating "locusts and wild honey" (1:6), evoking by his diet memories of a nomadic life. This "voice of one crying out in the wilderness" (Mark 1:3; cf. Isa. 40:3) announced the coming rule of God as judgment, judgment against those who fail to share what they have and judgment against those who use their power to enrich themselves at the expense of others (Luke 3:10-14). Jesus takes up the message and, indeed, the call to repentance, but it becomes in his life and words "good news to the poor" (Luke 4:18; cf. Matt. 11:4 and Luke 7:22). Jesus was no ascetic, quite in contrast to John the Baptist. Those who rejected John and his message of a judgment called his asceticism madness (Matt. 11:18; Luke 7:33); those who rejected Jesus and his gospel accused him of being "a glutton and a drunkard" (Matt. 11:19; Luke 7:35; cf. Deut. 21:20). Jesus did not glorify poverty any more than he glorified wealth. He glorified God. And he announced the coming sovereignty of God — also in the economic world. He called all Israel to pray for the coming of that kingdom and to begin to live in accord with it — also in the economic order.

The Lord's Prayer and the World of the Economy

The prayer Jesus taught those who would follow him is remembered and cherished by the churches — but its economic associations are too frequently forgotten or ignored.

The prayer begins with an invocation, simply "Father" in Luke's Gospel, "Our Father who art in heaven" in Matthew (Matt. 6:9 RSV).[15] The association here, of course, is familial, and the invocation of God as "Father" suggests family intimacy and the trust of little children toward one who cares for them.[16] But the association in the first century would also certainly have been economic, for the "father" was head of the household in that patriarchal world and in the economic world of the peasant. The "father" could be expected to pro-

---

15. It is generally agreed that Luke's shorter version of the prayer is closer to the original in length, if not in wording. See Joachim Jeremias, *The Prayers of Jesus* (London: SCM Press, 1967), pp. 85-94.

16. Especially, perhaps, if the Aramaic word behind the Greek is *Abba;* see Jeremias, *Prayers of Jesus,* pp. 95-98.

vide (cf. Matt. 6:26; 7:9-11; Luke 11:11-13). To invoke God as "Father," then, suggested provision and evoked a sense of dependence and trust that one's needs would be met in the household of God. A peasant household pooled resources and shared those resources with its members, determining membership in the family or clan on the basis of who could be counted "Father." To invoke God as "Father," then, would also evoke a sense of responsibility to share resources with all God's children. It challenged and finally subverted the attempt to hold on to what one had by restricting kinship obligations.[17] For, if God is "Father," then all are kin (Matt. 23:8-9). It is as John Calvin said: "if one father is common to us all . . . , then there ought not to be anything separate among us that we are not prepared gladly and wholeheartedly to share with one another."[18]

After the invocation the prayer asks that God establish cosmic sovereignty: "Father, hallowed be thy name. Thy kingdom come" (Luke 11:2 RSV).[19] These are petitions modeled after the Kaddish, the prayer for the conclusion of worship in the synagogue.[20] Like the Kaddish, this prayer is a cry from a world where God's cause and power are profaned, from a world where God's rule is challenged by evil and sin — and greed. Like the Kaddish the prayer pleads for God to act, to end the rule of sin and death and to establish God's own good future, "speedily and soon."

Those who make such petitions recognize that the kingdom Jesus proclaimed is God's work and not their own. It is God's power that establishes it and not their own. Even so, to make such petitions forms dispositions to hallow God's name and to welcome that kingdom, a courageous readiness to enlist on the side of God's power, and to resist whatever challenges God's cause or usurps God's rule, a willingness to shape life in the anticipation of that good future.

And the next petitions, the petitions for bread and for forgiveness, are best understood as that anticipation. Having asked God to establish that good

---

17. It ought to be observed that, although images are taken from the world of patriarchy and the economic world of peasantry, those worlds — with their hierarchical power and economic inequities — are challenged and finally subverted (e.g., Matt. 23:8-9).

18. John Calvin, *Institutes of the Christian Religion,* III.xx.38.

19. Matthew's addition here, "Your will be done, on earth as it is in heaven" (Matt. 6:10), reflects the confidence of the Christian church after Easter that God has acted, that Jesus *is* enthroned in the heavens, and it pleads for the full disclosure of that divine triumph on earth as well.

20. The Kaddish is "Exalted and hallowed be his great name in the world which he created according to his will. May he let his kingdom rule in your lifetime and in your days and in the lifetime of the whole house of Israel, speedily and soon." Jeremias, *Prayers of Jesus,* p. 98.

future, the prayer boldly petitions God for a foretaste of it. Already now in this sad and profane world, a taste, a foretaste, of God's good future is what those who pray this prayer request: already now in this world of hunger a taste of the eschatological banquet, already now in this world of guilt a foretaste of being brought safely through the final judgment.

Given the economic associations of invoking God as "Father," it is no surprise that the first petition is for bread. God provides — and God's household shares — our bread. And such bread is a foretaste of the kingdom of God.

"Give us this day our daily bread" (Matt. 6:11)[21] does not seem particularly oriented to the great messianic banquet. The marginal reading, however, which identifies the bread as "our bread for tomorrow" (Matt. 6:11 margin; Luke 11:3 margin), points in the right direction, namely, toward the future. Behind both translations, "daily" and "for tomorrow," is a curious Greek word *epiousios*. It occurs only here, so scholars cannot determine its meaning from other contexts. It puzzled Origen already in the third century, for he could find no other instance of the word in *any* Greek text (*de Oratione* 27.7), and it continues to puzzle commentators. Etymology is not of much help either.[22] Joachim Jeremias argued — persuasively, I think — that since the *Gospel of the Nazarenes* (an apocryphal gospel based on Matthew) used the Aramaic word *mahar*, and since at that point the author of that gospel would simply provide the text for the prayer as it was and had been used in Aramaic worship, the original Aramaic word used by Jesus was probably *mahar*. *Mahar* means "for the morrow," and the sense of the petition would be, as Jerome (342-420) said in his comment on this gospel, "Our bread for tomorrow — that is, our future bread — give us today."[23]

When one considers other gospel passages that associate God's provision of bread and food with God's kingdom, then the case begins to be not only plausible but also compelling. Notice, for example, Luke 14:15: "Blessed is anyone who will eat bread in the kingdom of God" and Luke 6:21: "Blessed are you who are hungry now, for you will be filled." (See also Matt. 8:11; Luke 22:29-30; Rev. 7:16.) When one joins such passages to the eschatological character of the Lord's Prayer, the petition for "bread" becomes the bold request for a foretaste of God's heavenly banquet.

21. Luke's "Give us each day our daily bread" (Luke 11:3) emphasizes continuous action both by the present tense rather than Matthew's aorist and by "each day." I agree with most scholars who take Matthew's wording here to be closer to the tradition they both received. See, e.g., Jeremias, *Prayers of Jesus*, pp. 91-92.

22. See Werner Foerster, *"epiousios," Theological Dictionary of the New Testament*, ed. Gerhard Kittel, trans. Geoffrey W. Bromiley, vol. 2 (Grand Rapids: Eerdmans, 1964), pp. 590-99, on the possible etymologies.

23. See Jeremias, *Prayers of Jesus*, pp. 100-102.

There is nothing ascetic about such a request. It is not hard to understand that the one who taught such a prayer would delight in fellowship about a table and indeed be charged as a glutton and a drunkard. But there is also nothing selfish about such a request. It is *our* bread for which we pray, not *my* bread, and it hardly signals the messianic banquet unless it is shared.

There is another association that is helpful and important here: manna, God's provision for Israel in the wilderness. There in the wilderness the Lord "gave them the grain of heaven" (Ps. 78:24), "a day's portion every day" (Exod. 16:4 RSV). There could be no hoarding, and no one went without (Exod. 16:18). Moreover, manna had become an eschatological symbol. In the Apocalypse of Baruch, for example, the promise is that manna will again fall to the earth in the day of salvation (29.8).[24] The coming of the kingdom would be the coming of the bread of heaven as well. Such bread would be worthy of an eschatological banquet.[25] To pray for a foretaste of this bread was to pray as well for a foretaste of a manna economy, an economic world where hoarding was futile and none went hungry.

The next petition asks for forgiveness, for a foretaste of being brought safely through the final judgment, but it too has economic associations: "Forgive us our debts, as we also have forgiven our debtors" (Matt. 6:12). We frequently overlook the financial and commercial character of the words "debts" and "debtors," caught up as they are in the religious and moral significance of our transgressions against the Law and our failures to meet our obligations to the Lawgiver and to our neighbors. Luke's Gospel ought to be enough to remind us of the economic significance of these words, for he uses another term for our failures in relation to God and then returns to the commercial language to deal with communal obligations: "Forgive us our sins, for we ourselves forgive everyone indebted to us" (Luke 11:4). The petition for forgiveness of sins is joined to a readiness not to demand payment on a loan, a readiness not to insist upon our economic rights when a neighbor is in need.

When one considers other gospel passages, the case for an economic reading of this petition becomes also not just plausible but compelling. Consider Luke 6:35: "lend, expecting nothing in return," or the magnificent parable of Matthew 18:23-35, which tells the story of a great and generous king whose servant owed him an enormous debt. The king "forgave him the debt" (Matt.

24. See further R. Meyer, *"manna," Theological Dictionary of the New Testament,* vol. 4 (Grand Rapids: Eerdmans, 1967), p. 464.

25. This image is capitalized upon by John 6:32-59, which moves from the bread God gave, manna (6:31-32a), to the bread God gives, Jesus, the bread of life (6:32b-51a), to the bread Jesus gives, his flesh, the Eucharist (6:51b-58).

18:27), but the same servant insisted that one of his fellow servants pay him the little he owed him. The "unforgiving servant" wanted nothing more to do with the economy of mercy and forgiveness that is like the kingdom of God, and he was brought back to judgment and condemnation. That Matthew uses this parable of the forgiveness of debts to call the community to the forgiveness of sins "seventy times seven" times (Matt. 18:22 RSV) does not detract from its economic significance. The bold request for a foretaste of God's mercy and forgiveness does not leave economic dispositions unaffected.

The forgiveness of debts has another association in the memory and hope of Israel: Jubilee. One need not claim, as John Howard Yoder did,[26] that Jesus called for observance of a Jubilee year in 26 C.E. (If he did, it is striking that there is in the tradition no appeal to the legislation of Leviticus 25, no legal argument given.) One need not even claim that the Jubilee was observed in any regular cycle after the return to the land from exile.[27] Jubilee was remembered as a sign of God's sovereignty over Israel and hoped for as a signal that God would establish the kingdom.[28] And, whether in memory or in hope, Jubilee required changes in the economic world; jubilee required that the poor, those pushed to the margins of the economic world, be restored to full participation in the life of the community. To announce such a future was surely to "preach good news to the poor"; to pray for it was to long for and to envision a jubilee economy in which the poor are blessed by God and their debts forgiven. It is not hard to imagine that the poor heard Jesus gladly and prayed his prayer earnestly, although they might stumble in resentment at forgiving the sins of a rich neighbor. The rich, too, might pray this prayer eagerly and plead for the forgiveness of their sins, longing for a foretaste of a future in which they would be brought safely through the judgment; but to pray this prayer earnestly permits no return to business as usual, and they might stumble in anxiety or in greed at forgiving the indebtedness of a poor neighbor. To pray this prayer is to want to be part of the economy of mercy and the society of forgiveness that is like the kingdom of God.

The Lord's Prayer is at once eschatological and economic. It forms a way of life, a way of being in this world — and in this economic world — while we watch and pray for another, for God's good future. And Jesus called all Israel not only to pray for the kingdom but also to begin to live in accord with it.

26. John Howard Yoder, *The Politics of Jesus* (Grand Rapids: Eerdmans, 1972), pp. 65-66, 76, following André Trocmé, *Jesus-Christ et la revolution non-violente* (Geneva: Labor et Fides, 1961).

27. See further Sharon Ringe, *Jesus, Liberation, and the Biblical Jubilee* (Philadelphia: Fortress, 1985), pp. 26-28.

28. Ringe, *Jesus, Liberation, and the Biblical Jubilee*, p. 32.

To Live in Accord with the Kingdom: Jesus' Wisdom about Wealth

Jesus came proclaiming the kingdom of God. He did not come with a social
program or a new set of laws for the economic world or even with a new legal
reading of the old laws of Moses. But he did come inviting people to live in
accord with the kingdom, to repent before it and to celebrate the present
signs and symptoms of its future power. But what does it mean to live in accord with it? And if that rich farmer of the parable was a "fool," what is the
shape of wisdom?

Three things, I think, are fundamental to the memory of Jesus here: two
captured in the commands to "be not anxious" and to "give" and a third caught
curiously in the observation, "You always have the poor with you."

1) "Do not be anxious" (Matt. 6:25 RSV; Luke 12:22). To be carefree — this
is wisdom. To anxiously and vainly attempt to secure one's life and identity by
one's possessions — this is foolishness. The instruction, in good wisdom fashion, is supported by an appeal to nature, to God's care for the birds and the lilies
(Matt. 6:26, 28-30; Luke 12:24, 27-28). But it is hardly a "commonsense" appeal.
Birds and wildflowers are short-lived and hardly the sort of creatures to relieve
the anxieties of those whose lives and identities are secured upon an abundance
of possessions. Their lives are cheap and brief according to the conventional
standards, but God's care is lavished upon them. These words of the gospel
contain an implicit challenge to conventional standards and an implicit appeal
to secure one's life and identity upon the care and power of God.

It is wisdom, then, but hardly conventional wisdom. It is an eschatological wisdom, joined to the command, "seek first the kingdom of God" (cf. Matt.
6:33; Luke 12:31). Conventional wisdom grounded and tested its advice in experience; careful attention to nature and to life allowed the sage to comprehend
the principles operative in the world that are quite beyond the reach of human
control; to those principles it was both prudent and moral to conform. The eschatological wisdom of Jesus also comprehended some basic principles at work
in the world, but they are the eschatological intentions of God. They are known
in experience, to be sure, but in the particular experience of the coming rule of
God already making its power felt. They are articulated in conventional wisdom forms — in beatitudes, "Blessed are you who are poor" (Luke 6:20); in
comparisons, "It is easier for a camel to go through the eye of a needle than for
someone who is rich to enter the kingdom of God" (Mark 10:25); and in imperatives, "Be not anxious!" But in these conventional forms it is God's future salvation and judgment that are announced and already brought to bear upon the
present. God will reign, and God is already at work, and to live in accord with
God's work and will is both prudent and moral.

The failure of the rich fool is clear in this context. He was not a fool just because he was rich. He was not a fool because he had earned his fortune in some dishonest way; apparently he acquired his treasures by hard work and the farsighted vision of a good businessman. He was a fool because he was anxious about his possessions, and he was anxious about his possessions because he thought life consisted in the abundance of possessions. He was a fool because he thought money the measure of value and the guarantee of security. Money equals value — it is a simple equation, a yuppie axiom, conventional wisdom. But Jesus turned the conventional wisdom on its head: "One's life," he said, "does not consist in the abundance of possessions" (Luke 12:15). What does life consist of, then? It consists of welcoming the reign of God. And what is Jesus' wisdom about wealth? "Be not anxious."

Such wisdom, it should be said plainly, is *not law!* "Be not anxious" is foolish as a law, only capable of increasing anxiety. The imperatives of Jesus are not given (or remembered) as parts of a moral code or as parts of a systematic ethical treatise that stands by itself. They are not part of some new Torah to be applied deductively to conduct, not the basis of a new Christian *halakah*. The imperatives stand alongside others like "watch" and "pray" because the imperatives are not primarily concerned with morality *per se* but with the response to and the anticipation of the reign of God.

As eschatological wisdom this advice assumes and relies upon — indeed welcomes and celebrates — the coming reign of the God who blesses the poor and lifts up the powerless. A response to the command "be not anxious" is a response to Jesus who had "nowhere to lay his head" and who preached good news to the poor. And a response to this command is also a response to the coming reign of God whose care extends even to those who, according to the standards of this age at least (and conventional wisdom), are neither valuable nor secure. To confront this command is to confront, already now, a choice between the present age and the age to come, between serving Mammon or serving God (Luke 16:13), between trusting the conventional patterns of privilege and power and prestige and security or trusting God. We can *either* say and live by the proposition that a person's life consists in the abundance of possessions *or* we can say and live by the proposition that a person's life consists in welcoming the reign of God who anointed Jesus to preach good news to the poor. The first is finally foolishness, although it passes for wisdom. The second is really wisdom, though it looks for all the world like foolishness.

Such wisdom surely looked like foolishness in the economic worlds of patronage and peasantry. A client could hardly be carefree about the continuing favor of a patron. What if the patron called for payment of a loan? What if the patron himself lost favor with his patron? What if some rival promised one's

270

benefactor a greater advantage? Anxiety and suspicion ruled, at least until one could learn to trust the greatest benefactor, the one whose coming reign is a rule of mercy. A peasant farmer, anxiously holding on to what he had lest he fall out of membership in the community, could hardly be carefree about subsistence, unless he learned to trust and to invoke a "Father" whose household includes the poor and whose coming rule means blessing to them.

The second thing about living now in accord with the coming kingdom is captured in the concrete command to "give." The carefree attitude toward riches forms in Jesus' followers a disposition, a readiness, to give generously to help the poor. Such a readiness is the other side of welcoming the eschatological blessing upon the poor, for to welcome that reign is to bless the poor already, to share what one has with them.

The command is expressed, of course, in a variety of cognate forms in the tradition: to the rich young ruler, "Sell all that you own and distribute the money to the poor" (Luke 18:22); to those who were already among his disciples, "sell your possessions, and give alms" (12:32), without any hint of a requirement to sell *all* they had; to Pharisees, "give for alms" (11:41), without the hint of requiring the selling of anything; or simply "lend, expecting nothing in return" (6:35), without the hint of a requirement even to give. The different forms make it quite clear again that Jesus is not legislating, not providing some timeless moral code or some new and extremely rigorous *halakah*.

The coming kingdom puts merely external and legal observance in crisis because the whole person is called to welcome and celebrate the reign of God. Jesus does not want grudging external observance of a law, no matter how rigorous it is. He wants repentance, the joyful turning of the whole self to welcome the kingdom of God. What does life consist of? A person's life consists of welcoming already the coming kingdom of God. And what then is Jesus' wisdom about money? Be generous.

The failure of the rich fool is also clear in this context. He was not a fool just because he was rich. He was a fool because his attempt to secure his own life and identity by his possessions made it impossible for him to be generous. His answer to his question, "What should I do, for I have no place to store my crops?" (Luke 12:17) featured his own ease and luxury and strikingly ignored the person in need who might be helped by the gleanings. He probably did manage a kind of nitpicking and grudging observance of the Law, leaving just that measure required by the rabbis' latest interpretation of Deuteronomy 24:19 unharvested at the edges of the field. But he did not see in his wealth an opportunity of gratitude to God for God's deliverance and for the gift of the land. He did not see in his wealth the opportunity to rejoice in God's mercy by being generous himself. He did not see in his wealth the opportunity for

271

celebrating the coming reign of God by already blessing the poor. And so, he was a fool.

Jesus does not legislate; he gives no new law; he forms character and nurtures the disposition to give joyfully and generously. But, for all that, it is not less stringent or demanding. To help the poor with self-forgetful generosity is to welcome God's coming reign (Luke 19:8-9), and not to help them is to expose oneself to God's coming judgment. There are a variety of concrete forms such self-forgetful generosity might take: almsgiving, to be sure, but also feeding the hungry, giving the thirsty drink, practicing hospitality, visiting the sick and imprisoned, and many other "works of love." It is not that wealth is evil or poverty a good. A person's life does not consist in an abundance of possessions — or in the absence of possessions. A person's life consists in welcoming the reign of God, and welcoming the reign of God is gestured and made manifest in great and simple generosity with what we have, be it great or simple.

Such generosity challenged and judged the economic world of patronage and provided a surprising extension to the obligations of kinship in the economic world of peasantry. The patron gave, to be sure, but always looking for a return, for some reciprocal favor, at the very least to be acknowledged as patron, as benefactor. The gifts of patrons were calculated to establish relationships of inequality and involved the conceit of philanthropy even where a return is expected. It is not to be so among those who follow Jesus and welcome the kingdom he proclaimed. He calls people to give without looking for a return, to give "in secret" (Matt. 6:4), to lend "expecting nothing in return" (Luke 6:35), to practice hospitality to those who cannot invite you "in return" (Luke 14:12-14). It is true that such generosity looks for a reward "at the resurrection of the righteous" (Luke 14:14), but not by way of calculation — as though one might succeed in making God one's client. Rather, God is acknowledged as the benefactor, and uncalculating generosity is simply the eschatological wisdom of living in accord with God's will and way and in anticipation of God's good and generous future. Ever and future recipients of God's mercy, those who celebrate God's coming rule make "friends," not clients, through their generosity (Luke 16:9). There can be no conceit of philanthropy where all acknowledge their greater indebtedness to God. Equality, not deliberate inequality, marks the giving of gifts in the new community.

Such generosity was closer to the obligations of kinship in the economic world of peasantry, but it could hardly be contained by that world. The uncalculating hospitality of peasant dinners for friends and neighbors was closer by far to the generosity Jesus called for, and indeed such dinners were images for heavenly joy (Luke 15:7, 10, 23, 24). But there is joy in heaven over a sinner who repents, and peasant dinners only image that heavenly joy by hospitality to those on the margins of village life. The obligations of kinship may not be limited to full participants in the life of the village; they were extended by Jesus to those on the margins. This "friend of sinners" received those whom the village had exiled to the margins. To receive Jesus and the kingdom he announced was to receive these marginalized people, to practice hospitality and kindness to them, not to distance oneself from them in an anxious attempt to hold on to what one had.

The third thing to notice is the word of Jesus, "you always have the poor with you" (Matt. 26:11; Mark 14:7; John 12:8).[29] These words were part of a rebuke of the disciples for their accusation against a woman who had wasted a costly ointment. They have often been used to counter attempts to put economic problems on the church's agenda. Here, it is suggested, Jesus set priorities for the life of the church. Here, it is said, Jesus focused our attention on himself rather than on futile attempts to alleviate poverty or to correct economic injustice. Here, it is claimed, Jesus elevated spiritual needs above physical needs.

It is true, of course, that Jesus rebuked the disciples here, and it is true that he focuses attention on himself. But he did *not* rebuke the disciples for being concerned about the poor. He did not focus attention on himself at the expense of the poor. Quite the contrary, as Jesus' citation of Deuteronomy 15 should make clear.

There, in the midst of the covenant law that gave the community the responsibility to eliminate poverty and to correct injustice, the blessing of God was announced: "there will be no poor among you" (Deut. 15:4 RSV). That blessing, however, was contingent upon the community's obedience (15:5). So, the presence of poverty was enough to call forth God's judgment, enough to condemn a community's grudging tight-fistedness toward the poor. But in the passage and in the patience of God, the fact that "the poor will never cease out of the land" (Deut. 15:11 RSV), that "you always have the poor with you," becomes not only judgment but also the occasion for the continuing invitation to repent of tight-fistedness and to "open your hand to the poor and needy neighbor in your land" (Deut. 15:11).

The word of Jesus, then, "you always have the poor with you," recognized the not-yet character of first-century existence and of its communities. The very presence of poverty called forth judgment on Israel and demonstrated that it is not yet God's unchallenged reign. The community was not yet what it was to be and to become: a community that welcomes and blesses the poor. So Jesus re-

---

29. On this passage, see Bruce C. Birch and Larry L. Rasmussen, *Bible and Ethics in the Christian Life*, revised and expanded ed. (Minneapolis: Augsburg, 1989), pp. 177-79.

buked the disciples with these words, not for being concerned about the poor, but for self-righteously singling out this woman, for presumptuously condemning her when the presence of poverty condemned the whole community. The disciples were casting stones at the woman in Israel's glass house.

The word of Jesus, then, was also curiously a word of invitation to "open your hand to the poor and needy neighbor," for while their existence and their communities were *not yet* God's unchallenged sovereignty, still there was Jesus already preaching good news to the poor and already making its power felt even as he approached death for the sake of God's cause in the world. So Jesus called attention to himself — but not away from the poor. This woman's devotion, her carefree lavishing of ointment on Jesus, will be remembered, he said. Her carefree generosity was her celebration of the coming reign of God and its presence in Jesus. And in the absence of Jesus the same freedom from the tyranny of possessions will be turned toward generous care for the poor and justice for them in the communities that remember both her and Jesus.[30]

"You always have the poor with you" does not dismiss poverty from the agenda of those who would follow Jesus. It calls them to watch for God's unchallenged sovereignty and, until it comes, to share his passion, to remember this woman and her carefree generosity, to open wide one's hands to the poor, to be a community which demonstrates already the generosity and justice of God. Such a community may even learn to see in the poor the presence of Jesus in his absence so that deeds of carefree generosity and of kindness done for the poor are done, as it were, unto him (Matt. 25:40, 45).

The failure of the rich fool is clear again. He was not a fool just because he was rich. He was a fool because he wanted to be on his own, looking out for number one, as though there were only one, himself. He was a fool because he had no sense of community, surely no sense of a community with the poor. He didn't see his own indebtedness to the work of the day laborers in the field or the craftsmen who built his barns. In his anxious and vain attempt to secure his life and his possessions, he probably didn't even see the poor in the land, and if he did, he could see them only as a threat to his possessions and to his security. He did not see his wealth as an occasion to express his gratitude for his dependence upon the gifts and skills of others, as an opportunity to nurture and sus-

30. Ringe, *Jesus, Liberation, and the Biblical Jubilee*, p. 64, calls attention to the parallelism which equates the woman's generosity to Jesus with a continuing generosity to the poor:
- A. "You always have the poor with you,"
- B. "Whenever you will, you can do good to them,"
- A1. "You will not always have me,"
- B1. "She has done what she could."

tain community with the poor on whom God's eschatological blessing rests. Therefore, he was a fool.

"You always have the poor with you" was judgment upon the economic worlds of patronage and peasantry, for in those worlds the poor remained poor and usually grew poorer. With these words Jesus reminded his hearers of the memory and hope of Israel, and that memory and hope judged those who would co-opt the tradition in their own economic interest. That judgment is of one piece with Jesus' judgment against the priestly aristocracy who used their power and status in the temple to enrich themselves (Mark 11:15-17, par.; John 2:13-17). It was linked with his judgment against those whose scribal authority to interpret Torah was available to the highest bidder among possible patrons (Matt. 23:25; Mark 12:40; Luke 11:39-41). These "neglect justice and the love of God" (Luke 11:42), and so, allowing their concern for temple and Torah to be co-opted by the economic interests of patronage and peasantry, they betrayed both God and the poor.

Jesus' word here, however, was spoken not to patrons or priests, not to peasants or scribes, but to the disciples, to the little community already gathered around Jesus. They were not free from temptations to forgetfulness in the economic worlds of their time; they were not beyond the risk of infidelity, of betraying both Jesus and the poor themselves. The judgment falls on them when they fail to live in accord with Jesus, when they fail to live in anticipation of a coming economic world, when they do not celebrate carefree generosity, and when they fail to acknowledge communal responsibility for the poor.

To live in accord with the kingdom did not mean, in the wisdom of Jesus, rigorous asceticism or rigid legalism. That is not the way God's good future makes its power felt. It makes its power felt where there is carefree trust in God, in characters ready to give generously and to practice kindness to the needy, and in communities which do not neglect justice but exercise their responsibility to help the poor.

CHAPTER FOURTEEN

Remembering the Early Church
Remembering Jesus

Jesus came announcing God's good future. He invited those who would follow him to pray for it and to live in accord with it — also in their economic worlds. Economic motives and behaviors were formed by the memory of this Jesus and by the hope for the good future that he announced and made present. What had passed for economic wisdom was challenged by an announcement of a great reversal in which the last would be first and the first last, and in which God could be trusted to provide. In place of the conventional economic wisdom the disciples had learned an eschatological wisdom, a wisdom tested by their experience of Jesus as the one who makes known God's future. The axioms of that eschatological wisdom for economic life included "Be not anxious," "Give," and (as a reminder of communal responsibilities) "You always have the poor with you."

Jesus was put to death on a Roman cross, but God raised him up, and the Spirit was poured out. The Spirit was poured out, and a community was formed in memory and in hope, struggling to revision all of life — including economic life — with Jesus exalted to God's right hand. They loved to tell the story — and they struggled to live it. As witnesses to that struggle, and as participants in it, we turn our attention in this chapter from remembering Jesus to remembering the early church remembering Jesus.

The Community of Goods

The earliest church, as Luke tells the story (Acts 2:1-42), was formed in Jerusalem by the power of God at Pentecost. The Spirit of God came to the disciples like fire and like wind. In a comic reversal of the Tower of Babel, Jewish pilgrims to Jerusalem from all over the world were able to understand the disciples. When Peter was called upon to give some explanation of these strange events, he first repudiated the suggestion of some that people were drunk. "It is only nine o'clock in the morning," he said (2:15). This was not some fraternity party; this was God's party. "This is what was spoken through the prophet Joel," Peter said, when God promised "in the last days" to pour out the Spirit upon all flesh (2:16-17). Peter then reminded his hearers of Jesus of Nazareth, who had lived among them, who had been put to death in an act of judicial murder, but whom God had raised up in triumph over the power of death (2:22-24). God had vindicated this Jesus and exalted him to "God's right hand." And having received the Spirit from the Father, the risen and exalted Jesus shared it, pouring the Spirit out upon the earth (2:32-33).

Many welcomed Peter's message — and God's triumph — and were baptized (2:41). That was the beginning of the church. And in that Spirit-formed community, as Luke tells the story, people "devoted themselves to the apostles' teaching and fellowship, to the breaking of bread and the prayers" (2:42). They lived their lives and their common life in glad response to the triumph of God, the vindication of Jesus, and the gift of the Spirit. The new reality reached into their economy; these people, Luke said, "had all things in common" (2:44). In memory of Jesus and in the power of the Spirit, this earliest church held possessions in common, selling what they owned and distributing the proceeds "as any had need" (2:45).

Two chapters later Luke gives another (and longer) account of this practice of the early church.

> Now the whole group of those who believed were of one heart and soul, and no one claimed private ownership of any possessions, but everything they owned was held in common. With great power the apostles gave their testimony to the resurrection of the Lord Jesus, and great grace was upon them all. There was not a needy person among them, for as many as owned lands or houses sold them and brought the proceeds of what was sold. They laid it at the apostles' feet, and it was distributed to each as any had need. (Acts 4:32-35)

This community of goods in the Jerusalem church has sometimes been read as a normative pattern — in monastic communities, in sixteenth-century Munster, in Bruderhof communities, to name a few. It has been sometimes been read as a noble experiment which must be tried again whenever the gospel is heard and wherever the Spirit transforms human and communal — and eco-

277

nomic — life.[1] On the other hand, it has sometimes been read as a failed experiment, as well motivated, perhaps, but as deeply flawed from the beginning.[2]

It is clear that Luke regards the experiment positively. He sets his first description of this community of goods in the context of his celebration of the church's life in its beginnings and when it was first continuing (Acts 2:43-47). And his second description provides a little envelope for Luke's memory of the power and grace of the message of the resurrection (note verse 33 in the context of Acts 4:32-35).

One should not forget here at the beginning of the church Luke's story of the beginning of Jesus' ministry (Luke 4:16-21). There in a synagogue in Nazareth Jesus read from the scroll of Isaiah, "The Spirit of the Lord is upon me, because he has anointed me to bring good news to the poor . . . ," and having returned the scroll, he said (in the shortest sermon on record), "Today this scripture has been fulfilled in your hearing." Here in Jerusalem that same Jesus, vindicated now by God in the resurrection as Lord and Christ (Acts 2:36), the anointed one, pours out the Spirit of the Lord upon the church, and the scroll of Isaiah is fulfilled here too. As Luke tells the story, the early church remembered Jesus and responded to the Spirit in this community of goods. In memory of Jesus and in celebration of his vindication by God and his gift of the Spirit they pooled their possessions and used them to respond to the needs of the poor. The Spirit of the Lord was upon them, and the Spirit still prompted good news to the poor.

The Gospel of Luke

The whole of Luke's Gospel is relevant here, not just the sermon at Nazareth. It is to Luke, after all, that we are indebted for this memory of the early church remembering Jesus. From the very beginning of his Gospel, Luke re-presented Jesus as associated with the poor and re-presented the cause of God as blessing the poor. It was shepherds, not the magi of Matthew's Gospel, who came to visit

1. See, for example, Karl Barth, *Church Dogmatics*, IV/2, trans. G. W. Bromiley (Edinburgh: T. & T. Clark, 1958), p. 178: "it will always be inevitable that there should be impulses in this direction wherever the Gospel of Jesus is proclaimed and heard."

2. So, for example, Luke T. Johnson, *Sharing Possessions: Mandate and Symbol of Faith* (Philadelphia: Fortress, 1981). Johnson not only says that "to read these passages in Acts as providing the ideological legitimation for such a structuring of the Christian community is to misread them" (p. 129); he also finds fault with any experiment in a community of goods, including the experiment of the Jerusalem church. It located the problem in property itself rather than in human desire (pp. 124-25), and it was, as such experiments inevitably are, tied to social authoritarianism (p. 124; see also pp. 131-32). Johnson proposes "almsgiving" as the better model for the sharing of possessions.

Jesus in Luke's remembering (Luke 2:8-20; cf. Matt. 2:1-12) — and in an animal stall, not in a house (as in Matthew). His parents offered the sacrifice of the poor (Luke 2:22; cf. Lev. 12:6-8a). As in all the gospels John the Baptist prepared the way for Jesus. In Luke, however, the crowd asked him the question to be asked again at Pentecost of Peter, "What then should we do?" (Luke 3:10; cf. Acts 2:37). And John's reply prepared the way both for Jesus and for the new common life of the church in Jerusalem; he exhorted the multitudes to share food and clothing, "Whoever has two coats must share with anyone who has none; and whoever has food must do likewise." He told tax collectors not to abuse their power by extortion, and soldiers not to abuse their power by pillaging. And then he told them of one who would baptize them with the Holy Spirit (Luke 3:11-16; note also Acts 1:5).

In Luke's account of the inauguration of Jesus' ministry in that synagogue in Nazareth, as we have seen, Jesus himself announced that he is the Christ, the anointed one, the preacher of good news to the poor (Luke 4:16-21). And then, in the Beatitudes at the beginning of the Sermon on the Plain, Luke displayed this Jesus, this anointed one, announcing good news to the poor. The good future of God was made present in words of blessing to the poor and hungry. Luke made no attempt to "spiritualize" the Beatitudes or to turn the blessing into a commendation of certain character traits. "Blessed are you who are poor," Jesus said, and "Blessed are you who are hungry now" (6:20-21). In Luke's account Jesus simply announced the great reversal of God's coming cosmic sovereignty; it would be (and was) good news to the poor. The flip side of these blessings upon the poor, of course, is the "woes" announced upon those who are rich and full (6:24-25). Such woes are not presented as fate, however, but as a call to repentance, as an invitation already to welcome God's future as good. So, in Luke's account, the Beatitudes introduce Jesus' invitation to turn from a way of life formed by violence and reciprocity and to practice love and generosity, even toward those who cannot be expected to reciprocate. To welcome God's future entails doing good to one's enemy, practicing carefree almsgiving, and lending without expecting a return (6:27-36).

Luke's "travel narrative" (9:51–19:28), a long teaching section set in the form of a journey to Jerusalem, contains a number of parables only found in Luke. There is, for example, hard on the heels of the commandment to love God and neighbor,[3] the parable of the Good Samaritan (10:25-37). In answer

---

3. In Luke this is one commandment. There is one verb and two objects; "You shall love the Lord your God . . . and your neighbor as yourself" (Luke 10:27). By this subtle editing of his source (Mark 12:28-34) Luke suggests that there is no love of God that is not also love of the neighbor.

to the question "Who is my neighbor?" (or, "Whom must I love?") Jesus told this story of a Samaritan who responded to the needs of a stranger with compassion and unstinting generosity. Those who heard this story not only learned to count the stranger (and enemy) as a neighbor; they also learned that the recognition of their neighbors as neighbors was much more likely to come by caring for them, by being neighborly to them, than at the conclusion of a tidy exegetical or sociological argument. Jesus turned the initial question around, answering the question with a question, "Who was a neighbor to the man in need?" (or, "Who loved?"); and, given the obvious reply, he said, "Go and do likewise."

There is also, of course, the parable of the Rich Fool (12:13-21), the parable I found when I was looking for my mother's maxim about a fool and his money. Luke follows that parable with sayings of Jesus that urge his followers not to be anxious but to sell their possessions and give alms (12:22-34). There is the parable of the Great Banquet (14:15-24), with its reminder of God's hospitality toward (and eschatological blessing upon) "the poor, the crippled, the blind, and the lame." Luke prefaces that parable with instructions to hosts to practice a similar hospitality (14:12-14).

And to refer to just one more of the parables in this travel narrative, there is the parable of the Rich Man and Lazarus (16:19-31). Lazarus was a poor man, reduced to begging for the scraps from the table of the rich man. He died, "and was carried away by the angels to be with Abraham." The rich man died, too, of course — not as soon, but he died — and he went straight to Hades. From the flames of Hades he begged for mercy. "Father Abraham," he said, "have mercy on me, and send Lazarus to dip the tip of his finger in water and cool my tongue." Abraham replied that the justice of God was not only poetic but also final; God had blessed poor Lazarus and pronounced woe upon the ungenerous rich man. Then the rich man asked that, at least, Lazarus be sent to warn his rich brothers. "They have Moses and the prophets," Abraham replied; "they should listen to them." The rich man replied that they might repent if one were to be sent to them from the dead. And Abraham's final word was to doubt that they would listen and repent "even if someone rises from the dead." Luke knows, of course, that someone has been raised from the dead, this Jesus anointed to preach good news to the poor. And in Acts he tells a story of his own of some people in the Jerusalem church who did repent, and who in repentance and remembrance "had all things in common" and distributed "to all, as any had need" (Acts 2:44-45).

Near the end of his travel narrative Luke tells the story of Zacchaeus (Luke 19:1-9). The song my children used to sing captures part of the story quite nicely: "Zacchaeus was a wee little man, a wee little man was he. He climbed up in the sycamore tree, the Lord Jesus Christ to see. And he said,

Zacchaeus, 'you come down, for I'm going to your house today.'" But the song omits what Luke presented as crucial features of the story. First, as a tax collector Zacchaeus may have been wealthy, but he would also have been regarded as an outsider, as a "sinner" (v. 7). Second, and still more important, Zacchaeus's hospitality to Jesus was expressed in his commitments to give half of his goods to feed the poor and to restore fourfold what he had cheated anyone (v. 8). And Jesus said, "Today salvation has come to this house." God's good future made its power felt in Zacchaeus's readiness to give generously and to do justice.[4]

It seems clear that Luke remembers this early community remembering Jesus positively. Moreover, it will not do to regard Luke's concern for the poor in his memory of Jesus — or in his memory of the early church remembering Jesus — merely as "a social prejudice,"[5] or to hint that it can best be left to one side in order to understand Luke. Luke's memory of Jesus was intimately related to his concern for the poor, and both were intimately related to the great reversal wrought by God. That reversal was important to Luke's understanding of both the significance of Jesus as the Christ and the shape of the moral life, and it was important in both ways at the same time. Witness the Magnificat: "He has brought down the powerful from their thrones, and lifted up the lowly; he has filled the hungry with good things, and sent the rich away empty" (Luke 1:52-53). Witness the inaugural sermon (4:16-21). Witness the Beatitudes and the woes (6:20-26). Witness the saying, "For all who exalt themselves will be humbled, and those who humble themselves will be exalted" (14:11). Witness the parable of the Rich Man and Lazarus (16:19-31). Witness the key testimony text: "The stone that the builders rejected has become the cornerstone" (Ps. 118:22; cited in Luke 20:17 and Acts 4:11). Witness Jesus' words at the Lord's Supper, "I am among you as one who serves" (Luke 22:27). And witness, above all, the resurrection of the crucified Jesus (Luke 24). The crucified one has been raised, and to greet his resurrection with joy is to remember and repent, to welcome the reversal he announced in his words, anticipated in his deeds, and established in his cross and resurrection — also in the economic world(s).

---

4. The same focus continues in Acts. Besides the picture of a community of goods in the early church, all of the heroes in Acts are generous to the poor. Cornelius gives alms (Acts 10:1-4); Paul brings relief funds to the poor in Judea (11:27-30; 24:17); Peter and John have no money to give a crippled beggar, but they give him something better (3:1-10).

5. Eric Franklin, *Christ the Lord* (Philadelphia: Westminster, 1975), p. 171.

Money as Illustrative — and More than Illustrative

It is true, as Jack T. Sanders says, that "the use of money is picked up as an illustration of something else" in Luke's Gospel.[6] But it does not follow that Luke's interest in money is *merely* illustrative, "as a commonplace and no more than that."[7] The "something else" of which possessions are, for Luke, illustrative is one's response to the good future that Jesus announced and that was established in his resurrection and ascension. The use of money and possessions is a primary symbol of human existence,[8] and in Luke it is always a sign and symptom of one's response to the presence and promise of the kingdom. Witness Zacchaeus, that wee little man; when he gave half his goods to feed the poor and restored fourfold what he had cheated anyone, it was indeed "illustrative" of something else. It was illustrative of the fact that Zacchaeus "received [Jesus] joyfully" (19:6 RSV). And when Jesus said, "Today salvation has come to this house," he indicated that Zacchaeus's generosity and justice were illustrative also of the good future of God, but not *merely* illustrative, for they anticipated the future reality to which they pointed, and already participated in it.

Similarly — to return at last to the church in Jerusalem — when the first Christians shared a community of goods, it was indeed "illustrative" of something else, but it was not *merely* illustrative, for it participated in the reality to which it pointed. Luke's memory of this church remembering Jesus was illustrative, and more than illustrative. The community of goods illustrated the repentance of these early Christians, their turn from the social and economic values of a "crooked generation" (Acts 2:38-40 RSV). It illustrated that this community received the Spirit "joyfully," as Zacchaeus had received Jesus. It illustrated their devotion to the fellowship, to the *koinonia* (Acts 2:42). It pointed to the fulfillment of Jewish and human hopes within the economic order.

That Luke presented the community of goods as the fulfillment of Jewish hopes and divine promises would have been clear to any reader who knew the book of Deuteronomy. When Luke said, "There was not a needy person among them" (Acts 4:34), he alluded to the promise of Deuteronomy 15:4: "There will ... be no one in need among you." Their liberal and ungrudging gifts fulfilled the command of Deuteronomy 15:10-11.[9] The care for the needy in this Jerusa-

6. Jack T. Sanders, *Ethics in the New Testament* (Philadelphia: Fortress, 1975), pp. 36-37.

7. Sanders, *Ethics in the New Testament*, p. 37.

8. See the account of "the symbolic world of possessions" in Johnson, *Sharing Possessions*, pp. 37-43.

9. Luke does not include Mark's story of the woman who anointed Jesus for burial (Mark 14:3-9), although he does include a different story of a sinful woman who anointed

lem church illustrated, in Luke's memory of it, the reformation and restoration of Israel,[10] the fidelity of a Jewish community to its covenant, both with God and with the poor. And it participated in the reality to which it pointed: the fulfillment of God's intentions for Israel. As the devout and aged Simeon had said when Jesus was presented in the temple, he would bring "glory to your people Israel" (Luke 2:32).

Jesus brought, however, not only "glory to your people Israel," but also "a light for revelation to the Gentiles," as Simeon also saw (Luke 2:32). John the Baptist had described the coming of the Lord by saying that "all flesh shall see the salvation of God" (Luke 3:6, citing Isa. 40:5), and Peter had described the coming of the Spirit by saying that "in the last days it will be, God declares, that I will pour out my Spirit upon all flesh" (Acts 2:17, citing Joel 2:28). That Luke presented the community of goods as the fulfillment of human hopes in the economic order would have been clear to any reader who was familiar with the proverbial wisdom of the Greeks. When Luke described the community of goods by repeating the phrase "[they] had all things in common" (Acts 2:44; 4:32), and when he described the community as "of one heart and soul" (Acts 4:32), he alluded not to the Hebrew Scripture but to Greek proverbial wisdom. Aristotle already had cited "'[friends have] one soul,' 'friends hold in common what they have,' 'friendship is equality,'"[11] as proverbial wisdom. By his use of such proverbial wisdom Luke identified the community created by the Spirit as a community of friends in an economic world of patrons and clients. And their community of goods illustrated a new economic order, an economic order of

---

Jesus (Luke 7:36-50). In Mark's story, after the disciples had rebuked the woman for waste, Jesus rebukes the disciples by citing Deuteronomy 15:11. Jesus rebukes the woman's accusers, but not for their concern for the poor; he rebukes them, as we said in the previous chapter, for self-righteously judging this woman for an act of self-forgetful generosity when the very presence of the poor is a judgment against the whole community. Luke omits that story, but he cites Deuteronomy 15 in describing the community of goods. He sees in the Jerusalem church a restored Israel, an Israel that keeps covenant, an Israel that practices the generosity for the poor that Moses had commanded in Deuteronomy 15. (Cf. Luke 16:29-31, where Moses and the prophets are cited as sources for the duty of generosity to the poor.)

10. This account of the community of goods confirms the thesis of Jacob Jervell that Acts tells the story of the mission to the Gentiles *not* on the basis of a Jewish rejection of Jesus but *rather* on the basis of a Jewish acceptance of Jesus and the restoration of Israel in the Jewish Christian community. Jervell, *Luke and the People of God: A New Look at Luke-Acts* (Minneapolis: Augsburg, 1972); see especially pp. 41-74. Jervell, however, does not mention this passage.

11. Aristotle, *Nicomachean Ethics*, bk. 9, ch. 8, 1168b, trans. Martin Ostwald, The Library of Liberal Arts (New York: Bobbs-Merrill Company, 1962), p. 260.

friends. Moreover, this economic order of friends was part of the distant memories and dim hopes of the Gentiles, for there were stories of communities long ago that "held all things in common" and distributed "to each according to his need."[12] The community of goods illustrated not only the restoration of Israel but also the restoration of the world, and it pointed to the fulfillment of human hopes, not just Israel's hopes.

The community of goods pointed to the fulfillment of Jewish and human hopes for an economic order that met the needs of the poor and that modeled the relationship of friends rather than of patrons and clients. But Luke locates the basis for that fulfillment in Jesus, now raised from the dead and exalted to God's right hand, and in his gift of the Spirit. They remembered Jesus, and the memory freed them from the anxious and vain attempt to establish their lives and their identities on their possessions or on the conventional standards of prestige and privilege in Roman society. The community of goods was an embodied testimony that a person's life does not consist of an abundance of possessions, but rather in welcoming the good future of God. The early church joined rich and poor in a community of goods. They remembered Jesus, and the carefree disposition toward wealth that they learned from him enabled them to give generously. They remembered Jesus, and their generosity enabled them to form a community which itself signaled the presence of God's good future, for there was not a "needy person among them" (Acts 4:34). In memory of Jesus and in the power of the Spirit this community was a restored Israel, a foretaste and an earnest of a new humanity.

More than Illustrative — But Not Legislative

The memory of this church first remembering Jesus was illustrative, and more than illustrative, but it was not legislative. Luke gave no legal rulings; he provided no social program. In Luke's account Jesus refused to adjudicate a legal dispute about inheritance (12:13-14). Moreover, the commands of Jesus with respect to possessions in Luke's Gospel are impossibly inconsistent if they are regarded as legislative. There is, for example, the command to the rich ruler, "Sell all that you own and distribute the money to the poor" (Luke 18:22; cf. Luke 14:33; 5:11, 28). The similar command to "sell your possessions, and give alms" (12:33) does not require that "all that you own" be sold and given away. Moreover, elsewhere Luke has Jesus say to the disciples, "Give to everyone who

12. Strabo, *Geography,* 7, 3, 9, trans. H. L. Jones (Loeb Classical Library); cited in Martin Hengel, *Property and Riches in the Early Church* (Philadelphia: Fortress, 1974), p. 5.

begs from you" (6:30), without the hint of a requirement that they should sell anything. Again, there is the command to "lend, expecting nothing in return" (6:35), but lending presupposes continuing possession, and the command to lend requires neither selling nor giving. And Zacchaeus, of course, as praiseworthy as his generosity and justice were, sold and gave away less than all that he possessed.

Similarly, while Luke remembers the practice of a community of goods in the early church positively, he also consistently praises the practices of almsgiving and hospitality (e.g., alms: Acts 9:36; 10:2; 11:29; 24:17; hospitality: Acts 10:23-33; 16:14-15; 16:32-34; 28:7-10). To give alms presupposes that one has something to give, that some possessions continue to be held, and to provide hospitality presupposes that one has a home.[13] The memory of Jesus and of the early church remembering Jesus does not provide in Luke a legal order with respect to possessions or a social program.

The early church's community of goods was not legislation for the continuing church. It was not remembered or represented that way by Luke himself. Unlike the community of goods practiced at Qumran, the Jerusalem church's sharing was not defined by statute, fixed by community regulation, or protected by sanctions.[14] The community of goods in Jerusalem was voluntary. "The decisive thing was *koinonia,* not organization."[15] It was an expression of friendship, not a legal order.

The churches Luke addressed probably did not practice a community of goods, and Luke does not require them to establish the practice in their communities. He does not legislate for his audience; he does ethics by way of reminder. He tells the story of Jesus and of the early church. And for Luke's community to own this story as its story is to own it as constitutive for identity and as determinative for discernment. Luke does not require of them the anachronistic pretense that they lived in Galilee or in Jerusalem in the first third of the century, but he does invite his readers to remember Jesus and to remember the early church remembering Jesus. He does invite them to regard the memory of Jesus as "holy" and to set all the stories of their life (including the stories of their economic life) alongside the remembered story of Jesus that they may be made new, "sanctified," by it. He does invite them to "fidelity," to live in ways

13. Johnson, *Sharing Possessions,* p. 20.

14. On the community at Qumran see 1QS (The Manual of Discipline) 1.11f.; see also Hengel, *Property and Riches,* pp. 32-33. The judgment on Ananias and Sapphira (Acts 5:1-11) was not prompted by a violation of some law requiring full divestiture, but by their conspiracy in deception against the Spirit (5:3).

15. Hengel, *Property and Riches,* p. 32.

that are faithful to the identity provided by the story, but because fidelity requires "creativity," he refuses to legislate, to fix the community of goods as a legal order. The memory of Jesus, however, is not less demanding by not being legislative. On the contrary, to read Luke's Gospel well was (and is) to be "disciplined" by it, to read it over-against their (and our) economic worlds. To read Luke's Gospel discerningly was (and is) to exercise "discernment" concerning how our lives and the common life can be made more "fitting," more worthy, of this story of good news to the poor.

Luke's memory of Jesus and of the early church remembering Jesus has nurtured and sustained the creative and faithful efforts of Christian communities to exercise a carefree generosity and to form a common life that protects the poor, practices hospitality toward them, and seeks justice for them. The story rebukes those who make stingy and tightfisted responses to the needs of the poor and those who are complacent with a common life and an economic order that serve the interests of the rich while the poor watch and pray for God's good future.

As Luke Johnson has said, "To read these passages in Acts [i.e., the passages describing the community of goods] as providing the ideological legitimation for such a structuring of the Christian community is to misread them."[16] Johnson seeks to discredit the community of goods as a model for the Christian community; he instead privileges the mandate for giving alms by "praising the theological roots of almsgiving."[17] He says that he does not intend "that one should replace the other as a unique form of sharing possessions."[18] Even so, one may wonder whether Johnson's admirable contribution to the moral discernment of the Christian community is sufficiently critical of the ways in which almsgiving, or individual acts of charity, can be (and has been) co-opted by an "ideological" legitimation of laissez-faire capitalism. And one may wonder whether he is sufficiently attentive to the theological roots of communal responsibilities for meeting the needs of the poor. Fidelity will not require that we play Jerusalem church, but it will not permit us to be complacent with an economic order that still creates patrons and clients rather than friends, that still ignores the covenantal and communal responsibilities to meet the needs of the poor. We may not be required to have a community of goods in the church or in the economic world, but we may not be satisfied with the sort of almsgiving that leaves the rich rich and with an easy conscience while it leaves the poor poor and with little hope. Remembering the community of goods

16. Johnson, *Sharing Possessions*, p. 129.
17. Johnson, *Sharing Possessions*, p. 138.
18. Johnson, *Sharing Possessions*, p. 138.

should make us suspicious of being satisfied with almsgiving as a response to poverty (and especially suspicious of self-satisfaction with our own little gifts); it should make us attentive to the needs of the poor also when we are considering the shape and policies of our common life. To make this story one's own still forms both identity *and community.*

The Pauline Churches

There once was a consensus that the early church was drawn from the ranks of the poor. The consensus was formed in part from Paul's own description of the Corinthian church, "not many of you were wise by human standards, not many were powerful, not many were of noble birth" (1 Cor. 1:26). Partly on the basis of this verse the Marxist historian Karl Kautsky claimed that early Christianity was essentially a proletarian movement, its converts moved by economic and social distress.[19] Adolf Deissman agreed that the early Christians were poor, but he provided a romantic, rather than a Marxist, portrait of their poverty.[20]

Recently, however, that consensus has been challenged, and a new consensus has emerged. When Paul says, after all, that "not many" of the Corinthians were from the upper strata of Greek and Roman society, he suggests that some were. Consider Crispus, for example, whom Paul baptized (1 Cor. 1:14); he was a ruler of the synagogue (Acts 18:8), a position which suggests considerable means and significant standing in the Jewish community, if not necessarily outside the Jewish community. Or, consider Erastus, whom Paul identified as "the city treasurer" in Romans 16:23. In the same verse Gaius, whom Paul also baptized (1 Cor. 1:14), was identified as "host to me and to the whole church," which suggests again considerable means and property.[21] Evidently in Corinth and elsewhere the early church included some members who were associated with wealth and numbered among the upper classes. There is now considerable agreement that the early Christians came from a broad spectrum of social levels and that the early church was more nearly a cross section of society than either Kautsky or Deissman thought.

This is the more remarkable because of what Ramsay MacMullen calls the

---

19. Karl Kautsky, *The Foundations of Christianity,* trans. H. F. Mins (New York: S. A. Russell, 1953). The work was originally published in 1925.

20. Adolf Deissman, *Light from the Ancient East,* trans. Lionel R. M. Strachan, fourth ed. (Grand Rapids: Baker Book House, 1965), pp. 465-67.

21. See further Gerd Theissen, *The Social Setting of Pauline Christianity* (London: T&T Clark, 1982), pp. 73-96.

"verticality" of Roman society.[22] There was in Roman society an oppressive and pervasive sense of "high" and "low" social standing. Social rank was intimately connected with wealth, even though it was not altogether identical with it. MacMullen describes the situation as "a very steep social pyramid." At the top of the pyramid in any given city stood the aristocracy of the city, who themselves were far down the slope from the Roman senatorial class. At the bottom were the totally indigent, most free but also slaves. Most associations were formed along socially homogeneous lines, but the early church joined in one community both "high" and "low," both rich and poor. The social integration of the early churches was remarkable — but it was not easy to transcend the hierarchical and "vertical" patterns of Roman society.

The Corinthian Church and "Remembrance"

It was not easy in Corinth, at least. The tension between social classes was probably related to the "divisions" and "quarrels" that beset the Corinthian church (1 Cor. 1:10, 11).[23] Surely this much is clear: the "verticality" of Roman society made its power felt in the Corinthian church when it gathered for the common meal associated with the Lord's Supper (11:17-33-34). The church divided along social lines; the division between "high" and "low," between rich and poor, was only too obvious at what was meant to be a communal meal. Some went hungry, while others stuffed themselves and got drunk (11:21).

Hospitality and fellowship (or *koinonia*) around a table had been a part of the common life of the church from the beginning. When Luke characterized the first church, he said that they "devoted themselves to the apostles' teaching and fellowship, to the breaking of bread and the prayers" (Acts 2:42). "Day by day," as Luke remembered it, "they broke bread at home and ate their food with

---

22. Ramsay MacMullen, *Roman Social Relations: 50 B.C. to A.D. 284* (New Haven: Yale University Press, 1974), pp. 88-120.

23. Gerd Theissen's account of the social stratification in Corinth and in the Corinthian church is quite successful. His efforts to trace *all* of the problems in Corinth to this social stratification, however, are not as convincing. The tensions in the Corinthian church were surely related to social stratification, but they should not be reduced to it. Theissen's account of the conflict between "weak" and "strong" about eating meat sacrificed to idols, in particular, seems insufficiently attentive to the theological differences between these groups in Corinth. This problem, too, would surely have been exacerbated by the social stratification of Corinth, but it should not be reduced to it. On the divisions at the Lord's Supper, however, Theissen is quite convincing (see *Social Setting of Pauline Christianity,* pp. 145-74).

glad and generous hearts" (Acts 2:46). There was no sharp distinction between breaking bread in remembrance of Jesus and the meals they shared in fellowship *(koinonia)*. It is plausible that many of the poor in the early church found these meals important to their subsistence. Table fellowship was one more way in which the early church celebrated the good future of God as good news to the poor. It soon became, of course, one of the ways the church embodied the good future of God as "one new humanity" of Jew and Gentile. When Paul rebuked Peter for his separating himself from table fellowship with the Gentiles in Antioch, he made it plain that "the truth of the gospel" was at stake in the social significance of the table fellowship of Jews and Gentiles (Gal. 2:14). And now in Corinth, where the fellowship had been broken by the verticality of Roman society, where the *koinonia* had suffered the division of rich and poor, Paul made it plain that the truth of remembering Jesus was at stake in the social significance of the communal meal of rich and poor.

The precise circumstances of the meal are not entirely clear, but it seems likely[24] that the owner of the house would invite Christians of all social classes to share a simple meal of bread and wine. Perhaps the affluent hosts of the Corinthian church invited those Christians who shared their social standing to a more sumptuous meal to be enjoyed before the poor arrived at the end of a day of work. The rich would eat and drink before the Lord's Supper and continue with their own meal, larger in quantity and better in quality, after the common meal had begun. From the perspective of the rich, they were being generous, and they were, after all, providing bread and wine for the poor. Moreover, they might suppose that, by providing bread and wine, they were being faithful to the tradition they had received from Paul. From the perspective of the poor, however, the meal had the effect (if not the intention) of reminding all participants where they stood on the steep slopes of the Corinthian social pyramid.

Paul had heard of the "divisions" at their communal meals (1 Cor. 11:18), and far from commending them for maintaining the traditions that they had received from him (11:2), he rebuked them. The Corinthian practice, with its division of rich and poor, he said, "show[s] contempt for the church of God" and "humiliate[s] those who have nothing" (11:22). Paul clearly privileged the hermeneutical perspective of the poor; he saw the situation, as they did, from the underside of the social pyramid. For him, too, the Corinthian practice served to illustrate and embody not the memory of Jesus, nor the fellowship of the body of Christ, nor the hope for God's good future, but the social hierarchy of Corinth. Such a practice, he said, "is not really to eat the Lord's supper"

---

24. This account of the circumstances follows the suggestions of Theissen, *Social Setting of Pauline Christianity*, pp. 145-74.

(11:20). It is to eat the bread and to drink the cup "in an unworthy manner" (11:27).

Their practice is not *koinonia*. Paul had just reminded them in another context of the fellowship with Christ and with each other in the Lord's Supper: "The cup of blessing that we bless, is it not a sharing [*koinonia*] in the blood of Christ? The bread that we break, is it not a sharing [*koinonia*] in the body of Christ? Because there is one bread, we who are many are one body, for we all partake of the one bread" (1 Cor. 10:16-17). Their practice does not display their fellowship in the body of Christ; it reflects the "verticality" of Corinthian society.

Their practice does not point to the good future of God. It does not anticipate that good future or welcome already the coming sovereignty of the one who blesses the poor. And because they "eat and drink without discerning the body" (11:29), the one body that they are in Christ (see also 12:12-27), the future Paul anticipates for them is judgment (11:27-34). That future, to be "condemned along with the world" (11:32), can be avoided by judging themselves (11:31), by pleading guilty, and by turning from such a practice to one that honors rather than humiliates the poor. They are to "wait for one another" and to eat a genuinely common meal (11:33-34). The rich Corinthians' conceit of providing a little stale bread and a little cheap wine for the poor and counting that as hospitality, while they ate and drank too much, fell under the judgment of God.

Fundamentally, however, it is not the Lord's Supper that they ate, because they did not remember Jesus. Paul reminded them of Jesus' word, "Do this in remembrance of me" (11:24, 25). And the memory of Jesus should form communities less anxious about securing their identities by their social status, more carefree with their possessions, less conceited in their philanthropy, more liberal in their sharing (their *koinonia*), readier to see things from the perspective of the poor, and readier to resist the verticality of Roman society. At the very meal that Christians celebrated "in remembrance" of Jesus, this Christian community was formed by "the world" (which stands under judgment, 11:32); their common life was structured by the social hierarchy of Corinth, not by the memory of Jesus. They did not remember Jesus. It was not the Lord's Supper that they ate.

Paul and the Memory of Jesus

Paul, of course, as is well known, seldom appealed directly to the memory of Jesus' words. And the contrast between Paul's words on wealth and those of Jesus has often been pointed out. Paul makes no mention of an apocalyptic reversal of social status. He provides no beatitude for the poor. There is nothing as radical as "Go, sell what you own, and give the money to the poor" (Mark 10:21).

On the topic of wealth Paul seems closer to the Stoics than to Jesus. He emphasizes *autarkeia,* the self-sufficiency, or autonomy, or contentment, so highly valued by Cynics and Stoics.[25] He told the Philippians, "I have learned to be content [*autarkēs*] with whatever I have. I know what it is to have little, and I know what it is to have plenty. In any and all circumstances I have learned the secret of being well-fed and of going hungry, of having plenty and of being in need" (Phil. 4:11-12; cf. 1 Tim. 6:6-10). He exhorted the Thessalonians to work diligently in order to provide for themselves and to "be dependent on no one" (1 Thess. 4:11-12; cf. 2 Thess. 3:7-12). Each one, in order to maintain independence, *autarkeia,* should have enough to care for his own needs and be "content" with what he has. Paul himself had worked with his own hands, as he more than once reminded his churches.[26] Paul's language echoes the usage of the Cynics and Stoics.[27]

But Paul sets the language of the Stoics in the context of the church's memory of Jesus, and the concepts are qualified, modified, transformed. Paul's "contentment" is hardly the ascetic and individualistic self-sufficiency of the Cynics. Paul knows, he says, how to be *autarkēs* when he has "plenty" (*perisseuein,* Phil. 4:12). And although Stoics like Epictetus and countless Cynics would have claimed self-sufficiency in the midst of having "little," no Stoic or Cynic would have used the word that Paul uses here (*tapeinousthai,* Phil. 4:12). Paul knows, he says, how to be humbled, but humility (*tapeinophrosunē*) is a vice for the proud Stoic, not a virtue as it is for Paul.[28]

Paul's contentment stands in a different moral context than the contentment of the Stoics. The root of Stoic contentment was willing whatever happened; that was the way one participated in the great reason that was at work in the world. The root of Paul's contentment was remembering the eschatological

---

25. On Paul's stress on self-sufficiency, *autarkeia,* and on his modification of this Greek philosophical ideal, see Hengel, *Property and Riches,* pp. 54-59, and Nils A. Dahl, "Paul and Possessions," *Studies in Paul* (Minneapolis: Augsburg, 1977), pp. 23-25.

26. He reminded the Corinthians that he paid his own way as a "defense to those who would examine me" (1 Cor. 9:3), and he reminded the Thessalonians of his work as an object lesson (2 Thess. 3:7-12). See also Acts 20:33-35.

27. And Paul's practice of supporting himself as a tent maker may echo the practice of some Cynics. See Ron F. Hock, *The Working Apostle: An Examination of Paul's Means of Livelihood* (Ph.D. Dissertation, Yale, 1974), pp. 163-65.

28. See further Allen Verhey, "Humble, humility," *The International Standard Bible Encyclopedia,* rev. ed., vol. 2 (Grand Rapids: Eerdmans, 1982), pp. 775-78.

act of God in Jesus Christ. He remembers the cross and resurrection of Jesus and reminds his readers that they have owned that story, that cross and resurrection, as their own. They participate, not in cosmic reason, but in Jesus' cross and resurrection. Because they remember Jesus, they may also hope. The Lord Jesus, Paul tells them, "will transform the body of our humiliation [*tapeinōseōs*] that it may be conformed to the body of his glory" (Phil. 3:21). And because they remember Jesus and hope, Paul exhorts them to "stand firm in the Lord. . . . The Lord is near. Do not worry about anything" (Phil. 4:1, 5, 6). The shape of Paul's contentment is the confidence that "I can do all things through him who strengthens me" (Phil. 4:13). Paul's "contentment" is in the last analysis a good deal closer to Jesus' eschatological wisdom of freedom from anxiety, of being carefree, than to the Stoics. A person's life is not secured by rigorous observance of the Law nor by ascetic severity to the body nor by philosophical theories about cosmic reason nor by an abundance of possessions, but by the grace of God in Jesus Christ. The just shall live by faith.

Similarly, in his advice to the Thessalonian church concerning the "loafers" in their midst Paul does not simply appeal to *autarkeia* as a freestanding philosophical principle. He sets the admonition to "be dependent on no one" (1 Thess. 4:12) not in the context of the virtue of independence but in the context of community, in the context of his reminder that "you yourselves have been taught by God to love one another" (1 Thess. 4:9). To live in community is not to disown financial responsibilities like the loafers at Thessalonica. It is rather to work for a living (2 Thess. 3:12), not that possessions might be accumulated and an identity secured, but — as Paul's own practice of work displayed — that the community might not be burdened (2 Thess. 3:8). The fault in the loafers is not simply that they violate *autarkeia,* or independence, but that they violate the *koinonia,* the fellowship. It is fitting, therefore, in Paul's view, that they should not be allowed at the common table: "Anyone unwilling to work should not eat" (2 Thess. 3:10).

Luke may be called as a witness to Paul's view of working for a living. He reports that Paul also reminded the Ephesian elders that he had supported himself by working with his own hands. It was, Paul said, "an example that by such work we must support the weak, remembering the words of the Lord Jesus, for he himself said, ' It is more blessed to give than to receive'" (Acts 20:35). To live in community is to work, not only that one will not burden the community, but also that one may give in remembrance of Jesus.

In the letters Paul himself never quotes the words of Jesus on wealth. He does not call for a community of goods. But he does call his readers to be generous and to live together in a community — and to eat together as a community — where the poor are welcomed and blessed. Paul evidently expects the wealthy in the congregations not only to be carefree about their possessions but also to be generous in freedom and in fellowship. He expects them to contribute to the needs of the poor, to practice hospitality (Rom. 12:13; cf. 16:23), to use their gifts, including their financial gifts, as members of one another because they are one body in Christ (Rom. 12:4-8). Such generosity and community are part of the "obedience of faith."

So, although Paul does not appeal to the memory of Jesus' words, he does remember Jesus, and creatively and faithfully he continues a tradition concerning wealth and poverty that reaches back to this Jesus. In memory of Jesus he qualifies and transforms the Stoic principle. In the hope born of memory he envisions a new economic world, an economic world that would practice generosity and community across the divisions of Roman society, across the division of slave and free, across the divisions created by the "verticality" of the Roman social order, across the division of conventional patronage, and across the division of Jew and Gentile. The Pauline churches — with the help of Paul's reminders — did sometimes live in memory of Jesus. The collection for the poor in Judea may provide the most vivid testimony to the truth of that claim.

The Collection

The collection for the poor in Judea seems to have been part of Paul's mission almost from the beginning. Acts tells the story of an early collection for the poor there. A certain Agabus, a "prophet" from Jerusalem who visited the church at Antioch, had foreseen a period of famine (and, as Luke says, he was right); the church at Antioch took a collection and appointed Paul and Barnabas to deliver it (Acts 11:27-30; 12:25). The chronologies of Acts and Paul's letters are notoriously difficult to correlate (or harmonize), but Paul's part in that early offering may be one reason why, a little later, when those "who were acknowledged pillars" in the church at Jerusalem affirmed Paul's ministry among the Gentiles, "they asked only one thing, that we remember the poor" (Gal. 2:9, 10). And Paul, as he told the Galatians, "was eager to do" it (Gal. 2:10).

The procedures for the collection are described in response to a question of the Corinthians "concerning the collection" (1 Cor. 16:1-4):

> On the first day of the week, each of you is to put aside and save whatever extra you earn, so that collections need not be taken when I come. And when I arrive, I will send any whom you approve with letters to take your gift to Jerusalem. If it seems advisable that I should go also, they will accompany me.

These are, as Paul says, the same directions he gave to the churches of Galatia and presumably to the other churches as well. On Sunday, the day of resurrection, the day of remembrance and hope, members of the Pauline congregations all over the Roman Empire set aside what they could as a gift for the poor in Judea. It is not difficult to imagine the concerns such an offering would prompt, and Paul clearly wants to assure the Corinthians that it will be handled with appropriate care and with unimpeachable honesty (cf. also 2 Cor. 8:20-21). It is also not difficult to imagine how this novel practice might (re)form the attitudes of the Gentile Christians toward both money and those Jewish strangers they nevertheless are taught to regard as "brothers" and "sisters" and "friends."

The significance of the collection is described in Paul's effort to encourage the Corinthians to give generously to it (2 Cor. 8, 9). In that effort, it ought to be observed, Paul utilizes what were evidently ancient fund-raising techniques. He begins by informing the Corinthians of the quite remarkable generosity of the churches of Macedonia (8:1-6); surely the Corinthians would not want to be less generous than the poor churches of Macedonia. Later he informs them that he had used the same technique with the churches of Macedonia. He had told the Macedonians about the "zeal" of the Corinthians for the collection — and quite successfully (9:1-2). Surely the Corinthians would not want Paul — or themselves — to be humiliated because their generosity did not match Paul's boasting about it (9:3-4). I leave it to the reader to decide whether to be amused or embarrassed by Paul as a fund-raiser. Even within these sections, however, something of the significance of the collection for Paul and the Pauline churches is suggested. The collection is a work of God's grace (*charin*, 8:1); the joy and generosity of the Macedonians is the work of God's grace. And the Macedonians beg Paul for "the privilege," or the grace *(charin)*, and "the sharing," or the community *(koinonian)*, of this "ministry [*diakonias*] to the saints" (8:4).[29]

When Paul turns from these fund-raising strategies to his more profound appeal to the Corinthians, he reminds them of Jesus. The collection is in memory of Jesus. "For you know," he says (2 Cor. 8:9), "the generous act [or the grace *(charin)*] of our Lord Jesus Christ, that though he was rich, yet for your sakes he became poor, so that by his poverty you might become rich." To remember Jesus is to be disposed to give generously. To remember Jesus and to own that story as their own is to participate in this grace (2 Cor. 8:7: *charin*; "in

---

29. See further Sondra Ely Wheeler, *Wealth as Peril and Obligation* (Grand Rapids: Eerdmans, 1995), pp. 80-81. For an illuminating list of the words and phrases Paul uses to refer to the collection, see Nils Dahl, "Paul and Possessions," pp. 37-38.

this generous undertaking"). Paul does "not say this as a command" (8:8); he proceeds by way of reminder. To remember Jesus is to have the "desire" to give generously. That desire, or "eagerness," is the critical thing in Paul's view; "for if the eagerness is there, the gift is acceptable according to what one has — not according to what one does not have" (8:12). The Corinthians are permitted to give this gift as a glad expression of their remembering Jesus. Paul permits nothing else, of course, and he encourages them now to match their eagerness — and to express it — by completing the offering according to their means (8:10, 11).

Paul does not infer from the memory of Christ or from the disposition of generosity that the Corinthians are to give everything away. The desired result is not that "others should be eased and you burdened" (2 Cor. 8:13 RSV). Rather, Paul commends the standard of "equality" (*isotēs*, 8:13, 14). There are different kinds of "equality," of course; Aristotle had distinguished, for example, the "equality" of distributive justice, the "equality" of rectification, and the "equality" of friendship,[30] but there can be little doubt that Paul is commending the "equality" of friendship with the poor in Judea.

As we have already observed, equality and friendship were proverbially linked; "friendship is equality."[31] One is reminded of the community of possessions in Jerusalem, not because Paul here or anywhere calls for a common purse, but because Paul envisions a community of friends. As the community of possessions in Jerusalem was an illustration of the *koinonia* of that early church, so the collection was an illustration of the *koinonia* of Gentile and Jewish Christians. That community was created by the great grace of God. God is the great benefactor, and the gifts of the Gentiles are simply gift answering to gift. Where God is the benefactor, there can be no "conceit of philanthropy." There is no hint in Paul's appeal of a division of the church into generous benefactors and needy beneficiaries. The community is marked not by the economic relationship of patrons and clients but by friendship. Where God is the benefactor, everyone is a client, and the gifts of each are not so much patronage as gift answering to gift. That is why Paul can say that "the rendering of this ministry not only supplies the needs of the saints but also overflows with many thanksgivings to God" (9:12) and why Paul concludes his appeal with the exclamation, "Thanks be to God for his indescribable gift!" (9:15).

The community was created by the grace of God, but it was expressed, illustrated, in the collection. The "equality" of Jew and Gentile was a gift of God in Jesus Christ, and their own gifts both welcome that good future of God es-

---

30. See Aristotle, *Nicomachean Ethics*, 1131b31, 1157b36, 1158b29, 1162a35.
31. Aristotle, *Nicomachean Ethics*, bk. 9, ch. 8, 1168b8, p. 260.

tablished in Christ and make it present. Paul urges them both to act "from equality" (*ex isotētos,* 8:13) and to act so "that there may be equality" (*hopōs genētai isotēs;* 8:14). Those two references to "equality" create a little envelope for Paul's hope that the "present abundance" among the Gentiles may meet the needs of the poor in Judea and that "their abundance" may supply the needs of the Gentiles (8:14); that is to say, as the Gentiles share what they have with the Jews, so the Jews share what they have (the promises to Israel) with the Gentiles. That is why the gift of the Gentiles expresses gratitude to God and "will produce thanksgiving to God through us" (9:11). And that is why Paul's appeal can include the promise of a "harvest of your righteousness" (9:10) and the promise that "you will be enriched in every way for your great generosity" (9:11). The point is not that they should give in order to get. The motive is not so self-serving as that. The point is rather that in this *koinonia* of Jew and Gentile the Gentiles not only give to the Jews but also by God's grace receive, for they share in the heritage and hope of the Jews. By receiving this gift the Jews will recognize and celebrate "the surpassing grace of God that he has given you [Gentiles]" (9:14).

Paul says something very similar when he reports to the Romans that he is on his way to Jerusalem to deliver the collection (Rom. 15:26-27):

> Macedonia and Achaia have been pleased to share their resources with the poor among the saints at Jerusalem. They were pleased to do this, and indeed they owe it to them; for if the Gentiles have come to share in their spiritual blessings, they ought also to be of service to them in material things.

And when he asks the Romans to pray that the collection be "acceptable to the saints" (15:31), he acknowledges the risk that the Jews will not welcome the "equality" of Jew and Gentile, the friendship that God has created and commanded by the grace of the Lord Jesus Christ.

The collection was gift answering to gift in memory of Jesus. It was an expression of the equality of Jew and Gentile that God had created and commanded in Christ. And it was illustrative — and more than illustrative — of a new economic order. It was illustrative of a community of friends, not clients and patrons. And it was illustrative of what may be called "a manna economy." After Paul has reminded the Corinthians of Jesus and commended "equality," he corroborates his argument by reminding them of God's provision of manna. "The one who had much did not have too much, and the one who had little did not have too little" (2 Cor. 8:15; Exod. 16:18). Manna was a familiar eschatological symbol, as we have observed, and Paul did not empty the story of its economic associations. In a "manna economy" hoarding is futile, loafing is foolish, daily needs are met, and God is trusted to provide. Such a "manna economy" illustrates and participates in God's good economic future.

To remember Jesus is to hope for a manna economy. It is to participate in a community of friends that transcends the verticality of Roman society and the divide between Jews and Gentiles. It is to share in a community of voluntary fellowship where the needs of any are met out of the abundance of others (2 Cor. 8:14). To remember Jesus is to be a community where the poor are already blessed, already welcomed, included, and honored.

James and a Church of "The Poor"

The church of which and to which the author of James writes is identified with "the poor." There is considerable disagreement, however, about how to understand this identification. Some, calling attention to the self-designation of other Jewish groups who felt oppressed as "the poor,"[32] have suggested that "the poor" are in James, as in these other groups, really "the pious," that "the rich" are really unbelievers or outsiders, and that these terms really say nothing about the economic status of Christians or the moral status of wealth.[33] Others construe these associations of "the poor" with "the righteous," on the one hand, and of "the rich" with "the wicked," on the other, as an expression not only of the material poverty of this community but also of its resentment against the wealthy. It is better, however, to understand this community's identification with the poor neither as a purely rhetorical identification of themselves as "pious" nor as a "proletarian" class-consciousness and hatred. That James returns again and again to real problems caused by real poverty (James 2:1-9, 15-16; 5:1-11) is enough to discredit the first of these views. And that this church of "the poor" included at least some wealthy members[34] is enough to render the second suspect.

How should this identification with the poor be understood? The key is in the verses which introduce the topics of wealth and poverty in the book, James 1:9-10, "Let the believer who is lowly boast in being raised up, and the rich in being brought low...." The background for these verses surely includes the memory

32. The community at Qumran is a good example of this identification of "the poor" and "the pious." See, e.g., 1QpHab 12:3, 6, 10; 1QpPs37; 1QM 11:9. But Qumran is by no means the only example.

33. See, for example, James Moffatt, *The General Epistles* (London: Hodder & Stoughton, 1948), p. 33.

34. See Peter H. Davids, *The Epistle of James* (Grand Rapids: Eerdmans, 1982), p. 46.

REMEMBERING JESUS IN THE WORLD OF ADAM SMITH

of Jesus' announcement of "good news to the poor."[35] Jesus had announced an eschatological blessing upon the poor and had made that good future felt; he had,
in Luke's memory at least, announced a corresponding "woe" upon the rich. Jesus
had proclaimed a coming future in which "many who are first will be last, and the
last will be first" (Mark 10:31) and where "all who exalt themselves will be humbled, and all who humble themselves will be exalted" (Matt. 23:12). Jesus had invited those who heard this announcement to "repent," to turn from conventional
values, to be formed and transformed by the anticipation of such a future. "Whoever wants to be first must be last of all and servant of all" (Mark 9:35; cf. also
Matt. 20:26, 27; 23:12; Mark 10:43-44; Luke 22:26; John 13:2-17). Jesus himself
identified with the poor; he identified himself as "one who serves" (Luke 22:27; cf.
also Matt. 20:28; Mark 10:45; John 13:2-17). Now the exalted Lord still promises
and works that reversal, and he still calls the church to welcome it by identification with the poor. This is not to glorify poverty. It is to take the side of those who
are so often beaten down and crushed by it. So, let the poor glory in that they are
"exalted"; and let the rich glory in that they are "humbled," in that they are in this
community not as proud patrons and conventional benefactors but as those who
serve, in that they have identified with "the poor."

This reading of James 1:9-10 is not undisputed. Some scholars believe
that "the rich" are the unbelievers. They call attention to the fact that James refers in 1:9 to "the believer who is lowly" while 1:10 simply refers to "the rich."
Because "rich" is an adjective, however, the construction requires that we supply a noun that is being modified, and the natural reading would be to supply
the noun from the previous clause, that is, "[the believer] who is rich."[36] They

35. Although James does not explicitly cite Jesus, it is clear both that he knew the
tradition of Jesus' words and that he utilized it. Davids, *The Epistle of James,* pp. 47-48, lists
thirty-six close parallels between James and the synoptic tradition and nine "more general
parallels in thought." James, too, does ethics "by way of reminder," consistently reminding
the congregation of what they already know (1:3; 3:1; 4:4; 5:20). He remembers Jesus, even
if he does not cite him, and with the help of his reminders, the congregation remembers
Jesus and discerns the shape of life — and a common life — that fits the remembered and
exalted Jesus. Moreover, while it must be admitted that James does not present a well-
developed Christology, there is a Christology. Jesus is Lord, or *kurios,* a title used eleven
times in the epistle, sometimes with reference to God, sometimes with reference to Jesus
Christ, and sometimes ambiguously. Jesus is Lord of the church, and the tradition of his
sayings still guides the church. He is "the Lord of glory" (2:1 RSV) who will come again
(5:7). Meanwhile, the congregation remembers and hopes, and remembering and hoping,
fashions a common life worthy of the Lord.

36. Moreover, the one verb of these two clauses (*kauxasthō,* "boast") would need to
be read in its plain sense in the first clause and then, when it supplied for the second, quite
ironically.

call attention to the "harsh words of 1:10-11,"[37] which offer no hope to the rich. These "harsh words," however, simply remind the rich of their mortality. The reference to the flower of the field that withers and dies would be familiar enough from both Hebrew Scripture (e.g., Ps. 37:2; 90:5-6; 103:15; Isa. 40:6-8) and the memory of Jesus' words (Matt. 6:28-30); it serves to remind the wealthy not only of the transient character of possessions but also of human dependence upon God. These "harsh words" hardly require us to identify "the rich" of James 1:10 with unbelievers. It is true, as they point out, that in James 2:6-7 "the rich" *are* unbelievers, but that passage seems a slender reed to support their interpretation of James 1:10, especially when the context of the passage suggests that there were wealthy members of (and visitors to) the congregation. The interpretation of James 1:10 as "Let [the Christian] who is rich glory in that he is humbled, made last of all and servant of all" is confirmed by the parallel passage in James 4:10, "Humble yourselves before the Lord, and he will exalt you."[38] So, let the poor glory in that they are "exalted"; and let the rich glory in that they are "humbled" before the Lord.

The wealthy members of the congregation who have learned to glory in being humbled, in being made servants of "the poor," are no longer identified with "the rich" but with "the poor." They find their identity in Christ, in "the name that was invoked over [them]" in baptism (2:7). Of course, there is a struggle between the way of life of "the rich" and the way of life faithful to Christ and to the poor. When they practice favoritism within the congregation, honoring those who come to their assembly "with gold rings and in fine clothes" (2:2) more than the poor, then their behavior expresses the conventional social attitudes of "the rich" rather than the reversal of values wrought by and taught by the Lord Jesus Christ. When they boast about their futures, thinking that they have secured their future by "doing business and making money" (4:13), then they do not boast in being humbled; then their boasting is the boasting of "the rich" and not a boasting in the Lord; "all such boasting is evil" (4:16).

The way of life of "the rich," from which the wealthy in this congregation of "the poor" have separated themselves (but against which they still struggle) is denounced in James 5:1-6.[39] The passage reiterates Jesus' announcement,

---

37. P. Maynard-Reid, *Poverty and Wealth in James* (Maryknoll, N.Y.: Orbis, 1987), p. 41, cited by Wheeler, *Wealth as Peril*, p. 102. My response to this claim is indebted to her fuller response.

38. Consider also the parallel passage in 1 Peter 5:6, where it is associated with freedom from anxiety, which in turn is associated with the saying of Jesus about the "lilies of the field" (cf. James 1:10-11).

39. On this passage see the very helpful remarks of Wheeler, *Wealth as Peril*, pp. 91-106.

"woe to you who are rich" (Luke 6:24), but develops it with an indictment that renders the coming judgment just. The first charge of the indictment is that the rich hoard their wealth, letting it sit idle, allowing it to rot and rust, thinking foolishly to secure their futures by their treasury (5:2, 3; cf. Matt. 6:19-20; Luke 6:37 12:33). The second charge is that the rich have acquired their wealth by oppressing those who worked for them; the laborers have not been dealt with fairly (5:4; cf. Lev. 19:13; contrast the generosity of the owner of the vineyard in Matt. 20:1-16). These rich fools do not see in their wealth either their indebtedness to others or their opportunity (and obligation) to share what they have with those on whom they depend. The third part of the indictment is that "the rich" live "in luxury and in pleasure" (5:5), self-indulgent while surrounded with the poverty of others. The indictment may remind us of Luke's story of the rich man and Lazarus — and of the question of whether the rich would practice justice and generosity even if someone were raised from the dead (Luke 16:19-31). The fourth charge is that "the rich" are guilty of the judicial murder of "the righteous one" (5:6; cf. Acts 3:14; 7:52; 22:14). It is no stretch to identify this "righteous one" with Jesus, who came announcing the good future of God and calling for repentance. The poor heard him gladly and welcomed the future he promised; some of the rich, too, welcomed that future and repented, boasting not in their wealth but in their being humbled. But some had to find a way to subdue and silence this preacher of good news to the poor.

The rich indicted in this passage are surely to be regarded as "fools" as well as villains, and the remedy for foolishness, of course, is wisdom. Wisdom is, indeed, another of the themes to which James returns again and again: "If any of you is lacking in wisdom, ask God, who gives to all generously and ungrudgingly" (1:5). God is the giver, moreover, not only of wisdom but also of every good gift (1:17). Gifts in this community, too, are simply gift answering to gift. But the greatest gift is "the wisdom from above." Such wisdom is, among other things, "full of mercy and good fruits, without a trace of partiality or hypocrisy" (3:17). Such wisdom is displayed in works, not just words, of compassion and mercy; it is "to care for orphans and widows in their distress" (1:27) and to meet the "bodily needs" of the poor (2:15-16). It is displayed in hospitality to the poor (2:1-7). It is displayed in humbling oneself before the Lord (4:10), in resisting the temptations in the way of life of "the rich" (5:1-6) and in enduring patiently the trials caused by that way of life (5:7-11). Don't be a fool!

It is an eschatological wisdom, of course, hardly based on observance of the regular patterns of nature and history, hardly recognized as wisdom when judged by the conventional standards of society. It is wisdom in view of the coming great reversal, but in view of that future it is the foundation for what is both prudent and moral. Such wisdom will, in the end, yield "a harvest of righteousness" (3:18). In the meantime, however, such wisdom yields in the congregation a "first fruits" of that future harvest. "In fulfillment of his own purpose [that is, compassion and mercy (5:11)] he gave us birth by the word of truth, so that we would become a kind of first fruits of his creatures" (1:18).

The coming great reversal establishes already a new social reality in which those who are lowly according to the world's standards are exalted and those who are exalted according to the world's standards — the rich — are humbled. The new social reality is an eschatological one, to be sure, but it already has and must have some effect in the communities James addresses. If there is cause for boasting, it is surely not in the arrogance of the rich (4:13) but in God and in that new social reality (1:9-11). James calls upon the whole community to welcome and to anticipate that reality, to "humble yourselves before the Lord" (4:10). In memory and in hope both rich and poor in the congregation of "the poor" challenge conventional standards of prestige and security, the foolish reliance upon wealth, and the proposition that a person's life consists of an abundance of possessions (5:5). Memory and hope form characters disposed to acts of concrete generosity (1:17; 2:15-17) and to justice (5:1-4). Memory and hope fashion a community marked by its identification with "the poor," eager to be hospitable to the poor and to honor them, marked by mutuality and fairness rather than by the "distinctions" and "verticality" of Roman society (2:1-9).

Revelation: Memory and Hope
in the Economic Hardship of Persecution

Remember also the churches of Asia Minor enduring the petty persecution of Domitian (81-96) and remembering Jesus. Their experience of alienation and oppression gave rise — as it had before, of course — to apocalyptic literature, specifically to the book of Revelation. In the midst of petty persecution, which evidently included economic hardship (13:17), these churches were reminded of Jesus, the Lamb who was slain, and that memory enabled them to envision a world where this slain Lamb is enthroned (5:6-14). For a time Satan and Caesar may continue to assert their doomed reign. For a time the story of Roman power and wealth may continue to deceive. Finally, however, judgment will be revealed against a variety of rich fools, against "the kings of the earth and the great men and the generals and the rich and the strong" (6:15 RSV) who refuse to welcome the reign of a Lamb.

The vision of the fall of Rome (or Babylon) recognizes the great wealth and splendor of that city. But wealth provides no security against the judgment of God. Even cities and empires can be rich fools evidently. The fall of Rome is

lamented only by those who are powerful and wealthy according to its standards and with its aid — "the kings of the earth" (18:9-10) and "the merchants," especially the slave traders (18:11-19). A voice from heaven calls for an
exodus from the city before its fall, "Come out of her, my people" (18:4). The
exodus is a spiritual exodus, of course, an exodus from the pride of power and
the greed that marked Rome's life and justified its doom (18:3). It is an exodus
that is undertaken not only in the expectation of Rome's fall but also in the
hope of a new world and a new city, a world and a city where God dwells and
reigns.

Still, the idea that people or cities or empires — or churches — can secure
their lives and futures by their possessions is a seductive idea, and the churches
of Asia Minor are warned against it. Consider, for example, the letter to the
church at Laodicea (3:14-21). That "lukewarm" church stands at risk of God's
wrath, John says, because they say, "'I am rich, I have prospered, and I need
nothing'" (3:17). They think themselves rich and, therefore, secure. John tells
them that they are really "poor" and that their security will be discovered in repentance, in welcoming the reign of Christ who turns conventional judgments
of wealth and poverty upside down.[40] A person's life — or a community's life
— does not consist in the abundance of possessions, and it cannot be secured
by accommodating the claims of Domitian and so living comfortably. A person's life consists rather in celebrating the enthronement of the Lamb who was
slain. Such a celebration frees the Christian person and community from conventional standards of prosperity and power, frees them to be not anxious and
to be generous, and frees them to dream — at least — of a good future where
justice dwells. It frees them for "patient endurance." "Patient endurance" is not
passivity; it is the moral heroism of a countercultural existence, in the world of
finance as in other areas of life.

In memory of Jesus and in hope the author of Revelation invites the
churches of Asia Minor to endure the petty persecution of Domitian with patience and heroism. The churches express their memory and hope not only in
their words of worship but also in subordinating their economic interests to the
sovereignty of Christ.

---

40. Consider also the letter to the church at Smyrna. "I know . . . your poverty, even
though you are rich" (Rev. 2:9).

The Churches of Timothy and Titus:
Memory and Hope in More Prosaic Circumstances

Compared to the book of Revelation the Pastoral Epistles are quite dull, at least prosaic. The danger here is not the greed and power of empire, not some seven-headed beast; the danger is heresy. What is required is not moral heroism in the face of Rome's power but "sound doctrine" and sound morality in resistance to the claims of the heretics. Against the asceticism of some of these heretics (e.g., 1 Tim. 4:1-5) and against the libertinism of others of them ("rejecting conscience," 1 Tim. 1:19; cf. Tit. 1:15-16), the Pastoral Epistles soberly reinforce mundane obligations, also in the economic world.

The Pauline tradition of contentment, or the Pauline qualification of the Greek tradition of contentment *(autarkeia)*, is retrieved (1 Tim. 6:6-10). And, faithful to Paul, contentment does not require asceticism; it requires moderation *(sōphrosunē)*. It is the love of money that is renounced, not money itself (6:10). The churches of Timothy and Titus evidently included some "who in the present age are rich," and these individuals are told — following a reminder of Jesus (6:13-16) — not to be fools, not to set their hope on their possessions instead of on God: "Command them not to be haughty, or to set their hopes on the uncertainty of riches, but rather on God. . . ." The implication is not asceticism, for they are to set their hopes "on God who richly provides us with everything for our enjoyment." But the implication is generosity: "They are to do good, to be rich in good works, generous, and ready to share" (6:17-18).

More interesting — but no less prosaic — is the evidence here of a recognition that caring for the poor is a communal responsibility, not just an individual responsibility. Of course, individual Christians ought to respond with an openhanded generosity to the suffering of another, but the community addressed here evidently recognized the hardships of the widows among them[41] and provided a programmatic response to their needs. There was a "list" of widows, and those women on the economic margins could enroll to receive regular support from the community (5:3-16).

The account of this program in the Pastorals, however, remains prosaic. There is nothing more prosaic than limited resources. And the advice concerning the widow list assumed both the significance of this communal and institutional response to the needs of poor widows and the reality of scarce resources

---

41. Not until Justinian did Roman law provide that widows were to receive a quarter of their husbands' estate. See Gustav Stahlin, "chera," *Theological Dictionary of the New Testament,* vol. 9 (Grand Rapids: Eerdmans, 1974), pp. 441ff. Widows were economically on the margins, without resources or hope.

for the program. The Pastorals are concerned with the mundane realities of the management of these resources. Prudent management of the fund required that family members not utilize the list to relieve themselves of the responsibility of caring for relatives, handing the burden off to the congregation (5:8, 16), and it required that the list be limited, that only certain widows be included on the list (5:9).

Compared to the uncalculating generosity of the Good Samaritan (Luke 10:25-37)[42] this calculating management of the widows' list in the Pastorals seems almost stingy. But what would the Good Samaritan do in conditions of scarcity? Suppose, for example, that there were more injured travelers along that road between Jerusalem and Jericho than the Samaritan had bandages, more than his donkey could bear, more than even the most hospitable innkeeper could keep. In conditions of scarce resources and great need, the Good Samaritan would have to begin to make some tough and unwelcome choices. Motivated by the same compassion that moved him to respond to the single crisis, he would look for some programmatic response, some institutional reform — better police protection, perhaps, or a cadre of volunteers to provide aid to the injured, or at least some additional resources to provide places at the inn. And the Good Samaritan — or a friend — will face the mundane tasks of managing limited resources in ways that are both fair and prudent.[43] The story cannot be reduced to policy, of course, and no particular program is simply given with the story, but the story required and requires some communal and programmatic response to the needs of the poor.

If there were time enough and space enough, we could continue to read the New Testament in this effort to remember the early churches remembering Jesus in the world of the economy. We have not yet, for example, attended to the exhortations in Hebrews to practice hospitality, to be content, to share (Heb. 13:2, 5, 16). But this at least is clear: In many and diverse ways the early churches remembered Jesus and his wisdom about wealth. Creatively and faithfully they reminded Christians that they need not be anxious, that they should be generous, and that the care of the poor is a communal responsibility. Creatively and faithfully, they called for discipleship and exercised discernment in their economic worlds.

---

42. See Wolfgang Schrage, *The Ethics of the New Testament,* trans. David E. Green (Philadelphia: Fortress, 1988), pp. 266-67.

43. See chapter twenty in this volume for an application of this thought experiment to a Christian response to the scarcity of medical resources.

CHAPTER FIFTEEN

The Continuing Church and a Continuing
Tradition of Justice and Generosity

Down the centuries Christians continued to ask the question of the Jerusalem converts at Pentecost, "What should we do?" (Acts 2:37) — and to ask it also within the economic worlds in which they lived. They did not answer that question by insisting on the community of goods practiced by those Jerusalem converts. They did not answer it by mining Scripture to discover hidden in it some definitive and timeless economic theory. The question — and the answer, too — was always in some sense *ad hoc,* related to particular contexts and concrete problems. Such questions invited discourse within the community, and such discourse required deliberation, the giving and hearing of reasons. The reasons given in the Christian community, of course, frequently resembled the reasons for economic choices given within other contemporary communities. In Christian community, however, such deliberation required Christian discernment; economic choices and the reasons for them had to be tested by their appropriateness not only to the circumstances but also to the memory of Jesus.

Christians have never been able simply to snap their fingers to create a new economic order — or to recreate an older one. And they have never been able to be content with the economic realities that crush the poor and divide people. But they, like those Jerusalem Christians, could — and did — insist that the Jesus they remembered had been exalted as Lord over their economic world no less than over their worlds of sickness and sex. The economic order was not regarded as autonomous; the claims of the sovereign Christ extended over it. Gladly and boldly they told the story of Jesus as the story of their economic life as well. The memory of Jesus — and the memory of the churches remembering

305

Jesus — formed character and community in the continuing church. Memory and hope formed a tradition of generosity and justice.

The tradition ran along the centuries in countless warnings against anxiety. "Do not be anxious," Jesus had said, warning against the effort of the rich fool to secure his identity and his future by his wealth (Luke 12:15-34). The invitation to trust God and the warning against an idolatrous confidence in Mammon has echoed down the years. Gladly the church has delighted in its confidence that God could be trusted to care; boldly the church has warned against living one's life as though its worth could be tested by the accumulation of possessions.[1] To be sure, sometimes the tradition was distorted by asceticism, and often the tradition has been misrepresented as a consolation for the poor in a world where nothing needs to be (or can be) changed. But when the whole community reads the whole Scripture and remembers Jesus, neither distortion can long endure. The community celebrates not poverty but a carefree confidence in the good future of God. And that good future is given token not in asceticism but in sharing, not in cheap consolation but in genuine help for the needy. It is given token in justice and generosity.

The tradition stretched along the years in "one long line of injunctions"[2]

---

1. See, to give just one example, Cyprian (third-century bishop of Carthage), "On Works and Alms," *The Ante-Nicene Fathers,* vol. 5 (Grand Rapids: Eerdmans, 1951), pp. 476-82. After citing the words of Jesus on anxiety, Cyprian says,

> You are afraid lest perchance your estate should fail, if you begin to act liberally from it; and you do not know, miserable man that you are, that while you are fearing lest your family property should fail you, life itself, and salvation, are failing; and whilst you are anxious lest any of your wealth should be diminished, you do not see that you yourself are being diminished, in that you are a lover of mammon more than of your own soul; and while you fear, lest for the sake of yourself, you should lose your patrimony, you yourself are perishing for the sake of your patrimony. . . . You are the captive and slave of your money; you are bound with the chains of covetousness; and you whom Christ had once loosed, are once more in chains. . . . You heap up a patrimony which burdens you with its weight; and you do not remember what God answered to the rich man, who boasted with a foolish exultation of the abundance of his exuberant harvest: "Thou fool," said He. . . .

2. Adolf Harnack, *The Mission and Expansion of Christianity in the First Three Centuries,* trans. James Moffatt (New York: Harper Torchbooks, Harper & Row, 1962; first German edition, 1902), p. 154. See his still useful treatment of "The Gospel of Love and Charity" in ch. 4, pp. 147-98. See also the excellent introduction to the "patristic social consciousness" by William J. Walsh, S.J., and John P. Langan, S.J., "Patristic Social Consciousness — The Church and the Poor," in *The Faith that Does Justice: Examining the Christian Sources of Social Change,* ed. John C. Haughey (New York: Paulist, 1977), pp. 113-51.

to generosity. "Give," Jesus had said, inviting those who heard him to welcome the good future of God in concrete acts of self-forgetful kindness and generosity, to feed the hungry, to give the thirsty water, to practice hospitality, to clothe the naked, to visit the sick and imprisoned (Matt. 25:31-40). The invitation to individuals to practice such almsgiving and acts of kindness to the poor has also echoed down the years. Gladly the church has delighted in the gifts of God, and boldly it has insisted that the gifts be shared. To be sure, sometimes the tradition was distorted by "the conceit of philanthropy," dividing the church or the world into patrons and clients, into virtuous benefactors and needy beneficiaries. But when the whole church reads the whole Scripture and remembers Jesus, that distortion cannot long endure. We remember, in remembering Jesus, both our common neediness and God's great gift. Our little gifts are set, then, in the context of God's immeasurably greater gift; they are no less a response to God's great gift than a simple prayer of thanksgiving (cf. Matt. 18:23-35). We remember, in remembering Jesus, that we are friends, and friends share what they have.

The tradition was embodied, finally, in a variety of institutional responses to the needs of the poor. "You always have the poor with you," Jesus said, citing Deuteronomy 15, reminding those who heard that caring for the poor was a communal responsibility. The very presence of the poor testified to the moral failure of the community. The continuing church acknowledged this communal responsibility and nurtured a sense of it both in the churches and in the other communities in which they had a voice.

Very quickly there was a common fund in the churches from which the needs of the poor were supplied. Justin Martyr, for example, in the second century described such a common fund in the Roman churches. The fund was supplied by the voluntary offerings of Christians at the Sunday Eucharist, was administered by the president, and was used to help the poor.[3] A century later Bishop Cornelius reported that the fund in Rome supported more than fifteen hundred people in the distress of poverty.[4]

In the first few centuries, of course, the church had no voice in the empire. Here and there, however, a lonely voice would be raised against the injustice of the society within which they lived. When Demetrius, proconsul of Africa in the

---

3. Justin, *First Apology,* 67.5-6. Among the beneficiaries of the fund Justin mentions orphans and widows, those in want due to sickness or any other cause, the imprisoned, strangers, and any others in need. A half-century later Tertullian tells of a similar fund in Carthage; to Justin's list of beneficiaries he adds that the fund was used to feed and to bury the poor (Tertullian, *Apology,* 39.5-7).

4. In Eusebius, *Ecclesiastical History,* 6.43.

third century, blamed the Christians and their refusal to worship the gods of the Romans for the evils of the day, Cyprian, the bishop of Carthage, raised his voice not only to defend the church against the charges but to trace the tragic social conditions of the empire in the third century to the greed of the wealthy.[5] The avarice of the rich and powerful within the empire was more of a threat to it, he said, than the barbarians from outside. The tightfisted refusal to provide for the poor and hungry was a greater problem, he said, than drought.

The church put the empire to shame by its care for the poor. Ironically, the best evidence of the extent and success of the church's program of charity toward the poor may be provided by the one remembered as "the Apostate." Julian, nephew of Constantine and raised as a Christian, abandoned the Christian faith and embraced the worship of the traditional Greco-Roman gods after he became emperor in 361. He appointed Arsacius to be high priest of Galatia in his effort to restore the ancient rites of Hellenism and to strip the Christian church, the church of the "Galileans," of its power and influence. In a letter to that pagan high priest, Julian the Apostate instructed Arsacius that the effort to restore Hellenism would require that they notice and copy the Christian practices of hospitality to strangers, attending to the proper burial of the poor and feeding the hungry, whether Christian or not.[6] Julian's effort was not successful, of course, but even in the effort to supplant the church a communal sense of responsibility for the poor was nurtured a little.

To be sure, the word of Jesus that "You always have the poor with you" has sometimes been used to dismiss care for the poor from the church's agenda, or at least from the forefront of that agenda. When the whole church reads the whole Scripture and remembers Jesus, however, that distortion cannot long endure. The community that gathers around Scripture in memory of Jesus will identify with Jesus and with the poor. It will pray for a kingdom in which there will be no more poverty. It will regard the presence of the poor as a cause for common confession and for a common effort to meet their needs and to provide some small token of God's good future.

In many and diverse ways the memory of Jesus and of his unconventional wisdom has informed the churches' discourse, deliberation, and discernment concerning questions of wealth and poverty. And in many and diverse ways it

5. Cyprian, "Treatise V, An Address to Demetrianus," in *The Ante-Nicene Fathers*, vol. 5, ed. Alexander Roberts and James Donaldson (Grand Rapids: Eerdmans, 1975 [repr. from Edinburgh edition)], pp. 457-65.

6. Julian, "Epistle 22: To Arsacius, High-Priest of Galatia," in *The Works of the Emperor Julian*, trans. Wilmer Cave Wright, vol. 3 (Cambridge, Mass.: Harvard University Press, 1953), pp. 67-73.

still does — and still must. We live in the world of Adam Smith, but we do not live in this world in memory of Adam Smith. We live in it in memory of Jesus and in hope. We may not proceed as if the economic order has a second and a different Lord than the one who was raised from the dead and set above every other power and authority. The greatest danger is still forgetfulness.

The discourse of the church with respect to the economic order is usually — and properly — *ad hoc.* It is prompted by the question of the faithful, "What should I do . . . about this?" or "What should we do . . . about that?" That was the rich fool's question, you may remember. It is not, however, the fool's *question* that must be avoided; that question was also asked by those who heard John the Baptist preach in anticipation of Christ and by those who heard Peter preach in memory of Christ on Pentecost. It is not the fool's question that must be avoided but his answer.

"What should I do about this or that feature of my participation in the economic order?" is a question we each must ask in Christian community, and "What should we do about our share in this economy?" is a question every Christian community must answer. The questions — and the answers, too — will be *ad hoc.* But the answers will always bear some resemblance to this simple advice, "Don't be a fool!" "Don't be a fool; a person's life does not consist of the abundance of things he possesses." "Don't be a fool; welcome the coming of a kingdom in which the humble are exalted, the hungry are fed, and the poor are blest." "Don't be a fool; there are Lazaruses in our midst — and one has been raised from the dead." "Don't be a fool; be a person who remembers the story of Jesus and who owns it as constitutive of identity and community and as determinative for discernment."

We may as well face it, though. We live in a nation of fools. We live in cities of fools. And — if we're going to be completely honest about it — you and I have often thought and acted like fools ourselves. We have acted as though our lives consisted of the abundance of our possessions. We have been tightfisted. It is not yet God's unchallenged reign; we are not yet a community where there are no poor.

Nevertheless, the Scripture is still read in Christian community; the story is still remembered; and here and there it is still performed. In spite of the forgetfulness of the world of Adam Smith, a tradition of generosity and justice in memory of Jesus still continues. It continues wherever the continuing church continues to remember Jesus and to watch for him in the economic world. It does not continue in any particular economic system. It does not continue in any particular impartial account of justice. Yet, it continues — here and there.

Working for a Living in Memory of Jesus

Here and there, I say, a tradition of justice and generosity in memory of Jesus continues. It continues, for example, in the voluntary poverty of some Christians — whether for a lifetime or for some limited time — for the sake of Christ and for the sake of those whose poverty is not voluntary. But it can — and sometimes does — also continue among those who work for a living, among those who work to secure the things necessary for living, to earn their daily bread and a little more. And because most of us do work for a living, let's focus on that.

"Working for a living" can be marked by the memory of Jesus and by hope for the coming reign of God. The author of the Epistle to the Ephesians says as much in exhorting the Christians of Asia Minor "to be renewed . . . and to clothe yourselves with the new self, created according to the likeness of God in true righteousness and holiness. . . . Thieves must give up stealing," he says. "Rather let them labor and work honestly with their own hands, so as to have something to share with the needy" (Eph. 4:23-24, 28).

That advice commends work without glorifying it. Work itself is a good thing, but it is not god. Some of us are tempted to make it a god, anxiously staking our identities upon it, making it the center and foundation of our lives. And some of us are tempted to make *ourselves* gods in our work, as if we were Messiah and our labor messianic. Against such temptations it is important to be reminded that there is a God and that our job is not it, that there is a Messiah and that we are not it. Work — whether religious work or secular work — can be "sacred" not because work is god but because work can be the gift and calling of the God invoked in prayer and known in the reading of Scripture.

Work is not god, but it is good. Some of us are tempted to regard it as evil, as a necessary evil, to be sure, if we are to earn a living, but as an evil nonetheless. Work, in this view, is something we endure in order to have enough money to escape from work, to do something — anything — else. This is the view (for reasons that we can understand and ought to work to correct) of some who work under brutalizing conditions for an insufficient wage. But it is shared by many more in our culture. There are teachers, it seems, who regard their time with students as something to be endured in order to make enough money to get away from work. There are doctors, it seems, who regard their patients as consumers and those patients' weaknesses as opportunities for profit; they, too, want to escape from work. Against this temptation, it is important to be reminded that work can be good, that it can engage and express our creativity, our energy, and our vocation to serve God and the neighbor.

When we regard work as evil, if a necessary evil, we are left with no way to judge good work — or the good worker — except on the basis of its commercial success. We do make such judgments, of course. The "successful" entrepreneur is the one who can retire at forty. The "good" book is the bestseller. The rich and famous are respected, admired, and envied because they can live in leisure. Such judgments are in accord with the view of work as something to be endured in order to make enough to quit and with the yuppie axiom that money equals value. Most of us, however, know better than that. Most of us — even if, sadly, we do not enjoy our own work — have had some experience that has taught us how much we depend on those persons who regard the integrity of their work as more important than the fact that they get paid enough to escape it. There was that teacher who took extra time and effort with our child when he needed it. There was that automobile mechanic five hundred miles from home who fixed the car for a few dollars when we were anticipating a major problem. The purely commercial standard is, frankly, foolishness.

To be sure, some work is not good. The author of the letter to the Ephesians used what was already evidently a timeworn expression, "honest work" (Eph. 4:28: "work honestly with their own hands"). Christian discernment will hardly insist that, to be good or "honest," work must be done "with one's hands" rather than with one's brain, but neither will it regard intellectual work as somehow better than work with one's hands. In Lubbers Hall, where I work, those who would boast that their work is academic should remember that without the honest work of janitors and secretaries their own work would be considerably less pleasant and efficient. All work takes some effort, all work takes place in community, and all work should be oriented toward some service to others.

Still, some work is not honest work, not good. The text in Ephesians itself suggests that not all work is good or worthy of the gospel. Thieves might regard themselves as "working for a living," but when they are renewed by the gospel, they should, as the text says, "give up stealing." And the Christian community has recognized, as the Heidelberg Catechism says (in commenting on the commandment), that "theft also includes cheating and swindling our neighbor by schemes made to appear legitimate, such as: inaccurate measurements of weight, size, or volume; fraudulent merchandising; counterfeit money; excessive interest. . . ."[7] Theft always takes some kind of power. The power accessible to the poor is violence. The rich, however, have access to subtler forms of power with which to steal: powers to market and measure and extend credit, for example. And the power to hire and fire can be exercised in stealing the energy and

7. The Heidelberg Catechism, Q&A 110 (Grand Rapids: Board of Publications of the Christian Reformed Church, 1975).

creativity of the poor and desperate in jobs that brutalize both cell and soul. Sweatshops and child labor, too, are forms of theft. In memory of Jesus any use of power against a neighbor, and especially against a poor neighbor, for the sake of one's own advantage counts as theft. And "working for a living" is no excuse for it.

The discourse and discernment of the Christian community will caution its members against some kinds of work and against some practices of some work as incoherent with the memory of Jesus. It will counsel young people (and all its members) to look for work consistent with God's cause and the neighbor's good, to find work in which and through which they can exercise their fundamental calling to be a disciple. It will counsel those who have found work to conduct themselves in their work as responsible not only to their employer but also to their craft, to their neighbors, and to God.

The text, finally, orients "working for a living" in memory of Jesus toward having "something to share with the needy." There is nothing here about working in order to accumulate the possessions on which a rich fool can finally secure an identity and a future. To work for a living in memory of Jesus is to work without being anxious; it is to work in order to provide for one's daily bread and a little more, in order to share.

"Working for a living" is a good thing, but it can tempt us to forgetfulness in this economic culture. Earning our daily bread may prompt us to forget that it remains a gift from God. And earning "a little more" can tempt us to foolishness. It is easy — especially easy in a culture of affluence — to suppose that a little more yet would be better yet. It is tempting — especially if one watches any television ads — to suppose that a person's life consists of an abundance of possessions, that human flourishing depends on having this or that car, or this or that brand of clothes, or just this or that. The yuppie axiom, money equals value, still passes for wisdom, but it is still foolishness. The disease caused by such foolishness in our culture could be called "affluenza."

The best remedy for affluenza is still a dose of grace. Grace is not cheap, of course. The grace of God is free, but it is not cheap. Otherwise, the thief could argue, "I like committing crimes. God likes forgiving them. Really the world is admirably arranged."[8] And to Paul's rhetorical question, "What then are we to say? Should we continue in sin that grace may abound?" (Rom. 6:1), the answer would have been, "I guess." Paul's answer to that question, of course, is "By no means!" The grace of God does not provide a rationalization for doing what we know is wrong or for neglecting what we know to be good or right or fitting. It

---

8. W. H. Auden, *For the Time Being: A Christmas Oratorio*, in *Religious Drama/1* (Cleveland: Meridian, The World Publishing Company, 1957), pp. 11-68, p. 60.

makes us free — not free to do nothing, not free to do anything we like, but free to live in memory of Jesus and in the hope of God's good future. It makes us, as the Heidelberg Catechism says, "whole-heartedly willing and ready from now on to live for him."[9]

The remedy for affluenza is grace because this pathology is not fundamentally a problem of the weakness of our intellect, as if we could not figure out a way to live more simply or to give more generously. It is, rather, a weakness of the heart and of the will. The problem is that we lack the personal resources to resist the seductions of a culture in which more is always better and in which status is measured by possessions. The problem is not that we lack the financial resources to be much more generous than we are. The problem is that we lack the spiritual resources to *want* to give more generously. We need the grace of God. We need to remember the glad announcement of God's good future, and those who are rich need grace to boast not in their possessions but "in being brought low" (James 1:10). We need the grace of God to repent, to turn from our folly and weakness, to be reoriented to a future ruled by the generosity of God. Then we may yet learn to delight already in that future and in the blessing of God upon the poor spoken and signaled even now. We may learn to pray for (and to work for) the good future of a gracious God. We may learn by God's grace that hoarding is folly and that sharing is a simple expression of remembrance and hope. We may even be healed of our affluenza.

We need grace. It is, of course, no easy thing to live in accord with it. And although the fundamental problem here is not an intellectual problem, there are a host of issues that require our best intellectual gifts. For two millennia the church has struggled with the task of discernment in the world of the economy. The memory of Jesus does not give tidy rules for the stewardship of our economic opportunities, but the community must continually attempt to formulate rules for its own times and places, and it must continually test these rules — and the practices formed by them — to see whether they are worthy of the memory of Jesus, whether they accord with the demanding grace of God.

I do not have rules to recommend. That is, I think, a matter for communal deliberation, and it requires all the diverse gifts with which the community is equipped. I do, however, want to challenge the conventional wisdom that my money, how I earn it, and what I choose to do with it are no one's business but my own. Such matters are my personal responsibility, to be sure, not to be surrendered to the group, but they are not simply private matters. To regard them as simply private matters puts Christian identity and community at risk. Personal responsibility is best protected not by pretending that our stewardship is

9. Heidelberg Catechism, Q&A 1.

no one else's business but by exercising that responsibility within a community that remembers Jesus well and faithfully. The assumption that these are simply private matters risks surrendering identity to a culture of affluence; it risks sacrificing the tradition and vocation of a community of moral discourse before the shrine of privacy; it risks amnesia.

I do not have rules to offer, but I can point to some places, here and there, where Jesus is remembered and the tradition continues. Jesus is remembered when those who work for a living are not anxious and when the "living" they work for is not simply an abundance of possessions. The tradition continues in generosity, when "a little more" than daily bread is regarded as an opportunity to share. Jesus is remembered when those who work for a living by being managers and CEOs acknowledge the indebtedness of the prosperous to those who work for them by rewarding such work and sharing such prosperity.[10] The list could go on, of course, but permit me to add one more thing: The tradition continues wherever hardworking parents teach their children not just a proverb from Poor Richard but also the story of Jesus. Jesus is remembered when such parents live that story — and urge their children to live it — with carefree and generous lives and as part of families and communities that are hospitable to the poor.

Being the Church in Memory of Jesus

So far, we have considered choices individuals face within the community. We must also consider some of the choices faced by our communities. As personal choices were neither to be surrendered to the group nor treated as simply "private" matters, so communal choices are neither to be simply surrendered to some ecclesiastical authority nor regarded as settled by the generally accredited economic wisdom of some broader community. Churches need to read Scripture together and remember Jesus in the world of Adam Smith. They need to set Scripture aside as *holy* and then set the story of their economic life alongside the remembered story so that they can be challenged and made new (or *sanctified*) by it. They need to be *faithful* to the identity they own when they own that story as their own, to the community formed by that story. Fidelity requires *cre-*

10. The Herman Miller Company, for example, introduced the Scanlon Plan in 1950, rewarding employees with company stock. For an account of employee ownership at Herman Miller and its importance to the success, financial and human, of the company see Max DePree, "Who Owns This Place?" *Leadership Is an Art* (East Lansing, Mich.: Michigan State University Press, 1987), pp. 87-94. "The capitalist system cannot avoid being better off by having more employees who act as if they own the place" (p. 94).

ativity, of course, and they may not simply and anachronistically pretend that they live in some other economic world. They need to read Scripture over-against themselves, ready to be *disciplined* by it. And they need to exercise *discernment,* asking how their choices can "fit" the story they love to tell, how their lives and their common life can be rendered "worthy" of the gospel. They need to think and talk and pray about their corporate responsibilities in the world of Adam Smith — in memory of Jesus.

In memory of Jesus let the churches ask regularly whether their life as the body of Christ is a blessing upon the poor. When a congregation is contemplating a new building, let it ask in memory of Jesus whether a new building is the best stewardship of its economic opportunities to bless the poor. If the church decides to build, let it ask whether the new building will be hospitable to the poor and how. If it needs a loan to build, let it not regard the choice of lender as being settled simply by the application of the conventional economic wisdom that one should look for the lowest rate of interest. Let the church examine the lending practices of institutions, and let it refuse to borrow from institutions that refuse to lend to the poor or to minorities.

When a congregation is thinking about evangelism, let it remember Jesus. Let the church remember that it is *his* mission the church is privileged to share, and then let it ask whether it can countenance strategies for "church growth" that proceed along socially homogeneous lines.[11] Let it acknowledge that the growth the church should be concerned about is its growth into "the measure of the full stature of Christ" (Eph. 4:13), and let it ask whether that stature can be reached with a strategy of social homogeneity. Let it acknowledge that the full stature of Christ requires a community that transcends the social and economic divisions of patron and client, of rich and poor, and let it ask whether that stature can be displayed if the poor are not blessed. Church growth along socially homogeneous lines puts mortar in the walls that divide people, the very walls that it was Christ's mission to break down. The remembered Jesus, the exalted Lord, "has broken down the dividing wall, that is, the hostility between us" (Eph. 2:14). In memory of Jesus the church will include Jew and Gentile, slave and free, client and patron, poor and rich, and in memory of Jesus they will grow to be friends.

11. The church growth movement founded by Donald McGavran observed that church growth frequently did occur along socially homogeneous lines. That sociological observation was then turned into a methodological strategy for evangelism. See especially the work of his successor, C. Peter Wagner, entitled (revealingly) *Our Kind of People* (Atlanta: John Knox, 1979). For a view of evangelism more fitting to the memory of Jesus as one who "preached good news to the poor" see Richard Mouw, *Political Evangelism* (Grand Rapids: Eerdmans, 1973).

Friends gather around a table, and when the church gathers around the table of the Lord, when it hears again the words, "Do this in remembrance of me," let it remember Jesus. And let Christians ask whether they bear any resemblance to the Corinthian Christians who feasted while the poor went hungry (1 Cor. 11:17-22). Let them ask whether they are truly "sharing in the body of Christ" (10:16) if they do not express that *koinonia,* that "sharing," economically. "Examine yourselves," Paul said (11:28). The Eucharist should be a time for thanksgiving, for the sort of thanksgiving that sees wealth as an opportunity to give generously. The Feast should be a time of hospitality. The foretaste of the eschatological banquet should give us a taste for, a hunger for, justice and generosity. In the meantime, therefore, "until he comes" (11:26), let the church remember and "proclaim [his] death." Let it discern his broken body in the bread — and in "the least of these" who are hungry and homeless, beaten down by poverty. The bread from heaven still points toward "a manna economy" in which God can be trusted, in which hoarding is foolishness, in which none have too much and none too little.

In the church a community of friends reaches across the earth. Friends should not be out of touch with one another forever. Let the churches in developed countries ask whether they bear any resemblance to those Gentile Christians in Macedonia and Greece who acknowledged and celebrated their unity with Jewish Christians in Judea by the collection for the poor. Let them ask whether they remember "the generous act of our Lord Jesus Christ, that though he was rich, yet for our sakes he became poor" (2 Cor. 8:9). Generosity was not — and is not — a "command" (8:8); it is a glad response to the remembered Jesus. And such generosity allows no "conceit of philanthropy"; it is a generosity which is itself a response to gift. It creates no divide between rich benefactors and needy beneficiaries; it acknowledges and celebrates the grace of God that makes us one community of friends.

In memory of Jesus let the church ask regularly whether its life as the body of Christ is a blessing upon the poor. And let it ask whether, if the church as a community does not live the story it loves to tell, it can honestly engage in encouraging and exhorting individual members to do so. Let it ask how, if the church as a community does not live in accord with its memory and hope, it can ask governments to do so. Let the church acknowledge the persistence of poverty — "you [still] always have the poor with you" (Mark 14:7) — and let it repent. But let it also celebrate gladly and boldly those places, here and there, where Jesus is remembered well and faithfully in our economic world and where the tradition of justice and generosity lives.

Here and there the church does, *ad hoc,* generously meet the needs of the poor in the church and in the community and in the world. Here and there food is provided: in emergency relief, in construction of irrigation systems, in agricultural development. Here and there shelter is given: in homeless shelters, in subsidized housing programs joined with education and edification. Here and there safe drinking water is supplied: wells are dug, and water purification systems are constructed. Here and there medical attention is given to those otherwise without access to it: health clinics are built and staffed. Here and there economic development is provided as part of spiritual development: work that is not brutalizing or insufficiently rewarded is provided, work that is good is nurtured, markets (and transportation to them) are found, vocational training is provided. Here and there loans, or investments, are made with the intention that the poor be blessed. Here and there debts are forgiven in remembrance of Jesus. Here and there a voice calling from the margins for economic justice is attended to and echoed in the churches. And here and there the churches, even in their work of development in "undeveloped" countries, acknowledge that the "good life" cannot be reduced to material goods, that it includes goods like friendship, simplicity, and faith; they may even acknowledge that such goods, such gifts, are sometimes in richer supply among the "undeveloped" and frequently received from those to whom they would give the gifts of development. Here and there churches do grow a little into the measure of the full stature of Christ: communities are formed in which the rich learn something of the "good life" from the poor and the poor are blessed by the rich; communities are formed in which rich and poor are friends. No church can meet all the needs of all the poor, of course, but here and there the needs of some are met — not only for food and shelter, but also for being welcomed and honored in a community. And there the tradition continues.

Economic Deliberation Today

Christians live in the world of Adam Smith, but we do not live in this world in memory of Adam Smith. We live in it in memory of Jesus and in hope for God's good future — as those who work for a living, as members of the church, and also, finally, as participants in the larger economic world, in the world of corporate and public economic policy.

Those concerned about the poor will not be unconcerned about economic policy. The Good Samaritan responded compassionately to the single victim of violence and theft, but, as we noted, there could have been many victims, more victims than he had bandages or more victims than his donkey could bear, and in that case one can imagine that his compassion would prompt attention to more programmatic responses and to policy issues. He might work, as a student once suggested, for better streetlights on the Jericho road, or he might enlist volunteers to provide security for those who travel alone. And he would, in his attention to programmatic responses and policy, soon face the mundane task of managing limited resources in ways that are both fair and prudent. The same compassion that drove him to extraordinary generosity when one was hurt would prompt attention to policy when many were hurting.

The story of the Good Samaritan — and the story of Scripture — cannot be reduced to policy, of course, and no particular economic policy is simply given with the story, but the story will prompt attention to policy and to the complex and specialized questions policy almost inevitably involves. Reading Scripture and remembering Jesus provide no alternative economic system, no economic theory as an alternative to the capitalism of Adam Smith. Scripture is, frankly, silent on the questions of "political economy" and economic policy. And the economic worlds of Jesus, whether the subsistence economy of the peasant farmer or the patron-client relationships of the empire, seem quaint and strange in our economic world. Moreover, even if there were a "revealed" economic system, we could not magically and anachronistically live in it. Like it or not, we live in an economic world fashioned in part by the vision of Adam Smith, and we must deliberate concerning corporate and public policies within that world.

In its consideration of policy, to be sure, the church that reads Scripture and remembers Jesus in the world of Adam Smith will raise up a prophet now and again. Here a Dorothy Day, "pounding at the locked door behind which the powerful mock the powerless with games of triage."[12] There a Martin Luther King Jr., echoing Amos's cry, "Let justice roll down like waters," and dreaming of God's good future. Here and there countless other voices raised in memory of Jesus and in hope, crying out that this is not the way it is supposed to be.[13]

Prophets protest injustice; they beat against oppression with their words. Prophets spot — and condemn — the idolatry that stands behind anxiety and greed (Col. 3:5). They irritate, embarrass, and denounce the smug and complacent. They uncover corruption, whether at the scales of the marketplace or at

12. So Daniel Berrigan, S.J., describes Dorothy Day in the introduction to her autobiography, *The Long Loneliness: The Autobiography of Dorothy Day* (San Francisco: Harper & Row, 1952, 1981), p. xxiii.
13. Indeed, all Christians have a prophetic vocation. We should speak no less of the "prophethood" of all believers than of the "priesthood of all believers." How could it be otherwise? We remember one who read Isaiah and said of himself, "The Spirit of the Lord is upon me, because he has anointed me to bring good news to the poor . . . to let the oppressed go free" (Luke 4:18, citing Isa. 61:1), and that same Spirit came "upon all flesh" at Pentecost (Acts 2:17, citing Joel 2:28).

the scales of justice. They unveil the foolishness masquerading as wisdom. But they save their harshest words for those who name God's name without caring about justice, without providing for the poor. They remember the past and they envision God's future. In the world of Adam Smith the church that remembers Jesus will nurture the voices of the prophets, will attend to them, and will speak sometimes in a prophetic voice itself. It is not yet God's good future, after all. The presence and persistence of poverty are enough to remind us of that. "You always have the poor with you" remains a judgment against our communities, too, and against policies that produce simultaneously both demeaning poverty and conspicuous consumption.

The church that remembers Jesus in the world of Adam Smith will nurture the voice of prophets, but the tasks of deliberation and discernment concerning economic policy require that it must also nurture faithful managers and policy-makers if the poor are to be blessed.[14] Prophets seldom make good managers or policy-makers. The true prophet sees clearly the distance between the present situation and God's good future, and reminds us all of it. The faithful manager, on the other hand, attends to the differences between the real choices available in the present situation. The real choices are limited and attended by ambiguity in an economic world that is still not God's good future. The real choices and their consequences in the world of Adam Smith will fall short of the prophet's vision. None of the real choices will usher in that future "where righteousness [or justice] is at home" (2 Peter 3:13). None of the real choices is likely to eliminate poverty, or idolatry, or anxiety, or greed completely. Nevertheless, the real choices — and the differences between them — are important to the vocation to serve both God's cause and the poor in the world of Adam Smith. The real choices may provide an opportunity for some

14. Indeed, all Christians have a management vocation. We should speak no less of the "royalty" of all believers than of the "priesthood" and "prophethood" of all believers. As Christ is remembered as "the anointed one," anointed to be priest, prophet, and king, so Christians "share in his anointing" (Heidelberg Catechism, Q&A 32). All Christians are called to leadership, to be "kings." Because the sign of royalty in Israel and in Jesus is humility, being "anointed" to be "king" is to be called to humble service. See Mark 10:41-44. In memory of Jesus the calling of Christians in management is to "servant leadership." For an account of "servant leadership" see Robert Greenleaf, *Servant Leadership* (New York: Paulist, 1977). Moreover, as the hymn says, "the crown awaits the conquest" ("Lead On, O King Eternal"). The cross is lifted over us; we journey — also economically and managerially — in its light. The crown awaits the day when Christ says to those who have given food to the hungry and shelter to the homeless, "Come, you that are blessed by my Father, inherit the kingdom prepared for you" (Matt. 25:34; one of the "proof texts" for the Heidelberg Catechism, Q&A 32).

to escape poverty; they may preserve some little (but real) human good where people work for a living; they may nudge the economic order just a little closer to something worthy of the gospel.

Managers and economists bring to their deliberation and to their decisions knowledge and skills that are critically important to identifying and understanding their real choices and the consequences of those choices. There are "sciences" of management and of economics that have been developed over the last few centuries, and along with them methods of empirical economic research and a specialized language. Faithful managers and economists do not disown these sciences and skills; they put them to work in memory of Jesus and in hope, in service of the neighbor in this economic world. They put these sciences and skills to work — but not without discernment. These sciences and skills are not to be regarded as "value-free" tools that can be innocently used within any and every normative framework. If the church is to nurture faithful managers and economic leaders, it must sponsor a continuing inquiry concerning the relation of these sciences and skills to the memory of Jesus.

Moreover, for the sake of its own communal deliberation and discernment about economic issues in the world of Adam Smith, the church must sponsor such inquiry. Economic deliberation has become increasingly complex and specialized in the world of Adam Smith, and the task of discernment is a daunting one. Complex economic questions are not answered well simply by reading Scripture and remembering Jesus; they will be answered well only if the diverse gifts and skills present in the community of memory and hope are brought to bear on it, including the gifts of managers and the skills of economists. Economic deliberation requires realistic analysis, not utopian pretense; it demands not wishful thinking but the specialized knowledge and training that allow plausible (but still uncertain) predictions of the consequences of actions and policies. Managers and economists bring to communal discernment their sciences and skills. The church may not simply disregard these sciences and skills, but neither may it simply surrender communal discernment to them. It may not treat these sciences either as a substitute for the wisdom of Jesus or as a value-free set of tools with which to supplement its memory of Jesus. It will invite economic analysis as a part of the deliberative process, but it will continue to test the reasons given in deliberation by its memory of Jesus. It will listen to the voices of managers and economists, but it will also listen to the voices of the prophets and to the voices of the poor. Indeed, it will (like Paul in Corinth) privilege the interpretation of the poor; it will insist that their experience of the economic order be expressed, and that their hope for a blessing be heard. Complex economic questions will not be answered well without the contributions of managers and economists within the Christian community, but neither will they be answered well without the other gifts and other skills of other members of the Christian community. The managers and the prophets in the Christian community will not always get along.[15] Nevertheless, it is important that they talk together and listen to each other, lest those who style themselves prophets in this economic world put at risk its little (but real) accomplishments by an indiscriminate criticism of the real choices, and lest the managers risk amnesia.

For the sake, then, of its own communal deliberation and discernment concerning the world of Adam Smith in memory of Jesus, and in order to nurture faithful managers and economists, the church needs to sponsor a continuing inquiry concerning the relation of the new sciences of management and economics to the memory of Jesus. There is too little of such inquiry, too few such conversations.[16]

Moreover, most of us are not well equipped for such conversations. Theological education — or, for that matter, a liberal arts education — seldom requires an introduction to economic theory, and an education in business and economics usually brackets religious convictions as irrelevant. Those brackets may be the place to begin the conversation.

The Relevance of Memory

In the moral discourse of the church about economic policy, religious convictions may not be bracketed as irrelevant. If the remembered Jesus is Lord, then he is Lord of the economic world as well. The church's deliberation about the strange world of our economic order must be undertaken in memory of Jesus. The Christian community may not proceed in deliberation about wealth and poverty as if economic questions were altogether independent of its memory of Jesus of Nazareth. It may not proceed with the Enlightenment assumption that in consideration of economic questions, objective and scientific inquiry must displace religious convictions. In the churches, surely, the brackets should be removed.

Not just in the churches, however, but also in the larger conversations the

15. The ancient kings and the prophets did not always get along either, after all. Moreover, this tension is an internal one, since all Christians, as we said (see notes 13 and 14), are called to be prophets and kings.

16. There are, however, some promising signs of conversation. The excellent anthology edited by Max L. Stackhouse, Dennis McCann, Shirley J. Roels, and Preston N. Williams, *On Moral Business: Classical and Contemporary Resources for Ethics in Economic Life* (Grand Rapids: Eerdmans, 1995), is one such sign.

brackets should be removed. They are more like blinders than brackets. If the economic world is emptied of religious and moral significance, then there will be no resources in it to resist the destruction toward which human greed and envy always tilt humanity. The point is not, however, that religious and moral convictions are to be tested by their utility to the economic project. The point is rather that the economic world inevitably expresses a larger view of the way things really are, inevitably displays something like religious convictions.

Adam Smith himself may be called upon to testify to the significance of religious convictions. We noted earlier his confidence that, when individuals are freed from traditional and ecclesiastical constraints, their pursuit of individual self-interest in the marketplace would increase the wealth of a society. We noted as well that as a moralist he did not advocate egoism but the impartial perspective of an objective observer. And we noted that as an "objective observer" he saw (or thought he saw) an "invisible hand." He claimed that there was a power that bears down on our economic life and sustains it, an "invisible hand" governing the marketplace to fashion conflicting interests into a socially beneficial harmony. Smith's belief and confidence in this divine (if natural) providence can only be regarded as religious. Faith in this "invisible hand" licensed — and indeed, required — individuals to pursue their self-interest in the economic world. Responsible *to* that power, that providence, that god at work in the market, human beings were rendered responsible only *for* making as much money as possible. By faith one could trust that providence, that "invisible hand," to order conflicting interests toward the common good; in the meantime such faith permitted and required pursuing one's self-interest. Responsibility *to* that divine presence rendered human beings responsible only *for* acting in their economic self-interest.

Adam Smith ground the prescription lens through which people learned to see themselves and their tasks differently. Prescription lenses, however, can distort as well as correct our vision, and a myopic focus on the creation of wealth requires some correction. Reading Scripture and remembering Jesus, the church may craft another set of lenses and a corrective vision for economic deliberation. The memory of Jesus suggests a different view of the way things really are. The memory of Jesus renders us responsible to the God whose cause he proclaimed — also in the economic order — and our responsibility *to* that God renders us responsible not only *for* creating wealth but also *for* achieving other economic goals as well. The conversation might continue, therefore, by considering the goals of political economy.

The Goals of Political Economy

Adam Smith trained our vision to focus on the creation of wealth. He taught us to see the importance of freedom, efficiency, and (realistically) self-interest to the creation of wealth. In memory of Jesus the church will not deny the importance of the creation of wealth. Poverty is not God's cause, and the creation of wealth can play a significant role in the project of blessing the poor. Moreover, until Jesus comes again, self-interest will not be eliminated, and efforts to order self-interested behaviors to the common good should not be abandoned. Until that time when Jesus comes again, however, self-interest does not "naturally, or rather necessarily" (to use Smith's words) serve the common good. It will take both wisdom and work. It will require a corrective vision. The memory of Jesus will grind the lens a little differently, permitting (and requiring) us to see economic opportunities and responsibilities a little differently.

Although the church will acknowledge the importance of the goal of creating wealth, the memory of Jesus will resist extravagant (and idolatrous) expectations of the creation of wealth. The life of a person — or a corporation or a nation — does not consist in the abundance of possessions. To pretend otherwise is perilously close to idolatry, rendering "economic progress" (or wealth creation) the equivalent of salvation history. The fault that runs through our lives, including our economic lives, is not just scarcity but also sin. Scarcity is a problem, of course, but Mammon is not the Messiah, and wealth is not our salvation. Moreover, scarcity is a problem associated with our finitude, and relative abundance will not eliminate finitude. Because our finite resources can be increased, the creation of wealth is an important goal; because abundance will not eliminate our finitude, the creation of wealth cannot be the only goal of economic life.[17]

The church will acknowledge, then, the importance of the goal of creating wealth, but it will not regard that as the single goal of economic life — whether of persons or of corporations or of nations. In addition to the creation of wealth, there are other economic goals,[18] goals that the creation of wealth itself should serve, not violate. Let me comment briefly on three of them: bless-

17. See further the excellent essays by Jon P. Gunnemann, "Thinking Theologically About the Economic," in *Christian Ethics: Problems and Prospects,* ed. Lisa Sowle Cahill and James F. Childress (Cleveland: Pilgrim, 1996), pp. 315-33, and by James M. Gustafson, "Interdependence, Finitude and Sin: Reflections on Scarcity," *Journal of Religion* 57, no. 2 (April 1977): 156-68.

18. Daniel Rush Finn, "Self-Interest, Markets, and the Four Problems of Economic Life," in *The Annual of the Society of Christian Ethics: 1989,* ed. D. M. Yeager (Washington, D.C.: Georgetown University Press, 1989), pp. 23-54, identifies four general goals of economic life: production, equity, sustainability, and the quality of relations.

ing the poor, sustaining the quality of human life, and sustaining the finite resources for the economic project.

In memory of Jesus it should be a goal of economic life to bless the poor. The creation of wealth should be ordered toward a blessing upon the poor. Smith himself, of course, regarded the common good as a natural consequence of the creation of wealth. He did not, however, regard a blessing upon the poor as a goal or intention appropriate to the economic life. His confidence in an unseen providence permitted single-minded attention to the creation of wealth, the parochial focus on one goal. His faith in an invisible hand, however, is a creed ripe for doubt. If our economic life is to be a blessing to the poor, we are going to have to aim at it, intend it, and direct policy and performance toward the benefit of the poor. To be sure, the creation of wealth should make it easier to share, but when the creation of wealth is regarded as the single goal of economic life, we create not only wealth but also an anxiety that renders us and our policy tightfisted and stingy.

The creation of wealth should, moreover, sustain the quality of human life, of human common life, and of human work; it should not reduce human beings — or their work — to marketable commodities. The market is a good instrument for distributing many good things and for rewarding much good work. But the market is not a good instrument for distributing everything. Some things should not be regarded as marketable commodities. The sphere of commerce may abut every other sphere of our lives, but the market's sphere should be limited. It is not difficult to come up with examples of points at which we think the market should be limited. We do not want a market in persons; we do not want slavery, or babies sold at auctions. We do not want a market in criminal justice; we do not want judges' decrees or juries' verdicts to be bought and sold. We do not want a market in political power and influence; we do not want citizens or their representatives to sell their votes. We do not want a market in labor where people are desperate; we do not want sweatshops and child labor. We do not want a market in body parts; we do not want the sale of organs, even the organs of the dead. Such practices might create great wealth for some, but they violate the goods the creation of wealth should serve. The market is a good instrument; nevertheless, some things ought not to be marketable. Some questions, then, are unavoidable. How is a line to be drawn? And where? And how should it be enforced?[19] Such questions are not even raised,

19. See Margaret Jane Radin, "Market Inalienability," *Harvard Law Review* (1987): 1849-1937. For an effort to consider the risks of commodification in reproductive medicine (or "the infertility industry") see Allen Verhey, "Commercialization, Commodification, and Embodiment," *Women's Health Issues* 7, no. 3 (May/June 1997): 132-42.

however, where the creation of wealth is regarded as the single goal of economic life and where the marketplace exercises a tyrannical hold on our imagination. Moreover, the market needs not only to be limited but also to be ordered toward the sustaining of the quality of human life, of human common life, and of human work.

The creation of wealth should also not put at risk the natural and social resources that permit its creation. The creation of wealth should not despoil the creation or the community. We put these things at risk first in the imagination when we reduce these "resources" to their economic utility. Even if we bracket the question of whether our imagination has been corrupted, it remains folly to create an economy that cannot be sustained, and it remains an economic goal to sustain the physical and social environment. Those who took to the streets in protest against the World Trade Organization in Seattle in 1999 did not have all the answers to questions of economic policy, and their violence may not be condoned, but they were right to challenge a myopic and shortsighted focus on the creation of wealth that neglected environmental and social issues. We should not hide our heads in a ledger while forests shrink, glaciers melt, species disappear, and coral reefs die.

These four goals — creating wealth, blessing the poor, sustaining the quality of human life, and sustaining resources — cannot always be pursued together. The meeting of the World Trade Organization in Seattle was evidence enough of that. There are sometimes trade-offs to be made. We hear often enough, for example, of the risk to the creation of wealth if the community pursues one or another of the other goals. And we are frequently reminded of the risks to the poor, to the quality of life (and work), and to the environment if the community licenses an unregulated and self-interested pursuit of wealth.

The trade-offs are real, but they should not be exaggerated. Sometimes the pursuit of one of these goals helps to sustain the pursuit of the others. The creation of wealth can, as we said, make sharing and sustaining both the quality of life and the environment more "affordable." But it is no less important to observe that the creation of wealth depends on these other goals as well. The support does not just move in one direction, as though the creation of greater wealth is always prior to blessing the poor, to preserving the quality of human life (and work), and to sustaining the resources on which the economic project depends. The blessing upon the poor that recognizes their membership in our communities,[20] for example, is important to both political and economic sta-

---

20. Michael Walzer has observed that recognition and membership in the community are the chief social goods distributed by the community. Michael Walzer, *Spheres of Justice: A Defense of Pluralism and Equality* (New York: Basic Books, 1983).

bility. It is important to recognize not only the trade-offs and ambiguities but also the mutual support of these different goals.[21] It is not my claim that in trade-offs the other goals should always trump the creation of wealth. It is my claim that, in memory of Jesus, the creation of wealth should not always trump these other considerations.

Beyond an Impartial Perspective

Adam Smith was, as we said, no egoist. He did not simply pronounce a moral benediction upon self-interest. He licensed self-interest in the marketplace because, as an "objective observer," he was confident that an unseen providence would order conflicting interests toward the common good. The mechanism for the restraint of self-interest was competition. To give him his due, he was in the right against the "mercantilism" of his day. This "mercantilism" created monopolies for the sake of "efficiency," but the monopolies simply licensed the unrestrained self-interest of the wealthy. The rich profited from state support, and the poor got poorer. And to give him his due again, he did not celebrate competition as the mechanism of the "survival of the (economically) fittest"; he was not a social Darwinist. To regard Adam Smith as a social Darwinist would be an anachronism, of course, but it would also be an injustice. Adam Smith envisioned a future economy marked not by savage competition but by moral progress. He expected science and reason to lead the way not only to economic progress but also to a wiser and better politics, to an increasingly cooperative and inclusive community. In that community individuals would admire the work of the unseen providence and form collective judgments in tune with the judgments of impartial and objective observers.

The failure of capitalist societies to make such spontaneous moral progress has made regulation both necessary and a constant challenge. The impartial perspective of Smith — and of Rawls and Nozick — has neither altogether failed nor altogether succeeded in developing strategies to achieve justice for the poor. It has not succeeded in forming a *character* other than the enlightened and self-interested "fool." It has not succeeded in forming a *community* other than the contractual relationships of self-interested individuals. It has not succeeded in forming a *discourse* about the good economic life, for the good life is regarded as a private matter, and only the right to pursue such private visions of the good life may be talked about publicly.

The memory of Jesus forms a character that cannot be reduced to ratio-

21. Finn, "Self-Interest, Markets, and the Four Problems," p. 50 *et passim*.

nally self-interested agency. It creates a community that cannot be reduced to the contractual ties between those self-interested agents. And it inspires a discourse that cannot be reduced to utility calculations or preference satisfactions. In memory of Jesus complex economic questions are not rendered somehow less complex, but they are asked and answered by people who are not anxious about securing their identities through possessions, who are disposed to give generously, and who are disposed to form communities that welcome and honor the poor.

The impartial perspective may succeed in forming certain regulations to protect the poor from oppression, or to protect the quality of human life and work, or to sustain the environment. But when the story we tell of the economic world in which we live is that self-interested behaviors lead naturally to the common good, then we should not be surprised that we form characters that look out for number one and regard the regulations as unwelcome restraints. Such managers may yield some grudging obedience to the regulations (having calculated the economic costs and benefits of compliance). Like the Jewish farmer who left unharvested only that measure of the crop required by the rabbis' latest ruling, the manager formed by the marketplace story will resent the restraints. The farmer who remembered a story he recited at the feast of first fruits and was formed by it left a generous part of his crop for the gleaners. Managers formed by the memory of Jesus will not resent the regulations as an unwelcome restraint on their self-interest. They will share profits with workers generously, honor the good work of their employees, protect and preserve the environment. They will be wise stewards of their economic opportunities and of their resources to bless the poor and to create communities of friends. They will admit to the partiality of their perspective and privilege the hermeneutical perspective of the poor in the interpretation of economic opportunities and problems. They will remember Jesus.

In memory of Jesus the poor in our midst and on the margins come into focus. With corrected vision we see them. The poor are with us still. And the presence of poverty remains, in memory of Jesus, a sign that the community and political economy are not yet God's good future. With corrected vision we see their presence as a call to communal responsibility, to faithful management and policy.

Against the temptations to forgetfulness in the world of Adam Smith, the Christian community reads Scripture — and remembers. We remember a story with Jesus of Nazareth in the center and with God's good future at the end. It is a good story, a story we love to tell. And it is a true story; and on the truth of the story we stake our claim to knowing something of God's way and cause. We remember the story and, gladly and boldly, set all the stories of our life, including

327

the stories of our economic life, alongside of it to be judged and made new by it, to be shaped into something fitting to the story, worthy of it. Reading Scripture and remembering, we struggle to live our lives and our common life in ways that are faithful to the remembered story. Fidelity requires creativity, of course, and will not permit us to pretend that we live in the Jerusalem or the Corinth of the first century or in the economic worlds of the first century. That story forms character and conduct; it is acknowledged as decisive for identity and determinative for discernment. The community discourses and deliberates and discerns what they ought to do in memory and in watchfulness. There are no fixed social programs, no revealed rules or statutes or sanctions, no sanctified theory of justice. But there is a memory and a hope, and there are communities whose members are gifted with skills for economic analysis and management, with sympathy and compassion, with knowledge of people and knowledge of impediments and obstacles, with experience of oppression or hardship and, yes, with money.

The tradition of justice and generosity does not continue in elegant theories of justice. It continues — and is embodied — here and there. Here in the moral discernment of communities that remember Jesus and watch for him. There in the announcement that one has been raised from the dead and in attention to the Lazaruses in our midst because one has been raised (cf. Luke 16:31).

Here and there. Here when the church raises its voice against the forgetfulness that can attend "working for a living," when it raises its voice against making our story one of competition, of an economic struggle for the survival of the fittest. There when the church raises its voice against an authoritarian and self-interested bureaucracy, whether it's a corporate bureaucracy or a party bureaucracy. Here and there when the church raises its hands to help and to defend the poor and powerless.

Here and there. Wherever people remember the story of Jesus anointed to preach good news to the poor and repent. Wherever people watch for Jesus and for a manna economy, an economy in which together we trust God and know hoarding to be foolish, an economy in which each has enough, none too little, none too much.

Here and there. Here where some are freed to rest from their work because they are not anxious. There where some are generous. Wherever a community includes and welcomes and honors the poor. Wherever Christians are reminded creatively and faithfully that they need not be anxious, that they should be generous, and that the care of the poor is a communal responsibility.

Economic deliberation in memory of Jesus will not pretend to have the last word on complex economic questions. It will not claim to have in its possession a revealed economic program, or some timeless set of economic rules and statutes, or even a tidy theory of justice. It will not claim to have the economic order under its control, as if it were now possible to create by fiat a wholly new economic order — or to recreate an older one. But it will insist that the consideration of economic choices and policies be set in the context of the memory of Jesus. It will insist that a critical test for our choices and policies is whether they are worthy of the gospel, whether they fit a story of "good news to the poor." It will insist that any notion of economic justice be informed by the story of God's work and way — and formed by the generosity and justice of God's good future. It will insist that this old economic order be acknowledged as flawed as long as poverty still grinds down the lives and the hopes of the poor, destroying both cells and souls. It will reflect not the folly of that rich farmer but the wisdom of Jesus. It will proceed "by way of reminder," boldly and gladly remembering Jesus.

PART FIVE

REMEMBERING JESUS
IN THE STRANGE WORLD OF POLITICS

*Revisiting Theocracy — A Continuing
Tradition of Justice*

CHAPTER SIXTEEN

Theocracy as a Four-Letter Word

"Theocracy" is a four-letter word. Or, at least, many people think of it as one. It is simply not considered appropriate for public discourse. Try it sometime. The next time someone asks whether you are a Republican or a Democrat, try saying, "I'm a theocrat." The reactions will be different from different people, of course, but many of them will be similar to those prompted by the use of a four-letter word in polite company. There will almost certainly be a double take. People will not quite believe that you have said what you said. The double take may be followed by a dirty look, suggesting that you should be ashamed of yourself. Or perhaps it will be followed by a little head wagging, indicating that efforts to have a serious conversation with you are hopeless. Or perhaps it will be followed by the sort of embarrassed giggle that violations of polite conventions sometimes prompt.

There are reasons, of course, for such reactions. "Theocracy" conjures up images of ancient and contemporary tyrannies, made more tyrannical by their claim to be holy, authorized by God. "Theocracy" reminds us of violence legitimated as divinely sanctioned, of "holy war," of inquisition and persecution, and of wars of religion like those that plagued Europe in the late sixteenth and early seventeenth centuries. We may all be grateful for the religious minorities and frustrated peacemakers who helped put a stop to those wars by looking for ways to think and act politically without invoking their religious disagreements. As long as members of particular religious communities were prepared to fight one another to the death, there was little hope for a just or lasting peace. It was prudent in that context to think and to act politically as if God were not a given, to provide a secularized account of political life, and to render theological disagreements politically irrelevant.[1] Little wonder, then, that the modern world worries that peace and justice are put at risk by talk of God as politically relevant — indeed, as politically sovereign. "Theocracy" has become a dirty word.

Problems with Scripture in the World of Politics

We may admit again — and we must — that there are problems when we read Scripture as somehow normative for the moral life. Indeed, the problems are magnified when we read Scripture as relevant to the world of politics. It is not that Scripture is *silent* about politics. We read of pharaohs and judges and kings and procurators, of civil disobedience and rebellion, of taxation and conscription, of laws and punishments, of wars of liberation and of conquest, of empire and of exile. Scripture *is* silent, of course, about many of the questions contemporary Christians find themselves asking in the middle of another season of political campaigns, questions about gun control or campaign reform or access to health care or, for that matter, representative democracy.

The silence of Scripture concerning the questions that dominate our political dialogue, however, seems a small problem compared to the *strangeness* of Scripture. The political worlds of Egyptian pharaohs, Jewish kings, and Roman emperors are foreign to us. Our interest in them is largely antiquarian. They are political worlds that we have happily left behind. Nevertheless, these various forms of royal despotism are less strange to many of us than the theocratic assumption that God is politically sovereign. We may indeed regret the loss of political worlds in which the violence of war was done with chariots and spears, but there is no doubt that we no longer live in that world. It is a strange world to us, made stranger still by the assertion that God sponsored such violence.

There is, moreover, the problem of *diversity* within Scripture's account of politics, a diversity that can be traced in part to the diverse political contexts of the people of God within Scripture. The stories of Abraham are set in a context of the political world of nomads. When the people were slaves in Egypt, they lived as an oppressed and politically powerless minority. They were liberated from oppression by Moses and by the hand of God. With the blessing of God

---

1. See Quintin Skinner, *The Foundations of Modern Political Thought*, 2 vols. (Cambridge: Cambridge University Press, 1978), 2:310-50. It is worth observing that this turn from a theological account of politics was offered first not by Enlightenment thinkers of the eighteenth century but by religious minorities and peacemakers. The Huguenots, for example, those French Calvinists who endured the massacres of the late sixteenth century, did not lack religious convictions, but they wanted (and needed) a way to talk to others who did not share them. See Skinner, p. 322.

and with violence they took possession of the land of Canaan. They established there a loose confederation of tribes that was regarded as authorized by covenant. The tribal league gave way to nationhood, and the rule of the charismatic figures called "judges" gave way to the political world of monarchy and royal despotism. The transition to a monarchy was contested by those who regarded it as apostasy from the faith that God was king, but it was celebrated by those who regarded the king as God's anointed. There was a short period of empire under David and Solomon. Then secession and civil war led to a division between the kingdoms of Judah and Israel and to weakened political stature among the nations. Israel, the Northern Kingdom, was defeated by the Assyrians and disappeared from the political landscape. Judah — and its Davidic dynasty — was defeated by the Babylonians a little more than a century later. Exiled from the land, many lived as aliens in the political world of Babylon. When Cyrus, king of the Persians, defeated the Babylonians, he permitted the exiled Jews to return to the land, where they lived the life of a vassal state. Many Jews remained in Babylon, and many others would establish Jewish settlements elsewhere outside of Palestine, giving rise to the quite different political realities of the Diaspora. These Jews lived the life of resident aliens. Back in Palestine Alexander the Great pushed the Persians out on his march to conquer the world, and the political world there and elsewhere was shaped to fit his Hellenistic vision. When Alexander died, his empire was divided among his generals, and Israel fell first to the Ptolemies in Egypt and then to the Seleucids in Syria. When the Seleucid ruler Antiochus IV Epiphanes attempted to enforce Hellenism by prohibiting Jewish practices and by turning the temple in Jerusalem into a temple for the worship of Zeus, the Jews responded, first with civil disobedience and then with rebellion. The surprising success of the revolt was credited not only to the clever and courageous Maccabees but also to God. A short period of independence ended when Pompey entered Jerusalem to put an end to a bloody conflict over succession to the throne and established Roman control over the land. The Romans, with their puppet kings and procurators, dominated the political landscape at the time of Jesus and the early church.

The diversity of Scripture can be traced not only to these major changes in the political landscape, but also to different responses to the same landscape. There are quite different responses to the authority and power of the Roman Empire, for example. Paul called the Roman churches to be subject to the rule of the emperor, and he defended that advice with the theocratic observation that "there is no authority except from God" (Rom. 13:1). A quite different — but no less theocratic — vision was provided by the author of Revelation, who saw the emperor as a "beast" who had received his "authority" not from God but from Satan, the dragon (Rev. 13:2; cf. 12:9). In his vision this dragon and his beast were locked in unholy combat against God and against the Christ of God.[2]

We could add to this list of problems, of course, the *difficulty* of Scripture. Neither Romans 13 nor Revelation 13 is easy to understand, and they have been read in a variety of ways. The greatest problem, however, is not the difficulty of Scripture; if we are quite honest, the greatest problem is not even the silence of Scripture or the strangeness of Scripture or the diversity of Scripture. The greatest problem is not with Scripture but with the readers of Scripture. The greatest problem is the *pride* of readers, the interpretative arrogance, which leads to the *abuse* of Scripture — and to the abuse of people that follows in its train. Scripture has been used to silence the criticism of kings who rule by "divine right." It has been used to unleash violence for the sake of some "holy war." It was used to justify slavery and to defend apartheid. Paul's advice concerning subjection to the young Nero has been used to demand obedience to tyrants like Hitler. The images of Revelation 13 have been used to demonize political opponents. Such uses of Scripture may be — and, I think, are — abuses of Scripture, but such abuses may rightly make us a little suspicious when we hear appeals to Scripture in political argument. And because such abuses of Scripture often involve the theocratic assumptions of Scripture, conscripted to serve the political interests of those in (or seeking) power, we may also be a little suspicious of theocracy.

There are problems, then, when we would read Scripture in Christian community as relevant to political life. Given the problems with both Scripture and our reading of it in this context, it is tempting to compartmentalize our lives, to live our lives like *TIME* magazine, keeping "politics" tidily separated from "religion." It is tempting to separate our political life from our religious commitments, and to regard Scripture as relevant to personal morality but not to political decisions, to private rather than to public matters. Such a compartmentalization of our lives ought to be regarded, however, not only as tempting but also as a temptation. If Jesus is Lord, then he is Lord of all of life, personal and communal, private and public. There are not two Lords. Christians respond to the one Lord in all their personal and political reflection and responsibilities. If Jesus is Lord, then he is Lord of our politics, too.

2. This diversity, too, of course, may be traced to the different political contexts of the letter to the Romans and the book of Revelation. Paul wrote Romans before Nero turned tyrant, while the political prisoner who wrote Revelation saw and suffered the petty persecution of other emperors a half-century later. The point is simply that, however the diversity is explained, it is real enough for any careful reader of Scripture and creates a problem for the contemporary appropriation of Scripture to politics.

A Political Life "Worthy of the Gospel"

In Christian community political discourse may not simply be surrendered to some other community or tradition. The church should not regard political choices as properly settled simply by the application of the generally accredited political wisdom of some other tradition or some larger "public." In the early church, there was a temptation to regard decisions about the ordering of their common life and the ordering of their relationship with other communities as properly settled by the conventional wisdom of life in the Greek city, the polis. Paul urged, however, that the Philippians live their lives — more literally, their political lives, their lives as citizens — "in a manner worthy of the gospel of Christ" (Phil. 1:27; *politeuesthe* means "behave as citizens"). The moral tradition of the polis did function in the discourse and deliberation of the early church, of course, but it was always to be tested against and qualified by the memory of Jesus.

Today, the temptation is to regard political decisions as properly governed by the widely accredited political assumptions of the Enlightenment. The Enlightenment regarded public order as properly founded upon rational and universal principles, such as utility or maximum freedom, rather than upon the particular traditions of specific communities. It established the ironic tradition that we can and should think without the aid of a tradition. It established the expectation that Christians and other religious people should treat their religious convictions as publicly irrelevant. It insisted, to use the words of Hobbes, that Scripture be read as addressed to the "inward man" about the inward man.[3] Thus the Enlightenment undercut the public significance of both Scripture and religion. There are reasons to be grateful, as we have noted, to those religious minorities and frustrated peacemakers who tried to put a stop to the religious wars of the sixteenth and seventeenth centuries by looking for ways to think and to act politically without invoking their religious disagreements. We are all indebted to these pre-Enlightenment thinkers and to their Enlightenment heirs. The point is not that appeals to this political tradition (and to its standards of a social contract and utility) are inappropriate to the continuing discourse and deliberation of Christian communities.[4] The point is rather that

---

3. Thomas Hobbes, *Leviathan* IV, ch. 47 (Harmondsworth: Penguin Books, 1968), pp. 710-11.

4. Even if the churches in contemporary Western culture wanted to eliminate appeals to the tradition of the Enlightenment in their political discourse, they probably could not. The elimination of the tradition of the Enlightenment is no more possible for contemporary Christians than the elimination of the conventional wisdom of the Greek city was possible for Christians in the first century.

such appeals must always be tested and qualified by the memory of Jesus; Christians are still called to a political life "worthy of the gospel of Christ."

Granted, then, that there are problems when Christians read Scripture as relevant to politics; even so, if Christians are to think and act politically in ways that are "worthy of the gospel of Christ," then we will read Scripture and remember Jesus. To neglect Scripture when thinking and talking about political life is to risk forgetfulness. To surrender political decisions to the wisdom of the Enlightenment is for Christians to risk amnesia and the loss of a public identity.

When Christians read Scripture as somehow relevant also to politics, we encounter a theocratic perspective on politics. If we would read Scripture and remember Jesus in the strange world of our politics, then we will have to come to terms with this strange notion of theocracy. Moses was a theocrat, and Samuel, and David, and the long line of the prophets. Jesus was a theocrat, and so were those who first remembered him. If we do ethics by way of reminder, if we read Scripture and remember Jesus as decisive for identity and determinative for discernment, then we will, I think, find ourselves called to be theocrats ourselves, to "say among the nations, 'The LORD is king!'" (Ps. 96:10; 1 Chron. 16:31).

If it is necessary in reading Scripture and remembering Jesus to retrieve the notion of "theocracy," it is also necessary to retrieve this notion with all due repentance. The history of religious violence and tyranny is not a pretty one, and it dishonors the name of God. If Christians find it necessary in remembering Jesus to retrieve a theocratic perspective on politics, let us not forget the manifold ways in which the notion of "theocracy" has been distorted and abused by the religious and/or political pride of Christians. Indeed, if we would retrieve a notion of "theocracy," let us do so without forgetting or dishonoring also those Christians who bracketed their particular convictions about God's sovereignty in order to serve what they saw to be the cause of God in the context of the wars of religion.

What Theocracy Is Not

To retrieve the notion of theocracy — or to defend it — is not, of course, to defend any or all of the political positions that have sometimes been associated with it. Indeed, quite the contrary. Since the notion of theocracy has sometimes been easily and sensationally discredited by confusing it with other notions, a defense of theocracy must undertake at least briefly to distinguish it from some of the political positions sometimes thought to be entailed by it.

Theocracy has sometimes been confused with hierocracy, with the political rule of a priestly or clerical hierarchy. But theocracy does not entail hierocracy, as the power of judges and kings in Israel makes quite plain. The theocratic vision makes political rulers responsible to God, not to priests or clerics. In theocracy, religious leaders are neither identified with political leaders nor given authority over them.

Theocracy has more often and more recently been confused with bibliocracy, with the legislation and enforcement of the positive law found in Scripture. Theocracy, however, ought *not* to be identified with the Reconstructionist Movement of R. J. Rushdoony and Greg Bahnson and the rest. Reconstructionists (or "theonomists") envision a state where the law of Moses is the law of the land, where unrepentant adulterers will be executed, where homosexual conduct will be a capital crime, where restitution in kind will be mandatory, even if it means a period of slavery. Theonomists are theocrats, but theocracy is not "theonomy." One can reject theonomy as a right-wing and reactionary political movement; one can reject the anachronistic eccentricity of the (ab)use of Scripture by the Reconstructionists; but one should not therefore suppose one has discredited either theocracy or the relevance of Scripture to the political life of Christians. Theocracy does not entail any particular legal code, and Christians must not suppose the Bible provides a timeless set of civil rules.[5] Theocracy is not to be identified with the enforcement of any of these particular codes nor the sum of them.

Theocracy has often been confused with historical instances of self-conscious attempts to reflect and institutionalize God's reign. But if neither Israel's amphictyony nor her monarchy are necessarily entailments of theocracy, it need hardly be said that neither Calvin's Geneva, the Massachusetts Bay Colony, Penn's "holy experiment" in Pennsylvania, Van Raalte's "colony" in Holland, Michigan, Leo XIII's *Rerum Novarum,* nor any such example is to be identified and confused with theocracy itself. To defend theocracy is not to defend, say, Calvin's Geneva or to propose that a contemporary state ape Penn's "holy experiment."

---

5. The laws and codes of the Old Testament were not something static, settled once for all in eternity, but rather something constantly modified to bring new situations under the reign of God and to nudge the common life toward something more fitting to the story of Israel. Consider, for example, the development of the laws concerning the release of slaves. In the Covenant Code, the oldest of the collections in Torah, the law requires the release of the male Hebrew slave (but not the female slave) at the end of six years (Exod. 21:1-6). In the Deuteronomic Code the law requires the release not only of the male slave but also the female slave at the end of the sixth year, and it requires not only release but also provision, "giving to him some of the bounty with which the LORD your God has blessed you. Remember that you were a slave in the land of Egypt . . ." (Deut. 15:12-17). By the time of the Holiness Code there is a prohibition against enslaving a fellow Israelite (Lev. 25:39-46).

To distinguish "theocracy" from some of the positions often confused with it may be enough to defend "theocracy" from certain easy and sensational accusations. But the exercise seems to have left "theocracy" open to the easiest and most sensational accusation of all, the accusation that "theocracy" is an empty cipher without any meaning at all. To defend theocracy against that accusation, however, requires a positive account of its meaning. It is to such an account that I now turn. In the first part of what follows, I will try to show that every state has a "theocratic" dimension. In the next few chapters I will proceed by way of reminder, reviewing the theocratic tradition within which Jesus stood, remembering Jesus and his proclamation of God's reign (or theocracy), and remembering the early church remembering Jesus in the strange world of first-century politics. Finally, I will suggest something of the political relevance of the church's memory of Jesus for the pluralistic world in which we live.

The Theocratic Dimension of Politics

Every state has a "theocratic" dimension. There is faith at work in all politics. As H. Richard Niebuhr said, "Faith as human confidence in a center and conserver of value and as human loyalty to a cause seems to manifest itself almost as directly in politics . . . as it does in religion."[6] Indeed, in that sense all people and all human communities "live by faith."

The importance of confidence and loyalty to communities, including political communities, can hardly be denied. States rely on and seek to elicit confidence in and loyalty not only to the executive, legislative, and judicial functions of government but also to "the cause" they seek. Nation-states do not typically rely on brute force; they seek to legitimate that power by some "mission." Czarist Russian presented itself to its subjects and to the world as Holy Russia, a servant of Orthodoxy. Communist Russia, for all its atheism, was no less devoted to a cause that transcended it. France and the United States present themselves as devoted servants of democracy and human rights. Every nation-state seeks to secure the confidence and loyalty of its citizens to itself by presenting itself as loyal to some cause that evokes that confidence and loyalty. "My country, right or wrong" is at best a fragile substitute for "My country because it is a servant of the right."

That there is hypocrisy in this is patent, for nations often act in simple self-interest rather than in the interest of any cause that transcends them. But

6. H. Richard Niebuhr, *Radical Monotheism and Western Culture* (New York: Harper & Row, 1960), p. 64. The next three paragraphs are indebted to pp. 64-68.

hypocrisy always pays its subtle tribute to the good, and here no less than elsewhere hypocrisy involves the admission that the cause is good and binding, even if we are not sufficiently devoted to it.

Any government's failure to act in ways coherent with the cause to which its citizens are loyal can result in a crisis of confidence. Confidence in government is not unrelated to confidence in the cause. But faith as confidence involves more than mere devotion to the cause. It also involves (often implicit) assumptions about the nature of persons and their communities, about the faults in persons and/or their communities, and about their prospects and destiny. These beliefs may support and sustain loyalty to a cause, but they also affect policy designed to further the cause. If citizens have confidence that truth is an ally of justice (or of a worthy order or a decent common life) and not an enemy, then and only then will they have confidence in a government that protects freedom of speech and inquiry. If citizens believe that technological innovation provides the remedy for personal and social ills, then they will confidently seek technological solutions for what may not be technological problems. Truth or technology may or may not in these cases become "the cause," but these assumptions are sure to influence whatever policy is formulated to pursue the cause, and they will affect whether or not citizens have confidence that their government is serving the cause.

I have, up to this point for the sake of emphasis, used the singular, "the cause," to speak of that to which nation-states are loyal. It is not as simple as that, of course, at least not often. There are various causes which lay claim on a nation's loyalty and confidence and on the loyalty and confidence of its citizens. And those various causes cannot all be served at once, at least not often. The cause of peace and the cause of justice both claim loyalty and confidence, but they sometimes seem to require different political policies and actions. The cause of freedom and the cause of order often seem to make conflicting legitimate claims. We can talk about the cause of a "just peace" or an "ordered freedom," but such locutions do not hide the necessity of relating distinct causes and establishing priorities. The theocratic dimension of statecraft points in the direction of many causes, many "goods" to which a state is loyal and in which it has confidence. But the point remains that every state has a theocratic dimension, not that they all acknowledge one god or the one true God.

To that observation may be added another. In many places — notably and ironically in "consensual" states, and surely in the United States — there is precious little public consensus. There is little consensus either about a cause that transcends the nation, to which the citizens are loyal and because of which they are loyal (or not) to the government, or about the assumptions concerning the nature of, the faults in, and the prospects for the human and social condition.

341

The cause can then become "pluralism" itself, or the freedom to pursue and practice different faiths, different loyalties and confidences. No doubt, that cause has won important victories over real and vicious injustices. But besides providing very little guidance for public decisions, it is always in danger of reducing the public good to an additive result (or balance) of multiple private goods and special interests, and of reducing public morality to tolerance.

It is worth pausing to suggest that a theocratic perspective need not — and should not — deny the importance of religious freedom. We sometimes easily assume that a theocracy must be an enemy of religious freedom. To be sure, many of the historical examples people often think of when they hear the word "theocracy" were not hospitable to religious freedom. And to be sure, a theocratic perspective will need to deny one of the contending accounts of the basis and significance of religious freedom. A theocrat will deny the account of religious freedom according to which a sovereign state grants religious freedom on the condition that religion be regarded as a private matter. In such an account sovereign states (or individuals in some hypothetical contract) grant religious freedom as a strategic choice in order to achieve unity and political stability in the context of religious pluralism. Religion is, on this account, a private matter, or at least it must be publicly regarded as a private matter. Loyalties to God must, on this account, be regarded as irrelevant, or at best secondary, to the public loyalties and choices of citizens. As long as people can be counted on to be loyal to the state and to the cause of the state, and as long as they agree to keep their religious loyalties and confidences to themselves, private, they may be permitted their religious preferences. Even this account has a "theocratic dimension": fundamental loyalties are formed and claimed, and certain assumptions undergird both the confidence and suspicion of such states. The primary loyalty belongs to the state, or to the cause of peaceable "pluralism" that the state serves. It is suspicious of religion as divisive. So, it tolerates religion as long as it is private rather than public, as long as it remains concerned with some other world, some spiritual world, wholly separated from the world of politics. Such an account of religious freedom will be suspicious of the theocrat because the theocrat regards loyalty to God as of public significance, and for the same reason, of course, a theocrat will be suspicious of such an account of religious freedom.

Such an account, however, is not the only plausible account of the basis and significance of religious freedom, and theocrats need not be opposed to religious freedom because they are opposed to a certain account of it. A second account, a theocratic account, regards religious freedom as important precisely because loyalty to God is more fundamental than loyalty to the state. A person's loyalty to God is not secondary but primary. Religious loyalties create allegiances more inclusive than national allegiances and loyalties more fundamen-

342

tal than particular political loyalties. On this account the state must, therefore, acknowledge and assure a person's rights to such loyalty. The state must acknowledge the limitations on its own sovereignty; it must acknowledge the secondary character of the loyalty of citizens that it can and does claim for itself. Because the primary loyalty belongs to God, the state acknowledges the limits of its sovereignty over the religious loyalties of citizens.[7]

Some Theocratic Soundings

The fundamental premise of theocracy is that the cause we must serve politically — and the cause the nations must serve — is God's cause. This premise, of course, is a long way from the formation of policy. To move from this premise to a more concrete political stance will require that we specify what God's cause is, or what God's causes are. That is not a simple task, of course. Perhaps we can identify God's cause with God's glory. But then, how shall we specify God's glory? Shall we identify God's cause and glory with the good of human persons or with the well-being of the whole creation? In either case, "good" and "well-being" are complex ideas. Moreover, however sophisticated our analysis of these ideas may be, our specification of God's cause will stand in need of correction. As God transcends our attempts to talk of God, so God's cause transcends our efforts to identify it and to discern concrete political positions worthy of it.

That, perhaps, is the first sounding worth taking and the first measure worth noting. God's cause transcends any and every political program or position. And because theocrats recognize *God's* cause as alone worthy of their ultimate loyalty and confidence (and of their nation's ultimate loyalty and confidence), they remain attentive to the ways in which they (and their nation) have failed to serve the cause of God politically. Such a theocratic posture should nurture the precious capacity for self-critical political reflection and for discourse, deliberation, and discernment. To remind ourselves and the nations of the transcendence of God's cause is part of what it means to "say among the nations, 'The LORD is king!'" — and it is no small contribution to the public good.

But if God's cause transcends our efforts to talk of it and to serve it politically, if it is presumptuous to identify and to limit God's cause self-assuredly, it does not follow that we know nothing of that cause. And it does not follow,

7. See Niebuhr, *Radical Monotheism*, pp. 69-71. For an example of this argument see John Milton, "A Treatise of Civil Power in Ecclesiastical Causes" (1659), in *John Milton: Selected Prose*, ed. C. A. Patrides (Harmondsworth: Penguin Books, 1974), pp. 296-326.

either, that we cannot serve God or the cause of God politically. God has not left God's cause without witness in the world. God and the cause of God are not totally unknown. We remember Jesus, the one who announced the coming kingdom of God and already made its power felt, and we know something of God and of the cause of God. We remember Jesus, and we know, for example, that God's cause is life, not death; health, not disease. We remember Jesus, and we know, for example, that God's cause is human freedom and human community, neither simply the individual liberty that can make contracts but is ignorant of covenant, nor simply the common good that treats differences as deviancy. We remember Jesus, and we know, for example, that God's cause is to feed the hungry, to protect the powerless, and to bless the poor. We remember Jesus, and we know that God's cause is peace; we know that God's cause is justice; we know that God's cause is the flourishing of the whole creation; we know many goods that belong to God's cause.

God's cause transcends our ability to think of it and our capacity to act for it, but our problem is not that we know nothing of it. The problem, rather, to put it oddly, is that we know too much of God's cause. Many goods belong to God's cause; there are many and diverse "causes" which do not fall automatically into place and priority. That is not to say, however, that any or every political cause has a place within loyalty to the God who raised Jesus from the dead, and it is not to say that any or every cause that has a place may be given prominence of place or priority. The international superiority of the Aryan race can hardly claim any place in God's cause. In Vietnam "national honor" could not finally claim priority over "peace" or "justice." The transcendence of God does not render deliberation or discernment concerning particular political choices impossible, as though every political "good" were equidistant from the transcendent cause of God. The Christian theocrat can and must select and exclude, relate and order, the diversity of political "goods," even though a simple unitive understanding of God's cause is beyond his ken.

The first sounding, the first measure, of theocracy is the warning against simply identifying a political cause or a set of political causes with God's cause. The second sounding worth taking, the second measure worth noting, is that political discernment requires of theocrats the selecting and excluding, the relating and ordering, of political causes in the light of God's transcendent cause. It is not an easy task, of course, and in a world that is not yet God's good future, part of what we know to be God's cause can conflict with another part of what we know to be God's cause. Political choices are sometimes tragic. Evils gather and cannot all be avoided. Goods conflict and cannot all be chosen. Political discernment is no easy task, but in memory of Jesus it can be and must be undertaken. Political discernment in the light of God's transcendent cause is a sec-

ond part of what it means to "say among the nations, 'The LORD is king!'" —
and a second contribution to the public good.

The transcendence of God and of God's cause does not mean that we
know nothing of the cause or that a faithful political discernment is impossible.
That was the point just made, but it needs now to be said and underscored that
the transcendence of God and of God's cause does not mean that we cannot
serve God or the cause of God politically. It does not mean that a faithful use of
political means and processes is impossible.

To be sure, Christian theocrats in memory of Jesus — who was, after all,
crucified by Roman authorities — will have modest expectations and make
modest claims for political power and process in their service to God's cause.
Indeed, they will be suspicious of any extravagant claims; they will be ready to
laugh derisively at political pride and the pretenses of power. No political party
or state is the faithful savior; no political movement or process is the messianic
inauguration of God's reign. But the suspicion of political pride is not for
Christian theocrats an excuse for political sloth. Devotion to the cause of God
in a world not yet God's cosmic sovereignty will not disown political responsibility; it will rather humbly own such responsibility. Political power — including the powers to vote and dissent and express and legislate and judge and administer — will be construed as an opportunity for some modest service to the
cause of God. The political process will be seen as an earthen vessel, which is
nevertheless serviceable to the preservation of some small but genuine goods
and to the protection against certain great and genuine harms. So the Christian
theocrat may and must be politically responsible.

The memory of Jesus and the hope for the coming kingdom that he made
present not only illuminate political discernment but also energize political activity. That is the third sounding worth taking, the third measure worth noting.
Theocratic political activity will sometimes take the shape of prophetic protest,
the shape of a bone crossways in the throat of power, but sometimes — and
more often probably — it will take the shape of humble participation in the art
of the possible. That, too, is part of what it means to "say among the nations,
'The LORD is king!'" — and a third contribution of a Christian theocrat to the
public good.

Our earlier analysis of the theocratic dimension of all statecraft showed
that certain beliefs and assumptions about the nature, faults, and destiny of persons and their communities could nurture and sustain loyalty to a nation's cause
and also affect the formation of a nation's policy. To deal adequately with Christian beliefs and assumptions about the nature, faults, and prospects of human
beings and their communities would demand a full-scale political theology in
the light of the churches' memory of Jesus. In lieu of that, let me briefly and illus-

tratively contrast some of the assumptions of the Christian theocrat with the beliefs and assumptions of an important contemporary rival, the technocrat.

Technocrats assume that persons are by nature "tool-makers," that they transcend nature by controlling it, and seek by curiosity and inventiveness to do so more and more. For technocrats the fault that runs though our world and through our lives is located in nature, not in persons. Human beings are beset by nature; it is nature that keeps them from getting what they need or want. The prospects for human beings and their communities, however, are bright as long as human curiosity and inventiveness are unencumbered by the fears of those without a taste for them. Technology provides mastery over nature and the path to what we want. Whatever the cause, the way to achieve it is provided by technology, until the cause itself becomes technological innovation. If and when the consequences of certain technologies become threatening, then a technological solution is sought. Technology is the faithful savior, the object of trust and finally of loyalty. "Better living through chemistry." Such assumptions prompt us to look for technological solutions to what may not be technological problems. They prompt us to test public education by its production of scientists and technicians — and, of course, to attempt to improve it by technological innovations. They prompt us to rely on the technical experts for political decisions — or simply to surrender political decisions to the experts. And, of course, they make it difficult to challenge politically any kind of scientific research and technology; *laissez innover!*

The Christian theocrat believes that human beings are by nature creatures of God, a part of God's creation and along with it dependent on God. Humanity as it comes from God is always fellow-humanity, and the dominion over nature given with God's creation is always responsible dominion. Human persons are responsible to God for the use and abuse of nature, for the effects of their dominion on both nature and their fellow humans. The fault is neither in nature nor in human dominion over nature but in human pride and sloth, human folly and greed. The prospects for persons and their communities — and their technologies — always tilt toward darkness when human pride, sloth, folly, and greed are not reined by law and tempered by a sense of finitude and, yes, of sin. But God is always active not only as creator and judge but also as redeemer of God's world and creatures. God is always creating new possibilities of restraining evil and promoting well-being. And the prospects for persons and their communities sometimes tilt toward splendor when people tend the creation and care for their fellow humans. Such assumptions would plainly not cohere with a cavalierly and naively anti-technological spirit, but they would not look to technology as the "faithful savior" either. Such assumptions would prompt us to test public education by its initiation of children into a tradition of civility and care, by its capacity to draw out from young people their gifts and to encourage the use of those gifts in a public-spirited way. They prompt us to attend to the common life and to the manifold mundane routines and decisions that make up a common life. And it might even be possible, with such assumptions, to say "no" to some kinds of research and technology that most threaten the creation and humanity's stake in it or are most liable to become instruments of human pride or folly or greed.

The fourth sounding worth taking, then, and the fourth measure worth noting, is that the Christian theocrat will attempt to form public policy and the common life in accord with Christian convictions about the creation, fault, and destiny of persons and their communities. This, too, is part of what it means to "say among the nations, 'The LORD is king!'" — and a fourth contribution of a Christian theocrat to the public good.

It begins to appear that our second, third, and fourth soundings point toward "the enforcement of morals" (to use the title of Lord Devlin's book on morality and law).[8] And there is a sense in which no theocrat could or would disown that task. But a Christian theocrat will have very good grounds for qualifying and restricting that task. The first and fundamental reason for qualifying "the enforcement of morals" is a healthy respect for freedom. It is a theocratic conviction, nourished and sustained by the story of creation and redemption, that one cause of God, one part of the complex and transcendent cause of God, is freedom. Truly to serve God's cause is to serve it freely. Never mind now the arguments based solely on reason and upon an impartial perspective (and such arguments can be made for freedom and may not be finally ignored by theocrats). The point now is that God is the source, preserver, and destiny of human freedom. Freedom does not become a negligible value, then, even when it is used paradoxically to deny its own source and destiny. Freedom remains a public good, and its preservation and protection a theocratic obligation. It is as Calvin himself said, "Indeed, the magistrates ought to apply themselves with the highest diligence to prevent the freedom (whose guardians they have been appointed) from being in any respect diminished, far less violated."[9] Freedom, of course, may not be unlimited; the result would be anarchy. But it must be protected and preserved, and that is the first qualification on the theocratic "enforcement of morals."

The Christian theocrat also knows that morality outreaches the grasp of legal sanctions. Morality is concerned with dispositions and character as well as with actions. Law and its sanctions focus on external actions. It is true, of

---

8. P. A. Devlin, *The Enforcement of Morals* (London: Oxford University Press, 1965).
9. John Calvin, *Institutes*, IV.xx.8.

course — and no theocrat would wish to deny — that certain habits of mind and action may be influenced by public law. But it is also true that the "habit" of respect for the law is diminished when laws and sanctions are imposed where there is no discernable connection between the law and broader social interests and where there is little possibility of adequate or equitable enforcement. That is a second qualification on the theocratic "enforcement of morals."

Morality outreaches law, moreover, not only in that it is concerned with character as well as with conduct, but also in the kinds of actions it prescribes and prohibits. Jesus did not tell the story of the Good Samaritan in order to make this point about morality and law, but I want to use it to illustrate the point. Jesus commended the behavior of the Samaritan, and he commanded those who heard the story to act likewise. But there is no hint that legal sanction would be appropriate against those who failed to act with the same sort of selfless generosity. The priest and the Levite may deserve to be blamed, but they are not to be fined or imprisoned. The brigands who assaulted and robbed the man also deserve to be blamed and, indeed, deserve legal punishment. If the Good Samaritan found people assaulted and left for dead again and again along that road from Jericho to Jerusalem, his selfless concern for others would motivate political action. He could, for example, advocate increased police protection along the road to enforce the laws against theft and assault. (Or he might write the procurator requesting the creation of a "Good Samaritan statute," which would encourage others to help by protecting them against legal consequences or subsequent litigation if they gave emergency aid to a stranger.) The point here, however, is not simply that selfless generosity can motivate political responsibility; it is rather that certain actions, like the selflessly generous actions of the Good Samaritan, are beyond the reach of law to enforce. The best the law can do is to encourage them. Enforced generosity is paradoxical, for generosity means that one gives beyond what anyone else has a right to expect. Leave aside for now the important question of what one has "a right to expect"; the distinction between generosity and what is due another is an important one. To give a stranger fifty dollars is generous and may deserve high praise. Not to give a stranger — even a needy stranger — fifty dollars would warrant low blame, if blame at all. To return fifty dollars to someone I had borrowed it from is only giving her her due, and it deserves low praise, if praise at all. To fail to repay my debt would deserve high blame. The first kind of act is beyond the competence of law; the second is within it. Law must deal with what will inevitably seem to morality to be "minimal standards," prohibiting actions which deserve high blame, not those deserving low blame, and enforcing actions which deserve low praise, not those deserving high praise. This is a third qualification on the theocratic "enforcement of morals."

With these qualifications, then, the Christian theocrat will own the vocation of the "enforcement of morals." Law and its sanctions may be used to enforce certain "minimal standards" when their enforcement is both possible and equitable and is consistent with the protection and preservation of freedom. That is the fifth sounding worth taking, the fifth measure worth noting, and the fifth contribution of a Christian theocrat to the public good. Those qualifications, it may as well be acknowledged, are as abstract as the problems they are intended to deal with are concrete. "The enforcement of morals" is never just that exactly, but always the prohibition or prescription or regulation of certain acts, for the sake of avoiding particular public evils or achieving particular public goods, by means of sanctions which are real and finite, and involving the sacrifice of specific liberties.

It is important, finally, to return to the first sounding, to allow it the last word in this section. God's cause transcends our attempts to talk about it and surely to "enforce" it. The "minimal standards" will always fall short of the "love, joy, peace, patience, kindness, generosity, faithfulness, gentleness, and self-control" that are "the fruit of the Spirit" (Gal. 5:22) and, like the Spirit, the first fruits of God's coming cosmic sovereignty. Such a higher righteousness will never allow us to identify the nation's order as the cause of God or the "minimal standards" as the fulfillment of morality. Indeed, one great contribution of the theocrat is to resist and challenge the reduction of morality to legality and legality to the rights of self-interested individuals. But neither will that higher righteousness allow us to despise the "minimal standards" as unrelated to God's cause. The Christian theocrat will be prepared to tend to sores in the body politic with remedies considerably less winsome than the Christian *charismata*. Loyalty to God and to the cause of God sustains the responsibility and the capacity to attend without self-righteousness both to the preservation of small but genuine goods and to the avoidance of considerable and genuine harms in the common life of nations, all while we wait and watch and pray for the good future of God. That is the vocation of the Christian theocrat, and the defense of theocracy. God reigns and will reign. That may neither be reduced to its political implications nor emptied of them. If "theocracy" is a four-letter word, so is "hope."

We have distinguished "theocracy" from some of the positions often confused with it; we have noticed the theocratic dimensions of all politics, and we have taken some initial soundings of a Christian theocratic perspective. Enough has been said, I hope, to warrant a closer look at the theocratic tradition of Scripture. To that task we turn in the next three chapters, reading Scripture and remembering Jesus, examining the theocratic assumptions within the Hebrew Scriptures, in the story of Jesus, and in the early church and its political

349

life in memory of Jesus. It will be important, of course, to recognize that the political world in which we live is quite different from the political world of Jesus and the early church. The final chapter will attempt, in memory of Jesus and in hope of the kingdom he proclaimed, to retrieve a notion of theocracy and to provide a constructive (and less abstract) theological account of its significance for Christian political discernment in the pluralistic world in which we live.

CHAPTER SEVENTEEN

A Theocratic Tradition

The word "theocracy" is constructed from two Greek words, *theos* and *kratein*. The fundamental sense of the word, therefore, is "the rule of God" or "the reign of God." It bears some obvious resemblance to the notion of "the kingdom of God," the *basileia tou theou*, that was at the center of Jesus' proclamation. Jesus never paused to define "the kingdom of God," but he made it known. He made it known, as we have said before, in his works of healing and in his words of blessing. When the sick were healed, when demons were cast out, when the poor had good news preached to them, when children were blessed, when women were regarded as equals, when the humble were exalted, and when the proud were humbled, then he made the kingdom known. And he made it known, as we hope now to show, also politically.

That the kingdom of God would be made known politically would hardly be surprising to the people of the first century. The danger in the first century — indeed, the temptation (Matt. 4:8-10) — was to reduce "the kingdom of God" to a conventional political realm or empire. The kingdom of God, however, was not to be seized, and the conventional political means of violence were powerless against it. It was not to be used as a tool of political ambition, neither the ambition of the one who would be God's servant nor the ambition of those who would make him king. Such a mistake was understandable enough in the first century (see John 6:15), and it has bedeviled theocrats throughout history. The danger now, however, is quite different. The danger now — indeed, the temptation — is to reduce "the kingdom of God" to some otherworldly sovereignty over individual souls, to empty it of its political significance. There are not, however, two Lords, one for private lives and one for the common life. The announcement that the kingdom of God was at hand would hardly be understood in the first century to exempt politics, as if God were about to act to establish sovereignty over everything except politics. Jesus came announcing "the rule of God," theocracy, over politics, too. Jesus was a theocrat.

That is hardly surprising. Jesus stood in a theocratic tradition. That God reigns was a central affirmation of Israel's account of the relation of God to the world, including the political world, and of God's activity within it.

Exodus and the Great Suzerain

It could hardly be otherwise. The story the people owned as their own was a story of God's rule. It was a story familiar in ritual and written finally in Torah. God had chosen them as a people, liberated them from their slavery in Egypt, made a covenant with them at Sinai, and brought them to the land. That covenant, moreover, was a "suzerainty treaty," familiar enough in the ancient Near East in the pledges exchanged between kings and their vassals.[1] In those pledges the gods were frequently called upon to witness the promises and to guarantee their fulfillment. At Sinai, however, God was not just a witness to the covenant; God was a party to it. God was the great suzerain, the great king who had rescued them from slavery, who provided them with Law, and who promised them land. And they were the people of God, a people created by God, a people constituted by the covenantal pledge of allegiance to God as their king.[2]

Because God was king, political authority among the people was derived from God — and answered to God! Political responsibility was a responsibility *to* God, to the God whose works and ways were remembered in the community of faith, to the God who heard the cries of the slave, who loves justice, and who intends the security and peace of the land God gives. That responsibility to God

---

1. See, e.g., G. E. Mendenhall, *Law and Covenant in Israel and the Ancient Near East* (Pittsburgh: Biblical Colloquium, 1955).

2. Oliver O'Donovan, *The Desire of the Nations: Rediscovering the Roots of Political Theology* (Cambridge: Cambridge University Press, 1996), pp. 36-49, examines the notion of God's kingship by identifying some of the "leading political terms that are habitually grouped with it" (p. 36), "salvation" *(yeshuah),* "judgment" *(mishpat),* and "possession" *(nachalah).* O'Donovan sees in these word groupings "three affirmations which shape Israel's sense of political identity and define what is meant by saying that Yhwh rules as king: he gives Israel victory; he gives judgment; he gives Israel its possession" (p. 45). To these three political terms he adds "praise," and to the three affirmations he adds a fourth, that "Yhwh's rule receives its answering recognition in the praises of his people" (p. 47). The story Torah tells confirms O'Donovan's affirmations (and helps to explain, I think, why the word groupings to which he calls attention exist).

formed a theocratic tradition that shaped Israel's political thought and common life through a variety of political circumstances and institutions. The test for political discernment remained always this affirmation of covenant that "God is king" joined with the memory of God's works and ways.

God's Rule in Conquest and Settlement

One reading of the book of Joshua is that Israel took possession of Canaan by violence — with the help of the Lord.[3] A better reading, however, may be that God took possession of Canaan by violence — and with little help from Israel's military establishment. Both sides of this revision are worthy of note.

First, the tradition of theocracy included the affirmation that God the king was a "warrior" (Exod. 15:3). It was a primary function of kings to fight for the liberation and defense of the people, and God surely did. Some of the earliest materials of the Hebrew Bible depict God as a warrior and celebrate his victories over

---

3. There are diverse theories of the conquest. Martin Noth, rejecting the account of the book of Joshua, suggested that semi-nomadic people gradually settled into the agricultural lands of Palestine. The settlement was largely peaceable, but there were tensions and sometimes violence between herdsman and farmer. John Bright accepts the general picture of the book of Joshua, finding it confirmed by archaeological evidence that there was a conquest of parts of Palestine. The army from the wilderness, however, was joined, in Bright's view, by kindred people already in the land. George Mendenhall and Norman Gottwald have proposed a third theory. In their view a group of fugitive slaves entered Palestine from Egypt, bringing with them a remarkable story of their deliverance from bondage by the God Yahweh and an equally remarkable social structure of covenant. They were hardly welcomed by the Canaanite city-states, but they were welcomed by the *Habiru* in the countryside. The *Habiru* were those who had been driven (or had withdrawn their loyalty) from the political system within which they had lived. They were alienated and marginalized; when the term is found in ancient Near Eastern texts, it can usually be translated "outlaw." These *Habiru* made the story of these fugitive slaves their own, making common cause with them in a revolt against the Canaanite city-states, and making covenant with this God Yahweh who overturned the established social and political structures. Thus was formed in southern Palestine a new political-religious entity called Israel, constituted by its loyalty to God as king, while Canaanites remained loyal to the city-state kings and to the religious and political structures that supported them. See Martin Noth, *The History of Israel*, rev. ed. (New York: Harper & Brothers, 1960); John Bright, *A History of Israel*, third ed. (Philadelphia: Westminster, 1981); George E. Mendenhall, "The Hebrew Conquest of Palestine," in *Biblical Archaeologist Reader 3*, ed. Edward F. Campbell and David Noel Freedman (Garden City, N.Y.: Doubleday, 1970), pp. 100-120; and Norman Gottwald, *The Tribes of Yahweh: A Sociology of the Religion of Liberated Israel, 1250-1050 B.C.E.* (Maryknoll, N.Y.: Orbis, 1979).

the Egyptians and the Canaanites. Note, for example, the Song of Miriam: "Sing to the LORD, for he has triumphed gloriously; horse and rider he has thrown into the sea" (Exod. 15:21). Or consider the Song of Deborah (Judg. 5), or the Song of Moses, which celebrated the victories of God the "warrior" not just over Egypt but also, if anachronistically, over the Canaanites, and which concluded with an affirmation of God's "reign" (Exod. 15:1-18). In Joshua's recital in the covenant renewal ceremony of Joshua 24, it is God who won the victories of exodus and conquest, and the people agree in their renewal of loyalty to God as king.

But the second side of this revision is equally important to the theocratic tradition: the people were not warriors! It is a stunning feature of the exodus narrative that the Israelites did nothing to bring about the destruction of the Egyptians. Moses told the people not that they should take up arms but that they should not be afraid; "stand firm," he said, "and see the deliverance that the LORD will accomplish for you today. . . . The LORD will fight for you, and you have only to keep still" (Exod. 14:13-14).[4] The Israelites, of course, did more than "keep still" against the Amalekites (Exod. 17:8-13; 1 Sam. 15:1-9) and against the other nations that resisted their pilgrimage to and settlement in the land. Even so, the role of the people in battle is consistently minimized, subordinated to the role of God in battle. Consider, for example, the siege of Jericho, which seems more like a liturgy than a military strategy (Josh. 6:1-21). Or, consider those cases where victory depended upon the forces of nature (e.g., Josh. 10:11). Or, consider God's instruction to Gideon to send some of the troops home, lest Israel say, "My own hand has delivered me" (Judg. 7:2).[5]

4. See John Howard Yoder, *The Politics of Jesus* (Grand Rapids: Eerdmans, 1972), pp. 79-89. Yoder followed this verse in entitling a chapter "God Will Fight for Us." He properly called attention to the requirement of reliance upon God, but he inferred too much (as we shall see below) when he concluded that "Wars are the outworking of the unwillingness of Israel . . . to trust Jahweh" (p. 83).

5. This subordination to God as "king" and "warrior" of Israel helps to explain the tradition of "holy war" in Israel. "Holy war" is not a biblical term, but if the term is taken to mean that both the power and the victory belong to God, then there is warrant for describing Israel's reflection concerning war as belonging to a "holy war" tradition. *Herem* is a biblical term; it refers to the grim practice of "the ban" in which no property is taken and no person taken captive; all is "devoted to destruction" (Josh. 6:21). As awful as the practice is, it should be observed that this practice, too, must be understood in the context of Israel's subordination to God. Since God wins the victory, to God belong the spoils of war. War was not to be fought for the sake of the booty. As awful as this practice is, it should also be observed that it puts a limit on the intentions appropriate to warfare. Finally, if the tradition of "holy war" means that the power and victory belong to God, then, as prophets more than once reminded kings, the ambition to be self-sufficient by military might and the exercise of that might in self-serving ways is not "holy."

There was no glorification of war itself in the conquest and settlement, surely no reliance upon the military might of the Israelites as the foundation of either its liberation or its possession of the land. On the other hand, there was no prohibition of war; pacifism as a code of conduct was not inferred from the celebration of God as "king" and "warrior" or from Moses' permission to "keep still" while God does the fighting. God was a "warrior," to be sure; one could hardly be "king" in that culture of violence without also being "warrior"; but this "warrior" took the side of the slave, of the oppressed, of the weak. God overturned the conventional measures and structures of power. Pharaohs and kings were defeated; slaves were delivered, made a people, and provided with a land. The people learned to fight, of course, but they also learned not to trust military power itself but the God whose story they told.

In the land Israel's allegiance to this king took the political form of an amphictyony, a loose federation of Israelite tribes united by covenant (Josh. 24). There was no central government, no standing army, and no king but God. In the exodus and gift of the land God had undone the conventional political and military power of the nations. Memory and loyalty made the people suspicious of the power of pharaohs and kings, suspicious of military establishments, and suspicious of the royal despotism that had ground them down and oppressed them. The covenant, after all, had established God as the great king, and some thought that theocracy required amphictyony. That vision of covenantal theocracy was voiced in Gideon's defiant rejection of the invitation of some that he should become king; "I will not rule over you, and my son will not rule over you; the LORD will rule over you," he said (Judg. 8:23). The suspicion of monarchy was expressed in Jotham's famous fable of the trees in search of a king (Judg. 9:7-15). And it found a voice in Samuel's warnings that a transition to monarchy was apostasy and that it would bring not only taxation and conscription but also a return to the old story of slavery and oppression (1 Sam. 8:10-18).

This suspicion of conventional political power, of course, did not eliminate political tasks in the land: Laws needed to be made and made known. Judgments needed to be rendered. The land and the people needed to be defended against attack. These tasks were undertaken in Israel's amphictyony by a motley collection of charismatic figures called "judges."[6] The record of the amphictyony was, at best, mixed. Their rejection of conventional power structures did not eliminate political ambition in the land (Judg. 9:1-6) or corrup-

---

6. The stories in Judges emphasize, of course, the military exploits of the judges, but there can be no doubt that at least some of those named (and probably others unnamed) provided something like legal review and judgment (see, e.g., Judg. 4:4-5; 1 Sam. 8:1-3).

tion (1 Sam. 8:3) or oppression or violence. The absence of mediating structures to represent the reign of God with some continuity gave free rein to chaos and anarchy. "In those days there was no king in Israel; all the people did what was right in their own eyes" (Judg. 21:25).

The record, however, was not quite as bad as that summary (from a later and monarchical perspective) suggests. There is, after all, the little collection of laws known as the Covenant Code (Exod. 20:22–23:33), which is to be dated to this period. It evidently borrowed from existing legal traditions of the ancient Near East, but it also set those traditions in the context of the conviction that God was king and lawgiver.[7] That context modified the existing traditions in at least one striking way: the prevailing concern of the Covenant Code is to protect and to provide for the oppressed, the poor, and the weak.

> You shall not wrong or oppress a resident alien, for you were aliens in the land of Egypt. You shall not abuse any widow or orphan. If you do abuse them, when they cry out to me, I will surely heed their cry. (Exod. 22:21-23)

> For six years you shall sow your land and gather in its yield; but the seventh year you shall let it rest and lie fallow, so that the poor of your people may eat. . . . You shall do the same with your vineyard, and with your olive orchard. (Exod. 23:10-11)

Theocracy revised legal traditions in service of the story of God's deliverance, covenant, and gift of the land. And it could also revise its institutions in service of the same story.

The Transition to Monarchy

The amphictyony gave way to monarchy. Judges gave way to kings. But make no mistake, God remained king in Israel. The stories of 1 Samuel 8 to 12 preserve the memories of a national debate about the transition from amphictyony to monarchy — and about the meaning of theocracy.

In 1 Samuel 8 it was the people who demanded a king. The demand displeased both Samuel and the Lord, who tells Samuel that the people have "not rejected you, but they have rejected me from being king over them" (1 Sam. 8:7). Samuel reported the Lord's displeasure and warned the people of the con-

7. See Paul D. Hanson, "The Theological Significance of Contradiction within the Book of the Covenant," in *Canon and Authority*, ed. George W. Coats and Burke O. Long (Philadelphia: Fortress, 1977), pp. 110-31.

scription and taxation and oppression that would be certain to mark "the ways of the king." The people refused to listen to Samuel and demanded a king, that they might "be like other nations" (8:20). The story had its origin, clearly, among those who thought that theocracy required amphictyony, who thought that to support a monarchy in Israel was apostasy, a turning back to the politics of Pharaoh and enslavement.

In 1 Samuel 9, however, a quite different story is told. Here it was God who appointed a king, God who initiated the transition from amphictyony to monarchy. Here it was not the apostasy of the people but God's own reign that brought about the reign of kings in the land. The transition to monarchy was God's way of responding to the Philistine threat, of bringing deliverance. God told Samuel to anoint Saul to be king; "He shall save my people from the hand of the Philistines; for I have seen the suffering of my people, because their outcry has come to me" (1 Sam. 9:16). The story clearly had its origin among those who had supported the transition to monarchy, who saw it not as the apostasy of the people but as the deliverance of God. As God had seen their suffering and heard their cry when Pharaoh oppressed them, so now God saw their suffering and heard their cry when the Philistines oppressed them. And as God took them from Egypt and gave them a land, so now God gave them a king in the land to secure both it and them.

The story of the transition continues in the next few chapters, and it continues to weave together contrasting dispositions to monarchy, as if apostasy were the warp and deliverance were the woof of the story woven. The ambiguity of political power is highlighted in the contrast between victory of Saul over the Ammonites, in which the deliverance of the Lord is provided (1 Sam. 11:5-15), and the farewell discourse of Samuel, in which the warnings about royal despotism are revisited (12:1-25).[8]

I have had students complain that the editors here seem unable to decide which story to tell. But that, I take it, is precisely the point in a way. There is no telling in the beginning whether monarchy would be a story of apostasy or of deliverance. The story of monarchy might be a story of deliverance if the king

8. That the ancient debate was preserved in Israel is itself remarkable. The Deuteronomic Historian, of course, has his own reasons for presenting the transition to monarchy as both apostasy and deliverance. He made considerable use of more ancient records and traditions in his address to the exilic community. That the traditions suspicious of monarchy were preserved through the long period of monarchy (and available to him) is remarkable. One may be confident that the monarchs would have preferred it if the ancient voices accusing monarchy of apostasy and tyranny had been silenced. The prophets, however, kept such voices alive. (And the work of the Deuteronomic Historian, of course, which includes Joshua, Judges, Samuel, and Kings, is also known as the "former prophets.")

exercised authority in the land under God, if the king did not exalt himself but the poor and powerless, if the king kept faith with both God and the people. But the story would be a story of apostasy if the king regarded his power as self-sufficient and used it to exalt himself. The concentration of power and the continuity of power in the office of a king could remedy anarchy within the land and respond to threats like that of the Philistines, but such power was not only gift but also temptation. And it was a temptation one could hardly expect a king to resist.

The advocates of the amphictyony were right in this: Because God is king, political authority among the people is derived from God — and answers to God! There should be no return to the royal despotism and absolutism of the pharaohs and kings from whom God provided deliverance. But they were wrong in thinking that theocracy required amphictyony, as if the rule of God depended on it, as if God's reign could be reduced to it. And they were wrong in thinking that the amphictyony was an unambiguous institutionalization of God's rule, as if its chaos and corruption were consistent with the cause of God. God's reign transcended both amphictyony and monarchy; the form of political life was less important than fidelity and faithfulness within it.

The advocates of the transition to monarchy were right in this: The cause of God could be served by the continuity and stability of power that monarchy could provide. Because God is king, monarchy, too, can find its origin in God's deliverance and be answerable to God. Let a king, therefore, be anointed, and commissioned to perform the reign of God. But they were wrong in confusing the authority of the king with the authority of God — and in thinking that a king could be trusted against the temptations of despotism and absolutism. Let the king, therefore, and the power of the king be restrained by other institutions, by law and prophecy, which are independent of the king even as they, too, are dependent upon God.[9] God's reign may transcend the particular form of political life, but it nevertheless bears on it. Fidelity and faithfulness to God attended also to the forms of political life — and finally insisted on institutional restraints on the power of the king. Theocratic reflection rejected absolutism.

God remained the great king. The king of Israel ruled under God. The sign of royalty in Israel was, therefore, not the pride of power but humility. The point was made positively in the midst of the narratives of the transition. "I am only a Benjaminite," Saul said, "from the least of the tribes of Israel, and my family is the humblest of all the families of the tribe of Benjamin" (1 Sam. 9:21). God made the least greatest. That was the sign of God's reign. And under God, the king — or any other political authority — was called to perform such a

9. See further Oliver O'Donovan, *The Desire of the Nations*, p. 65.

358

reign, to protect the poor and the powerless in the land and to provide for them. Theocrats were prepared to celebrate such a king.

God remained the great and real king of Israel. The king of Israel ruled under God. Hard on the heels of the transition to monarchy, the point was made negatively. When Saul's disobedience led to the selection of David to rule in his place (1 Sam. 13–16), King Saul and all the people learned soon enough that the king in Israel was answerable to God. And hard on the heels of the prophet Nathan's oracle that God would establish David's throne forever (2 Sam. 7:8-17),[10] when David used his power to have Uriah, husband of Bathsheba, killed in battle, the same prophet announced the judgment of God against him (2 Sam. 12). He told David a story of a rich man who had oppressed a poor man, and when David angrily insisted on being told the identity of the unjust and unpitying scoundrel so that he could be punished, Nathan said, "You are the man!" (12:7). This was not just a personal rebuke. Because David (or any king) ruled under God, he was required to exercise compassion and act with justice; he was not to permit the power of pride or the pride of power to tempt him to become an oppressor himself. When kings were proud or unfaithful to the covenant or oppressive, theocrats would bravely remind them that they were answerable to God — and to the Law and the prophets.

Monarchy

This was the warp and woof of theocratic reflection concerning the monarchy: Let a king be anointed and commissioned to perform the reign of God. But let the king and the power of the king be restrained by the independent authority of God's Law and prophets. The warp was emphasized in the royal psalms and by the storyteller scholars call the Yahwist. The woof was represented by the prophets. The fabric of faithful theocratic reflection during the monarchy required both.

The Politics of the Yahwist

The theocratic hope for a king anointed and commissioned to perform the reign of God was voiced in the prayer that was probably part of the cultic anointing of the king (or of the anniversary of his accession), Psalm 72:

10. To which David replied humbly, "Who am I . . . that you have brought me thus far?" (2 Sam. 7:18).

Give the king your justice, O God,
   and your righteousness to a king's son.
May he judge your people with righteousness,
   and your poor with justice.
May the mountains yield prosperity for the people,
   and the hills, in righteousness.
May he defend the cause of the poor of the people,
    give deliverance to the needy,
    and crush the oppressor. . . .
In his days may righteousness flourish
   and peace abound, until the moon is no more.
May he have dominion from sea to sea,
   and from the River to the ends of the earth.
May his foes bow down before him,
   and his enemies lick the dust. . . .
May all kings fall down before him,
   all nations give him service.
For he delivers the needy when they call,
   the poor and those who have no helper.
He has pity on the weak and the needy,
   and saves the lives of the needy.
From oppression and violence he redeems their life;
   and precious is their blood in his sight.
Long may he live! . . .
May all nations be blessed in him;
   may they pronounce him happy.
Blessed be the LORD, the God of Israel,
   who alone does wondrous things.

Psalm 72 is one of those "royal psalms," psalms associated with the life of the king.[11] Most of them, like Psalm 72, are intercessions on behalf of the king, because Israel's hope is not in the king but in God, not in the king's chariots and horses but in God (Ps. 20:7), not in the king's judgment but in God's justice, not in the king's dominion but in God's. The theocratic hope during the monarchy, however, is that, under God, the king will perform the deliverance, the justice, and the blessing of God.

    The Yahwist shared that hope.[12] During the empire of David and Solomon

11. The others include Psalms 2, 20, 21, 45, 89, and 110.
12. On the Yahwist see Hans Walter Wolff, "The Kerygma of the Yahwist," in Walter Brueggemann and Hans Walter Wolff's *The Vitality of Old Testament Traditions,* second ed. (Atlanta: John Knox, 1982), pp. 41-66. A second example of theocratic reflection

the Yahwist remembered and retold the ancient stories of Israel. It was the first installment of the great work that would become the Torah. The Yahwist did not write these stories down in order to preserve some objective historical record of an ancient history. He wrote to shape the life, including the political life, of the people of God at that particular moment in the history of Israel, to form a politics a little more worthy of the story of God's reign, of theocracy. He wrote not just to record Israel's history but also to shape that history, to give some direction to political life under the reign of God. Consider the story of the ancestors.

The Yahwist story of the ancestors starts with the call of Abraham (Gen. 12:1-4).

> Now the LORD said to Abram, "Go from your country and your kindred and your father's house to the land that I will show you. I will make of you a great nation, and I will bless you, and make your name great, so that you will be a blessing. I will bless those who bless you, and the one who curses you I will curse; and in you all the families of the earth shall be blessed."
> So Abram went, as the LORD had told him. . . .

The story is that God (or Yahweh, the LORD, for the Yahwist uses the name of God from the very beginning) came to Abram and said, "Pack up, man! It's time to go." And the story is that Abram went. It could not have been easy, and it was probably harder for Sarah, but they went. They packed up and went — and when they left, they were not exactly sure where they were going. This God of theirs had only said, "Go to the land that I will show you." It could not have been easy, but they set out on a journey in obedience to the God who called them and with faith in the God who promised to protect and bless them.

This little story of calling and obedience, of promise and hope, of course, is part of a larger story. The larger story begins, of course, "in the beginning" or at least "in the day that the LORD God made the earth and the heavens" (Gen. 2:4b).[13] It was a good beginning, a hopeful beginning. But Adam spoiled his

---

within Torah may be found within the book of Deuteronomy itself. The words and statutes of Deuteronomy, presented as the last words of Moses, are almost certainly to be ascribed to a reformer during the time of Josiah's reform, around 622 B.C.E. And that reformer insists that the reign of God puts limits on the authority of kings. Monarchy is not inconsistent with the rule of God in the land of promise, but royal despotism is. The king under God is to be marked not by greed or by pride but by humility, "neither exalting himself above other members of the community nor turning aside from the commandment" (Deut. 17:20). See pp. 369-73 in this volume.

13. Genesis 1:1–2:4a is priestly material, dating from the exile. Genesis 2:4b is the beginning of the story for the Yahwist.

chances by sinning. And hard on the heels of human sin came the curse (Gen. 3:14-19), which fell heavy on God's good creation.

Everything that's wrong with the world can be traced to that curse, and that curse can be traced to the horrible reality of human sin. Too proud to trust God, human beings tried to seize the blessing that could only be received. What they got was not blessing but the curse. It fell on the serpent, on the ground, on the woman and on the man, on their relationship, and on their children (Gen. 4:11). The signs of it were patriarchy and pain, shame and murder.

The curse was finally no less grasping than human pride. It reached out further and further to corrupt and destroy more and more. The curse laid claim not only to human hearts but also to human culture and to all the nations of the earth. The signs of it were everywhere: in enmity and pride, in a flood, and in the confusion of tongues at the Tower of Babel. The Tower of Babel (Gen. 11) is something of a climax to this story. Human pride repeated once more the sin of Adam, grasping at what can only be received, and the curse fell heavy on the nations, too. They could not understand one another; they could not make themselves understood. If they had known the limerick, they might have recited it:

God's plan made a hopeful beginning,
But man spoiled his chances by sinning.
   We hope that the story
   Will end in God's glory,
But at present the other side's winning.

That's the story up to this call of Abram. It's the story of a curse that finally claimed all the nations. It's a horrible story, a story of hatred and murder, a story of incest and rape, a story of hopelessness and homelessness. It's the story of the human alienation from God and from each other and from the creation itself. It's a story of life and of common life bereft of the blessing of God.[14]

But the curse was not the end of the story! God would not let sin have the last word, would not let the curse be the end of the story. And that's where the little story of the call and promise of God — and of the obedience and faith of Abraham and Sarah — comes in. It's a new beginning — and for the nations, too. God called Abram and Sarah to begin a journey and promised to bless them — and to bless "all the families of the earth" (Gen. 12:3) by them. God

14. It is surely no accident that the word for "bless" does not occur in the Yahwist materials in Genesis 2-11, but suddenly appears five times in the call of Abram in Genesis 12:1-3.

called Abram and Sarah to begin a project, and the project was to bless the nations!

It's a new beginning, but it's a long journey, and in the stories that follow the journey gets off to an unpromising start. In the chapters that follow you wonder sometimes, or at least you wonder whether Abraham and Sarah wondered sometimes, whether God's promises could really be counted on. God had promised them children, a nation of children, children like the sands of the beach, like the stars of the sky. But where are these promised children? When they are pushing one hundred, Abraham and Sarah count as their children an adopted slave and Ishmael, who was born of Hagar. God had promised them land, a great land. But when Sarah dies, the only land Abraham owns is that little plot of ground in which he buried her. God had promised them protection. But they must have felt vulnerable when famine forced them to go down to Egypt and to live there as aliens (Gen. 12:10-20). That's when Abraham told Sarah to lie about their relationship. "Tell these Egyptians that you are my sister," he said, "because if they think you are my wife, they will want me dead and you available." They must have had their times of wondering about this God of theirs and about the promises on which they staked their lives.

But if Abraham and Sarah wondered sometimes whether God could be trusted, God surely had reasons to wonder whether Abraham and Sarah could be counted on. That story of Abraham's deception in his effort to protect himself in Egypt, after all, comes hard on the heels of this little story of Abraham's obedience and faith. And when God assured Abraham that he and Sarah would have a child, Sarah laughed (Gen. 18:9-12). God must have scratched his head on days like those, wondering what he was thinking when he thought to begin a project of blessing the nations with this pair.

The new beginning was full of promises, but not very promising. Even so, God was faithful to the promises — and Abraham and Sarah did continue the journey God had put them on. Centuries later the Yahwist told these stories when Israel was an empire. He told the stories that the people might learn to count their blessings and to count them as the blessings of this promise-making God of Abraham and Sarah. Had God promised children to Abraham and Sarah? At the time of empire the children of Abraham and Sarah could hardly be counted. God keeps his promises. God had blessed them. Had God promised them land? The empire stretched from the Nile to the Euphrates (Gen. 15:18), a rich and good land. God keeps his promises. God had blessed them. Had God promised them security? The empire was (or seemed) invulnerable. God keeps his promises. God had blessed them. But the Yahwist orients these promises and their fulfillment to another promise. He tells the stories to orient the continuing journey of faith and obedience to this last promise, "in you all the families of the earth shall be blessed."[15]

There were some in the empire, you may be sure, who regarded the story as having reached its conclusion in the conquest and in empire. There were some who would have been content to celebrate the blessings of God upon the children of Abraham and to forget the promise that all the nations would be blessed by them. But that promise was the project of God. God would not let it be forgotten. And neither would the Yahwist.

Abraham and Sarah were put on a journey toward a blessing to all the nations. Israel was blessed so that it could be a blessing to all the nations, including and especially those now under their power, under their dominion. That promise of God, that project of God, that calling, may not be forgotten or neglected. And the Yahwist reminded the people of it not just by this story of the call of Abraham and Sarah, but again and again and yet again.

There is the Yahwist's story of Sodom and Gomorrah (Gen. 18–19). God had just announced that the aged Sarah would have a baby and was about to leave Abraham to carry out the destruction of Sodom and Gomorrah. Just then, however, God pauses and asks himself, "Shall I hide from Abraham what I am about to do, seeing that Abraham shall become a great and mighty nation, and all the nations of the earth shall be blessed in him?" (Gen. 18:17-18; notice the Yahwist's reminder that Abraham is to be a blessing to all the nations). And when Abraham hears of the plan to destroy the cities, what does he do? What he does *not* do is say, "It's about time!" He does not say, "Good! I'll bring marshmallows." He argues with God. He tries to talk God out of this plan. He intercedes on behalf of Sodom and Gomorrah. He does not delight in this project of destruction. It is no accident that at the end of the story, after Lot has escaped, we hear of the births of Moab and ben-Ammi, and it is no accident that we are told that they are the ancestors of the Moabites and Ammonites "to this day" (Gen. 19:37, 38). There were people "in that day," in the day of empire, who would have delighted in the destruction of the Moabites and the Ammonites! There were people, probably people who had the ear of the king, who wanted to destroy them. But the story of Abraham set a different political agenda. If they were on a journey of faith and obedience like Abraham, they would not delight in the destruction of Moab and Ammon. They would intercede on their behalf. They would be their advocates. They would use their power to be a blessing to the nations, not to curse them.

Or consider the Yahwist's story of Isaac and Abimelech, king of the Philistines (Gen. 26). God repeats to Isaac the promises to Abraham, including

---

15. This promise is emphasized both by its position and by its grammar. (Only this last clause is in the perfect tense.) See further, Wolff, "The Kerygma of the Yahwist," pp. 47-49.

— lest the reader forget — this one: "all the nations of the earth shall gain blessing for themselves through your offspring" (26:4). In the middle of the chapter
Isaac lives his father's story in one way. Afraid that the Philistines might kill
[him] for the sake of [his wife] Rebekah," he tells "the men of the place" that she
is his sister (26:7). But at the end of the chapter he lives his father's story in a
better way. Although the Philistines sent him away and stole his wells, Isaac does
not seek revenge. He makes a peace treaty with the Philistines, a covenant to do
no harm. Thus he is a blessing to the Philistines. It is no accident that Abimelech
is here identified as the king of the Philistines. It is not historically accurate, but
it is no mistake. The Philistines were not yet around when Isaac was alive. They
entered the land from the sea about the same time that the Jews were entering
the Promised Land by crossing the Jordan. Nevertheless, this is no mistake by the
Yahwist. The Philistines were there in the days of empire. David had put an end
to the Philistine threat, and the Philistines had been subjugated to the empire.
You may be sure that there was no little resentment about the ways the
Philistines had treated Israel in the past. It was a history of economic oppression,
of political quarrels, and of military conflict. There were people "in that day," in
the days of empire, who wanted revenge against the Philistines. There were people, probably people who had the ear of the king, who wanted to push them back
into the sea (but without their boats). The story of Isaac and the Philistine king
set a different political agenda. If the promises of Abraham were handed down
to them as they had been to Isaac, and if they took up the journey of faith and
obedience like Abraham and Isaac, then they would not simply seek revenge
against the Philistines. They would seek a covenant of peace with them. They
would do them no harm. They would bless them. They would use their power to
be a blessing to the nations, not to curse them.

Or, consider the story of Jacob, who was a blessing to Laban, the Ara-
mean. Laban said it himself, "The LORD has blessed me because of you" (Gen.
30:27). Jacob was a blessing to Laban, first, by his famous skills with livestock,
and then, after Laban had exploited him, by his willingness to make a covenant
of peace (31:51-52). The promise and the calling to be a blessing to the nations
extended to Jacob and to all the descendents of Abraham and to Laban and to
the Arameans and to all the nations touched by Israel's power.

Or, consider the story of Joseph. By his administrative skill he was a blessing not only to the Egyptians but to all the nations of the earth. When seven
years of abundant harvest were followed by seven years of drought and famine,
people were going hungry all over the world. But Joseph had stockpiled grain,
and all the nations were fed. The project of God to bless the nations made a little headway against the curse of drought and famine through Joseph's skill and
obedience.

Such stories were told by the Yahwist in the time of empire to remind the people of God of God's promise and calling. The people of God were ready to celebrate the blessings bestowed on them and on their king, but they too often and too easily forgot that God's *blessing* was also a *calling* to bless the nations, that God's *promise* was also a *vocation* to bless the nations. The journey of faith and obedience that began with Abraham and Sarah does not delight in the destruction and trouble of others. It does not seek revenge. It does not hoard or waste. The calling is to bless the nations. That is the political vocation of God's people: to intercede for the nations, to be their advocate, to use our skills and powers for their good, not to their harm, to seek peace, and to feed the hungry of all nations. That was God's project in calling Abraham and Sarah. It was, the Yahwist said, God's project in the blessings upon the empire. And it remains God's project until it is completed, until the end of the story, until that day in God's good future when the curse is finally and fully lifted from the earth (Rev. 22:3). In the meantime, God's people still journey on with obedience and hope toward that future, remembering the promise and the project of God to bless the nations — also politically.

The Prophets

The vision of the Yahwist was worthy of the memory of Israel, but the monarchy proved unworthy of the Yahwist's vision. The empire took its lessons from those "other nations" admired by the advocates of monarchy long ago (1 Sam. 8:5), not from the Yahwist. David and Solomon increasingly followed the patterns of royal absolutism learned from Egypt, Phoenicia, and the Canaanites. There were reasons for theocrats to celebrate the achievements of David and Solomon: the deliverance from the oppression of the Philistines, the prosperity of empire, the security of possession of the land, not to mention David's songs and Solomon's wisdom. But there were also reasons for theocrats to remind both the king and the people that God was the great king of Israel and that they remained answerable to God: Royal absolutism had licensed oppression within Israel, most notably perhaps in the forced labor Solomon used in his building projects (1 Kings 5:13-18; 9:15-22). The prosperity was not shared; Jerusalem and the royal court prospered while the poor lost possession of their land; a royal census even eliminated the old tribal boundaries that secured a share in the possession of the land in favor of districts more efficient for taxation and conscription (2 Sam. 24; 1 Kings 4:7-19). The security fashioned by royal absolutism was quickly threatened by rebellion and resentment (2 Sam. 15–18, 20; 1 Kings 1–2). When Solomon died and Rehoboam quite deliberately threatened to continue a policy of oppression and absolutism (1 Kings 12:1-14), the tribes of the north would have no more to do with David's line. The land was broken into north and south, Israel and Judah. The tragedy of division was followed by the greater tragedy of the continuing neglect of the political implications of the story of exodus and Sinai and the gift of the land. Royal absolutism brought not a blessing upon all the nations but the threat of judgment against Israel and Judah.

The theocratic demand that the king and the power of the king should be subordinated to — and not identified with — the reign of God was given voice most eloquently by the prophets. In the prophets "the reign of God" was both assumption and promise. "Thus says the LORD . . . ," they said, adopting a form taken from the language of diplomacy; they were couriers delivering the message of the great king. The prophets were — and were called to be — an independent voice of the rule of God in Israel. They proceeded by way of reminder, remembering the ancient stories of exodus, of covenant, of the gift of the land, and even (in the south, at least) of the way and will of God with David and Zion. They remembered the stories over-against royal despotism and injustice, challenging readings of the story that licensed complacency and injustice.[16]

Prophets confronted the kings with their reminder of God's sovereignty. Nathan rebuked David because he had no pity (2 Sam. 12:6). Gad, known as "David's seer" (2 Sam. 24:11), courageously condemned the census.[17] Elijah confronted Ahab after Ahab had seized the vineyard of Naboth for a palace vegetable garden (1 Kings 21). Again and again the prophets reminded kings of a greater king, the King of kings. Again and again they announced the judgment of God against the king. "Listen, O house of the king! For the judgment pertains to you" (Hos. 5:1). Again and again they insisted that the sign of royalty was humility and that the sign of legitimate authority was the protection of the poor and powerless.

It was not just the kings whom prophets reminded of the reign of God, of course, nor kings alone to whom the judgment applied. Many others were indicted for infidelity to covenant, especially the beneficiaries of royal despotism who had exchanged responsibility to God for the benefits of the king's patron-

---

16. See, for example, the turn Amos gave to the tradition of exodus and election, a tradition that had probably been used to assure the blessing of God regardless of political and social injustice. "Hear this word that the LORD has spoken against you, O people of Israel, against the whole family that I brought up out of the land of Egypt:

You only have I known of all the families of the earth;
therefore I will punish you for all your iniquities." (Amos 3:1-2)

17. It is noteworthy that the punishment of plague was averted when David insisted on paying for an offering instead of simply seizing it (2 Sam. 24:18-25).

age. The prophets condemned the priests who put the worship of God in the service of the king, and they mocked the ceremonies that pretended to worship God without prompting justice in the land (e.g., Isa. 1:12-17; Jer. 7:21-23; Hos. 6:6; Amos 5:21-24; Mic. 6:6-8). The prophets derided those who claimed to be prophets while simply saying what the king wanted to hear (e.g., Jer. 8:11; 23:9-40; 28:1-17; Mic. 3:5-8). They denounced the judges who took a bribe and did not give the poor a hearing (e.g., Isa. 5:23, 10:1-4; Ezek. 22:12; Amos 5:10-15; Mic. 7:3). They announced the judgment of God against merchants who cheated the poor (e.g., Hos. 12:7-9; Amos 8:4-6; Mic. 6:11). They condemned the privileged who were complacent with injustice (e.g., Isa. 3:16-24; Amos 4:1-3; 6:1). They even heaped scorn upon the boasts of the mighty empires surrounding Judah and Israel (e.g., Isa. 10:5-19; 30; 31). They humbled the proud with their oracles of judgment and beat against injustice with their words.

The prophets announced not only the judgment of God but also, on the far side of judgment, the good future of God's reign. God was faithful to the project of liberation, justice, and security that had been made known in the exodus, covenant, and gift of the land. That project was to be David's project, too, and the prophets reminded the people not only of the ancient traditions of amphictyony but also of the hopes for David. "A shoot shall come out from the stump of Jesse," Isaiah said (Isa. 11:1). "The spirit of the LORD shall rest on him"; "with righteousness he shall judge the poor, and decide with equity for the meek of the earth"; and by his humble reign God will bless the nation and the nations, bringing peace to earth (Isa. 11:2-11; cf. also Isa. 9:2-7; Zech. 9:9-10; 12:1–13:1).

The prophets were neither revolutionaries nor policy-makers, but they reminded policy-makers of the story and of their theocratic responsibility to the great king. The prophets never led a movement to replace the monarchy or to return to the political forms of amphictyony.[18] They insisted on obedience to God, the great king, within the existing institutions. They recognized more clearly than most the ambiguity of power, but they did not repudiate political power because of its ambiguity; instead, they insisted more daringly than most on the accountability of power. The king was neither divinized nor demonized; he was called to account.

The oracles of judgment (and the words of promise) did not simply announce some fated future; they called for a response. The judgment might be

---

18. Ironically, prophecy had presided over the transition to monarchy (1 Sam. 9:15–10:16). Nathan had blessed the Davidic dynasty (2 Sam. 7:8-17). The revolt of Jeroboam, too, had been blessed by a prophet's words (1 Kings 11:29-39), although Jeroboam was later repudiated by the same prophetic voice (1 Kings 14:7-11).

avoided by repentance, and the promise might be forfeited by infidelity.[19] The repentance called for, and the fidelity demanded, was not simply a matter of certain cultic ceremonies; it was a matter of the performance of God's reign in the common life; it was a matter of rescuing the poor, judging justly, sharing the "possession" of the land, and blessing the nations.

Political Reform in Deuteronomy

Josiah repented. After the corruption and infidelity of the reigns of Manasseh and Amon, Josiah repented — and undertook a religious and political reform in Judah (621 B.C.E.). He humbled himself (2 Kings 22:11-20), renewed the covenant (2 Kings 23:1-3), and undertook to reform the common life of Judah. Some version of the book of Deuteronomy clearly played a significant role in Josiah's reform. The story, of course, is that "the book of the law" was discovered by Hilkiah the high priest, not that he wrote it. There probably was an earlier version, itself a reworking of still more ancient traditions, which was found and then edited in the service of Josiah's reform. At any rate, large parts of Deuteronomy seem to have been written in the service of the religious and political reform of Josiah, itself undertaken in the service of covenant renewal and the rule of God. Deuteronomy provides, therefore, a glimpse at political reform in the theocratic tradition.

Consider, first, the invitation to readers in the seventh century to imagine and to identify with the people about to enter the land for the first time, to make that story their own story. Deuteronomy presents itself as Moses' words to the people as they look across the Jordan toward their future. Moses sees there "the land that the LORD promised" (Deut. 8:1), "a good land" (8:7), a land of prosperity and plenty (8:8-10). He sees there the fulfillment of God's promise in election and in exodus, the fidelity of God to covenant, the end to the judgment of the wilderness, but he also sees there, in the gift of God, a great danger. Moses warns them, "Take care that you do not forget the LORD your God" (8:11). The prospect of entry into the land of promise and prosperity — and into political responsibility within the land — required that certain questions be faced: How shall we live in that land in memory of the liberation of slaves? How shall we display the salvation God worked and works for those on the margins of social life while we build a common life in this future? How shall

19. See Jeremiah 26:16-19 for an example of Jerusalem's avoidance of the judgment announced by Micah through the repentance of Hezekiah, and consider the forfeiture of Hosea's promise of the restoration of Israel by its refusal to turn.

we conduct ourselves in this land of promise in fidelity to covenant? How shall we reflect the justice of God in the exercise of the authority that derives from God and answers to God? How shall we secure this blessing of God, and how shall we share this possession? How shall the rule of God take effect in our praise and in our politics?[20]

Leave aside for a moment the particular ways Josiah's reform answered those questions. The adoption of this particular moment as the locus for political reflection is itself significant. Deuteronomy invited its readers to identify imaginatively with those rescued slaves and nomads about to enter the land of promise and political responsibility within it. As countless social contract theories have invited us to participate imaginatively in the original contract in order to test our political institutions and judgments, so Deuteronomy invited its readers to participate in the original covenant.[21]

The similarity is obvious enough: both the social contract tradition and this theocratic tradition of covenant look back to an original moment as somehow normative for political reflection, and as instructive concerning the meaning of justice. The contrasts, however, are no less obvious. The social contract tradition (ironically) wants to do without tradition. The theocratic tradition of covenant seeks to initiate people into a tradition. The social contract tradition seeks to liberate us from the particular communities and stories that form our character so that a rational, universal, and peaceable community may be founded. The theocratic tradition of covenant seeks to form a community of liberation and justice in memory of the story of exodus, covenant, and the gift

---

20. See the excellent essay by Gerald W. Schlabach, "Deuteronomic or Constantinian: What Is the Most Basic Problem of Christian Social Ethics?" in *The Wisdom of the Cross: Essays in Honor of John Howard Yoder*, ed. Stanley Hauerwas et al. (Grand Rapids: Eerdmans, 1999), pp. 449-71. Schlabach acknowledges the Constantinian problem and the power of John Howard Yoder's account of it, but he argues that the more basic problem for Christian social ethics is encountered in the question posed by the Deuteronomic situation. To make the Constantinian problem the basic problem, as many pacifists do, regarding Constantinianism not only as a fourth-century phenomenon but also as emblematic of Christian unfaithfulness and compromise with violence and coercion, nurtures a social ethic focused on the avoidance of evil. To make the Deuteronomic problem the basic problem focuses instead on "the challenge of embracing the good in a faithful manner" (p. 450).

21. Note the persistent repetition of "today" in Deuteronomy (e.g., 7:11; 8:19; 15:15; 26:17; 27:9, etc.) and passages like 5:2-3: "The LORD our God made a covenant with us at Horeb [the name for Mt. Sinai in Deuteronomy]. Not with our ancestors did the LORD make this covenant, but with us, who are all of us here alive today." The covenant at Sinai is not simply an event of some distant past. It is a present reality, constitutive of identity and determinative for discernment, for those addressed.

of the land and in hope of God's *shalom*. Both the social contract tradition and the theocratic tradition of covenant tell a story, a story in terms of which people make sense of the political world and understand their political responsibilities, but the stories are different.

The story of contract is told, for example, in John Rawls's narrative. The story is that rational and self-interested individuals, under a "veil of ignorance" concerning their particular identities and stories,[22] contract to secure their interests and freedom by limiting them. They contract, that is, to accept Rawls's two principles of justice: maximum freedom and presumptive equality.[23] This story of a social contract, like the stories it wants to eliminate, does form the character of those who own it as their story. If this is the story we tell, we should not be shocked when, by it, we form self-interested individuals, individuals who understand contracts but not covenant, individuals who will only ever experience justice as a boundary that they must not trespass in the pursuit of their own interests or as a weapon to protect themselves from those who are different from them. If this is the story we tell, we should not be surprised if, by it, we form a society of wary strangers, a society with tolerance, to be sure, but the sort of stingy and tightfisted tolerance that will let the stranger be as long as the stranger stays out of the way.

The theocratic tradition of covenant tells a different story, a story of exodus, covenant, and the gift of a land. God has created a people and continues to rule them. Political authority is derived from God, the great king; and political responsibility finally answers to God, the God who heard the cries of the slave, the God who loves justice, the God who intends the security and peace of the land God gives. Where this story is owned as the story of community, justice is not just a minimal constraint upon individual self-interest; it is a communal

22. There is something internally inconsistent about this story — this story that we can do without stories. Moreover, this story is pure fiction. None of us can simply step out of our identities, vacate our location in space and time, in order to adopt a rational, universal, and impartial perspective.

23. "Maximum freedom" is the principle that each is entitled to the maximum freedom compatible with a like freedom for all others. "Presumptive equality" is the principle that inequalities in distribution are to be considered arbitrary and, therefore, unjust unless there is equal opportunity and unless those inequalities work out in the long run to the advantage of the least well off. I like those principles, frankly, but others who stood in the tradition of the Enlightenment and social contract quickly challenged them. Robert Nozick, for example, was unconvinced, rejecting the principle of "presumptive equality." The debate between Rawls and Nozick went on so long and so interminably that new categories of people now need to be covered under the "veil of ignorance." Some will be Rawlsians, and some will be Nozickians — but who?

commitment to listen to the cry of the poor in the land, to lift those up who had been beaten down, to share the "possession" of the land.

In Deuteronomy the political reformers associated with Josiah invited Judah to identify with the original covenant. The great danger for those slaves looking across the Jordan to their future was forgetfulness, and the great danger for the Southern Kingdom several centuries later was forgetfulness. The test for political discernment remained always the memory of God's works and way, and that remembering shaped Israel's political thought and common life through a variety of circumstances and institutions into a theocratic tradition, a tradition which was at work in Josiah's reform.

For Josiah's reform to remember the covenant did not mean that the people should pretend to live in the amphictyony or ape the institutions of the past. Fidelity required creativity, and reform required something better than an anachronistic retrieval of some ancient code. So, we turn back briefly to the content of Josiah's reform. Deuteronomy did, after all, provide some particular answers to the questions prompted by the imaginative identification with those slaves and nomads looking across the Jordan to the land of promise. The answers provided by Deuteronomy, however, were not a timeless ideal, and the statutes provided by the Deuteronomic Code were not a timeless code. They were, rather, timely theocratic responses to new and pressing circumstances, to the idolatry and corruption of the reigns of Manasseh and Amon. The circle of reformers around Josiah revisited and reworked ancient theocratic traditions and laws. Like the makers of the ancient Covenant Code, they nudged the received legal tradition toward a code at once fitting to the circumstances and a little more worthy of the story of God's reign.

As a timely response to idolatry and forgetfulness (and unlike earlier law codes) Deuteronomy insisted that the practice of worship at the innumerable cultic sites in the land be forsaken and that the people gather for worship at Jerusalem (Deut. 12; contrast Exod. 20:24 and 1 Kings 3:4). In response to the corruption and injustices during the reign of Manasseh and Amon Deuteronomy insisted on institutions of justice that kept faith with God and the people (Deut. 1:16-18; 10:17-18; 16:18-20). There is, in memory of the story, a special concern for the weak, the poor, the disinherited, the sojourner, and for all those who have no power to press their claims. "[God] executes justice for the fatherless and the widow, and loves the sojourner, giving him food and clothing. Love the sojourner therefore; for you were sojourners in the land of Egypt" (10:18-19 RSV). Every seven years debts are to be forgiven, and one must not refuse a loan to a poor neighbor because the seventh year is approaching (15:1-11; cf. Exod. 23:10-11). In its revision of the law for the release of slaves in the seventh year Deuteronomy reminds its hearers of the exodus and demands that slaves be not only released but furnished "liberally" (Deut.15:12-18; cf. Exod. 21:2-11). And in provisions that would have been anachronistic at the time of conquest and settlement — and until the transition to monarchy — Deuteronomy demanded that the king be humble, that he serve God and the people, not "exalting himself above other members of the community" (17:14-20).

Such was the shape of political reform in Deuteronomy: a timely, faithful, and creative application of the theocratic tradition, not a timeless code. Josiah's reform, however, did not avert the catastrophes of the destruction of Jerusalem by Nebuchadnezzar of Babylon and exile (587 B.C.E.), events which would require enormous fidelity to endure and remarkable creativity to encompass within the theocratic tradition.

Theocracy in Exile

"By the rivers of Babylon — there we sat down and there we wept," the psalmist said (Ps. 137:1), giving voice to the pain of exile. "There we wept when we remembered Zion." Jerusalem had been destroyed; the temple, reduced to a heap of rubble. And the Babylonians mocked and teased and laughed at their pain; and God was mocked, too. "Sing us one of the songs of Zion!" the mockers said (137:3). The songs of Zion had announced God's perpetual protection of Jerusalem and its temple — but now they both lay in ruins and in ashes. "Sing that song about how 'God is in the midst of the city' and 'it shall not be moved'" (46:5). "Sing that one about walking about Zion, counting its towers and considering its ramparts, 'that you may tell the next generation' that your God is God indeed (48:12-14). Sing that one and consider the ramparts smashed and the towers leveled. And we and Marduk will laugh," they said.

Marduk, of course, was one of the gods of the Babylonians, the patron deity of Babylon, the king of the gods. There by the rivers of Babylon the Jews heard again and again — and must have half believed — that Marduk had won the victory over Yahweh. Is not Babylon the great city and Jerusalem a heap? Is not Marduk the great king of the gods, and the God of Abraham, Isaac, and Jacob a phony and a failure? And there by the rivers of Babylon they heard the Babylonians sing their own song, the *Enuma Elish*.[24] It is a song of creation, a song of Marduk's power and victory. It tells the story of how Marduk — primeval light, who makes his abode in the sun — became the champion of the gods against Tiamat, the watery forces of chaos, and of how the gods granted to

24. See James B. Pritchard, ed., *Ancient Near Eastern Texts Relating to the Old Testament* (Princeton, N.J.: Princeton University Press, 1950), pp. 60-72.

Marduk "kingship over the universe entire." It tells how Marduk subdued Tiamat in battle, how he cut Tiamat into two and divided the waters above from the waters below with a firmament, how he made an abode of dry land on the earth and stationed the stars as an abode for the gods. It tells how Marduk then made man from the blood of Kingu, Tiamat's consort, to be a servant to the gods. And it tells how Marduk then rested in Babylon, how he celebrated his victory in Babylon, where he still sits enthroned with Babylon's king. "Don't you love our songs?" they said. "Sing us one of yours."

Those were days of despair and anguish, nights of doubt and pain. And still, they remembered! They remembered Jerusalem and its temple (Ps. 137:5-6). They remembered the land and its goodness. They remembered the liberation of the exodus, and the presence of God in the wilderness. The memories themselves were sometimes painful in exile, but they taught their spirit to hope.

A New Story of Creation

There by the waters of Babylon a priest taught the exiles a new song of creation, and taught them to sing it in defiance of Marduk.[25] "In the beginning," it begins. In the beginning God — not Marduk, but God — created heaven and earth. The watery forces of chaos are there, but it is God who moves upon them, not Marduk who subdues them. And God said, "Let there be light," and there was light. The light is not divine; it is not Marduk of holy terror; the light is God's creature, too, the gift of day. "And God saw that the light was good." The light is not divine, but it is good. It was God — not Marduk, but God — who divided the waters in two, made a firmament to span the earth and called it heaven, made a dry land to appear and called it Earth. It was God who put the lights in the sky, who set sun and moon and stars in the firmament. They are just lights, not the abode of Marduk or of the astral powers that determine fates, just lights, but they are good. It was God who called forth the living creatures to fill the waters and the air and the earth. All of this is God's good pleasure, not Marduk's craft. And it was God who made us. And not from the blood of an evil god, but in God's own image! And not for slavery did God create us — but for freedom, for dominion, to be lords, not slaves! It was good, "very good." And on the seventh day God rested and celebrated. God blessed the day

---

25. Genesis 1:1–2:4a is widely recognized as part of P, or the Priestly Document, which was a literary product of exile. On P see Walter Brueggemann, "The Kerygma of the Priestly Writers," in Brueggemann and Wolff's *The Vitality of Old Testament Traditions*, pp. 101-13.

and called forth praise. It is the day of God's triumph, not Marduk's. God is, after all, the great king, "enthroned on the praises" of God's people (Ps. 22:3).

Jerusalem was a ruin, but the creation endured. And the whole creation is a reminder of the goodness and power of God. "This is our Father's world:/O let us not forget/That though the wrong is great and strong,/God is the ruler yet."[26] The temple was a heap, but the Sabbath remained. And the seventh day — a day of rest and gladness — remained a promise of God's *shalom*. So, even by the waters of Babylon, where nothing looked good or promising, the exiles learned to sing the Lord's song. It was a song of God's rule, of theocracy.

That God is king may be implicit in the creation story, but the association between the affirmation that God is king and the creation is unmistakable in the creation hymns (e.g., Pss. 29, 33, 104, 148; cf. also the enthronement songs, Pss. 93, 95–99). Theocracy may be implicit in the story, but the association is unmistakable in the story itself. When God grants "dominion" to humankind (Gen. 1:26), it is clear that human dominion is "under God" and that human beings remain answerable to God. Moreover, the gift of "dominion" is clearly linked to the creation of male and female as "the image of God" (Gen. 1:26, 27). As Mesopotamian kings installed little statues of themselves to indicate their claim to sovereignty in captive lands, so God created and installed humankind as the "image of God" in the creation to indicate God's claim to sovereignty. To exercise this dominion "under God" is to exercise authority (including political authority) in ways that serve God's cause and the creation's flourishing.

The exiles who made this story of the creation their own did so in spite of — and in defiance of — Babylon's idolatry and oppression. One cannot own this story and still think the light divine, or the stars astral deities, or the trees uncanny powers, or the beasts gods. One cannot sing this song and fail to see that the light and the stars and the trees and the beasts are good. Nothing God made is god, but all that God made is good. The story frees us from idolatry and frees us for a life of delight in and care for all God's creatures.

One cannot own this story as one's own and still think human beings are fit for oppression, fit for bondage. One cannot sing this song and fail to see that to make a man a slave is offensive to God, in whose image he is, or that to oppress a woman is offensive to God, in whose image she is. How can we be complacent with injustice? Human beings were not made from the blood of an evil god, not made to be slaves. The story frees us to respect each other and to care for each other.

One cannot own this story and still take the power and pride of Nebuchadnezzar altogether seriously. One can hardly fail to see that he, too, is

---

26. Mary Babcock Crawford, "This Is My Father's World," in *Psalter Hymnal*, #436:2.

finally answerable to God. The theocratic tradition continued, even in Babylon. God still reigned — and would reign.[27]

The Deuteronomic Historian

The Deuteronomic Historian[28] said as much. During the exile he surveyed the history that led to the exile. He retrieved the ancient stories of conquest and judges and kings, ordered them, and commented on them at important intervals. He found in that history the rule of God — and a recurrent cycle of apostasy, punishment, repentance, and deliverance.[29] It is clear that the exile was punishment — God's *just* punishment for the forgetfulness and unfaithfulness of the people and their kings. But it is clear also that, if there is repentance, there may yet be a new deliverance. If there is some renewal of obedience, there may yet be a future for Israel. God reigns, after all.

The Deuteronomic Historian sees the exile as punishment, but he does not see it as the end. His history was not written simply to preserve some objective historical record of an ancient history, nor simply to justify God's judgment.[30] It was a call to the people that they should repent. The call to repent was frequently reiterated in important speeches. Witness, for example, the obvious editorial addition to Solomon's prayer in dedication of the temple

27. On the other hand, one can own this story as one's own without thinking that the world is flat, or that the stars are fixed upon a firmament which divides the waters, or that the earth is the center of the universe, or that the project took six days. One can own this story without disowning the account of creation that follows it (Gen. 2:4b-24), with its different account of the order and manner and duration of God's creation.

28. "The Deuteronomic Historian" is the name given to the anonymous editor or editors who compiled Joshua, Judges, Samuel, and Kings, or "the former prophets." Judging from the last episode of this history, the work was completed during the exile, or more precisely, sometime shortly after "the thirty-seventh year of the exile of King Jehoiachin of Judah" (2 Kings 25:27), 560 B.C.E., when Jehoiachin was released from prison. Since there is no mention of the Edict of Cyrus (538 B.C.E.), the Deuteronomic History was almost surely completed before that date. The Deuteronomic Historian obviously made considerable use of more ancient records and traditions, but he put them in the service of his address to the exilic community. On the work and message of the Deuteronomic Historian see Hans Walter Wolff, "The Kerygma of the Deuteronomic Historical Work," in Brueggemann and Wolff's *The Vitality of Old Testament Traditions*, pp. 82-100.

29. Wolff, "The Kerygma of the Deuteronomic Historical Work," pp. 87-90.

30. Martin Noth, *The Deuteronomic History* (Sheffield: JSOT Press, 1981; English ed.), argued that the Deuteronomic History was composed to display the justice of God's judgment.

(1 Kings 8:46-50): when the people are "carried away captive . . . , if they repent with all their heart and soul in the land of their enemies, . . . then hear . . . their prayer . . . and forgive your people . . . and grant them compassion in the sight of their captors." And when the editor paused to meditate on the destruction of the Northern Kingdom, it is traced not so much to the people's initial apostasy as to their refusal to heed the prophets' call to "turn" (2 Kings 17:7-18).

The Deuteronomic Historian does not know what to expect on the other side of repentance. He expects deliverance, to be sure, but he does not know what shape that deliverance will take. The prayer of Solomon only looked for "compassion in the sight of their captors" (1 Kings 8:50). Amphictyony and empire are ancient history, and perhaps the monarchy is at an end. The Deuteronomic Historian had recorded Nathan's oracle (2 Sam. 7:12-16) with its promise concerning David's dynasty, but he had treated the promise as contingent upon obedience to the Law of Moses (e.g., 1 Kings 2:3-4; 9:4-9). If the covenant is abandoned, the promise to David is nullified. That King Jehoiachin is released from prison (2 Kings 25:27-29) is a little thing, to be sure, but it is a small ray of hope for the monarchy and for the Jews, an opportunity with which God can begin again. Israel's hope, however, is not in Jehoiachin but in God. Conquest and the possession of the land are also ancient history, and there is not in the Deuteronomic Historian any emphasis on a return to the land.[31] The possession emphasized by the Deuteronomic Historian is the possession of the Law, and it is around the Law, as God's gift and Israel's possession, that a new political order must be formed.

Theocracy remained the fundamental assumption. God reigned, whether in conquest or in exile, whether in amphictyony or in monarchy, whether Israel was an empire or separated into the two threatened nations of Judah and Israel. God reigned, even when Israel fell to the Assyrians, even when Jerusalem was destroyed by the Babylonians. And God would reign, and that was the hope of the people and of the nations.

"Seek the Welfare of the City Where I Have Sent You"

In Jeremiah's letter to the exiles in Babylon between the first deportation and the destruction of Jerusalem (Jer. 29), he cautioned them against the prophetic

---

31. The promise of a return to the land is emphasized by the Priestly materials. (See, e.g., Gen. 17:8 RSV, "And I will give to you, and to your descendants after you, the land of your sojournings, all the land of Canaan, for an everlasting possession; and I will be their God." See also Gen. 28:4; 35:12; 48:4; Exod. 6:4, 8.)

voices promising a quick return. "Build houses and live in them," he wrote, and "seek the welfare of the city where I have sent you into exile, and pray to the LORD on its behalf, for in its welfare you will find your welfare" (29:5, 7). They may acknowledge the political authority of Babylon — or of Persia or Egypt or any other city of their Diaspora — but they must also, of course, acknowledge the greater authority of God. The very practice of prayers for the foreign city and its rulers acknowledges the reign of God.

Faithfulness to covenant is called for, even in a foreign land, and fidelity requires nonparticipation in the idolatry and injustice of Babylon. The stories of Daniel reflect this separation from the idolatry and defilement of Babylon and its palace. But they also point in another direction, toward seeking the welfare of the city. Fidelity requires not just such separation but also participation, utilizing opportunities for political influence to bless the nations. Daniel was Nebuchadnezzar's best counselor, as Joseph had been Pharaoh's. His discernment was formed by attention to the reign of God, and, although a subject of the king, he had an independent mind — and an independent voice. His was a better service to Nebuchadnezzar than the obsequious subservience to which absolute rulers were accustomed. The story is that Nebuchadnezzar finally acknowledged the rule of God, "for his sovereignty is an everlasting sovereignty, and his kingdom endures from generation to generation . . . and he is able to bring low those who walk in pride" (Dan. 4:34, 37). This triumphant outcome is balanced by the constant peril of Daniel and his friends. The stories leave no room for simple optimism about the efforts of God's people to "seek the welfare of the city" or about the willingness of rulers (foreign or domestic) to serve God's cause. Hope, however, is not optimism about empires or emperors; it is a lively confidence in the reign of God.

The prophets reminded the exiles of the covenant; they defended Yahweh's claim as the legitimate suzerain; and they announced that God would be faithful to the cause of God made known in Judah's past. They remembered the exodus, and promised a new one (e.g., Isa. 43:16-21). They remembered the covenant, and promised a new one, with the Law written on their hearts (e.g., Jer. 31:31-34). They remembered David, and promised a new one (e.g., Ezek. 34:23-24). All of the great prophets of exile included oracles of restoration in their prophecies.

The prophets knew, however, that the cause of God was bigger than Israel — and that the rule of God extended far beyond the borders of Judah. All the nations stood under God's sovereignty; it was God's righteousness, not their power, which was finally decisive. Nebuchadnezzar was God's "servant" (Jer. 25:9; 27:6); Cyrus was God's "shepherd" (Isa. 44:28), his "anointed," commissioned to serve God's cause (Isa. 45:1-8). These titles, of course, were familiar titles for Israel's kings. All the nations stood under God's judgment. Amos, of course, had already known as much, as he announced God's judgment on the nations around Israel (greeted, no doubt, by the cries of his hearers, "Amen, brother! Preach it, Amos") before he announced God's judgment on Israel (greeted, I suspect, with the guilty silence that can make no reply without invoking a double standard) (Amos 1:3–2:8). The judgment of God was announced "in the midst of the gods" (Ps. 82:1), and while it was familiar to Israel, it was a vocation for the politics of the nations, too:

> "How long will you judge unjustly
>   and show partiality to the wicked?
> Give justice to the weak and the orphan;
>   maintain the right of the lowly and the destitute.
> Rescue the weak and the needy;
>   deliver them from the hand of the wicked". . . .
> Rise up, O God, judge the earth;
>   for all the nations belong to you! (Ps. 82:2-4, 8)

All the great prophets of exile included oracles of judgment against the nations (e.g., Jer. 46–51; Ezek. 25–32; see also Isa. 13–23) as well as promises of Israel's restoration. But God's judgment and Israel's restoration meant the welfare of the nations, too.

The theocratic vision of God's blessing upon the nations was not just an idiosyncrasy of the Yahwist. It continued to be the hope of the prophets that Israel would be "a blessing in the midst of the earth" (Isa. 19:24; see also Jer. 4:2). Even in exile this tradition continued — not, of course, in the political policies advocated by the Yahwist for empire, but faithfully and creatively in the expectation that the nations would learn from the judgment and restoration of Israel (e.g., Ezek. 36:23). The tradition continued most famously (and most creatively) in "the servant songs" of Isaiah (Isa. 42:1-4; 49:1-6; 50:4-11; 52:13–53:12). The mission of the servant, equipped with God's Spirit, is to bring "justice to the nations" (42:1). The nations "wait for his law" (42:4 RSV). He is a "light to the nations, that my salvation may reach to the end of the earth" (49:6; cf. also 42:6). There was nothing triumphalist about this mission; it meant enduring oppression and judgment (53:7-8); it meant intercession for the transgressors (53:12; like Abraham in the Yahwist stories and like Jeremiah in the letter to the exiles). But the "new thing" (42:9)[32] is that the humiliated will be exalted; "my servant shall prosper; he shall be exalted and lifted up" (52:13). "So he shall startle many

---

32. This "new thing" is really an old thing. There follows (42:10-13) a revisiting of the tradition of God as "warrior," rescuing the weak and helpless.

nations; kings shall shut their mouths because of him; for that which had not been told them they shall see" (52:15). The "new thing" is an old thing: once more God's politics are revealed. God exalts the humiliated and humbles the exalted. The humiliated and exiled people shall be lifted up — but now in the sight of the nations and as an object lesson to the nations. The pride of power and the power of pride will be challenged by Israel's restoration. "A family of humble nations will creep out from under the wreckage of the empires, and Israel's own humiliation and recovery will provide a kind of paradigm for the fate of others, if they will accept the evidence of Yhwh's hand at work."[33] Israel itself, and the prophetic voice within it, was a testimony to the nations that all political authority was "under God" and answerable to a God who defended the weak and the oppressed. Kings were not to pretend to be above the law or to use their power to serve their own interests. They were to serve God's cause.

The Restored Community

When Cyrus, king of Persia, defeated the Babylonians in 537 B.C.E., he wrote an edict permitting their return to the land (537). It seemed to some — and to the Chronicler (2 Chron. 36:21) — to fulfill the word of Jeremiah (Jer. 29:10) that the exile would last "seventy years" and then God would restore the people to the land, and the land to the people. The tolerance — and even the patronage — extended by the Persians, however, still felt like "bondage" to others — and to Ezra (Ezra 9:8-9).[34]

A "Day of Small Things"

It was a "day of small things" (Zech. 4:10). In the midst of small things, with a foothold in the land, the Israelites faced those Deuteronomic questions again: How shall we live in the land in memory of the liberation of slaves and of exiles? How shall we display the salvation God worked and works for those on the margins of social life while we rebuild institutions in this future? How shall we conduct ourselves in this land of promise in fidelity to covenant? How shall we reflect the justice of God in the exercise of the authority that derives from and answers to God? How shall we secure this blessing of God,

33. Oliver O'Donovan, *The Desire of the Nations*, p. 71.
34. Daniel's reading of the Jeremiah text would extend the figure to "seventy weeks of years" (Dan. 9:24), or 490 years, to the end of Seleucid oppression.

and how shall we share this possession? How shall the rule of God take effect in our praise and in our politics? How shall we live in the land in a way that fits the rule of God?

There were no easy answers. Haggai and Zechariah (and evidently the Chronicler) hoped that Zerubbabel would revive the Davidic dynasty and rule an independent kingdom when the Persian Empire fell, but Darius seized the Persian throne, and Zerubbabel vanished (at least from the record). The temple was rebuilt, but there was no renewal of the Davidic dynasty and splendor, and there was no new international order in which empires recognized and served the reign of God to defend the weak.

Nehemiah and Ezra were theocrats under the authority of the Persian king; they were appointed by the Persian king to govern, but they recognized that they were finally answerable to God. The recognition of dual authorities was not a new thing for theocrats. It can be found, of course, in Jeremiah's letter to the exiles, but it can also be traced to the transition to monarchy when Saul was made king "under God." God remained "the great king." They sought the reformation of a Jewish province within the Persian Empire, not independence, but they sought a reformation that served the covenant and the reign of God. They established a hierocracy, centered around cultic observance and governed by priests (and representatives of a distant Persian king). "The former governors . . . laid heavy burdens on the people. . . . Even their servants lorded it over the people. But I did not do so, because of the fear of God," Nehemiah said (Neh. 5:15). The sign of authority in theocracy remained humility. Nehemiah used his authority to achieve a redistribution of property, a more just sharing of the land of promise, and he put a stop to the rich taking advantage of the poor in the land who found themselves in economic trouble (Neh. 5:1-13). The cause of God remained the defense of the poor and powerless. Ezra came with a copy of the Law of God (Ezra 7:6, 14). He gathered the people together to hear it (Neh. 9:3), and the people made an oath to keep it (Neh. 10:28-29). Ezra and Nehemiah were servants of a Persian king and of God. It is somewhat ironic that these servants of a Persian king were unsympathetic to the claims of foreigners who had settled in the land or who lived around Jerusalem. They called for a separation so that Israel could purify itself, forbidding intermarriage (Ezra 9; Neh. 13:23-27) and even calling for divorce from foreign wives (Ezra 10). The experience of exile may have required such separation, but it was not clear to everyone that either the circumstances or the Law of God required it.

The story of Ruth is probably to be dated to this post-exilic period. It testifies not only to a more generous attitude toward intermarriage but also to a performance of the Law which is even more clearly oriented toward the protection and redemption of the poor and powerless. And the story of Jonah, which is also probably to be dated to this period, displays the inclusive mercy of God while it mocks the exclusivism of the prophet Jonah — and of Ezra.

There were no easy answers, but the theocratic questions remained important. Different voices were heard in the community — and would make their way into the canon. There was not one timeless code, whether the Covenant Code or the Deuteronomic Code or Ezra's law, to which the theocratic tradition could be reduced.

When the Persian Empire did finally fall, it remained a "day of small things" (Zech. 4:10) in Judah. The prophets still hoped for a humble king who would come triumphantly to Jerusalem, "riding on a colt, the foal of a donkey" rather than on a warhorse, and bringing peace with his dominion rather than violence (Zech. 9:9). But there was still not yet any renewal of the Davidic dynasty and its splendor, and the fall of the Persians to Alexander the Great brought the world no closer to a new international order of justice and peace than the fall of the Babylonians had.

"An Abomination that Desolates" and Apocalyptic Theocracy

Alexander the Great fell, too — to death, in 323 B.C.E., shortly after his victory over the Persians. The world empire he had established did not last long. It quickly broke into three independent — and hostile — kingdoms. The kings of Macedonia, Alexander's home, kept control of part of the empire, but the rest of the territory was divided between two of Alexander's generals, Ptolemy in Egypt and Seleucus in Mesopotamia. The rival powers were each Hellenistic; the world empire had fallen, but Alexander had established many Greek outposts to manage trade throughout the East, and the culture he had brought with him and established there remained. Palestine was once more a disputed buffer between rival kingdoms, now between the Ptolemies and the Seleucids, and the ill-defined but unfriendly border between them separated also the Jews of the Diaspora in Egypt and Babylon. Until about 200 B.C.E. most of Palestine was under the rule of the Ptolemies, who did not directly interfere with the hierocracy in Jerusalem. Shortly after 200 B.C.E., however, the Seleucid king Antiochus III seized Syria and Palestine from the Ptolemies. The Seleucid Empire was large but fragile, in danger of disintegration from overextension. The Seleucid kings sought to resist disintegration by insisting that the many different particular cultural and religious traditions (which were often linked to movements of national independence) be surrendered and that Hellenism be adopted. Antiochus IV Epiphanes pursued this policy with a vengeance in Palestine. He prohibited possession of the Torah, observance of the Sabbath and dietary laws, and the practice of circumcision. He erected a statue of Zeus in the temple of Jerusalem and desecrated the temple by offering swine upon its altar.

This was no "day of small things." This was the season of "an abomination that desolates" (Dan. 9:27). In times of such hopelessness and helplessness, the theocratic tradition endured as an apocalyptic hope and as a political help to Israel, as apocalyptic protest against the brutality (and bestiality) of tyrants, and as the promise of a future in which God's cause will be accomplished.

Apocalyptic thought[35] divided history into two ages, this age and the age to come, this time and the time to come. This present age is ruled by sin and death, by powers in rebellion against the rule of God. It runs its course to its certain end, a course traced in dreams and visions along the paths of empire. At the end of this age God will act to end the rule of sin and death and empire and to establish God's own cosmic sovereignty. There is a great gulf between the two ages. No historical process links them. Only God can establish the good future of God's unchallenged sovereignty, but God certainly can and certainly will. "[On that day] the LORD will become king over all the earth" (Zech. 14:9). God will reign not only over the nations, bringing a reversal of Israel's fortunes, but also over the whole cosmos, shattering the rule of sin and death. Little wonder that the beginning of that age would be accompanied by cosmic signs and portents, by judgment and the resurrection of the dead. Apocalyptic expectation combined despair about the evil character of this age with profound hope for the future.

To the crisis provoked by Antiochus IV Epiphanes the apocalyptic visions of Daniel replied. In the vision of Daniel 7, for example, the empires of Babylon, the Medes, the Persians, and the Greeks appear as beasts, and Antiochus IV Epiphanes appears as the "little horn" of the last beast ("speaking arrogantly"; Dan. 7:8). But then Daniel saw "an Ancient One" take his throne and "one like a human being, coming with the clouds of heaven. . . . To him was given dominion and glory and kingship, that all peoples, nations, and languages should serve him. His dominion is an everlasting dominion that shall not pass away, and his kingship is one that shall never be destroyed" (7:13-14). The faithful who bend their knee before God the king need not fear the beasts. They may live in the confident and courageous expectation of God's good future — even through this season of "an abomination that desolates." Daniel was confident that God was about to act to end the reign of beasts and to establish cosmic sovereignty (and thereby to restore dominion to humanity and humanity to do-

---

35. On apocalyptic literature and thought see further Paul D. Hanson, *Old Testament Apocalyptic* (Nashville: Abingdon, 1987).

minion). It would be God's victory, signaled by the resurrection of the dead (12:2). It was not the result of some political program, but it could hardly be considered irrelevant to politics. Daniel's vision provided courage to act with integrity in the face of Antiochus IV Epiphanes. It has been called "non-violent resistance literature,"[36] but it was consistent with the resistance movement begun by the Maccabees even if it did not sponsor it, and it seems to refer to the Maccabees as "a little help" to the pious of Jerusalem (11:33-35).

The theocratic tradition prompted first disobedience to the tyrannous edicts of Antiochus IV Epiphanes, and then resistance, and finally rebellion. Devout and holy Jews, like the old priest Mattathias, were prepared to choose martyrdom rather than disloyalty to God the king. Their zeal for the covenant and its Law drove them to resist both Antiochus's commands and his enforcers. And such resistance in the face of the equal zeal of Antiochus and his agents led to violence and rebellion. 1 Maccabees invoked the memory of Phinehas in telling the story of Mattathias (1 Macc. 2:15-28; cf. Num. 25:7-11). And Mattathias himself, the story goes, reminded his sons of Phinehas as he encouraged them to "show zeal for the law, and give your lives for the covenant of our ancestors" (1 Macc. 2:50-69). Violence, even the breaking of the Law (namely, the law of Sabbath; 1 Macc. 2:29-48), was permitted in order to defend both the Law and themselves, to resist the tyrant, and to put an end to the abomination.

The revolt led by the Maccabees succeeded, quite beyond human expectations.[37] The temple was purified, and Jewish independence was established under the sons of Mattathias in the Hasmonean dynasty.[38] Almost as soon as

36. A. A. Di Lella and L. F. Hartman, *The Book of Daniel*, Anchor Bible (Garden City, N.Y.: Doubleday, 1978), p. 67.

37. 2 Maccabees emphasizes the "miraculous" success of the rebellion, and accordingly deemphasizes the military successes of the Maccabees. Moreover, while 1 Maccabees celebrates the Hasmonean dynasty, 2 Maccabees celebrates temple observance. Nevertheless, the contention of Jonathan Goldstein in the Anchor Bible, vol. 41, *I Maccabees* (Garden City, N.Y.: Doubleday, 1976) that the authors of these works were "bitter opponents" (p. 33), that 1 Maccabees represents the war party and 2 Maccabees a pacifist (or submission) party seems to go too far. See also Jonathan Goldstein, Anchor Bible, vol. 41A, *II Maccabees* (Garden City, N.Y.: Doubleday, 1983).

38. The account of the glorious days of Simon as king in 1 Maccabees 14:4-14 revisits many theocratic hopes.

He established peace in the land, and Israel rejoiced with great joy. All the people sat under their own vines and fig trees, and there was none to make them afraid. No one was left in the land to fight them, and the kings were crushed in those days. He gave help to all the humble among his people; he sought out the law, and did away with all the renegades and outlaws. (1 Macc.14:11-14)

independence had been restored, however, some of the pious Jews who had supported the Maccabean struggle grew disaffected with the ambition, violence, and luxury of the Hasmoneans. The brief period of independence came to an end in quarrels over the throne, quarrels settled by the arrival of Pompey and the Romans in 63 B.C.E.

Psalms

"God is king"; wherever one turns in the Hebrew Scriptures, one is confronted by this theocratic affirmation — and claimed by it. God's authority was established in deliverance; it was exercised in the righteousness of God's Law and judgment; it promised security and blessing upon Israel and the nations; and it evoked the loyalty and praise of the people.[39] "God is king"; the affirmation ran down the centuries in the praise of the people. In Israel's songs of worship the people celebrated God's reign; indeed, God is "enthroned on the praises of Israel" (Ps. 22:3).

Psalm 47, for example, invites "all peoples" to give praise to God (47:1). And the reason is simply the confident and joyful assurance that God is "a great king over all the earth" (47:2, 7, 8). The psalm closes with the great theocratic vision, a cause for great joy: "God sits on his holy throne. The princes of the peoples gather as the people of the God of Abraham" (47:8-9). The promise to Abraham is fulfilled!

Psalm 98 invites Israel to praise God for deliverance, but then audaciously issues a second invitation, this time to "all the earth" — and every creature in it — to join in Israel's praise "before the King, the LORD . . . for he is coming to judge the earth. He will judge the world with righteousness and the peoples with equity" (98:4-9; cf. 96:13). This king is a "lover of justice" (99:4). On the basis of this theocratic faith and hope the psalmists exhort Israel not only to praise God but to "say among the nations, 'The LORD is king!'" (96:10). These theocrats had the whole world and the future on the horizon. They were oriented toward a future in which the Lord would come to judge and to save, to establish his universal reign beyond ambiguity and challenge and corruption, to establish a politics in which justice and peace "will kiss each other" (85:10).

The memory of God's works and ways determined the significance of the claim that God was king. God is the mighty creator of this world, and its ruler. This "lover of justice" set humanity within the creation as "the image of God," as the token of God's own sovereignty in it, as apt for "dominion" but not for

---

39. See footnote 2 of this chapter.

bondage. God holds back the waters of chaos. This great king would not let sin and the curse have the last word in his world. The Lord called Abraham to be a blessing to all the nations, delivered some slaves from tyranny and oppression to display his justice and gave them a land and a Law. This ruler makes people free, makes the last first, protects the weak. Judges and kings were called to be humble servants of the people, to perform God's reign. Prophets were called to be an independent voice in the kingdom. Lawgivers were to render the law worthy of God's reign. The people were called to remember. Together, and as a sign of God's good future, they were called to theocracy.

The theocratic tradition of Israel regarded political power as accountable to the God made known in the story. The nation — and the nations — were to serve God's cause, the cause that was also made known in the story. Every political structure and policy was to be tested by its service to the cause of God. The transcendent cause of God, made known in Israel's past, was always there in its future, calling the nation to repentance and reform. The theocratic tradition honored the authorities because they had their authority from God, but it joined to honor a suspicion of the authorities because they so frequently served their own interests rather than God's cause. Theocratic political discernment recognized the ambiguity of power, and would not let go accountability to God.

In the amphictyony the suspicion of conventional politics, the politics that had enslaved and oppressed the slaves of Egypt, prompted reliance upon a charismatic leadership, but the judges could not withstand the threat of chaos. The transition to monarchy displayed both Israel's suspicion of royal despotism and Israel's hope that a humble king might perform God's reign and serve God's cause. The monarchy itself provided a context for both the political vision of the Yahwist (and the royal psalms) and for the prophetic oracles of judgment against royal despotism and a politics in the service of the rich. The prophets reminded both the king and the people of the covenant of the great suzerain, of the cause of the great king, and of their accountability. They called for repentance and reform, and the lawmakers sometimes heeded their call by revisiting the received legal tradition and revising it to make it "fit" the old story (and the new circumstances) a little better. In exile the theocratic tradition continued to honor the authorities, to pray for them, and to "seek the welfare" of the city where God had sent them. Even the Babylonians got their authority from God. But also in exile the theocratic tradition continued to join suspicion to honor. It recognized the inhumanity (the bestiality) of a politics of oppression and enslavement, and did not let go — even in exile — the conviction that the authority of kings and emperors is "under God" and accountable to God. Theocracy required both separation from the injustice and violence of Babylonian power and political participation to serve the welfare of others and the cause of God. In the restored community the theocratic tradition learned not to despise "small things" but not to confuse them with the cause of God either. Sometimes "small things" politically and certain legislative "minimal standards" can both secure genuine (if small) goods and give some little token of God's good future. That future, as apocalyptic reminds us, will not be a political accomplishment; God's cause is transcendent. But that future is nevertheless relevant to both our suspicion of political authorities and our honoring them, to both political discernment and political participation.

CHAPTER EIGHTEEN

The Theocratic Politics of Jesus

It was a difficult time, a time of crisis. The glories of the independent kingdom of the Hasmonean dynasty had long since departed. Roman rule had been imposed at first indirectly (but quite effectively) through the long reign of Herod the Great. He was, in the view of Augustus, an able administrator in a tough job; Augustus gave him the title "King of Judea" and added territory to his domain. Herod's reign was marked both by great building projects and by great brutality. Among his many building projects was the rebuilding of the temple in Jerusalem. Even that, however, did not win him the favor of the Jews. He was, after all, not a Jew himself, this so-called "King of Judea," but an Idumaean. And Herod's building projects came with the price tag of heavy taxes. Moreover, Herod's jealous violence against his rivals, even against those within his own family whom he saw as rivals, led in the last years to a reign of terror.[1] The land was impoverished by Herod's reign; the population was demoralized by his arbitrary violence;[2] and the Jews did not mourn his death in 4 B.C.E.

---

1. Herod killed his two sons by Mariamne and finally Mariamne herself. He killed other members of his family, too, when he grew anxious that one or another was a threat to his hold on the Jewish throne. Augustus, knowing Herod's character and conduct (and knowing also about Jewish scruples about pork) is reported to have quipped that he would rather be Herod's pig (his *hyn*) than Herod's son (his *huion*). Macrobius, *Saturnalia*, II.f.ii, cited by Everett Ferguson, *Backgrounds of Early Christianity* (Grand Rapids: Eerdmans, 1987), p. 330. There is no independent confirmation of Matthew's account of Herod's violence against the children of Bethlehem after the birth of Jesus (Matt. 2:16-18), but such violence would not have been out of character.

2. See further Joachim Jeremias, *Jerusalem in the Time of Jesus* (Philadelphia: Fortress, 1969), p. 125.

Although a Jewish delegation to Rome made it clear that they wanted nothing more to do with the Herodians, Herod's realm was divided among his sons, Herod Antipas, Philip, and Archelaus. Herod Antipas ruled in Galilee until 39 C.E.; Philip ruled territories north and east of Galilee until 34; but Archelaus ruled only briefly over Judea, Samaria, and Idumaea. He was deposed by Augustus in 6 C.E. and banished for his incompetence and corruption. Augustus turned his territory into a province under the direct control of Rome and administered it by a series of procurators, governors directly responsible to the emperor.[3] With this shift to direct Roman rule came the imposition of Roman taxes, the census necessary to take them, and the insult of still less independence.

The signs of crisis were all around Palestine: the protests of reform movements like those of Qumran and the Pharisees, the violence of revolutionary movements like that led by Judas the Galilean, the criticism of solitary charismatic figures like John the Baptist, the prevalence of beggars and vagabonds in Jerusalem, and random acts of violence by *lēstai*, or "robbers" (which were prompted, probably, not so much by some revolutionary design as by a general breakdown of respect for law).

The Jews did preserve a measure of independence under the Romans. The great council in Jerusalem contained seventy-two members taken from the ranks of three groups, the high priests, the elders (from the aristocratic families of Jerusalem), and the scribes (experts on Jewish Law). The high priest presided — and was named and deposed by the Romans. The council represented the ruling class in Jerusalem, a ruling class whose power and privilege depended in no small measure on the patronage, or at least the tolerance, of Rome.

The Jewish Parties

At the time of Jesus at least four parties were contending in the land, promoting their policies and positions. Most of them had their origin during the Hasmonean dynasty, but all of them had to come to terms with the Roman occupation. We will take a brief look at each of the parties, the Essenes (as found in the community at Qumran), the Pharisees, the Zealots, and the Sadducees. Each was theocratic, but each in its own way.

The community at Qumran apparently began in protest against the Hasmoneans' use of the title "high priest" even though they were not from the

---

3. Pontius Pilate, the most famous of them because of his role in the death of Jesus, was the fifth procurator, 26-36 C.E.

line of Zadok, whom Solomon had appointed (1 Kings 2:35).[4] And because this community regarded the priests of Jerusalem as illegitimate, they also judged worship in the temple to be corrupted. These theocrats despaired of the leadership in Jerusalem, withdrew into the wilderness, and established there a community of strict discipline awaiting the vindication of God. They hoped for the restoration of the priesthood and of the temple, but in the interim they would have nothing to do with the politics of Jerusalem. This dissident movement outlasted the Hasmonean dynasty, but when the Romans put Herod on the throne and ruled indirectly through the Jewish aristocracy, including the priests, the Essenes at Qumran were hardly disposed to reenter Jerusalem. They remained in the wilderness until their destruction by the Romans in C.E. 68. At the time of Jesus they remained a renewal movement marked by the withdrawal prompted by their despair concerning the political and religious leadership in Jerusalem. The community was also characterized by strict observance of the Law and by the people's expectation of God's vindication of "the sons of light." That vindication, of course, was to be their vindication, and it would bring with it the condemnation of all others. It was a self-consciously theocratic movement, a countercultural experiment sustained by apocalyptic hope for the reign of God.

The Pharisees probably also had their origins in the pious reaction to the Hasmoneans. Unlike the community at Qumran, however, the Pharisees respected the institutions of the temple and the priesthood and remained within Jewish society. For a time the Pharisees were involved in political intrigue. Their vigorous dissent from the policies of Alexander Jannaeus, the Hasmonean ruler from 103-76 B.C.E., was met with ruthless violence. On his deathbed Alexander urged his wife Salome Alexandra to make peace with the Pharisees, and she did. Pharisees became more and more influential in the council, being numbered among the scribes, the experts in Jewish law. Not all of the scribes were Pharisees, but most were. And not all Pharisees were scribes; many were devout lay people who devoted themselves to observance of the Law and to the practices of prayer, fasting, and almsgiving. The pharisaic scribes functioned politically as something like a magisterium of the Torah, and within the council they came to have great power as interpreters of the Law. Within Jewish society

4. In Ezekiel 40–48 the priestly ministry is assigned to the sons of Zadok (40:46; 43:19; 44:15; 48:11). The Zadokite high priests, however, had not distinguished themselves under Antiochus IV Epiphanes; the high priest Jason was a Hellenizer. The Hasmoneans took over the office of high priest after the Maccabean revolt. The group of priests who gathered around the Teacher of Righteousness to form the community at Qumran called themselves "Sons of Zadok, the priests who keep the covenant" (1QS V.2.9). See further E. Lohse, *The New Testament Environment* (Nashville: Abingdon, 1976), pp. 74-75.

the Pharisees emphasized obedience to the Law of God, both the written Law and the oral Law, while patiently waiting for God to intervene on behalf of his people. They opposed the Roman takeover in 63 B.C.E., but not by force.[5] Here the theocratic tradition prompted patience and nonviolent resistance. They persistently opposed anyone, including Herod and the procurators, who would violate the Law of God. They refused, for example, to swear a loyalty oath or to allow images in the city. They were content, however, to leave liberation in the hands of God, accommodating themselves to Roman rule, refusing only to render to Caesar and his law the sort of obedience due solely to God and God's Law.[6]

Some of the pious Jews, however, including some of the Pharisees, grew impatient with Roman rule and joined the cause of the freedom fighters.[7] Judas the Galilean (mentioned in Acts 5:37) ignited Jewish passion for liberation from the Romans in C.E. 6, after the exile of Herod's son Archelaus, the imposition of direct Roman rule, and an initial census for the taking of taxes. Judas upbraided his countrymen "as cowards for consenting to pay tribute to Rome and tolerating mortal masters, after having God for their lord."[8] The radical theocratic vision of Judas called for zealous observance of the Law (including the social legislation of the Jubilee year)[9] and zealous violence against the Romans and any who collaborated with them. Judas was an early victim of the

5. See, e.g., *The Psalms of Solomon*, trans. H. E. Ryle and M. R. James (Cambridge: The University Press, 1891), a first-century B.C.E. writing which originated from within pharisaic circles. It refers derisively to Pompey's sacrilegious entry into the Holy of Holies and hopes for a Davidic king (not a Hasmonean!) to deliver God's people and land from the Romans. This Davidic messiah relies on God, not on an army: "For he shall not put his trust in horse and rider and bow, nor shall he multiply unto himself gold and silver for war, nor by ships shall he gather confidence for the day of battle. The Lord himself is his King, and the hope of him that is strong in the hope of God" (*The Psalms of Solomon* 17:37-38; cf. Zech. 4:6).

6. The thesis of Jacob Neusner, *Politics to Piety* (Englewood Cliffs, N.J.: Prentice-Hall, 1972-73), that the Pharisees gradually became a pietistic and nonpolitical movement is probably overstated. On the Pharisees see also Ellis Rivkin, *A Hidden Revolution* (Nashville: Abingdon, 1978).

7. The Zealots probably had their origin among the Pharisees; at least they attracted Pharisees as early supporters. The first person to join Judas the Galilean in his organized rebellion was identified by Josephus as a Pharisee, R. Saddok (Josephus, *Jewish Antiquities*, XVIII.4).

8. Josephus, *The Jewish War*, II.118, trans. Thackeray (Loeb edition, 2:369).

9. When the Zealots took control of Jerusalem in 66 C.E., under the leadership of Menahem, the son of Judas the Galilean, they burned the city archives, effectively destroying the records of indebtedness (Josephus, *The Jewish War*, 2:427).

violence, but his story was celebrated among the young, and his cause gained support among the peasants and the poor until the Zealots, as they came to be called, were able to push moderation aside and begin the revolutionary struggle of C.E. 66-73.[10]

The Sadducees were not sympathetic toward any of these movements for reform or revolution. They had their origins in the priestly and aristocratic families of Jerusalem. Not all Sadducees were priests or members of the aristocracy but most were. The ancient Zadokite dynasty of high priests had been terribly compromised under Antiochus IV Epiphanes, when Jason took office by bribery and then used the office to promote Hellenism. When the Maccabean revolt was successful and the Hasmoneans, in spite of the fact that they were not from the line of Zadok, took over the office of high priest, some of the Zadokites and other aristocratic families supported them in an effort to protect their vested interests in Jerusalem and its temple. When the Romans occupied Jerusalem, some of these families remained loyal to the Hasmoneans, but more of them prudently calculated that their interests and positions could be best served by accommodation and collaboration with the Romans. In their positions as high priest and as members of the Sanhedrin these Sadducees were willing to serve as puppet authorities for the Romans in order to preserve their positions, their properties, and their control of the temple, including its considerable treasury. (The temple had revenues from the temple tax, tithes, gifts and alms, sales of sacrificial animals, and the exchange of the money of pilgrims into temple currency.) They were theocrats — after a fashion. God's rule is found in the temple. And the priests, of course, should profit from it. They profited considerably. The Sadducees acknowledged the Torah as canon but rejected the oral Law, the prophets, and the writings. They were more interested in preserving the status quo and their privileged position within it than in any

10. The question of whether there was a Zealot "party" at the time of Jesus is much debated. Martin Hengel, *The Zealots,* trans. David Smith (Edinburgh: T. & T. Clark, 1989), argues that the Zealots were "a relatively exclusive and unified movement . . . between 6 and 70 A.D." (p. 5). Richard Horsley, on the other hand, has argued that there was no Zealot "party" until the Jewish Revolutionary War; Horsley, *Jesus and the Spiral of Violence: Popular Jewish Resistance in Roman Palestine* (New York: Harper & Row, 1987). Whether there was a Zealot "party" or not, there surely was a lively memory of Phinehas (e.g., 1 Macc. 2:26, 54, where Phineas is the model for Mattathias and the Maccabees), a lively hope for deliverance from the Romans, and a "zeal" for God's rule that was ready for both violence and martyrdom. There was a "Zealot" tradition at the time of Jesus even if there was not a Zealot "party." See William Klassen, "Jesus and the Zealot Option," in *The Wisdom of the Cross: Essays in Honor of John Howard Yoder,* ed. Stanley Hauerwas et al. (Grand Rapids: Eerdmans, 1999), pp. 131-49.

apocalyptic vision of God's reign.[11] The destruction of Jerusalem and its temple in c.e. 70 sealed their doom as surely as it did that of the Zealots, whose call for rebellion they had opposed.

These four parties — the Essenes, Pharisees, Zealots, and Sadducees — were contending for their policies and positions, and for their versions of the theocratic tradition, at the time of Jesus. Procurators and puppet rulers contended for Rome — and for the favor of Rome — at the same time. In that political world Jesus came announcing the coming of the kingdom of God. He revisited the theocratic tradition, and he announced the rule of God as the good future for Israel and the nations. The other parties, of course, had also revisited that tradition; indeed, Jewish political reflection in the first century was unthinkable apart from that tradition. Jesus revisited the tradition within the context of the apocalyptic conviction that God was about to act to establish God's own cosmic sovereignty against all that resisted it. That, too, did not make Jesus politically unique; the Zealots, Qumran, and the Pharisees seem to have shared that apocalyptic conviction. Still, the politics of Jesus may be distinguished from the other Jewish parties of the first century.

Obviously Jesus was not a member of the community at Qumran. He did not withdraw from the common life of Israel into the desert with his followers, there to wait and watch for God to act. He did not reject the institutions of Israel, although he surely criticized them. His was a reform movement within Israel, not removed from it. He did not look to construct purity by separation from the temple with its corrupt priests or from Jerusalem and its heathen rulers. His politics were not separatist.

No less obviously, Jesus was no Zealot — the views of S. G. F. Brandon (and Pontius Pilate!) notwithstanding.[12] There was something quite irenic in Jesus' announcement of the kingdom. He rejected the vengeful use of the *lex talionis* (the law of "a tooth for a tooth") to license, even as it limited, personal retaliation (Matt. 5:38-41), and that rejection of retaliation evidently extended to political dispositions. He rejected, moreover, the vengeful nationalism of much contemporaneous apocalyptic expectation. The "enemy" was to be loved, not destroyed. The Zealot desire for revenge belonged to the old age. Jesus did

---

11. They denied, for example, the characteristic doctrine of apocalyptic, resurrection. See Mark 12:18 and Acts 23:8.

12. That Jesus was condemned to die by Pontius Pilate as a pretender to the Jewish throne has been the starting point for nearly all those who, like S. G. F. Brandon, *Jesus and the Zealots* (New York: Scribner, 1968), would understand Jesus as a Zealot, a political revolutionary committed to the liberation of the land from the Romans. The thesis that Jesus was a Zealot has been discredited; see Martin Hengel, *Was Jesus a Revolutionist?* (Philadelphia: Fortress, 1971).

not proclaim theocracy as a call to a holy war of national liberation. He did not divide those around him into "children of light" and "children of darkness" and urge or welcome the destruction of the latter (Luke 9:52-56). On the contrary, he was a friend of Samaritans, tax collectors, a Roman centurion, and other "enemies." When he entered Jerusalem he rode no warhorse but an ass (Matt. 21:1-9; Mark 11:1-10; Luke 19:28-40; John 12:12-19). That self-conscious fulfillment of Zechariah 9:9, with its vision of a humble king, did not point toward any nationalistic "holy war" but toward "peace to the nations" (Zech. 9:10).

He was no Zealot, then, but he was no Sadducean collaborator either. The cleansing of the temple is enough to distinguish Jesus from the priestly aristocracy who had accommodated the Romans in order to preserve their position, their property, and their control of the temple and its treasury. The Sadducees had provided benediction and endorsement of the Romans. They had used their authority in the temple to make themselves clients of Rome and to make themselves rich at the expense of pious pilgrims and the poor. When Jesus drove out the moneychangers and the merchants, whose commerce had enriched the priestly aristocracy (Matt. 21:12-13; Mark 11:15-17; Luke 19:45-46; John 2:13-17), it was surely — even if not solely — a political judgment against the Sadducees. Using Jeremiah 7:11, he even accused them of being the *lēstai*, the robbers (Mark 11:17). Unlike the Sadducees, Jesus regarded the prophets as well as the Torah as the word of God, and unlike the Sadducees, he cherished the apocalyptic hope for God's coming cosmic sovereignty and for resurrection (Mark 12:18-27).

Moreover, Jesus did not pander to the Roman authorities with whom the Sadducees collaborated. He called Herod Antipas "that fox" (Luke 13:32), and he condemned the Gentile rulers who "lord[ed] it over" their subjects (Mark 10:42). Such politics belong to the old age. The famous — but notoriously difficult — saying of Jesus about the tribute money, "Give to the emperor the things that are the emperor's, and to God the things that are God's" (Mark 12:17), is no Zealot call to arms. But neither is it the sort of compartmentalization of "two realms" that would leave the Herodians, Sadducees, and other collaborators with an easy conscience. Jesus does not assign to Caesar an unchallenged sphere of secular authority.[13] Jesus was neither a collaborator nor a Zealot, neither a secularist (and compartmentalizer) nor a revolutionary. He did not recognize a permanently twofold locus of authority, only a transitory duality which belonged to this age, a duality between the coming and the passing orders. In the theocratic tradition of Jesus all political authority is from God and accountable to God. It

13. See Oliver O'Donovan, *The Desire of the Nations: Rediscovering the Roots of Political Theology* (Cambridge: Cambridge University Press, 1996), pp. 91-92.

joined suspicion to honor when dealing with kings and emperors, and it would not let go the conviction that political authority is "under God." And in the context of Jesus' proclamation of God's cosmic sovereignty, there can be no question about what things do and do not belong to God. All things will belong to him, the claims of Caesar notwithstanding, and even now Jesus' hearers (in this context the Herodians, not the Zealots, incidentally) are called to welcome that coming sovereignty of God, to give their whole allegiance to God and to the cause of God. The collaborators are called to repentance, to political — even if not merely political — repentance.

Jesus was closest to the reform movement of the Pharisees, but the polemic in the gospels leaves no doubt that he is not to be numbered with that party either.[14] The Pharisees emphasized observance of the law of God while they patiently waited for God to intervene on behalf of his people. In Jesus' teaching, however, because the kingdom was at hand, merely external and legal observance was regarded as (at best) insufficient. The imminent sovereignty of God demanded something more than an external and conventional righteousness based on observance of statutes. His politics was not simply a politics of obedience to the Law; his was a politics of response to God and to the cause of God. He set the Law in the context of response. He would not allow external observance of the Law to substitute for the required response to God's good future. And he would not allow God's Law to be co-opted by those who would use it to boast about their own righteousness and to exclude those on the margins of Israel's life. Jesus condemned (and parodied) a casuistry that aimed at ensuring external observance while it left the heart untouched (Matt. 15:2-9, 16-20; 23:25-28; Mark 7:5-7, 18-23). The coming kingdom forced something more radical than the labored application of legal precepts to external behavior, something more penetrating than certain legal limits on the expression of lust, deceitfulness, vengefulness, avarice, and pride. The promise of the prophets, after all, was that God would write the Law upon their hearts (Jer. 31:31-34; Ezek. 11:19-20). God's good future was making its power felt, not in tortured interpretations of ancient legal texts, but in the hearts and lives of those who welcomed that future and repented. Personal and social righteousness was finally the work of God; the effort of the Pharisees to construct it by their attention to external limits was no more likely to be successful than the Zealot effort to achieve it by throwing out the Roman tyrants.

---

14. The polemic in the gospels is frequently directed against the Pharisees. The explanation for this is not that the Pharisees were further from Jesus than the Essenes, Zealots, or Sadducees. The explanation is, rather, that when the gospels were written, the Pharisees were the only other Jewish party to have survived the Jewish Revolutionary War.

The politics of Jesus, then, are not to be identified with any of the parties
— nor, for that matter, with a rejection of one of the parties, as though it were
sufficient to observe, for example, that Jesus rejected the Zealot option. But
what, then, were the politics of Jesus? What was Jesus' theocratic vision for the
common life of Israel?

Apocalyptic Theocracy — and the Politics of Jesus

The place to begin is, once again, the church's memory of Jesus as one who
came announcing the "kingdom of God." "The time is fulfilled," he said, "and
the kingdom of God has come near; repent, and believe in the good news"
(Mark 1:15). That announcement stood in the context of the theocratic tradition, and within that theocratic tradition it stood closest to the tradition of
apocalyptic literature and thought.

Against the background of apocalyptic thought it is clear that Jesus did
not announce the reign of God as an ideal political order whose coming was
contingent upon human striving or political strategy. Its coming was contingent not on human activity but on the decisive act of God, the apocalyptic,
world-shattering, and world-renewing act of God which would bring both final
judgment and final liberation and salvation. Its coming was not something human political action could either hasten or delay; its coming was something for
which people could only pray. And pray they did, both in the Kaddish and in
the prayer Jesus taught his disciples.[15]

Against that apocalyptic background, however, it is equally clear that Jesus did not announce the kingdom as limited to God's sovereignty in the mysterious region of the soul. The scope of God's reign was nothing less than cosmic. Jesus nowhere narrowed the scope of apocalyptic expectation to the
mystical or pious or "existential" surrender of the heart to God.[16] He came with

15. The Kaddish was an Aramaic prayer used at the close of the service in the synagogue (and with which Jesus was undoubtedly familiar): "Exalted and hallowed be his great
name in the world which he created according to his will. May he let his kingdom rule in
your lifetime and in your days and in the lifetime of the whole house of Israel, speedily and
soon." Joachim Jeremias, *The Prayers of Jesus* (London: SCM Press, 1967), p. 98.

16. Luke 17:21b, "The kingdom of God is among you" (NRSV; Gk. *entos hymōn
estin;* KJV: "The kingdom of God is within you"), has sometimes been read to defend such
a view of the kingdom. R. E. O. White, for example, uses it to defend the view that the
kingdom of God *"means* the reign of God within each soul living under the divine sovereignty" (*Biblical Ethics* [Atlanta: John Knox, 1979], p. 78). *Entos hymōn* is indeed ambiguous; it could mean either "within you" or "among you." The Aramaic preposition which

no political program to establish the kingdom, but the kingdom he announced was no less political than personal.

Jesus did not simply revisit the apocalyptic tradition, however. He fulfilled it. And, in fulfilling it, he broke through to something new, to the future present. Apocalyptic had divided history into "two ages" and fixed a great gulf between them. Jesus bridged the gulf. In his works and words the good future of God — while it remained future — was already present; in him the kingdom of God already made its power felt. The future remained future, and it remained fundamental to Jesus' proclamation, but Jesus unveiled it, performed it, in the present.[17]

---

very likely lies behind it has the same ambiguity (according to T. W. Manson, *The Sayings of Jesus* [London: SCM, 1949], pp. 303-4). Since the meaning cannot be settled on linguistic grounds, it is necessary to look at the immediate context. In Luke 17:20b-21a Jesus disowns attempts to calculate the time and place of God's decisive act by attention to "the signs of the times." Luke 17:21b stands as an antithesis to such attempts. Moreover, a parallel construction follows in Luke 17:23-24, where Luke 17:23 warns against efforts to calculate and predict and the following clause, Luke 17:24, stands as its antithesis, insisting that the disclosure of the "Son of Man" will be sudden and universal. On the basis of the antithetical structure and on the basis of the parallel with the following verses, the meaning of Luke 17:21b is plain: the time and place of the kingdom cannot be calculated; it "will (suddenly) be in your midst" (Joachim Jeremias, *New Testament Theology* [New York: Scribner, 1971], p. 101; Manson, *Sayings of Jesus*, pp. 303-4). If the *estin* (the "is") seems to stand in the way of such an interpretation, it may be observed that in the Aramaic of Jesus there would have been no copula, no *estin*. The *estin* is in Luke, of course, and it coheres with his tendency to emphasize a more "realized" eschatology. Even in Luke, however, the verse cannot be used to defend the sort of reading White and others provide, for Luke sets these verses in the context of a response to a question from the Pharisees, and Luke would not have Jesus say that the kingdom of God is "within" the heart of the Pharisees. Instead, Luke seems to have Jesus reject the calculations of the Pharisees with the claim that the kingdom is (already) "among" them or "in their midst" in the person and ministry of Jesus. At any rate, there is no basis in Luke 17:21b for construing the kingdom as an inner and purely "spiritual" reality in the soul of believers. The kingdom is not something that enters people; it is something that people enter.

17. In his healing ministry, for example, the future triumph of God over disease and death was performed. In his exorcisms the victory over Satan and his hosts was anticipated (Luke 11:20). He taught with an "authority" associated not with the Law but with God's coming sovereignty (Mark 1:22, 27). In his "woes" — and in his forgiveness — the future judgment was already announced (Matt. 11:21-24; 23:13-36; Luke 6:24-26; 11:42-52). And in his Beatitudes, the future salvation of God was made present (Matt. 5:1-12; Luke 6:20-22; 7:23; 11:28). Meals with him were foretastes of the heavenly banquet. The "consistent eschatology" of Albert Schweitzer, with its single focus on the imminent future of the kingdom of God and its interpretation of Jesus' moral teachings as "the special ethic of the interval before the coming of the Kingdom" *(Interimsethik)*, must be regarded as a misun-

The present, therefore, was critical. "The time [the *kairos*] is fulfilled" (Mark 1:15a), he said; the moment of truth had arrived. A response was required. Apocalyptic thought, because of its determinism and pessimism about this age, had sometimes construed human action as fruitless and inconsequential. (At its best it reinforced a sober and fierce obedience to the Law while waiting for God to act.) But Jesus, like the prophets before him, called the people to "repent," to turn.[18] He summoned cities (e.g., Chorazin, Bethsaida, and Capernaum; Matt. 11:20-24), a generation (Matt. 12:38-42), and nations (Matt. 25:32) to repentance. The repentance called for was not *merely* political, but it was, nevertheless, surely political. Against the background of apocalyptic thought Jesus can hardly be understood as an idealistic optimist announcing slow and steady human progress toward a perfect social order, but he broke through apocalyptic pessimism to call for a response. While human action does not establish the kingdom, it is nevertheless again called for, and called for as the eschatologically urgent response to the reign of God, which is at hand and already making its power felt.

---

derstanding, for it neglects the present effectiveness of God's future. See Albert Schweitzer, *The Quest of the Historical Jesus* (New York: Macmillan, 1961), p. 354. But C. H. Dodd's "realized eschatology," which emphasizes the present reality of the kingdom to the point of dismissing Jesus' proclamation of the future act of God, is at least equally mistaken. The future remained fundamental, for even in the deeds and words of Jesus it was the *future* rule of God that made its power felt. See Dodd, *The Parables of the Kingdom* (London: Nisbet, 1935). Both the future act of God and its present impact are part of Jesus' teaching and ministry. See Norman Perrin, *The Kingdom of God in the Teaching of Jesus* (Philadelphia: Westminster, 1963), pp. 74-78 and 83-84 for a convenient summary of the evidence for the kingdom as present and future in Jesus' ministry.

18. On "repentance" see Behm and Wurthwein, "*metanoeō, metanoia,*" *Theological Dictionary of the New Testament*, ed. Gerhard Kittel, trans. Geoffrey W. Bromiley, vol. 4 (Grand Rapids: Eerdmans, 1967), pp. 975-1008. It should be noted that the words "repentance" and "repent" do not often appear on the lips of Jesus in the gospels. Some have even doubted the authenticity of the summons to repentance (e.g., E. P. Sanders, *Jesus and Judaism* [Philadelphia: Fortress, 1985], pp. 106-13). As Behm says, however, "The whole proclamation of Jesus . . . is a proclamation of *metanoia* even when the term is not used" (Behm, "*metanoeō,*" p. 1002). Along with Mark 1:15 — and the majority of New Testament scholars — we may allow "repentance" as a summary of Jesus' teaching. Even so, we should not infer too much from the word; the meaning of repentance, the shape of it, must be inferred from the whole of the story, not from a word study. Repentance is not merely an uneasy conscience prompted by introspection or meditation on the Law. It is surely not merely the external gestures of sackcloth and ashes (Matt. 11:21). It is rather a radical turning from the old securities and a joyful turning toward God and God's future. See Allen Verhey, *The Great Reversal: Ethics and the New Testament* (Grand Rapids: Eerdmans, 1984), pp. 16-21.

Apocalyptic thought expected God to turn the world upside down, to shake it, to put an end to the rule of sin and death, to judge and to save, to liberate and to secure *shalom*. And so did Jesus. But Jesus revised the material content of apocalyptic expectation as well as its form. He still expected a great reversal of this present age, but the nationalistic hope for Israel's revenge against the nations is strikingly absent.[19] The great reversal announced by Jesus was captured and condensed in axioms like "Many that are first will be last, and the last will be first" (Matt. 20:16; Mark 9:35; 10:31; Luke 13:30)[20] and "All who exalt themselves will be humbled, and all who humble themselves will be exalted" (Matt. 23:12; cf. Matt. 18:4; Luke 14:11; 18:14).

That great reversal was not only announced by Jesus; it was also performed by him. Those who did not count for much in Israel counted with Jesus — and in his politics. Those on the margins of Israel's common life were at the center of Jesus' ministry — and of his politics. He made the last first. He blessed the poor, healed the lepers, ate with "sinners," taught women, lifted up a Samaritan as a moral example. And those who exalted themselves — the rabbis who insisted on the best seats in the synagogue (Mark 12:38-40), the priests who used temple observance to enrich themselves (Mark 11:15-17), "that fox" Herod Antipas (Luke 13:32), and the Gentile rulers who "lord[ed] it over" their subjects (Mark 10:42) — did not count for much with Jesus. They belonged to the present evil age and fell under judgment, along with the self-assertiveness of empires and the conventional politics of pomp and protocol, prestige and privilege.

The coming reign of God called into question the present order; in the crisis of the times, the political implications of his announcement of the kingdom and of the great reversal it brings could hardly be lost or overlooked. Jesus practiced the great reversal he announced also by his presence among the disciples "as one who serves" (Luke 22:27; cf. Matt. 20:28; Mark 10:45; John 13:2-17). Jesus revisited the ancient theocratic image of the humble king. And the only fitting response to this coming reign of God — and to this Jesus — is captured in the command to "be last of all and servant of all" (Mark 9:35; cf. Matt. 20:26, 27; 23:11; Mark 10:43-44; Luke 22:26; John 13:12-17). It was a response required especially, of course, of those who "would be first," of the leaders of Israel's common life.

19. See Joachim Jeremias, *Jesus' Promise to the Nations* (Naperville, Ill.: A. R. Allenson, 1958), pp. 41-46.

20. In addition to the biblical references, see also Pap. Oxyrhynchus 654, ar. 3, and the Gospel of Thomas 4.

Liberation and Exorcism

Apocalyptic literature had been preoccupied with visions and speculations about the signs of the times as this age runs its course toward the end. But Jesus did not indulge in such speculations. Indeed, he warned against them (Luke 17:20-30; even "the apocalyptic discourse" is hedged about by warnings against calculation and speculation, Mark 13:5-6, 21-22). Jesus emphasized the suddenness of the end, its unpredictability. He "saw" only "Satan fall from heaven like a flash of lightning" (Luke 10:18). That was apocalyptic vision enough. He not only "saw" that future, however; he also performed it. In his exorcisms that good future made its power felt; he brought as well the promised liberation from the power of Satan and his hosts. As he said, "If it is by the finger of God that I cast out the demons, then the kingdom of God has come upon you" (Luke 11:20).

Contemporary readers who assume a tidy distinction between the spiritual and the political may conclude from Jesus' vision and practice of exorcism that he was apolitical, but that was not the assumption of the first century. Indeed, it was more reasonable in the first century to conclude that, because Jesus "saw" Satan fall, Caesar too would fall from his throne, and that, as Jesus made the future power of God felt in exorcisms, so he would make the future present by casting out the Roman army. That conclusion, it should be repeated, was not unreasonable. It cohered with the intimacy of the spiritual and the political worlds in apocalyptic literature, with the social significance of possession, and with at least one of Jesus' exorcisms.

First, the spiritual world and the political world were not neatly distinguished in the apocalyptic world of Jesus. The book of Daniel, where the angel Michael is God's champion (and Israel's) against the patron angels of Persia and Greece (Dan. 10:13, 20-21; 12:1), is sufficient evidence that the spiritual and political worlds were intimately connected in apocalyptic.[21] Daniel's vision provided courage to act with integrity in the face of Antiochus IV Epiphanes. The book of Daniel was at least consistent with the resistance movement begun by the Maccabees, even if it did not sponsor it, and indeed, it seems to refer to the Maccabees as "a little help" to the pious of Jerusalem (Dan. 11:33-35).

Second, exorcism had social significance. Consider Paul Hollenbach's sociological account of possession. Possession, he says, was frequently found in contexts of social tension: "class antagonism rooted in economic exploitation, conflicts between traditions where revered traditions are eroded, colonial domi-

---

21. See also 1 Enoch 37–71.

nation and revolution."[22] He uses Frantz Fanon's study of mental illness during the Algerian war of revolution against France, *The Wretched of the Earth*, to illustrate his point. The oppressed find themselves in a schizophrenic spot; they are the oppressed, but they dream of becoming the oppressor. Divided against themselves, they are driven to mental illness, which may be seen, then, "as a socially acceptable form of oblique protest against, or escape from, oppressions."[23] It is a form of protest where people see no other way to cope with their conditions but fear provoking the oppressors too much.

Exorcisms in such an apocalyptic — and oppressive — context were charged with political significance. Consider, finally, therefore, the political connotations of the exorcism in Mark 5:1-20. They are hard to miss or to ignore. Jesus encountered one possessed, a man who "lived among the tombs," a man whom no one could restrain (v. 3). The name of the demon was Legion, "for we are many" (v. 9). A legion, of course, was a Roman cohort of soldiers, four thousand to six thousand men; a legion was the sign of Roman power and possession of the land. Jesus casts out "Legion," and then "Legion" "begged him earnestly not to send them out of the country" (v. 10). So Jesus permits the "Legion" to enter a herd of swine, which promptly rush into the sea and are drowned (v. 13). It was every Jewish revolutionary's dream: the legion cast out of the land, driven into the sea. The man was restored to himself, to self-control, and to his community, to his friends. The people, however, "were afraid" (v. 15) — afraid perhaps that such an exorcism would provoke Rome.[24]

The conclusion of some, therefore, that Jesus' vision of Satan's fall might initiate revolution was not unreasonable, but it *was* wrong. Jesus did not violently cast the Roman legion into the sea; he did not cast Caesar down from his throne, not yet anyway (cf. Rev. 12:9). Two related things stood in the way of such a political performance: Israel's possession and Jesus' vision of the future.

Israel was possessed not just by Roman colonialists and oppressors but by its envy of them, by the schizophrenic desire of the oppressed to be the oppressors themselves, by the wish to lord it over those who had lorded it over them

---

22. See Paul W. Hollenbach, "Jesus, Demoniacs, and Public Authorities: A Socio-Historical Study," *Journal of the American Academy of Religion* 99 (1981): 567-88, p. 573.

23. Hollenbach, "Jesus, Demoniacs, and Public Authorities," p. 576. Hollenbach also observes (p. 577) that the connection between deviancy and possession can lead to accusations of possession as a way to silence social protest. The observation is relevant, of course, to the Beelzebul incident (Mark 3:22-30).

24. Luke Timothy Johnson makes a strong case that this man reappears in Mark 16:1-8 as the young man dressed in a white robe at the right hand of Jesus' tomb. If so, and if Mark was written to Roman Christians following Nero's persecution, then the fear of provoking Rome would have special significance for Mark's audience.

— or at least to lord it over some. And that demon would not be exorcised by violence. Satan's fall did not spell revenge against Rome; it spelled an end to both oppression and the desire for revenge. Israel needed liberation from the "strong man," to be sure, but the "strong man" was not so much Caesar as Satan himself (Mark 3:23-27). In the temptation narrative Satan could offer "all the kingdoms of the world and their splendor" (Matt. 4:8), but to accept that offer would not exorcise Satan from Israel's politics. Jesus served God, not Satan (Matt. 4:10), and he called Israel to welcome God's reign and to be free from its "possession." The violent overthrow of Rome sponsored by Israel's revenge and resentment would not cast out its demons. The overthrow of Rome would not guarantee a politics in Israel worthy of God's reign. The politics of Israel itself, not only its colonial dominion by Rome, was alienating and provisional.

The good future of God did not entail a Jewish empire on the model of the Roman; it meant the fulfillment of the old theocratic vision of an international order of blessing for both Jews and Gentiles (e.g., Matt. 8:11; Luke 13:29; cf. Isa. 25:6-7; 49:12).[25] It meant an end to the bestial politics of empire and resentment.

But if it will not do to conclude from Jesus' vision and from his exorcisms that he was apolitical, disinterested in the politics of the land, and if the conclusion is not a Zealot call to arms, what is the political conclusion? We have seen it already, of course. There is a "great reversal" for political power itself.

> You know that among the Gentiles those whom they recognize as their rulers lord it over them, and their great ones are tyrants over them. But it is not so among you; but whoever wishes to become great among you must be your servant, and whoever wishes to be first among you must be slave of all. For the Son of Man came not to be served but to serve, and to give his life a ransom for many. (Mark 10:42-45)

To welcome already the coming reign of God, to celebrate already the apocalyptic vision of Satan's fall, and to remember Jesus as the one who makes that future present is to construe political power as a vocation to humble service. Politics is not disowned but liberated from the hold of the demonic in Jesus' vision and practice. Political power is not to be construed or used as an opportunity to lord it over others or to seek revenge; it is, rather, a vocation to humble service.

---

25. See further Jeremias, *Jesus' Promise to the Nations*, pp. 51-73.

The Authority of Jesus

Jesus made the good future of God present in his exorcisms — and also in his exercise of authority. Indeed, his exorcisms (and all his miracles) were part of that exercise of authority *(exousia)*. Both his words and his deeds expressed his authority, for they unveiled the coming reign of God. The future rule of God made its power — and its authority — felt in both works and words. Jesus' authority was the authority of one in whom God's authority was at work.

The crowds recognized the authority of Jesus both in his teaching, "for he taught them as one having authority, and not as the scribes" (Mark 1:22), and in his exorcisms, for "he commands even the unclean spirits, and they obey him" (Mark 1:27). The authority of Jesus was recognized, moreover, not just by the Jewish crowds but also by that representative of Roman authority, the centurion (Matt. 8:5-13; Luke 7:1-10).

That representative of empire recognized the authority, the *exousia,* of Jesus in an unmistakably political way. It is the ability to command that is *exousia,* and Jesus has it, and because he has it, he need not be personally present in order to guarantee the execution of his commands. The centurion used his own experience of authority as an analogy to the authority of Jesus. "I also," he said, "am a man under authority, with soldiers under me" (Matt. 8:9). He was "in authority" by being "under authority." He was authorized, and so was Jesus, of course. And the deference to Jesus' *exousia* by the centurion is striking: "Lord, I am not worthy to have you come under my roof; but only speak the word, and my servant will be healed" (8:8). Jesus need not condescend so much as to make a special visit. It would be neither necessary nor altogether fitting, unnecessary because Jesus had the authority to command, not altogether fitting because the authority of Jesus was greater than his own and because the one who authorized Jesus was greater than the one who authorized the centurion.

Jesus granted the petition of the centurion and healed his servant. Jesus exercised his authority to bless this Roman official, not to curse him, to grant to him a foretaste of God's blessing upon Gentiles (8:11), not to take revenge against him. But it is also noteworthy that the Roman official used his own power to care for those under him, for his servant. Here was no tyrant, but a humble ruler, one who looked out for those who were least in his household. No pride of power kept him from making a humble request for the sake of his servant.[26]

---

26. In Luke's Gospel, moreover, it is not only implicit that the centurion cares for his slave but also made explicit — by some Jewish elders — that "he loves our people" (Luke 7:5).

Jesus exercised his authority, the authority of God's coming rule, also in driving from the temple those who sold animals for sacrifice and exchanged Roman coins (stamped with the image of the emperor) for Jewish coins to pay the temple tax (Mark 11:15-17; John 2:13-17). Such practices were not illegal, and they might even have begun as a convenience to pilgrims, but by the prices they charged and the rate of exchange they exacted, the priestly aristocracy enriched themselves at the expense of the pious poor. And, by exploiting the poor, they profaned the temple. Citing Jeremiah 7:11, Jesus accused the temple authorities of running a "den of robbers" (Mark 11:17). Moreover, this commerce in the court of the Gentiles effectively prevented the one place in the temple that was open to the Gentiles from being a place of prayer. Jesus would not allow it. Citing Isaiah 56:7 he reminded his hearers of the theocratic hope of a temple that would be "a house of prayer for all nations" (Mark 11:17). Certainly Jesus' cleansing of the temple was more a prophetic or symbolic action than the programmatic inauguration of a revolution;[27] even so, it was a symbolic action that invoked the notion of "authority" (Mark 11:28) and involved the use of force rather than a personal appeal to conscience.[28]

Finally, Jesus "taught . . . as one having authority, and not as the scribes" (Mark 1:22). Jesus amazed his hearers — and scandalized some of them — because he spoke with authority. Again the apocalyptic background is important. In apocalyptic literature the seer sees in the future some new and superior revelation of God and God's cause.[29] In Jesus this revelation is no longer provided under a pseudonym; it is provided by Jesus himself. And that new revelation of God and of God's cause is no longer merely future. It already makes its power felt — and its claims — in Jesus himself and in his words.

In Jesus' words of judgment the coming judgment of God was anticipated, and in his words of blessing the coming salvation of God was made known. But upon whom did the judgment rest? Upon those who liked to regard themselves as the "first" of the nation, upon the proud and wealthy, upon the governing classes and the cities who refused to repent, who refused to welcome the announcement of God's rule, who refused hospitality to the reversal theoc-

27. Even Brandon, who emphasizes the temple cleansing in his portrayal of Jesus, acknowledged that the action of Jesus "appears to have been of a more symbolic character" than the seizure of the temple by the Zealots in C.E. 66 (*Jesus and the Zealots*, p. 338).

28. In John's account Jesus not only drove the merchants and the money changers out, but used a whip to do it (John 2:15).

29. See, e.g., *Ethiopian Enoch* 37.4; U. Wilckens, "The Understanding of Revelation within the History of Primitive Christianity," in *Revelation as History*, ed. Wolfhart Pannenberg (London: Macmillan, 1968), pp. 57-82, p. 70.

racy promised (or threatened).[30] And if judgment fell on them, to whom did the coming salvation come? Salvation came to the crowd; Jesus "had compassion for [the crowd], because they were like sheep without a shepherd" (Mark 6:34; cf. Matt. 9:36). And with the authority of God's coming reign, Jesus announced already God's salvation and blessing to those who were "last," to those who did not count for much in Israel's politics, to women and children, to the poor and weak — and to any who repented, even tax collectors like Zacchaeus (Luke 19:1-9) and even Roman centurions.

Jesus came announcing that something new was at hand, that the good future of God was at hand and already making its power felt. That new thing was the final and decisive revelation of God and of the will of God, and Jesus spoke as one authorized to make it known. Jesus was not simply a pious interpreter of the ancient code, like the scribes; he spoke rather on his own authority "under God." Indeed, he set his own authority over-against the authority of the Law as interpreted by the scribes: "You have heard that it was said. . . . But I say to you . . ." (e.g., Matt. 5:21, 27, 31, 33, 38, 43).[31] It was Jesus' teaching, not the Torah, that provided the foundation for a life — and a common life — able to stand in the judgment of God (Matt. 7:24-27; Luke 6:47-49). Moreover, given the new thing God is doing, the Law and the prophets belong decisively to the past, to the old age (Matt. 11:12, 13; Luke 16:16). Jesus called for a response to God's good future, for repentance. His ethic was fundamentally an ethic of response rather than an ethic of obedience to the Law.

The Authority of Jesus and the Law

Still, the questions of Jesus' attitude toward the Law and his interpretation of it can hardly be neglected if we are to understand the politics of Jesus, for the Law, as we have seen, was critically important to the theocratic tradition.[32] When the

30. See, for example, the woes (e.g., Luke 6:24), the judgments upon the cities (e.g., Matt. 23:37-38), and the polemic against the scribes (e.g., Matt. 23:1-36).

31. The form of the "antitheses" is probably the work of Matthew, but it is faithful to a memory of Jesus who set the authority of his words over-against the *halakah* of the scribes; see, e.g., Mark 10:2-12.

32. The question of Jesus' attitude to the Law is complicated by the presence of apparent discrepancies in the tradition. Some texts seem to disclose an almost rabbinic attachment to the Law (e.g., Matt. 5:17-19; 18:16; 23:2-3; Mark 1:44; 7:9-10; 10:18-19; Luke 5:14; 16:27-31); others seem to reject the Law (e.g., Matt. 5:38-41; Mark 2:18–3:6; 7:14-23; 10:2-12; Luke 13:10-17). It is complicated further by the fact that the evangelists evidently interpreted and communicated the attitude of Jesus to the Law in their own distinctive

Covenant Code articulated the shape of social life appropriate to the social life of a theocratic amphictyony, it nudged the received legal tradition in the direction of something worthy of a story of the liberation of slaves. The Deuteronomic Code was an instrument of social reform. Ezra took Torah to Jerusalem and put it at the center of the restored community. Whether Persians, Greeks, or Romans ruled, the Law had an unassailable political authority for the Jews. All of life was to be directed by the commandments of Torah. It was the Law of God, and by it God governed Israel. When the Seleucids prohibited Torah and its observance, civil disobedience and finally rebellion became unavoidable. The Romans did not prohibit Torah or its observance, and for many Jews, including many of the Pharisees, the political independence of the nation was less important than the integrity of a culture formed by observance of Torah. Theocracy was compatible with Roman occupation of the land but not with lawlessness.

Torah was the fundamental authority for the common life, for the politics of Israel. It was the professional responsibility of the scribes and rabbis to preserve, interpret, and apply Torah. They stood, according to the Pharisees, in a long and authoritative tradition, the so-called oral Torah, which had been passed down and supplemented by a succession of teachers reaching from Moses and Joshua to their own rabbis and teachers.[33] A more serious responsibility could hardly be imagined, for God's Law was the foundation of Jewish life.

The Torah, of course, contained both statutes and stories, both laws and narratives, and the oral Torah, the tradition of authoritative interpretation, did, too. Commentary on the statutes was regarded as *halakah,* or "walk," as rules for behavior. Carefully following exegetic rules attributed to Hillel (first century, B.C.E.),[34] the rabbis made the ancient statutes relevant to new and concrete questions of conduct. Commentary on the remainder of Torah was called *haggadah,* from the verb for "relate" or "tell." *Haggadah* was more spontaneous, and in it the narratives were elaborated and stories added for the sake of edifying the community. *Halakah* was regarded as the more important of the modes of interpreting Torah.

---

ways. In Mark's story of Jesus, for example, Jesus is quite carefree about observance of the Law. In Matthew's story, on the other hand, Jesus is quite concerned about such observance: the Law holds and Jesus is its best interpreter. The contrast between Matthew and Mark can be seen quite clearly in Matthew's redaction of Mark 2:23-28 in Matthew 12:1-8. See further Robert J. Banks, *Jesus and the Law in the Synoptic Tradition* (London: Herder & Herder, 1965), and Verhey, *The Great Reversal,* pp. 83-85. Some things about Jesus' attitude to the Law, however, can be said confidently.

33. See *P. Aboth* 1.1.

34. *Tosephta Sanhedrin* 7.11, quoted in C. K. Barrett, *The New Testament Background* (New York: Macmillan, 1957), p. 146.

This devotion to the Law, it should be observed, was not alien to apocalyptic thought. Indeed, one can find in apocalyptic literature assertions about the centrality and the eternal validity of the Law (e.g., Jub. 3:31; 6:17). While waiting patiently for God to act, the pious Jew will keep the Law. Nevertheless, apocalyptic was oriented toward a future act of God which would establish God's cosmic sovereignty beyond any challenge, and for apocalyptic it was that future act which would be finally and genuinely decisive — not any event of Israel's past, not even Sinai. The vision and hope of the apocalyptic teacher was something new, something incomparably superior to all previous revelation, something final.

In the teachings of Jesus this new thing, this good future of God, this final revelation, was already making its power felt. The people "were astounded at his teaching, for he taught them as one having authority, and not as the scribes" (Mark 1:22). Notice, however, that although he did not teach them "as the scribes," still he taught them, like the scribes, in the synagogue, that house of study of the Torah, and on the Sabbath. Jesus did interpret Torah, and the interpretation of Torah was fundamental to his politics, but he interpreted the Law in a way authorized by God's good future. In his interpretation the Law became an instrument of God's future judgment and a token of God's future salvation. Jesus did not destroy the Law or the prophets; he fulfilled them (Matt. 5:17-18; Luke 16:17). He brought the Law — and the whole theocratic tradition — to eschatological fruition.

The imminent sovereignty of God demanded something more than an external and conventional righteousness based on observance of statutes. Jesus shifted the emphasis from *halakah* to *haggadah,* from rules for conduct to the formation of character. He parodied, as we have noted, a casuistry that aimed at ensuring external observance while it left the heart untouched (Matt. 23:25-28; Mark 7:5-7), and he condemned a casuistry co-opted by the powerful and made to serve their interests. He put the Law in the service of the poor. These observations warrant further comment and illustration.

Notice, first, that Jesus shifted the emphasis from *halakah* to *haggadah,* from statute to narrative, from rules for external conduct to the formation of character by the story. As we have seen, the lawgivers of Israel had set the statutes in the context of the story, and, as we have also observed, they had fashioned and refashioned the received legal tradition in order to make it more fitting to the story. And so did Jesus. He set the Law in the context of a story that began with creation, continued in covenant, and was about to climax in God's unchallenged reign. The welcome due the kingdom outreaches the grasp of legal sanctions and *halakah.*

Consider, for example, the controversy about divorce. There was a great debate about the *halakah* concerning divorce. The rabbis had agreed that the relevant statute was Deuteronomy 24:1-4, but interpretation ranged from Rabbi Shammai's refusal to permit a man to divorce his wife unless there was unchastity to Akiba's allowance for divorce if the husband finds some other woman more to his liking.[35] The Pharisees invited Jesus to join the debate (Mark 10:2), but in Mark's account at least Jesus refused the invitation to debate *halakah*. He set the statute aside as having been written "because of your hardness of heart." It belonged to the old age. Instead, Jesus appealed to the creation story, to Genesis 1:27 and 2:24, and concluded, "Therefore, what God has joined together, let no one separate." Not the statute but the story is decisive; it is time for the fulfillment of what had been God's intentions from the beginning. Jesus does not provide a new legal requirement here; it is not some new and rigorous *halakah*. It is not *halakah* at all; it is *haggadah,* and it forms a disposition not to divorce even when a self-serving interpretation of the Law would permit it.

Matthew's account is a little different. The stress still falls on *haggadah,* on the story of creation, but in Matthew's Gospel (Matt. 19:3-9) Jesus does not use *haggadah* to set aside the statute but to interpret it. The statutes are set in the context of the story and interpreted in the light of it. In Matthew Jesus finally returns to the debate about *halakah,* to the statute (still recognized as related to their "hardness of heart"), and he gives a ruling like that of Rabbi Shammai. In Matthew, Jesus does enter the debate, and the *halakah* is, in agreement with Rabbi Shammai, that men may only divorce their wives where there has been "unchastity."

The contrast is striking, if typical: Mark's Jesus sets aside the statute; Matthew's Jesus holds to the statute and is its best interpreter. Still, the agreements are also striking, and typical of Jesus' attitude toward the Law. In both Mark and Matthew Jesus shifts the emphasis from *halakah* to *haggadah,* from statute to narrative, from rules for external conduct to the formation of character by the story. In Mark — and for Mark's Gentile audience — the memory of Jesus' emphasis on *haggadah* is retrieved in the context of Gentile freedom from the Jewish statutes. In Matthew — and for Matthew's largely Jewish Christian audience — Jesus' emphasis on *haggadah* is used, not to set aside *halakah,* but as crucial to the proper interpretation of the statutes. And in both the statutes were given because of the hardness of heart. The statutes of Torah belong to the age of hard hearts. In the good future of God hearts will be softened, and on them will be written the law of God.

---

35. Mishnah, *Gittin* IX.10 preserves something of this debate. See further Allen Verhey, "Divorce in the New Testament," *The International Standard Bible Encyclopedia,* rev. ed., 1:315-19.

In the meantime, however, while hearts remain hard, the statutes remained important to the common life of Israel, and political reform in Israel still engaged the interpretation of the statutes of Torah. The coming reign of God required something more than external observance of the Law, but it was no license for lawlessness. The reign of God may not be reduced to a political program or to a set of "minimal standards," but the Law remained important. And political authorities should be prepared to tend to sores in the body politic with remedies considerably less winsome than patient persuasion in order to protect the poor and powerless, just as Jesus dealt with the extortion in the temple. Such a political posture construes authority as a vocation to humble service; it does not reject it. Political reform itself, however, required dispositions and virtues that the statutes by themselves could not provide. It required a response to the announcement of God's good future. Moreover, the Law could be co-opted by the powerful and read in hard-hearted and self-serving defense of their interests. Notice, also, therefore, that Jesus rejected the self-serving use of the Law.

Consider, for example, the controversy concerning the vow of "Corban" (Mark 7:6-13).[36] There was a well-developed casuistry concerning vows, based in part on the statutes of Numbers 30 and Leviticus 27, and later set down in the Mishnah tractate *Nedarim*. Making a vow was not regarded as a religious obligation, but the fulfilling of a vow validly made was. To make a vow that something was "Corban" was to declare that it was dedicated to God. It did not require that the thing actually be offered up in the temple, but only that it be withdrawn from ordinary use. It could be simply a legal fiction. One could vow something to God, not so that it might be given to God, but so that some other person would not receive it. This legal fiction, of course, was easily abused. One could refuse to share one's food by declaring that the portion hospitality might suggest was "Corban," or, as in the case Jesus brings up, one could refuse to provide for a parent by saying, "What you would have gained from me is Corban" (Mark 7:11 RSV). Hard-hearted sons could use the Law to renege on their natural (and legal!) obligations to their parents, and if the vow were validly made, it would be enforced by the rabbis. Or, they might utter "Corban" hastily and in anger, and when their hearts softened, they might seek to have the vow annulled, but the tradition made no allowance for annulling a valid vow on account of the honor that was due parents.[37] And because the tradition made no

36. See T. W. Manson, *The Teaching of Jesus* (Cambridge: Cambridge University Press, 1967), pp. 315-19.
37. The tradition did make allowance for annulling vows uttered in bargaining, vows to confirm obviously exaggerated statements, vows made under a misapprehension,

such provision for annulment, hard-hearted rabbis would still enforce the vow. The rabbis, it should be observed, did not typically treat obligations to parents cavalierly, but they were powerless against a self-serving use of the Law and captured by their devotion to the tradition.

Halakah by itself could not provide the virtues and dispositions critical to a decent common life or to a decent use of the commandments. It could be co-opted by the hard-hearted and read in self-serving defense of their interests. Jesus rejected such self-serving casuistry and its hard-hearted enforcement against the poor and powerless. The authority to interpret the Law was a critical form of social authority in first-century Palestine, and that authority, too, is not disowned by the politics of Jesus but construed as a vocation to serve the poor and powerless. Let the Law be read and interpreted in the light of the whole story, the end of which is at hand in a great reversal of first and last. Let it be read and enforced in the light of God's cause and in the interest of those who are least. When, in more than one dispute with the Pharisees, Jesus appealed to Hosea 6:6, "I desire mercy and not sacrifice" (Matt. 9:13; 12:7), he disclosed a rule for interpretation that was not found in Hillel's list of rules for *halakah*. It was a hermeneutical key for the interpretation of the Law.[38] The Law was to be read and performed in the interest of the needy, the sick, and those on the margins of Israel's life. The coming kingdom condemns the pride of power and gives direction for the enforcement of "minimal standards." The cause of God — the protection of the weak, the blessing on the poor, the inclusion of those on the margins — must be served with political authority, including the political authority to interpret Scripture. The hermeneutical privilege of the poor, so important to Catholic social thought, was important first to Jesus' theocratic politics.

Notice also, therefore, that Jesus set the interpretation of the Law in the service of the poor, appealing to the Law and interpreting it in their interests. When, for example, he quoted Deuteronomy 15:11, "You always have the poor with you" (Mark 14:7), he reiterated the ancient judgment against the politics of Israel that it had forgotten the covenant and reminded those who heard him

---

and vows that turned out to be impossible to fulfill because of the pressure of other circumstances (*Nedarim* iii.1).

38. It should be observed that the explicit reference to Hosea 6:6 is only found in Matthew, but this hermeneutical key is implicit in all the disputes about the Sabbath (see Mark 2:23-28; 3:1-6; Luke 13:10-17; 14:1-6; John 5:1-18; notice the repetition of the question concerning "doing good" on the Sabbath in Mark 3:4, Luke 14:3, and the similar question in John 7:23). Moreover, it is also implicit in the parable of the Good Samaritan. The priest and Levite are on their way to participate in temple observance, and so they fail to act with compassion, but Jesus counts compassion more important than sacrifice.

of the ancient command to "open your hand to the poor and needy neighbor in your land" (Deut. 15:11). And when he invited his hearers to "lend, expecting nothing in return" (Luke 6:35), he quite clearly cites Deuteronomy 15:8.[39] Deuteronomy 15 is legislation concerning the Sabbath year, and it contains provisions for the release from debt (vv. 1-6), for lending to the poor (vv. 7-11), and for freeing slaves (vv. 12-18).

It was the provocative thesis of John Howard Yoder[40] that the "platform" for the politics of Jesus was the proclamation of the year of Jubilee in C.E. 26. The year of Jubilee came every fifty years, after seven Sabbath years (Lev. 25). It may be too much to claim that Jesus called for the enforcement of the year of Jubilee.[41] It is, however, surely part of the church's memory of Jesus that, when he announced the good future of God, he reminded his hearers of images of Jubilee, the forgiveness of debts, the liberation of the enslaved, and blessings upon the poor — and Jesus did not empty those images of their social and political significance.[42] The politics of Jesus were Jubilee politics even if he did not call for enforcement of a Jubilee year. He summoned the people to acknowledge the reign of God, theocracy; he drew out the implications of blessings upon the

---

39. See Robert B. Sloan Jr., *The Favorable Year of the Lord: A Study of Jubilary Theology in the Gospel of Luke* (Austin, Tex.: Schola, 1977), p. 134.

40. See John Howard Yoder, *The Politics of Jesus* (Grand Rapids: Eerdmans, 1972), pp. 64-77. Yoder acknowledges his indebtedness for this thesis — and for this third chapter — to André Trocmé, *Jesus and the Nonviolent Revolution*, trans. Michael H. Shank and Marlin E. Miller (Scottdale, Pa.: Herald, 1973).

41. Sloan, *The Favorable Year of the Lord*, maintains that the Jubilee was an "eschatological metaphor" indebted more to Isaiah 61 than to Leviticus 25. See pp. 171-72: "The 'subject of the text' [Luke 4:14-21] . . . is *not*, as Yoder suggests, the Mosaic jubilee. The *subject* of the text . . . is the advent . . . of the *Eschaton*. . . ." Sharon H. Ringe, *Jesus, Liberation and the Biblical Jubilee* (Philadelphia: Fortress, 1985), reaches a similar conclusion.

42. Sloan, for example, acknowledged that "the *Eschaton*" was "pre-eminently described in terms of the 'release' ordinances of the Mosaic 'year of jubilee'" (*The Favorable Year of the Lord*, p. 172). While I agree with Sloan and Ringe that there is no evidence that Jesus called for the enforcement of a Jubilee in C.E. 26, I am suspicious of Sloan's positing an "either/or" between "eschatological metaphor" and political practice. Yoder himself regarded political practice as "prefiguring the 'reestablishment of all things'" (*Politics of Jesus*, p. 76). Yoder also acknowledged that the Jubilee "platform" was mediated through the use of prophetic texts rather than legal texts in Luke 4:16-21. It may also be observed that, when Yoder (or Trocmé) calls attention to the authority of these materials for the continuing church, he uses the Jubilee not as a basis for contemporary rules but as a backing for certain "dispositions" (*Politics of Jesus*, p. 77). This way of using Scripture seems right to me but curiously inconsistent with Yoder's reading of texts concerning nonviolence.

poor and release from all that enslaves; and he announced judgment against the powers that resisted the performance of God's reign.

Finally, notice what was put first above, that the coming kingdom required something more radical than the labored application of legal precepts to external behavior, something more penetrating than certain legal limits on the expression of human anger, lust, deceitfulness, vengefulness, avarice, and enmity. Consider, for example, the antitheses of Matthew's Gospel (Matt. 5:21-46). Matthew quite deliberately compares the righteousness of the scribes, focused on external observance of the Law, with "the surpassing righteousness" that Jesus demands (Matt. 5:20). The Law forbids murder (5:21), prohibits adultery (5:27), restricts divorce (5:31), condemns swearing falsely (5:33), restricts revenge (5:38), and commands love of (some) neighbors (5:43). Jesus did not reject those ancient laws, but what he did reject was any scribal interpretation that was satisfied with external limits on the expressions of anger, lust, deceit, revenge, and self-centeredness. Such scribal righteousness left the moral agent untouched by its attention to the limits on conduct, so that even observance of the Law would be grudging and external. By announcing the coming kingdom, Jesus is the best interpreter of the Law; he presses beyond external restrictions to the heart upon which the Law finally will be written and claims the whole person for the rule of God. The promise of the prophets, after all, was that God would write the Law upon their hearts (Jer. 31:31-34; Ezek. 11:19-20). The good future was making its power felt, not in tortured interpretations of ancient legal texts, but in the hearts and lives of those who welcomed that future and repented.

In the righteousness that exceeds "that of the scribes" (Matt. 5:20) people will be disposed to reconcile with their neighbors, not to be angry with them (5:21-26). They will be disposed to chastity, not to reduce the neighbor to a sexual object (5:27-30). They will be eager for fidelity, not for divorce (5:31-32). They will be disposed to truthfulness, not eager to deceive (5:33-37). They will be eager for peace, not for revenge (5:38-42). And they will be ready to love even the enemy, even the one who is hardly ready to return their kindness (5:43-47). So they will "fulfill" the Law and the prophets (5:17); so they will be "children of your Father in heaven" (5:45), the "light of the world," and that most political of images, "a city built on a hill" that "cannot be hid" (5:14).

Jesus, in the memory of Matthew, does not provide in the antitheses a new and more rigorous *halakah*. He claims and forms character and community. To be sure, the character is sometimes described in terms of the ways that it breaks into surprising behaviors, such as turning the other cheek or going the second mile (5:39, 41). Such behaviors are indeed signs and symptoms of the "surpassing righteousness" that Jesus demands, and, of course, the character and community Jesus formed must find positive and external expression, but Jesus did not provide here a code for external conduct. Perhaps the clearest evidence that he did not is that, if he did, then he violated his own code, for Jesus called the scribes and Pharisees "fools" (23:17; cf. 5:22) and allowed oaths, even as he attacked the pettifoggery surrounding them (23:16-22; cf. 5:33-37).

The Politics of Jesus and Violence

The antithesis concerning revenge (Matt. 5:38-48) is sometimes taken to be a key to the politics of Jesus and to require the rejection of violence.

> You have heard that it was said, "An eye for an eye and a tooth for a tooth." But I say to you, Do not resist an evildoer. But if anyone strikes you on the right cheek, turn the other also; and if anyone wants to sue you and take your coat, give your cloak as well; and if anyone forces you to go one mile, go also the second mile. Give to everyone who begs from you, and do not refuse anyone who wants to borrow from you. (5:38-42)

The pattern of the antitheses is repeated. The ancient law, here the famous *lex talionis*, is given first, followed by a word spoken with Jesus' own authority. As in the other antitheses, it is not the ancient law itself that is rejected, but a scribal interpretation of the law that is satisfied with merely external observance. The *lex talionis* set a limit on revenge, it did not sanctify it. The limit still stands, and as a minimal standard it remains effective against revenge where hearts remain hard. But Jesus rejects a scribal interpretation that permits people to seek revenge up to that limit. With the authority of God's coming rule, Jesus' word reaches to the heart and commands a disposition not to return insult for insult[43] or blow for blow, a readiness not to insist on one's rights over-against the neighbor, even if the neighbor is an enemy. And the pattern also holds in that the word of Jesus is not given as *halakah*, not given as a legal requirement. As there was a context within which Jesus called the scribes "fools," so there might be a context within which Jesus would call for resistance to the evildoer.

Jesus clearly addresses the situation that ignites our incendiary desire for revenge, the situation in which we have been treated unjustly. But he does not here address the situation in which we are to defend a neighbor against an attack or against some other form of injustice. Or to make the point differently, he does

---

43. David Daube, *The New Testament and Rabbinic Judaism* (London: Athlone, 1956), pp. 260-63, argues that to be struck "on the right cheek" is to be struck with the back of the hand, an insult rather than an injury.

not demand of the police officer that he never interpose himself and his authority between an attacker and the one attacked. He does not require of a judge that
he turn a deaf ear when a victim of assault brings a charge before him.

Richard Hays thinks to defend the pacifist reading of this passage by citing Deuteronomy 19:15-21, where the *lex talionis* does have a prescriptive function. In that passage, as a deterrent to false witness, judges are commanded to
"do to the false witness just as the false witness had meant to do to the other."
And it concludes, "Show no pity: life for life, eye for eye, tooth for tooth. . . ."
Hays's comment on this passage is this:

> But where Deuteronomy insists, "Show no pity," Jesus says, "Do not resist
> an evil doer." The Law's concern for maintaining stability and justice is sup-
> planted by Jesus' concern to encourage nonviolent, long-suffering generos-
> ity on the part of those who are wronged. This extraordinary change of em-
> phasis constitutes a paradigm shift that effectually undermines the Torah's
> teaching about just punishment for offenders.[44]

I should think, however, that precisely *where* the judge is concerned about
maintaining stability and justice is *not where* Jesus says, "Do not resist an evildoer." Those who are wronged should not seek revenge, but those who are
charged with protecting the innocent should not, on the pretext of "pity," renege on their obligations, under God, to hear the case of the widow (cf. Luke
18:1-8) or to see that justice is done for the powerless. Jesus' word does *not*
"supplant" or "undermine" the Law's concern for maintaining justice and stability in the land.

The good future of God frees us from the need to assert the sort of tightfisted justice that looks out for number one, that protects self-interest, that licenses tit-for-tat when we have been hurt or offended, and that limits compassion to those from whom we can legitimately expect reciprocity. The good future
of God provides a taste of a better justice, a justice that belongs to theocracy, a
justice that frees the slaves and protects the poor and powerless. That good future makes its power felt in parabolic gestures like turning the other cheek —
and in parabolic gestures like overturning the tables of the moneychangers in
the temple when the priests are growing rich at the expense of the poor. It makes
its power felt, surely, in peacemakers (Matt. 5:9), for in the peace they make we
see a token of the *shalom* God promises. *And* it makes its power felt in those who
hunger and thirst for justice (Matt. 5:6 *New Living Translation*), for in the justice
done for the weak and powerless we have a foretaste of God's future.

44. Richard B. Hays, *The Moral Vision of the New Testament* (Grand Rapids: Eerdmans, 1996), p. 325.

The question of Jesus' pacifism does not rest on a single verse, of course. The church remembers Jesus as one who "suffered under Pontius Pilate." When he was insulted, he did not return the insult. When they struck him and reviled him, he did not look for revenge. He characteristically "turned the other cheek." When he was arrested, he did not resist; and when one of his disciples drew his sword and struck one of the arresting party, Jesus told him to put his sword away (Matt. 26:52; Luke 22:51; John 18:11).

Moreover, he consistently rejected violence as a messianic strategy, as a means to achieve the good future of God. After he fed the crowds, they acclaimed him "the prophet who is to come" and were ready to "take him by force to make him king," but Jesus would have none of it and withdrew (John 6:14, 15). He would not be co-opted by a popular movement of a politically destructive sort, restless, dissatisfied, resentful, disregarding justice and genuine community. He would not be "possessed" by a popular movement drawn to power itself rather than to the kingdom of God. Such a movement would be itself "possessed" by a spirit of resentment and envy, a spirit hostile to the kingdom of God. Jesus would not have his power and authority used as a means to achieve the political ends of such a movement. He would serve the cause of God. He sought peace — and judged the Zealot desire for revenge; he sought justice — and judged the Sadducean collaboration in exploitation and extortion. And when Jesus told Pilate, "My kingdom is not of this world" (John 18:36 NIV), he differentiated his politics from a politics based on coercion and violence. God's rule is not by violence and oppression. Violence and injustice are marks of the not-yet character of Rome's politics and Israel's politics — and of ours!

One cannot read this story of Jesus, or own it as one's own, and celebrate violence. In memory of Jesus the church will be suspicious of violence. God's good future will not be wrought by violence, and the church will reject violence as a messianic strategy, as a means to achieve the good future of God. But while hearts remain hard, while it is still not yet the good future of God, Christians may discern that political authority is necessary not only to organize and orchestrate a common life but also to restrain evil. They may discern that sometimes political authority may need to resort to force, to coercion, and even to violence in order to resist injustice and violence. Such at least has been the conclusion reached by the Christian tradition of "just war."

Jesus was no Zealot, but the inference to be drawn from both his statement about revenge and his story is not an absolute prohibition of force or coercion or violence. Jesus did not make pacifism a legal requirement of those who would follow him; pacifism is not the new *halakah*. Nevertheless, peace, *shalom*, is the new *haggadah*, the new story. Jesus told — and lived — a story

415

that reached back to the peaceable difference of the creation and forward to a peaceable kingdom, and that story forms the character and community of those who would follow him. They will not delight in violence; they will delight in peace. They will not seek violence, limited only by the restrictions of the latest scribal account of a just war. While hearts remain hard, while it is still not yet the good future of God, Christians will discern how hard their own hearts often are, and they will recognize how infrequently violence softens hearts. Christians will look for political alternatives to violence, alternatives that protect both justice and the neighbor while keeping the peace.[45] They will be peacemakers, hungering and thirsting for justice; they will be justice-makers, hungering and thirsting for *shalom*. They will be and form an international community that reaches across the boundaries and across the enmity of violence, correcting misinformation (or dis-information), rejecting the demonization of the enemy, repenting from their own sins, loving the enemy.

They will not, however, reduce God's good future and the *shalom* it promises to the absence of hostilities.[46] They will hope for — and already respond to — a future in which justice and peace "will kiss each other" (cf. Ps. 85:10). It is not yet that future, of course, and in this sad world sometimes justice and peace come into conflict. Those who would follow Jesus need not, I think, require the absolute foreswearing of force or coercion or even violence in the defense of justice and peace. When John the Baptist was asked by some soldiers, "What should we do?" he did not tell them to foreswear force or to put off their weapons but to foreswear the unjust uses of their power. "Do not extort money from anyone by threats or false accusation, and be satisfied with your wages" (Luke 3:14). When Jesus commended the centurion (Matt. 8:5-13; Luke 7:1-10), he did not make the commendation contingent upon the centurion's renunciation of military service. When he confronted the injustice of the priests in the temple (Mark 11:15-19 par.), it was not a coup attempt, but it was hardly an exercise in persuasion. When he exercised political authority and called his disciples to leadership, it was not as the Gentile rulers who "lorded it over" their subjects, but it was still political authority and leadership.

Violence may be compared to divorce. No Christian may delight in divorce. It is not God's cause. But sometimes, in this sad world, divorce is neces-

45. Here it is appropriate to commend the excellent collection of essays in *Just Peacemaking: Ten Practices for Abolishing War,* edited by Glen Stassen (Cleveland: Pilgrim, 1998). The collaborators include both pacifists and just war theorists; the essays articulate ten practices to serve both peace and justice.

46. See Nicholas Wolterstorff, *Until Justice & Peace Embrace* (Grand Rapids: Eerdmans, 1983), pp. 69-72.

sary to protect either marriage itself or one of the marriage partners. Even then, it may only be done with tears and repentance. Analogously, no Christian may delight in violence. It is not God's cause. But sometimes, in this sad world, violence is necessary to protect peace and justice. Sometimes, in this world of tyrants and bullies, it is necessary to protect the one who is "least" from the one who is great and the ones who are most vulnerable to violence and oppression from the strong.

Any judgment that violence is justified should be made (or reviewed) in Christian community gathered around Scripture, remembering Jesus. To that conversation people will bring different gifts and passions, a gift and passion for peace, a gift and passion for justice. In that conversation deliberation and discernment will be served by attention to the questions important to the tradition of just war:[47] Is there a *justifying cause* for violence? Is the violence undertaken with *right intentions?* Is it undertaken under the auspices of a *legitimate authority?* Is violence a *last resort?* Has there been an *announcement* of the intention to begin hostilities? Is there *a reasonable hope of success?* And in the midst of violence, is due *proportion* preserved, does the good to be accomplished or preserved outweigh the harm being done in violence? Is *discrimination* between combatants and noncombatants preserved? The point of such questions is not to sanctify violence up to the limit permitted by just war doctrine. The point is rather to discern the path of discipleship in the ambiguities of this sad world, remembering and following one who loved both peace and justice, who loved both the weak and the enemy.

The kingdom that is not "of this world" or "of this age" (John 18:36) is, nevertheless, of political relevance in this age, too. The kingdom of God, theocracy, will not be achieved by violence or by injustice, but it already breaks into this age as "good news to the poor." It already makes its power felt in the prophetic summons to turn from a politics that "lords it over" those who are least in the land. That future is present in a law written upon the hearts that even the "enemy" is to be loved and blessed. It was signaled when Jesus entered Jerusalem to confront the political and religious authorities riding on a colt, not on a warhorse, fulfilling the hope of Zechariah for a "humble" king who would lead the people toward "peace to the nations" (Zech. 9:9, 10), not into any national-

47. This list is taken from Ralph B. Potter, *War and Moral Discourse* (Richmond, Va.: John Knox, 1969), which remains a very thoughtful and accessible account of just war; see pp. 43-44. Many others give a similar list; for example, Thomas Kennedy, "Can War Be Just?" in *From Christ to the World: Introductory Readings in Christian Ethics,* ed. Wayne G. Boulton, Thomas Kennedy, and Allen Verhey (Grand Rapids: Eerdmans, 1994), pp. 436-41.

istic holy war. And it will make its power felt also in the communities that remember Jesus and, remembering him, do justice and make peace. It will make
its power felt in churches prepared to "say among the nations, 'God is king!'"

CHAPTER NINETEEN

The Politics of the Early Church
in Memory of Jesus

It is not implausible that Jesus should have been considered dangerous by those who refused to repent, who refused to welcome the coming reign of God — dangerous enough to kill. So Jesus was put to death as a pretender to the throne, and the ironic title on the cross, "The King of the Jews" (Mark 15:26), claimed to be the last word concerning Jesus of Nazareth. The last word, however, belonged to God. God raised this Jesus up and enthroned him at God's right hand, "far above all rule and authority and power and dominion" (Eph. 1:21). God raised him up, and the New Testament remembered him and proclaimed that he was no pretender, that God has vindicated him as Messiah. The New Testament with one voice joins the "loud voices in heaven, saying, 'The kingdom of the world has become the kingdom of our Lord and of his Messiah, and he will reign forever and ever'" (Rev. 11:15). The early church was no less theocratic than Israel had been. And it said among the nations, "God reigns."

The early church faced again the Deuteronomic question: Now that we have received this kingdom, how shall we live in it? How shall we live a common life, a politics, which displays the lordship of Christ? And since they were not a nation but the light of the nations, they faced a second question as well. How shall we live with the politics of Rome? The early Christians talked together about such questions, deliberated about them, retrieving elements of the theocratic tradition of Israel, and exercised discernment in memory of Jesus. There was more than one voice in that conversation, of course, and more than one voice found its way into the New Testament canon in memory of Jesus.

Mark: Heroic Discipleship in the Counter-Empire

Mark was the first "Gospel" to be written. That he calls his creation a "Gospel" (Gk. *euangelion*) may itself reveal something of his political posture in memory of Jesus. The word, of course, was a familiar one in the vocabulary of Christian proclamation, but it was also used within the cult of the emperor to refer to the announcements of good news to the empire. There was an implicit contrast between kingdom of God, hidden in mystery and in proclamation, and the empire of Caesar, apparent in its strength and power.

The community to which Mark wrote has traditionally been identified as the Gentile Church in Rome during or shortly after Nero's persecution, a community that confronted Roman claims to sovereignty from a position of apparent powerlessness. Mark wrote his "Gospel" to remind that community of Jesus, to remind them that Jesus came proclaiming the kingdom of God and that he was the agent of that kingdom in his suffering. He wrote to call this community to discipleship.

The call to discipleship is set immediately after the summary of Jesus' preaching (Mark 1:16-20), as if to identify the meaning of repentance and believing the gospel. And as if to identify the meaning of discipleship, in the central section of the Gospel, after the first of three passion predictions, Mark reiterates Jesus' call to discipleship, now addressed to "the multitudes." "If any want to become my followers, let them deny themselves and take up their cross and follow me" (8:34). The meaning was clear and painfully relevant to those tyrannized by Nero: to believe the gospel is to follow Christ, and to follow Christ is to be willing to suffer with him.[1]

That was, however, precisely what the disciples could not or would not understand, according to Mark. Mark did his best to help the Roman church understand it. Immediately after each of the passion predictions, Mark called attention to the failure of the disciples. First, Peter, so important to the Roman church, "began to rebuke" Jesus for his talk of suffering. Peter wanted the journey to end with lunch at Pilate's palace, not at a cross. And Jesus "rebuked Peter," that preeminent leader of the church, saying "Get behind me, Satan!" (8:32-33).

Then, when the disciples fail to understand the second passion prediction (9:31-32), Mark turns immediately to the story of their quarrel concerning "who was the greatest" (9:33-34). Into that narrative setting Mark puts a little collection of sayings beginning, "Whoever wants to be first must be last of all

---

1. Perhaps the miracle traditions, which play such an important role in the first part of Mark's Gospel, had — when they circulated independently — prompted triumphalism, but Mark ties them inextricably to the story of the cross.

and servant of all" (9:35).[2] Mark takes this saying, so important to the "great reversal" Jesus announced, and — creatively and faithfully — sets it in this particular narrative setting. It was a rebuke to leaders in the church who were still quarreling about who was the greatest. The politics of this community was to be marked by mutual service, not by quarrels about rank. And if we, with Mark, include the remainder of the little collection, then the common life of this community is also to be marked by hospitality to children (9:36-37), tolerance (9:38-40), pastoral care for the "little ones" (9:42), moral vigilance (9:43-48), and peace (9:50). And with Mark, we should also include in the responsibilities of discipleship fidelity and equality in marriage (10:2-12), blessing the children (10:13-16), and a carefree generosity with possessions (10:17-31).[3]

Finally, after the third passion prediction (10:32-34), Mark includes the request of James and John to be given places of preeminence in the kingdom (10:35-37). Jesus replies by reminding them that they are called to a heroic discipleship, and perhaps to martyrdom, to "drink the cup" that Christ will drink and to be "baptized" with the baptism that Christ will undergo (10:38-40). The cup and baptism are familiar to the community of Mark (even if they would not have been clear to the disciples) as images of sharing in the death of Christ. How can the Christians in Rome claim to share in Christ's death in the Supper and in baptism if they refuse to share it when Nero's lackeys come? When the other disciples hear of the ambition of James and John, there is another quarrel, and Jesus calls for a politics of service that stands in obvious contrast to the politics of the tyrant Nero.

> You know that among the Gentiles those whom they recognize as their rulers lord it over them, and their great ones are tyrants over them. But it is not so among you; but whoever wishes to become great among you must be your servant, and whoever wishes to be first among you must be slave of all.

---

2. The little collection of sayings is found in Mark 9:35-50. It is marked as a collection from the oral tradition by the introductory formula, which does not fit very well with the setting provided by Mark, and by the fact that the sayings are linked together by the presence of key words rather than topically. See Paul Minear, *The Commands of Christ* (Nashville: Abingdon, 1972), pp. 84-87, and Allen Verhey, *The Great Reversal: Ethics and the New Testament* (Grand Rapids: Eerdmans, 1984), p. 53.

3. That Mark intends to form the common life of the community by the material from 9:35–10:31 as a unit is displayed by the envelope he created for this material. The first word to the quarreling disciples, the first saying of the little collection, was the command "Whoever wants to be first must be last of all and servant of all" (9:35). The last word of this unit repeats the thought, now in the form of the eschatological promise, "But many who are first will be last, and the last will be first" (10:31).

For the Son of Man came not to be served but to serve, and to give his life a ransom for many. (10:42-45)

The failures of the disciples climaxed in the passion narrative, when "all of them deserted him and fled" (14:50). Again, the reader's attention is directed to Peter, that hero of the Roman churches. He followed Jesus to the courtyard of the high priest but then denied him (14:66-72). After his denial Peter "broke down and wept." He was a broken man, a crushed "Rock," broken and crushed by his own infidelity and cowardice. Mark's readers knew, of course, that Peter's tears were tears of repentance and that the grace and power of God would restore him. They knew that Peter would learn well what he learned so slowly. Peter learned that to follow Christ was to suffer with him, and he followed Christ, finally, all the way to a Roman cross of his own. Peter learned that leadership in this community required the readiness to suffer with and for others. It required humility and courage. It required "watchfulness."

Three times at the end of the apocalyptic discourse Jesus told his disciples to "watch" (NRSV: "keep alert" [13:33]; "keep awake" [13:35, 37]). No one knows the "day or hour" of the end (13:32), but the community knows that the end will come. Jesus has won the victory, and he will return to complete it. In the meantime the patience and courage of the community were tested by the petty persecutions of Jewish and Roman authorities; the followers of Jesus were betrayed by members of their own families, and some were put to death (13:9-13). That "night" of testing (13:35) is parallel to the night in Gethsemane when the disciples failed to "watch" (14:32-41). And the three times they failed are parallel to the three exhortations to "watch" at the end of the apocalyptic discourse. But now the command to watch comes to "all" (13:37). All are called to a watchful discipleship, to heroism in the face of Nero's tyranny, to a politics of service.

Mark underscores the authority of Jesus (e.g., 1:21-28, set immediately after the first call to discipleship), and the authority of Jewish religious leaders and Roman political authorities seems meager in comparison. He portrays the "authorities" in a consistently unfavorable light. He mocks the power of "King Herod" even as he records the execution of John the Baptist and foreshadows the death of Jesus and of Christians at the hands of the authorities (6:14-29). In Mark's Gospel the Herodians and the Pharisees are curious collaborators (3:6; 8:15; 12:13). Peaceful coexistence with the established authorities was never an option for Jesus, for the established authorities were suspicious and jealous of Jesus' authority from the beginning. Jesus' followers, Mark's community, could expect nothing different. No truce had been called. Watchful discipleship in such circumstances called for the church to be a counterculture, a new covenant community, marked by its care for those who did not count for much to the authorities. The politics of watchful discipleship stood in contrast to both the synagogue and the empire; it was the word and work of Christ that was authoritative, not the legalism of the scribes, nor the tyranny of Nero. Watchful discipleship did not eliminate positions of authority within the church, and it did not disown power, but it construed authority as responsible to Christ the Lord, and as a form of discipleship of the one who was among us as one who served.

Mark proceeded by way of reminder, remembering Jesus. As we said, Mark's "Gospel" is offered in implicit contrast to the "gospels," the *euangelia* of the emperor, the announcements of the birth of an heir or of a victory in battle. And nowhere is the contrast more vividly drawn than in the memory of Jesus' own contrast between politics "among the Gentiles," where ruling is tyranny, and politics "among you," where authority is a vocation to humble service.

Matthew

The author of Matthew used almost all of Mark,[4] but he used it creatively and faithfully to address a different community facing different concrete problems in its common life and in its relationships with other communities. The Christian community to which Matthew was written was largely Jewish, and the problems it faced included the crisis of having been recently excluded from the synagogue. The author reminded that community of Jesus, and called it to discipleship. The tradition, including Mark's Gospel, served the good of remembrance, but Matthew could not simply repeat Mark's Gospel. It had been written in and for a different social and historical context. The remembered story of Jesus was the story that made the people a community and gave them an identity. It was the story that illumined, judged, and transformed all the other stories of their lives. The tradition was used faithfully and creatively to enable discipleship and discernment in this Jewish Christian community. To a largely Gentile church confronting Nero, Mark had emphasized that Jesus is the Christ as the suffering one and that discipleship requires a heroic readiness to suffer with him. To the Jewish Christian community expelled from the synagogue, Matthew emphasized that Jesus is the Christ as the one who fulfills the Law and the prophets, the one who brings the story of covenant to its eschatological fruition. And discipleship requires, therefore, a righteousness that also fulfills the Torah, a righteousness that does not fall short of the righteousness of the synagogue but surpasses it.

4. He used over 600 of Mark's 661 verses.

A Politics of Law in Response to the Kingdom

From the opening words of the Gospel, the reader is reminded of the Torah: "An account of the genealogy of Jesus the Messiah, the son of David, the son of Abraham" (Matt. 1:1).[5] The story of Jesus was part of a larger theocratic story, a story of creation and covenant, a story of the promises to Abraham and to David. Jesus brought that story to its eschatological conclusion. In his story one can see the faithfulness of God to the covenant. The birth stories in Matthew underscore the theme of fulfillment even as they describe the one born in Bethlehem to be ruler in Israel (2:6).[6]

Jesus appeared proclaiming that "the kingdom of heaven has come near" (4:17) and already made its power — and the authority of that kingdom — felt in his words and in his works. Matthew collected some of those words of Jesus into the first discourse of Jesus in Matthew's Gospel,[7] the Sermon on the Mount (5–7), and "the crowds were astounded at his teaching, for he taught them as one having authority, and not as their scribes" (7:28-29; cf. Mark 1:22). In the narrative that follows (Matt. 8-9) Matthew collected some of the mighty works of Jesus, and again used them to display the authority of Jesus. Jesus has the authority of one authorized by God, as the Roman centurion acknowledged (8:8-9); he has the authority to rebuke the threatening waters of chaos (8:23-27), to cast out demons (8:28-32), and to heal the sick and forgive sins (9:2-8). He spoke and acted as one authorized by God; here was the agent of God's coming reign, of theocracy.

The theocratic politics of this Jewish Christian community were a response to this ruler born in Bethlehem and to his authority under God. The authority of Jesus, however, did not bring the authority of the Torah to an end. Torah remained critical to the common life of Israel. In a key verse of the Sermon on the Mount, a verse found only in Matthew, Jesus insisted that he did not come "to abolish" Torah but "to fulfill" it (5:17).[8] He did not destroy Torah;

---

5. The opening words might more literally be translated "a book of the generations of . . ." (Gk. *Biblos geneseōs*). Any pious Jew familiar with Genesis would recognize the allusion to the formula that occurs eleven times in Genesis, "These are the generations of . . ." (Hb. *tôlēdôt*), (e.g., 2:4; 5:1; 6:9; 10:1; 11:10; 11:27; 25:12; 25:19; 36:1; 36:9; 37:2).

6. Each of the stories refers to the fulfillment of prophecy (1:23; 2:6, 15, 18, 23).

7. Matthew's Gospel generally follows the order of Mark, but the author self-consciously imposed on it a pattern of five narrative sections and five discourse sections set between the birth stories and the passion narrative, each narrative section followed by a discourse. That the pattern was self-conscious may be seen in the concluding formula that stands at the end of each of the discourse sections (Matt. 7:28; 11:1; 13:53; 19:1; and 26:1).

8. On this topic see Gerhard Barth, "Matthew's Understanding of the Law," in *Tradi-*

he established it; he fructified it. This is a matter of first importance to Matthew and to his community. The politics of this community were organized around the authority of Jesus — and around the Torah as interpreted by Jesus.

The Law still held for Matthew's community. The whole Law held; even the least of the commandments was to be taught and done (5:18-19).[9] In the controversies about the Law, the issue in Matthew (in contrast to Mark) is never whether the Law holds; the issue is rather who truly performs the Law and who is its best interpreter.[10] That is the issue between the synagogue and the church. Matthew complains bitterly against the scribes and Pharisees (see, e.g., 23:3-36), but he never complains about their devotion to the Law. He complains that they do not know the meaning of Hosea's "I desire mercy, not sacrifice" (Hos. 6:6; Matt. 9:13; 12:7), that they condemn the "guiltless" (Matt. 12:7), that "they do not practice what they teach" (23:3), that they lay "heavy burdens on the shoulders of others" (23:4), that they love the perks of leadership but do not serve (23:7-12), that they focus on minutiae and neglect "the weightier matters of the law: justice and mercy and faith" (23:23).[11] And in a stinging rebuke he complains repeatedly that they are "blind guides" (23:16, 17, 19, 24, 26). They claimed to lead the community by their interpretation of Torah, but they were blind to the real will of God. They refused to welcome the good future of God, and they refused to read the Law in the light of it. They rejected the good news of the coming theocracy. So, their guidance was hardly trustworthy.

Still, the scribes and Pharisees — and the synagogue — at least honored the Law. In this they were better than the "false prophets" within the Christian community. The "false prophets" called upon the name of the Lord, prophesied in his name, cast out demons, and did other mighty works, but they were to be

---

tion and Interpretation in Matthew's Gospel, ed. Gunther Bornkamm, Gerhard Barth, and H. J. Held (Philadelphia: Westminster, 1963), pp. 58-164 [and pp. 64-73 on Matthew 5:17], and J. P. Meier, *Law and History in Matthew's Gospel* (Rome: Biblical Institute Press, 1976).

9. Even the commandments concerning kosher and Sabbath still held. Note, for example, that Matthew both omits Mark 7:19, "Thus he declared all foods clean," and adds to Mark 13:18 ("Pray that it [the flight on the occasion of the desolating sacrilege] may not be in winter") the phrase, "or on a sabbath" (Matt. 24:20). Indeed, even the oral Law still held. In a passage found only in Matthew Jesus was reported to have said that "the scribes and the Pharisees sit on Moses' seat; therefore, do whatever they teach you and follow it; but do not do as they do, for they do not practice what they teach" (23:2-3).

10. See, for example, Matthew 9:9-13 (and Mark 2:13-17), Matthew 12:1-8 (and Mark 2:23-28), Matthew 12:9-14 (and Mark 3:1-6).

11. Notice in 23:23 that this focus on "the weightier matters" is not an excuse for neglecting the lighter matters: "It is these [the weightier matters] you ought to have practiced without neglecting the others."

condemned as "evildoers" (Gk. *anomian*; 7:22-23), as workers of "lawlessness" (NKJV), because they do not honor or observe the Law of Moses. The common life is to be formed both by the authority of Jesus and by the Law as interpreted by Jesus. This community is not to fall below the standards of the synagogue; it is not to abolish the Law; on the contrary, it is to surpass the righteousness of the scribes and Pharisees (5:20).

The Sermon on the Mount gives an account of such righteousness. The Beatitudes (5:1-12) announce the good future of God, but they also form community and character. This community will bless and exalt the humble, for the humble will be exalted in the kingdom of heaven. It will bless and comfort those who mourn, any who ache now because it is not yet God's good future, for they will be comforted in God's kingdom. It will praise those with a taste for justice, for justice is a foretaste of God's reign. It will hail the merciful, for in their mercy they see something of God's rule. It will bless the peacemakers, for in the peace they make there is a token of the *shalom* God promises. It will sustain those who endure evil for the sake of God's cause. It will bless those whom Jesus blessed, and in blessing them it will nurture those dispositions and habits of the heart that welcome the future he promised and made present.

In the antitheses (5:21-48) the authority of Jesus stands in contrast to the authority of the scribes; and the righteousness of the community of his disciples, to the righteousness of the scribes. The Law holds, but this community will not be content with a common life marked by the vices the Law restrains. In token of the good future of God, when the law of God will be written on the hearts of Israel, it is called to character and community marked by the readiness to be reconciled with a neighbor (5:21-26), by chastity (5:27-30) and fidelity (5:31-32), by truthfulness (5:33-37), by a readiness to forgive and to give (5:38-42), and by loving even the enemy (5:43-48). So it will surpass the righteousness of the scribes. So it will be "the light of the world" (5:14).

Members of this community will engage in the practices of piety, in almsgiving, prayer, and fasting, no less than the Pharisees, but they will not engage in such practices that others may attend to them but that they may attend to God (6:1-18). So they will surpass the righteousness of the Pharisees. Finally, attention to God and to the cause of God disclosed in Jesus forms both their hearts and their politics. To "strive first for the kingdom of God and his righteousness" (6:33) provides and requires freedom from anxiety about earthly possessions (6:19-21, 25-34); it calls for repentance and disdains self-righteous severity in judging others (7:1-5). The last word of the Sermon before the trio of warnings at the end (7:15-27) is the golden rule, "In everything do to others as you would have them do to you; for this is the law and the prophets" (7:12). Just so they fulfill the Law and form "a city built on a hill" (5:14).

A Politics of Care for the Little Ones: Communal Deliberation, Reconciliation, and Forgiveness

Matthew turned Mark's account of Peter's confession into the founding of the church (16:13-20; cf. Mark 8:27-30) and vested Peter with the authority to make judicial rulings and judgments, to "bind" and to "loose" (16:19). Matthew does not spell out Peter's authority in this passage, but he does return to the issue of governance in this community in the eighteenth chapter, the fourth section in which Matthew compiles Jesus' words to create an extended discourse.

It begins with the inquiry of the disciples, "Who is the greatest in the kingdom of heaven?" (18:1). Mark's Gospel had told the story of a quarrel among the disciples concerning who was the greatest in order to rebuke the quarreling leadership of the Roman church (Mark 9:33-37). Matthew handled that tradition artfully to shift the point of the story from a rebuke to instruction concerning the responsibilities of leadership in the community. By omitting the reference to the quarreling among the disciples, the question "Who is the greatest?" became an honest inquiry about rank within the community. It is the question, "Who counts?" And by moving immediately to the child whom Jesus set in the midst of the disciples (Matt. 18:2-5), Matthew answered that question. Children count. The little ones count. The last count as first. Those who do not count for much in other politics count in the kingdom of heaven, and they command the attention of leaders. The disciples' inquiry was, however, not just the question, "Who counts?" It also raised the issue about the nature of leadership in the kingdom of heaven. The question is "What is the character of greatness?" And by the child set in the midst of them Matthew answered that question, too. The child provided a model of humility. Leaders are to count themselves servants. Authority is not abolished any more than the Law had been, but in this community it is to be exercised in response to Christ and in service to those who are least. "Whoever becomes humble like this child is the greatest in the kingdom of heaven. Whoever welcomes one such child in my name welcomes me" (18:4-5).

The twin points are reiterated in the parable of the lost sheep (18:10-14; cf. Luke 15:3-7). Matthew introduced the parable with the admonition, "Take care that you do not despise one of these little ones" (18:10), and he set as the conclusion of the parable a reminder of God's care for "these little ones" (18:14). Little ones count, and leadership — like the shepherd — humbly cares for the last of the sheep. The politics of this community should reflect the great reversal of the kingdom, a politics where the last are first, and where leaders humbly serve.

It is not just sheep that sometimes "go astray" (18:12). And Matthew turns next to some guidelines for how to respond "if another member of the church sins against you" (18:15-18). You are not to seek revenge, of course, or retaliate in kind, returning insult for insult or injury for injury (5:38-39). You are to seek reconciliation with your brother or sister. You are to forgive, of course, for the Lord taught you to pray, "Forgive us our debts, as we also have forgiven our debtors" (6:12), a point Matthew had underscored both in the context of that prayer (6:14-15) and in the context of this discourse (18:21-34). To forgive, however, is not simply to ignore the offense — or to ignore the offender, treating the brother or sister as a stranger. The guidelines insist both on the offended individual's responsibility to undertake the process of reconciliation and on the church's responsibility for communal discernment and judgment.

Jesus authorized the offended party to go to the offender and admonish him, to seek reconciliation rather than continuing the quarrel, to nurture and encourage a common discipleship. The offense that prompted resentment is first to be reported privately to the offender. Perhaps the private conversation will reveal that it was just a misunderstanding, that there was no real offense. But perhaps it will reveal that there was an offense, and then the private conversation provides an opportunity for repentance and forgiveness. One hopes for a readiness to repent in the offender, a readiness to forgive in the offended, and an eagerness for reconciliation in both. The desired outcome is that "you [will] have regained" a brother or a sister (18:15). If, however, the private conversation is unsuccessful, then the guidelines call for a slightly larger conversation; "take one or two others along with you" on this mission of reconciliation (18:16). And if you are still unsuccessful, then you are to bring the matter to the attention of the church. Here Jesus vested the church with the authority to make judicial rulings and judgments, to "bind" and to "loose" (18:18; cf. 16:19). Jesus authorized the church to engage in mutual admonition and discipline, to hear the case, to deliberate about it, and to exercise discernment in memory of Jesus.

This practice of communal discernment is itself sustained by the practice of prayer (18:19). It is not that prayer is a means to get some help for the exceptionally difficult case. Prayer is not a technology, not magic. Prayer is simple attention to God, but in attending to God we learn to attend to all else in a new light, and respond to all things as all things are related to God.[12] In prayers of confession we learn humility, and we are freed from the compulsive need to defend our own little righteousness. In prayers of thanksgiving we learn to be

12. See pp. 62-66 in this volume.

grateful for the gifts of God, and we are freed from both our envy of the gifts of others and our conceit about our own. In gratitude for the forgiveness of God, we are called and formed to be forgiving ourselves (18:23-35). And in petition as a form of attention to God we learn to govern both our requests and our lives by the cause of God.

The desired outcome of this "binding" and "loosing" remains reconciliation in a common discipleship, and forgiveness remains a given. But if — and only if — the offender adamantly "refuses to listen" to the admonition and instruction of the community, then he or she is to be regarded as a stranger, "as a Gentile and a tax collector" (18:17), as an enemy. Of course, this community responds to Jesus and follows him also by its openness to the stranger, to Gentiles and tax collectors, and by its love of the enemy. If someone refuses to participate in this politics of forgiveness and reconciliation, however, if someone refuses either to forgive or to be forgiven, then that person excludes himself from this community, and that exclusion can only be recognized by the community.

There is much to learn from Matthew's account of a politics of reconciliation and forgiveness, and too often in contemporary churches we fail to trust that politics. Too often we prefer to treat offenses as merely private matters and to treat those with whom we have differences as merely strangers. That ought to be recognized as a temptation, and as a failure to trust both our brothers and sisters and the Lord who authorized such politics. And too often in contemporary churches some leader is too ready to condemn, too eager to "lord it over" those regarded as "sinners," too disposed to exclude them. Such leaders cannot wait for the lament of one who has been injured or insulted or offended that the offender had refused reconciliation. And they do not listen either to the whole community of sinners gathered in the name of Jesus or to the one prematurely regarded as stranger and enemy. They do not remember that Jesus authorized a politics of reconciliation and forgiveness, a politics where reconciliation and forgiveness are not only the desired end, but also practices that characterize the community and its politics.

As we noted, Jesus had authorized Peter and vested him with the authority to "bind" and to "loose." But Peter's authority is exercised in discipleship. As leader, he is to be among the community as one who serves, humbly attending to the least among them. No conventional hierarchy was authorized. Jesus authorized not just Peter but each member of the community to engage in the practices of reconciliation and forgiveness, to speak and to listen to others. And he authorized the community as a whole and vested it with the authority to "bind" and to "loose." Peter's authority is not a substitute for the community's moral discourse, deliberation, and discernment in memory of Jesus as the Christ. Leadership in this community serves the community's discernment, nurturing it by remembering Jesus and his vocation to care for the least and for sinners, sustaining it by reminding it of the goals and practices of reconciliation and forgiveness, gathering it in the name of Jesus for prayer and study.

The contrast with conventional politics is not overlooked in Matthew. He repeated Mark's account of Jesus' rebuke of Gentile rulers who "lord it over" their subjects, who count greatness as an opportunity for tyranny (20:25; cf. Mark 10:42). And he repeated the vocation, in the light of the great reversal, to a different politics. "It will not be so among you . . ." (20:26-28; cf. Mark 10:43-45). Matthew, however, seems more interested in drawing the contrast with the politics of the scribes and the Pharisees. These "blind guides" who "love to have the place of honor," lording it over the synagogue, were hardly better than those Gentile rulers. It is not to be so among the followers of Jesus. Such leadership belongs to the old age. It is no accident that Matthew inserted into "woes" against the scribes and Pharisees the refrain of reversal, "The greatest among you must be your servant. All who exalt themselves will be humbled, and all who humble themselves will be exalted" (Matt. 23:11-12). Matthew draws a startlingly egalitarian implication in memory of Jesus and the reversal he promised, "You are not to be called rabbi, for you have one teacher, and you are all students" (23:8). The kingdom, however, does not abolish authority any more than it had abolished the Law; it transforms it — and shares it.

In Matthew's final discourse, the apocalyptic discourse (24:1–26:1), he follows Mark 13, but by adding a series of parables to Mark (24:45–25:46) he effectively shifts the focus of "watchfulness" from heroic discipleship, ready to suffer with Jesus, to the performance of God's future judgment and salvation. The climactic and final parable in this series, of course, is the parable of the judgment upon the nations (25:31-46). "When the Son of Man comes in his glory . . . , then he will sit on the throne of his glory . . ." and he will judge the nations by their treatment of "the least of these." As we wait and watch for the king, we can find him already in the humiliated, in those beaten down and crushed by life, in the hungry, in the thirsty, in the stranger, in the naked and the sick and imprisoned. If we serve and help them, we serve and help the King of kings, the Lord of lords. And if we do not serve and help them, then we turn our backs upon the Lord, whether we watch for him or not, whether nations acknowledge him or not. That, too, is part of Matthew's account of the politics of Jesus.

Luke–Acts

Luke, like the author of Matthew, made extensive use of Mark's Gospel, and, again like the author of Matthew, he used it creatively and faithfully to address a different community facing different concrete problems in its common life and in its relationships with other communities. The Christian communities for whom Luke wrote included both Jewish and Gentile Christians. For Jew and Gentile to be members of one community was problem enough to prompt creative and faithful remembrance of the story of Jesus. Luke proceeded by way of reminder, calling Jew and Gentile to discipleship. It was the remembered story of Jesus that made them a community and gave them an identity that transcended their being Jewish or not. To a largely Gentile church confronting Nero, Mark had emphasized the sufferings of Jesus and shown that discipleship requires a heroic readiness to suffer with him. To the Jewish Christian community expelled from the synagogue, Matthew emphasized Jesus' fulfillment of the Law and the prophets and revealed him as the one who brings the story of covenant to its eschatological fruition. Discipleship required, therefore, a righteousness that also fulfilled the Torah, a righteousness that did not fall short of the righteousness of the synagogue but surpassed it. To churches made up of both Jews and Gentiles, Luke emphasized that Jesus is the Christ as the universal Savior and as the one who proclaimed "good news to the poor." And discipleship, then, required that Jews and Gentiles respect one another and that the poor be blessed. The old theocratic vision of an international order of peace and liberation of the oppressed is the vision also of this Gentile evangelist.

For the most part Luke follows the order he found in Mark, but he takes the episode of the rejection at Nazareth and puts it at the very beginning of Jesus' ministry. He does not put it first because of some concern for chronological accuracy;[13] he puts it first and expands on Mark's memory of it because it is fundamental to his understanding of Jesus and of the common life of the churches. The story is that Jesus went to the synagogue on the Sabbath, "as was his custom" (4:16, a gloss added by Luke). He was a pious Jew (and the Gentiles must not forget it). There he read from the prophet Isaiah, "The Spirit of the Lord is upon me, because he has anointed me to bring good news to the poor . . ." (Luke 4:17-19; Isa. 61:1-2). He followed the reading with the shortest sermon on record — and the most provocative. "Today this scripture has been fulfilled in your hearing," Jesus said (Luke 4:21). The people of Nazareth were "amazed" — and provoked — at his words of grace. The reading of Isaiah had stopped short of mentioning "the day of vengeance of our God" (Isa. 61:2b), the day of God's vengeance against the Gentiles. It was evidently that omission

13. Luke 4:23 refers to the miracles at Capernaum as having already happened, as they had, of course, in Mark's order. See Mark 1:21-38, the parallel to which is found in Luke 4:32-43, after the episode at Nazareth.

that provoked them.[14] At any rate, in the ensuing discussion Jesus reminded them of the gracious work of Elijah and Elisha among the Gentiles (Luke 4:25-27), and those who heard him "were filled with rage" (4:28). If one is to enter into the story of Jesus for Luke, one must enter through this narrative. Jesus is the Christ, the "anointed" one, as the one who brings "good news to the poor" and as the Savior of both Jews and Gentiles.

A Politics in Memory of One Who Preached Good News to the Poor

We have already attended to Luke's story of Jesus as the one "anointed to bring good news to the poor" — and to his story of the common life of the Christian community in memory of Jesus.[15] Here it is enough simply to recall two things: In the common life of the early church, in her *koinonia*, Luke saw the fulfillment of Israel's covenant, for "there was not a needy person among them" (Acts 4:34; cf. Deut. 15:4). In that same community he saw also the fulfillment of human hopes, human hopes for a politics of friendship in place of a politics of patron-client relationships, hopes for a community that shared both power and possessions.

A Politics in Memory of a Universal Savior: Mutual Respect of Jew and Gentile

Jesus was not only, for Luke, the one who brought good news to the poor. He was also the universal Savior; "repentance and forgiveness of sins is to be proclaimed in his name to all nations, beginning from Jerusalem" (Luke 24:47; cf. Acts 1:8). That statement is programmatic for the book of Acts, but it is also typical of Luke's insistence upon both the Jewish origins of the gospel ("from Jerusalem") and the inclusion of the Gentiles ("to all nations"). For the Gentile Christians who made this story their own there can be no repudiation of the Jewish heritage — or of Jews. And for the Jewish Christians who make this story their own there can be no repudiation of the Gentile mission — or of Gentiles. Discipleship entails a politics of peaceable difference, a politics of friendship and equality between Jews and Gentiles.

14. See Joachim Jeremias, *Jesus' Promise to the Nations*, trans. S. H. Hooke (Philadelphia: Fortress, 1982), pp. 44-46.

15. See pt. four, ch. 14, pp. 276-87 in this volume.

It is true that the mission to the Gentiles does not begin until Acts 10,[16] but from the beginning of Luke's Gospel, right alongside his emphasis on the Jewishness of Jesus and of the gospel, there is a foreshadowing of the mission to come. The angels themselves announced to the shepherds the birth of this Jewish and universal Savior; the "good news of great joy for all the people" is that there "is born this day in the city of David a Savior, who is the Messiah, the Lord" (Luke 2:10-11). When Jesus was presented in the temple as "customary under the law" for firstborn sons (Luke 2:27; cf. 2:22-24; Lev. 12:2-8), Simeon, the devout old priest, celebrated God's universal salvation, "a light for revelation to the Gentiles and for glory to your people Israel" (Luke 2:32). The old theocrat "looking forward to the consolation of Israel" (Luke 2:25) retrieved the language of the servant songs of Isaiah (Isa. 42:6; 49:6), and so did Luke (cf. Acts 13:47). As in all the gospels, John the Baptist used Isaiah 40:3, "The voice of one crying out in the wilderness: 'Prepare the way of the Lord,'" but only in Luke's Gospel did he continue to the fifth verse, "and all flesh shall see the salvation of God" (Luke 3:3-6; cf. Matt. 3:1-3; Mark 1:2-3; John 1:23). Luke traces the ancestors of Jesus all the way back to Adam, that other human being in whom all are united (Luke 3:23-38). And in the beginning of Acts, long before the Gentile mission begins, Peter quotes the prophet Joel in his Pentecost sermon to say that God has poured out his Spirit "upon all flesh" (Acts 2:17).

The Gentile mission did not begin until Israel was restored, until "the dwelling of David" was rebuilt (Acts 15:16-17). The story Luke told in the beginning of Acts was not that Israel as a whole rejected the gospel or that the mission turned to Gentiles because of Israel's rejection. On the contrary, many Jews believed (2:41; 4:4; 5:14; 6:1-7, etc.), and those who did constituted a restored Israel.[17] Only after that was the old theocratic vision of blessing upon the Gentiles and of a new international order of peace also fulfilled through the Gentile mission. When that mission did begin with Peter's visit with Cornelius (10:1-48), Peter was hardly an eager evangelist. The inclusion of the uncircumcised was clearly God's rule, not Peter's idea. By visions, heavenly messen-

---

16. Indeed, Luke omits the large section of Mark's Gospel (Mark 6:45–8:26, between Luke 9:17 and 18) which presents "the Gentile mission" of Jesus.

17. See further Jacob Jervell, *Luke and the People of God* (Minneapolis: Augsburg, 1972), pp. 41-132. Not all the Jews believed, of course. Those who did not excluded themselves from the restored Israel. They waited "for another" (Luke 7:19). They did not see in Jesus or in the community of his followers the promise of God's good future. Israel is restored — and divided. It is through the restored Israel that the project of God to bless the nations goes forward. The division continues throughout Acts, and in some cities where Jews take offense at Paul's gospel, that becomes the occasion for Paul's "turning to the Gentiles" (e.g., Acts 13:46; 18:5-6).

gers, and the gift of the Spirit God made it plain to Peter that "what God has made clean, you must not call profane" (10:15; cf. 11:9; 15:9) and that "God shows no partiality" (10:34; cf. 11:12; 15:9).

The lesson was not an easy one to learn, not for Peter, and not for the early church. But through the practice of communal discourse, deliberation, and discernment, they did come to see and affirm the reign of God in the inclusion of Gentiles. First, when some Christians were offended by Peter's fellowship with Cornelius, they confronted him privately. Peter told them the story (Acts 11:4-17), and they were reconciled. There was no need for repentance or for forgiveness; instead, they praised God for the salvation of the Gentiles (11:18). Later, when some Christians were offended by Paul's mission among the Gentiles, they could not reach an agreement together, and the Council of Jerusalem met to consider the matter and to make a judgment (15:1-29).[18] There was "much debate" (15:7). But after Peter told the story of Cornelius one more time,[19] and after Barnabas and Paul testified to God's work upon the Gentiles, James saw the agreement between their stories and the promises of a restored Israel and God's blessing on the Gentiles (15:13-18). He saw the "fit" between their stories and the story of Scripture. He saw that the inclusion of the Gentiles as Gentiles was worthy of the gospel. His judgment, which won "the consent of the whole church" (15:22), was that the Gentiles should be welcomed, not burdened.[20]

18. See Luke Timothy Johnson, *Decision Making in the Church: A Biblical Model* (Philadelphia: Fortress, 1983).

19. Here Peter also asserts the equality of Jew and Gentile in a strikingly Pauline way: "we believe that we [Jews] will be saved through the grace of the Lord Jesus, just as they will" (Acts 15:11).

20. Three other things are worthy of note in the decision of the council as Luke describes it. First, although the council did not require circumcision or observance of the Jewish law, it did require that the Gentiles "abstain . . . from things polluted by idols and from fornication and from whatever has been strangled and from blood" (Acts 15:20; cf. 15:29; 21:25). These requirements are taken from Leviticus 17 and 18, where they are identified as requirements not only upon Jews but also upon the strangers who dwell among them. (See Ernst Haenchen, *The Acts of the Apostles* [Philadelphia: Westminster, 1971], p. 449.) It was evidently proposed as a *modus vivendi* for the fellowship of Jewish and Gentile Christians. And it was subject, of course, to modification in the continuing process of deliberation and discernment in the churches. (Note, for example, the question of eating meat sacrificed to idols in 1 Corinthians 8-10. Note also that some later copyist rendered the ritual commands into a summary of morality; the Western text may be translated, "abstain from idolatry and fornication and blood[shed] and whatever you would not have your neighbor do to you.")

Second, the requirement was consistent with Luke's account of the authority of Torah. For Luke there is an "indissoluble connection between Israel and the law" (Jervell,

The lesson was not an easy one for the churches who first read Luke's Gospel, either. Some of the Jewish Christians had continued to condemn the Gentiles as "sinners," and some of the Gentile Christians had continued to despise the Jews as self-righteous legalists. Luke proceeded by way of reminder. For these churches the memory of Jesus and of the early church remembering Jesus was not merely a matter of historical interest. It was fundamental to their identity as a community. They were a community that acknowledged Jesus, the Jewish Messiah, as the universal Savior, a community that had its origins in a restored Israel and its destiny in the reign of God that brings blessing also to the Gentiles. They were a community of disciples, and discipleship required a politics of peaceable difference. It did not require uniformity. Jewish Christians were not required to act like Gentiles, and Gentile Christians were not required to act like Jews. But it did require friendship and respect, unity and equality. Jewish Christians were to welcome Gentile Christians *as Gentiles,* demanding neither circumcision nor observance of the Jewish law. They were not to use the Law to condemn the Gentiles or to repudiate God's blessing upon them. Gentile Christians were to love the Jewish Christians *as Jews,* respecting their pious observance of the Jewish law.

The whole story is critical, of course, but parts of the story provide apt paradigms for Jews and Gentiles in their new relationship. Notice, for example, Luke's version of the story of the healing of the Roman centurion's servant (Luke 7:1-10; cf. Matt. 8:5-13). In Luke's version this Gentile "sent some Jewish elders" to Jesus (7:3), and the Jews interceded on his behalf (7:4-5). The centurion is a model for Gentile believers. He recognized that his access to the salvation Jesus works came only through the Jews; he recognized the Jewish origins

---

Luke and the People of God, p. 141). In the restored Israel, the Law was kept! And then the promise (to Israel!) of blessings upon the Gentiles was also kept. But the Gentiles remained Gentiles. There was not the same "indissoluble connection" between Gentiles and the Law. Gentiles need not observe the Jewish law, but they did need Jews to observe it. In the church there is now an "indissoluble connection" between Gentiles and Jews. See further Jervell, pp. 133-51, and Donald Juel, *New Testament Literature* (Nashville: Abingdon, 1978), pp. 215-35.

Finally, James calls attention to the continuing contribution of the Jewish synagogue. James did not agree with the argument of the pharisaic Christians that the Gentile Christians should be circumcised, but he did acknowledge the force of their argument that the whole Law was important to Gentiles, too. James observed in effect that Gentiles have ample opportunity to learn the whole law of Moses, "For in every city, for generations past, Moses has had those who proclaim him, for he has been read aloud every sabbath in the synagogues" (Acts 15:21). In spite of the division of Israel, in Luke's view the synagogue retains its identity as a community that proclaims the covenant; *contra* Richard Hays, *The Moral Vision of the New Testament* (San Francisco: HarperSanFrancisco, 1996), p. 421.

of the gospel. Moreover, he did not despise the Jews; on the contrary, as the elders said, "he loves our people, and it is he who built our synagogue for us" (7:5). The elders are a model for the Jews. They did not condemn the Gentile for being a Gentile or uncircumcised; on the contrary, they interceded on his behalf and doubtlessly delighted in the blessing Jesus brought to him. Or, notice again the story of Peter and Cornelius (Acts 10). Jewish Christians ought to join Peter in welcoming, not judging, the Gentiles, and in acknowledging, not resisting, God's decision to include them as Gentiles: "What God has cleansed, you must not call common" (10:15 RSV). And Gentile Christians, like Cornelius, should acknowledge "the message [God] sent *to the people of Israel,* preaching peace by Jesus Christ — he is Lord of all" (10:36; italics added). The common obligation was that they should "repent and turn to God and do deeds consistent with repentance" (26:20). Such turning to God and to God's good future included surely a common life, a politics, that delighted in good news to the poor and in the unity of Jews and Gentiles.

Luke and the Anti-Jewish Polemic of the Tradition

Before we leave Luke's narrative politics of peaceable difference and mutual respect, we should observe something that is *not* there. It is hard, of course, to see what is not there, but it is, I think, terribly significant in this particular case. What is not there is the polemic against "the Jews." What is not there is Matthew 27:25, "Then the people as a whole answered, 'His blood be on us and on our children!'" What is not there is John 8:44, "You [who claim to be children of Abraham] are from your father the devil, and you choose to do your father's desires. He was a murderer from the beginning. . . ." One may well wish, of course, that such texts were not in Matthew and John either. The history of the reading and the use of such texts in Christian communities is ugly and damnable. Gentile Christians have taken such texts as a license for their anti-Semitism, for enmity and violence against the Jews and against the synagogue, for the Holocaust. May the God of Abraham forgive us!

One may — and must — ask what such texts (and others like them) are doing in Christian Scripture. Jesus himself was a Jew, of course, and an observant Jew! Christianity began as a reform movement within Judaism, one of the many with a theocratic vision for the renewal of Israel. The first Christians were Jews, and neither they nor other Jews supposed that they had converted from one religion to another. To be sure, some Jews, like Saul of Tarsus, regarded some Christians as apostate, but most Christians continued to go to temple and to synagogue. When the temple was destroyed in 70 c.e., it created an identity crisis within Judaism — and a family quarrel concerning "authentic" Israel. Matthew and John can only be understood in the context of that family quarrel — and in reaction to its outcome in the decision of the synagogue to exclude Christians.

Family quarrels, of course, are frequently ugly, and they were in this case. The authors of Matthew and John were both Christian Jews, and their readers were Christian Jews. They were engaged in sibling rivalry with the synagogue about the identity of Israel, about who could claim to be the true heir of the ancient tradition. And they lamented their exile from the synagogue. John referred at least three times to the exile of Christians from the synagogue (John 9:22; 12:42; 16:2, with obvious anachronism). The polemic against "the Jews" is not anti-Semitic in Matthew and John. In John, for example, where "the Jews" occurs some seventy times, mostly in pejorative contexts, the contrast is never between "the Jews" and "the Gentiles."[21] The contrast is rather between "the Jews" and "the Jews who had believed" (8:31). Indeed, only one Gentile figures in John's narrative — Pilate — and John makes it clear that he is an outsider (18:35). The criticism of "the Jews" is from within the family. That does not make the polemic any less ugly, but family quarrels should be kept within the family. If anyone said to one of my brothers some of the things I said to them when I was younger, I would have thoroughly resented it.

Meanwhile, the Christian church went through an identity crisis of its own. The very success of the Gentile mission had put at risk the Jewish identity of the Christian church. Matthew, with his condemnation of the "false prophets" who do "lawlessness," disclosed a concern also about this identity crisis within the Christian movement. By 140 c.e. Marcion would visit Rome with a thoroughly anti-Jewish "gospel." When Gentiles became dominant in the church, they all too eagerly made the polemic of Matthew and John against "the Jews" their own; in the mouths and hearts of Gentiles, of course, this polemic *was* anti-Semitic. To read such passages humbly, to read them prayerfully, to read them over-against ourselves instead of in self-serving judgment of others, to read them discerningly, should prompt regret about the family quarrel — and repentance for an anti-Semitic reading and performance of such texts.

Luke, the only Gentile author within the New Testament, may be helpful to Gentile readers here. Not only because such ugly polemical texts are absent. Not only because discipleship requires a politics of peaceable difference among

---

21. Indeed, Gk. *ta ethnē* never occurs in the Gospel of John. John is the only major New Testament work in which it does *not* occur. Note, moreover, the contrast between the way John and Paul treat that old image for Israel, the vine (John 15:1-8; Rom. 11:17-24). John has no interest in the "grafting in" of "wild branches," or Gentiles.

Jews and Gentiles within the church. Not only because Luke reminds us so emphatically of the Jewishness of Jesus and of the early church. Not only because he represents the inclusion of the Gentiles as the fulfillment of the promise made to Jews. Luke tells a story of the cross less liable to anti-Semitic distortion. Jesus prays for the forgiveness of those who crucify him, both Roman soldiers and the Jewish crowd, presumably, "Father, forgive them; for they do not know what they are doing" (Luke 23:34). It is "the leaders" and the soldiers who mock Jesus on the cross, not the crowd (23:35-38; cf. Mark 15:29-32). Jesus makes the evening prayer of the pious Jew on the cross, "Father, into your hands I commend my spirit" (23:46; cf. Ps. 31:5). And finally, in Luke's story "when all the crowds who had gathered there for this spectacle saw what had taken place, they returned home, beating their breasts" (23:48). Jesus' prayer and that lament in Luke's Gospel should silence Gentile accusations against the Jews.

Luke's Attitude toward Roman Authorities

Luke and Acts are sometimes read as an apology to Roman officials, defending the early Christian movement against the charges brought against them and claiming the status of *religio licita* (licit religion) in the Roman Empire. There are, indeed, passages that emphasize the political innocence of Jesus (Luke 23:2, 4, 14, 22) and of Paul (Acts 18:12-15; 21:37-39; 25:24-27; 26:30-32). Luke's attitude toward the authorities, however, is too carefree to be styled apologetic. His confidence (like that of the early church that he described, and like that of the rabbi Gamaliel, whom he quoted [Acts 5:33-39]) was in God, and that confidence kept him free to criticize — even to ridicule — political officials.

In Luke's Gospel Jesus called Herod Antipas "that fox" (13:32). But that epithet is less revealing than Luke's use of Psalm 2 to describe the political leadership. When Luke reported that Herod and Pilate became friends in their conspiracy against Jesus (23:12), he alluded to the psalm. When he reported the Sanhedrin's opposition to a restored Israel, he reminded his readers (through the prayer of the early church to "the sovereign Lord") of Pilate and Herod and cited Psalm 2:1-2, "Why did the Gentiles rage, and the peoples imagine vain things? The kings of the earth took their stand, and the rulers have gathered together against the Lord and against his Messiah" (Acts 4:24-30). Their hopeless conspiracy is doomed; the church continues confidently and boldly without the support of the political authorities. "[The sovereign Lord] who sits in the heavens laughs; the LORD has them in derision" (Ps. 2:4). There is a touch of that "derision" in Jesus' epithet for Herod and in some of Luke's other descriptions of political officials.

In Acts 12 Luke derides the pretentious but powerless power of Herod Agrippa. In spite of the extraordinary security measures with which Herod Agrippa had imprisoned Peter, by the more extraordinary power of God Peter escaped (12:6-10). Then in the very midst of public acclaim and royal pretense, "because he did not give God the glory" (12:23 RSV) Herod Agrippa fell over dead. The Lord reigns, and rulers who neglect it or deny it do so at risk to themselves (cf. Ps. 2:10-12). There is a theocratic dimension to politics for Luke. Luke ridiculed the Philippian magistrates for trying to avoid the public embarrassment of their unlawful treatment of Paul (Acts 16:35-40). He derided the procurator Felix for seeking a bribe (24:26), the procurator Festus for sending Paul a prisoner to Rome without knowing what charges to indicate (25:27), and other officials for other self-serving postures and acts.

Luke's attitude to civil authority, however, was not unremittingly critical. He ridiculed the corruption, the pretensions of power, the incompetence, and the hopeless conspiracy against God and against the cause of God. But he praised the proconsul of Cyprus, Sergius Paulus, as "an intelligent man" (Acts 13:7), and Paul did appeal to Caesar (25:10-12). If the "most excellent Theophilus" (Luke 1:3; cf. Acts 1:1) was a Roman official, there is nothing in Luke or Acts that would suggest he should resign. And when Luke recorded the conversion of Sergius Paulus (13:12), he said nothing of any resignation from office. Luke could be critical, even derisive, but he did not reject the vocation of political authority. There is nothing in Luke to support the view of John Howard Yoder that "the function exercised by government is not the function to be exercised by Christians."[22]

Confidence in God and a theocratic vision warranted Peter's words to the Sanhedrin, "We must obey God rather than any human authority" (Acts 5:29; cf. 4:19-20; 26:19). And they gave Paul the boldness to remind the procurator Felix of "justice, self-control, and the coming judgment" (24:25). When one bends the knee before God the great king, one may stand boldly before a tyrant.[23] In stark contrast to Paul's boldness Luke set the obsequious subservience of his accuser Tertullus (Acts 24:1-8). This is hardly the stuff of conventional apology; it is a bold assertion of the theocratic vision of Psalm 2 and of Jesus of Nazareth.

22. John Howard Yoder, *The Politics of Jesus* (Grand Rapids: Eerdmans, 1972), p. 199.

23. Cf. Thomas Macaulay's comment on the Puritan: "He prostrated himself in the dust before his Maker; but he set his foot on the neck of his king" (Herbert Augustine Smith, ed., *Macaulay's Essay on Milton* [Boston: The Athenaeum Press, Ginn & Company, 1898], p. 53). It was a favorite line of Henry Stob, my teacher of blessed memory.

Paul

Romans 13:1-7: Loving the Neighbor
in a World Not Yet God's Good Future

Paul's advice to the Roman churches in Romans 13 seems pedestrian in comparison to his bold talk of "justice" to Felix. It is, nevertheless, the *locus classicus* for Christian consideration of political responsibility. Whenever Christians think about political responsibility, they turn to Romans 13:1-7.

> Let every person be subject to the governing authorities; for there is no authority except from God, and those authorities that exist have been instituted by God. Therefore whoever resists authority resists what God has appointed, and those who resist will incur judgment. For rulers are not a terror to good conduct, but to bad. Do you wish to have no fear of the authority? Then do what is good, and you will receive its approval; for it is God's servant for your good. But if you do what is wrong, you should be afraid, for the authority does not bear the sword in vain! It is the servant of God to execute wrath on the wrongdoer. Therefore one must be subject, not only because of wrath but also because of conscience. For the same reason you also pay taxes, for the authorities are God's servants, busy with this very thing. Pay to all what is due them — taxes to whom taxes are due, revenue to whom revenue is due, respect to whom respect is due, honor to whom honor is due.

The passage has a sad history in the churches. It has been piously used sometimes to support great injustices. Christians can and sometimes do use Scripture itself to shirk their duties, rather than to discover them, to evade their responsibilities rather than to discern them. Some Christians in Hitler's Germany appealed to Romans 13 to justify their obedience to and support of the Third Reich. More recently some Christians in the United States used the passage to condemn those who, like Martin Luther King Jr., refused to obey unjust laws requiring segregation. And more recently still, some used it to condemn those who refused to be drafted to fight what they considered an unjust war in Vietnam. When it has been read as timeless law, it has sometimes been used to justify uncritical obedience to the state, no matter how unjust or pernicious the regime.

The response to this sad history has sometimes been to treat Romans 13 as a white elephant.[24] You know what a white elephant is. Go to any garage sale,

24. Victor Paul Furnish, *The Moral Teaching of Paul: Selected Issues,* second ed. (Nashville: Abingdon, 1985), pp. 18, 117.

and you will find numerous examples. A white elephant is obsolete, outmoded, and frequently a little ridiculous. And in response to the way this passage has been used by some, others have treated Paul's teaching here as obsolete, outmoded, and a little ridiculous.

Both of these views are wrong, however. Romans 13 was not a timeless law requiring obedience to any and every law of any state, however unjust. It was, rather, a timely contribution to the deliberation and discernment of the Roman churches. Paul wrote letters, not codes or treatises. The letters were the means of Paul's presence to the churches in his absence, and whether he was present or absent, he nurtured communities of moral discourse, deliberation, and discernment; he proceeded by way of reminder, not by way of legislation. And when the church acknowledged these letters as canon, it canonized them *as letters*. To read them in the context of Christian community is to read them as canon, as somehow authoritative for us, but it is not to read them as timeless law. It is to read them as script to be performed and — in service to such performance — to read them as scripted, as written, by an author, for an audience, doing certain things with the words and traditions at the author's disposal. To read them as scripted, as written, requires exegetical care and attention to the historical and literary context. That effort, important as it is, remains only one contribution to the community's effort to understand and perform the text. Given the sad history of the use of this text, it is important to remind ourselves again that we are to read it *humbly,* listening to other members of the community, and especially to those who have been oppressed by a government or by governments. The Christian community must read this text grateful for the diverse gifts within the community, grateful that some bring a prophetic longing for justice to the community and to the text, grateful that others bring a patient readiness to suffer wrong rather than to inflict it, and grateful that still others bring a sage reasonableness. The Christian community will set this text in the service of remembrance, exercising together the standards of excellence for the reading and performing of Scripture, holiness and sanctification, fidelity and creativity, discipline and discernment. It will read this text prayerfully, invoking the God who was and shall be and is the great king, confessing its sins (including its interpretative arrogance), thanking God for the diverse ways God chooses to govern the world, and saying, "Your kingdom come." In such prayer we may learn to govern our petitions, our reading of Scripture, and our political lives by the cause of God.

We return, though, to the effort to read this text as scripted, as written. We return to the modest but important contribution that attention to its historical and literary context might make to the community's effort to perform this text with fidelity and creativity. Paul wrote the letter during the early reign

441

of Nero (54-68), not during the latter part of that reign. Nero, of course, would become infamous as a tyrant. The church would reach this judgment after he persecuted the Christians in Rome after the disastrous fire of 64, and it was not only Christians who regarded the later Nero as a tyrant. Ten years earlier, however, there was considerable hope that the young Nero would conduct his administration with justice and humanity.

In that historical context Paul reminded the Roman Christians of a lively theocratic tradition that already existed among Greek-speaking Jews concerning political responsibilities. The tradition may be traced to the letter of Jeremiah to the exiles, encouraging them to "seek the welfare of the city where I [the LORD] have sent you" and to "pray to the LORD on its behalf" (Jer. 29:7). Greek-speaking Jews had taken that advice. The roots of the tradition reached also into the ancient wisdom tradition and its political advice. Proverbs 8:15, for example, says of wisdom — or has wisdom say — "By me kings reign, and rulers decree what is just." In the first century B.C.E. the Wisdom of Solomon expressed that tradition in its advice to rulers (6:1-11). It reminded rulers that their dominion was given by God — and under God. Rulers were "servants" of God and of God's "kingdom." And it warned rulers that the failure to "rule rightly" would bring the judgment of God.[25] The same tradition reminded the people of the prudence of obedience to the authorities (e.g., Prov. 24:21; cf. 1 Peter 2:17).

Paul evidently reminded the Roman churches, especially the Jewish Christians, of the tradition that had formed their political posture in the past as they talked together about the controversy concerning taxes.[26] Paul's advice is

25. The tradition found another voice, closer still to the time of Paul's letter to the Romans, in the work of Philo, the great Jewish philosopher of Alexandria. When the Jews of Alexandria were being persecuted in 37 C.E., Philo visited the emperor Caligula (37-41 C.E.) to protest. He recorded his mission in his essay, *Embassy to Gaius* (trans. F. H. Colson; Loeb Classical Library, 1962). The tradition of respect for the emperor under God is once again expressed. It was fully consistent with protest against injustice and with disobedience to unjust commands. Indeed, when Gaius (or Caligula) demanded that offerings be given in Jerusalem's temple *to* him, the Jews refused, disobeyed his order, and persisted in their policy of giving sacrifices *for* Gaius *to* the Lord God. This tradition was probably familiar and instructive for the Greek-speaking Jewish Christians in the Roman churches. On Philo in connection with Romans 13 see further Furnish, *Moral Teaching of Paul*, pp. 121-22.

26. Furnish argues convincingly that Romans 13:1-7 was meant to address the issue of taxation, acknowledging his own indebtedness to the work of Johannes Friedrich, Wolfgang Pohlmann, and Peter Stuhlmacher, "Zum historischen Situation und Intention von Rom. 13:1-7," *Zeitschrift fur Theologie und Kirche* 73 (1976): 149ff. The two main taxes in the Roman Empire at this time were direct and indirect. The direct taxes were paid to government officials; the indirect taxes, largely harbor fees and taxes on exports and imports, were paid to companies of Roman knights. There was, during Nero's early reign,

quite at home within the wisdom tradition of Greek-speaking Jews when he says that rulers are appointed by God (Rom. 13:1-2), that they are "God's servants" (13:4, 6), that they are instituted to protect the innocent and to punish the evildoer (13:3-4), and that those who desire a well-ordered community life ought, therefore, to render them due honor and taxes (13:5-7).[27] These were commonplaces of that tradition, and Paul reminded the people of them. This theocratic tradition, with its advice to "be subject" and its reminder that the emperor is subject to God, did not underwrite imperial arrogance. It limited it. The Jews in exile and the Christians in Rome were not invited to condone absolutism and despotism.[28] They did not give the worship that some emperors claimed. They gave appropriate civil obedience. Theocracy did not require the amphictyony or a Jewish monarchy, but it would not permit anarchy and chaos.

---

widespread unrest concerning the corruption of these companies and their exploitation of the public. In 13:7 Paul mentions both Gk. *phoros* ("taxes") and Gk. *telos* ("revenue"), terms which are the Greek equivalents of the official Latin terms for direct and indirect taxes. Paul advises the Romans that it is both prudent and moral to pay both kinds of taxes, prudent because it is dangerous not to, and moral because it is a sign of respect for the governing authorities whose responsibility it is to punish wrongdoers like the corrupt Roman knights.

27. When this tradition and this passage call the authorities "God's servant" (vv. 4, 6), they do not presume that the authorities are incapable of injustice. That they are "God's servants, busy with this very thing" (v. 6) does not mean that government is God's servant *because* it inevitably attends to the protection of the innocent and the punishment of criminals. It means, rather, that government is God's servant *in so far as* it attends to the protection of the innocent and the punishment of criminals. Either (i.e., causally or conditionally) is a possible way to translate the participle *proskarterountes* ("attending to"; NRSV: "busy with"), but I do not believe that Paul was naive about the evil a tyrant could do or had recently done in the empire. He knew from his own experience that the authorities did not always protect the innocent. He knew that they did not always attend to justice. The government is called to justice as God's servant; its injustices are not to be whitewashed. And he called the Roman Christians to submit to the authorities in terms of their vocation to do justice, not in terms of some naive assumption that they always do justice.

28. There was a debate about imperial kingship among the Romans themselves. One view bore a resemblance to the Jewish tradition reiterated by Paul. It emphasized *clementia*, clemency or benevolent rule. On this view, according to M. Sordi, "The king is first and foremost custodian of the laws he makes and his *potestas* (power, authority) finds its own limits in the *potestas* of God, to whom he too is *subditus* (subject) and to whom he owes his empire" (Marta Sordi, *The Christians and the Roman Empire*, Eng. trans., second ed. [New York: Routledge, 1994], p. 172, cited by J. Ian H. McDonald, *The Crucible of Christian Morality* [London and New York: Routledge, 1998], p. 179). This view was taken by Augustus, Claudius, and Tiberius. The other view emphasized the deity of the emperor; it was the view taken by Antony, Caligula, the later Nero, and Domitian.

Paul set that traditional advice, however, in the context of a new discernment. In memory of Jesus he set it in the context of his appeal to the Roman churches not to be conformed to this age, ruled as it is by sin and death, but to "be transformed by the renewing of your minds, so that you may discern what is the will of God" (Rom. 12:2). He set it alongside the Christian tradition surrounding the command "Do not repay anyone evil for evil" (12:17).[29] The rejection of vengeance (12:17-20) reminds us of Jesus' word in the Sermon on the Mount concerning the *lex talionis* (Matt. 5:38-48) even though no "Word of the Lord" is quoted. And what was said concerning that passage is even clearer here, where it is set alongside Romans 13:1-7. Those who are wronged should not seek revenge, but those who are charged with protecting the innocent should not, on the pretext of either piety or pity, renege on their obligations, under God, to protect the oppressed or to punish the wrongdoer.[30] Love for enemies is not inconsistent with a concern for maintaining justice and stability in the land.

On the contrary, Paul sees political responsibility as an implication of the duty to love the neighbor in a world not yet God's good future. Paul set the traditional material in the context of reminders of the obligation to love the neighbor (Rom. 12:9-10; 13:8-10) and of the eschatological situation (12:2; 13:11-12). Political responsibility, which was circumscribed in Paul's time to submission, is set in the context of the more urgent duty to love our neighbor while we wait for and pray for God's reign. We must love the neighbor — even the remote neighbor, even the neighbor we don't know or care to know — in a world where that neighbor is still threatened by violence, theft, deception, and oppression. That duty grounds and *requires* political responsibility; it does not *repudiate* it. Paul puts our political responsibility in the context of our greater obligation to love the poor, the hungry, the oppressed.

In a world like this one love requires that justice be done for the neighbor, and not just some tightfisted justice that protects self-interest, but a justice that reflects God's ancient concern for slaves, for the poor, for the least. That justice is the vocation of government, and where the government is not just "them" (as it was for Paul and the early church) but "us" (as it is where the people are not just ruled but also rule), it is *our* vocation. Because of our duty to love the

29. See E. G. Selwyn, *The First Epistle of St. Peter* (London: Macmillan, 1947), pp. 406-19, especially Tables VIII A, pp. 408-10, and VIII C, p. 416, for the identification of this tradition. Selwyn calls attention to the parallels among Romans 12:3-20, 1 Thessalonians 5:12-22, and 1 Peter 3:8-12, 4:7-11, and 5:1-5. With Romans 12:17 compare 1 Thessalonians 5:15 and 1 Peter 3:9. See also Verhey, *The Great Reversal*, pp. 66-67.

30. See pp. 412-18 in this volume.

neighbor we can and must support and respect and submit to — and participate in — government as the servant of God in so far as justice is sought and done *for the neighbor.*[31]

Love for the neighbor requires a concern for maintaining justice and stability in the land, but it will not be satisfied with it. Civil justice remains a minimal standard. And, of course, the Christian called to love the neighbor may not use justice as an instrument of self-interest against the neighbor. The law of *lex talionis* was not to be used, Jesus said, as a license for revenge (Matt. 5:39-42). We did not read that text as discounting the place of the law (or the Jewish authorities) in maintaining a measure of stability and justice in Jewish society. In Romans 13:1-7 Paul sees civil authority, even the Roman authorities, as important to a measure of justice and stability in the Mediterranean. But we must not read this text as a license to use the authorities (or Roman law) to pursue personal self-interest at the expense of the neighbor. As we have seen, Paul himself set this text alongside the tradition concerning nonretaliation (12:3-20). And in 1 Corinthians 6:1-8 Paul chided the Corinthians for the practice of bringing civil suit against each other in the Roman courts.[32] "Why not rather be wronged? Why not rather be defrauded?" he asked (6:7).

1 Corinthians 6:1-8: A Community of Discernment and Reconciliation

It is striking, of course, that in 1 Corinthians the civil authorities are not identified as "servants of God" (as in Romans 13) but as "the unrighteous" (6:1). It is possible to take "the unrighteous" simply as a reference to unbelievers, rather than as a moral judgment. Bruce Winter has argued, however, following an examination of the practices of civil litigation in Corinth, that when Paul referred

31. Think of a family. In a family, love sometimes requires the careful calculation of rights and duties and the equitable apportioning of them. Every parent of three children who has just two candies will testify to that. Love demands justice. Every parent knows that. No system of justice is perfect. Every child knows that. Imperfect structures of justice can be improved and made more tolerable by the spirit of love. Every healthy family knows that. It is not so different in any larger society. And as love tells me not to demand my own way within the family, so love tells me not to protect my own interest in politics but to look out for those of my neighbor, to insist that justice be done, especially for the poor and oppressed.

32. See Bruce W. Winter, "Civil Litigation in Secular Corinth and the Church: The Forensic Background to 1 Corinthians 6:1-8," in *Understanding Paul's Ethics: Twentieth-Century Approaches,* ed. Brian Rosner (Grand Rapids: Eerdmans, 1995), pp. 85-103.

to "the unrighteous," he was indeed rendering a moral judgment on the judges and juries who heard and decided civil cases.[33] Winter called attention to the injustices of the system of civil litigation. There were financial qualifications for jury service, there was a bias in favor of those with status and wealth, and there was outright bribery.[34] Moreover, the proceedings themselves involved the rhetoric of vituperation, or personal attack on the character of one's opponent. The proceedings involved not a dispassionate inquiry but strife and enmity, and the result was usually further enmity.[35] The jurors, I suggest, were "servants of God" who failed their vocation to justice and were *therefore* regarded as "unrighteous."

Paul did not surrender the task of justice to civil authorities. Justice was the work of God's reign, of theocracy. The authorities were the "servants of God." They maintained order against chaos and required some minimal justice. But when they were unfaithful to their calling, they faced the judgment of God and the judgment of the people of God. Moreover, Paul would not surrender the churches' task of communal deliberation and discernment to the Roman authorities. He made it clear that when one Christian has "a grievance against another," it should be made a matter of the politics of friendship within the church, not a matter of the politics of enmity in the Corinthian system of civil litigation. It should be made a matter of the politics of forgiveness and reconciliation, not the politics of strife and division. It should be heard within the community where slave and free, male and female, Jew and Gentile, rich and poor, "high" and "low" have both a voice and ears to hear, not within a system where only those with status have standing.

The church was — and was called to be — a community of deliberation and discernment in memory of Jesus and in hope for his coming. We need not repeat here what was said in part one of this volume about Paul's vision of the internal politics of the church as a community of discourse, deliberation, discernment, and memory. The Christians in Corinth, no less than the Christians in Rome, were "full of goodness, filled with all knowledge, and able to instruct one another" (Rom. 15:14), but they did not live up to their calling. Their failure to be reconciled with one another was, Paul said, "a defeat for you" (1 Cor. 6:7). The failure of some members of the Corinthian church to bring their grievances before the community was a violation of the politics of discourse and discernment, of reconciliation and forgiveness. And the failure of the community to hear them and to resolve them in memory of Christ was forgetful-

33. Winter, "Civil Litigation in Corinth," pp. 89-90 *et passim.*
34. Winter, "Civil Litigation in Corinth," pp. 91-94.
35. Winter, "Civil Litigation in Corinth," pp. 94-96.

ness; it was to surrender decision and judgment to the conventional standards
of the broader community (and in the case of civil litigation in Corinth, to unjust standards). Ironically, in this community of spiritual enthusiasts there was
a failure of nerve, a failure to live in anticipation of God's coming reign, when
with Christ "the saints will judge the world" and "the angels" (1 Cor. 6:2, 3).
This alone should reveal the presumption of those church members who
boasted that they were already fully spiritual. Their politics was the politics of
Corinth, not the politics of Christ; it was marked by resentment and elitism,
not by reconciliation and communal discernment. Both the "unrighteous" authorities and the presumptuous and divided Christians of Corinth had been
unfaithful to their political vocation from God.

The Corinthian church had also been unfaithful to their political vocation in their failure to deal with the "sexual immorality" among them, immorality "of a kind that is not found even among pagans" (1 Cor. 5:1). They should
have been grieved by this, confronted the offender with their grievance, and if
the man had been unwilling to repent, they should have brought the matter to
the church for discernment and discipline. Instead, they were arrogant and
boasted (5:2, 6), presumably seeing that as evidence that "all things" were "lawful" to them (6:12). Paul here asserted his apostolic authority. He had to, lest the
libertine assumptions of some of the spiritual enthusiasts corrupt the freedom
of Christians into license and the politics of peaceable difference into moral indifference. But he did not substitute his authority for the community's deliberation and discernment. He wrote boldly, by way of reminder, calling them to a
politics "worthy of the gospel of Christ."

Philippians 3:20: Citizenship in Heaven

That is Paul's own language, of course, in Philippians 1:27 (where Gk. *politeuesthe* is translated "live your life" but might more literally be translated "live
your political life" worthy of the gospel of Christ). He followed up that advice
to the Philippian church with the reminder that "our citizenship [Gk. *poli-
teuma*] is in heaven, and it is from there that we are expecting a Savior, the Lord
Jesus Christ" (Phil. 3:20). As the city of Philippi was a colonial outpost of the
Roman Empire, so the church in Philippi was a colonial outpost of the empire
of the Lord Jesus Christ. The point of having citizenship in heaven was not that
one could "go home" some day. Rome did not establish colonies so that the citizens of those colonies could one day go home to Rome. On the contrary, Rome
established colonies so that Roman civilization could be extended across the
empire. The colony of the empire of the Lord Jesus Christ had similarly been

established to extend the way of life associated with Christ. And like the Roman colonies that could rely on the emperor to rescue and liberate his subjects in desperate times, so the Philippian church expected a liberator, a Savior, from heaven. Paul's image here provides an opportunity to summarize our reflections concerning the politics of Paul.

"Citizenship in heaven" is an unmistakably theocratic image. Paul, too, was a theocrat.[36] God reigns in heaven — and Christ, the one to whom God gave "the name that is above every name, so that at the name of Jesus every knee should bend, in heaven and on earth and under the earth, and every tongue should confess that Jesus Christ is Lord, to the glory of God the Father" (Phil. 2:9-11). The "gospel" that Paul preached was not a new way of being "religious," at least not in the sense in which the Enlightenment taught us to use the word. It was the good news (and the costly claim to allegiance) that the crucified Jesus was the Messiah of Israel and the Lord of all. It was the fulfillment of those ancient theocratic hopes for a king who would bring glory to Israel and blessing to the Gentiles (e.g., Rom. 15:12), for a king to whom all things — and all kings — would be subject (e.g., 1 Cor. 15:24-28, citing the royal Psalm 110). The "gospel" was political.

Paul's theocratic vision, his political gospel, did not require any Roman citizen in the Christian community to disown his Roman citizenship. Paul did not renounce his own. It required Roman subjects to "be subject," but it set obedience to the emperor in the context of obedience to God. The civil authorities are "God's servants" in so far as stability and justice are served in a world where chaos and violence still threaten the neighbor. The authorities can, however, be unfaithful to that vocation, and then they must be recognized as "unrighteous." Political discernment in memory and hope was neither simply opposed to everything that the Roman authorities accomplished nor a quisling.[37] The Christian church was never to be merely a subversive movement. It was to recognize and celebrate "whatever is true, whatever is honorable, whatever is just, whatever is pure, whatever is pleasing, whatever is commendable" (Phil. 4:8), and to recognize and celebrate these things "worthy of praise" wherever they were found. But it was never to compromise its loyalty to Christ the king. It is God who is to be worshipped, not Caesar, and it is God's cause that must be served, also by rulers.

Paul's theocratic vision, his political gospel, required a political life

---

36. See further Dieter Georgi, *Theocracy in Paul's Praxis and Theology* (Philadelphia: Fortress, 1991).

37. N. T. Wright, "Paul's Gospel and Caesar's Empire," *CTI Reflections*, vol. 2 (Princeton: Center of Theological Inquiry, Spring 1999), pp. 42-65, p. 58.

within the Christian church that was "worthy of the gospel of Christ." Humility remained the sign of royalty (Phil. 2:6-11), and of the common life of the community. "Let each of you look not to your own interests, but to the interests of others" (2:4). It was to be a politics of discourse, deliberation, and discernment in memory of Jesus. It was to be a politics of friendship, of peaceable difference, of reconciliation and forgiveness. The citizens of heaven included both Gentile and Jew, both slave and free, both women and men, and there were no second-class citizens. It was to be a politics that modeled a justice and peace that transcended traditional racial and cultural divisions. The Roman Empire boasted of such a justice and peace, of course, but its "justice" and "peace" were built upon oppression and coercion. It was to be a politics of a restored humanity, itself a foretaste of God's good future. Of course, it was not yet that good future, and there were failures in the politics of the church. There was still pride, and there was still resentment; there were temptations to forgetfulness; and even where Jesus was remembered, the practice of discourse, deliberation, and discernment sometimes left them muddled and confused. Even so, they were colonial outposts of a heavenly empire, and it was from there that they awaited a savior, a liberator, a victor over the powers of this age (3:20).

Ephesians: Pax Christi

No account of the politics of the early church should be considered adequate if it ignores the little treatise we call the letter of Paul to the Ephesians. The questions of authorship and audience and date are much disputed, and I will not resolve them here. I read it with C. H. Dodd against the background of the animosity of the Jewish Revolutionary War in 66-73 c.e.[38] The enmity of Jew and Gentile had deep roots and broke out periodically in repression or rebellion. Moreover, it was regarded as a "holy enmity" on both sides. To the Jew, the Gentile was an idolater; to the Roman, the Jew was an atheist, refusing to acknowledge the gods or the divine authority of Caesar. The Jewish rebellion of 66 was followed by a war that was no polite reassertion of Roman dominion; it was a blood bath. And the animosity of the war spread into parts of the empire besides Palestine. There were anti-Jewish riots in several cities, including Alexandria, Caesarea, and Antioch. This political situation threatened the accomplishments of Paul's mission, and the unity of Jew and Gentile that he preached was

38. C. H. Dodd, "Christianity and the Reconciliation of the Nations," in his *Christ and the New Humanity* (Philadelphia: Fortress, 1965), pp. 11-13.

in jeopardy again. This crisis prompted the little encyclical known as the letter to the Ephesians. Whether written by Paul (and dating it to the Jewish Revolutionary War would suggest that it was not) or by a faithful and creative interpreter of Paul, the letter reminded Jewish and Gentile Christians of their identity in Christ. It remembered Jesus and reminded its readers that they had owned that story as their own story in baptism.

"He is our peace," the author says (Eph. 2:14). In Jesus there is "one new humanity in place of the two, thus making peace" (2:15). The "dividing wall" has been broken down. The "hostility" is ended. The Law that had separated Jew and Gentile, dividing "the righteous" from "the sinner," has been "abolished" (2:15). Ephesians simply echoes Galatians and Romans here, of course, with their announcement of justification by grace through faith.[39] There, too, the talk of justification by grace through faith was not an answer to the question of an introspective conscience, "How can I get right with God?" There, too, it was an answer to the social question of the Pauline churches, "How can Jew and Gentile live in one community?"[40] And it is no accident that "by grace you have been saved through faith" is repeated here in Ephesians (2:8) to underscore the creation of "one new humanity" of Jew and Gentile.

This "one new humanity" is anticipated in the church, where both Jews and Gentiles "have access in one Spirit to the Father" through Christ (2:18). Jews and Gentiles are together "citizens" (2:19) of that heavenly kingdom. More than that, Jews and Gentiles share in Christ's rule over "the principalities and the powers" (3:10 RSV). God had "raised him from the dead and seated him at his right hand in the heavenly places, far above all rule and authority and power and dominion . . ." (1:20-21), and God had "raised us up with him and seated

---

39. Note especially Galatians 2:15-21 and Romans 3:1–7:6. In Christ (and in their baptism into Christ) the Jews have "died to the law" (Rom. 7:4; Gal. 2:19), and in Christ the Gentiles have "died to sin" (Rom. 6:1-14). It is not that the Law is evil; on the contrary, "the law is holy" (Rom. 7:12). But when it is used to divide, to boast about "our righteousness" and to condemn "them" as "sinners," then it has been co-opted by the powers of sin and death. The Law itself discloses that all, both Jew and Gentile, are "under the power of sin" (Rom. 3:9), that all are "sinners." "But now, apart from the law, the righteousness of God has been disclosed, and is attested by the law and the prophets, the righteousness of God through faith in Jesus Christ for all who believe. For there is no distinction . . ." (Rom. 3:21-22). "All have sinned . . . [and] they are now justified by his grace as a gift" (Rom. 3:23-24).

40. Krister Stendahl, "Paul and the Introspective Conscience of the West," in his *Paul among Jews and Christians* (Philadelphia: Fortress, 1976), pp. 78-96; also Nils A. Dahl, "The Doctrine of Justification: Its Social Function and Implications," *Studies in Paul* (Minneapolis: Augsburg, 1977), pp. 95-120.

us with him in the heavenly places" (2:6).[41] Christians are "above" the political animosity and racial enmity that marked the times. The "powers," however, seem not to recognize the theocracy wrought by Christ. They take no notice. They continue to assert their own presumption of sovereignty. But the victory has been fought and won. The issue has been settled "in the heavenly places." On earth, however, the struggle continues, and it continues even in the church. Their struggle, the author of Ephesians says, is "not against enemies of blood and flesh, but against the rulers, against the authorities, against the cosmic powers of this present darkness, against the spiritual forces of evil in the heavenly places" (6:12). They are exhorted to "take up the whole armor of God" against such foes and to "stand firm" (6:13). This is a "spiritual" struggle, but no less political because of that. They are called to be a colonial outpost of a new humanity, resisting the culture of racism and resentment, resisting Rome's oppression and Judah's resentment, anticipating the peace that is the cause of God. It is the prayer (and subtle exhortation) of the author that "through the church the wisdom of God in its rich variety might now be made known to the rulers and authorities in the heavenly places" (3:10). This church of Jew and Gentile is the first fruits of God's good future, of the new humanity, of "the mystery" (3:3-9), and both Paul and the church are God's instruments to make it known, also to the "principalities and powers." They are called to model an

---

41. This concept of "the principalities and the powers," of course, was not invented by the author of Ephesians. It was familiar to both Jews and Gentiles. Among the Gentiles there was what C. D. Morrison called "the Graeco-Roman concept of the State" with its astral and cosmic powers. Among the Jews there were, for example, "the gods" (Ps. 84), the "holy ones" (Ps. 89:6-8) in the divine council, and of course, the "angels" of Daniel with their national assignments and their association with the beasts of the empires. The concept appeared in the indisputably Pauline letters (Rom. 8:38-39; 1 Cor. 2:8; 15:24-26). It appeared also in Colossians, where "the powers" are described as created "through him and for him" (1:16) and "disarmed" in the victory Christ won over them on the cross (2:15). "The powers" were evidently regarded as the spiritual beings that structure and influence life on earth, also politically. *As created* they have positive functions to order and sustain life. They share, however, in the fallenness of the creation, and *as fallen* they are tyrannical and enslave. Christians made the eschatological and theocratic claims that "the powers" had been made subject to God's sovereignty in the exaltation of Christ (e.g., Col. 2:15; Eph. 1:20-21), and that they continue to assert their own doomed sovereignty — and will — until Christ appears in glory. The emphasis on principalities and powers and "spiritual rulers" in Ephesians occurs not because the epistle is so "spiritual" but because it is so oriented to the political situation. See further Hendrikus Berkhof, *Christ and the Powers* (London: SPCK, 1966); G. B. Caird, *Principalities and Powers* (Oxford: Clarendon, 1956); Clinton Morrison, *The Powers That Be* (Naperville, Ill.: A. R. Allenson, 1960); Richard Mouw, *Politics and the Biblical Drama* (Grand Rapids: Eerdmans, 1976), pp. 85-115.

end to the hostility, called "to lead a life worthy of the calling to which you have been called, with all humility and gentleness, with patience, bearing with one another in love, making every effort to maintain the unity of the Spirit in the bond of peace" (4:1-3). While the *pax Romana* crumbled, the author announced the good news — and the obligations — of the *pax Christi*.

Revelation: Sovereignties in Conflict

Consider, finally, the theocratic vision of Revelation. Revelation (Gk. *apocalypsis*, 1:1) is surely to be counted as apocalyptic literature, and like most apocalyptic literature it springs from a community's experience of alienation and oppression. It was written as a protest against oppression and as consolation for the oppressed. It was not written to provide a basis for computing the date of Armageddon or for calculating the days left before Christ's return. It was written to exhort and encourage the Christians of Asia Minor who found themselves victims of the petty persecutions of the emperor.[42] Revelation called for watchfulness, not calculation; for courage, not computation.

The theocratic claim comes already in the greeting where Jesus Christ is identified as "the faithful witness, the firstborn of the dead, and the ruler of the kings of the earth" (1:5). A symbolic world is constructed for the readers which makes intelligible both their faith that Christ is Lord and their daily experiences of injustice at the hands of Caesar. The material for that construction comes largely from the theocratic tradition of Jewish prophets and seers. There is a holy war going on. There are "sovereignties in conflict."[43] On the one side are God, his Christ, and those who worship them; on the other are Satan, his vice regents, the beasts and "the kings of the earth," and those who prostrate themselves before them. The victory has been won by Christ, as the reader is assured in the first vision (1:12-20) of "one like the Son of Man" living, though he was slain, and reigning. The resurrection is God's vindication of the authority of this one, and the church acknowledges his authority and celebrates it in its wor-

42. Revelation was probably written during the reign of Domitian (81-96 c.e.). Nero's persecution did not evidently extend to Asia Minor. During the reign of Domitian the imperial cult was vigorously promoted and enforced in Asia Minor. See Elisabeth Schüssler Fiorenza, *Invitation to the Book of Revelation* (Garden City, N.Y.: Image Books, 1981), pp. 61-67. Revelation self-consciously adopts the letter format for its apocalyptic visions; it has an epistolary address and greeting (1:4-5) and an epistolary closing (22:21), and it contains seven letters to the seven churches of Asia Minor (2:1–3:22).

43. See further Paul Minear, "Sovereignties in Conflict," in *I Saw a New Earth* (Washington, D.C.: Corpus, 1968), pp. 228-34.

ship. Satan and his minions still battle on, still act like tyrants, still threaten and destroy, but their doom is sure.

The Christ of that opening vision commands John to write to the seven churches of Asia Minor, and in the seven letters that follow (2:1–3:22) the same Christ commends or censures the churches and issues his commands to them. Each letter closes with a promise to the church of a share in Christ's victory if they continue in the struggle (2:7, 11, 17, 26-28; 3:5, 12, 21; and each of these images of victory returns in the last two chapters). The "conflict of sovereignties" is not "a cosmic drama which one may view"[44] as though the seer is engaged in a spectator sport; it is an eschatological battle for which one must enlist.

"After this . . . in heaven a door stood open!" (4:1). The language of the vision that followed (4:1–5:14) is both political and liturgical. Heaven is portrayed as a throne room, and in it God sits enthroned. The heavenly court, instead of acclaiming Domitian as "worthy" and as "Lord and God" (4:11), sings its praise to God. Then "the Lion of the tribe of Judah, the Root of David" is identified as the one who "has conquered" and "can open the scroll" of history (5:5). When John looks, he sees "a Lamb standing as if it had been slaughtered" (5:6), but the Lamb *is* the Lion of Judah, and he has won the victory. That a slain Lamb is counted worthy to reign stands in obvious contrast to the conventional and imperial understanding of power. The heavenly court/choir sings "a new song" (5:9; cf. Ps. 96:1; 98:1), and they are joined by more and more until "every creature" (5:13) sings praise to the Lamb. The church already participates, of course, in the songs of praise, which are the very songs it sings in its worship "on the Lord's day" (1:10). More than that, it understands itself politically as God's empire, as God's kingdom — in Domitian's empire, as a counter-empire. Those in the church are heralds of theocracy; they are the voice for now of the whole creation, of all that is abused and oppressed by the false sovereignty of imperial power.

The Lamb that is the Lion opens the scroll with its seven seals, and the seer sees, first, the four horsemen, four "aspects of Roman power and rule"[45] — military conquest, civil war, inflation that robs the poor of sustenance, and death (6:1-8). The opening of the fifth seal unveils another aspect of Roman power in its image of the martyrs who cry out, "How long?" (6:9-11). The sixth seal discloses the beginnings of the judgment (6:12-17), but it is held back until Israel is restored (7:1-8) and "a great multitude . . . from every nation" is gathered (7:9-17). The salvation promised them answers not only the pleas of the martyrs but also the destruction wrought by the horsemen, for the victory of

---

44. So Jack T. Sanders characterizes the apocalyptic vision of Revelation in *Ethics in the New Testament* (Philadelphia: Fortress, 1975), p. 114.

45. Schüssler Fiorenza, *Invitation to the Book of Revelation*, p. 84.

God will bring complete well-being (7:16-17). When the seventh seal is opened, there was "silence in heaven." The climactic vision is put off for a time, and instead we see another cycle of seven visions. Six angels blow their trumpets, and the wrath of God is poured out upon the earth (8:1–11:14). When the seventh angel blew his trumpet, "there were loud voices in heaven, saying, 'The kingdom of the world has become the kingdom of our Lord and of his Messiah, and he will reign forever and ever" (11:15). The old theocratic hopes are about to be fulfilled. "The nations raged, but your wrath has come" (11:18; cf. Ps. 2:1, 5). The time has come for the final judgment, "for rewarding your servants . . . and for destroying those who destroy the earth" (11:18).

In the visions that follow (11:19–20:15) the seer sees eschatological holy war. Satan is cast out of heaven (12:10), but upon the earth he continues the battle. He summons first a beast from the sea (13:1-10) and then a beast from the land (13:11-18). Without attempting to identify these beasts exactly, it is clear that they are related to the imperial cult (13:4, 12-15) and that they use political power (13:5-7) and economic power (13:16-17) to persecute and oppress. Satan's battle initiative upon the earth, summoning the imperial power with its totalitarian and religious claims, requires a response not of violence (13:9-10) but of "endurance" (13:10) and "wisdom" (13:18). This is a holy war that "the LORD will fight for [them], and [they] have only to keep still" (Exod. 14:14). They "sing the song of Moses . . . and the song of the Lamb" (15:3-4).

The vision of Babylon/Rome and its fall (17:1–19:10) displays the splendor of Rome but also Rome's flaunting of wealth and power, its injustice. There are those who lament its fall, those who are powerful and wealthy according to Rome's standards and with Rome's aid, "the kings of the earth" (18:9-10) and "the merchants" (18:11-19). But the people of God, who have been called out of the city in a spiritual exodus, leaving behind the pride of power and the greed of that city's life (18:4), rejoice, joining in the heavenly "hallelujah" (18:20; 19:1, 3, 6).

The victory is won finally by the one whose name is "King of kings and Lord of lords" (19:16). And the outcome is "a new heaven and a new earth," no longer threatened by the waters of chaos (21:1). The outcome is a "new Jerusalem" (21:2–22:5), where God dwells and reigns and blesses. The outcome is God's good future, "all things new" (21:5) — the liberation of all things (including politics) from the rule of sin and death, the renewal of covenant (21:7), and "the healing of the nations" (22:2). The outcome is theocracy.

In the meantime Revelation commends "patient endurance" (e.g., 1:9; 2:2, 19; 3:10; 13:10; 14:12), but "patient endurance" is not passivity.[46] To be

46. Contrary to Jack Sanders's characterization of "patient endurance" as "a retreat from the ethical dimension" in *Ethics in the New Testament*, p. 114.

sure, this resistance movement, this counter-empire, does not take arms to achieve power. It does not plot a coup to seize economic and political control. But it is a resistance movement, and the author knows the inside of a prison on Patmos. The Christian churches of Asia Minor are to resist the pride of power and power of injustice. They must resist the bestial politics of empire. No one can live in the symbolic world of Revelation and be content with the injustice of this age. They must give testimony to the reign of God, to the victory of the Lamb, and to the transformation of political and economic power that was wrought by him. In their worship they remember Jesus and join their voices to the heavenly chorus, singing praise to the Lamb. In their life, including their political life, they celebrate the coming reign of God, singing "We shall overcome."[47]

There are a variety of political perspectives in the New Testament in memory of Jesus. They are all, however, theocratic. The continuing church will not simply repeat any one of them. It will read Scripture, remembering Jesus, not pretending to live in the Asia Minor of Domitian's empire or in the Rome of Nero's early reign any more than in Pilate's Jerusalem. Fidelity requires creativity. The continuing church is ready to be disciplined by the remembered story and is called to the discernment of its political responsibilities, both internally and in relationship to the politics of the city where God has sent it (cf. Jer. 29:7). Christians are people who form a community of faith and who want to live in all their other communities "by faith." They remember Jesus and say among the nations, "The Lord reigns — and will reign." That theocratic vision is non-negotiable for the church, as it is for the church's Scriptures. That theocratic vision may not be reduced to its political implications, but neither may it be emptied of them. God's reign is not merely political, but it is nevertheless surely political. And that brings me, finally, to some modest suggestions for contemporary theocrats in the pluralistic polis and politics of our culture.

47. As Richard Hays observes in *The Moral Vision of the New Testament* (pp. 183-84), that anthem of the civil rights movement was based upon the refrain of promise in the seven letters (in the King James version).

CHAPTER TWENTY

A Continuing Theocratic Tradition

The early church had a lively sense of being "a people." They were "a chosen race, a royal priesthood, a holy nation, God's own people" (1 Pet. 2:9). Indeed, even their opponents called them the "third people."[1] Christians themselves, however, did not simply set themselves in contrast to the Jews and the Romans; they were a "new humanity in place of the two" (Eph. 2:15). The old ways of distinguishing and dividing people had been cancelled, and not only national but social and sexual distinctions had been transcended (Gal. 3:28; Col. 3:11). They were "a new creation" (Gal. 6:15).

The Continuing Church

The continuing church did not cross some Jordan to take possession of a piece of real estate. They were, as Tertullian insisted, "a people of the whole world," and national boundaries were insignificant to them.[2] Nevertheless, they still faced those theocratic questions Moses had raised for the people of God ready to enter that land. Now that we have been made a people and given "an inheri-

---

1. Tertullian, *ad Nationes*, I.viii. See further, Adolf Harnack, "Christians as a Third Race," in *The Mission and Expansion of Christianity in the First Three Centuries*, trans. James Moffatt (New York: Harper Torchbooks, 1961; the German original was published in 1908), pp. 266-78.

2. Tertullian, *Apology*, 37. Consider also the famous line in *Apology*, 38: "[N]othing is more foreign to us than the state. One state we know, of which all are citizens — the universe"; in Tertullian, *Apology and De Spectaculis*, trans. T. R. Glover, Loeb Classical Library (Cambridge, Mass.: Harvard University Press, 1931).

tance" (1 Pet. 1:4) that surpasses the imagination, how shall we live? How shall we live a common life, a politics, which displays the lordship of Christ? And since they were not a nation but the light of the nations, they faced a second question as well. How shall we live with the politics of Rome?

The conviction that they were in fact "a people" was not just an abstraction for the early church. It entailed also a lively sense of political independence. They were not simply a part of some other people; they were not first of all or fundamentally answerable to some other nation or empire or its ruler. They were ruled by Christ, the ascended Lord. They were under his authority, and, under his authority, they were authorized to rule themselves. Their citizenship was in heaven (Phil. 3:20). They were, as their Thessalonian opponents had claimed, ruled by "another king named Jesus" (Acts 17:7). They had — or were called to have — a common life, a politics, "worthy of the gospel of Christ" (Phil. 1:27).

As the *Epistle to Diognetus* said, it is not that Christians live in cities of their own or speak a language of their own or dress differently or eat differently, but they nevertheless display that "their citizenship is in heaven."[3]

> They marry like all other men and they beget children; but they do not cast away their offspring. They have their meals in common, but not their wives. They find themselves in the flesh, and yet they live not after the flesh. Their existence is on earth, but their citizenship is in heaven. They obey the established laws, and they surpass the laws in their own lives. They love all men. . . . They are reviled, and they bless; they are insulted, and they respect.[4]

The early church displayed its citizenship and said among the nations, "God is king," by caring for the sick, by living sexual lives of chastity and fidelity, by feeding the hungry, and by helping the poor. The early church displayed its citizenship and said among the nations, "Jesus is Lord," in a politics of mutual instruction and discernment, of reconciliation and forgiveness, and of peaceable difference. This was not a politics of force or of lording it over a neighbor; it was a politics of "persuasion, not force: for force is no attribute of God."[5] The apol-

---

3. *Epistle to Diognetus*, 5, in *The Apostolic Fathers*, ed. J. B. Lightfoot and J. R. Harmer (Grand Rapids: Baker, 1984), p. 506.

4. *Epistle to Diognetus*, 5, p. 506.

5. *Epistle to Diognetus*, 7, p. 507. See also *Epistle to Diognetus*, 10, p. 509:

> For happiness consisteth not in lordship over one's neighbours, nor in desiring to have more than weaker men, nor in possessing wealth and using force to inferiors. . . . But whosoever taketh upon himself the burden of his neighbour, whosoever

ogists never tired of pointing out the way of life of these communities or of comparing it to the politics of the empire.

How, then, those in the early church wondered, should they relate to the politics of the empire? Their sense of political independence provided the freedom to disobey the authorities when obedience to Christ and to the cause of God required it. They told and lived the story of the martyrs, after all. But it also provided the freedom to honor the Roman authorities. And in ordinary circumstances their political responsibility as citizens of heaven included such honor and submission. As "servants of God" they were to live "as free people," but that freedom was not anarchy; "as free people" they were to "accept the authority of every human institution" and to "honor the emperor" (1 Pet. 2:13-17). The early church joined suspicion of political authorities to the honor due them in ways that were familiar to the theocratic tradition.

The earliest political writings of the continuing church were from the apologists, who undertook the task of defending the early church against the charges brought against it, including the charge of being a subversive movement. Understandably, this genre emphasized the honor and submission that Christians gave to the emperor. This genre of apologetic literature developed into anti-pagan polemic, of which Augustine's *City of God* is the crowning achievement, and within which the theocratic dialectic between suspicion and honor finds clearer expression. The writings against heresy within the church were a quite different genre, of course, but no less important politically. Gnosticism, Marcionism, and Manichaeism all threatened the church's link with the Jewish tradition and the identification of the God and Father of Jesus with the God of creation and covenant in the Hebrew Scriptures. Against the heretics it was necessary to defend the theocratic political tradition of Israel and of Jesus, a tradition "wrung from experience on the underside of world politics,"[6] a tradition of God's judgment against the bestial politics of empire but, at the same time, a tradition of God's blessing upon the nations.

The sense of political independence required that the church confront the empire "as a foreign power."[7] It did not require, however, the denial of whatever

---

desireth to benefit one that is worse off in that in which he himself is superior, . . . he is an imitator of God.

6. Oliver O'Donovan and Joan Lockwood O'Donovan, eds., *From Irenaeus to Grotius: A Sourcebook in Christian Political Thought, 100-1625* (Grand Rapids: Eerdmans, 1999), p. 5. This whole paragraph is indebted to the analysis there of the genres within which early Christian political thought appeared, and the whole book is a splendid resource for Christian political thought.

7. O'Donovan and O'Donovan, eds., *Irenaeus to Grotius,* p. 6. The O'Donovans add

was good and true and just within that "foreign power." They were the people of God, but God, after all, was the creator of all and (whether recognized or not) Lord of all. The emperor could do some good; the pagan philosopher could speak the truth; local customs were not to be summarily dismissed; and "the Samaritan" could still put "the righteous" to shame. "Whatever is true, whatever is honorable, whatever is just, whatever is pure, whatever is pleasing, whatever is commendable" (Phil. 4:8) is not to be denied but credited to God and counted as God's gifts to humanity. To many of the apologists — and surely to Clement of Alexandria and Origen — Christ was the powerful and creative Word of God, present in the creation and in history, the *logos* who has always generated the good and the true. The audacious claim of these apologists was that whatever goodness and truth and justice existed was the work of Christ. The wisdom of other peoples could and did enter the deliberations — and the political deliberations — of Christians. The final test, however, for reasons given and heard in the church remained the story of Jesus. Discernment — and political discernment — was still to be exercised in memory of the Christ, who is Lord of all.

The Constantinian Church

The dialectic of suspicion and honor was not easy to preserve, and it did not get easier with the conversion of Constantine, his victory over Maxentius, and the Edict of Milan in 313. Eusebius surely spoke for many other Christians in his celebration of these events and in praise of Constantine. One can understand the enthusiasm. Only a decade before, in 303, the emperor Diocletian had issued a series of edicts requiring that Christian churches be destroyed, that their Scriptures be burned, and finally that all Christians should be put to death. Hard on the heels of Diocletian's persecution came this remarkable reversal. Suddenly, the emperor was a Christian!

One can understand the enthusiasm. For nearly three centuries they had been saying that Christ was Lord, that he had ascended to the right hand of God, and that he would return to judge and to save. In their mission to all nations they had been saying, "The Lord is king!" They had envisioned a future emptied of tyranny, filled with peace. Many had heard them gladly, but the more the people responded, the more the rulers had opposed them. Now, suddenly, the ruler was on their side. It was the victory of Christ!

---

parenthetically, "even when the emperor was a Christian." They also observe that this inference from the meaning of the church's *politeia* was less clear in the East than in the West.

The Inordinate Praise of Constantine

That was, of course, the explanation Eusebius gave in his praise of Constantine. One can understand Eusebius's enthusiasm, but his praise was still inordinate. He claimed too much when he claimed to see in Constantine's accession an end to the "despotic violence" of emperors.[8] He claimed too much when he claimed to see in Constantine's victories the fulfillment of the ancient oracles of peace.[9] He claimed too much when he claimed to see in Constantine "a transcript of the divine sovereignty" and "the semblance of heavenly sovereignty."[10] It was almost as if the accession of Constantine were the *parousia*. The reign of God was identified too uncritically with the reign of Constantine. Honor was due Constantine as emperor, and what Christian would not be glad at his conversion, but Eusebius undercut the suspicion of conventional politics that had been part of the theocratic tradition since the amphictyony. (Constantine himself claimed too much when he claimed to be a bishop, if only over external matters in the church. In the *politeia* of the church he should have been regarded as another member.) Against the enthusiasm of Eusebius the church would need to struggle to recover its sense that this, too, was not yet God's good future, to retrieve its capacity to confront the empire as "a foreign power" (even when the emperor was a Christian), and to articulate the boundaries between the church as a new humanity and the empire as the old order.[11]

The Inordinate Criticism of "Constantinianism"

Eusebius went too far in his celebration of Constantine. Critics of "Constantinianism," notably John Howard Yoder and Stanley Hauerwas, sometimes go too far, too.[12] One can understand their concerns. I share many of those con-

8. Eusebius, "From a Speech for the Thirtieth Anniversary of Constantine's Accession," in *Irenaeus to Grotius,* ed. O'Donovan and O'Donovan, pp. 60-65, p. 62.

9. Including Psalm 72:7-8 and Isaiah 2:4. Eusebius, "From a Speech on the Dedication of the Holy Sepulchre Church," in *Irenaeus to Grotius,* ed. O'Donovan and O'Donovan, pp. 58-59, p. 59.

10. Eusebius, "From a Speech for the Thirtieth Anniversary of Constantine's Accession," in *Irenaeus to Grotius,* ed. O'Donovan and O'Donovan, pp. 60-65, p. 60. Even so, it ought to be noted that Eusebius began his praise of Constantine with praise of God, the "Great Sovereign."

11. It is a long — and continuing — story. It is told with great insight in Oliver O'Donovan, *The Desire of the Nations* (Cambridge: Cambridge University Press, 1996), pp. 199-242.

12. See John Howard Yoder, "The Constantinian Sources of Western Social Ethics,"

cerns, and I am deeply indebted to them both, especially for their emphasis on the politics appropriate to the common life of the Christian community; but they go too far in their criticisms of "Constantinianism," construing it, it seems, as "the fall of the church." Consider, for example, the litany of complaints in Yoder's "The Constantinian Sources of Western Social Ethics."[13]

One can understand his concern that the church after Constantine included many who were only nominally Christians, since it was no longer dangerous to be named a Christian.[14] But he claimed too much when he said, "After Constantine, the church was everybody," and when he took the persecution of pagans and heretics to be a necessary result of Constantine's conversion and rule.[15] The Edict of Milan (313) did not make Christianity the official religion of the empire; indeed, it did not even give Christianity a preferred position; it recognized religious pluralism. It was not until Theodosius I that the assemblies of heretics and the rituals of pagans were prohibited, and not until the Theodosian Code of 438 that Theodosius II ordered the death penalty for heretics and decreed that pagans could not serve in the army. A Theodosius was not a necessary successor of Constantine. A Christian emperor could have and should have protected religious freedom — not because religion is a private matter, not because religion should be publicly regarded as irrelevant, or at best as secondary, to the public loyalties of citizens, and not because religious freedom signals that one's primary loyalty belongs to the state. A Christian emperor could have and should have protected religious freedom precisely because loyalty to God is more fundamental than loyalty to the state. The emperor could have and should have acknowledged the limitations on his own sovereignty, the limits on that secondary loyalty of citizens that he could claim for the empire. There are good theocratic reasons to protect religious freedom.[16]

The celebration of Constantine had confused Constantine's conversion with the final victory of God and confused the empire with the kingdom of God and the emperor's authority with the reign of God. Those are important concerns, named by Yoder as concerns about "the new eschatology" and "the new 'servant of the Lord,'"[17] but they are more appropriate to Eusebius's inordinate celebration than to Constantine's conversion and accession. Yoder

---

in *The Priestly Kingdom: Social Ethics as Gospel* (Notre Dame: University of Notre Dame Press, 1984), pp. 135-47; and Stanley Hauerwas, *After Christendom?* (Nashville: Abingdon, 1991). They regard Constantinianism as "the fall of the church."

13. Yoder, *The Priestly Kingdom*, pp. 135-47.
14. Yoder, *The Priestly Kingdom*, pp. 135-36.
15. Yoder, *The Priestly Kingdom*, pp. 135-36.
16. See ch. 16, pp. 342-43 in this volume.
17. Yoder, *The Priestly Kingdom*, pp. 136-39.

claimed too much when he said, "Ethics had to change because one must aim one's behavior at strengthening the regime."[18] That was not the aim of most Christians, as happy as they might have been about Constantine's conversion. And if they expected the emperor to be a (rather than *the*) "Servant of the Lord," there were resources for such an expectation not only in the political reflections of the Yahwist and the royal psalms but also in the political reflections of Paul and others long before Constantine's conversion.

Yoder claimed too much when he complained that "after Constantine" moral deliberation was reduced to "universalizability" and "effectiveness."[19] It was almost as if the Enlightenment, with its Kantian and utilitarian theories of ethics, was the direct descendent of Constantine. It may be admitted that "Constantinians" were interested in identifying moral agreements where they could be found, but the apologists of earlier centuries, as we have observed, had already celebrated moral truth and goodness wherever they found it. Such moral truth was still regarded as the work of the *logos* in creation and history, the very *logos* revealed finally and decisively in the Christ whose story is told in Scripture. And the memory of Jesus could remain the test for appeals to such moral commonplaces in the deliberation of apologists (and "Constantinians").

It may also be admitted that "Constantinians" were interested in effectiveness. This is a charge that Yoder repeated often. "The prevailing assumption, from the time of Constantine until yesterday, [was] that the fundamental responsibility of the church for society is to manage it."[20] Yoder was surely right to claim that the "fundamental" responsibility is not management but mission, but he goes too far in the claim that Christians should have no interest in the consequences of their acts and nothing to do with "managing the world." A theocrat will have to disagree.[21] To be sure, there are limits to our efforts to predict and calculate the consequences of our actions, but the moral life requires some such effort. Could we drive a car morally without making such an effort? And if God gave human beings "dominion" in the world (Gen. 1:26, 28), it is

18. Yoder, *The Priestly Kingdom,* p. 137. See also Hauerwas, *After Christendom?* p. 39, and the charge that the church took up "Rome's project."

19. Yoder, *The Priestly Kingdom,* pp. 139-40.

20. John Howard Yoder, *The Politics of Jesus* (Grand Rapids: Eerdmans, 1972), p. 248. In "The Biblical Mandate," *Post-American* (April 1974), p. 25, Yoder made the same point with another memorable phrase, that we should "see our obedience more as praising God, and less as running the world for Him." If it were simply a matter of "less" and "more," there should be no objection to this claim, but for Yoder Christians have no business running the world.

21. Yoder sees an association of the "theocratic" and Calvinist traditions; see his *The Christian Witness to the State* (Newton, Kans.: Faith and Life Press, 1964), pp. 64-65.

not self-evident that the refusal to "manage" the world is appropriate. Of course, one should not use that power to oppress and enslave. (That story of creation was written against the tyranny of the Babylonians, as we have seen.) But Joseph and Daniel and Nehemiah served in Egyptian, Babylonian, and Persian governments. The judges and kings and prophets and lawmakers of Israel used their capacities to consider and predict the outcomes of their actions and policies. If these managed and calculated, then it does not seem that Christians should always refuse to participate in managing a society or to consider the effects of actions and policies.

Against "Constantinianism" Yoder set the story of Jesus, and particularly the story of his obedient "powerlessness" on the cross.[22] Yoder did ethics "by way of reminder," too. He is right to set the stories of our lives alongside the story of Jesus so that our lives may be judged and made new by the memory of Jesus. And he is right about this: our common life is still possessed by demons that will not be exorcised by violence. But he goes too far. We need not repeat here what was said earlier concerning the story of Jesus — discussion about his power and "authority" in exorcism (or about the social and political significance of exorcism), about the "authority" he displayed in cleansing the temple, about the "authority" of his words (or about the saying concerning nonretaliation). Let it simply be said again that soldiers and a centurion and scribes were not called to give up their power; they were called to construe and use their power to protect and to serve those who were least. Constantine and "Constantinians" have plenty to repent of here, but they need not repent of power or authority itself. They may not be tyrants. They may not "lord it over" those who are subject to them. They may not pursue policies that only serve the interests of the rich and powerful. Jesus and the theocratic tradition neither divinized nor demonized political authority in the context of a common life; they called it to account; they called it to respond to the vision of a humble king and to that king's announcement of God's good future. Neither Constantine nor any Christian politician is the Messiah, but they are all called to remember that there is one, and to exercise authority as a form of discipleship. The Christian communities of which they are a part are called to remind them of that.

Finally, Yoder claimed too much when he drew so sharp a distinction between the pacifism of pre-Constantinian Christians and the post-Constantinian Christians who "considered imperial violence to be not only morally tolerable but a positive good."[23] To be sure, there is a clear distinction, but both sides of Yoder's contrast are overstated. We know that there were Christians serving in

22. Yoder, *The Politics of Jesus*, pp. 244-48.
23. Yoder, *The Priestly Kingdom*, p. 135.

the Roman army from the second century on.[24] Tertullian, whose pacifist credentials were as good as any, defended the church against the charge of being "useless" by telling the provincial proconsul of Carthage that "we sail with you, and fight with you, and till the ground with you."[25] Moreover, he reported with pride that the army of Marcus Aurelius was saved from drought by the prayers of the Christians within it.[26] More significant, however, is the other side of Yoder's contrast.

Not even Eusebius saw Constantine's violence as a positive good; he celebrated his victory as a victory in the war *against* violence, his rule as the *end* to the "despotic violence" of emperors.[27] In this he was naive, of course, but he hardly regarded violence as a positive good. The emergence of the Christian accounts of "just war" did not make of violence a positive good; on the contrary, they were motivated by their recognition of the evil of violence to attempt to limit it and to restrain it.

The Old Word in a New Situation

There can be no doubt that the situation of the church changed with the conversion of the emperor, but the Christian emperor should be confused neither with Christ nor with the anti-Christ. The theocratic tradition had undergone revision in the light of new circumstances before, its creativity and fidelity tested before. The tradition continued, and so did the memory of Jesus in the church. Consider Lactantius. He lived through the persecution of Diocletian, and he ended up serving as a scholar in the court of Constantine. Early in his life he had written *Divine Institutes.* It was a pearl of the apologetic tradition. He saw the church as a new humanity, as citizens of heaven, responding to the Christ of blessed memory and glorious hope and bringing a new civilization to the world.

Lactantius was the first Christian thinker to work through the notion of "justice," but he did it *before* the conversion of the emperor.[28] His Christian ac-

24. See Roland Bainton, *Christian Attitudes toward War and Peace* (Nashville: Abingdon, 1960), pp. 68-69.

25. Tertullian, *Apology,* 4, cited by Lisa Sowle Cahill, *Love Your Enemies* (Minneapolis: Fortress, 1994), p. 47.

26. Tertullian, *Apology,* 5, cited by Cahill, *Love Your Enemies,* p. 47. Origen, *Contra Celsum,* 8.73, also insisted that Christians had helped the emperor in battle by praying on behalf of his armies.

27. Eusebius, "From a Speech for the Thirtieth Anniversary of Constantine's Accession," in *Irenaeus to Grotius,* ed. O'Donovan and O'Donovan, pp. 60-65, p. 62.

28. Stanley Hauerwas goes too far in *After Christendom?* pp. 45-68, when he suggests that "justice is a bad idea for Christians" and that a concern for it is "Constantinian."

count of "justice" is shaped by the memory of Jesus, especially by Jesus' double love commandment and his announcement of the reign of a God who humbles the exalted and exalts the humble. Like the apologist he was, Lactantius set this justice, a justice displayed (if imperfectly) in the common life of the Christian community, at once polemically over-against the civilization of the Greeks and Romans and apologetically as the very fulfillment of their (and all) human hope for justice.

Justice was, he said, constituted by piety and equality. Here he echoes the commandment to love God and the neighbor. Piety is the worship of God, and it is the "originating impulse" of justice. Anticipating Augustine, Lactantius insisted that without piety there can be no genuine knowledge of justice. "The second constituent part" and the "energy and method" of justice is equality, "treating others as one's equals."

> With him [God] there is no slave or master. Since we all have the same father, so we are all alike his freeborn children. No one is poor in his eyes, except for want of justice; . . . no one has the title "Excellency" without accomplishing all the stages of moral growth. And that is why neither the Romans nor the Greeks could sustain justice, since they had so many levels of disparity in their societies, separating poorest from richest, powerless from powerful, the obscure from the most elevated dignities of royal state. . . . But someone will say, "Don't you have poor and rich, slave and master, in your community? Aren't there distinctions between one member and another?" Not at all! That is precisely the reason that we address one another as "Brother," since we believe we are one another's equals. . . . [S]laves are not slaves to us, but we treat them and address them as brothers in the spirit, fellow slaves in devotion to God. Wealth, too, is no ground of distinction, except insofar as it provides the opportunity for preeminence in good works. To be rich is not a matter of *having* but of *using* riches for the sake of justice. . . . What security is there in rank, wealth, or power, when God can bring even kings lower than the low? And so among the commands which God took care to give us, he included this in particular: "Whoever exalts himself will be humbled, and whoever humbles himself will be exalted" (Matt. 23:12).[29]

This was written *before* Constantine's conversion. His conversion and the new freedom of Christians in the empire might be taken, of course, as an empirical correlate of that axiom of reversal. The humble were suddenly exalted. But it

---

29. Lactantius, *Divine Institutes*, bk. V, sections 14-15, in O'Donovan and O'Donovan, *Irenaeus to Grotius*, pp. 52-53.

was not taken as the completion of that project, as if those now exalted could exalt themselves. The new situation still required the old word, lest the reign of God be forgotten. And when the popularity of *Divine Institutes* required a second edition, it was republished *after* Constantine's conversion — and with a new dedication to Constantine! The old word was republished in and for a new situation. There may be gratitude for a little vindication of the martyrs within history as well as at the end of history. But there should be no triumphalism. And the greatest danger is still forgetfulness. In memory of Jesus the church continued to serve God's cause by telling the old story and by living it, by saying among the nations, "The LORD is king!" and by reminding the emperor that the humble will be exalted, and the one who exalts himself will be humbled.

The Contemporary Church

Christians are still people who form communities of faith and who want to live in all their other communities "by faith." We still face those theocratic questions that Deuteronomy suggested Moses had raised for the people of God ready to enter their future. Now that we have been made a people, how shall we live as one? How shall we live a common life, a politics, which displays the lordship of Christ? And since the church is not a nation but the light of the nations, how shall we live with the politics of the cities and nations in which we live? Those are questions, of course, which call for the deliberation and discernment of the whole community gathered around the whole of Scripture, remembering Jesus. And the greatest danger is still, as Moses had said, forgetfulness.[30]

30. Politics tempts us to forgetfulness in a variety of ways. Some of the temptations are as old as humanity. Politics still tempts us to use our power and authority to protect our own interests at the expense of our neighbors' interests, to "lord it over" others if we can. Contemporary pluralism, however, tempts the church to forgetfulness in at least two other ways. (See ch. 2, pp. 39-40 in this volume.) In the midst of moral differences, one can understand the enthusiasm of some for the Enlightenment project of identifying and applying certain universal moral standards, moral principles that are independent of any particular community and tradition. The enthusiasm for a moral Esperanto, for a universal moral language, however, neither permits nor requires religious commitment to be anything more than a private matter; it silences the voices of those who would speak publicly with religious conviction, and it tempts us to forgetfulness. And in the midst of many and diverse goods, the church sometimes gathers around a loyalty to some particular good in addition to its loyalty to God in Christ. Robert Wuthnow, *The Restructuring of American Religion: Society and Faith Since World War II* (Princeton: Princeton University Press, 1988) has identified the disturbing trend that people today join churches in order to be associated with other people who share their particular social class and interests. A church

Thankfully, the remedy for forgetfulness remains close at hand. The remedy for forgetfulness is still to tell the old, old story, and to struggle to live it — also in our political life. The contemporary church can still read Scripture with saints and with strangers, and, reading Scripture, it can remember Jesus. The memory of Jesus can form in the churches a common life, a politics, "worthy of the gospel of Christ" (Phil. 1:27), and it can form in the churches a voice that is ready to say among the nations, "The Lord reigns — and will reign."

The practice of reading Scripture in Christian community aims at remembering, and it has been the burden of this book to do Christian ethics boldly and gladly by way of reminder. That practice of reading Scripture in Christian community, as we have often repeated, invokes certain standards of excellence: holiness and sanctification, fidelity and creativity, discipline and discernment. Holiness requires that we privilege the Scripture as "holy," as the rule for our faith and life — and for our politics. There is a theocratic tradition in Scripture and in the memory of Jesus that is non-negotiable for the church. Sanctification requires that we set the remembered story alongside the stories of our life, including the story of our politics, until the stories of our life are made new by it. Reading Scripture and remembering Jesus, we also hope and pray and work for the renewal of our politics. We struggle to perform this "script" as well as to study these writings as "scripted," to live a politics "worthy of the gospel of Christ." That performance will require creativity and fidelity — and creativity *in order to be* faithful, for we do not live in the Jerusalem of David or in the Jerusalem of Jesus or in the new Jerusalem of John's vision. Discipline is the readiness to be disciplined by the story, to read it over-against ourselves and not just in self-serving defense of our political interests. Discernment is the standard of excellence in reading Scripture that is able both to see how parts of Scripture "fit" the whole and to see how our choices, including our political choices, "fit" or are "worthy of" the story of Scripture.

From the very beginning of this book we have emphasized Paul's account of the church at Rome as a community "full of goodness, filled with all knowledge, and able to instruct one another" (Rom. 15:14). That commendation was, we said, also a vocation to be a community of moral discourse, deliberation, and discernment in memory of Jesus. We have seen that vocation confirmed in our examination of the politics of the early church in memory of Jesus. It was there in the practice of communal deliberation, reconciliation, and forgiveness

---

can then find its vision of God's good future reduced to the triumph of some particular (if genuine) good or to the fulfillment of the interests of a particular group. Such provincialism can tempt the church to forgetfulness. The greatest danger is still forgetfulness, and the contemporary church needs to recover its memory and identity, also politically.

in Matthew's community. It was there in the politics of peaceable difference in Luke's Gospel. And it was there, of course, in Paul's call to the Corinthians to exercise communal discernment and reconciliation.

Church Politics

If we circle around once more to the choices we face, let the first choice be to nurture this political tradition and vocation of the church, to sustain and strengthen the practice of talking together about our choices, of reasoning together, and of exercising discernment together in memory of Jesus. There is enough work to be done on the renewal of the internal political life of our churches to keep all Christians busy for a while. The church is not yet conformed to its memory of Mark's remembering Jesus and calling for a heroic and watchful community. It does not yet measure up to its memory of Matthew's call for a surpassing righteousness. It does not yet live a politics worthy of Luke's memory of Jesus as one who brought good news to the poor. Its common life does not fit Paul's vision of a colony whose citizenship is in heaven. It does not yet image the *pax Christi* Ephesians hoped it would make known to the principalities and powers. There is plenty of work to be done on the politics of the Christian community itself in memory of Jesus. That work will require, of course, a renewal of the practices — and the politics — of discourse, deliberation, and discernment, of repentance, reconciliation, and forgiveness, and of peaceable difference. And it will require, of course, the reformation of identity and community in memory of Jesus.

There is much work to be done if the churches are to live a common life, a politics, which displays the lordship of Christ. But the other question, the question about how we should live with the politics of the cities and nations in which we live, will not go away. And because the lordship of Christ is not limited to the church but extends over the whole cosmos, the church that would display the lordship of Christ may not ignore or neglect it.

Theocracy in the Context of Pluralism

That brings me, finally, to attempt a constructive account of theocracy in the context of pluralism. It may be useful to revisit briefly some of the territory we have traversed. I began by defending theocracy. The defense of theocracy had to begin by distinguishing theocracy from some of the political positions that have sometimes been associated with it. To defend theocracy is not to defend

468

hierocracy, the political rule of a priestly or clerical hierarchy. The theocratic vision makes political rulers responsible to God, not to priests. To defend theocracy is not to defend bibliocracy, the legislation and enforcement of the positive law found in Scripture. Theocracy does not entail any particular legal code, whether the Covenant Code or the Deuteronomic Code or any other; it entails nudging the received legal tradition in the direction of a politics worthy of the rule of God. And to defend theocracy is not to propose that a contemporary state ape any "theocracy" of history — not Israel's amphictyony nor her monarchy, not Calvin's Geneva, the Massachusetts Bay Colony, or even Van Raalte's "colony" in Holland, Michigan.

To defend "theocracy" by distinguishing it from some of the positions often confused with it, however, left it open to the accusation that "theocracy" is an empty cipher without any meaning at all. Against that accusation I attempted to defend theocracy by a positive but (admittedly) abstract account of the meaning of theocracy. I tried to show that every state has a "theocratic" dimension, that all human communities "live by faith." All states rely on a measure of confidence in and loyalty to a cause that transcends them. Moreover, policy is always formed within assumptions about the nature of persons and their communities, about human "fallenness" (the fault that runs through our world and through our common life), and about the prospects and destiny of people and groups.

We took some initial theocratic "soundings" in an attempt to provide an initial account of the meaning of theocracy. Then, as we read Scripture and remembered Jesus, as we attended to the theocratic tradition in which he stood and to the politics of those who remembered him, we developed that account and made it more concrete.

The fundamental premise of theocracy, we said, was that the cause we must serve politically and the cause the nations must serve is God's cause. Political authority derives from God, and it is answerable to God! Along the way we have seen something of God's cause, or causes. We saw, for example, that it was God's intention to protect and provide for the oppressed and the poor and the weak — not only in the exodus, but in the complaints of the prophets and in the work of the lawgivers, and climactically in Jesus' announcement of a great reversal. We saw that it was God's intention to bless the nations with prosperity and peace — not only in the stories of the ancestors told by the Yahwist, not only in the visions of the prophet Isaiah, but climactically in Jesus, who is celebrated as the humble king who brings peace to the nations.

God's cause, however, transcends our political institutions and programs, even the best of them. That was the first "sounding" we took, and along the way it has been confirmed again and again. The reign of God could not be reduced to amphictyony nor, then, to monarchy. The prophets reminded the king and the people of the transcendent cause of God. It was there in Israel's past, made known there but never captured there, and it was there in its future, calling the nation to repentance and reform. Apocalyptic reminded us not only that God's future rule is surely political but also that it will not come as a political accomplishment; God's cause is transcendent. And Jesus reminded both Pilate and us that his kingdom is "not of this world," that his genuinely political authority was not to be co-opted to serve some cause other than the transcendent cause of God. The theocratic tradition honored the authorities because they had their authority from God, but it joined to honor a suspicion of the authorities because they so frequently served their own interests rather than God's cause. Theocratic politics recognized the ambiguity of power, and it would not let go accountability to God. It neither divinized nor demonized rulers; it called them to account. This recognition of the transcendence of God's cause should nurture among theocrats capacities for humble and self-critical political reflection and for an independent and prophetic voice.

Christ's kingdom is "not of this world," but it is nevertheless made its power felt "in" this world, and it is relevant to our political choices. We do not know enough about God's cause to be able to identify any certain policy unequivocally *as* God's cause, but the transcendence of God's cause does not mean that we know nothing of it or that faithful political discernment is impossible. The transcendence of God does not render deliberation or discernment concerning particular political choices impossible, as though every political "good" were equidistant from the transcendent cause of God. That was the second "sounding" of theocracy, and we have seen it confirmed in our reading of Scripture.

The amphictyony began in suspicion of conventional politics, the politics that had enslaved and oppressed the slaves of Egypt, but when the charismatic leadership could not withstand the threats of anarchy and chaos (or Philistine oppression), a new political order was required. And discernment was exercised in exalting the humble Saul to be king so that he could protect the land from threats within and without. There was ambiguity in this transition to monarchy, to be sure, but discernment was exercised in preserving an independent voice for the prophet and the lawgiver against royal absolutism. In the court of the empire the Yahwist exercised discernment concerning the ways a humble king might perform God's reign and serve God's cause, calling for policies to bless the nations, not to curse and destroy them. And the prophets exercised discernment in their oracles of judgment against royal despotism and against a politics in the service of the rich. They called for repentance and reform, and the lawmakers sometimes heeded their call by revisiting the received legal tradition and exercising discernment, revising the code to make it "fit" the old story

470

(and the new circumstances) a little better. And when Jesus issued his own call for repentance and reform, he exercised discernment. He judged the priestly aristocracy for policies that served their own interests but exploited the poor; he judged the lawyers and scribes who did not use their authority to interpret the Law in order to protect the weak or provide for the poor. Paul exercised discernment, and called upon the church to exercise its own, on the question of taxes during the reign of the young Nero and on the question of civil suits in Corinth. And John of Patmos exercised political discernment in calling for an uncompromising and patient endurance of Domitian's oppression.

Such political choices were seldom unambiguous, and no political choice simply ushered in God's reign, but political discernment was still a possibility and a calling. God had not left God's cause without witness; it was not totally unknown. The theocratic tradition of Israel regarded political power as accountable to the God made known in the story. The nation — and the nations — were to serve God's cause, the cause that was also made known in the story. Every political structure and policy was finally to be tested by its service to the cause of God and by its "fit" with the story. Political discernment remains both a possibility and a calling in the contemporary church. We read Scripture in Christian community, remembering Jesus, and we talk together about politics in memory of Jesus. Not every political cause has a place within loyalty to the God of creation and covenant who raised Jesus from the dead, and not every cause that has a place can be given prominence of place or priority. The Christian theocrat can and must select and exclude, relate and order, the diversity of political "goods," even though a simple unitive understanding of God's cause is beyond his ken. This second "sounding" should encourage political discourse and discernment in memory of Jesus.

And if we can know something of God's cause politically, then we must also serve that cause politically. The transcendence of God and of God's cause does not render political means and processes inappropriate instruments in the service of God and that cause. That was the third "sounding" of theocracy. To be sure, in memory of Jesus theocrats will have modest expectations of the service government can render to the cause of God. The apocalyptic tradition of Israel and of Jesus is enough to remind us that no political strategy will usher in the new heaven and the new earth. Politics cannot be messianic, but it can be watchful. Theocrats will be suspicious of the extravagant claims for political power and authority, ready to laugh derisively at political pride and at the pretenses of power. We have heard testimony enough of that — in the prophets, in the apocalyptic caricature of empires as beasts, in Luke's depiction of the incompetence and corruption of Roman officials in Acts, and in the echo of God's derisive laugh in Psalm 2 when Herod Antipas and Pontius Pilate cooperate "against the Lord and against his Messiah" (Acts 4:26). But the suspicion of political pride is not for Christian theocrats an excuse for political sloth. Devotion to the cause of God in a world not yet God's cosmic sovereignty will not disown political responsibility but, rather, modestly own it.

Moreover, in memory of Jesus theocrats may sometimes act politically by separating themselves from politics as usual. The amphictyony was in some sense intended to separate Israel from the conventional politics that was marked by exploitation and oppression. (The tasks of politics did not go away, of course, nor the risk of chaos.) In exile the people separated themselves from the Babylonian politics of oppression and enslavement. Jesus refused participation in a popular movement that would have followed him against Rome in the hope of vengeance. Paul insisted that the Corinthians separate themselves from the injustices of the civil court in Corinth. And John called for a spiritual exodus from Rome and from the politics of Rome under Domitian. Such refusal of participation is itself a political act, or can be. And if it is not a political act, then it is political sloth and no part of faithfulness.

The pacifism of John Howard Yoder — and of many pacifist communities from early monasticism to the Amish — has sustained the Christian story of peace and peaceableness when it was threatened by forgetfulness, and it has refused participation in "secular" politics as a political act. Such pacifism has rejected any continuity between the reign of God and the politics of this world and every confusion of the politics of this world and the politics of discipleship. It has withdrawn from the confusion and the ambiguities and the compromises of politics. Such withdrawal is a "witness" — when it is performed well — to the uncompromising judgment of God and to the great good future of God. It is to be honored as a performance of the story from which others who would live the story have much to learn. Nevertheless, there are at least four reasons not to regard pacifism and withdrawal as the only way or as the most faithful way to live the story.

First, there is the story itself. We need not repeat here our reading of the gospels, but we may repeat the conclusion that the church's memory of Jesus did not make pacifism a new *halakah*, a legal requirement of Jesus' politics.

Second, withdrawal as a political strategy lives in the neighborhood of despair. The image of exile is a powerful one — and a biblical one. Christians are "aliens and exiles" (1 Pet. 2:11). But exiles should not spend all of their time in lament, sitting and weeping "by the rivers of Babylon" (Ps. 137:1). Lament itself, by its attention to God, should give birth to hope. Ironically, hopelessness is tempted to violence, as the horrific conclusion of that psalm may remind us. Exiles have work to do, especially since they are a colony of heaven, not just eager to "go home" but eager to extend the realm of the great King. They are to "seek the welfare of the city." They, like Daniel and Nehemiah, are to take opportunities for humble political service, also in exile.

Third, the story we love to tell and long to live is not a tribal story. It is the story of all nations and of every person. It was not just the Jews who were made in the image of God, who were made fit to rule but unfit for bondage. And it is not just those who tell that story of creation who confront the image of God when they confront a neighbor. It is a true story, and because it is a true story, whether one names the other "image of God," he may sense something that evokes respect and even awe. Jesus *is* the Messiah, and the Messiah is — and will be recognized as — Lord of all (Phil. 2:9-11). Fidelity to the story does not call us to withdraw from the "secular" any more than it calls us to pronounce a priestly benediction on the pride of empire. We are called to sustained and constructive engagement with the world, not to leave the story to one side when we discuss politics or to withdraw from "secular" political discernment and action for the sake of protecting the story. If the story is true, then it is publicly and politically true. If the story is true, then the very notion of a "secular" politics is suspicious; politics is mixed up with creation and sin and the cause of God.

Finally, those who choose to withdraw from politics are at risk of underestimating the goodness of God's work in human power and authority and of neglecting the not-yet character of their choice of powerlessness. If the story is true, then power is not to be simply identified with violence. Not all power is violence. Not all power is "lording it over" others. Sometimes power is in the hands of a great conductor who humbly serves both music and musicians. Sometimes power is exercised by a college administrator who humbly seeks to help a faculty become the best teachers and scholars they can be. Sometimes power is in the mayor's office, exercised in hospitality to those who are advocates of the city's poor.

Politics is an earthen vessel, but it is nevertheless serviceable to the preservation of some small but genuine goods and to the protection against certain great and genuine harms. In memory of Jesus Christians may and must be politically responsible. This third "sounding" of theocracy was confirmed in our reading of Scripture. The royal psalms looked for the king to act politically, to perform the reign of God, to serve God's justice and peace. The prophets acted politically by preserving their independence, limiting and protesting against royal despotism and absolutism. It was confirmed in the stories of the political service of Joseph in the Egyptian government, of Daniel in the Babylonian government, of Nehemiah in the Persian government. Even in exile the call to be separate from the injustice and idolatry of Babylon's politics was joined to an understanding that there was a place for participation in the politics of Babylon. When there was an opportunity to "seek the welfare of the city" (Jer. 29:7) and to serve God's cause, to insist "in the midst of the gods" that justice be done (Ps. 82), then that opportunity is a responsibility. It was confirmed when John the Baptist told the soldiers not to quit the army but to act responsibly and when Jesus affirmed the faith of the centurion without insisting upon his resignation. Political authority comes from God, and it is accountable and responsible to God. It is called to respond to the announcement of a great reversal for political power itself. In memory of Jesus and in hope of the good future he promised, political authority was not disowned; it was called to humble service, to seek the interests of those who are least. And it was confirmed, of course, when Paul set political responsibility in the context of the Christian's duty to love the neighbor, even the neighbor we do not know, while it is not yet God's good future, while that neighbor is still threatened by violence and greed. Theocratic political activity will sometimes take the shape of prophetic protest, the shape of a bone crossways in the throat of power. But sometimes — and more often, probably — it will take the shape of humble participation in the art of the possible. Political power includes the powers to vote and dissent and express and legislate and judge and administer, and all of it is to be construed as an opportunity for humble service to God and the neighbor.

The fourth initial "sounding" of the meaning of theocracy was that political discernment should be informed by Christian convictions about the nature of persons and their communities, about the fault that runs through our common life, and about the destiny of all things in God's good future. It was confirmed at several points along the way of our review of the theocratic tradition. The story of creation in Genesis 1 was told, we said, against the oppression and idolatry of Babylon. Christians believe that human beings are by nature creatures of God, part of God's good creation and along with it dependent on God, that humanity as it comes from God is always fellow-humanity, and that the dominion given with God's creation is always responsible dominion. Human persons are authorized to govern, to exercise political power, already in the creation, and they are answerable to God. Human beings are not made "fit" for oppression and slavery. They are made "fit" for freedom and fellow-humanity.

The story of the curse that rests heavy on humanity and upon its politics was told by the Yahwist as background for the theocratic hope of a blessing on all the nations. The fault that runs through our lives and through our politics is traced neither to nature nor to human dominion. The problem is not human freedom, which is, after all, the good gift of God the creator, but sin. The fault is traced to human pride and sloth, to human folly and greed. The curse followed hard on the heels of human sin, and it left its mark everywhere. The prospects for persons and their communities still tilt toward darkness when human pride, sloth, folly, and greed are not reined by law and tempered by a sense of finitude and, yes, of sin.

But God would not let sin and the curse have the last word. That is, of course, the rest of the story. God is always active not only as creator and judge but also as redeemer of God's world and creatures. God is always creating new possibilities for restraining evil and promoting well-being. Jesus came announcing the good future of God, and a new destiny was revealed and made its power felt. The church was made, by the power of the Spirit, the first fruits of a "new humanity," a community of peaceable difference. The equality and mutuality of Jew and Gentile, of slave and free, of male and female were marks of this new people (Gal. 3:28) — and of the destiny of all people. That equality and mutuality was to mark the common life of the churches, and those churches were to make it know to "the principalities and powers in the heavenly places" (Eph. 3:10 RSV). None of this is to be reduced to politics, but it bears on our political responsibility. The prospects for persons and their communities sometimes tilt toward splendor when they tend the creation and care for their fellow humans, but there is nothing triumphalist about the theocratic tradition in Scripture. The servant songs of Isaiah are evidence enough of that, and the story will not let us forget that the humble king who served God's cause died on a Roman cross.

The final "sounding" observed that the theocrat would not shrink from the task of "the enforcement of morals," but would insist on certain qualifications and restrictions upon that task. The first qualification was a healthy respect for freedom. It could not be otherwise, for freedom was the cause of God — or more accurately, a part of the complex cause of God — from the very beginning. This King of kings made people free. It was the story of creation and the story of exodus. The prophets preserved an independent voice against royal absolutism, and the visionaries condemned the inhumanity, the bestiality, of empires and their readiness to enslave and oppress. And it was the story of Jesus; "for freedom Christ has set us free" (Gal. 5:1). He did not coerce allegiance or use violence to claim the throne. He announced the good future of God and invited a response. To serve God's cause truly is to serve it freely. God is the source, preserver, and destiny of human freedom. Freedom does not become a negligible value, then, even when it is used paradoxically to deny its own source and destiny. Freedom remains a public good, and its preservation and protection a theocratic obligation. Freedom, of course, may not be unlimited; the result would be anarchy. But freedom must be protected and preserved. That was the first qualification on the theocratic "enforcement of morals."

The Christian theocrat also knows that morality outreaches the grasp of legal sanctions. Morality is concerned with dispositions and character as well as with external actions. Law and its sanctions focus on external actions. The story of exodus, for example, formed identity and community in ways that were reflected in law but could never be fully captured by law. The codes of Israel and their periodic revisions nudged the legal tradition in the direction of the story, toward something a little better "fit" to the rule of God, but they always failed to capture it. The Law might command, for example, that a certain portion of the harvest be left for the poor to glean (e.g., Deut. 24:19-21). The Law reflected Israel's story and the care of God for the poor (Deut. 24:22), but if the farmer's dispositions and character did not reflect the story of Israel, then obedience to the Law would be grudging and resentful, and the farmer would instruct his laborers to leave as little as legally permitted. The point was confirmed in Jesus' attention to *haggadah*, his focus on the formation of character by story. He parodied a legal casuistry that insisted on a nit-picking observance of the Law while characters remained hard-hearted and selfish, and he condemned a casuistry that had been co-opted by the rich and powerful. Nevertheless, the Law — and the interpretation of the Law — remained important to the politics of Jesus. It is true, of course — and no theocrat would wish to deny — that certain habits of mind and action may be influenced by public law. But it is also true that the "habit" of respect for the law is diminished when laws and sanctions are imposed where there is not the possibility of adequate or equitable enforcement. That was the second qualification on the theocratic "enforcement of morals."

Morality outreaches law, moreover, not only in that it is concerned with character as well as with conduct, but also in the kinds of actions it prescribes and prohibits. Law must deal with what will inevitably seem to morality to be "minimal standards." That was the third qualification upon a theocratic "enforcement of morals." Again the ancient codes of Israel confirm the point. They could not simply create an Israelite common life out of nothing. They nudged the existing legal traditions toward the story. *At the very least* a community that remembers its own liberation from Egypt's slavery should have a law to let a slave go free after seven years (Exod. 21:2). And later the law was nudged a little. *At the very least* that community should have a law that the freed slave not be sent out "empty-handed" (Deut. 15:13). And later the law was nudged a little more. Morality should never be reduced to "the very least," but it will insist "at least" that such protections and provisions be made for the poor and the powerless. And it will work politically to make sure of it. And again the point was confirmed in the teachings of Jesus and in his call for a "surpassing righteousness," a righteousness that goes beyond law or its authority for the politics of Israel. In the restored community the theocratic tradition learned not to despise "small things" but not to confuse them with the cause of God either. Sometimes "small things" politically and certain legislative "minimal standards" can both secure genuine (if small) goods and give some little token of God's good future.

With these qualifications, then, the Christian theocrat will own the vocation of the "enforcement of morals." Law and its sanctions will not be confused with God's good future, but neither will they be despised as an insignificant service to the cause of God and to the neighbor's good. It is still "a day of small things." Such a politics is not messianic, but watchful. Law and its sanctions may be used to enforce certain "minimal standards" when their enforcement is possible and equitable and consistent with the protection and preservation of freedom. "The enforcement of morals," of course, is never just that exactly, but always the prohibition or prescription or regulation of certain acts, for the sake of avoiding particular public evils or achieving particular public goods, by means of sanctions which are real and finite, and involving the sacrifice of specific liberties.

In memory of Jesus Christians will engage in discourse, deliberation, and discernment about the politics of the city and the nation in which they live. They will not necessarily always agree, of course, but they will be instructed by each other. And sometimes they will come to an agreement, and see something new about the shape of a life — and a common life — in memory of Jesus. Sometimes they will see something else about how they may "say among the nations, 'The LORD reigns.'"

Access to Health Care[31]

There is, for example — at least at the level of denominational statements — considerable agreement about access to health care. Let's consider this issue, not in an effort to provide the last word about the choices our society faces here, but as a constructive illustration of the possible contributions of the theocratic tradition in the context of pluralism.

The Consensus

The first thing I want to do is simply to call attention to the fact that there is a consensus. There is an extensive literature within the Roman Catholic tradition on access to health care. The American bishops' "Pastoral Letter on Health and Health Care,"[32] is representative when it announces as its first principle that

31. This section is a revision of Allen Verhey, "A Protestant Perspective on Access to Healthcare," *Cambridge Quarterly of Healthcare Ethics* 7, no. 3 (Summer 1998): 247-53.
32. "Pastoral Letter on Health and Health Care," *Origins* XI (1981): 396-402.

"Every person has a basic right to adequate health care." In recent years most mainline Protestant churches have also issued statements calling for health-care reform and for guaranteed access to adequate health care. American Baptists called for legislation that would assure "access to and funding for quality health care for all persons."[33] Episcopalians demanded "adequate health care for all";[34] they emphasized prevention and acknowledged the possible necessity of rationing. Lutherans have identified access to health care as a "substantive entitlement."[35] Methodists advocated a national health-care plan that would "provide comprehensive benefits to everyone."[36] Presbyterians insisted that "free markets alone cannot provide for the adequate supply and equitable distribution of [medical] resources," and they urged "all groups of society, including government, . . . to insure equal access to [basic] health services."[37] These statements

33. Cited in Paul Simmons, "Baptist-Evangelical Biomedical Ethics," in *Bioethics Yearbook: Volume 3. Theological Developments in Bioethics: 1990-1992*, ed. B. Andrew Lustig (Dordrecht: Kluwer Academic Publishers, 1993), p. 258.

34. The Standing Commission on Health, "Report of the Commission," in *The Blue Book: Reports of the Committees, Commissions, Boards, and Agencies of the Episcopal Church, 1991* (New York: Episcopal Church Center, 1991), p. 186. See further Judith A. Granbois and David H. Smith, "The Anglican Communion and Bioethics," in *Bioethics Yearbook: Volume 3. Theological Developments in Bioethics: 1990-1992*, ed. B. Andrew Lustig, pp. 100-102.

35. C. C. Van Dehsen Klein, *Politics and Policy: The Genesis and Theology of Social Statements in the Lutheran Church in America* (Minneapolis: Fortress, 1989) p. 218. See also the Social Statement of the Lutheran Church in America, 1980, "Economic Justice: Stewardship of Creation in Human Community," cited in Paul Nelson, "Bioethics in the Lutheran Tradition," in *Bioethics Yearbook: Volume 1. Theological Developments in Bioethics: 1988-1990*, ed. B. Andrew Lustig (Dordrecht: Kluwer Academic Publishers, 1991), pp. 119-43.

36. The General Conference of the United Methodist Church, "Universal Access to Health Care in the United States and Related Territories," in *The Book of Resolutions of the United Methodist Church — 1992* (Nashville: The United Methodist Publishing House, 1992), pp. 395-98. See further Ronald L. Shelton, "Biomedical Ethics in Methodist Traditions," in *Bioethics Yearbook: Volume 3. Theological Developments in Bioethics: 1990-1992*, ed. B. Andrew Lustig, pp. 222-23.

37. *Minutes of the 201st General Assembly of the Presbyterian Church (USA), 1989* (Louisville: Presbyterian Church [USA], 1989), p. 524. See also "Christian Responsibility and a National Medical Plan," *Minutes of the 203rd General Assembly of the Presbyterian Church (USA), 1992* (Louisville: Presbyterian Church [USA], 1992). See also Kenneth Vaux, "Biomedical Ethics in the Reformed Tradition," in *Bioethics Yearbook: Volume 1. Theological Developments in Bioethics: 1988-1990*, ed. B. Andrew Lustig, pp. 201-13; W. E. Weist, ed., *Health Care and Its Costs: A Challenge for the Church* (Lanham, Md.: University Press of America, 1988).

warrant, I think, the claim that there is a consensus among Christian churches about access to health care.

I would not overstate the case. There are Protestants who disagree vigorously with these denominational statements. Witness, for example, Pat Robertson and the Christian Coalition. Moreover, there is not a consensus about any particular policy proposal. Nevertheless, there is a consensus — a consensus that one critical test for any policy and for any policy proposal is whether it guarantees universal access to good health care, a consensus that the current practice of health care in the United States fails to meet that standard, and a consensus that finite resources will require of proposals for health-care reform that they contain costs and acknowledge limits.

The Consensus Is Not Accidental

The second thing I want to do is to claim that this consensus among the churches is no accident. Although it is not easy to tell from the brief excerpts I have quoted, most of the statements cited are supported by appeals to Scripture and especially to the gospels. And even where the appeals to Scripture are not explicit, the practice of reading Scripture in Christian community is in the background.

The stories of Jesus as healer have formed in many of those who read them a virtue of compassion toward the sick and a vision of health care as a vocation, as a form of discipleship of the healing Christ. This Jesus, moreover, was not only a healer but also a preacher of "good news to the poor" (Luke 4:18; 7:22). Luke, the physician among the evangelists, makes the point elegantly. One who has read, for example, Luke's story of the Rich Man and Lazarus (Luke 16:19-31) will hardly be content when the poor must scavenge and beg for crumbs from the richly supplied tables — or the richly supplied medicine chests — of the rich. One who has heard the story of the Good Samaritan can hardly be complacent when some who lie hurting and "half dead" today are passed by. One who knows the story of the Sheep and the Goats (Matt. 25:31-46) has a peculiar set of spectacles through which to see in the sick and poor and powerless the very image of the one called "Lord," and to see in what is done to them conduct done, in the Lord's words, "unto me."

It is not shocking, then, that there should be a consensus in the churches' statements on access to health care. The "old, old story" — and stories — that Christians love to tell they also long to live, to practice, also when they consider the public and political issue of access to health care. To own such stories as one's own — whether in the vocation of health care or in the vocation of policy formation — is to be concerned that the sick poor receive good health care.

479

Moreover, the Christian struggle to live the stories they love to tell has produced a tradition with which this consensus coheres. We reviewed that tradition of health care for the poor in the second part of this book, and we need not repeat all of that here.[38] It is a rich and catholic tradition. I may be forgiven if I simply itemize some of my favorite pieces of that tradition. In the sixteenth century in Calvin's Geneva the poor were guaranteed access to both the hospital and a physician.[39] In the eighteenth century John Wesley supplemented his evangelism in America with a little medical care, and when, returning to England, he witnessed the sickness and suffering of the poor, he undertook a more regular practice. His desire to identify remedies available to the poor led to the publication in 1747 of *Primitive Physick*.[40] In the nineteenth and twentieth centuries Catholics and Protestants responded to appeals to build hospitals, hoping to follow Jesus by their care for the sick poor.[41] And about a century ago Walter Rauschenbusch, in an effort to help doctors and nurses avoid becoming "hirelings" who served only for money, penned a little prayer for them, petitioning for them a sense of their work as a "holy calling," as a form of discipleship to the saving Christ, and petitioning of them a sense that the sick child of poor immigrants is no less precious than the child of the rich.[42] Given Scripture and such a tradition, the consensus in Protestant statements is no accident. To make and to defend that claim was the second thing I wanted to do.

The Consensus and Public Policy

The third thing I want to do is to ask what this consensus can contribute to both public consideration of access to health care and efforts to increase such access. To pursue this third item in my agenda, permit me to return to the story of the Good Samaritan.[43]

38. See ch. 6, pp. 130-31 in this volume.

39. See John Calvin, "Draft Ecclesiastical Ordinances," in *Calvin: Theological Treatises,* trans. J. K. S. Reid, The Library of Christian Classics, vol. XXII (Philadelphia: Westminster, 1954), p. 65. See further J. H. Smylie, "The Reformed Tradition: Health and Healing," in *Health Care and Its Costs: A Challenge for the Church,* ed. W. E. Weist, pp. 182-83.

40. See further E. B. Holifield, *Health and Medicine in the Methodist Tradition* (New York: Crossroad, 1986), pp. 32-33.

41. See, for example, Holifield, *Health and Medicine,* pp. 53-57.

42. Walter Rauschenbusch, *For God and the People: Prayers of the Social Awakening* (Boston: Pilgrim, 1925 [1909]), pp. 81-82; see pp. 79-80 in this volume.

43. The following paragraph is a summary and paraphrase of Luke 10:30-37. Some

Once upon a time, on the road between Jerusalem and Jericho a man was mugged and left half dead by the side of the road. Some passed by on their way to Jericho's market or to Jerusalem's temple, but one who saw him had compassion. A Samaritan it was who bent over the man and tended to his care, pouring oil and wine upon his wounds and bandaging them. Then he gently lifted the man and brought him to an inn. When he could stay no longer himself, he gave the innkeeper two denarii, with instructions to care for the man and with the promise to pay for whatever the wounded man required.

It's a good story, a story we still love to tell. And we do tell it. We tell it in the name we give the statutes designed to protect and to encourage such behavior, the so-called "Good Samaritan laws." We tell it in the name of every hospital that calls itself Good Samaritan. And Christians tell it, of course, in the churches, where it is acknowledged as part of Scripture, part of the larger story by which Christians test the faithfulness of their conduct and character.

On the other hand, it's an old story and — in the context of modern medicine — an odd story. Compassion leads to costly care. That we understand well enough, perhaps better than the Samaritan did, for we have today an assortment of technologies to help and to heal that make donkeys, oil and wine, and the binding of wounds seem simply quaint. Moreover, costs are attached to these technologies which make the Samaritan's two denarii seem laughable (even if it was two days' wages for an agricultural worker).

The Good Samaritan seems no longer so apt an image for the care of those who hurt, and the reason is simple. The Samaritan did not face the issue that health-care providers and health-care policymakers are forced to face today, the issue of scarcity. The *limitless* compassion of the Samaritan makes his story seem more odd than exemplary; unlimited care seems not a real option.

But suppose the oil and the wine and the stay at the inn left the wounded man in the story only "half alive." Would the Samaritan continue to pay for his care? Or suppose he encountered another neighbor on the side of the road when he returned to pay the bill for the first traveler. Would he do the same for the second neighbor? Suppose he encountered not just one other but more than his donkey could bear, more than his purse could afford, more than even the most hospitable innkeeper could receive. What would he do then? And could he continue to be a *good* Samaritan?

---

of the commentary on this passage was published previously and developed more fully in Allen Verhey, "The Good Samaritan and Scarce Medical Resources," *Christian Scholar's Review* XXIII, no. 3 (1994): 360-73. See also James F. Childress, "Love and Justice in Christian Biomedical Ethics," in *Theology and Bioethics*, ed. Earl Shelp (Dordrecht: D. Reidel, 1985), pp. 225-44, especially pp. 225-26.

Suddenly he seems a tragic figure, forced to make unwelcome choices. Introduce scarcity into the story, and it no longer seems quite so old and so odd. But introduce scarcity, and it no longer seems quite the same story. Let this be the thought experiment for a theocratic contribution to consideration of access to health care: Can we continue to tell this story of the Good Samaritan as an image of care for those who hurt *and* acknowledge the limits of our resources? Can we still be Good Samaritans? Can we still be Good Samaritans — or Fair Samaritans — in the midst of the tragic choices imposed by scarcity? The answer, I think, is "Yes, we can still be Good Samaritans — but not without attention to public policy."

To be "good," a Samaritan who encountered stranger after stranger left "half dead" by the side of the road would finally have to give some attention to public policy. The Good Samaritan's compassion, his charity, would finally, as we have noted before, insist on some consideration of policy, perhaps increased police protection on the Jericho Road, but also, perhaps, a health-care policy that would assure the needy access to an inn or at least not penalize a hospitable innkeeper. The very compassion, or charity, that moved the Samaritan to care for *one* who hurt would motivate attention to policy when *many* hurt.

A contemporary Good Samaritan should be attentive to policy. Let me quickly mention, however, two caveats. First, no particular policy about access to health care is simply given with the story. The details of policy are not magically provided by compassion. And the consensus among Christians formed by Scripture and the tradition does not guarantee unanimity about policy. Second, the story and the tradition cannot be reduced to policy. The story is lived and the tradition continues not just in policy formation, but in the formation of health-care ministries among the poor, in parish nurse programs and in neighborhood ministries among the poor, in neighborhood clinics staffed by contemporary Good Samaritans. The story is lived and the tradition continues not just where public programs are instituted, but where doctors and nurses learn to see their work, as Rauschenbusch prayed, as a "holy calling," as a form of discipleship that attends to the needs of the sick poor.

Although no policy is simply given with the story, and although the story cannot be reduced to policy, those who tell the story and delight in it should not neglect it when they consider public policy. The story not only *motivates* attention to policy; it also *forms* that attention to policy.

It forms, first and most obviously, a prophetic protest against public policies that lead to injustice in access to health care. The story is lived and the tradition continues when theocrats say among the nations, "The LORD is king," when they work to combat injustice in health care, and when they encourage people to test policy recommendations not just against some standard of im-

482

partial rationality but against the plumb line of "good news for the poor," including especially the sick poor. Theocrats contribute, then, to public attention to access to health care by speaking sometimes prophetically, raising their voices against injustices in health-care delivery. Prophetic indictments of policy are significant contributions to public deliberation, but prophets do not necessarily make good managers. Prophetic voices are appropriate and important, but insufficient to policy formation.

The story also forms, however, the virtues and vision that policy cannot supply, but that are critically important to the formation of good policy and on which the success of any policy may depend. Can we still be Good Samaritans? Yes, we can — but not without attention to policy. And the contemporary Samaritan attentive to policy will require virtues besides compassion to be "good." The first of them is *truthfulness,* the readiness to acknowledge the truth about our world and our medicine, about the limits imposed by our mortality and by the finitude of our resources. The twin of truthfulness is *humility,* the readiness to acknowledge that we are not gods but the creatures of God, finite and mortal creatures in need, finally, of God's care, and watching finally for God's future. Joined to both is *gratitude,* thankfulness for opportunities within our limits, opportunities to care for one regarded as among "the least of these." We have come around again to *compassion,* to care. The Samaritan will never be good without compassion, without charity, but let it be said again: The Samaritan will never be good with just compassion.

That is, of course, precisely the wrong way to put it. The contemporary Samaritan will never be good with *only* compassion, but *just* compassion is indeed required. The virtue of *justice* is essential to those who would be good in the midst of scarcity. A readiness to do justice and to insist that justice be done is required of anyone who would be (even) a *fair* Samaritan. Theocrats, then, can contribute to public attention to access to health care by reminding their members and society of the virtues required of life in a mortal body and in a community, virtues like truthfulness and humility, gratitude, compassion, and justice.

Let me underscore the significance of story to policy here by attending briefly to other stories. Consider, first, that wonderful story of the frontier, so regularly invoked in medicine.[44] According to the story, we have continuously encountered new frontiers and are constantly overcoming new obstacles and securing new horizons. It's an optimistic story, and it forms an optimistic character. But the story also helps to explain something of what's wrong with our

44. See further Allen Verhey, "The Health Security Act: Policy and Story," *The Christian Century,* 26 Jan. 1994, pp. 74-77.

health-care system. The story of the frontier does not train those who tell it to be content with limits and leads to boundless medical expectations, creating problems when discontent with limits spills over onto the limits of human mortality and finite resources. The story of the frontier celebrates the rugged individualist, alone against nature and the odds, and it celebrates the technical innovations that extend human mastery over nature and help one beat the odds. The frontier knows justice, of course, but it is a tightfisted justice that looks out for number one. And it knows tragedy, the sad story that in the battle against nature and the odds we sometimes lose, but it tells us to respond to tragedy by battling on.

Or, consider the omnipresent American story of the marketplace. In this story the seller gets rich by supplying what the buyer wants. This story shapes character too. It frequently creates incentives for productivity and creativity and molds our characters so that they demonstrate those qualities, and that can advance the interests of everyone in society. When the marketplace is the story of medicine, however, then medicine becomes a commodity like cookies or cars. Marketplace medicine tends to become a medicine for the rich and powerful while the weak and poor watch and pray. Moreover, the marketplace story of medicine will not sustain the dispositions of care and trust that have sometimes marked the covenant of physician and patient.

If these are the stories we tell, then the policies we make will understandably be formed by our discontent with limits, by our individualism and tightfisted sense of justice, by our suspicion of nature and our confidence in technology. It will be the same old story.

Obstacles and new possibilities remain of course, and there remain markets. But the story is lived and the tradition continues in humble and truthful acknowledgment of limits, and in gratitude for opportunities within those limits to care. For we are not just strangers but neighbors and are known to be such in compassion. We are to acknowledge the limits but also to share, to care, and to do justice. And the theocratic test for justice is not a pinched view of individual entitlement but the care given to the poor and weak.

These notions of care, or charity, and justice introduce a third contribution of the story to policy deliberation about access to health care. The story nurtures prophetic voices; it sustains a vision and virtues important to policy; but it also informs the moral analysis of the notions we bring to consideration of access to health care. No one doubts, I suppose, that charity and justice are relevant to our deliberations about access to health care. But what is "charity"? And what does "justice" mean?

I remind you that the story of the Good Samaritan follows the commandment to love God and the neighbor. Jesus was asked, "But who is my neighbor?"

and he replied with a story and with a question, "Who was a neighbor to the one left half dead?" Note two things here: First, the Samaritan was a neighbor, not just stranger, not simply enemy. According to the story, we *are* neighbors to each other, even to those we do not know or care to know. Second, the answer to the question, "Who is my neighbor? To whom do I owe the duties of charity?" comes indirectly, not so much by theoretical analysis as by a readiness to care for another as though she or he *were* a neighbor.

Or, consider "justice." In John Rawls's *A Theory of Justice*[45] "justice" means "maximum freedom" and "presumptive equality." I like those principles, frankly, but there is a story there too, a story of a social contract of strangers, a story of an "original position" and a "veil of ignorance" in which self-interested individuals consent to certain constraints on their liberty and entitlements for the sake of protecting themselves. In this story justice can only be felt as a restraint, as a limit to my pursuit of individual interest. There is a different story of justice in Scripture, a story of God's justice, a story of one who hears the cries of those who hurt and rescues them, a story of exodus and the liberation of slaves, a story of manna and an economy in which none had too little and none had too much, a story of a community in which people were friends, not just clients and patrons. That's the story theocrats own and tell when they say among the nations, "The LORD is king." And to own that story was — and is — to celebrate that justice and to own the vocation to do justice, to hear the cries of those who hurt, and to form a policy attentive to them.

Theocrats contribute to the deliberation about access when they nudge the analysis of moral notions in the direction of the story they love to tell and struggle to live. The contemporary Good Samaritan will be attentive to policy. Let me repeat, however, the first caveat: No particular policy is simply given with the story. The story nurtures prophetic protest. It sustains a vision and virtues important to policy. But it does not simply provide policy.

Policy is always developed within particular conditions.[46] Policy-making remains the art of the possible. The good and the right are always relevant, but always relevant under the constraints of the possible. The story is lived and the tradition continues not only when theocrats speak prophetically, not only when they speak sagely, and not only when they speak analytically of moral notions. The story is lived and the tradition continues when theocrats speak politically,

45. John Rawls, *A Theory of Justice* (Cambridge, Mass.: The Belknap Press of Harvard University Press, 1971).

46. See James M. Gustafson, "Varieties of Moral Discourse: Prophetic, Narrative, Ethical, and Policy," in *Seeking Understanding: The Stob Lectures, 1986-1998* (Grand Rapids: Eerdmans, 2001), pp. 43-76.

using policy analysis and compromise to preserve or to accomplish some little good for those who hurt and to avert some great harm toward which selfishness always tilts a society.

There is a consensus on access to health care. The consensus is not accidental. The theocratic contribution to deliberations about access is formed by the story it loves to tell and struggles to live. So, let the conclusion of this section be the conclusion of the story of the Samaritan: "Go and do likewise."

And let that also be the conclusion of my effort to do ethics by way of reminder.

A Theocratic Account of Public Education:
Moral Formation — and Difference

Amy Rife, a Hope College student who helped me think through this book, was kind enough to say that she thought the issue of access to health care did illustrate the possible contributions of a theocratic perspective; but she also complained that the issue was "too easy." "The hard case," she said, "would be public education. How would a theocrat deal with the problem of moral formation in the context of the public school, especially when the public school is set in the context of a pluralistic society?" It was a terrific question, of course, and we had an interesting conversation about it. About the same time Gordon VanWylen, the president emeritus of Hope College who was serving as the director of the Van Andel Education Institute, asked me to talk to a group of school superintendents, principals, and teachers from across the country gathered in Holland, Michigan, for two weeks in the summer. He wanted me to speak about moral formation in the context of our culture's pluralism. Because any good teacher learns by responding to the challenges of his students (and because it is hard to say "no" to Gordon VanWylen), I gave the following talk to the Van Andel Education Institute in the summer of 1998.[1] I add it here as an appendix because I think it provides another illustration of a theocratic perspective on public issues.

1. It was previously published as Allen D. Verhey, "Moral Formation — and Difference: A Theological Perspective," in *K-12 Education: The Cultural Context* (Grand Rapids: The Van Andel Education Institute, 1999), pp. 121-44. Thanks to Gordon Van Wylen for the invitation and to the Van Andel Institute for permission to republish the piece in this volume.

Moral Formation — and Difference

It is an old conversation we enter today. Long ago Meno asked Socrates, "Can you tell me, Socrates, whether virtue is acquired by teaching or by practice; or if neither by teaching nor practice, then whether it comes to man by nature, or in what other way?"[2]

Socrates replied, of course, in good Socratic fashion, with questions of his own. Meno learned at least that there was no simple answer to his question. The question of acquiring virtue, or moral formation, quickly runs to other questions.

There are questions about the *responsibility* for moral formation. Who is responsible for the moral formation of young people? And to whom (or to what) are they responsible? There are *normative* questions about moral formation. What sort of conduct or character is the goal of moral formation? What virtue or virtues are to be acquired by the young? And there are, of course, *pedagogical* questions. How is virtue acquired? How does moral formation take place? Is virtue a kind of knowledge, that it can be taught?

These are not easy questions, and there are clearly different ways of answering them. Socrates and his young friends at what Aristophanes mockingly called the "Thinking-shop"[3] puzzled over such questions without reaching many certain conclusions. Toward the end of the dialogue, however, Socrates made an intriguing suggestion. Perhaps, he said, "virtue is a gift of the gods."[4]

"Virtue Is a Gift of the Gods"

That suggestion is not developed in the dialogue, and it is frequently not taken very seriously. Perhaps the remark was simply Socrates' way of admitting that there was no good answer to Meno's question — as if he had said, "God only knows how moral formation takes place." More likely, I think, it was Socrates' way of acknowledging the role of "luck."[5] The acquisition of virtue is not entirely under any individual's control. Things happen, things that a child or a parent or a teacher does not choose to happen, but things that, nevertheless, affect a child's moral formation. There are no guaranteed recipes for moral formation.

2. Plato, *Meno,* Jowett translation, 70A.
3. Aristophanes, *The Clouds.*
4. Plato, *Meno,* 87C-99E.
5. See further Martha Nussbaum, *The Fragility of Goodness: Luck and Ethics in Greek Tragedy and Philosophy* (Cambridge: Cambridge University Press, 1986), pp. 318-72.

Whatever Socrates meant exactly, I take his suggestion to be an invitation to theological reflection about moral formation. Therefore, let "Virtue is a gift of the gods" be the text for my remarks.

On Corrupting the Young

Before we leave Socrates, however, it may be good to remember how his story ends. He was, you recall, sentenced to death on charges that included the accusation that he had corrupted the young people of Athens. If he was uncertain whether or how young people could be taught virtue, his fellow citizens were nevertheless confident that young people could be corrupted.

The case for the prosecution was not without merit, it should be admitted. Socrates had taught the young to question cherished Athenian traditions, to question just about everything. He was, moreover, known to be a foe of democracy, accusing it of honoring numbers more than reason.[6] To protect and defend the old virtues of Athens it was necessary to get rid of Socrates. Or so, at least, it seemed to a majority of Athenian citizens in 399 B.C.E. Socrates chose death rather than exile, and he chose to drink the hemlock rather than to escape.

The trial and death of Socrates should give educators pause. We may be happy enough to be reminded by him that moral formation is an ancient enterprise and that the questions surrounding it are complex and enduring. And I, at least, am glad for the suggestion that "virtue is a gift of the gods." But his trial and death make it a little too clear that teaching is a risky business, at least if it involves moral formation, and it inevitably does. Moral formation is a risky business — also, and perhaps especially, in a democracy, for all of its presumed tolerance of difference. One who undertakes such a task is liable to the charge of corrupting the youth.

Indeed, I suspect you could all be accused of "corrupting the youth." You

---

6. The case against Socrates was made more compelling by the circumstances of Athens. The Athenians had lost the Peloponnesian War to the more sternly nurtured Spartans, who still threatened to prey upon the city. An oligarchy known as "The Thirty" had recently for a short and miserable time supplanted the democratic institutions of Athens. One of "The Thirty" had been Critias, known to be an associate of Socrates. The city was threatened. Even the idea of city, of a polis, of a community, seemed threatened by the individualism of the Sophists. Some of the citizens of Athens doubtlessly were simply nostalgic for the Athens of old; they wanted to return to the good old days when the gods and goddesses of Olympus were honored and trusted. So, never mind that Socrates had fought bravely in the war. Never mind that he was innocent of the cruelty and violence of "The Thirty." Never mind that he was not a Sophist.

have evidently managed to avoid the hemlock. But, if there were a trial, how would you plead? And, if you pled "not guilty," what would your defense be?

Let me take you off the hook. Let me simply admit that I am liable to the charge of corrupting the young people who are entrusted to my instruction.

There was that young man who was evidently being groomed to take over the family business; he ended up being a religion major, and his vocation took a different direction. I didn't think that I had corrupted him. In fact, his moral formation seemed to me "a gift of God." But I suspect his father might have accused me of having corrupted his boy.

There was that young woman who learned from me to be suspicious of the traditional reading of certain biblical texts about women, and I wondered recently whether the Southern Baptists might accuse me of having corrupted that young woman. Of course, if I had failed to teach her to be suspicious of the traditional reading of those texts, certain feminists might also have accused me of corrupting that young woman.

There seems no escape from our liability to the charge of corrupting the youth. There is no escape because teaching inevitably involves moral formation and because we teach in the context of moral pluralism, in the context of moral difference.

So, what are my options?

The Options

One option, of course, is to quit teaching. Skip that one. It's a not a real option; teaching is too much fun.

A second option is to continue teaching but to quit the task of moral formation. We might skip this one, too, for teaching, we said, inevitably involves moral formation. This option does, however, have its advocates. The modest claim is that schools should leave moral formation to the parents. The slogan is a quotation of Sergeant Friday, "Just the facts, ma'am." That may be easier in some areas of instruction than in others, but it is finally impossible in all of them.

Consider this "fact": "Columbus discovered America," and consider whether Native Americans find that "fact" free of moral formation or innocent of corrupting the young. One Native American wrote a poem called "Columbus Day." It read in part,

In school I was taught the names
Columbus, Cortez, and Pizarro and

A dozen other filthy murderers. . . .
No one mentioned the names
Of even a few of the victims . . .
Let us then declare a holiday
For ourselves, and make a parade that begins
With Columbus' victims and continues
Even to our grandchildren who will be named
In their honor.
Because isn't it true that even the summer
Grass here in this land whispers those names,
And every creek has accepted the responsibility
Of singing those names? And nothing can stop
The wind from howling those names around
The corner of the school.[7]

The facts are inevitably ordered somehow, interpreted in the light of some larger story, and marshaled toward some end thought worthy of a person's humanity.

Perhaps I should also mention the advocates of "values clarification" in this context. They do not want teachers to engage in moral formation; they want teachers to help students clarify their values, not cultivate or change them. Teachers are required to provide support and acceptance of each student's moral tastes, and they are prohibited from forming the morality of their students. Of course, such a program forms students to regard values as a matter of taste — and of private taste at that. Life is a banquet; eat what you like. One is entitled to one's own preferences, which are to be discovered, not cultivated or improved. The very relativism of "values clarification" makes it liable to the charge of corrupting the youth.[8]

So, I won't give up teaching, and if I continue teaching, I cannot avoid the task of moral formation. But how can I undertake the task of moral formation in the context of so much diversity of values, in the context of so many different communities, in the context of moral pluralism?

---

7. The author is Jimmie Durham, a Cherokee. The poem is cited in full in Stanley Hauerwas, *After Christendom?* (Nashville: Abingdon, 1991), pp. 155-56.

8. On "values clarification" see Sidney B. Simon, Leland W. Howe, and Howard Kirshenbaum, *Values Clarification: A Handbook of Practical Strategies for Teachers and Students* (New York: Hart, 1972), and Sidney B. Simon, "Values Clarification vs. Indoctrination," in *Moral Education: . . . It Comes with the Territory,* ed. David Purpel and Kevin Ryan (Berkeley: McCutchan, 1976). On the charge of corrupting the youth, see Richard A. Baer Jr., "Value Education as Indoctrination," *The Educational Forum,* Jan. 1977.

The Enlightenment Option — and Its Problems

A third option takes its inspiration from the Enlightenment. Those who lived during the Enlightenment were painfully aware of difference and of the violence difference could prompt; rival creeds had made it clear that they were willing to fight each other to the death. And they knew that moral relativism simply surrendered the resolution of differences to violence. Enlightenment thinkers sought peace. And to achieve that peace and to secure it, they sought to found morality on human reason alone. They sought a universal morality, a morality that transcended all of our differences, including our religious differences.[9] They sought to liberate people from the contingency — and the tyranny — of particular traditions and communities, including religious traditions and communities.[10]

Lawrence Kohlberg has been an influential advocate of this option in moral education.[11] Children begin with what Kohlberg calls a "pre-conventional morality" in which they are motivated by their individual needs and desires, responding to threats of punishment and promises of reward. Then — usually by the time they are eleven years old — they develop quite naturally what Kohlberg calls a "conventional morality" in which they recognize and appreciate the rules of the community to which they belong. Socialization has taken place; children at this stage have internalized the moral expectations of the group.[12] But Kohlberg identifies moral maturity with a third level, which he calls "post-conventional morality" and which he says children sometimes (but infrequently) achieve when they reach adulthood. At this "post-conventional level"

9. Witness Kant's first formulation of the "categorical imperative": "Act only on that maxim whereby thou canst at the same time will that it should become a universal law" (Immanuel Kant, *Fundamental Principles of the Metaphysic of Morals*, trans. Thomas K. Abbott [New York: Liberal Arts Press, 1949], p. 30).

10. On the "Enlightenment Project" see Alasdair MacIntyre, *After Virtue: A Study in Moral Theory* (Notre Dame: University of Notre Dame Press, 1981), and Jeffrey Stout, *The Flight from Authority: Religion, Morality, and the Quest for Autonomy* (Notre Dame: University of Notre Dame Press, 1981). For this paragraph see especially Stout, *Flight from Authority*, pp. 235-38.

11. See Lawrence Kohlberg, *Essays on Moral Development*, vol. I: *The Philosophy of Moral Development* (New York: Harper & Row, 1981); vol. II: *The Psychology of Moral Development* (1984).

12. Socialization takes place along the lines described by social learning theories, for which, however, "conventional morality" is the final stage reached. On social learning theory see, e.g., B. F. Skinner, *Beyond Freedom and Dignity* (New York: Knopf, 1971), and Albert Bandura, *Social Learning Theory* (Englewood Cliffs, N.J.: Prentice-Hall, 1977).

people return to "the standpoint of the individual," thinking and acting as free agents, treating others as equally free agents.

The process of moral maturation depends in part on cognitive development, but Kohlberg thought schools could facilitate the process by democratic discussions of ethical quandaries. In such conversations children would see for themselves when the proposals of others were more rational and universal, and we would have moral development without indoctrination and without relativism.

Maturity is autonomy, and morality at this highest stage is identified with the autonomous acceptance of a social contract and the principle of justice. At this highest stage, everybody is entitled, in Kohlberg's words, to "the maximum freedom compatible with the like liberty of others."[13]

It is the Enlightenment project for moral development. In Kohlberg's account of "moral maturity" and in Kant's account of ethics, persons must be rational and autonomous, must transcend the particular communities to which they belong, and must affirm the universal principle of justice, which respects the freedom of others. And in both accounts there is the promise of a society of free people who may hold very different conceptions of the good life and still live together justly and peaceably.

It sounds innocent enough, as American as apple pie, and it surely has been influential, but there are serious problems with this option, and it puts us at risk, frankly, of corrupting the youth.

Let me attempt to illustrate both the problems and the risk by considering briefly the notion of justice. Justice is, after all, Kohlberg's basic principle and the best candidate for being the sort of universal and rational principle that would enable us to live together justly and peaceably.

13. Lawrence Kohlberg, "The Cognitive-Developmental Approach to Moral Education," in *Moral Education: . . . It Comes with the Territory,* ed. David Purpel and Kevin Ryan (Berkeley: McCutchan, 1976), p. 183. Rousseau had suggested that human beings pass through an age-related sequence of stages in reaching moral maturity (Jean-Jacques Rousseau, *Emile* [New York: Dent, 1911 (1762)]). Jean Piaget had provided the first empirical study of the relation of cognitive development to moral development (Jean Piaget, *The Moral Judgment of the Child* [New York: The Free Press, 1965 (1932)]). John Dewey had described three levels of moral development. In the first stage, physical needs and desires motivate the individual. In the next stage group customs and standards are accepted with little critical reflection. And in the third stage, finally, action is based upon one's own thought and judgment (John Dewey and James H. Tufts, *Ethics* [New York: Henry Holt, 1932], p. 7). Kohlberg assigns two "stages" to each of the three levels: (1) obedience and punishment, (2) reward and reciprocity, (3) conformity, (4) law and order, (5) social contract, and (6) universal principles.

As soon as one attempts to give some content to the notion of justice, however, differences reappear, and we have to ask, like Alasdair MacIntyre, "Whose justice? Which rationality?" There does not seem to be any purely rational foundation even for the notion of justice. There seems to be no "moral Esperanto," no universal moral language. Or if there is, then the sad little joke about Esperanto, that no one really speaks it, seems confirmed.

Consider what is surely one of the most intriguing recent efforts to defend a particular notion of justice as rationally persuasive. John Rawls asks us to imagine ourselves charged with the task of creating for ourselves a social contract,[14] a set of rules that will govern our life together. Some of us are male; some are female. Some of us have African ancestors; some have European ancestors; some have Native American or Asian or other ancestors. Some are Christians; some are Jewish; some, Buddhist; some belong to some other religious community, or to none. Given these differences, Rawls says, we are unlikely to reach agreement about a social contract. Our different communities and traditions, our different stories, our particular visions of what it means for human beings to flourish, will prevent agreement. But let a "veil of ignorance" fall on us. Under this "veil of ignorance" no one knows who he (or she) is. When the veil is lifted, some will be male, but who? Some will be white, but who? Some will be Christian, but who? Rawls claims that under the veil of ignorance we will be able to reach a consensus about justice. Equipped only with our reason and self-interest, we will all consent to two principles of justice. The first principle is "maximum freedom," Kohlberg's principle that everyone should be entitled to the greatest freedom compatible with a like freedom for all others. The second principle of justice is "presumptive equality," or the principle that inequalities are to be considered arbitrary and unjust unless those inequalities meet two conditions. Inequalities must be attached to positions that are open to everyone, and they must work out in the long run to benefit those who are least well off in our society.

Now, I like those principles, frankly, but others who stood in the tradition of the Enlightenment quickly challenged them. Robert Nozick, for example, was unconvinced, rejecting the principle of "presumptive equality."[15] The debate between Rawls and Nozick went on, as we have noted before, so long and so interminably that new categories of people now need to be covered under the "veil of ignorance." Some will be Rawlsians, and some Nozickians, but who?

Justice seems not to be a candidate for the Esperanto dictionary, after all;

14. John Rawls, *A Theory of Justice* (Cambridge, Mass.: Harvard University Press, 1971).

15. Robert Nozick, *Anarchy, State, and Utopia* (New York: Basic Books, 1974).

there does not seem to be one account of justice that wins the universal consent of the rational and "mature." Differences remain.

And not only do differences remain; so do stories. The Enlightenment project seeks to transcend differences by ignoring them and the stories that give rise to them. It seeks to liberate us from the particular communities and stories that form our characters and our identities, so that a rational and universal and peaceable community may be founded. It trains us to forget our stories for the sake of morality. But there is a story here. The story the Enlightenment trains us to tell is that we can do without stories. It is the story retold in Rawls's narrative of social contractors upon whom a "veil of ignorance" descends.

There *is* a story. There remains a narrative in terms of which we make sense of the moral life. This story, however, is internally inconsistent, this story that we can do without stories. Moreover, this story is purely fiction. None of us can simply step out of our identities, vacate our location in space and time, in order to adopt a rational, universal, and impartial perspective.

There is a story to the Enlightenment project, an internally inconsistent fiction, but notice also that this story, like the stories it wanted to eliminate, does form the character of those who own it as their story. The story is that we are all fundamentally rational and self-interested individuals. If this is the story we tell in the effort to eliminate stories, then we should not be shocked if, by it, we form self-interested individuals, individuals who understand contracts but not covenants, individuals who will only ever experience justice as a boundary they must not trespass in the pursuit of their own interests. If this is the story we tell, then we risk corrupting the young.

If this is the story we tell in the effort to create a peaceable community in the midst of difference, we should not be shocked if, by it, we form a society of strangers, a social contract of individuals who use the notion of justice like a weapon to protect themselves from those who are different from them. They may practice tolerance, but it will be the sort of stingy and tightfisted tolerance that will let the stranger be as long as the stranger stays out of my way. If this is the story we tell, then we will create a society of wary strangers.

Let it be admitted that such a stingy tolerance was — and remains — a historical achievement in the context of violence about differences. But let it also be admitted that such tolerance is a very thin account of the moral life. My point is not that the Enlightenment project has altogether failed; my point is that is has been pretentious about its successes. My point is that the impartial perspective of Kohlberg and the Enlightenment can provide only a *minimal* account of the moral life, and if we do not acknowledge that it *is* a minimal account, then we distort and corrupt the moral life. My problem is that Kohlberg identifies moral *minimalism* with moral *maturity*.

495

The minimalism of the impartial perspective can be seen in the account it gives of relationships of covenant and community. The relationship between husband and wife, for example — or between parent and child, or between teacher and student — can from an impartial perspective only be construed as a *contractual relationship* between autonomous individuals. Now there are contractual features to these relationships, to be sure. My wife and I sometimes talk about the rights and duties of our contract. You can imagine the context. Such a conversation frequently takes place in the middle of an argument. We can be glad, I think, for the language of contract, but if that's the only language Phyllis and I have for talking about our marriage, we are in some trouble. Marriage and family life and other covenanted relationships are not constituted or nurtured as contracts between self-interested individuals. The impartial perspective does not build or sustain *community.*

The minimalism of the impartial perspective can be seen in a second way. The effort to adopt an impartial perspective requires of people a certain alienation from themselves, from the passions and loyalties that give them moral character, and from the histories and communities that give them moral identity. It is legitimate, indeed, salutary, for people to attempt to see themselves as objectively as they can, as others see them. No one, however, can *live* that way, transcending their links with others in time and place, denying their moral identity — at least, no one can live that way with integrity. The impartial perspective will not build or sustain or nurture *character.*

Notice also that the impartial perspective finally handles our differences by asking not "What should be decided?" but "Who should decide?" That is a very important question, to be sure, but if "Who should decide?" is the only question we ask, then we never get around to a moral conversation about what should be decided. Unless we acknowledge the minimalism of the impartial perspective, we will not even be able to sustain or nurture a moral *conversation.*

So, I should not give up teaching. That was the first option. I should not surrender the task of moral formation. That was the second option. And for that task of moral formation I cannot — even in the context of moral differences — be satisfied with the third option, the Enlightenment option. None of us should deny our stories and communities in order to pretend to have a purely rational and impartial perspective.

I spent considerable time on the Enlightenment project not only because it has been so influential, but also because its influence effectively deafened us to the suggestion of Socrates that "virtue is a gift of the gods." By sundering the unity of life into a private realm of autonomy and arbitrary preferences and a public realm of justice and impartial reason, the Enlightenment muted the voices of those who thought theology relevant to the public concerns about moral formation and difference. The Enlightenment was tolerant, of course, of persons with religious convictions — as long as they stayed in their place, as long as they did not claim that their convictions were relevant to public matters like education or the effort to achieve a certain civility in the midst of our differences.

I hope I have shown that the Enlightenment project is (at least) insufficient for the task of moral formation in the midst of difference and that it (at least) puts us at risk of corrupting the young. If I have, then we may look for another option. I return, therefore, at long last, to Socrates' suggestion that "virtue is a gift of the gods," and I take up his invitation to theological reflection on moral formation and difference.

"Virtue is a Gift of the Gods": Life as Mystery

When Socrates said that virtue is a gift of the gods, he said in effect that moral formation is a *mystery,* not merely a puzzle. Given enough time, you can figure out a puzzle or solve a problem, but mystery transcends our puzzling over it. Mystery eludes our figuring and our control. Mystery evokes not just curiosity but wonder and awe.[16]

We live in a world full of mystery. We make our way through life surrounded not only by puzzles but by mystery. Each encounter with another human being is an encounter with mystery. And at the depths and the heights of our lives, at the beginnings and the ends of them, and at the center of them, there is the Ultimate Mystery, whom we call God. There is no escaping this mystery.

Little wonder, then, that human beings are so incorrigibly religious, that spirituality is as natural to human beings as breathing. We live in God's world, and we encounter mystery. Mystery evokes among us senses of its presence and power. Mystery evokes a sense of dependence upon some dimly known but reliable order, a sense of gratitude for the givenness (the gifts) of life and health, a sad sense of a tragic flaw that runs through our lives and through our world, a hopeful sense of new possibilities just over the horizon — and it evokes a keen sense of responsibility to the inscrutable Mystery who sustains the order, gives the gifts, judges the flaw, and promises hope.[17] Moral educators do not create

---

16. On "mystery" see Craig Dykstra, *Vision and Character: A Christian Educator's Response to Kohlberg* (New York: Paulist, 1981), pp. 34-44.

17. This account of a "natural piety" (or what John Calvin identified as the *sensus divinitatis*) is indebted to James M. Gustafson, *Ethics from a Theocentric Perspective: Theology and Ethics,* vol. I (Chicago: University of Chicago Press, 1981), pp. 129-36.

that sense; it is evoked by the mystery. It is a gift of God, a gift to which we must in some way respond. It is a gift which makes claims upon us and which renders us responsible to the Mystery, to God.

There is, of course, an obvious problem here. It is the problem of difference. The world is full not only of mystery, but also of different ways of naming it. If we are responsible to the mystery, how shall we name it? If we are responsible to God, to which god? The problem for human beings is not whether to be spiritual or not; the problem is how to name the mystery, how to interpret its presence, how to direct these senses. And there is no purely rational foundation for talking about mystery any more than there is for talking about morality. There is no religious Esperanto, either.

I am a Christian. I know of no other way to talk faithfully about the mystery at the heart of our world than as a Christian. I know of no other way to make sense of these senses than as a Christian. Of course, it is easy to be presumptuous here, easy to claim to know too much. Even so, as a Christian, I dare to claim that all of our responses to mystery are in fact responses to the God whose story is told in Scripture.

One can do worse, I think, than to name the mystery wrongly. One can respond to mystery by ignoring it — and the senses evoked by it — or by refusing to trust and honor it or to acknowledge it. When, in teaching the young, we empty the world of wonder, when we eliminate mystery in our quest for mastery, then we distort their vision and their lives.

One can do worse, I say, than to name the mystery wrongly. Those who can name the mystery aright can still be guilty of refusing to trust and to honor God. Christians sometimes respond to the mystery by reducing God to a giant puzzle or by attempting to domesticate God, rendering the inscrutable not only scrutable but serviceable to their own projects, to their own individual or communal causes. Those who know enough to say "Lord, Lord" have sometimes been guilty of domesticating God, drafting God into the service of this army or that one, of this race or that one, of this denomination or that one. Both the mystery, however, and a commandment prohibit the effort to domesticate God.

One can do worse, I say, than to name the mystery wrongly, but name it we must if we are to begin to interpret its presence, if we are to orient those senses of dependence and gratitude, of remorse and hope, and of responsibility. We experience those senses, of course, always already oriented toward someone or something, toward mothers or friends or teachers or nations or technology. And sometimes we think to name the mystery after one or another of those persons or things. One way or another, we do learn to name the mystery, and the moral life is a response to the mystery — so named.

Mystery and the Christian Story

As a Christian, I dare to claim that all of our responses to mystery are in fact responses to the God whose story is told in Scripture. And as a Christian, I also dare to claim that moral formation occurs as we respond to God's gifts, as we learn to relate to all things in ways appropriate to the relations of all things to the God whose story is told in Scripture.

Creation

The story begins with the creation of all things. "In the beginning" God was there and called a cosmos out of chaos. God made all things out of nothing. The point of the story is not to form some theory about the order or the duration of our beginnings. The point is to form our response to mystery.

Notice, first, that if God made all things out of nothing, then all that God made is good. God says as much in the story, of course. The creation, in all of its wonderful variety, is good. Difference is good — and peaceable — in this beginning.

Notice, moreover, that, if God made all things out of nothing, then nothing God made is god. God alone is God. Nothing in God's creation or in ours is God. None of our differences may be made the object of our ultimate loyalty or confidence. There is a radical monotheism in this beginning.

Notice, also, a third implication: If God called a cosmos out of chaos, and called it good, then goodness is there prior to our discovery of it. Moral formation is a gift of God in this beginning. At the depth of our sense of dependence is the reliability of the Creator. And at the height of our sense of gratitude is the goodness of God; whenever we discover something of goodness, whether in ourselves or in another, we may and should give thanks to God.

The Fault in Our World

Before the story continues, it is important to face a very important, if obvious, question: Can this really be a true story? Never mind how long it took or whether it involved natural processes, can it really be true that all things are good, that difference is peaceable?

The counterevidence is all around us. The world is dripping with blood. There is clearly something wrong with it. To make our way in the world evokes not only senses of dependence and gratitude but also a sense of remorse. There

499

is a fault that runs through our lives and through our world and through our differences.

The story of Scripture does not deny the reality and the power of evil. On the contrary, it confirms it. While it says and says plainly that "in the beginning" God made all things and made all things good, it continues with the story of the human sin and of the curse that followed in its train. It traces the fault in our world not to God but to human sin, to the human refusal to trust God or to give thanks to God.

Sin was a free act, but the problem with Adam's world — with our world — is not freedom. Human freedom was — and is — a gift of God. It is the good gift by which God would form humanity for voluntary fellowship with God and with each other. It is a prerequisite for moral maturity, but it should not be identified with maturity as the goal of moral formation, and it can be deformed. The solution for our world is not to eliminate freedom. To coerce faith or fellowship violates the freedom God gives. The problem is human sin. And the solution is repentance, the sense of remorse that responds humbly to God's judgment and trusts God to forgive and to make things new. In a world like this one, marked and marred by sin, moral formation requires such humility and trust before the mystery. In Adam's world — and in ours — the path to moral maturity leads through repentance.

Sin left an ugly mark on our world — and on our differences. Male and female had been created for mutuality and equality, but sin left the "curse" of patriarchy in its wake. Hard on the heels of the story of the first sin is the story of Cain and Abel, a paradigmatic story of envy and violence in the context of difference (Gen. 4:1-16). Cain was a farmer; Abel was a herdsman. Cain's sacrifice had somehow gone badly; Abel's sacrifice had been pleasing to God. For all of their differences, however, they were brothers, made for affection. Cain's envy did not see a brother. It saw a rival, an enemy. And it moved Cain to violence and murder.

The problem with Cain's world — with our world — is not difference. The solution for Cain — and for us — is not eliminating difference (violently or otherwise). The solution for Cain — and for us — is not regarding some difference as god or as demon. The problem is envy and enmity, pride and resentment. And the solution is repentance, a repentance formed in humble acknowledgement that we are all sinners, a repentance formed in the trusting recognition that God made us siblings, a repentance that reforms our attitudes into something like love, the sort of love that is patient and kind, that is not envious or boastful or arrogant or rude, that does not insist on its own way, that is not irritable or resentful, that does not rejoice in wrongdoing, but rejoices in the truth. That love is, as Paul says in 1 Corinthians 13, a gift of God, the greatest gift of the Spirit of God. And, as he also makes clear, that love is the mark of moral maturity. It is, in fact, the mark of God's good future and of our destiny. God makes things new. Moral formation is a gift of God. The sort of tolerance that leaves us strangers to each other is at its best a pale reflection of that love, a mark not of moral maturity but of our distance from the good future of God.

A New Beginning

But I have gotten ahead of the story. Before God requires such love, God gives it. Before God requires repentance, God makes possible hope for a new beginning. Human sin might have smashed the world back to chaos, but God would not let evil have the last word, would not let "the fall" — or the flood — be the last word.

God formed for himself a people. They were and were to be a distinctive people, different from the rest; but from the beginning, they were and were to be a sign and a promise of God's intention to bless "all the nations." Their story is a story of some slaves who cried out to God in hope against hope that there was someone there to hear their cries. It is the story of a God who heard those cries and answered them with a promise. With that promise God formed a people and set them on a journey toward freedom and justice and a blessing upon all the nations.

That story formed the memory and the hope of Israel. It formed the Israelites' worship — and their life. It formed lawmakers who made and remade the statutes to fit both circumstances and the story, institutionalizing kindness to the slave, to the poor, and to strangers in the land. It formed prophets who envisioned peace and justice and who beat against injustice with their words. It formed kings who were lovers of justice and friends of the poor (Ps. 72). It formed farmers who left the edges of the field unharvested for the poor. It formed parents who told the story to their children and modeled the sort of life that fit the story. And it formed children who heard the story and owned it as their own. For this people moral formation was a gift of God.

Sometimes the people very nearly forgot the stories — or forgot to tell them — and very nearly lost their memory and their identity. Sometimes they forgot the promise to all nations, and regarded the promise as their possession rather than their vocation. And sometimes, although they remembered the story and the promise of God within it, they refused to live the story, refused to be formed by it. But the remedy for forgetfulness was always to hear again the old, old story, and the remedy for their refusal to be formed by it was always repentance.

The center of the Christian story, of course, is Jesus of Nazareth, son of

Mary. He came to Israel and to the world announcing that God would keep God's promise, proclaiming that the good future of God was "at hand," and inviting all who heard him to repentance. In God's good future there will be peace, he said. To repent, therefore, to be formed already by that future, is to be a peacemaker. In God's kingdom, the poor will be blessed, he said. To repent, therefore, to be formed already by that future, is to be generous. In God's good future, sinners will be forgiven. To repent, therefore, to be formed already by that future, is to be forgiving. In God's coming cosmic sovereignty there will be a place for Samaritans and Gentiles and sinners and women and for others who do not count in the world's estimation. To repent, therefore, to be formed already by that future, is to be hospitable to those who are different, to love the enemy.

God's good future formed his life, and it formed the stories he told. You remember the stories, I expect. You remember the story about a good Samaritan who had compassion on an enemy, the story about a heavenly banquet to which those who don't count for very much were invited, the story about a forgiving king who insisted only that the forgiven be forgiving.

Remember the one about a prodigal son and a waiting father (Luke 15:11-32)? Consider it for a moment as the story of the elder son whose pride and envy prevented him from joining the celebration at the prodigal's return. It is the story of Cain and Abel revisited, the paradigmatic story of conflict over difference revisited. Here, however, there is the father's reminder that the boy who returned is the elder son's brother. "It [is] fitting to make merry and be glad," he said, "for this *your brother* was dead, and is alive" (v. 32 RSV).

The parable ends there. We are not told whether the elder brother is persuaded to join in the joy. But this, it seems to me, is crucial to the pedagogy of moral formation. Should the elder brother rejoice? And why? Is it because the father has *commanded* him to rejoice? But how does anyone command joy? One might command tolerance, grudging acquiescence, but not joy. And yet, it is joy that the father calls for. He could hardly expect the elder son to comply — "to make merry and be glad" — unless his words had struck some resonant chord, unless they had evoked a sense already present — however deeply suppressed — in the heart of the elder brother that this unworthy prodigal was his brother and not a rival.

The father's authority is by itself insufficient to form repentance or joy. All that the father can command is a hearing, but a hearing he certainly can command. There is no guarantee that through hearing his father the elder brother will repent of his pride and envy and join in the rejoicing. But he may. He may discover in the hearing his brother's true identity; he may see his brother as his brother. And if he does, then he also discovers his own true identity.

I said that this story revisits the story of Cain and Abel. Consider this:

502

Cain took his brother to the field and killed him. The curse on Cain was that he became a "fugitive and a wanderer." The elder brother is "in the field" when he first appears in Jesus' story. And when he hears that his brother "was dead, and is alive," he is given a chance to end his own status as a wanderer and to come home. To see his brother as his brother, to repent of his pride and envy, to join in the joy would be his own homecoming. Perhaps the elder brother never did join in the rejoicing. We are not told (quite deliberately, I think). But we know this: he would be welcomed by his father.

The pedagogy is not commandment, not coercion. The truth about our world and about ourselves is encountered as a mystery to which we come home. Moral formation is a gift of God, to which we may and must respond.

There was no guarantee for the waiting father, and there was none for Jesus either. His story, like Socrates', includes a trial on charges of having corrupted the people. And, as with Socrates, the trial leads to conviction and to death. The envy and pride of religious and political leaders conspired to kill this Jesus.

Except, of course, that the story does not end there. His story continues. The story is that God raised him up, that God vindicated this teacher and healer, that God acted, as Jesus said he would, to end the rule of sin and death and to establish God's own good future. Jesus was raised in our world and in our history, and our world and our history have, happily, no escape.

The Gift of the Spirit: Moral Formation and Peaceable Difference

The story is that God raised this Jesus up, the firstborn from the dead, and poured the Spirit out, the first fruits of God's good future. It is not yet that good future, of course, but while we wait and watch for it, the Spirit provides a fore-taste of it. The Spirit is a gift for moral formation and peaceable difference in a world not yet God's good future.

Note, first, that on the day of Pentecost the presence and the power of the Spirit overcame the division of languages that had been the curse on humanity since the Tower of Babel. People were suddenly and quite remarkably capable of understanding each other. It was a gift, of course, but a gift that may establish certain assumptions for dealing with difference.

The Enlightenment assumed that we need to be able to locate universal and rational principles before we can talk together peaceably in the midst of our differences. It settled for a tolerance that leaves us strangers to each other and nurtures a freedom capable of contracts but empty of covenant. Post-modernism assumes that our values are simply incommensurable, that we cannot really talk together. It settles for a celebration of difference and of freedom that is ever only a step away from violence.

Pentecost teaches us to assume that in the presence and the power of the Spirit, who is never under our control, who comes always and only as a gift to the world, people can talk together even if there is no moral Esperanto. Pentecost trains us to hope that in such conversations people may discover in a stranger not only a rival and an enemy but a friend and a sibling. Pentecost evokes a sense of new possibilities for people to discover both themselves and a peaceable community in the context of difference.

Throughout the Roman Empire in the first century the Spirit formed communities of peaceable difference. It formed communities that included both Jews and Gentiles, and it formed these communities in spite of traditional animosities and suspicions. They were "one new humanity of Jew and Gentile." The Spirit formed communities that included men and women as equals, communities where the curse of patriarchy was being lifted. It formed communities that included both slaves and masters, and it taught them to regard each other as "beloved brother[s] — . . . both in the flesh and in the Lord," as Paul said to Philemon (16).

It was not easy, and there were no guarantees. But in the presence and the power of the Spirit they learned to welcome one another, to be hospitable to differences, to love one another. The Jew was not required to become a Gentile, or to speak like one, in order to be a member of this community and to have a voice in it. But the Jew was required not to condemn the Gentile for being Gentile. The Gentile was not required to become a Jew or to talk like one, but the Gentile was required not to despise the Jew for being Jewish.

The Spirit formed communities of peaceable difference neither by imposing an authoritarian hierarchy nor by nurturing moral indifference, but by forming communities of moral discourse and discernment. In the presence and the power of the Spirit they learned to talk to each other and to listen to each other. They became communities of mutual encouragement and admonition. To use Paul's wonderful compliment to the Roman churches, they were "able to instruct one another" (Rom. 15:14). That, too, was a gift of the Spirit, and it engaged the diversity of gifts present in the congregations. They needed each other, including and especially the stranger, the outsider, the one who was different, in order to discern a life and a common life that was worthy of the gospel, appropriate to the story "according to the Spirit."

They talked together about many questions, about eating meat that had been sacrificed to idols, about the collection for the poor in Judea, about marriage and divorce, about this and that. And you can bet that they talked about the limits of acceptable diversity and the limits of acceptable unity.

Acceptable Unity

Permit me to say a word about each of these. First, consider acceptable unity. The unity and peace the Spirit gives was not the unity and peace of the so-called *pax Romana*. That unity and peace was imposed and coerced, and it built upon oppression of the weak and the poor. Such unity, such a peace, was not acceptable. The unity and peace the Spirit gives is not imposed but received as a gift. The unity and peace that is response to that gift must not oppress the weak and poor, but practice a justice formed by the story of God's care and a generosity formed as gift answering to gift.

The unity and peace the Spirit gives is not the unity and peace of the Enlightenment either. That unity and peace settles for too little. Response to the gift of the Spirit calls us to be hospitable, not just tolerant, to be in community, not just in contractual agreements. The Spirit would give a maturity measured "according to the full stature of Christ," not a maturity measured by autonomy, which could be simply "an opportunity for self-indulgence" (Gal. 5:13) and a form of immaturity. The communities formed by the Spirit sought a conversation about what should be decided, not just about who should decide. They sought to recognize the stranger and the rival as a sibling, not just to protect themselves from the violence of strangers and rivals. They sought to come home.

Acceptable Diversity

Consider also, finally, the limits of acceptable diversity. In the presence and the power of the Spirit these communities sought and celebrated diversity. The Spirit formed them to love the enemy, to be hospitable to the outcast and the "sinner." They were normatively inclusive communities. How could there be a limit?

I suggest that there were — and are — two limits. The first is this: if love is to be the mark of such communities, then they must abhor what destroys and thwarts it. Remember that what thwarts love is not difference. What thwarts love is envy and pride and greed and self-centeredness. To such "works of the flesh" neither love nor a community formed by the Spirit will be hospitable. The response of love to such "works of the flesh" is to call for repentance. When the Afrikaner churches of South Africa began to exclude certain ethnic groups from their fellowship and from their tables, then many other churches quite properly said that they had crossed the limits of acceptable diversity and called them to repentance.

The second limit is this: idolatry. We may not give ultimate allegiance to things that are less than ultimate. In the church this limit is expressed positively in the requirement of ultimate allegiance to the God whose story is told in Christian Scripture. The church calls those who confuse God with the nation or the race or the family to repentance.

The church, of course, is not the world, nor is the world the church. Civil society may not express this limit positively; it may not require allegiance to the God of Abraham, Isaac, and Jesus as a condition of membership in community, as a limit to acceptable diversity. It is prohibited from doing so by the limits of acceptable unity. The unity the Spirit gives is not built on coercion but on voluntary response to gift.

Even so, civil society may and should express this limit minimally — in the acknowledgment that there is a mystery and that the state and its interests are not it. The state expresses this limit by its refusal to claim the ultimate allegiance of its citizens.

The church and the world are different, but the same mystery is at work in both the church and the world. The Spirit is present to both church and world, evoking and forming the senses of dependence, gratitude, remorse, hope, and responsibility.

"Virtue is a gift of the gods," Socrates said. Or, as I have read the text, "Moral formation and peaceable difference are gifts of the Spirit." Socrates also identified certain questions, you may recall, and we may return to them in closing.

The gifts call for response, and it is the gifts that make us able to respond. The gifts make us response-able. To the question of responsibility, then, the simple but demanding answer is that we are all responsible. Parents, teachers, clergy, neighbors, we are *all* responsible. And we are all responsible *to* God, to the mystery at the heart of our world.

That responsibility *to* God shapes an answer to the normative question, to the question of what we are responsible *for*. Without forgetting that moral formation and peaceable difference are gifts of God — indeed, in response to those gifts — we are responsible for challenging the envy and pride that turn siblings into rivals. We are responsible for practicing the kind of hospitality that is only gift answering to gift but that alone is capable of establishing trust. We are responsible for nurturing and training the senses of dependence, gratitude, remorse, hope, and responsibility toward a maturity that is ready to forgive and to love the enemy. It is not just "tolerance" toward which we must aim. It is not just a self-serving "freedom" by which we should measure moral maturity. And, although we must surely aim at "justice," the story we tell of it should be richer by far than the story that a veil of ignorance fell on self-interested individuals forced to live together.

506

To the pedagogical questions, the answer remains a mystery. A mystery, however, is not a puzzle we have not yet figured out. There are no guarantees. Moral formation and peaceable difference are not simply under our control or at our disposal. Still, there are some pedagogical hints. With all due respect for the stages of cognitive development, we have seen something of the importance of stories, stories that one can own as one's own, stories that leave open the possibility of repentance, stories that are not merely dilemmas or quandaries or puzzles.[18] We have seen something of the importance of evoking and developing certain moral senses.[19] We have seen something of the importance of modeling hospitality. We have seen something of the importance of communities of mutual admonition and encouragement.[20] And we have seen, at least if these remarks have made any sense at all, something of the importance of refusing to empty our lives and the lives of our children of mystery, the importance of refusing to eliminate or to domesticate the mystery that is at the heart of our lives.

18. Such a hint might suggest that Robert Coles is on the right track. See Robert Coles, *The Moral Life of Children* (Boston: Houghton Mifflin, 1986).

19. That hint might suggest the wisdom of some of what Martin Hoffman recommends in Martin Hoffman, "Affect and Moral Development," in *New Directions in Child Development: Emotional Development*, ed. D. Ciccheti and P. Hesse (San Francisco: Jossey-Bass, 1982), pp. 83-103.

20. This hint suggests the promise of Kohlberg's "just communities," where a richer account of justice and maturity would be operative.

Index of Subjects and Names

Index of Scripture and Other Ancient Texts

1:10-11	299	**1 John**		11:18	454
1:17	300, 301	3:16	28	11:19–20:15	454
1:18	301	4:1-2	11, 18	12:9	335, 401
1:21	195			12:10	454
1:27	300	**Jude**		13	336
2:1-9	297, 300, 301	5	22	13:1-10	454
2:2	299			13:2	335
2:7	299	**Revelation**	147, 301-2,	13:10	454
2:6-7	299		452-55	13:11-18	454
2:15-16	297, 300, 301	1:1	452	13:17	301
3:17	300	1:4-5	452n.43	14:4	222n.8
3:18	301	1:5	452	14:12	454
4:10	299, 300, 301	1:9	454	15:3-4	454
4:13	299, 301	1:10	453	17:1–19:10	454
4:16	299	1:12-20	452	18:3	302
5:1-6	299-300	2:1–3:22	452n.43, 453	18:4	302, 454
5:1-11	297	2:2	454	18:9-10	302, 454
5:2-3	300	2:7	453	18:11-19	302, 454
5:4	300	2:11	453	18:20	454
5:5	300	2:17	453	19:1	454
5:6	300, 301	2:19	454	19:3	454
5:7-11	300	2:26	453	19:6	454
5:11	301	2:28	453	19:16	454
5:14	122, 301	3:3	22	21:1	454
5:15	122	3:5	453	21:2–22:5	454
		3:10	454	21:4	97, 114, 117, 144
1 Peter		3:12	453	21:5	71, 454
1:4	457	3:14-21	302	21:7	454
1:14	223	3:17	302	22:2	454
1:15-16	223	3:21	453	22:21	452n.42
2:1	195	4:1	453		
2:9	456	4:1–5:14	453		
2:11	472	4:11	453	**EARLY CHRISTIAN**	
2:11-18	223	5:5	453	**LITERATURE**	
2:13-17	458	5:6	453		
2:17	442	5:6-14	301	**Augustine**	
3:15	143	5:9	453	*The City of God*	
3:21-22	23	5:13	453	10.9	124n.11
5:5	209	6:1-8	453	14.3	125n.17
		6:9-11	453	22.22	125n.17
		6:12-17	453	"Against Lying"	18, 36,
2 Peter		6:15	301		127n.23
1:12	22	7:1-8	453	"On Patience"	18, 147
1:13	22	7:9-17	453		
2:13–3:8	206-10	7:16-17	454	*Epistle of Barnabas*	
3:1	22	8:1–11:14	454	21:4	15
3:13	319	11:15	419, 454